Leadership, Talent, and Human-AI Collaboration

Don Ashley
https://orcid.org/0009-0009-2950-0029
Wayland Baptist University, USA

Manjari Sharma
https://orcid.org/0000-0003-1459-165X
Christ University, India

Sharad Gupta
https://orcid.org/0000-0002-4994-3523
Christ University, India

IGI Global
Scientific Publishing
Publishing Tomorrow's Research Today

Vice President of Editorial Melissa Wagner
Director of Acquisitions Mikaela Felty
Director of Book Development Jocelynn Hessler
Production Manager Mike Brehm
Cover Design Jose Rosado

Published in the United States of America by
IGI Global Scientific Publishing
701 East Chocolate Avenue
Hershey, PA, 17033, USA
Tel: 717-533-8845 | Fax: 717-533-7115
Website: https://www.igi-global.com E-mail: cust@igi-global.com

Library of Congress Cataloging-in-Publication Data

LCCN: (CIP Data Pending)
ISBN13: 9798260025413
Isbn13Softcover: 9798260025420
EISBN13: 9798260025437
British Cataloguing in Publication Data
A Cataloguing in Publication record for this book is available from the British Library.

Table of Contents

Detailed Table of Contents

Moving beyond the post-heroic era of human-AI symbiosis, this chapter looks at artificial intelligence-augmented leadership as a paradigm shift from the conventional heroic, individualistic models toward one of cooperation between humans and machines. While humans have irreplaceable talents in moral judgment, empathy, contextual complexity, creativity, and moral imagination, AI shines in quick data processing, pattern recognition, and efficiency. Using Upper Echelons Theory and complementarity models, the study maps the development of AI across assistive, cooperative, and agentic phases, reinterpreting transformational, servant, adaptive, and emerging agentic leadership styles for hybrid settings. It looks at the paradox of augmentation-automation, and also at how psychological contracts are changing, how digital resistance is addressed, and how to make governance to be ethical and trustworthy. Effective AI-augmented leadership calls for careful orchestration: encouraging superagency by ongoing learning, balanced human-AI loops, value-aligned overrides, and human-centered safeguards.

This chapter examines AI-augmented leadership as a distinct organisational phenomenon in which artificial intelligence systems actively participate in functions such as strategic planning, resource allocation, and performance management. Drawing on leadership theory, decision science, sociotechnical systems theory, and technology ethics, the authors synthesise disparate traditions into an integrated framework for understanding distributed agency in human–AI systems. A typology of leadership configurations ranging from decision support through collaborative partnership to autonomous agency clarifies governance and accountability implications of each. The chapter analyses how centralised, distributed, and hybrid decision-making architectures shape information flows and authority distribution. Behavioural consequences including leader identity transformation, follower perceptions, and cultural adaptation are examined alongside ethical considerations such as algorithmic bias, epistemic opacity, and accountability. Implementation requirements and a future research agenda are presented.

Artificial intelligence (AI) is changing organizational behavior by defining the way in which employees cooperate, innovate, and feel at work differently. Although AI contributes to the improvement of the efficiency of algorithms, it also increases burnouts, surveillance issues, and psychological pressure in tech-oriented work environments. This chapter discusses the potential of AI-human cooperation to transform organizations into systems that focus on efficiency to human flourishing systems. The results obtained indicated that AI systems can lead to innovation, trust, and engagement under mediation by empathetic and ethically transparent leaders, but they will cause psychological safety to be eroded when they are seen as tools of surveillance. The research proposes a socio-technical concept of empathetic digitization, according to which the AI potential is aligned with human dignity, and the notion of well-being is a strategic determinant of sustainable organizational performance.

The prevalent incorporation of artificial intelligence (AI) in organizational schemes has meaningfully transformed work mechanism, practices in leadership, and design of performance. The study an effort to explore the effect of AI, human collaboration, Artificial intelligence, readiness of AI infrastructure, oriented leadership, employee behavioural adaptability, and AI, enabled performance on organizational change. Quantitative research design has been used on collected data based on Likert scale from 270 respondents. Collected data has been analysed applying descriptive methods, ANOVA, regression analysis and correlation analysis supported by diagnostic tests to confirm the reliability and validity of the research model. The outcomes of the study reported the strong explanatory power of proposed model with performance

This chapter discusses the increasing use of artificial intelligence in the recruitment, selection, and performance management systems and the implications of this on the current talent strategy. It employs a theoretical perspective to evaluate the way the Artificial Intelligence-driven sourcing systems, machine-based screening solutions, predictive evaluation devices, and workforce-analytics systems are transforming the organizational hires systems across the globe. Simultaneously, this chapter stresses the persistence of the role of human judgment in interpreting the outputs of algorithmic, protecting a fairness factor, and maintaining institutional legitimacy that subsequently enhances the chances of the candidates to get employed in the spheres of their interests. This chapter is based on an integrated approach to the understanding of AI-driven talent management by synthesizing technological, behavioral, and strategic perspectives. The conclusion will include the description of the managerial implications and the perspectives of future research field of AI.

The chapter shows artificial intelligence (AI) technologies have been adopted by organizations to improve their recruitment procedures of job applicants based on data from recent surveys conducted in both the United States and the United Kingdom. The majority of respondents believe AI will shape the future of recruitment: 61% in the U.S. and 58% in the UK believe applicants should use AI in ways that remain hidden to others, while 56% (U.S.) and 52% (UK) believe candidates will need AI assistance to complete application processes. Additionally, 55% of U.S. and 52% of UK respondents think non-users will face disadvantages. People from Millennial (78% U.S.; 79% UK) and Gen Z (71% U.S.; 62% UK) groups show the highest adoption rates of technology, while office workers in both countries report an 82% technology usage rate. The most commonly used tools by users include ChatGPT

Preface

The emergence of artificial intelligence (AI) has ushered in a profound transformation in the ways organizations lead, manage talent, and cultivate collaboration between humans and intelligent systems. No longer confined to automating routine activities, AI has become an active participant in strategic decision-making, leadership processes, talent acquisition, workforce development, and employee experience. As organizations navigate increasingly dynamic and digitally enabled environments, the challenge is not merely to adopt new technologies but to create systems in which human capabilities and artificial intelligence complement one another in ways that enhance organizational effectiveness and human flourishing.

Leadership and talent management are among the areas experiencing the most significant changes as AI technologies continue to evolve. Leaders are being called upon to balance efficiency with empathy, innovation with ethics, and technological capability with human judgment. Similarly, organizations are rethinking traditional approaches to recruitment, workforce analytics, employee well-being, and career development through the lens of human-AI collaboration. These transformations raise important questions concerning trust, accountability, fairness, psychological safety, and the future of work itself. Consequently, understanding the behavioral and organizational implications of AI-enabled systems has become an imperative for scholars, practitioners, and policymakers alike.

It is within this rapidly changing context that Leadership, Talent, and Human–AI Collaboration has been developed. This volume brings together contributions from researchers across diverse disciplines and geographical regions who examine the intersection of artificial intelligence, leadership, organizational behavior, and human capital management. Through theoretical frameworks, empirical investigations, and conceptual analyses, the chapters collectively provide insights into how AI is redefining leadership roles, decision-making structures, talent systems, and employee well-being. The volume seeks to offer readers a comprehensive and forward-looking perspective on the opportunities and challenges associated with building intelligent, ethical, and human-centered organizations.

CHAPTER OVERVIEW

Chapter 1, "AI-Augmented Leadership: Forging Adaptive Strategies for Organizational Transformation," explores the emergence of AI-augmented leadership and examines how human capabilities and machine intelligence can coexist within hybrid organizational environments. Drawing upon leadership theories and complementarity models, the chapter highlights the importance of ethical governance, continuous learning, and human-centered safeguards in fostering sustainable AI-enabled leadership.

Chapter 2, "AI-Augmented Leadership and Digital Decision-Making Models," investigates AI as an active participant in strategic planning, resource allocation, and performance management. The chapter develops an integrated framework for understanding distributed agency and analyzes how different decision architectures influence authority, organizational culture, and accountability in human-AI systems.

Chapter 3, "From Algorithmic Efficiency to Human-Centered Leadership in AI–Human Collaboration: Implications for Organizational Behavior," examines the behavioral consequences of AI integration and proposes a socio-technical framework of empathetic digitization. The authors demonstrate that ethical and transparent leadership is essential for promoting trust, innovation, and employee well-being in technology-intensive workplaces.

Chapter 4, "AI Human Collaboration and Organizational Performance: An Empirical Study of Behavioral Leadership and Performance Dynamics," presents empirical evidence on the relationships among AI readiness, behavioral leadership, employee adaptability, and organizational performance. The findings reveal the critical role of AI-enabled leadership and infrastructure readiness in driving organizational transformation.

Chapter 5, "Cognitive Alignment Protocols: Designing Harmonized Decision Systems for Ethical AI-Human Collaboration in Organizations," introduces the concept of Cognitive Alignment Protocols as a framework for synchronizing human judgment, organizational values, and algorithmic decision systems. The chapter emphasizes transparency, ethical congruence, and behavioral alignment as key determinants of trust and responsible AI adoption.

Chapter 6, "From Automation to Augmentation: The Transformative Role of Artificial Intelligence in Human Capital Management," discusses the growing influence of AI across human capital management functions, including recruitment, workforce analytics, employee engagement, and performance management. The chapter offers a balanced perspective that positions AI as an enabler of human expertise rather than a substitute for it.

Chapter 7, "AI in HRM – Transformative Talent Management Strategies in Organizations," examines how AI technologies are revolutionizing talent acquisition, development, assessment, and retention. The authors highlight the strategic importance of AI-driven systems in enabling organizations to identify and nurture talent in increasingly competitive environments.

Chapter 8, "Human–AI Collaboration in HRM: Leveraging the HAC Model to Promote Employee Well-Being in AI-Enabled Indian IT Workplaces," explores how hybrid approaches to human resource management can enhance employee well-being and organizational effectiveness. Using the HAC model, the chapter demonstrates how ethical AI policies and data-driven practices can support healthier and more adaptive workplaces.

Chapter 9, "AI-Human Collaboration in Talent Decision Systems: Transforming Recruitment, Selection, and Talent Acquisition," analyzes the growing integration of AI into talent management systems. The chapter emphasizes the continuing importance of human judgment in ensuring fairness, institutional legitimacy, and strategic decision-making while leveraging the advantages of AI-enabled recruitment tools.

Chapter 10, "The Evolution of Job Applications Through Artificial Intelligence Technologies," investigates changing patterns in job application processes and applicant behaviors. Drawing upon survey evidence from the United States and the United Kingdom, the chapter highlights generational differences in AI adoption and examines the implications of AI-assisted recruitment for the future workforce.

Collectively, these chapters reveal that leadership and talent management are undergoing a paradigm shift shaped by collaborative intelligence. While artificial intelligence offers unprecedented opportunities to enhance efficiency, decision quality, and workforce development, the contributors consistently emphasize that technological progress must be accompanied by ethical governance, empathy, transparency, and a commitment to preserving human dignity. The volume thus advances a vision of organizations in which AI serves not as a replacement for human capabilities, but as a catalyst for more adaptive, resilient, and people-centered systems.

CONCLUSION

As editors, we extend our sincere gratitude to all contributing authors for their scholarly dedication and valuable contributions to this volume. Their expertise and diverse perspectives have made possible a collection that reflects the multidimensional nature of leadership and talent management in the era of AI-human collaboration. We also acknowledge the efforts of reviewers, editors, and publishing professionals whose support has been essential throughout the development of this work.

We hope that this book will serve as a meaningful resource for researchers, educators, organizational leaders, human resource professionals, and policymakers seeking to understand and navigate the profound changes brought about by artificial intelligence. The frameworks and insights presented throughout the volume offer both conceptual guidance and practical implications for building organizations that are innovative, ethical, and sustainable.

Finally, we believe that the future of work will be defined not by the competition between humans and machines, but by the quality of their collaboration. As AI technologies continue to evolve, the challenge facing organizations will be to cultivate leadership models and talent systems that empower people while responsibly leveraging the capabilities of intelligent technologies. It is our hope that this volume will contribute to ongoing scholarly discourse and inspire future research aimed at fostering workplaces that are inclusive, trustworthy, and capable of promoting both organizational excellence and human well-being.

Don Ashley
Wayland Baptist University, USA

Manjari Sharma
Christ University, India

Sharad Gupta
Christ University, India

Chapter 1
AI-Augmented Leadership:
Forging Adaptive Strategies for Organizational Transformation

Ramakrishnan Ramachandran
http://orcid.org/0000-0001-8712-7677
Vivin Consultants, Chennai, India

Sruthi Pillai
http://orcid.org/0009-0003-1325-3090
Al Injaz International Private School, Oman

ABSTRACT

Moving beyond the post-heroic era of human-AI symbiosis, this chapter looks at artificial intelligence-augmented leadership as a paradigm shift from the conventional heroic, individualistic models toward one of cooperation between humans and machines. While humans have irreplaceable talents in moral judgment, empathy, contextual complexity, creativity, and moral imagination, AI shines in quick data processing, pattern recognition, and efficiency. Using Upper Echelons Theory and complementarity models, the study maps the development of AI across assistive, cooperative, and agentic phases, reinterpreting transformational, servant, adaptive, and emerging agentic leadership styles for hybrid settings. It looks at the paradox of augmentation-automation, and also at how psychological contracts are changing, how digital resistance is addressed, and how to make governance to be ethical and trustworthy. Effective AI-augmented leadership calls for careful orchestration: encouraging superagency by ongoing learning, balanced human-AI loops, value-aligned overrides, and human-centered safeguards.

DOI: 10.4018/979-8-2600-2541-3.ch001

1. INTRODUCTION: THE POST-HEROIC LEADERSHIP ERA

Artificial intelligence (AI) and leadership have come together to create a time when the usual heroic models based on personal charm, vision, and making decisions on your own aren't good enough anymore. This chapter explores artificial intelligence-enhanced leadership as a way of creating adaptive strategies for organizational transformation.

From the heroic, individualistic models of the past to a cooperative, post-heroic age when human intuition enhances machine accuracy, the incorporation of artificial intelligence (AI) into organizational leadership signals a great change.

The post-heroic leadership era is defined by distributed responsibility, Human-AI collaboration, machines handle cognitive loads once considered exclusively human, while uniquely human, qualities remain irreplaceable, marking a shift from 'great man' narratives to collective, technology-enabled orchestration (Bolden, 2011) .

As businesses navigate this landscape in 2026, leaders must coordinate Human-AI symbiosis to generate transformation. Leaders have to navigate a landscape in which certain human abilities become even more critical, and harder to coordinate, as AI penetrates high-level decision-making.

1.1 Overview of AI's Disruptive Role in Leadership

Hambrick and Mason (1984) suggest in the Upper Echelons Theory (UET) that the traits of the top-level management determine the outcomes of the organization. Upper echelons theory implies that effective top leaders excel at optimally combining organizational resources.

Technological intervention in the past few decades has made tremendous changes to leadership and the organization. Artificial intelligence is one such technological intervention, that is dominating the entire business world. It plays a vital role in the strategic decision-making process by reshaping the business models and boosting the agility of the business.

By integrating AI in business, organizations can navigate easily through the environmental complexities of the business and allowing them to focus on a higher-quality decision-making process. AI's ability to process the large set of data and predicting the patterns has helped many businesses to take effective decisions (Kaggwa et al., 2024) .

Bevilacqua et al. (2026) suggests that it is important for the top management team to develop an open mind set towards the integration of AI in the decision-making process. This involves developing critical thinking and continuous learning along with hands on experience on varied AI tools. A strong knowledge of the various

AI tools for operational, organizational, and strategic needs will help the leader to choose the right tool to be used.

1.2 Capabilities and Constraints

Artificial intelligence is no longer optional, but rather fundamental for competitive existence by becoming an integral part of every business. However, people lack trust due to the perception that AI cannot grasp emotional context or interpret nuances the way humans do (Barabadi et al., 2026) .

Machine learning identifies and classifies the patterns within a data. Historically pattern recognition was associated with statistical patterns. With the introduction of AI, the patterns are determined using data processing, neural networks and advanced algorithms. The most important application of pattern recognition are speech recognition, anomaly recognition and financial forecasting.

But at the same time, we should accept the fact that pattern recognition of AI is highly dependent on the quality of input data received. It is seen that interaction plays a major role during the process of learning new things.

Human learning and reasoning happen by interacting with the environment. On the other hand, AI which is trained by human does not interact with the environment exactly in the way how it should be. It uses machine algorithm to understand the pattern and makes the prediction based on the changes happening with the pattern (Holzinger et al., 2023) .

Felin and Holweg (2024) argue that AI with the help of machine learning works backward. It takes lots of trained data to predict the next pattern or word. The outputs are often combinatorial remixes rather than true novelty.

Whereas, human intelligence works in forward direction by applying logics, enabling interventions and experimentation, which provide the actual output necessary for the decision making. But then Korteling et al., (2021) argue that human intelligence does not perform well in comparison to AI due to lack of memory storage, inefficiency in processing large data and poor multitasking.

The complementary character of human-AI strengths shown in the table1 below explains why coordination is so important.

Table 1. AI and Human Capabilities in Leadership Decision-Making

Dimension	AI Capabilities	Human Capabilities	Leadership Implications
Data Processing & Pattern Recognition	At much higher speed, scale, and accuracy	Limited capacity; prone to fatigue and bias	AI handles analytics; humans provide interpretation
Speed & Efficiency	Instantaneous responses	Slower, reflective processing	AI for rapid decisions; humans for deliberation
Moral Reasoning & Ethics	Rule-based; lacks empathy	Contextual nuance, empathy, justice orientation	Humans must lead ethical judgments
Contextual Subtlety	Limited to trained data; struggles with ambiguity	Intuitive grasp of social/ cultural dynamics	Human-AI collaboration required for nuanced contexts
Creativity & Innovation	Pattern-based generation	True novelty, intuition, hope	Humans drive breakthrough innovation

Source: Compiled by authors

Table 1's complementarity helps to explain why deliberate orchestration rather than simple adoption is required of AI-augmented leadership. AI's faster speed and scope let leaders in data processing and pattern recognition move from hand analysis to interpretive supervision—interpreting results in complex settings where human instinct shines.

Empirical data from current research confirms this: high-performing companies use artificial intelligence for quick pattern recognition while humans manage ethical subtlety and contextual nuances (Singla et al., 2025).

Over-reliance on the rule-based moral reasoning of artificial intelligence can cause dehumanized decisions, as shown in situations where algorithmically outputs neglect cultural dynamics; therefore, calibrated cooperation is necessary.

Leadership has great repercussions: AI frees people for deliberative, value-driven decisions by handling instantaneous efficiency for operational decisions (e.g., real-time forecasting). Artificial intelligence creates pattern-based concepts (e.g., combinatorial remixes) in innovation and creativity, but revolutionary novelty demands human insight and hope—characteristics that propel transforming change.

As Zárate-Torres et al. (2025) observe, shared accountability produces above-average results, only if leaders promote ethical integration. Organizations without this, run the risk of unethical misbehavior or inhumane practices.

Examples include healthcare predictive analytics (AI detects disease risks) matched with human judgment on patient impact or fintech anomaly detection (AI flags fraud patterns). Ultimately, Table 1 reveals the augmentation-automation conundrum: Artificial intelligence commoditizes conventional cognition, hence strengthening human strengths and need symbiotic models for long-lasting benefit.

Research reveals that good Human-AI teamwork produces above-average results, only when leaders encourage shared responsibility and ethical integration (Zárate-Torres et al., 2025) . Organizations run the danger of unethical failures or in humanized procedures without this.

1.3 The Core Contradiction and New Psychological Contract

At the heart of AI-augmented leadership, there is a basic paradox. Enhancing AI competence increases the need for human skills. This contradiction results from artificial intelligence commoditizing everyday cognition, hence raising unique human attributes amid uncertainty.

Technology offers unheard-of efficiency and foresight, yet it calls on leaders to abandon conventional control to promote true Human-AI symbiosis. Leaders struggling with the conflict between augmentation, where artificial intelligence improves human capabilities, and automation, where it risks replacing or over-reliance on them, manifest this contradiction, creating interdependent yet opposing dynamics that vary across time and contexts (Raisch & Krakowski, 2021).

Though its dependence on statistical correlations, instead of genuine contextual knowledge can lead to skewed results, decreased responsibility, or decreased human inventiveness, AI's faster strategic changes thanks to its better pattern recognition and speed enable fast strategic adaptation. By means of algorithmic humility, leaders must foster a balanced Human-AI symbiosis that preserves ethical integrity and revolutionary innovation while exploiting machine capabilities (Islami, & Mulolli, 2024).

As companies negotiate implied expectations, the new psychological contract shows itself: While leaders undertake to increase teams' AI literacy and ethical governance, workers exchange regular cognitive tasks for positions stressing relational skills, innovation, and monitoring. This agreement depends on openness, common agency, and ongoing learning to make sure artificial intelligence helps to improve rather than replaces human agency in quest of adaptive change.

Altering the psychological contract, the integration of artificial intelligence transforms from conventional relational or transactional models toward more fluid, technology-mediated systems. Employees may suffer in the artificial intelligence age, marked by feelings of disconnection, decreased job security, and weakened trust as automation affects human contact and autonomy (Braganza et al., 2021).

Empirical data reveals that as employees see changes toward surveillance, obsolescence of skills, or reduced agency, AI adoption may damage the favorable correlations between psychological contracts, job involvement, and organizational trust. Leaders have to solve this by rethinking artificial intelligence as a cooperative enabler instead of a menace. They must foster openness, reskilling, and ethical governance to restore psychological safety, reciprocal obligations, and shared value creation in hybrid settings (Kim & Kim, 2024).

1.4 Conceptual Framework & Chapter Structure,

Leaders use hybrid cooperation to increase production while maintaining human-centered values like compassion, ethical thinking, and contextual sensitivity. The conceptual framework for AI-augmented leadership advances a multidimensional model, that presents AI-augmented leadership as a dynamic interaction of human strengths (intuition, ethics) and artificial intelligence skills (data processing, pattern detection).

Combining upper echelons theory with Human-AI complementarity, it suggests that best results come from symbiotic decision loops whereby leaders organize rather than rule.

The chapter is structured as follows: Following this introduction, Section 2 conducts a systematic mapping of AI-Augmented Decision Models. Section 3 examines adaptive Leadership as a Non-Replaceable Skill before proceeding to Section 4 on Transformative and Servant Leadership in the Hybrid Age.

In section 5, it looks at Managing Resistance, Change, and Professional Identity and then proceeds to the Integration Challenge: Accountability, Governance, and Maturity in section 6. Section 7 concludes with future directions after synthesis and recommendations.

This chapter reviews interdisciplinary literature from organizational behavior, management information systems, leadership studies, and artificial intelligence ethics methodology. from prominent peer-reviewed journals, current conceptual models, and published industry studies, guaranteeing a balanced synthesis of theoretical basis and evolving empirical evidence.

2. SYSTEMATIC MAPPING OF AI-AUGMENTED DECISION MODELS

Systematic mapping of AI-enhanced decision models exposes a fast changing, fractured but still progressively important research environment. From helping strategic management to automating technical activities like requirements prioritization, these models concentrate on combining artificial intelligence (AI) with human decision-making in many fields.

2.1 Three Evolutionary Stages: Assistive, Collaborative, and Agentic AI

AI has emerged and evolved over a period of time from mere the replication of human like reasoning to self-sufficient tool. AI's foremost purpose in many organizations is clearly that of assistive role.

This assistive AI helps the organization to measure the reliability of the communication received or send, sources of data and monitoring knowledge about a scenario pertaining to the decision-making process (Gyöngyössy et al., 2024).

AI assists humans by predictions and explanation for the changes in the pattern. But there are three challenges put forward by Steyvers & Kumar (2023), when using AI for decision making assistance. AI can outperform humans in certain scenario which is called as complementarity. Humans should recognize /not overlook this complementarity strengths of AI.

Another challenge is that the AI model used to detect the expectations and the patterns of human need to be closely monitored to prevent the misuse of data by the third party. The third challenge in using assistive AI is that the interaction between human and AI requires the understanding of relevance of AI advice during a specific time span, confidence level of data processed and the amount of data fed.

Over the years, AI has become an inevitable part of the business. AI facilitates the decision makers by providing better choices. It integrates the human skills with the logical skills. Human creative can be enhanced by collaborating the tool and techniques of AI which can result in better productivity (Cariaga, 2025). The Human-AI collaborative decision making is dependent on two dimensions such as the level of interdependence and the nature of specialization.

This collaboration makes the organization to understand whether a sequential or parallel pattern is followed. The study conducted by Puranam (2021) opined that the Human-AI collaboration will work better only when the complementary strengths of both are analysed. Humans are good at judging in an ambiguous context whereas AI is better in pattern recognition and data processing.

Agentic AI is not just another AI which just answers the prompt. It senses the environment, decides on the possibilities of doing a task and assures that each step will lead to the achievement of goals. LLM (large language models) and RL (reinforcement learning) forms the basis of agentic AI (Bandi et al., 2025). Agentic AI focuses more on the multistep reasoning, whereas it allows human to focus more on the strategic decisions. Bandi et al., (2025) identified the core components of agentic AI like:

Perception and world modelling: Perception gets the data from external sources in the form of text, events and sensors and convert them into a structured observation. Whereas, world modelling is more into internal representation of processing of data, which helps in prediction, consistency check and counterfactual simulations.

Memory: It provides the base for processing the data in the form of short-term memory and long-term memory. Short term memory focuses on the current context and exchange of data. Long term memory focuses on analyses semantic knowledge.

Planning and reasoning: This stage actually transforms the goals into actionable steps, helps in sorting out the best alternatives and helps in selecting the action which fits into long and short horizon.

Execution and actuation: Execution helps in bridging the impact. It helps in validating the outcomes in accordance to the expectations, which further assists the organization to move forward with the plan or to deviate.

Reflection and evaluation: This stage verifies the immediate or the final output and initiate selective replanning if required.

Orchestration: This stage supports in building up the communication between and AI, by providing a greater extent of transparency in data processing.

2.2 Core Components

AI's application is universally accepted in all the field of business, irrespective of the sectors. Most of the fintech companies uses AI to provide valued addition to the customers. Thus, more organization and countries are tended to invest on AI, since the technology will yield both financial and economic benefits.

AL and ML are widely used in areas such as risk management, detection of fraudulent activities, algorithmic trading, investment management and so on. Most of the banks are relying on AI analytics for creating added value in the areas such as customer acquisition, relationship management and in smart servicing (Kumar, 2024).

China was an early adopter of AI investing 1.66 billion for AI in 2016 (Yan, 2023) . AI techniques like ML, NLP and RPA (robotic process automation) helps the financial functions to convert a large set of data into actionable insights, in financial predictions and thus in decision making process. RPA uses bots to automate the repetitive tasks such as accounts payable and receivables, journal entry etc.,

Similar to fintech sector, AI is revolutionising the healthcare sector as well. The two major reasons for the AI to get popularized in healthcare sector is that: increase in population and the connectivity of people throughout the world with multiple devices (Ilyas, 2022).

The most common techniques that they use is predictive analysis, robotics and AI driven automation which help them to take informed decisions. Predictive analysis for instance, helps in detecting the early signs of a disease and helps in taking proactive measures, which in turn will save the lives of millions of people (Haque, 2025). The key point to be noted while implementing AI techniques in healthcare is that AI should just be used for improving the efficiency and effectiveness of the system not to replace human (Bajwa et al., 2021).

2.3 The Algorithmic Deference Trap and Trust Frameworks

With the advent of AI, decision-making based on algorithms is widely accepted in every phase of business. In recent past, algorithms are the tools which managers are highly dependent on due to its efficiency and its capability to optimize the data driven decision making. At the same time, the degree of trust, fairness and emotions associated with human and algorithm-based decision making is purely based on the perceptions the different people have (Lee, 2018).

Algorithmic decision making will some time causes a negative impact on the employee well-being. Study conducted by Zayid et al. (2024) highlighted that algorithmic decision making may lead to job insecurity and anxiety. Since algorithms do not validate the human emotions, employees fear that their performance is not being measured based on the actual context.

This decision-making system has two major consequences on the society as well. The first one is that over reliance on AI based algorithm will lead to unpredictable and unethical future development. The second problem arises when organizations start using it without completely understanding the way it has to be used and implemented (Breidbach, 2024).

Trust in AI is crucial for the diffusion of technology. Development and implementation of AI is highly dependent on the meeting the expectations and satisfaction of all the stakeholders of the organization. When we deal about the trust factor, we do not just expect it to be ethical, we also look for its performance, transparency, explainability and compatibility with the existing system (Afroogh et al., 2024).

Xu, Murthy & Jia (2025) identified four different strategies to understand the radical behaviour and trust on AI. The first strategy is contemporary role architecture which focuses on assisting the human decision rather than replacing it. The second strategy is adaptive user centered design which integrated AI into individual decision support system. The third is context-aware task allocation helps in assigning tasks based on various situation.

The last strategy is autonomous reliance calibration mechanism, which empowers the individual to control the over dependence on AI. These kinds of strategies will lead to the creation of trust framework which helps the organization to improve its performance. More innovation is encouraged in those organizations which encourages the culture of AI-human collaboration (Zhang et al., 2025).

2.4 Practical Integration Strategies

Modern leaders are not only required to become masters of AI but they should also excel in integrating the various tools of AI in decision making. Collaborating human intelligence and AI will help in inclusive and adaptive leadership. Leaders should integrate strategies in such a way that it will enhance the quality of decision making across various departments and thereby improves the organizational agility (Fantoni & Sasmita, 2025).

The AI literacy has become crucial for the leaders to improve the efficiency of the organization. The integration and implementation of AI presents both opportunities and challenges. A proper tool and effective model which supports AI-human collaboration will lead to the concept of augmented leadership (Mohammed, Bambale & Abdullahi, 2025).

3.ADAPTIVE LEADERSHIP AS A NON-REPLACEABLE SKILL

Adaptive leadership style focuses on mobilizing people to understand the tough challenges and finding out the way to tackle it. This creates an environment fostered with learning, innovation and context driven.

Adaptive leadership addresses human-centric challenges that require behavioral, cultural, and mindset shift, while AI can handle technical problems of known issues with known solutions.

3.1 Adaptive Leadership in the AI Era

Adaptive leadership takes the essence from complexity leadership theory and situational leadership theory (Boikanyo, 2025). It emphasizes leading through rather than around uncertainty by developing resilience, emotional intelligence (EQ), and the capacity to handle complicated, adaptive problems devoid of obvious solutions.

Increasing demand for AI implementation process expects the leaders to be adaptive and agile. Adaptive leaders will help the organization to be flexible in accordance with the strategic vision formulated. This leadership style is about being proactive and informed about the emerging technologies in business (Pandey, 2025).

Adaptive leadership forms the basis for ethical decision making. This ensures that the adoption of AI is done in such a way which aligns with the societal values. Adaptive leadership encourages continuous learning which will help the organization to address the challenges such as bias mitigation, transparency issues and accountability (Suffiyah et al., 2025).

3.2 Key Enablers

Adaptive leadership style is based on the principle of agility and learning based models with the focus on flexibility, experimentation and resilience. These leaders are capable to act in volatile situations and can take strategic decision in favour of innovative organizational culture.

The key characteristics an adaptive leader should possess is to have a strategic vision, strong communication skills, being agile during the change process and the capability of taking the right decision under uncertain condition (Hasanah & Rozi, 2025). One of the essential enablers of adaptive leadership style is organizational culture which prioritizes adaptability, encourages learning and openness to change.

3.3 Technology-Driven Challenges and Responses

Adaptive leadership style cannot be adopted if the regulations pertaining to AI is not proper. It is also mandatory that reskilling and upskilling is done in the organization which opens the door for innovation (Randriamiary, 2024) . If not done correctly, incorporating technology into any company presents difficulties. One of the challenges that AI implementation faces is lack of proper regulation.

Issues related to privacy, transparency and algorithmic bias also contributes to the improper implementation of AI in business. Lack of transparency creates a sense of doubt among the general public regarding the fairness, accountability and ethical issues. Lack of technological capacity might also hinder the adoption and implementation of AI in the organization (Renta-Davids et al., 2025).

Increasing reliance on AI will result in job displacement. This causes the distress among the employees and the productivity of the other employees might also get affected (Arora, 2024 .

The success of AI implementation is highly dependent on the data set received. If the quality of input data is not good, then the decision-making process associated with it will not help in adaptive leadership style. The cost and return on investment are another challenge faced by the organization in implementing AI (Badhurunnisa & Dass, 2023).

3.4 Measurement and Outcomes

Adaptive success can now be measured with precision previously unavailable. Developed by Raei (2018) in a doctoral dissertation, The Raei Adaptive Leadership with Authority Scale (RALWAS) specifically measures adaptive leadership exercised from positions of formal authority. It addresses a gap in measuring authority-based adaptive processes and underwent validation through mixed methods, focusing on reliability and construct validity for leaders in hierarchical roles.

Adaptive Leadership Questionnaire (ALQ), developed by Northouse (2021) is another. Often used for 360-degree input. This adaptive leadership framework is evaluated via this 30-item, scenario-based instrument across six fundamental dimensions.

Developed and validated by Nöthel et al. (2023), the Adaptive Leadership Behavior Scale (ALBS) is a unidimensional instrument of adaptive leadership behaviors in turbulent, VUCA settings. This 15-item scale spans three field studies using employee ratings of supervisors (Study 1: N=201; Study 2: N=311; Study 3: N=155 leader-follower dyads).

The ALBS helps to close a gap in scientifically evaluating adaptive leadership by allowing studies on its antecedents, mechanisms, and effects—including possible improvements through AI-augmented devices—in quickly changing organizational environments. ALBS offers an accurate, valid, and useful tool to empirically examine antecedents and outcomes of adaptive leadership in changing situations.

4. TRANSFORMATIONAL, SERVANT AND AGENTIC LEADERSHIP IN AI-ENABLED WORKPLACES

Burns' (1978) transformational leadership highlighted charisma and visionary impact, resonating during organizational change and globalization. Transformational leadership is a well-known phenomenon these days that is said to have a good effect on how much work is done and how happy the employees are.

Another popular model is Greenleaf's (1977) servant leadership with emphasis on care and moral responsibility that responded to increasing ethical corporate governance demands along with Authentic leadership model.

Still, as the digital revolution picked up speed, these systems showed their shortcomings in dealing with the complexity and speed of information flows that now define today's businesses.

4.1 Transformational Leadership Reimagined:

Transformational leadership has a particularly preeminent position among the pantheon of leadership theory mostly because of its strong empirical support. Its ability to motivate good change and raise follower happiness, production, and commitment has been demonstrated and is safe.

As we know it now, transformational leadership has demonstrated its capacity to create a good working environment distinguished by great motivational levels and employee performance (Avolio & Bass, 1995) . Its emphasis on intellectual stimulation has helped to improve organizational development.

With its emphasis on motivating change by means of follower empowerment and inspiration, transformational leadership has unmatched empirically supported capacity to impact positive organizational change.

Retaining its allure and influence in varied contexts, transformational leadership is generally regarded as a very appealing and powerful framework (Leong & Fischer, 2011) . Research results support this claim and help to advance the debate by showing that transformational leadership interventions directly cause better organizational performance and unique change management.

Transformational leadership has been the focus of criticism from growing circles of academic critics and disgruntled leadership practitioners (Ladkin & Patrick, 2022) mostly because of its erratic implementation and a conceptuality that has long been called amorphous and vague. Transformational leadership's charismatic and leader-centric character has also drawn criticism (Antonakis, 2012). Critics of transformational leadership say that it doesn't adapt to changes in the surroundings properly.

To highlight the limitations of this approach in changing workplace settings, Nielsen et al. (2022) questioned the veracity of statements about the broad efficacy of transformational leadership, especially with regard to its function in reducing the relationship between job satisfaction rating and work-related ambiguity. Transformational leadership is increasingly criticized, despite its obvious contribution.

In India, Tambe et al., 2019) examined the function of artificial intelligence in transformational leadership and its impact on organizational culture. The authors used a longitudinal study design to gather data from companies that had used AI-driven solutions to boost operational efficiency and look at how these technologies impacted leadership behaviors and staff engagement.

Hao, Lv, & Du, (2020) and Wijayati et al., (2022) have provisionally confirmed confidence in artificial intelligence's capacity to propel organizational transformation by positively influencing worker performance, work engagement, and finally generating good organizational outcomes.

Motivated by the emergence and enhanced accessibility of generative artificial intelligence, the study serves as an invitation to scholars and practitioners to rethink transformative leadership underwritten by large-scale language models ready and able to handle increasing organizational complexity and contextual unfamiliarity and addressing recognized gaps.

The focus is on closing a growing divide between the lofty goals of transformational leadership and its diminished actual-world effectiveness. Artificial intelligence (AI) offers a fresh and immediately actionable countermeasure that gives proponents of transformational leadership the means to answer growing criticism.

Early indications support projections about the justifiability of using artificial intelligence as a corrective tool, intended to improve the application of transformational leadership principles (Smith & Green, 2018), aided by its remarkable talent for pattern recognition, and well-demonstrated ability to supply actionable insights.

Including Artificial Intelligence (AI) into leadership techniques offers a fresh way to overcome the failings of transformational leadership. The criticisms of the model may be allayed by AI's promise in improving decision-making, adjusting to various environments, and producing data-driven insights. Research looking at leadership results produced by AI interventions show promising initial findings.

AI has evolved into a readily available and empowering tool that may help current leaders navigate a vista of apparently infinite possibilities. AI-assisted interventions' quality of decisions consistently lowers the bias that doggedly follows human efforts while also generating empirically verified improvements in correctness and success rates (Zhang & Zhang, 2023) .

By means of good reduction of risks connected with subjectivity in assessing leadership effectiveness, artificial intelligence offers a special chance to improve leadership performance by ongoing evaluations and detection of areas for development. Huang and Rust (2018) look at the bigger effects of artificial intelligence's impact in services, especially how it could replace or change the way things have always been done.

Dwivedi et al. (2021) caught the two sides of artificial intelligence rather nicely: it emphasizes the difficulties in attempting to match human traits using AI systems; ethical concerns, especially those about the societal effects of job loss and more obsolescence, exacerbate the technical limitations.

4.2 Servant Leadership

Servant leadership, which gives follower development, well-being, ethical responsibility, and community top priority, resonates especially strongly in the age of artificial intelligence, where automation threatens dehumanization.

Leaders' free humans for higher-order contributions like creativity, empathy, and purpose-driven work by consciously configuring AI as a “servant ally” rather than master (Hackl, 2025) . Emphasizing humility, listening, and stewardship, servant leaders guarantee that artificial intelligence builds rather than usurps human dignity.

Leaders center on empowerment, creating psychological safety, reestablishing trust among job insecurity, and encouraging inclusive growth as artificial intelligence takes care of mundane tasks. Empirical studies reveal that Servant leadership raises participation in AI-driven settings and reduces burnout by giving people over just efficiency priority.

In reality, servant leadership helps to resolve the paradox of augmentation: leaders anchor moral purpose and guarantee that technology enhances meaning and belonging while artificial intelligence aids leaders in scaling empathy (through sentiment analysis) and support.

This human-centered approach opposes estrangement and turns possible opposition into dedication, therefore situating servant principles as vital for ethical hybrid workplace AI innovation. Iqbal et al. (2022) contrasted the predictive validity of transformational leadership with servant leadership.

This review of the two separate approaches revealed that limiting leadership behavior to any one particular style is inappropriate. Rather, several leadership approaches are important since each one influences varying levels of change on several corporate outcomes, especially in terms of creative behaviour and employee performance variance.

4.3 Agentic Leadership

The development of the Agentic Leadership Model in 2025 shows a theoretical breakthrough. It sees artificial intelligence as an agentic colleague that actively improves leadership skills including empathy, openness, and empowered independence, as opposed to earlier theories of leadership that viewed technology as just a facilitator.

It suggests that leadership effectiveness today results from collaboration between people and artificial intelligence, in which humans anchor ethical vision and relational sensitivity while robots manage complex information, rather than from human capability alone.

The convergence of several current trends drives the necessity of thinking about Agentic Leadership:

Technological Convergence: Quick changes in generative artificial intelligence, natural language models, and affective computing mean that computers now work not just at the level of efficiency but also in relational and cognitive areas (Shrestha, Ben-Menahem, & von Krogh, 2019).

Worldwide Difficulties: Presently, leaders deal with problems including geopolitical instability, pandemics, and climate change, which call for quick synthesis of enormous volumes of data and flexible reactions outside the purview of human intuition alone (George et al., 2022).

Organizational requirements: The growth of hybrid and remote work environments have challenged conventional leadership structures. Today's leaders are expected to keep involvement and responsibility across digital channels, often depending on AI-driven insights into team morale, productivity, and psychological well-being (Chamorro- Premuzic, Wade, &Jordan, 2018).

Ethical Requisites: According to Rahwan et al., (2019) AI-driven transparency and fairness audits can provide mechanisms that are able to track and defend actions to address the increasing demand for open and honest government by public needs. these accountability challenges.

Thus, Agentic Leadership is a required framework for negotiating complexity in the twenty-first century rather than a futuristic conjecture.

The **Adaptive Leadership Competency Profile (ALCP)**, focusing on building capacity for change and congruent behaviors in the 21st century, is a 360-degree performance-assessment tool derived from qualitative data and literature, operationalizing 11 macro-leadership competencies (with 65 items) for adaptive leadership in complex systems. It underwent psychometric development and validation to measure macro-level adaptive competencies (Sherron, 2000).

Leadership agency during crisis is embedded in the social, cultural, and material context in which it is realized, and is reflected in the professional identities of its participants (Gordin Yoskovitz & Schechter, 2024) Liddicoat & Taylor-Leech, 2021).

Agentic leadership is a modern, forward-looking paradigm where leaders leverage Agentic AI—autonomous systems that can reason, plan, and take action—as a strategic partner to enhance organizational performance, speed, and innovation.

Agentic leadership differs from conventional leadership, which depends just on human judgment; it achieves objectives with little, high-level direction by coordinating a team of autonomous AI agents with human talent. Proactive, goal-oriented activity defines it; emphasis is placed on improving human skills (empathy, strategy) using technical accuracy.

4.3.1 Core Principles of Agentic Leadership

The leader focuses on high-level strategy, creativity, and empathy after setting goals and boundaries. AI agents analyze data, simulate situations, and identify patterns in real-time. to independently manage the day-to-day difficult tasks and data-intensive decisions.

Proactive Action: Unlike reactive technologies, agentic systems act to address problems including IT downtime or supply chain disruptions before consumers have to get engaged.

Scalability of Empathy: Using AI-driven sentiment analysis, leaders may track team morale and participation at scale and provide tailored assistance to geographically spread teams.

Key Characteristics of an Agentic Leader

Responsibility with initiative: Acting in uncertain circumstances while holding responsibility for the results, whether human- or AI-driven.

- Adaptability and curiosity: A commitment to ongoing learning and mental model updating as AI ability develops swiftly.
- Systems Thinking: Grasping how the interaction of technology, culture, and the environment produces a 360° cockpit of operations.

Setting and keeping an eye on safeguards to guarantee that automated systems fit with business values, fairness, and privacy defines Ethical Intelligence. Artificial intelligence is becoming a need for leadership as the digital age develops It views artificial intelligence as an agentic partner that actively improves leadership characteristics including empathy, openness, and empowered independence, unlike past leadership philosophies that saw technology only as a facilitator.

It suggests that current leadership effectiveness results from human–artificial intelligence collaboration, whereby people establish ethical vision and relationship sensitivity while robots manage complex data. It follows that leadership effectiveness today comes from human capability as well as co-created capability.

Modern leadership is more about collaborative creation and not control. Agentic Leadership reminds us that artificial intelligence is meant to assist us, rather than replace us. Tomorrow's leaders will have to shape environments in which people and artificial intelligence actually interact, not only manage teams. This mix of humanity and flexibility will distinguish great leaders. AI has grown from a calculator, as it can now decide, adapt, and act without waiting for command.

Agentic AI is a model, originally presented by Kashif Zaman in 2024, that reframes artificial intelligence as an amplifier of leadership rather than as a replacement.

> Artificial intelligence can decipher patterns but it cannot understand fear, hesitation, or silence yet. Empathy hence stays human still.
>
> Trust needs oversight: AI can act, but our responsibility is still fairness and ethics.
>
> Direction is still driven by purpose: AI can help to maximize efficiency, but leaders have to decide why the work is worthwhile.

Future leaders are those who work with artificial intelligence, rather than just apply it.

4.3.2 Hypothetical agentic leadership mini-cases

In healthcare, agentic leadership may comprise a hospital administrator establishing high-level patient outcome targets while agentic artificial intelligence driven by LLMs and reinforcement learning automatically tracks EHR data, forecasts readmission risks, simulates treatment path, and handles normal scheduling—alerting physicians only for ethical subtleties or abnormalities. Should artificial intelligence biases appear, the leader stresses empathy (e.g., family counseling) and aim equitable treatment, showing ethical intelligence and proactive behavior.

In fintech, while agentic systems sense market events, develop hedging plans, carry out trades, reflect on results, and orchestrate transparency reports, a risk manager defines boundaries for compliance. People interact on unclear rules and establish relational trust with customers.

These examples show the scalability of agentic leadership. AI manages multistep reasoning, lowering cognitive burden. Leaders retain human-centric vision, addressing scaling issues including data quality and trust (Bandi et al., 2025).

4.4 Comparative Analysis.

This table below highlights complementarity of the models. No single model suffices alone, Effective AI-augmented leadership integrates elements dynamically, with adaptive and agentic approaches addressing speed/complexity gaps in traditional models.

Table 2. Comparing the different models of Leadership

Leadership Model	Core Focus in AI Era	Strengths in Human-AI Symbiosis	Limitations in AI Context	Key Leadership Implications
Transformational	Visionary inspiration and intellectual stimulation	Motivates collective ambition; legitimizes disruption through shared purpose	Can become leader-centric; struggles with rapid, data-driven pivots without augmentation	Use AI for personalized motivation and scenario modeling to amplify inspirational reach while grounding vision in evidence
Servant	Prioritizing follower growth, well-being, and ethical care	Preserves psychological safety and dignity; reframes AI as "servant ally" to free humans for higher contributions	Risk of over-emphasizing consensus in fast-paced environments; may slow decisive action	Configure AI ethically to enhance empathy at scale (e.g., sentiment analysis) while leaders anchor moral responsibility
Adaptive	Mobilizing for complex challenges; agility and learning	Enables rapid response to AI-driven volatility; fosters continuous experimentation and resilience	Demands high cognitive load; can overlook long-term ethical anchoring without safeguards	Treat resistance as signal; orchestrate hybrid loops where AI accelerates adaptation and humans ensure contextual alignment
Agentic	Co-creating with autonomous AI partners; high-level orchestration	Extends reach via proactive, multi-step reasoning; scales empathy and execution	Over-reliance risks diminished human agency or ethical drift; requires calibrated trust	Leaders set boundaries and purpose; AI handles coordination while humans drive empathy, creativity, and ethical vision

Source: Compiled by authors

Table 2 reveals no single leadership model suffices in the AI era; effective augmentation requires dynamic integration. Visionary inspiration from transformational leadership inspires aspiration but runs the danger of leader-centrism. Leaders may use scenario modeling to base their vision in facts and so increase reach by not relying on artificial intelligence augmentation for data-driven changes.

By redefining artificial intelligence as a servant ally, servant leadership helps to preserve dignity while also improving empathy on a large scale by means of sentiment analysis and grounding moral accountability.

Adaptive leadership accelerates quick reaction to volatility but requires protections against ethical drift; AI speeds experimentation with humans guaranteeing alignment. Agentic leadership stretches orchestration via proactive AI collaborators, scale execution while humans lead purpose and empathy—essential as over-reliance causes reduced agency.

High achievers show this fusion and are three times more likely to redesign processes and show senior ownership by combining adaptive agility with agentic scaling (Singla et al., 2025). Implications include hybrid loops(e.g., Transformational spark ignites collective ambition, servant care mitigates resistance, adaptive pivoting handles uncertainty, and agentic coordination executes at speed). Organizations that master this complementarity produce transformational results and transform artificial intelligence from tool to symbiotic partner.

5. LEADING CHANGE AND MANAGING DIGITAL RESISTANCE

AI challenges expert identities and meaning-making processes. Resistance sometimes results from threats to signature abilities, fairness in computerized judgments, loss of narrative control like experts opposing tools that automate judgement defining their expertise/moral goal.

5.1 Frameworks for AI-Led Organizational Change

Traditional change frameworks like Kotter's 8-step model were designed for straight, human-paced change. Generative AI has rendered them obsolete in their original form, while simultaneously offering the means of their reinvention (Jacobs, 2025) .

A new generation of AI-augmented change models has emerged that compresses Kotter's steps from months to days and replaces static communication with adaptive, personalized messaging.

Generative artificial intelligence most commonly maps straight onto every traditional stage:

Shows how rivals' artificial intelligence advantage creates urgency by means of real-time scenario modelling
Build guiding coalitions via AI-matched skill-and-motivation profile.
Create vision with jointly authored artificial intelligence stories, and
Use hyper-personalized micro-videos made for each employee segment,
Empower action,
Produce short-term victories,
Integrate gains, and
Anchor fresh approaches

Empirical proof is quite remarkable. AI simultaneously identifies what works, and scales winning variations before resistance can organize, changing the dynamics of transformation from sequential waterfall to parallel sprints by running thousands of micro-change tests.

A self-accelerating transformation engine is created to change process itself, one that learns faster than the people experiencing it. The critical leadership task becomes curation from control, deciding which AI-generated interventions align with human values and merit amplification.

5.2 Identifying and Addressing Digital Resistance

Digital resistance in the AI era is rarely simple technophobia. Treating opposition as resistance is a leadership strategy that always fails. Effective approaches reframe resistance as diagnostic intelligence—the organization's early-warning system for misaligned change.

Golgeci et al., (2025) presents AI resistance as a multi-dimensional idea encompassing workers' anxieties, inefficiencies, and aversion to artificial intelligence. They propose a framework depicting a process. Causes/antecedents lead to manifestations of resistance, then to relieving mechanisms and results. It offers means of reducing resistance, through artificial intelligence accessibility, human-artificial intelligence augmentation, and artificial intelligence-technology legitimation,

According to them, individual, technical, and institutional elements all contribute to resistance as under:

Worries about job loss or less independence.
Insufficient openness in artificial intelligence (black box problems).
Perceived challenges to human uniqueness or professional identity.
Not enough help or education.
Ethical issues include fairness and bias.

The process framework of the article stresses proactive resistance reduction and confrontation by means of:

Creating organizational legitimacy (Showing value/transparency for artificial intelligence to legitimize it via communication, ethical governance, and leadership backing.)
AI accessibility (Making artificial intelligence cognitively and physically accessible),
Human-AI augmentation (Positioning AI as a complement/enhancer to human capabilities rather than a replacement)

Employees move to constructive contribution from defensive withholding, when they see their problems are treated seriously rather than ignored.

5.3 Best Practices in Change Management

Upskilling in the face of opposition calls for going beyond simple training programmes to very personalized learning journeys arranged by AI itself. Empirical data shows that generative artificial intelligence can generate leadership choices evaluated as more useful and practical than those from humans in blind tests, yet disclosure of the part AI plays often leads to lower acceptance, underlining identity-related resistance in AI-driven organizational change (Stock-Homburg, 2025) .

They expressly tackles challenges in AI-augmented leadership against resistance and identity. The results reveal that in blind evaluations, knowledge workers frequently prefer AI leadership for practicality and do not view it as subpar. But, overt disclosure of AI engagement causes a preference change toward human leaders.

Case studies of digital-journey reveal consistent patterns. Successful transformations have five non-negotiable behaviors:

(1) Every member of the C-suite must finish the same artificial intelligence training as frontline employees in executive role modelling.
(2) "Teach-back" demands whereby students right away use newly acquired knowledge to actual corporate challenges,
(3) Peer responsibility groups as opposed to personal tracking,
(4) Ongoing rather than milestone certification, and
(5) Incorporation of upskilling into performance goals so that learning is viewed as career advancement rather than remedial work (Jacobs, 2025); Brennan, 2024) .

Norton (2023) examines how Amazon employs leadership principles to promote accountability, efficiency, and high performance by means of structured systems to convert vision into results. Amazon's culture is based in its 16 Leadership Principles supported by five key mechanisms.

Amazon's development of its famous "Working Backwards" process, now the global gold standard perfectly shows AI-enhanced change management in action. The Working Backwards approach starts with the ideal client experience and goes backwards to determine what to construct.

Its main tool is the PR/FAQ, (Press Release/Frequently Asked Questions), a six-page narrative co-drafted with a randomly chosen frontline employee. This written story created before any designing, costing, or building work makes teams make their ideas clearer, question their assumptions, and make sure that they are putting the customer first.

Incorporation of generative artificial intelligence for draft versions, scenario simulations, and bias checks has reduced development cycles while preserving human oversight in 2025. For large-scale AI releases (e.g., inside agentic tools for supply chain), teams employ artificial intelligence to produce hyper-personalized micro-communications matching Kotter stages, hence lowering opposition through openness.

By ensuring customer/employee points of view to guide AI projects from the beginning resolves resistance by demanding disciplined iteration, early feedback, and truth-seeking in meetings, minimizing ego-driven ideas and generating group buy-in through customer-focused narratives instead than top-down imposition.

High performers like Amazon scale such practices enterprise-wide, redesigning workflows to embed AI as amplifier rather than replacement, aligning with McKinsey findings where workflow redesign is a key differentiator (Singla et al., 2025).

Using responses from 1,993 respondents spanning 105 countries McKinsey analysis of 2025 emphasizes extensive use of AI (88% of businesses use it often in at least one activity, up from 78% the previous year) fueled mostly by generative AI and emerging agentic AI, yet ongoing obstacles in scaling beyond pilots to enterprise-wide effect and value capture.

Though almost all businesses (88%) have adopted artificial intelligence, most are still in early stages without enterprise scaling, maybe showing resistance to identity changes and workflow adjustments. High performers counteract this by senior leader ownership and ambitious transformation targets, facilitating easier navigation of AI-driven change (Singla et al.,2025).

One trend is now clear across industries. Companies who see resistance as intelligence instead of rebellion not only lower opposition, but turn it into the main source of competitive edge.

5.4 Sustaining Long-Term Transformation

Maintaining AI-driven change calls for incorporating adaptability into the fabric of the company. Change is seen by the most adaptable companies as a constantly operating system rather than as a project with a completion date.

They institutionalize artificial intelligence inside the change process itself, sentiment engines that spot developing fatigue, predictive models that predict resistance pockets, and automatic celebration systems that support wanted behaviours at scale.

From a worldwide point of view, cultural background influences sustainability approaches. While North American businesses sometimes achieve velocity through rivalry and gamification (Zarifis, 2025). The McKinsey "Superagency in the Workplace" report (Mayer et al., 2025) provides compelling evidence that employees are far more ready for AI integration than leaders perceive, framing "superagency" as human amplification rather than replacement.

Generative AI (gen AI) can create "superagency"—a state where individuals, amplified by AI, dramatically enhance their creativity, productivity, and positive impact in a human-led, symbiotic partnership with technology. Employees self-report using generative AI for at least 30% of daily work at ~12–13% (three times leaders' estimate of 4%). Further, only 20% of leaders. expect this level within a year, compared to 47% of employees.

With 94% employee familiarity and high trust in employers (71%) for ethical deployment, resistance often stems from leadership misperception rather than workforce fears. As the report states: "C-suite leaders estimate that only 4 percent of employees use gen AI for at least 30 percent of their daily work, when in fact that percentage is three times greater, as self-reported by employees."

Leaders overestimate the barriers and underestimate actual usage (3× gap). This supports arguments that resistance often originates from leadership caution or misperception, not workforce identity fears framing AI as "superagency" (human amplification) reduces dehumanization concerns and fosters adaptive identities.

This perception gap highlights leadership as the primary barrier to maturity—only 1% of organizations reach high maturity, despite 92% planning increased investments. This gap shows how misaligned leadership can accidentally encourage resistance and identity issues in AI-driven change, whereas an inspiring "superagency" strategy reduces such risks by presenting AI as a human enhancer. Leaders must close these gaps by training, alignment, and bold deployment, reframing AI as enhancer to foster adaptive identities and reduce dehumanization concerns.

Superagency positions AI as a partner empowering creativity, productivity, and impact in human-led symbiosis. Employees anticipate significant transformation (nearly universal in two years), with optimists (59%) driving adoption. (Mayer et al., 2025). Resilience is ultimately measured by the organization's capacity to initiate the next transformation before the current one is complete

6. GOVERNANCE, ACCOUNTABILITY, AND MATURITY IN HUMAN-AI SYMBIOSIS

Compulsory human-in-the-loop for high-stakes decisions (e.g., career or customer-impacting), annual independent algorithmic audits, and Open disclosure of training data provenance are necessary for effective governance and accountability to make maturity in human symbiosis.

Employee confidence in company handling stresses the importance of accountability in sustainable symbiosis. Suggested actions include integrating artificial intelligence to magnify agency without compromising human supervision in creative/ethical domains, giving top priority to training, and closing perceptual gaps.

Leaders who actively promote ethical scaling enable Human-AI symbiosis to grow maturity. While investment surges, true maturity remains unusual (1%), according to McKinsey studies; governance maturity depends on leadership ownership, training expenditure, and trust-building mechanisms to allow 'superagency', where artificial intelligence enables human creativity and productivity under accountable, human-centered frameworks (Mayer et al., 2025).

Companies must create strong accountability systems in order to promote maturity in Human-AI symbiotic; Stock-Homburg (2025) demonstrates that although GenAI outperforms humans in perceived usefulness across leadership styles, sustainable symbiosis calls for transparent governance to counteract trust erosion upon revelation and maintain human accountability in relational domains.

Strong governance is necessary to advance maturity in Human-AI symbiosis. McKinsey's 2025 poll reveals that firms handling more hazards (average four) and great performers excel by means of human validation, leadership responsibility, and workflow redesign. This ensure responsible integration whereby AI drives innovation while preserving human oversight in relational and ethical dimensions (Singla et al., 2025).

Just about 6% of those who qualify as high performers (≥5% EBIT impact and notable value) are three times more likely to show senior ownership, restructure processes, and scale agents. Adoption of agentic artificial intelligence looks promising. 62% are experimenting, 23% are scaling in at least one function but just in one or two functions, with no function having more than 10% scaled deployment.

High performers stand out due to transformational intent (3.6 times more likely), workflow changes (almost three times), and leadership support, which is in line with governance maturity needs. Barriers comprise risk reduction with average four risks managed, one-third report on inaccuracy effects, and erratic scaling.

6.1 Variations in Cross-Cultural

Cross-cultural aspects shape resistance and AI maturity. While international surveys reveal somewhat better employee support outside the US, with comparable perception gaps, North American companies usually push velocity via competition/gamification (Zarifis, 2025).

Investments in industries like healthcare and technology top public sector expectations. To speed symbiotic maturity, leaders have to customize governance, by stressing ethical trust in societies with high trust.

6.2. Recommendations for Leaders and Organizations

- Before acting on every AI-influenced recommendation, set up weekly "decision-hygiene" rituals whereby it is stress-tested against clearly stated corporate values.
- Redesign leadership development around hybrid intelligence competencies: Prompt engineering, bias detection, ethical override discipline, and narrative translation of probabilistic outputs into human meaning
- Institutionalize overlapping change: Use AI itself to identify developing tiredness and resistance and start the following transformation wave while the current one is still building speed.
- Establish varied red-team councils with actual veto capability over important artificial intelligence implementation to guarantee that the voices most impacted by automation are likewise most powerful in its management.

  Organisations should go beyond voluntary responsible-AI statements at policy level to enforceable internal regulation.

Compensation structures should reward ethical stewardship by including significant bonuses for documented overrides of profitable but biased recommendations. Only when leaders are materially incentivized to protect human dignity will responsible innovation move from aspiration to default practice.

7. CONCLUSION

The preceding sections have followed a logical curve: AI-assisted leadership represents a radical re-architecture of power, knowledge, and ethical responsibility rather than only a minor enhancement to current practice.

From helpful instruments to agentic partners that expand human reach while also requiring fresh fields of calibrated trust and purposeful overriding, decision-making models have developed. AI-augmented leadership is essentially a total restructuring of moral responsibility, awareness, and power. Decision models go from supportive to agentic partners, which call for calibrated trust and conscious overrides.

Treating improvements as chances for experimentation, adaptive leadership rises as the meta-competence for non-linear acceleration. Through iterative, artificial intelligence-backed cycles, transformational vision inspires group ambition, servant care preserves dignity, and reinvented change architectures transform opposition into knowledge.

These parts fit together: complex models need flexible pivoting; adaptive legitimacy needs transformational spark and servant empathy; synergies scale only in perpetual-motion structures based on ethics—transparency, human responsibility, and preservation of moral imagination, empathy, and narrative sense-making.

Leaders have to promise dual fluency (technical questioning and moral judgment), weekly stress-testing of AI outputs that are aligned with values, development of hybrid intelligence (prompt engineering, bias identification, ethical override), permanent human-exclusive zones for identity-forming activities, overlapping change cadences, and different councils with veto power.

Companies following AI-augmented leadership could implement adjusted PR/FAQ procedures to synthesize adaptive strategies, starting from transformed stakeholder (e.g., employee/customer) experiences and working backward to guarantee ethical, efficient AI integration under ambiguity.

McKinsey's 2025 results offer a synthesis anchor. Although 88% embrace AI, actual value comes in the roughly 6% of high performers who seek transformation via leadership commitment, workflow modification, and risk-mitigated governance, thus recommending companies give this top priority for adaptive strategies.

Mayer et al. (2025) present a compelling vision of "superagency" as the aim of Human-AI symbiosis in synthesizing AI-augmented leadership; employees are ready and utilizing AI far more than leaders understand, recommending urgent leadership action via training, alignment, and bold deployment to maximize productivity while maintaining human centrality. Future directions should investigate means for sustaining this empowerment throughout maturity stages and changing AI capabilities.

At the organizational level, legal rules and human-in--loop mandates, provenance disclosure, audits, must promote ethical stewardship by means of pay linked to responsible overrides. Success measures not efficiency alone but human flourishing, making people more creative, connected, and purposeful. Organizations that master this do not diminish the human spirit, but liberate it for imagining futures worth inheriting together.

7.1 Guidelines for Future Research

By training and alignment, integrate superagency consequences: employees' readiness (3x usage gap) pushes leaders to act quickly to release $4.4 trillion productivity potential while maintaining human centrality.

Longitudinal studies tracking superagency development across maturity levels and agentic breakthroughs should be the focus of upcoming research. Key areas include agentic risks (e.g., hallucinations in multistep reasoning leading to bad decisions), cross-cultural scaling challenges; empirical studies of hybrid models (e.g., agentic + servant elements), and long-term effects on psychological contracts in light of job changes (92 million displaced vs. 170 million created by 2030). Such studies would improve symbiotic structures for long-lasting change.

7.2 Final Reflections

Future leadership is fundamentally both human and machine. It is neither entirely human nor completely computer generated. The organisations whose leaders understand the skill of symbiotic intelligence, those who can perform artificial cognition with the same subtle authority that an orchestra conductor brings to great soloists, are those that will define the next decade.

The best form of leadership in this future is making sure that computers never out-think mankind's most fundamental ideals, not out-thinking computers. Properly executed, artificial intelligence-assisted leadership frees the human spirit for its most crucial task: dreaming up futures worth living in, together. It does not degrade it.

History will recall the leaders who used those parameters to make people more human, businesses more equitable, and the future worth inheriting when it reflects on this decade. It will not remember the models with the most parameters. AI will handle intelligence and humans must master orchestration. Orchestration requires responsibility, structure, respect for process and calm execution under pressure

REFERENCES

Afroogh, S., Akbari, A., Malone, E., Kargar, M., & Alambeigi, H. (2024). Trust in AI: Progress, challenges, and future directions. *Humanities & Social Sciences Communications, 11*(1), 1568. Advance online publication. DOI: 10.1057/s41599-024-04044-8

Antonakis, J. (2012). Transformational and Charismatic Leadership. In Day, D. V., & Antonakis, J. (Eds.), *The Nature of Leadership* (pp. 256–288). Sage Publications.

Arora, M. (2024). Influence of artificial intelligence on organizational leadership: Challenges and opportunities. International Journal of Research in Human Resource Management, 6(2), 06–10. DOI: 10.33545/26633213.2024.v6.i2a.194

Avolio, B. J., & Bass, B. M. (1995). Individual consideration viewed at multiple levels of analysis: A multilevel framework for examining the diffusion of transformational leadership. *The Leadership Quarterly*, *6*(2), 199–218. DOI: 10.1016/1048-9843(95)90035-7

Badhurunnisa, M., & Dass, V. S. (2023). Challenges and opportunities involved in implementing AI in workplace. *International Journal for Multidisciplinary Research*, *5*(6). Advance online publication. DOI: 10.36948/ijfmr.2023.v05i06.10001

Bajwa, J., Munir, U., Nori, A., & Williams, B. (2021). Artificial intelligence in healthcare: Transforming the practice of medicine. *Future Healthcare Journal*, *8*(2), e188–e194. DOI: 10.7861/fhj.2021-0095

Bandi, A., Kongari, B., Naguru, R., Pasnoor, S., & Vilipala, S. V. (2025). The rise of Agentic AI: A review of definitions, frameworks, architectures, applications, evaluation metrics, and challenges. *Future Internet*, *17*(9), 404. DOI: 10.3390/fi17090404

Barabadi, E., Fotuhabadi, Z., Arghavan, A., & Booth, J. R. (2026). Comparing AI and human moral reasoning: Context-sensitive patterns beyond utilitarian bias. *Frontiers in Artificial Intelligence*, *8*, 1710410. Advance online publication. DOI: 10.3389/frai.2025.1710410

Bevilacqua, S., Ferraris, A., Matzler, K., & Kuděj, M. (2026). Strategic leadership at high altitude: Investigating how AI affects the required skills of top managers. *Journal of Business Research*, *205*, 115878. DOI: 10.1016/j.jbusres.2025.115878

Bolden, R. (2011). Distributed leadership in organizations: A review of theory and research. *International Journal of Management Reviews*, *13*(3), 251–269. DOI: 10.1111/j.1468-2370.2011.00306.x

Braganza, A., Chen, W., Canhoto, A., & Sap, S. (2021). Productive employment and decent work: The impact of AI adoption on psychological contracts, job engagement and employee trust. *Journal of Business Research, 131*, 485–494. DOI: 10.1016/j.jbusres.2020.08.018

Breidbach, C. F. (2024). Responsible algorithmic decision-making. *Organizational Dynamics, 53*(2), 101031. DOI: 10.1016/j.orgdyn.2024.101031

Brennan, R. (2024, October 16). The Future of Adaptive Leadership: Emerging Trends. Robert Brennan - Facilitation, Training & Coaching Services. https://robertbrennan.com.au/the-future-of-adaptive-leadership-emerging-trends/

Cariaga, R. (2025). Human-AI Collaboration in Decision-Making, Creativity, and Productivity: Systematic review. SSRN Electronic Journal. DOI: 10.2139/ssrn.5378095

Dwivedi, Y. K., Hughes, L., Ismagilova, E., Aarts, G., Coombs, C., Crick, T., Duan, Y., Dwivedi, R., Edwards, J., Eirug, A., Galanos, V., Ilavarasan, P. V., Janssen, M., Jones, P., Kar, A. K., Kizgin, H., Kronemann, B., Lal, B., Lucini, B., & Williams, M. D. (2021). Artificial Intelligence (AI): Multidisciplinary perspectives on emerging challenges, opportunities, and agenda for research, practice and policy. *International Journal of Information Management, 57*, 101994. DOI: 10.1016/j.ijinfomgt.2019.08.002

Fantoni, M. J., & Sasmita, J. (2025). Leadership in the era of Artificial Intelligence: Challenges, opportunities, and strategic transformation. *Journal Corner of Education Linguistics and Literature*, *5*(2), 220–232. DOI: 10.54012/jcell.v5i2.612

Felin, T., & Holweg, M. (2024). Theory is all you need: AI, human cognition, and causal reasoning. *Strategy Science*, *9*(4), 346–371. DOI: 10.1287/stsc.2024.0189

Golgeci, I., Ritala, P., Arslan, A., McKenna, B., & Ali, I. (2025). Confronting and alleviating AI resistance in the workplace: An integrative review and a process framework. *Human Resource Management Review*, *35*(2), 101075. DOI: 10.1016/j.hrmr.2024.101075

Gordin Yoskovitz, G., & Schechter, C. (2024). Agentic leadership: Principals' agency during the COVID-19 crisis. *Leadership and Policy in Schools*, *23*(4), 920–937. DOI: 10.1080/15700763.2023.2261039

Greenleaf, R. K. (1977). *Servant leadership: A journey into the nature of legitimate power and greatness*. Paulist Press.

Gyöngyössy, N. M., Török, B., Farkas, C., Lucaj, L., Menyhárd, A., Menyhárd-Balázs, K., Simonyi, A., Patrick, V. D. S., Ződi, Z., & Lőrincz, A. (2024). Assistive AI for augmenting human decision-making. arXiv (Cornell University). https://doi .org//arxiv.2410.14353DOI: 10.48550

Hackl, C. (2025, June 17). Ai as a servant leader: A new paradigm for human-centered transformation: Smartlab - The Digital Experience Platform. AI as a Servant Leader. https://smartlabservices.com/blog-posts/ai-as-a-servant-leader-a-new-paradigm-for -human-centered-transformation

Hambrick, D. C., & Mason, P. A. (1984). Upper echelons: The organization as a reflection of its top managers. *Academy of Management Review, 9*(2), 193–206. DOI: 10.2307/258434

Hao, M., Lv, W., & Du, B. (2020). The Influence Mechanism of Authentic Leadership in Artificial Intelligence Team on Employees' Performance. *Journal of Physics: Conference Series, 1438*(1), 012022. DOI: 10.1088/1742-6596/1438/1/012022

Haque, A. (2025). Responsible artificial intelligence (AI) in healthcare: A paradigm shifts in leadership and strategic management. *Leadership in Health Services (Bradford, England), 38*(4), 644–656. DOI: 10.1108/LHS-01-2025-0018

Hasanah, U., & Rozi, F. (2025). Adaptive leadership in the dynamics of business in the digital era. *International Journal of Public Administration and Policy, 1*(2), 39–44. DOI: 10.58290/ijpap.v1i2.138

Holzinger, A., Saranti, A., Angerschmid, A., Finzel, B., Schmid, U., & Mueller, H. (2023). Toward human-level concept learning: Pattern benchmarking for AI algorithms. *Patterns (New York, N.Y.), 4*(8), 100788. DOI: 10.1016/j.patter.2023.100788

Huang, M.-H., & Rust, R. T. (2018). Artificial intelligence in service. *Journal of Service Research, 21*(2), 155–172. DOI: 10.1177/1094670517752459

Ilyas, M. (2022). Augmented intelligence for advancing healthcare. Journal of Systemics, Cybernetics, and Informatics. *Journal of Systemics, Cybernetics and Informatics, 20*(6), 13–19. DOI: 10.54808/JSCI.20.06.13

Iqbal, A., Ahmad, M. S., & Nazir, T. (2022). Does servant leadership predict innovative behaviour above and beyond transformational leadership? Examining the role of affective commitment and creative self-efficacy. *Leadership and Organization Development Journal, 44*(1), 34–51. DOI: 10.1108/LODJ-01-2022-0016

Islami, X., & Mulolli, E. (2024). Human-artificial intelligence in management functions: A synergistic symbiosis relationship. *Applied Artificial Intelligence, 38*(1), 2439615. DOI: 10.1080/08839514.2024.2439615

Jacobs, S. (2025). 5 innovation trends reshaping leadership in 2025. Sheri Jacobs Consulting. https://www.sherijacobs.com/blog/5-innovation-trends-reshaping-leadership-in-2025

Kaggwa, S., Eleogu, T. F., Okonkwo, F., Farayola, O. A., Uwaoma, P. U., & Akinoso, A. (2024). AI in Decision Making: Transforming Business Strategies. *International Journal of Innovation and Scientific Research*, *X*(XII), 423–444. DOI: 10.51244/IJRSI.2023.1012032

Kim, B. J., & Kim, M. J. (2024). What an artificial intelligence-induced job insecurity shapes knowledge dynamics: The mitigating role of artificial intelligence self-efficacy. *Journal of Innovation & Knowledge*, *9*(4), 100590. DOI: 10.1016/j.jik.2024.100590

Korteling, J. E., Van De Boer-Visschedijk, G. C., Blankendaal, R. M., Boonekamp, R. C., & Eikelboom, A. R. (2021). Human- versus Artificial Intelligence. *Frontiers in Artificial Intelligence*, *4*, 622364. DOI: 10.3389/frai.2021.622364

Kumar, A. (2024). Redefining Finance: The Influence of Artificial Intelligence (AI) and Machine Learning (ML). *Transactions on Engineering and Computing Sciences*, *12*(4), 59–69.

Ladkin, D., & Patrick, C. (2022). Critiques of transformational leadership. *Leadership*.

Lee, M. K. (2018). Understanding perception of algorithmic decisions: Fairness, trust, and emotion in response to algorithmic management. *Big Data & Society*, *5*(1), 2053951718756684. Advance online publication. DOI: 10.1177/2053951718756684

Leong, L., & Fischer, R. (2011). Transformational leadership in diverse contexts. *Journal of Cross-Cultural Psychology*.

Liddicoat, A. J., & Taylor-Leech, K. (2021). Agency in language planning and policy. *Current Issues in Language Planning*, *22*(1-2), 1–18. DOI: 10.1080/14664208.2020.1791533

Mayer, H., Yee, L., Chui, M., & Roberts, R. (2025, January 28). Superagency in the workplace: Empowering people to unlock AI's full potential. Superagency in the workplace: Empowering people to unlock AI's full potential. https://www.mckinsey.com/capabilities/tech-and-ai/our-insights/superagency-in-the-workplace-empowering-people-to-unlock-ais-full-potential-at-work#

Mohammed, A., Bambale, S. A., & Abdullahi, U. (2025). AI-Driven Decision-Making in Leadership: Balancing automation and human judgment for optimal organizational performance. *Journal of Economics and Administrative Sciences*, *31*(150), 129–141. DOI: 10.33095/hv149002

Nielsen, M. B., Hetland, J., Harris, A., Notelaers, G., Gjerstad, J., & Einarsern, S. V. (2022). The impact of follower leadership position on transformational leadership as moderator of the association between work-related ambiguity and job satisfaction. *Frontiers in Psychology, 13*(970887), 970887. https://www.frontiersin.org/articles/10.3389/fpsyg.2022.970887. DOI: 10.3389/fpsyg.2022.970887

Northouse, P. G. (2021). *Leadership: Theory and practice* (9th ed.). Sage Publications.

Norton, A. (2023, April 18). How Amazon uses mechanisms to hone efficiency and execution: Volume One, the PRFAQ. Amazons Working Backward process for product ideation. https://www.linkedin.com/pulse/how-amazon-uses-mechanisms-hone-efficiency-execution-angus-norton

Nöthel, S., Nübold, A., Uitdewilligen, S., Schepers, J., & Hülsheger, U. (2023). Development and validation of the adaptive leadership behavior scale (ALBS). *Frontiers in Psychology, 14*, 1149371. Advance online publication. DOI: 10.3389/fpsyg.2023.1149371

Pandey, V. (2025). Leadership in the AI Era: Navigating and shaping the future of organizational guidance. *International Journal of Science and Research Archive, 15*(3), 1737–1747. DOI: 10.30574/ijsra.2025.15.3.1875

Puranam, P. (2021). Human–AI collaborative decision-making as an organization design problem. *Journal of Organization Design, 10*(2), 75–80. DOI: 10.1007/s41469-021-00095-2

Raei, M. (2018). Development and validation of the adaptive leadership with authority scale [Doctoral dissertation, Antioch University]. Antioch University Repository and Archive.

Raisch, S., & Krakowski, S. (2021). Artificial intelligence and management: The automation–augmentation paradox. *Academy of Management Review, 46*(1), 192–210. DOI: 10.5465/amr.2018.0072

Randriamiary, D. (2024). Reframing the role of leaders navigating the challenges and opportunities of tomorrow's workplace in the age of artificial intelligence. SSRN Electronic Journal. DOI: 10.2139/ssrn.4716033

Renta-Davids, A., Camarero-Figuerola, M., & Camacho, M. (2025). Navigating the challenges and opportunities of artificial intelligence in educational leadership: A scoping review. *Review of Education, 13*(2), e70101. Advance online publication. DOI: 10.1002/rev3.70101

Sherron, C. T. (2000). Psychometric development of the Adaptive Leadership Competency Profile [Doctoral dissertation, University of North Texas]. UNT Digital Library. https://digital.library.unt.edu/ark:/67531/metadc2697

Singla, A., Sukharevsky, A., Hall, B., Yee, L., Chui, M., & Balakrishnan, T. (2025, November 5). The state of AI in 2025: Agents, Innovation, and transformation. The state of AI in 2025: Agents, innovation, and transformation. https://www.mckinsey.com/capabilities/quantumblack/our-insights/the-state-of-ai

Smith, A. M., & Green, M. (2018). Artificial Intelligence and the Role of Leadership. *Journal of Leadership Studies*, *12*(3), 85–87. DOI: 10.1002/jls.21605

Steyvers, M., & Kumar, A. (2023). Three challenges for AI-Assisted Decision-Making. *Perspectives on Psychological Science*, *19*(5), 722–734. DOI: 10.1177/17456916231181102

Stock-Homburg, R. (2025). Unlocking the potential of AI in leadership: Can generative AI outperform human leaders. In Proceedings of the 58th Hawaii International Conference on System Sciences (pp. 1742-1751). https://hdl.handle.net/10125/109054

Suffiyah, Y., Ilias, M., Adami, C., Arukgoda, A., Lakshika, E., Barlow, M., Gunawardana, K., Awad, E., Dsouza, S., Kim, R., Schulz, J., Henrich, J., Shariff, A., Rahwan, I., Barocas, S., Hardt, M., Narayanan, A., Barocas, S., & Ilias, M. (2025). Navigating the Future: The impact of Artificial intelligence on adaptive and ethical leadership. *Personalia Pelajar*, *28*(1). Advance online publication. DOI: 10.17576/personalia.2801.2025.03

Tambe, P., Cappelli, P., & Yakubovich, V. (2019). Artificial intelligence in human resources management: Challenges and a path forward. *California Management Review*, *61*(4), 15–42. DOI: 10.1177/0008125619867910

Wijayati, D. T., Rahman, Z., Fahrullah, A., Rahman, M. F. W., Arifah, I. D. C., & Kautsar, A. (2022). A study of artificial intelligence on employee performance and work engagement: The moderating role of change leadership. *International Journal of Manpower*, *43*(2), 486–512. DOI: 10.1108/IJM-07-2021-0423

Xu, G., Murthy, S. V., & Jia, B. (2025). Enhancing Intuitive Decision-Making and reliance through Human–AI Collaboration: A review. *Informatics (MDPI)*, *12*(4), 135. DOI: 10.3390/informatics12040135

Yan, X. (2023). Research on financial field Integrating artificial intelligence: Application basis, case analysis, and SVR Model-Based Overnight. *Applied Artificial Intelligence*, *37*(1), 2222258. Advance online publication. DOI: 10.1080/08839514.2023.2222258

Zárate-Torres, R., Rey-Sarmiento, C. F., Acosta-Prado, J. C., Gómez-Cruz, N. A., Rodríguez Castro, D. Y., & Camargo, J. (2025). Influence of Leadership on Human–Artificial Intelligence Collaboration. *Behavioral Sciences (Basel, Switzerland), 15*(7), 873. DOI: 10.3390/bs15070873

Zarifis, A. (2025). *Leadership With AI and Trust: Adapting popular leadership styles for AI*. De Gruyter. DOI: 10.1515/9783111630137

Zayid, H., Alzubi, A., Berberoğlu, A., & Khadem, A. (2024). How do algorithmic management practices affect workforce Well-Being? A parallel moderated mediation model. *Behavioral Sciences (Basel, Switzerland), 14*(12), 1123. DOI: 10.3390/bs14121123

Zhang, J., & Zhang, Z. (2023). Ethics and governance of trustworthy medical artificial intelligence. *BMC Medical Informatics and Decision Making, 23*(1), 7. DOI: 10.1186/s12911-023-02103-9

Zhang, Q., Wang, F., Liao, G., & Li, M. (2025). How does AI trust foster innovative performance under paternalistic leadership? The roles of AI crafting and Leader's AI opportunity perception. *Behavioral Sciences (Basel, Switzerland), 15*(8), 1064. DOI: 10.3390/bs15081064

Chapter 2
AI-Augmented Leadership and Digital Decision-Making Models

Göran Roos
http://orcid.org/0000-0003-0943-3585
Adelaide University, Australia

ABSTRACT

This chapter examines AI-augmented leadership as a distinct organisational phenomenon in which artificial intelligence systems actively participate in functions such as strategic planning, resource allocation, and performance management. Drawing on leadership theory, decision science, sociotechnical systems theory, and technology ethics, the authors synthesise disparate traditions into an integrated framework for understanding distributed agency in human–AI systems. A typology of leadership configurations ranging from decision support through collaborative partnership to autonomous agency clarifies governance and accountability implications of each. The chapter analyses how centralised, distributed, and hybrid decision-making architectures shape information flows and authority distribution. Behavioural consequences including leader identity transformation, follower perceptions, and cultural adaptation are examined alongside ethical considerations such as algorithmic bias, epistemic opacity, and accountability. Implementation requirements and a future research agenda are presented.

INTRODUCTION

AI-augmented leadership refers to organisational arrangements in which artificial intelligence systems perform analytical, advisory, or autonomous functions that

DOI: 10.4018/979-8-2600-2541-3.ch002

directly influence leadership tasks such as strategic planning, resource allocation, performance management, and operational coordination. These arrangements do not merely introduce new tools into existing leadership practices; they reconfigure the fundamental architecture of decision authority, transforming leadership from a predominantly human cognitive process into a hybrid sociotechnical accomplishment distributed across human and algorithmic actors (Raisch & Krakowski, 2021; Shrestha et al., 2019). The construct of AI-augmented leadership therefore captures something qualitatively distinct from earlier conceptions of technology-mediated leadership: the algorithmic actor is not merely a passive instrument through which leaders act, but an active participant that shapes the problems presented to human judgement, constrains the solution space available, and in increasingly autonomous configurations, executes decisions without direct human involvement at the case level (Faraj et al., 2018; Kellogg et al., 2020; Raisch & Krakowski, 2021; Shrestha et al., 2019).

By leveraging AI's data-driven insights, predictive analytics, and automation capacities, leaders can make more informed decisions, anticipate market shifts, and personalise engagement with employees and stakeholders at a scale and granularity that exceeds unaided human cognitive capacity (Bankins et al., 2024; Brynjolfsson et al., 2018; Chowdhury et al., 2024; Davenport & Kirby, 2016). The productivity implications are documented across multiple sectors: AI augmentation reduces the time required for information synthesis, identifies patterns obscured by data volume or complexity, and enables consistent application of decision criteria across high-volume operational decisions (Raisch & Krakowski, 2021; Iansiti & Lakhani, 2020).

Recent causal evidence is convergent: Brynjolfsson, Li and Raymond's (2025) field experiment in a customer-support setting documented a 14 per cent average increase in problems resolved per hour from generative-AI assistance, with the gains concentrated among lower-skilled workers; Noy and Zhang's (2023) experimental study of generative AI applied to professional writing tasks recorded a 37 per cent reduction in time on task and a 0.45-standard-deviation improvement in output quality. Iansiti and Lakhani (2020) argue that the fundamental competitive shift of the current era lies not in the sophistication of individual AI systems but in the degree to which organisations successfully integrate algorithmic and human decision-making into coherent, accountable architectures. The evidence base has now extended into strategic-decision domains: Csaszar, Ketkar and Kim's (2024) study, using a leading accelerator programme and a startup competition as empirical settings, found that contemporary large language models can generate and evaluate strategies at quality levels comparable to human entrepreneurs and investors — a finding that complicates the conventional view that AI assistance is most valuable for operational rather than strategic decisions and that frames the typology question developed in the next section.

Effective augmentation requires that human leaders maintain ultimate discretion and responsibility, ensuring that technological inputs are balanced with human values, intuition, and ethical considerations (Davidovic, 2023; Floridi, 2019; Santoni de Sio & van den Hoven, 2018; Taddeo & Floridi, 2018). This balance—using AI to extend human cognition while preserving human oversight—distinguishes AI-augmented leadership from earlier forms of computerised decision support (Jarrahi, 2018). The theoretical distinctiveness of AI-augmented leadership thus rests on three properties absent from prior forms of managerial technology: adaptive learning from experience, recommendation generation under genuine uncertainty, and the distributed locus of agency that emerges when decision capacity is shared across human and computational actors (Jarrahi, 2018; Jordan & Mitchell, 2015; Raisch & Krakowski, 2021; Shrestha et al., 2019).

The imperative for AI-augmented leadership derives from escalating organisational complexity. Modern enterprises must contend with volatile markets, distributed workforces, and exponential data growth that consistently exceed the bounded rationality of individual human decision-makers (Raisch & Krakowski, 2021; Simon, 1955, 1957). Organisations that fail to augment human cognitive capacity risk decision quality degradation precisely when environmental demands are most severe. Yet the integration of AI into leadership processes is not without risk. Automation bias—the tendency to over-rely on algorithmic recommendations without adequate critical evaluation—introduces systematic error precisely through the mechanism intended to reduce it (Cummings, 2004; Parasuraman & Manzey, 2010). Epistemic opacity in machine learning systems means that leaders who cannot interrogate the reasoning behind algorithmic recommendations cannot reliably detect when those systems are operating outside their competence boundaries (Burrell, 2016; Pasquale, 2015). The governance challenge is therefore not merely technical but fundamentally organisational and ethical: how to preserve meaningful human agency and accountability within hybrid decision systems characterised by distributed authority and algorithmic complexity.

AI-augmented leadership addresses this by distributing cognitive load across human—machine networks, enabling leaders to transcend individual limitations while preserving the ethical reasoning, contextual interpretation, and value adjudication that remain distinctly human capabilities (Kolbjørnsrud, 2024). The result is a qualitatively different form of organisational intelligence—one that is neither purely human nor purely computational, but emerges from the governance of their interaction.

This chapter positions AI-augmented leadership within the broader discourse of human–AI collaboration, examining how this partnership reshapes organisational behaviour, governance frameworks, and leadership practice. The analytical approach integrates multiple theoretical traditions including leadership studies, decision science, human factors engineering, sociotechnical systems theory, organisational behaviour, and technology ethics. The chapter makes four principal contributions. First, it synthesises disparate theoretical traditions into an integrated framework for understanding distributed agency in human–AI leadership systems. Second, it develops a theoretically grounded typology of AI-augmented leadership configurations that clarifies the distinctive governance and accountability implications of each. Third, it provides a systematic analysis of digital decision-making architectures and their organisational consequences. Fourth, it identifies priority research gaps and develops a structured agenda for future empirical investigation.

These contributions are pursued through four corresponding investigative questions that structure the chapter's inquiry: How do established theoretical traditions require extension to accommodate non-human agency in leadership systems? In what ways do distinct AI augmentation configurations differ in their governance and accountability implications? How do digital decision-making architectures shape information flows, organisational performance, and the distribution of authority? And what behavioural, ethical, and implementation considerations determine whether AI augmentation delivers its intended benefits or generates new forms of organisational dysfunction? Each question is addressed substantively in the body of the chapter and synthesised in the conclusion.

The intellectual lineage of the augmentation framing in this chapter runs from Licklider's (1960) 'man-computer symbiosis' essay, which proposed that the most productive configuration of human and machine would be one in which routine analytic work was delegated to the machine while contextual judgement and goal-setting remained human, through Engelbart's (1962) augmentation framework and the long line of decision-support and knowledge-management research that followed (Sprague, 1980; Power, 2008), to the recent generative-AI inflection in which large foundation models bring previously human-only language tasks within the machine's effective reach. The chapter situates itself within this augmentation tradition rather than within the rival 'full automation' framing, under which the long-run trajectory is the substitution of human judgement by machine judgement. Brynjolfsson (2022) calls this rival framing the 'Turing Trap': the tendency in research, policy and corporate decisions to set machine performance against human performance on the same task, biasing investment toward substitution rather than augmentation even where the augmentation pathway would generate greater aggregate welfare. The reasons for the chapter's position against this trap are developed in the typology section below.

Three definitional contrasts are useful at the outset. First, AI-augmented leadership is distinct from AI-driven leadership: the former retains human decisional authority and uses AI as analytic, advisory or bounded-autonomous support, while the latter places decisional authority itself with the algorithm. Second, AI-augmented leadership is distinct from algorithmic management as that term is used in the platform-work literature (Lee et al., 2015; Möhlmann et al., 2021): algorithmic management refers to the use of algorithms to direct, evaluate and discipline workers, often at scale and with low transparency, while AI-augmented leadership is concerned with the support of leaders rather than the surveillance of subordinates — although the two practices can overlap in deployment and the EU Platform Work Directive (2024) treats them as related governance objects. Third, AI-augmented leadership is distinct from digital leadership: the latter is a broader concept encompassing leadership in digitally mediated environments without necessary reference to artificial-intelligence systems specifically.

The chapter proceeds as follows. Section 2 reviews the theoretical foundations underpinning AI-augmented leadership, examining how established frameworks in leadership theory, decision science, and sociotechnical systems theory require extension to accommodate human–AI configurations. Section 3 develops a typology of AI-augmented leadership models, articulating the distinctive characteristics, boundary conditions, and governance implications of each configuration. Section 4 analyses digital decision-making architectures, examining how centralised, distributed, and hybrid structures shape information flows, accountability, and organisational performance. Section 5 examines the behavioural and organisational consequences of AI integration, including effects on leader identity, follower perceptions, and cultural adaptation. Section 6 addresses ethical and governance considerations, with particular attention to accountability, algorithmic bias, and the regulatory landscape. Section 7 examines implementation considerations, and Section 8 develops a structured research agenda. The chapter concludes by synthesising normative, structural, and practical implications for leadership in the age of artificial intelligence.

THEORETICAL FOUNDATIONS

This section grounds the analysis in three established theoretical clusters — leadership theory, sociotechnical systems theory, and decision science — and shows how each requires extension to accommodate non-human agency. To analyse AI-augmented leadership rigorously, one must ground the phenomenon in established theoretical constructs that explain human cognition, agency, and decision-making in complex sociotechnical systems. Three clusters of theory prove especially illuminating: the evolution of leadership theory in technological contexts, established and emerging frameworks for decision-making under bounded rationality, and integrative sociotechnical frameworks that conceptualise human–AI systems as distributed configurations of agency and cognition. Each cluster contributes distinct analytical leverage; their integration generates insights unavailable from any single tradition.

Evolution of Leadership Theory in Technological Contexts

Leadership theory has progressed through successive paradigms, each revealing particular assumptions about human agency, situational contingency, and organisational structure. Trait-based approaches, originating in the 'great man' tradition, conceptualised leadership capacity as residing in stable individual characteristics (Stogdill, 1948; Judge et al., 2002). Despite their limitations, trait-based perspectives retain relevance in AI-augmented contexts: cognitive flexibility, learning agility, and epistemic humility—traits that enable leaders to calibrate reliance on algorithmic systems and interrogate their outputs—have emerged as differentiating characteristics among effective AI-augmented leaders (Chaleshtori, Ghaffari, et al., 2024a; Kolbjørnsrud, 2024; Korn Ferry Institute, 2025). The critical insight is that trait relevance has not diminished but rather shifted: the traits that matter most are those that govern human–algorithmic interaction rather than purely human-to-human influence.

Trait-based approaches further reveal a risk of algorithmic essentialism: where AI systems are deployed to identify leadership potential through pattern recognition across historical datasets, they may reify historically contingent leadership profiles into self-perpetuating selection criteria, perpetuating rather than correcting existing biases in leadership identification and development (Barocas & Selbst, 2016; Köchling & Wehner, 2020; Mehrabi et al., 2021; O'Neil, 2016).

Behavioural theories shifted analytical focus from who leaders are to what leaders do, identifying task-oriented and relationship-oriented behaviours as key dimensions of leadership effectiveness (Fleishman, 1953; Hersey & Blanchard, 1969). This taxonomy proves instructive in AI-augmented contexts, where behavioural repertoires must extend to include a third dimension: algorithmic orientation, encompassing the behaviours through which leaders engage with, interpret, challenge, and communicate about AI-generated outputs. Leaders who excel at task and relationship behaviours but lack algorithmic orientation risk becoming passive recipients of algorithmic recommendations rather than active architects of human–AI collaboration.

AI systems demonstrate markedly differential capabilities across task-oriented and relationship-oriented behavioural dimensions: whilst performing strongly in task-oriented functions such as data analysis, pattern detection, predictive modelling, and scheduling optimisation, AI systems remain substantially limited in relationship-oriented behaviours requiring empathy, moral reasoning, cultural nuance, and interpersonal trust-building (Chaleshtori, Aziz, et al., 2024b; Chaleshtori, Ghaffari, et al., 2024a; Vaccaro et al., 2024). The integration of AI-driven task execution with human-centred relationship management therefore emerges as a core competency for augmented leaders, representing a theoretically grounded division of labour between computational and distinctively human capabilities.

Situational leadership theory introduced contingency, arguing that effective leadership requires adapting style to follower readiness and task complexity (Hersey & Blanchard, 1969). The contingency principle translates directly to AI-augmented contexts, where effective human–AI collaboration requires situational calibration: matching the degree of AI autonomy to task characteristics, stakeholder sensitivity, and the AI system's demonstrated competence in the relevant domain. Inappropriate application of AI autonomy—delegating high-stakes, ethically complex decisions to autonomous systems or, conversely, applying excessive human oversight to routine high-volume tasks—generates predictable failures of either accountability or efficiency.

Distributed leadership extends the contingency tradition further, conceptualising leadership as emergent across organisational networks rather than concentrated in formal hierarchies (Gronn, 2002). AI systems function as non-human nodes within distributed leadership networks, influencing decisions through analytical authority even when formal authority remains human (Faraj et al., 2018; Kellogg et al., 2020). The distributed leadership lens reveals how AI integration creates new patterns of influence that may not align with formal organisational hierarchies: algorithmic recommendations may carry greater practical weight than those of formally senior human leaders, particularly in data-rich operational domains where AI competence is demonstrably superior. This divergence between formal and effective authority creates governance challenges that organisational design must explicitly address (Faraj et al., 2018; Shrestha et al., 2019).

The foundational conceptualisation of e-leadership was introduced by Avolio et al. (2000), representing the first systematic theorisation of leadership mediated by advanced information technology. E-leadership theory demonstrated that digital mediation alters not only the mechanics of communication but the phenomenology of leadership itself: how influence is experienced, how trust is established, and how accountability is perceived (Avolio et al., 2000; Bailey et al., 2022; Glikson & Woolley, 2020; Lee, 2018). These insights remain relevant to AI-augmented leadership but require substantial extension. Whereas e-leadership examined how technology mediates human-to-human leadership relationships, AI-augmented leadership introduces a qualitatively different challenge: technology not merely mediates but participates in leadership processes as a quasi-agent with its own decision logic, competencies, and failure modes.

The theoretical transition from e-leadership to AI-augmented leadership thus involves a qualitative shift in the role of technology within leadership processes. Earlier technologies primarily mediated communication between human actors; AI systems generate analytical outputs, make recommendations, and execute decisions autonomously—functions previously reserved for human agents. This shift demands theoretical frameworks that can accommodate non-human agency within organisational decision processes, a demand that classical leadership theories, designed to explain human social phenomena, cannot fully meet without significant extension.

Sociotechnical Systems Theory and AI-Augmented Organisations

The sociotechnical tradition begins with Trist and Bamforth's (1951) study of the Longwall method of coal-getting, which showed that mechanisation introduced into a productive system without redesign of the surrounding social organisation produced new pathologies — disrupted teams, increased absenteeism, deteriorated psychological wellbeing — even where the technology itself functioned correctly. The lesson the tradition has drawn from this for the past seventy years is that technical change and social organisation are jointly designed or they are jointly degraded. AI introduction into leadership systems sits squarely within this tradition. A complementary contemporary framing is Hutchins's (1995) distributed-cognition thesis, which treats cognition as a property of a system composed of humans, artefacts and environments rather than of an individual mind in isolation; AI-augmented leadership is, on this account, the contemporary instance of a distributed cognitive system whose units of analysis must include both human and algorithmic agents. Sociotechnical systems theory, originating with Trist and Bamforth's (1951) landmark analysis of coal-mining reorganisation, established that technological and social subsystems of work are jointly optimised rather than independently managed. The theory holds that technological design choices carry social consequences that, if unaddressed, undermine both productivity and worker wellbeing—and, conversely, that social system requirements impose constraints on technically feasible configurations. Mumford (2006) extended this tradition into the information systems domain, arguing that participative design processes—those engaging users in the specification and evaluation of sociotechnical arrangements—produce superior adoption, reduced resistance, and more contextually appropriate systems than technically imposed implementations (see also Baxter & Sommerville, 2011).

The relevance of sociotechnical systems theory to AI-augmented leadership is considerable. AI does not enter organisations as a neutral technological artefact; it reconfigures role relationships, redistributes cognitive labour, alters power dynamics, and reshapes the conditions under which meaning and accountability are produced (Faraj et al., 2018; Raisch & Krakowski, 2021). Leaders deploying AI systems without attending to these sociotechnical effects risk generating unintended consequences including skill erosion, reduced employee agency, coordination failures across human—machine boundaries, and governance vacuums where nominal oversight is insufficient to constitute *meaningful human control* (Bainbridge, 1983; Holm & Lorenz, 2022; Parasuraman & Manzey, 2010; Trist & Bamforth, 1951).Sociotechnical analysis provides a framework for designing AI deployments that optimise across both technical performance criteria and human experience dimensions, ensuring that augmentation genuinely enhances rather than merely redistributes the work of leadership (Trist & Bamforth, 1951; Mumford, 2006).

Decision-Making Theories and Digital Extensions

Herbert Simon's (1955, 1957) concept of bounded rationality established that human decision-makers operate under cognitive constraints that limit their ability to identify optimal solutions. Rather than maximising expected utility, bounded rational agents satisfice—selecting the first option that meets an acceptable threshold—because the cognitive costs of exhaustive search exceed its benefits. This framework remains foundational for understanding AI-augmented leadership, but requires extension in two directions. First, AI systems extend the effective boundary of human rationality by automating information search, pattern recognition, and option generation—enabling leaders to consider vastly larger solution spaces than unaided cognition would permit (Raisch & Krakowski, 2021; Vaccaro et al., 2024). Second, whilst AI expands informational processing capacity, it introduces new forms of boundedness. Epistemic opacity—the inability of human leaders to critically evaluate how algorithms derive their recommendations—creates a distinctive constraint on rational evaluation that differs fundamentally from the cognitive limitations Simon described (Burrell, 2016).

Epistemic opacity in contemporary machine learning systems, particularly deep neural networks, arises from the mathematical complexity of learned representations and the absence of explicit symbolic reasoning traces (Burrell, 2016; Rudin, 2019). Unlike a human expert who can articulate the reasoning behind a recommendation, a trained model produces outputs through computations that resist straightforward interpretation (Burrell, 2016; Pasquale, 2015). This opacity has profound implications for leadership decision-making: leaders who cannot interrogate algorithmic reasoning cannot reliably identify when AI systems are operating outside their competence boundaries, when training data reflects historical biases that should not govern current decisions, or when novel circumstances invalidate learned patterns. The explainability requirements embedded in the EU AI Act (European Parliament & Council of the European Union, 2024) reflect regulatory recognition that epistemic opacity is not merely a technical inconvenience but a governance challenge that undermines meaningful human control.

The field of explainable artificial intelligence (XAI) has developed substantial technical responses to the opacity problem, but with important limitations that governance frameworks must acknowledge. Rudin (2019) argues that for high-stakes decisions, post-hoc explanations of opaque black-box models are inherently inadequate because they approximate rather than reveal actual model reasoning; the appropriate response is to build interpretable models that are transparent by construction (Rudin, 2019; Barredo Arrieta et al., 2020). Barredo Arrieta et al. (2020) provide a comprehensive and widely cited taxonomy of XAI methods and their trade-offs, demonstrating that no single explanation approach is universally superior and that explanation needs vary systematically across different stakeholder groups—a finding implying that governance frameworks must specify what explanations are required for which audiences rather than treating explainability as a unidimensional technical property (Barredo Arrieta et al., 2020; Rudin, 2019). For leaders exercising oversight of AI systems in high-stakes domains, these contributions suggest that the demand for explainability must be operationalised in terms of the specific understanding required for effective oversight rather than the technically tractable outputs that AI systems most readily produce.

AI-augmented leadership thus does not straightforwardly extend human rationality; it reconfigures the cognitive boundaries within which leadership operates, replacing some constraints whilst introducing others that carry distinct and potentially more consequential properties. The epistemic relationship between human leader and algorithmic system differs qualitatively from earlier forms of decision support, in which the human could always interrogate the tool's logic; the opacity of trained models forecloses this interrogation precisely in high-stakes situations where its absence is most costly (Burrell, 2016; Pasquale, 2015).

Naturalistic decision-making (NDM) emerged from studies of experts operating in high-stakes, time-pressured environments, revealing that experienced decision-makers employ pattern recognition and mental simulation rather than systematic option comparison (Klein, 1993, 1998, 2008). The recognition-primed decision model shows that expert performance depends on accumulated experiential knowledge that enables rapid situation assessment and action selection without exhaustive deliberation. AI-augmented leadership intersects with NDM in complex ways. AI systems can support NDM by providing rapid pattern recognition across datasets that exceed expert experiential breadth (Agarwal et al., 2023; Brynjolfsson et al., 2018; Klein, 2008); simultaneously, AI delegation risks atrophying the human experiential base that makes NDM expertise possible (Endsley, 2017; Macnamara et al., 2024). Endsley (2017) argues that increasing automation can paradoxically degrade human situation awareness and decision-making capability over time, as reduced engagement diminishes the skill maintenance that expertise requires. This deskilling risk represents a long-term governance challenge that point-in-time performance assessments may systematically miss.

Empirical evidence for AI-induced skill atrophy is accumulating across multiple professional contexts. Macnamara et al. (2024) present evidence that AI assistance may accelerate skill decay among expert practitioners and hinder skill acquisition among learners—with the particularly concerning feature that this degradation may occur without performers' awareness, undermining the self-monitoring that would otherwise trigger compensatory maintenance efforts (Macnamara et al., 2024; Onnasch et al., 2014). Onnasch et al. (2014) conducted a meta-analysis of 18 experiments demonstrating the 'lumberjack effect': higher degrees of automation benefit routine performance but produce larger performance costs when automation fails, creating a systematic inverse relationship between automation-era performance gains and resilience to automation failure (Onnasch et al., 2014; Endsley, 2017). Holm and Lorenz (2022), analysing a large Danish employee dataset, found that AI enhances skills in high-skill occupations whilst increasing work-pace constraints and reducing autonomy in mid-skill occupations, with deskilling implications distributed inequitably across the skill hierarchy (Holm & Lorenz, 2022; Brynjolfsson et al., 2018). These findings collectively suggest that governance of AI-augmented leadership must include explicit mechanisms for monitoring human skill retention rather than relying solely on performance assessment during normal AI-augmented operation.

The ecological rationality programme developed by Gigerenzer and colleagues offers a complementary perspective. Rather than viewing cognitive limitations as deficiencies, ecological rationality recognises that heuristic decision-making is often effective precisely because it exploits the structure of the environment (Gigerenzer & Gaissmaier, 2011; Luan et al., 2019). Fast-and-frugal heuristics outperform complex analytical procedures in many ecologically valid conditions, particularly when data are noisy, sample sizes are small, or environmental structure is stable. This perspective complicates the assumption that AI augmentation necessarily improves leadership decision quality: in environments characterised by radical uncertainty, genuine novelty, or rapid structural change, the pattern-recognition logic of trained AI systems may be less reliable than human heuristics grounded in situational understanding (Gigerenzer & Gaissmaier, 2011; Jarrahi, 2018; Luan et al., 2019; Vaccaro et al., 2024). Effective AI-augmented leadership therefore requires not the wholesale substitution of human judgement by algorithmic processing, but the intelligent calibration of which cognitive mode—heuristic, deliberative, or algorithmic—is best suited to the decision at hand.

Sensemaking theory, developed by Weick (1995), contributes a further dimension to the theoretical framework. Sensemaking describes the process through which organisational actors construct interpretations of ambiguous situations sufficient to support action (Weick, 1995). In AI-augmented leadership contexts, algorithmic outputs become sensemaking resources that shape how leaders frame problems and interpret evidence. The danger lies in what we term algorithmic anchoring: AI-generated problem framings may constrain the interpretive diversity that effective collective sensemaking requires, channelling leadership attention toward statistically probable scenarios and away from the genuinely novel situations that often require the most urgent leadership response (Burton et al., 2020; Faraj et al., 2018). Leaders must therefore cultivate what might be termed algorithmic sensemaking literacy: the capacity to use AI outputs as inputs to sensemaking without surrendering interpretive agency to algorithmic framings.

Integrative Frameworks for Human–AI Leadership Systems

Human–AI leadership systems represent a distinct class of sociotechnical configuration characterised by distributed agency, where decision authority flows across human and algorithmic actors based on task characteristics, competence assessments, and governance design choices. Sociotechnical systems theory, developed by Trist and colleagues at the Tavistock Institute and subsequently elaborated by Baxter and Sommerville (2011), provides the conceptual foundation for analysing these configurations. The core insight of sociotechnical theory is that effective system design requires the joint optimisation of social and technical subsystems: neither can be designed in isolation without generating systemic dysfunction. In AI-augmented leadership contexts, this principle implies that AI system design, organisational structure, governance architecture, and human skill development must be approached as interdependent elements of a unified sociotechnical system rather than independent technical and managerial problems.

Shrestha et al. (2019) classify human–AI collaboration structures into three categories: full AI delegation, hybrid sequential collaboration, and aggregated human–AI decision-making. In full delegation the AI makes decisions autonomously within set parameters; in hybrid sequential structures AI provides input but humans retain decision rights; and in aggregated decision-making AI acts as a team member with its contribution weighted alongside human members. Each configuration carries distinctive governance requirements and accountability implications. Parasuraman et al. (2000) also identified four types of automation functions—information acquisition, information analysis, decision and action selection, and action implementation—each of which can be automated at different levels, providing scaffolding for systematic analysis of where human involvement adds value.

Recent scholarship has extended sociotechnical systems theory to accommodate the distinctive properties of AI systems. Kudina and van de Poel (2024) argue that AI systems require additional conceptual building blocks beyond traditional sociotechnical frameworks—specifically the recognition of artificial agents with autonomous, interactive, and adaptive properties that traditional sociotechnical artefacts do not possess—and that values co-evolve through deployment in complex sociotechnical contexts rather than being fixed at the design stage (Kudina & van de Poel, 2024; Baxter & Sommerville, 2011). Johnson and Verdicchio (2025) reinforce this position by arguing that the relationship between AI technology and organisational values is best understood through co-production: technology and society shape each other in ongoing, mutually constitutive processes that governance frameworks must monitor longitudinally rather than assess at a single design or deployment point (Johnson & Verdicchio, 2025; Raisch & Krakowski, 2021). Salwei and Carayon (2022) demonstrate through a clinical decision-support case study that performance and adoption outcomes depend critically on the alignment between AI system design, workflow integration, and the cognitive and organisational context of deployment (Salwei & Carayon, 2022; Baxter & Sommerville, 2011). These extensions have practical implications for AI governance in leadership contexts: they suggest that sociotechnical governance must be adaptive and ongoing rather than consisting of one-time compliance assessments, and that value alignment in AI-augmented systems requires continuous relational attention rather than static technical specification.

The development of integrative frameworks for human–AI leadership systems requires engagement with research on levels of automation, trust calibration, and cognitive load management. Parasuraman et al. (2000) proposed a foundational model identifying ten levels of human–machine interaction, ranging from full human control through complete automation, and four functional domains—information acquisition, information analysis, decision selection, and action implementation—across which automation can vary independently. This multidimensional framework reveals that real organisational AI deployments rarely apply uniform levels of automation across all functional domains: an organisation may employ near-autonomous AI for information acquisition and analysis whilst retaining full human authority over decision selection in high-stakes domains. The practical governance challenge is ensuring that these domain-specific automation levels are deliberately chosen and transparently governed rather than emergent from technical convenience.

Trust in automation research, synthesised by Lee and See (2004), identifies three dimensions of trustworthiness that shape human reliance on automated systems: performance (whether the system performs its intended function reliably), process (whether the system's operational logic is comprehensible and appropriate), and purpose (whether the system's goals align with the user's goals and values). Misalignment on any dimension generates trust miscalibration: over-trust when performance and purpose dimensions are visible but process opacity is high; under-trust when process opacity generates scepticism despite reliable performance. Hoff and Bashir (2015) extended this analysis by identifying dispositional trust (stable individual differences in automation trust), situational trust (context-dependent factors including task risk and time pressure), and learned trust (developed through specific experience with a particular system). This layered model has important practical implications: organisational interventions targeted at dispositional trust through training may prove less effective than interventions targeted at situational trust through interface design and governance protocols (Hoff & Bashir, 2015; Lee & See, 2004).

Calibrated trust—wherein trust levels appropriately match system capabilities—enables effective human–automation collaboration. Research consistently demonstrates tendencies toward both over-trust (automation complacency) and under-trust (automation disuse), each of which degrades system performance (Parasuraman & Riley, 1997). These tendencies are contextual phenomena shaped by interface design, task load, and experience with particular systems.

Quantitative synthesis of the trust-in-AI literature has substantially advanced this theoretical foundation. Kaplan et al. (2023) conducted the first meta-analysis targeted specifically at trust in AI as distinct from automation and robotics, examining 65 articles and finding that factors beyond AI system performance—including transparency, perceived anthropomorphism, and user AI experience—significantly shape trust independently of actual system reliability. This finding challenges performance-centred trust calibration models and implies that governance interventions targeting perceived AI characteristics may be as consequential as improvements in underlying system performance. Hancock et al. (2021) extended the meta-analytic tradition through sequential comparison of trust in robots and automation, identifying how the human–machine trust relationship evolves with accumulated interaction experience. De Visser et al. (2020) propose a theory of longitudinal trust calibration in human–robot teams that introduces the concept of relationship equity—an accumulated emotional resource predicting goodwill and collaboration readiness—alongside descriptive, predictive, and prescriptive models for trust calibration interventions across team development trajectories. Taken together, these contributions establish that trust calibration in AI-augmented leadership is a dynamic, multi-factorial, and time-varying phenomenon that static governance designs cannot adequately manage.

Recent empirical contributions substantially advance the theoretical and practical understanding of trust calibration in organisational AI contexts. Lee and See's (2004) canonical analysis frames the underlying problem as one of calibrated reliance — trust appropriately matched to AI capability — and shows that miscalibration in either direction (over-trust or under-trust) degrades joint human-AI performance. Building on this foundation, Zhang et al. (2020) established a finding of major governance significance: even when trust calibration is achieved—that is, when users correctly identify when the AI is reliable and when it is not—overall decision accuracy improves only when users possess complementary domain knowledge enabling them to identify and correct AI errors. Trust calibration is therefore necessary but insufficient; governance frameworks targeting calibration must also address the complementary capability required for humans to add value when overriding AI recommendations. Klingbeil et al. (2024) clarify a conceptual distinction with practical implications: trust is an attitudinal antecedent whilst reliance is observable behaviour, and the two frequently diverge—a finding with direct consequences for intervention design, as measures targeting subjective trust may not reliably produce appropriate reliance behaviour without accompanying situational and motivational support.

Bansal et al. (2021) identify the performance paradox in human–AI teams: whilst human–AI combinations generally outperform individual humans, they frequently underperform the AI system alone, primarily because humans fail to recognise when the AI is correct and instead override accurate recommendations (under-trust) or fail to intervene when the AI errs (over-trust). This paradox implies that the goal of human oversight is not simply to be present but to be appropriately calibrated, and that governance architecture must actively support the discriminative capability required for calibration to translate into performance benefit.

Vuori et al.'s (2026) four-configuration model maps onto the inverted-U of Figure 1, with full trust and blind trust producing the over-reliance arm, full distrust and (in part) uncomfortable trust producing the under-reliance arm, and the calibrated optimum lying between them; the authors identified four distinct trust configurations in an empirical study of organisational AI use: full trust (high cognitive and emotional trust producing productive engagement), full distrust (low on both dimensions producing disengagement), uncomfortable trust (high cognitive, low emotional trust producing data manipulation and withdrawal behaviours), and blind trust (low cognitive, high emotional trust producing uncritical acceptance). The uncomfortable trust configuration is particularly consequential for governance: employees who rationally understand AI capabilities but emotionally distrust the system may manipulate their inputs to influence AI outputs, creating feedback loops that degrade system performance and further erode institutional trust.

The concept of distributed agency, articulated by Taddeo and Floridi (2018), challenges assumptions embedded in traditional leadership theories. In an AI-augmented system, the capacity to act is not concentrated in any single human leader but distributed across multiple human and non-human actors with different capabilities, authority domains, and accountability relationships (see also Gronn, 2002). Hutchins's (1995) analysis of distributed cognition in complex organisational settings provides an empirical foundation for this theoretical position: cognitive work in complex systems is accomplished through coordinated interaction among human actors, artefacts, and structured environments rather than within individual minds. AI systems in leadership contexts function as cognitive artefacts with unprecedented analytical capacity—extending distributed cognition to a degree qualitatively different from prior technologies. The governance implication is that leadership effectiveness in AI-augmented systems cannot be assessed by evaluating individual human leaders in isolation from the algorithmic systems through which their decisions are made and implemented.

In an AI-augmented system, the distribution of agency across human and algorithmic actors creates a 'problem of many hands' regarding moral and legal responsibility: when multiple agents—human and artificial—contribute to an outcome, assigning accountability to any individual becomes analytically and normatively complex (van de Poel et al., 2012). Effective leadership in this context becomes the governance of distributed agency—ensuring that whilst execution may be shared, responsibility remains anchored to human intent and that governance structures preserve the traceability required for accountability. The leader in such a system acts as what Elish (2019) terms the 'moral crumple zone': the human actor who absorbs institutional liability for the actions of a distributed and often opaque cognitive network. This concept is not merely descriptive but normatively significant—it reveals how the design of human–AI systems can concentrate moral risk in ways that are unjust when the crumple zone human lacks genuine capacity to oversee, understand, or override the systems for which they nominally bear responsibility.

The theoretical foundations of distributed agency in AI-augmented systems have been substantially reinforced by recent work. Floridi (2025) extends the distributed morality and agency framework by proposing AI as agency without intelligence: systems that exercise functional agency in allocating actions across a sociotechnical environment without possessing the consciousness or intentionality traditionally associated with moral agents. This reconceptualisation has important implications for accountability: governance frameworks cannot assign responsibility solely to the AI system (which lacks moral agency) or entirely to individual human operators (who may lack practical control), but must distribute responsibility across the network of developers, deployers, overseers, and institutional structures that constitute the AI-augmented system (van de Poel et al., 2012; Santoni de Sio & Mecacci, 2021). Bailey et al. (2022) contribute, proposing that AI systems are best understood not as stable artefacts with fixed properties but as evolving relations constitutively entangled with organising and strategising processes—a perspective that challenges static governance frameworks and demands continuous relational governance attending to how human–AI relations evolve through deployment experience.

Automation bias—the documented tendency for human operators to favour algorithmic recommendations over contradictory evidence from other sources—represents perhaps the most consequential behavioural challenge in human–AI systems (Cummings, 2004; Parasuraman & Riley, 1997). Automation bias operates through two distinct mechanisms: omission bias (failure to notice system errors) and commission bias (uncritical acceptance of erroneous algorithmic recommendations). Parasuraman and Manzey (2010) synthesise empirical evidence demonstrating that automation bias is not a stable individual trait but a situational phenomenon that increases with cognitive load, time pressure, and confidence in system reliability. This situational sensitivity has important design implications: governance systems that reduce automation bias under normal operating conditions may prove insufficient when cognitive load peaks—precisely the high-stakes situations where bias has the greatest consequence. Effective governance architecture must therefore be calibrated to worst-case cognitive conditions rather than average operating environments.

The empirical basis for automation bias is well established across a range of contexts. Goddard et al. (2012) conducted the first systematic review of automation bias, identifying frequency, effect mediators, and mitigators; a follow-up empirical study (Goddard et al., 2014) found a 5.2% automation bias rate among NHS general practitioners in simulated prescribing scenarios, with professional experience providing no reliable protective effect. Lyell and Coiera (2017) synthesised 40 studies demonstrating that automation bias is most strongly associated with verification complexity and cognitive load rather than multitasking per se—a finding with direct implications for governance design in cognitively demanding leadership contexts. Khera et al. (2023) synthesise empirical evidence in clinical AI settings, demonstrating that automation bias in AI-assisted decision support constitutes a systemic risk when governance designs fail to structure verification obligations explicitly. In public sector settings, Alon-Barkat and Busuioc (2023) conducted three experimental studies demonstrating not only automation bias but also selective adherence: decision-makers were more likely to defer to algorithmic recommendations when decision subjects belonged to negatively stereotyped minority groups, revealing a compounding interaction between algorithmic authority and pre-existing human bias. Kupfer et al. (2023) demonstrated in an experimental study of AI-based personnel selection that informing decision-makers about potential system errors significantly increased verification intensity and reduced automation bias—providing empirical support for structured error-disclosure as a mitigation mechanism applicable to leadership decision contexts.

Several additional findings from recent empirical literature deepen understanding of automation bias mechanisms and mitigation strategies. Foundational experimental work by Skitka et al. (1999) demonstrated that participants in automated conditions made commission errors in 35% of opportunities where automated advice contradicted accurate gauge readings, with omission error rates significantly higher in automated compared to non-automated conditions—evidence that automation presence fundamentally alters monitoring behaviour independent of operator intention. A cognitive mechanism of particular relevance to AI-augmented leadership is signal dependence neglect: Agarwal et al. (2023) found that radiologists failed to recognise that their own visual analysis and the AI's analysis drew on the same underlying image data, thereby treating the AI's confirmation as an independent second opinion and double-counting correlated evidence. This mechanism suggests that performance gains from AI assistance require genuine informational complementarity between human and algorithmic inputs rather than mere co-presence of human and machine analysis.

Research on AI familiarity further reveals a Dunning–Kruger pattern: Horowitz and Kahn (2024) found a non-linear relationship between AI background knowledge and reliance tendencies, with individuals possessing moderate AI familiarity more susceptible to automation bias than either novices (who exhibit some aversion due to unfamiliarity) or highly knowledgeable practitioners (who approach calibrated reliance). This finding has direct implications for governance design: partial AI literacy may be more dangerous than none, suggesting that leadership development programmes must pursue genuine competence rather than surface-level familiarity. Agudo et al. (2024) demonstrated that the sequence in which AI recommendations are presented acts as a cognitive anchor: participants receiving AI assessments before forming their own judgements showed significantly higher compliance with incorrect AI recommendations compared to those who committed to an independent judgement first. This anchoring effect implies that decision process architecture—specifically, whether human judgement precedes or follows AI recommendation—constitutes a governance variable capable of substantially moderating automation bias without requiring changes to the underlying AI system.

Buçinca et al. (2021) provide complementary evidence that cognitive forcing functions—interface designs requiring users to commit to an independent assessment before viewing the AI recommendation—significantly reduce over-reliance relative to standard explainable AI approaches, though at the cost of user satisfaction, underscoring a governance design tension between effective bias mitigation and adoption acceptability. Figure 1 visualises the resulting Automation Bias–Trust Calibration Nexus, mapping how the calibration of human trust in AI advice traces an inverted-U relationship with decision-quality outcomes.

Figure 1. The Automation Bias–Trust Calibration Nexus

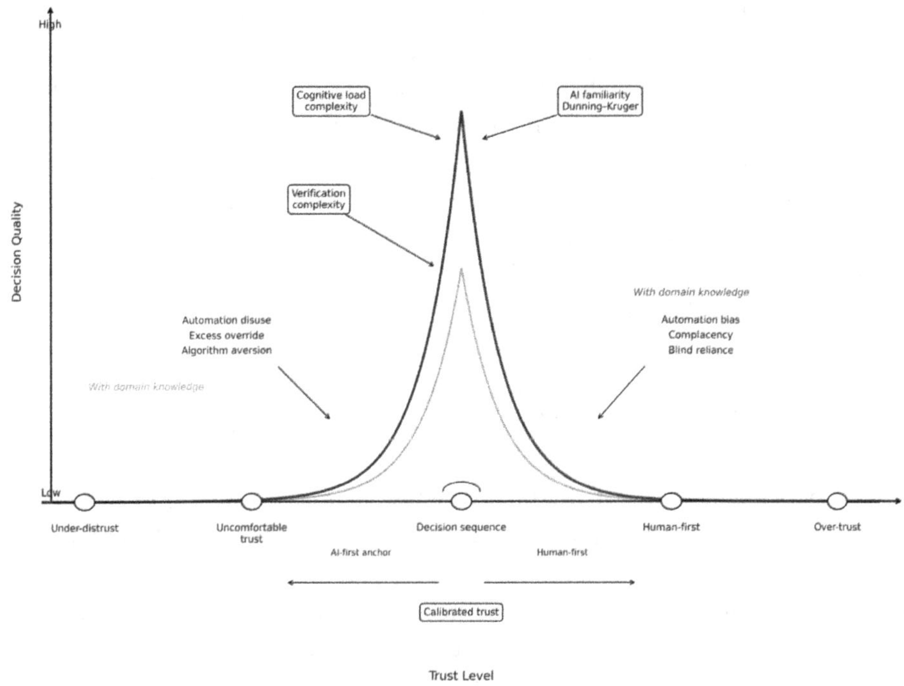

Note. Adapted to display the inverted-U relationship between trust in AI advice and decision-quality outcomes, with the optimum lying between under-reliance (algorithm aversion) and over-reliance (automation bias). The mediating role of explainability interfaces, error-recovery feedback and ecological validity of the AI signal is shown along the right-hand axis. Taken together, these theoretical traditions provide complementary lenses on AI-augmented leadership: leadership theory clarifies the contestation of authority, sociotechnical systems theory specifies the joint-optimisation problem, and decision science articulates the cognitive constraints on the human side of the augmentation relationship — all of which are extended rather than displaced by the entry of algorithmic actors.

Before settling on the typology developed in the next section, it is useful to mark the alternative framings against which the chapter's position is taken. A pure-automation framing treats AI-augmented leadership as a transitional condition on the way to full automation of leadership tasks, with the augmentation period understood as a function of present technical limitations rather than a settled equilibrium; this framing is influential in industry forecasting work but has limited empirical support in the organisational-behaviour literature and is in tension with the regulatory architecture documented in the ethics section below. An AI-as-tool framing treats AI systems as essentially passive instruments analogous to spreadsheets or dashboards, with no consequential transfer of agency from human leaders to algorithmic systems; this framing under-recognises the documented behavioural and identity effects of AI deployment surveyed in Section 4. A decision-augmentation framing — closest to the position adopted here — treats AI as a partial transfer of cognitive and sometimes decisional functions to algorithmic systems, with the consequent need for governance design that preserves meaningful human control.

An AI-as-co-worker framing, finally, foregrounds the relational and identity dimensions of human–AI collaboration and treats the AI system as a constructed organisational participant; this framing offers a useful complement to the decision-augmentation framing and is drawn on selectively in Section 4. The chapter's position is that the decision-augmentation framing best fits the empirical and regulatory landscape documented in the sections that follow, while the AI-as-co-worker framing supplies a vocabulary for the behavioural and identity dimensions that decision-augmentation alone does not address.

TYPOLOGIES OF AI-AUGMENTED LEADERSHIP MODELS

This section develops a tripartite typology — Decision-Support Tool, Collaborative Partner, and Autonomous Agent — that organises the heterogeneous landscape of AI-augmented leadership configurations by their governance and accountability implications. AI can augment leadership in qualitatively different ways depending on the role AI plays in the decision-making process, the degree of autonomy delegated to algorithmic systems, and the mechanisms through which human authority is preserved or exercised. Understanding these configurations is prerequisite to effective governance design: governance mechanisms appropriate for a decision support model are systematically insufficient for autonomous agent configurations, and governance designs calibrated to high autonomy may impose unproductive burdens on lower-autonomy deployments (Parasuraman et al., 2000; Shrestha et al., 2019). The typology developed here draws on Parasuraman et al.'s (2000) levels-of-automation framework, adapted to the specific governance and accountability demands of organisational leadership contexts. Shrestha, Ben-Menahem and von Krogh (2019) developed the canonical organisational-decision-making typology in this space, distinguishing full human-to-AI delegation, hybrid sequential decision-making, and aggregated human-AI decision-making, with each structure suited to different combinations of decision specificity, interpretability requirement, alternative-set size, decision speed and replicability. The Decision-Support Tool / Collaborative Partner / Autonomous Agent typology developed in this section is structurally aligned with Shrestha et al.'s framework while emphasising governance and accountability dimensions that their framework treats as exogenous.

These typologies are conceptually distinct but not mutually exclusive in organisational practice; organisations typically deploy multiple configurations simultaneously across different functional domains, using autonomous AI for high-volume routine decisions, collaborative AI for complex analytical tasks, and AI decision support for strategic choices requiring human accountability.

Levels of Automation in Leadership

Drawing from industrial control theory and human factors research, AI-augmented leadership can be categorised by levels of automation applied to management functions. Sheridan and Verplank (1978) introduced the foundational taxonomy that Parasuraman et al. (2000) subsequently elaborated into ten levels; for organisational leadership contexts, three analytically distinct configurations capture the most practically important variation. At the lowest level, AI functions as a decision support tool, providing information and recommendations whilst human leaders retain full decision authority and implementation responsibility. At an intermediate level, AI functions as a collaborative partner, engaging in iterative dialogue that co-shapes problem framing and solution generation. At higher levels, AI functions as an autonomous agent, executing decisions within defined parameters with human oversight operating at the meta-level of parameter setting and performance monitoring rather than individual case adjudication.

Industry practitioner surveys indicate that organisations are currently transitioning from the decision support to the collaborative partner configuration in operational domains, whilst strategic leadership largely remains at the decision support level (Kolbjørnsrud, 2024; Korn Ferry Institute, 2025; Raisch & Krakowski, 2021). This trajectory reflects the progressive maturation of AI capabilities in specific task domains alongside growing organisational confidence in AI system reliability. The governance imperative during this transition is ensuring that the expansion of AI authority is accompanied by commensurate expansion of transparency, accountability mechanisms, and human oversight capacity—rather than following technical capability growth with governance development as an afterthought.

For present purposes, a condensed five-level taxonomy captures the practically relevant range of AI integration in organisational leadership: Level 1 (Informational Support), wherein AI aggregates data without analytical interpretation; Level 2 (Decision Support), wherein AI generates options with humans retaining selection rights; Level 3 (Active Assistance), wherein AI suggests a single option for human approval; Level 4 (Management by Exception), wherein AI executes autonomously with human intervention on anomaly; and Level 5 (Autonomous Governance), the theoretical extreme of full AI autonomy. Practitioner surveys suggest that organisations are transitioning from Level 2 to Level 3 in operational domains, whilst strategic leadership largely remains at Level 1 or 2 (Korn Ferry Institute, 2025; Raisch & Krakowski, 2021). The EU AI Act's high-risk provisions impose particular requirements on Level 3 and above configurations (European Parliament

& Council of the European Union, 2024). Table 1 operationalises this five-level taxonomy by setting out, for each level, the division of labour between human and AI, an example leadership task at that level, the locus of accountability, and the most salient governance risk.

The five-level taxonomy itself extends the function-allocation framework of Parasuraman, Sheridan and Wickens (2000), who proposed that automation can be applied to four broad classes of function — information acquisition, information analysis, decision and action selection, and action implementation — and that each function can be automated to a different degree. The chapter's L1–L5 collapses this two-dimensional matrix into a single ladder for organisational decision-making applications, with the trade-off that finer distinctions in function-class automation are not represented at the cost of cleaner mapping to leadership tasks. A foundational caveat for the upper levels (L4–L5) is provided by Bainbridge's (1983) 'ironies of automation' argument: as automation reduces the operational role of the human to occasional intervention at exceptions, the human's capacity to recognise and respond to exceptions atrophies precisely because the routine practice that maintains it has been removed. The skill-atrophy risk flagged in Table 1 at L4 and L5 is therefore not a contingent failure mode but a structural property of high-automation regimes that organisational design must actively offset. Recent empirical evidence on this dynamic is provided by Gerlich (2025), who in a mixed-method study of 666 participants found a significant negative correlation between frequent AI-tool usage and critical-thinking scores, mediated by increased cognitive offloading; the effect was strongest in younger participants, consistent with the developmental hypothesis that early-career professionals are most vulnerable to the skill-formation pathway that L4–L5 automation removes.

Table 1. A Five-Level Taxonomy of AI Integration in Organisational Leadership

Level	Description	Human–AI Division of Labour	Example Leadership Task	Accountability Locus	Salient Risk
L1 - Informational Support	AI aggregates and visualises data; human formulates options and decides.	Human-led: full decision authority retained; AI as decision-input.	Strategic environmental scanning; competitor analysis dashboard.	Human leader (full).	Information overload; reliance on AI framing of the data.
L2 - Analytical Augmentation	AI generates ranked options; human selects, modifies or rejects.	Human-led with explicit AI advisory: human evaluates each AI proposal.	Resource-allocation choices; pricing decisions; portfolio prioritisation.	Human leader (full).	Anchoring on AI ranking; first-option bias.
L3 - Collaborative Decision-making	AI and human iterate jointly; decision emerges from interaction.	Joint authority within defined decision space; human retains override.	Project staffing in matrix organisations; cross-functional planning.	Joint, with human as ultimate accountable party.	Diffuse responsibility; the 'problem of many hands'.
L4 - Conditional Autonomy	AI decides within boundaries; human monitors and intervenes by exception.	AI-led under human-set rules; human authority restored at exceptions.	Dynamic pricing; supply-chain rebalancing; routine HR screening.	Human leader for boundary-setting; system designer for in-rule errors.	Skill atrophy; automation bias; delayed exception detection.
L5 - Bounded Autonomy	AI decides and acts without case-by-case human review.	AI-led; human role is design, audit and post-hoc review.	Algorithmic trading; real-time fraud blocking; some platform moderation.	System designer and organisation; attributability gap most acute.	Loss of meaningful human control; cascading errors; opacity.

Note. The taxonomy adapts Sheridan and Verplank's (1978) ten-level scale and the Parasuraman, Sheridan and Wickens (2000) refinement to organisational leadership tasks. The boundary between L3 and L4 marks the transition from human-led to AI-led decision-making and is the most consequential threshold for governance design.

AI as Decision Support Tool

In the decision support model, AI functions as an advanced analytical instrument that processes data, identifies patterns, and generates recommendations, whilst human leaders retain full decision authority and bear undivided accountability for outcomes (Parasuraman et al., 2000; Shrestha et al., 2019). This configuration preserves of leadership accountability whilst extending cognitive capacity through algorithmic processing. The AI system occupies the information acquisition and analysis functions of the Parasuraman et al. (2000) taxonomy without penetrating the decision selection or action implementation domains. Human override is therefore inherent to the model's design: every AI recommendation is a candidate for human acceptance, modification, or rejection, with the human leader retaining authority to act on reasoning that the AI system has not considered or cannot access.

The functional role of AI in this configuration is to enhance the leader's informational base and reduce cognitive burden in complex analyses, freeing human attention for the contextual interpretation, stakeholder relationship management, and ethical judgement that algorithmic systems cannot reliably perform (Davenport & Kirby, 2016; Jarrahi, 2018). Boundary conditions for this model centre on decision complexity, stakes, and the interpretive demands of context. For low-stakes, high-volume decisions—routine credit approvals, inventory management, scheduling optimisation—AI support accelerates processing without raising significant governance concerns (Davenport & Kirby, 2016; Jarrahi, 2018). For high-stakes decisions—significant personnel actions, novel strategic choices, decisions with pronounced ethical dimensions—the decision support model is most appropriate precisely because it preserves human authority and the full exercise of human judgement over consequential choices.

The primary risk in the decision support configuration is automation bias in its commission form: the tendency to accept AI recommendations without adequate critical evaluation (Cummings, 2004). When AI recommendations are accurate in the large majority of cases, selective attention constraints make it cognitively expensive to maintain critical vigilance—particularly under time pressure or high workload (Bainbridge, 1983; Parasuraman & Manzey, 2010). Governance mechanisms appropriate to this risk include structured decision review protocols that require explicit justification for AI-aligned decisions in designated high-stakes categories, explainability interfaces that surface the factors driving AI recommendations, and regular audits of human override frequency to detect patterns of excessive reliance (Barredo Arrieta et al., 2020; Okamura & Yamada, 2020; Rudin, 2019).

The risk of automation bias in decision support contexts is particularly acute in human resource management applications, where AI systems increasingly assist with candidate screening, performance assessment, and promotion recommendations. Kellogg et al. (2020) identify six mechanisms through which algorithmic control operates in organisational settings—restricting, recommending, recording, rating, replacing, and rewarding—each with distinctive implications for human authority and worker agency. In the decision support configuration, recommending and recording mechanisms are most prominent, with governance implications centring on how AI recommendations are documented, how the relationship between AI recommendations and actual human decisions is monitored, and how employees subject to AI-assisted decisions can access meaningful explanations and exercise appeal rights. Meijerink and Bondarouk (2023) advance the concept of the duality of algorithmic management, arguing that algorithmic control simultaneously constrains and enables human agency: effective governance must manage both dimensions, preventing the erosion of meaningful human oversight whilst preserving the agency-expanding benefits of algorithmic decision support.

Governance structures in the decision support configuration focus on validation and quality of AI-generated information—ensuring data accuracy and that analytical models are sufficiently transparent for critical evaluation (Barredo Arrieta et al., 2020; Glikson & Woolley, 2020; Shrestha et al., 2019). Boundary conditions centre on decision complexity and stakes. For low-stakes, high-volume decisions, AI support accelerates processing while human oversight handles exceptions. For high-stakes strategic decisions, AI enriches analysis but human judgement remains central. The model's primary limitation involves cognitive overload: leaders facing continuous AI recommendations may experience decision fatigue, defaulting to algorithmic suggestions without adequate critical evaluation (Hoff & Bashir, 2015; Parasuraman & Manzey, 2010; Pignatiello et al., 2020; Sakamoto et al., 2024).

AI as Collaborative Partner

The collaborative partner model positions AI as a quasi-peer in decision processes, engaging in iterative dialogue with human leaders to co-produce problem framings, explore solution alternatives, and refine judgements through recursive exchange (Kolbjørnsrud, 2024; Shrestha et al., 2019). This configuration extends beyond the information provision of decision support to encompass joint problem structuring, where AI systems contribute to defining what question is being addressed and what evidence is relevant—functions that shape decision architecture at a more fundamental level than recommendation provision. The collaborative model reflects the genuine intellectual division of labour that is possible when AI systems possess domain competence sufficient to contribute meaningfully to problem analysis alongside human contextual knowledge and value judgement.

Human override mechanisms become more nuanced in collaborative configurations. Rather than simple acceptance or rejection of AI recommendations, leaders engage in deliberative override—modifying problem parameters, challenging AI-generated framings, introducing contextual considerations that reshape AI outputs, and selectively integrating machine and human analytical contributions into composite judgements (Kolbjørnsrud, 2024). This mode of engagement requires what Kolbjørnsrud terms 'fusion skills': the capacity to intelligently interrogate AI systems, identify the boundary conditions of their competence, and integrate algorithmic and human analytical perspectives without surrendering interpretive authority to either.

Research on human–AI teaming suggests that effective collaborative partnerships require appropriate trust calibration, mutual predictability, and sufficient shared understanding for productive role differentiation (National Academies of Sciences, Engineering, and Medicine, 2022; Vaccaro et al., 2024). Research on shared mental models—aligned representations of system goals, task requirements, team member capabilities, and interaction protocols—demonstrates their centrality to effective team performance (Mathieu et al., 2000); this principle has been extended to human–AI teaming contexts, where shared understanding between human and algorithmic actors constitutes a critical determinant of collaborative effectiveness (National Academies of Sciences, Engineering, and Medicine, 2022). In the collaborative partner configuration, this implies that leaders must develop sufficient understanding of AI system capabilities and limitations to form accurate expectations about collaborative performance, whilst AI systems must be designed with sufficient transparency to support the human model-building that calibrated collaboration requires (Mathieu et al., 2000; National Academies of Sciences, Engineering, and Medicine, 2022).

Boundary conditions for the collaborative partner model involve task interdependence, genuine ambiguity, and the availability of human expertise for effective co-production. Collaborative models excel in complex, ill-structured problems where problem definition itself remains contested—strategic planning, innovation strategy development, complex stakeholder negotiations—and where AI analytical capacity complements human contextual expertise (National Academies of Sciences, Engineering, and Medicine, 2022; Vaccaro et al., 2024). The model is less appropriate decisions where the overhead of collaborative process exceeds its value, and for decisions where AI system limitations in contextual understanding, ethical reasoning, or stakeholder sensitivity make human authority without AI co-production more reliable.

Research on human–AI collaboration suggests that effective partnership requires appropriate trust calibration, mutual predictability, and shared mental models (National Academies of Sciences, Engineering, and Medicine, 2022). Vaccaro et al. (2024) found in a systematic review and meta-analysis that human–AI combinations generally outperformed humans alone but identified no evidence of consistent synergy wherein combined performance exceeded both human and AI performance individually. This finding directly challenges the assumption that human–AI collaboration is straightforwardly superior to either component independently and highlights the importance of task-specific calibration. Boundary conditions involve task interdependence: collaborative models excel in complex, ill-structured problems where iterative deliberation produces value, but struggle when AI systems lack domain-specific training or when time pressure precludes iterative dialogue.

AI as Autonomous Agent Within Defined Parameters

The autonomous agent model delegates decision authority to AI systems within circumscribed domains, with human leaders monitoring performance and intervening only when algorithmic systems exceed their competence boundaries, encounter novel circumstances outside their training distribution, or breach pre-established ethical or risk thresholds (Endsley, 2017; Parasuraman et al., 2000). This configuration represents from classical leadership models and raises the most acute governance challenges. The AI system penetrates to the decision selection and action implementation functions of the Parasuraman et al. (2000) taxonomy; human authority operates at the meta-level of system design, parameter setting, and performance governance rather than individual decision adjudication. The Chinese typology of agentic AI captured by CAICT and Huawei (2025) distinguishes a parallel ladder running from task-specific assistants to fully autonomous 'physical actors', supplying a non-Western reference framework for the boundary-setting decisions discussed in the next subsection. In terms of the five-level taxonomy presented in Table 1, the autonomous-agent configuration corresponds to Levels 4 and 5, where decision authority is delegated within rule-based boundaries and the accountability locus shifts from the human leader towards the system designer and the organisation collectively.

Human override mechanisms in the autonomous agent configuration operate at meta-level rather than case-level: leaders define decision parameters, risk thresholds, and escalation criteria, intervening only when systems breach these boundaries or when performance audits reveal systematic failure patterns (Endsley, 2017; Parasuraman et al., 2000). This architecture requires extraordinarily careful governance design, since the human decision-makers who set parameters in advance cannot anticipate all circumstances their systems will encounter, and the temporal gap between system operation and human review creates accountability challenges when autonomous decisions cause harm (Santoni de Sio & van den Hoven, 2018). The moral crumple zone phenomenon identified by Elish (2019) is particularly salient in this configuration: when autonomous AI systems cause harm, accountability tends to collapse onto human operators who were nominally responsible for oversight but who lacked practical capacity to prevent the specific failure.

Boundary conditions for the autonomous agent model are critical and contested. Decisions involving significant ethical implications, substantial stakeholder impact, novel circumstances, or reputational risk generally warrant human case-level authority rather than autonomous AI execution (Santoni de Sio & Mecacci, 2021). Current AI systems, despite impressive performance in well-defined domains, exhibit systematic limitations in handling distributional shift—circumstances that differ materially from training data—and in integrating ethical contextualisation into decision logic (Barredo Arrieta et al., 2020; Rudin, 2019). The EU AI Act's high-risk system category captures many contexts where autonomous AI deployment requires particularly stringent governance including human oversight mechanisms, transparency obligations, and regular conformity assessments (European Parliament & Council of the European Union, 2024). Organisations deploying autonomous AI in these contexts must treat governance architecture not as a compliance exercise but as a substantive component of responsible system design.

Accountability structures in the autonomous agent configuration bifurcate in important ways. Organisations bear responsibility for system design, parameter specification, and oversight architecture, whilst individual leaders face accountability for monitoring effectiveness and responsiveness to anomalies (Santoni de Sio & Mecacci, 2021; van de Poel et al., 2012). The 'moral crumple zone' dynamic identified by Elish (2019) is most acute in this configuration: the nominal human overseer bears institutional accountability for outcomes generated by systems whose internal logic they may be unable to fully comprehend or whose decision pace renders real-time intervention practically impossible. Decisions involving significant ethical implications, substantial individual stakeholder impact, novel circumstances, or reputational risk generally warrant human involvement regardless of AI capability.

Comparative Analysis and Implementation Implications

The three configurations differ across multiple governance-relevant dimensions: the location of decision authority, the mechanisms and frequency of human oversight, the accountability structures most appropriate to each, the skills required of human leaders, and the regulatory obligations triggered by each configuration in high-risk domains. Organisations must engage these dimensions deliberately when choosing among configurations for specific decision functions, recognising that the technically sophisticated option is not necessarily the governance-appropriate one.

As Table 2 shows, organisations commonly employ multiple configurations simultaneously for different functions—using autonomous AI for supply chain optimisations that meet volume, speed, and reversibility criteria; collaborative AI partners in product development processes that benefit from structured analytical support; and decision support AI for significant personnel actions where human authority and accountability are non-negotiable (Iansiti & Lakhani, 2020; Raisch & Krakowski, 2021). This portfolio approach requires governance systems capable of maintaining clarity about which configuration applies to which decision domain, preventing what we term configuration drift—a progressive tendency toward higher automation levels as organisational familiarity with AI systems grows, without commensurate expansion of governance infrastructure— ensuring that oversight capacity is sustained across all configurations in the portfolio (Bailey et al., 2022; Chaleshtori, Aziz, et al., 2024b).

Consistent with the diagonal axis in Figure 2, the three typologies differ not merely in degree but in kind across the dimensions of decision authority, accountability structure, human skill requirements, and governance burden. In the decision support model, authority and accountability are unified in the human leader; governance focuses on information quality and transparency of AI outputs. In the collaborative partner model, authority is shared and accountability is distributed across the human–AI dyad; governance requires documentation of joint deliberation and mechanisms for resolving disagreements between human and algorithmic judgements. In the autonomous agent model, execution authority resides in the AI system whilst oversight accountability rests with human designers and monitors; governance requires robust system specification, anomaly detection infrastructure, and escalation protocols. Organisations may—and typically do—employ multiple models simultaneously for different functions, using autonomous AI for supply chain optimisations, collaborative AI partners in product development, and decision-support AI for strategic planning. The governance challenge is therefore not only to manage each configuration appropriately but to maintain coherence across configurations as boundary conditions shift and as AI capabilities evolve. Figure 2 sets out a typology of AI-augmented leadership configurations along two axes — locus of decisional authority and governance burden on the human leader — that supports the comparative analysis developed in the subsections that follow. Table 2 lays out this comparison across seven governance-relevant dimensions, supporting the case that the three configurations are distinct design choices rather than positions along a single developmental path.

Table 2. Comparative Analysis of AI-Augmented Leadership Configurations

Dimension	Decision-Support Tool	Collaborative Partner	Autonomous Agent
Locus of decisional authority	Human-retained, full.	Shared within a defined decision space.	Delegated to AI within rule-based boundaries.
Governance burden on human leader	Light: AI literacy plus interpretation discipline.	Heavy: continuous calibration of when to override.	Front-loaded: boundary-setting, audit, exception design.
Accountability allocation	Human leader (full).	Joint, with human as ultimate accountable party.	Diffuse; organisation and designer co-implicated.
AI-literacy requirement	Functional: reading AI outputs critically.	High: understanding model assumptions and uncertainty.	Architectural: governance, audit and red-team competence.
Organisational-culture fit	Compatible with bureaucratic and professional cultures.	Requires deliberation-orientated culture and psychological safety.	Requires high-reliability culture with audit and learning routines.

continued on following page

Table 2. Continued

Dimension	Decision-Support Tool	Collaborative Partner	Autonomous Agent
Change-management implications	Incremental; tool adoption.	Substantial; role redesign and team-process redesign.	Transformational; redefined accountability architecture.
Salient failure modes	Algorithm aversion; under-utilisation.	Diffusion of responsibility; uncomfortable trust.	Automation bias; attributability gap; moral crumple zones.

Note. Configurations are stylised; in practice a single organisation may operate all three simultaneously across different functional domains. The 'governance burden on human leader' row captures the active oversight effort required; the 'accountability allocation' row captures formal responsibility for outcomes.

Figure 2. Typology of AI-Augmented Leadership Configurations

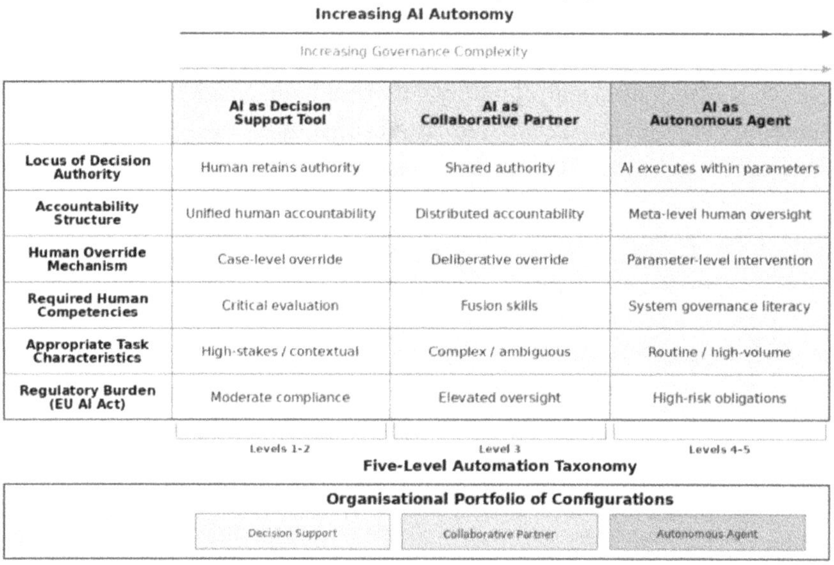

Note. The figure positions the three configurations along two axes: the locus of decisional authority (human-retained to AI-delegated) and the governance burden on the human leader (light to heavy). The diagonal arrow denotes the trajectory from Decision-Support Tool through Collaborative Partner to Autonomous Agent. The three configurations therefore do not represent a single development path along which organisations progress in lockstep; they are distinct design choices with different governance signatures, and a single organisation may operate all three simultaneously across different functional domains.

DIGITAL DECISION-MAKING ARCHITECTURES

This section analyses how AI-augmented leadership reshapes three structural features of decision-making in organisations: the centralisation–distribution balance, the temporal layering of decisions, and the architecture of information flows and feedback. The introduction of AI into leadership changes not only who makes decisions but how decisions are structured, sequenced, and implemented across organisations. AI-augmented leadership operates within digital decision-making architectures—the configurations of data infrastructure, algorithmic systems, information flows, human roles, and governance mechanisms through which decisions are made and executed. These architectures are not neutral technical arrangements but embody choices about authority, accountability, and organisational values that have profound consequences for leadership effectiveness, equity, and legitimacy. The architecture within which AI-augmented leadership operates shapes the choices available to human leaders as much as any individual competency or governance policy.

Centralised versus Distributed Decision Architectures

A critical consideration in AI-augmented leadership architecture concerns whether AI promotes the democratisation of analytical capacity or the consolidation of strategic control. Evidence suggests a complex dynamic: AI tends to centralise strategic authority by enabling top-level leaders to maintain oversight of vastly more information than was previously tractable, whilst simultaneously enabling decentralisation of operational decisions by providing local nodes with analytical capacity previously available only at organisational centres (Bloom et al., 2014; Shrestha et al., 2019).

In a centralised architecture, data, analytics, and AI-driven decisions are funnelled through a core hub. Strategic decisions and many operational decisions are made or approved by top leadership, informed by AI analysis applied to enterprise-wide data. Advantages include consistency in decision standards, concentrated expertise in AI system oversight, and clear accountability for system performance. However, centralised architectures may create bottlenecks that limit decision velocity in time-sensitive operational contexts, and may systematically underweight local contextual knowledge that front-line leaders possess but centralised AI systems cannot access (Bloom et al., 2014; Shrestha et al., 2019). The information asymmetry between local operating contexts and centralised analytical hubs represents a persistent governance challenge in centralised AI-augmented architectures.

In a distributed architecture, AI tools and decision rights are federated throughout the organisation. Different business units, regional teams, or individual team leaders have their own AI decision support systems tailored to local conditions, operating within organisation-wide governance frameworks that specify data standards, algorithmic fairness requirements, and escalation protocols. Distributed architectures enable greater responsiveness to local conditions and preserve the contextual knowledge of front-line leaders. The governance challenge is ensuring consistency across locally deployed systems and preventing the fragmentation of data infrastructure that can prevent organisation-level learning and audit. Wang et al. (2024) find that information flow patterns in AI-augmented organisations significantly affect both decision quality and organisational learning capacity, with network architecture choices having persistent effects on adaptive capability.

Hybrid architectures attempt to balance these tensions through dynamic authority allocation. Routine, low-risk decisions distribute to local nodes with AI support, whilst high-stakes strategic decisions are centralised with comprehensive AI analysis (Parasuraman et al., 2000; Raisch & Krakowski, 2021). Governance mechanisms specify the criteria that trigger escalation from distributed to centralised decision authority, the data integration requirements that enable centre-to-periphery learning, and the assurance mechanisms that verify local AI deployments operate within organisation-wide standards. Hybrid architecture design requires explicit governance of the allocation logic itself: how is it determined which decisions qualify for local versus central authority, and who has authority to revise these determinations as organisational circumstances evolve?

In a centralised architecture, a retailer might use a central AI system to set prices or allocate inventory for all stores, guided by parameters from senior management, enabling consistency but potentially reducing front-line agility. Front-line managers may feel disempowered when required to wait for central AI-driven directives in rapidly changing local conditions—a risk that requires explicit organisational design to mitigate through clear escalation pathways and local override protocols (Bloom et al., 2014; Kellogg et al., 2020).

Temporal Dimensions of Decision-Making

AI's capabilities for continuous data monitoring and rapid analysis compress decision timelines and enable a shift toward more real-time, event-driven decision-making. This temporal compression—what might be termed algorithmic velocity—is among the most consequential and least-discussed consequences of AI integration in leadership contexts (Iansiti & Lakhani, 2020; Kirilenko et al., 2017). In sectors like finance, logistics, and digital platform management, AI systems execute decisions at timescales measured in milliseconds, vastly outpacing human cognitive cycles (Cummings, 2004; Iansiti & Lakhani, 2020; Kirilenko et al., 2017). Even in less extreme contexts, AI-enabled analytics enable decision timescales that compress deliberation cycles from days to hours or hours to minutes.

This temporal compression forces leaders to shift from making discrete decisions to designing 'decision factories': systems that make decisions automatically within prescribed parameters (Iansiti & Lakhani, 2020). The construct of decision velocity thus becomes a governance variable as well as an operational one: the faster decisions are made, the less opportunity exists for meaningful human review, and the more critical becomes the quality of the initial parameter specification.

The temporal architecture of AI-augmented decision-making should therefore be understood as a tripartite structure. Real-time decisions—automated trading, dynamic pricing, immediate resource allocation—often require AI autonomy due to speed requirements that preclude human deliberation for individual instances; governance focuses on system specification and anomaly detection rather than case-by-case oversight (Cummings, 2004; Parasuraman & Riley, 1997). Near-term tactical decisions spanning hours to days typically accommodate human–AI collaboration wherein AI analysis informs human judgement within compressed timeframes; governance requires clear escalation protocols and override authority. Strategic decisions extending over months or years provide opportunity for extensive human deliberation even when informed by sophisticated AI analysis; governance emphasises the quality of the analytical foundation and the integrity of the human judgement applied to it. A coherent decision architecture requires that authority allocations be explicitly mapped to this temporal structure, ensuring that the degree of AI autonomy is proportionate to both the speed requirements and the stakes of each decision class.

The governance implications of algorithmic velocity are profound. When decisions occur faster than human deliberative capacity, meaningful human control at the individual decision level becomes structurally impossible—oversight must shift to parameter governance and post-hoc performance auditing (Hasanović & Muftić, 2025; Santoni de Sio & van den Hoven, 2018), with the attendant risks of moral crumple zones described by Elish (2019). The situations that most require the speed AI enables are often also those in which the consequences of AI error are most severe: market dislocations, operational crises, safety-critical events. Governance architecture must therefore address the paradox of algorithmic velocity: the same circumstances that make AI speed most valuable also make human override least feasible.

Longer-term temporal dynamics introduce additional complexity. As shown in Figure 3, real-time decisions, such as automated trading, dynamic pricing, or immediate resource allocation, often require AI autonomy due to speed requirements that preclude human deliberation for individual instances. Simultaneously, the aggregate pattern of autonomous decisions may produce system-level dynamics—price spirals, resource concentration, service inequality—that human leaders neither intended nor anticipated from individual decision parameters (Iansiti & Lakhani, 2020; O'Neil, 2016). This emergent aggregate effect represents a distinctive challenge for governance: human leaders are accountable for system-level outcomes they cannot directly control at the decision level, requiring governance mechanisms capable of detecting and correcting emergent patterns rather than merely governing individual decisions. Figure 3 renders the resulting Temporal Decision Architecture, distinguishing real-time, tactical and strategic decision layers and the associated division of labour between AI and human leader at each layer. A Finnish public-sector mapping of AI-supported decision-making finds that the compression of decision cycles by AI changes the cadence of leadership communication and accountability as much as it changes the substantive content of decisions (Sitra, 2025).

Figure 3. Temporal Decision Architecture

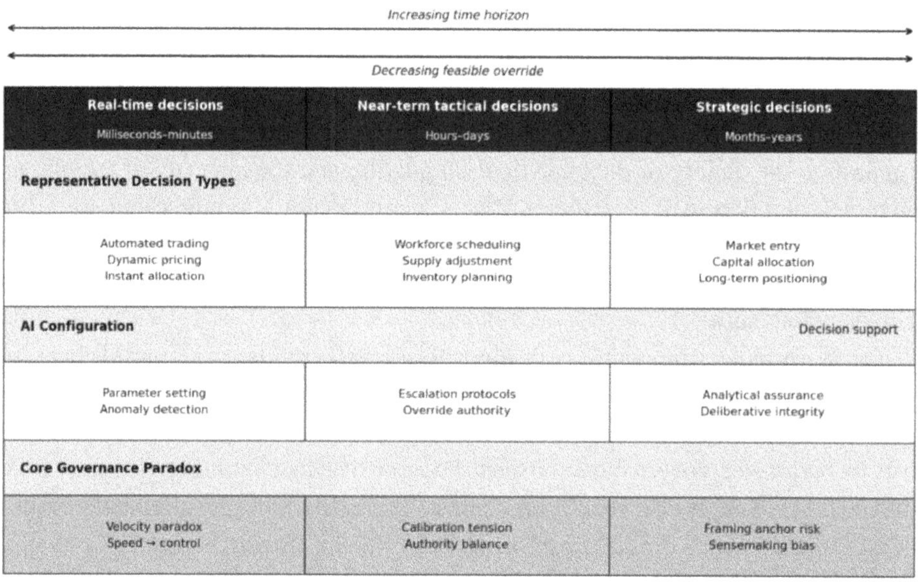

Note. The figure shows three temporal layers of decision-making (real-time, tactical and strategic) and the associated division of labour between AI and human leader at each layer. Real-time decisions are typically AI-led with rule-based human escalation; strategic decisions retain human primacy with AI providing scenario and option support.

Information Flow and Feedback Mechanisms

AI-augmented leadership requires rethinking how information flows through the organisation and how feedback is collected and utilised. AI has the capacity to reconfigure information flows into more networked, multidirectional patterns rather than hierarchical channels—enabling front-line operational data to inform strategic decisions in near real-time, and enabling strategic parameters to be communicated to operational systems with greater consistency than human instruction chains permit. Wang et al. (2024) demonstrate that organisations that redesign information flow architectures alongside AI system deployment significantly outperform those that graft AI onto existing information hierarchies.

Transparency mechanisms—dashboards, reporting systems, explainability interfaces—constitute critical infrastructure for human comprehension of algorithmic reasoning (Barredo Arrieta et al., 2020; Rudin, 2019). Leaders unable to understand how AI systems arrive at their recommendations cannot meaningfully evaluate those recommendations, maintain effective oversight, or fulfil the accountability obligations imposed by emerging regulatory frameworks (Burrell, 2016; European Parliament & Council of the European Union, 2024; Pasquale, 2015). Effective transparency infrastructure must be calibrated to the genuine informational needs of human overseers rather than representing the technically tractable outputs of AI system logging: a technically accurate but incomprehensible explanation does not constitute meaningful transparency for governance purposes.

Empirical research on explainability interfaces reveals a transparency paradox with direct implications for governance design. Buçinca et al. (2021) demonstrated that providing simple explanations for AI decisions paradoxically increased over-reliance because explanations generated an illusion of understanding that terminated further scrutiny; only cognitive forcing functions that introduced deliberate decision friction successfully interrupted heuristic processing. Rudin's (2019) foundational distinction is load-bearing here: explainability, in the sense of a post-hoc account of why an opaque model produced a given output, is not the same as interpretability, in the sense of a model whose internal logic is transparent by design; Rudin argues that for high-stakes decisions the latter should be preferred over the former because explainability methods can be unfaithful to the model they purport to describe and thereby provide governance assurance without governance substance. Building on this distinction, Schemmer et al. (2022) found that feature-based explanations increased willingness to follow correct AI advice but simultaneously increased acceptance of incorrect advice, with explanations functioning as a persuasion mechanism rather than a diagnostic tool—users could not evaluate the quality of the explanation itself and therefore treated its presence as a trustworthiness signal regardless of its accuracy.

Vasconcelos et al. (2023) further demonstrated across five experiments that explanation engagement is strategically determined by cost–benefit calculations: explanations reduce over-reliance only when tasks are sufficiently complex to justify the verification effort, implying that null effects in transparency intervention studies may reflect rational disengagement rather than explanation failure per se.

These findings collectively challenge the governance assumption that providing more explanation necessarily produces better oversight: transparency infrastructure must be designed to support genuine comprehension and calibrated verification rather than providing explanatory content that satisfies regulatory optics without improving decision quality.

Consistent with the anchoring evidence discussed in Section 2, Agudo et al. (2024) demonstrated that decision process architecture directly moderates transparency effectiveness: requiring human overseers to form an independent judgement before receiving the AI explanation significantly reduced automation bias relative to AI-first presentation sequences, suggesting that the sequence of information presentation constitutes a governance variable as consequential as explanation content itself. Similarly, Goddard et al.'s (2012) systematic review of automation bias identified that studies employing status displays showing AI system state information produced better-calibrated reliance than studies using command displays providing direct action recommendations, because those displays maintained active human engagement with the decision rather than enabling passive acceptance of automated directives.

Effective information flow mechanisms in AI-augmented organisations must address several interconnected challenges including the attribution of outcomes to specific decisions when causal chains traverse multiple human and algorithmic actors; temporal delays between decisions and observable consequences that complicate feedback loops; and confounding variables that make it difficult to isolate the contribution of AI augmentation to organisational outcomes (Faraj et al., 2018; Wang et al., 2024). Developing feedback architectures that support genuine organisational learning—rather than merely confirming prior beliefs through selectively attended performance data—represents a demanding governance design challenge that few organisations have yet systematically addressed (Uren & Edward, 2023; Wang et al., 2024; Faraj et al., 2018). The structural redesign of decision-making — across centralisation, temporal layering, and feedback mechanisms — is therefore not an incidental consequence of AI adoption but a primary site at which AI-augmented leadership is constituted in practice.

BEHAVIOURAL AND ORGANISATIONAL IMPLICATIONS

This section examines how AI augmentation reshapes leader identity, follower perceptions, and organisational culture, drawing on identity theory, social-information processing and recent empirical evidence on cross-cultural variation in AI adoption. Introducing AI into leadership structures produces far-reaching effects on human behaviours, relationships, and organisational norms that cannot be reduced to the technical properties of AI systems or the formal governance structures that govern them. The psychological and social dynamics of human–AI integration are themselves determinants of whether AI-augmented leadership delivers its intended benefits or generates new forms of organisational dysfunction. Leaders, followers, and organisations must work through these dynamics deliberately, drawing on emerging empirical evidence about how human actors respond to algorithmic authority, role transformation, and cultural change.

Leader Identity and Role Transformation

A philosophical premise underwrites this entire section. Polanyi (2009/1966) argued that human knowledge has an irreducibly tacit dimension — 'we can know more than we can tell' — and that the most consequential professional judgements rest on tacit knowledge that cannot be fully propositionalised, codified, or transferred to a system designed to compute over explicit representations. The leader-identity discussion that follows is, in this sense, an inquiry into what happens to the tacit dimension of leadership when explicit data and algorithmic recommendations expand to occupy the foreground of decision-making.

A complementary, longitudinal framing is offered by Roos (2026), who reads the empirical record of AI deployment as producing two diverging trajectories rather than a single average effect. On one trajectory — the erosion curve — passive AI dependency atrophies the capabilities that distinguish skilled leadership, with cognitive offloading degrading the very judgement that AI is supposed to augment; on the other — the amplification curve — intentional, friction-preserving AI partnership strengthens those capabilities by freeing human attention for the work that requires it. The leader-identity question, on this reading, is not which trajectory AI 'will' produce in aggregate, but which trajectory any particular organisational design selects for. Figure 4 represents this divergence: starting from a common baseline of capability at the point of AI introduction, the amplification trajectory rises as friction-preserving partnership routines build new competencies, while the erosion trajectory falls as cognitive offloading and skill atrophy compound, with the inflection at which the two trajectories separate determined by the organisational design choices examined in the remainder of this section.

Figure 4. The Erosion–Amplification Curves of Human Capability under AI Exposure

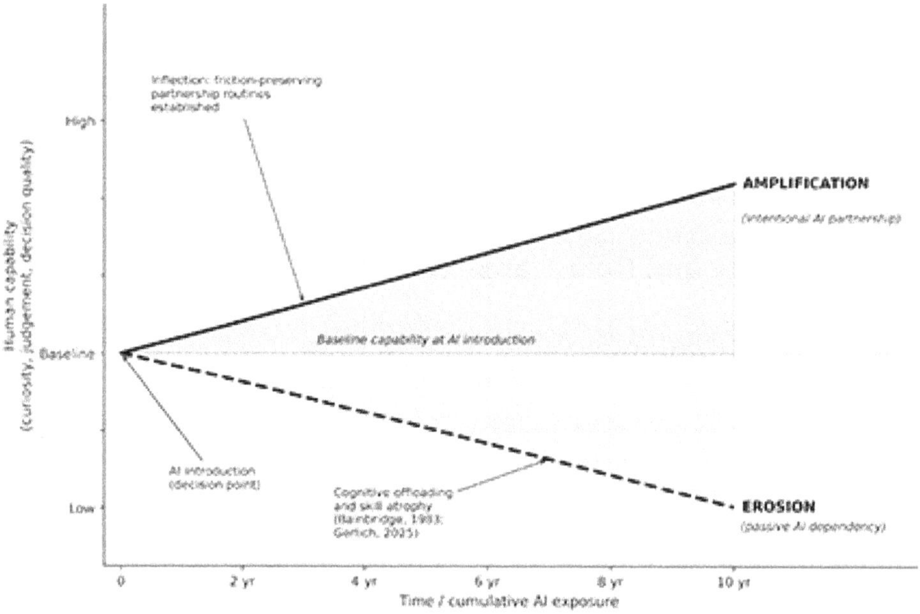

Note. Adapted from Roos (2026). The figure shows the two diverging capability trajectories produced by alternative organisational approaches to AI deployment. The amplification curve represents the trajectory under intentional, friction-preserving AI partnership in which routine tasks are delegated while contextual judgement, deliberate questioning, and reflection-in-action are protected; the erosion curve represents the trajectory under passive AI dependency in which cognitive offloading compounds over time, drawing on the evidence base assembled by Bainbridge (1983) on the ironies of automation and Gerlich (2025) on AI-mediated cognitive offloading. The two trajectories diverge from a common baseline at the moment of AI introduction; the inflection point at which routines stabilise is the consequential organisational-design variable.

The integration of AI into leadership processes precipitates significant transformations in leader identity and role conceptualisation. Traditional leadership identities emphasise decisional authority, expert judgement, and interpersonal influence as core constitutive elements (Judge et al., 2002; Stogdill, 1948). When AI systems assume functions previously central to these identities—analytical processing, option generation, performance evaluation—leaders may experience what Strich et al. (2021) document as identity threat: the perception that one's professional role and associated competencies have been devalued or rendered redundant. This threat is not merely psychological but has practical consequences for AI adoption: leaders who experience identity threat are more likely to resist AI implementation, to under-utilise AI analytical capacity, or to substitute AI delegation with performative human deliberation that adds cost without adding value.

Constructive navigation of identity transformation requires explicit reconceptualisation of leadership value-add in terms that acknowledge and integrate AI capabilities rather than competing with them—what Deb Biswas and Sengupta (2025) describe as role reframing through the cultivation of socio-technical and ontological adaptability. The emerging leadership identity in AI-augmented contexts emphasises meta-cognitive capabilities—the ability to evaluate AI system quality, identify its boundary conditions, and integrate algorithmic outputs with human contextual knowledge—alongside relational capabilities that algorithmic systems cannot replicate: empathy, trust-building, ethical courage, and the political navigation of complex stakeholder environments (Aboumoussa & Pfister, 2024; Kolbjørnsrud, 2024). Evidence suggests that leaders who successfully reframe their identity around these distinctive contributions are more likely to engage productively with AI tools and achieve effective human–AI collaboration (Deb Biswas & Sengupta, 2025; Zhang et al., 2025).

Research involving leaders across organisational contexts identifies a three-pillar model of leadership transformation in AI-augmented workplaces: anticipatory-ethical leadership (proactive engagement with AI's ethical implications), socio-technical reengineering (active redesign of human–AI work arrangements), and collective intelligence cultivation (building team-level capacity for effective human–AI collaboration) (Deb Biswas & Sengupta, 2025). This model implies that leadership development programmes for AI-augmented contexts must address not only technical AI literacy but the ethical, organisational, and relational dimensions of effective AI-integrated leadership practice.

Deb Biswas and Sengupta (2025) found that effective adaptation involves socio-technical reengineering and ontological shifts in leader identity that organisational design must explicitly support.

Follower Perceptions and Responses

Follower responses to AI-augmented leadership vary significantly based on decision domain, perceived fairness, transparency, and individual differences in automation trust. Lee (2018) found that algorithmic decisions were perceived as less fair than human decisions for tasks involving personalised assessment—performance evaluations, hiring decisions—but not necessarily for tasks involving objective calculation or standardised processing. This asymmetry reflects the 'algorithm aversion' phenomenon: followers extend greater tolerance for human inconsistency than for algorithmic error, because human error is attributed to situational factors whilst algorithmic error is attributed to fundamental system deficiency (Dietvorst et al., 2015; Starke et al., 2022).

The mechanisms underlying algorithm aversion have been systematically examined in empirical research that substantially enriches this theoretical foundation. The term itself originates with Dietvorst, Simmons and Massey (2015), whose experiments showed that participants exposed to an algorithm's errors lost confidence in it more sharply than they did in a human forecaster making errors of the same magnitude; the asymmetry held even when the algorithm continued to outperform the human. The follow-up paper (Dietvorst et al., 2018) demonstrated that allowing participants to modify the algorithm's output even slightly substantially restored use, a finding that has direct implications for the design of AI-augmented leadership tools. Burton et al. (2020) conducted a systematic review of 61 peer-reviewed articles identifying five distinct causes of algorithm aversion: false expectations of algorithmic perfection by decision-makers; decision-makers' lack of decision autonomy; absence of social or economic incentives for algorithm use; misalignment between human and algorithmic decision-making processes; and conflicting concepts of rationality between decision-makers seeking to minimise uncertainty and algorithms designed to reduce risk. This multifactorial taxonomy implies that interventions targeting only one source of aversion may prove ineffective when other sources remain unaddressed.

Longoni et al. (2019) identified a specific mechanism termed uniqueness neglect: resistance to AI in personalised domains was driven by concern that AI providers cannot account for individuals' unique characteristics and circumstances, a perception that was substantially attenuated when AI care was framed as personalised or when the decision concerned others rather than oneself. This finding is particularly relevant to AI-augmented leadership in human resources contexts, where follower perceptions of AI decision-making appropriateness may depend critically on whether the system is perceived as capable of individual sensitivity.

The counterpart phenomenon of algorithm appreciation, documented by Logg et al. (2019) across six experiments, demonstrates that lay people often prefer algorithmic over human advice, particularly for tasks perceived as quantitative or objective—a preference pattern that reverses for subjective, interpersonal, or values-laden domains. This task-type moderator implies that follower acceptance of AI-augmented leadership is not uniform but highly contextually contingent, making blanket communication strategies unlikely to be effective across diverse decision domains.

Jussupow et al. (2022) found through survey research that professional identity threat predicts resistance to AI across two dimensions—expert status and recognition, and role as autonomous professional—with deeper workflow integration increasing trust whilst individual accountability increased identity threat perceptions. This finding connects algorithm aversion to the leader identity transformation dynamics discussed above, suggesting that both leaders and followers may resist AI adoption through identity-protective mechanisms that governance design must explicitly anticipate and address. Mirbabaie, Stieglitz and Brünker's (2022) parallel investigation of collaboration with virtual assistants found that the perceived autonomy of AI agents triggers extended-self dynamics in which users either incorporate the agent into their professional identity (assimilation) or resist it as a threat to that identity (rejection); the empirical pattern suggests that organisational interventions that make AI assistance integral to the work — rather than peripheral to it — produce better assimilation outcomes than interventions that leave the relationship under-specified.

The relationship between transformational leadership and positive follower responses to AI augmentation is empirically supported by multiple studies. Zhang et al. (2025) demonstrate that transformational leadership activates employee AI trust, which in turn predicts employee AI crafting behaviours—proactive modifications of work arrangements to exploit AI capabilities more effectively. This mediation pathway suggests that AI implementation effectiveness is substantially determined by the quality of human leadership that surrounds it: technically sophisticated AI deployments led by transformationally disengaged or sceptical leaders may generate systematically worse outcomes than less sophisticated systems embedded in high-trust, vision-aligned leadership contexts (Robertson et al., 2025; Zhang et al., 2025).

Transparency regarding AI involvement in decisions critically affects follower responses. Research by Starke et al. (2022) indicates that disclosure of algorithmic involvement can either enhance or diminish perceived fairness depending on contextual factors including the domain sensitivity of the decision, the perceived competence of the AI system, and followers' prior beliefs about algorithmic versus human decision quality. The interaction of these factors suggests that transparency is necessary but not sufficient for legitimate AI-augmented leadership: transparency that surfaces AI involvement in algorithmically inappropriate domains may damage legitimacy more than strategic opacity—a governance dilemma that regulatory requirements for transparency do not fully resolve.

Follower technostress—anxiety regarding technological change, job security, and role displacement—represents a significant concern for AI implementation at scale (Tarafdar et al., 2007). Empirical evidence indicates that transformational leadership directly mitigates technostress by providing vision-based meaning frameworks that contextualise technological change within organisational purpose and individual development trajectories (Çiçek & Kılınç, 2021; Rademaker et al., 2025). Organisations that implement AI without simultaneously investing in leadership communication, psychological safety, and explicit workforce development commitments tend to underperform those that address the human dimensions of technology adoption alongside the technical dimensions (Robertson et al., 2025; Uren & Edward, 2023).

Organisational Culture and Normative Adaptation

Organisational culture profoundly mediates AI-augmented leadership effectiveness. Organisations that explicitly frame AI as augmentation technology rather than workforce replacement, coupled with genuine workforce investment and clear communication about AI's role limitations, tend to achieve substantially higher human–AI collaboration quality than those that deploy AI without cultural attention (Raisch & Krakowski, 2021; Robertson et al., 2025). The cultural framing of AI is not merely rhetorical: it shapes the psychological safety within which employees experiment with AI tools, the willingness to report AI system errors without fear of self-incrimination, and the organisational learning capacity through which human–AI collaboration continuously improves. Weick's (1995) framework of organisational sensemaking is directly relevant here: the introduction of AI into work routines is one of the equivocal events that sensemaking theory takes as its primary object, in which actors retrospectively construct accounts of what AI is, what it does, what it means for them and what it requires of them. The cultural adaptation that the chapter analyses in this section is, on this reading, an organisation-level instance of sensemaking under technological equivocality.

Cultural transformation toward AI-augmented ways of working requires explicit organisational design interventions rather than emergent change (Hinings et al., 2018; Schein, 2010). Communities of practice that enable employees to share experiences and develop collective understandings of effective human–AI collaboration generate more rapid and robust cultural adaptation than top-down change management approaches alone (Faraj et al., 2018; Wenger, 1998). Senior leadership visibility and explicit endorsement of human–AI collaboration—including leaders modelling productive AI engagement and transparent acknowledgement of AI limitations—prove essential for the cultural embedding of collaborative human–AI norms (Glikson & Woolley, 2020; Kotter, 1996).

Organisations must cultivate explicit norms around responsible AI use including transparency about algorithmic involvement, equity in AI-mediated resource allocation, and accountability for AI-influenced decisions (Jobin et al., 2019; Mittelstadt et al., 2016). The institutionalisation of these norms requires more than policy codification: it demands consistent behavioural modelling by leaders, formal mechanisms for raising concerns about AI system behaviour without retaliation, and regular cultural assessment to detect normative drift toward problematic patterns of AI reliance or evasion. Organisations that treat culture as a background condition rather than an active design variable in AI implementation consistently underestimate the cultural work that successful human–AI integration requires (Robertson et al., 2025; Schein, 2010). Leader identity, follower response and organisational culture are jointly the human-side conditions on which the success of AI-augmented leadership depends, and they cannot be treated as residual variables once the technical implementation is in place.

ETHICAL AND GOVERNANCE CONSIDERATIONS

This section addresses the accountability challenges, fairness concerns, and regulatory architecture that constrain AI-augmented leadership in practice, with explicit attention to the EU AI Act's phased application, the post-2025 US framework, and the Council of Europe Framework Convention. As organisations integrate AI into leadership and decision-making, they face profound ethical and governance challenges that extend well beyond technical compliance. The shift from governing people to governing processes, parameters, and protocols demands new governance architectures, new forms of professional expertise, and new normative frameworks for assessing the legitimacy of AI-augmented decisions (Dafoe, 2018; Jobin et al., 2019). The regulatory landscape is evolving rapidly toward more demanding requirements that treat algorithmic governance as a substantive organisational obligation rather than a technical formality. Organisations that approach governance as a minimum compliance exercise will find themselves inadequately equipped for the governance demands of advanced AI integration.

Accountability, Responsibility Attribution, and the Attributability Gap

AI-augmented decision-making systems generate a distinctive accountability problem that Zeiser (2024) terms the *'attributability gap'*: a structural separation between accountability (responsibility for outcomes) and attributability (the causal tracing of outcomes to specific decisions and agents). In traditional organisational structures, accountability and attributability are linked: identifiable human decision-makers can be held responsible because their decisions can be causally traced to outcomes. When decisions emerge from human–AI collaboration—where algorithmic analysis, human interpretation, governance parameter choices, and training data all contribute to outcomes—causal attribution becomes both technically demanding and legally contested. A complementary diagnosis is offered by Elish (2019), whose 'moral crumple zone' framework identifies an asymmetry in how blame attaches to humans whose role is residual oversight of an automated system: when the system fails, the human at the periphery absorbs the legal and reputational consequences disproportionate to the human's actual causal contribution. The framework names exactly the dynamic that Table 2 of this chapter identifies as a salient failure mode of the Autonomous Agent configuration.

The attributability gap is consequential even when human leaders remain formally accountable (Commission Nationale de l'Informatique et des Libertés, 2025): the proliferation of algorithmic recommendations can obscure the human value-judgements embedded in final decisions, making it difficult to assess whether human overseers exercised genuine deliberation or merely rubber-stamped algorithmic outputs (Pasquale, 2015; Zeiser, 2024). This distinction has direct regulatory significance under the EU AI Act and emerging accountability standards that distinguish substantive from theatrical human oversight (European Parliament & Council of the European Union, 2024; Hasanović & Muftić, 2025). This problem has a longer political-theoretical lineage than the AI-decision-making literature sometimes acknowledges: Thompson (1980) named it the 'problem of many hands' in his analysis of moral responsibility in the modern state, arguing that the standard responses — hierarchical responsibility flowing upward and collective responsibility flowing outward — both distort the underlying concept and that a properly causal-and-volitional account of personal responsibility remains the more defensible foundation. AI-augmented decision-making sharpens the problem rather than introducing it; the policy question is whether the institutional response can be sharpened to match.

Santoni de Sio and Mecacci (2021) identify four distinct responsibility gaps in AI systems: the problem of many hands (responsibility diffused across developers, deployers, operators, and users), the problem of the execution gap (human intentions not reliably translated into system behaviour), the problem of the learning gap (system behaviour evolving away from original design through machine learning), and the problem of the opacity gap (human actors unable to understand system behaviour sufficiently to detect or correct error). Each gap is independently capable of producing accountability failures, and each calls for a distinct institutional response: culpability gaps require clearer allocation of design responsibility and documentation of decision logic; moral accountability gaps require logging systems and audit trails; public accountability gaps require transparency mechanisms and regulatory reporting; and active responsibility gaps require governance structures that assign ongoing stewardship of AI system performance. In complex AI-augmented leadership systems, multiple gaps operate simultaneously, requiring multi-layered governance rather than single-point accountability assignment.

The concept of meaningful human control, developed by Santoni de Sio and van den Hoven (2018), provides a normative framework for maintaining accountability in AI-augmented contexts. Meaningful control comprises a tracking condition (the system tracks human moral reasons through its operation) and a tracing condition (the system's behaviour is traceable to an identifiable, properly informed, properly competent and properly authorised human). Operationalising the framework imposes three demanding requirements on human overseers: sufficient understanding to detect problematic patterns; sufficient authority to intervene effectively; and sufficient practical capacity — time, cognitive resources, and organisational support — to exercise oversight reliably under realistic operating conditions. Many current governance arrangements satisfy the authority dimension without adequately addressing the understanding and practical-capacity dimensions, creating formal accountability structures that cannot deliver substantive oversight (Busuioc, 2021; Wieringa, 2020). This framework provides the normative foundation for distinguishing substantive from theatrical human oversight — a distinction with significant legal and ethical implications under the EU AI Act and emerging accountability standards internationally.

Subsequent scholarship has substantially operationalised the meaningful human control framework for practical application. Cavalcante Siebert et al. (2023), in a paper co-authored with van den Hoven himself, translate the philosophical framework into four actionable engineering properties for AI system development: explicitly defined moral domains within which the AI system operates; appropriate representations that enable human overseers to understand system states and outputs; commensurate responsibility that aligns the level of human accountability with the degree of human control available; and explicit links between AI system actions and human decisions (Cavalcante Siebert et al., 2023). Veluwenkamp (2022) resolves an important ambiguity in the original tracking condition of the MHC framework by distinguishing between motivating reasons (the reasons that actually cause behaviour) and normative reasons (the reasons that should govern behaviour), arguing that meaningful control requires systems responsive to normative rather than merely motivating reasons (Veluwenkamp, 2022). Davidovic (2023) argues that MHC discussions commonly fail to identify the purpose behind calls for human control—a necessary clarification before oversight obligations can be meaningfully institutionalised—and that different purposes such as safety, accountability, and legitimacy generate different operational requirements for what effective human control must accomplish (Davidovic, 2023). These elaborations collectively transform MHC from a philosophical ideal into a governance specification framework applicable to the design and assessment of AI oversight mechanisms in organisational leadership contexts.

van de Poel et al. (2012) analyse the problem of many hands as a structural feature of complex sociotechnical systems where responsibility is diffused across chains of actors who each contribute to outcomes without any individual actor having full causal responsibility. This structural analysis suggests that individual-level accountability frameworks are fundamentally inadequate for AI-augmented systems and must be supplemented by systemic accountability mechanisms: organisational responsibility for system design quality, regulatory accountability for the adequacy of governance frameworks, and professional accountability for the exercise of technical and managerial roles within AI-augmented systems.

Practical accountability mechanisms for AI-augmented leadership include clear documentation of AI system capabilities and limitations at the point of deployment and throughout the system lifecycle; transparent logging of AI recommendations and human decisions that enables post-hoc audit of human–AI collaboration patterns; explicit protocols for escalating novel circumstances beyond system competence boundaries; and regular performance reviews that include assessment of AI system accuracy, bias, and boundary condition performance (European Parliament & Council of the European Union, 2024; National Institute of Standards and Technology, 2023). Elish's (2019) analysis of moral crumple zones warns against accountability structures that formally assign responsibility to human operators whilst practically preventing them from exercising effective oversight—a warning particularly relevant to high-autonomy AI configurations where the speed of algorithmic execution structurally limits human intervention.

Algorithmic Bias, Fairness, and Equity

Algorithmic bias represents perhaps the most extensively studied ethical concern in AI-augmented leadership contexts. Because AI algorithms learn from historical data, they can inherit the prejudices, inequities, and exclusions embedded in past organisational practices (Barocas & Selbst, 2016). In leadership contexts, this risk is acute: AI systems used for performance evaluation, promotion recommendation, or resource allocation may systematically disadvantage protected groups not because of explicitly discriminatory programming but because they extrapolate patterns from historically discriminatory organisational data (Kellogg et al., 2020; Köchling & Wehner, 2020). The technical mechanism of bias—training data that reflects historical discrimination—does not mitigate its ethical and legal consequences.

Chouldechova (2017) proved a fundamental impossibility result with far-reaching implications for AI fairness governance: multiple intuitive fairness metrics cannot be simultaneously satisfied except in the theoretically special conditions of equal base rates across groups. This mathematical result implies that there is no technically correct definition of algorithmic fairness that resolves all fairness concerns simultaneously; organisations must make explicit normative choices about which fairness dimensions to prioritise, with full awareness that these choices involve genuine trade-offs rather than resolvable technical problems. O'Neil (2016) documented the systematic inequities generated by opaque algorithmic systems deployed without adequate bias assessment across multiple social domains, demonstrating that the problem of algorithmic discrimination is not hypothetical but empirically prevalent.

Bias mitigation in AI-augmented leadership requires multi-layered approaches operating at different system stages. Pre-processing interventions rebalance training datasets to achieve more representative samples or to remove historically discriminatory variables; in-processing interventions incorporate fairness constraints directly into the learning objective; and post-processing interventions adjust system outputs to equalise outcomes across groups (Mehrabi et al., 2021; Pessach & Shmueli, 2022). No single intervention is sufficient across all contexts and fairness dimensions; effective bias governance requires combining technical interventions with ongoing monitoring, audit, and organisational accountability mechanisms that detect emergent bias in deployed systems (Mehrabi et al., 2021; National Institute of Standards and Technology, 2023).

The NIST AI Risk Management Framework (National Institute of Standards and Technology, 2023) provides comprehensive guidance on bias mitigation through its govern-map-measure-manage cycle, emphasising that purely technical mitigation proves insufficient: leaders must embed ethical judgement and human oversight into decision processes where algorithmic bias carries consequential implications for individuals and communities.

Regulatory Frameworks and Structural Governance Implications

The European Union's AI Act (European Parliament & Council of the European Union, 2024) represents the most comprehensive regulatory framework governing AI-augmented decision-making in organisational contexts (European Parliament & Council of the European Union, 2024; Roberts et al., 2023; Veale & Zuiderveen Borgesius, 2021). Taking a risk-based approach, the AI Act classifies AI systems according to their potential for harm, with the highest governance requirements applying to systems that pose unacceptable risk (prohibited) or high risk (stringently regulated). The high-risk category includes AI systems used in employment, education, creditworthiness assessment, and other domains where AI-augmented leadership decisions significantly affect individual life prospects.

The EU AI Act (European Parliament & Council of the European Union, 2024), which entered into force on 1 August 2024 and is being phased into application through 2 August 2027 for high-risk systems integrated into products regulated under existing EU legislation, with most high-risk Annex III obligations entering into force on 2 August 2026, classifies AI systems according to their potential for harm. Prohibited systems—those posing unacceptable risks—are banned outright; high-risk systems are subject to mandatory conformity assessments, transparency requirements, and human oversight obligations before market placement; limited-risk systems face specific transparency obligations; and minimal-risk systems are largely unregulated, though subject to voluntary codes of conduct. As of early 2026, the provisions governing high-risk AI systems in Annex III areas—including employment, critical infrastructure, education, and access to essential services—are entering application, substantially raising compliance requirements for organisations deploying AI in these domains (European Parliament & Council of the European Union, 2024; OECD, 2024).

Article 14 of the EU AI Act establishes specific requirements for human oversight of high-risk systems that operationalise meaningful human control in regulatory terms. Oversight must be effective and substantive rather than ceremonial: the regulation explicitly prohibits governance arrangements that nominally assign oversight responsibility without ensuring that overseers have the competence, authority, and practical support to exercise it. High-risk AI systems must be designed to enable human overseers to decide not to use the system, to override or reverse its output, and to intervene in or interrupt system operation through accessible control mechanisms (European Parliament & Council of the European Union, 2024). The implication for organisational governance is that AI systems cannot be designed for routine acceptance with override available only under exceptional circumstances; they must be designed with the assumption that human intervention is a normal and expected element of system operation.

The philosophical underwriting of this regulatory requirement is older than the technology it governs: what Article 14 demands is what Aristotle (1999) in Book VI of the Nicomachean Ethics called phronesis, the practical wisdom that arrives at the right action, in the right way, for the right reasons in the particular situation at hand. Phronesis is contextual and irreducibly human in a sense that procedural compliance alone cannot satisfy; an overseer who merely countersigns algorithmic recommendations is exercising what Aristotle would have called techne rather than phronesis. The contemporary operationalisation of this argument for autonomous systems is provided by Santoni de Sio and van den Hoven (2018), who formalise meaningful human control as the conjunction of two conditions: a tracking condition (the system tracks human moral reasons through its operation) and a tracing condition (the system's behaviour is traceable to a properly informed, properly competent, properly authorised human). Recent empirical work has begun to operationalise phronesis itself: McLoughlin, Thoma and Kristjánsson's (2025) multi-method study, using nationally representative UK and US samples, identified ten distinct internally reliable components of phronesis and constructed a Short Phronesis Measure with strong test-retest reliability, providing for the first time an empirically grounded instrument for assessing the practical wisdom that Article 14 presupposes.

A particularly rigorous peer-reviewed analysis of EU AI Act Article 14 in the academic literature is provided by Laux (2024), who proposes a taxonomy of human oversight roles distinguishing constitutive oversight (where human involvement defines the decision itself) from corrective oversight (where humans can intervene to modify or reverse AI decisions), and articulates six normative principles for institutionalising what he terms institutionalised distrust of AI systems (see also Veale & Zuiderveen Borgesius, 2021). Laux argues that effective oversight under the Act requires not passive monitoring but active scepticism institutionalised into governance design—a claim with significant implications for how organisations design review processes, escalation protocols, and override mechanisms for high-risk AI applications. The institutionalised distrust framework implies that governance architectures should assume AI system error as a baseline expectation rather than treating error as exceptional deviation from reliable performance, fundamentally reversing the default assumption that has characterised many early AI deployment governance designs; the French Conseil d'État's December 2025 Charter on AI use within the administrative jurisdiction provides a worked example of this design discipline by specifying that the judge always retains decisional responsibility regardless of the AI's recommendation (Conseil d'État, 2025) (Laux, 2024; Parasuraman et al., 2000).

The structural implications of the EU AI Act extend beyond individual system compliance to organisational governance architecture. The requirement that human overseers properly understand AI system capacities and limitations elevates AI literacy from a desirable leadership skill to a legal requirement for those exercising oversight responsibility over high-risk systems (Hasanović & Muftić, 2025). This has direct consequences for leadership development, personnel selection, and governance role design: organisations cannot assign AI oversight responsibility to individuals lacking sufficient technical literacy to perform it effectively and then claim to have satisfied Article 14 obligations.

Beyond the EU AI Act, comparable regulatory developments across jurisdictions converge on shared principles: meaningful human involvement in high-stakes decisions, transparency regarding algorithmic reasoning, systematic bias auditing and remediation, and robust accountability mechanisms. In the United States, the National Institute of Standards and Technology AI Risk Management Framework (2023) offers a voluntary governance architecture that many organisations are adopting as a de facto standard for responsible AI risk governance, organised around the functions of governing, mapping, measuring, and managing AI-related risks throughout the system lifecycle. The convergence of regulatory frameworks across jurisdictions toward common governance principles provides organisations with a relatively stable foundation for governance architecture development, even as the specific requirements of individual frameworks continue to evolve (Roberts et al., 2023; OECD, 2024).

The OECD AI Principles (originally adopted in 2019 and substantially revised in May 2024 to address generative AI, bias and information integrity; OECD, 2024) are adhered to by 47 jurisdictions, provide influential guidance emphasising transparency, explainability, accountability, and human oversight in AI deployment. In the United States, the regulatory architecture has shifted materially between 2023 and 2025. Executive Order 14110 on Safe, Secure, and Trustworthy AI (Biden, October 2023) was revoked on 20 January 2025 and replaced by Executive Order 14179 'Removing Barriers to American Leadership in Artificial Intelligence' (Trump, January 2025), with a more permissive orientation and a 180-day implementation deliverable issued in July 2025 as America's AI Action Plan. The National Institute of Standards and Technology AI Risk Management Framework (NIST, 2023) remains in force as voluntary guidance and continues to function as a de facto standard, organised around the govern-map-measure-manage cycle. Whilst the US framework now imposes fewer federal mandatory requirements than the EU AI Act, sectoral regulators retain authority over AI deployment in their domains — most directly relevant to AI-augmented leadership being the United States Equal Employment Opportunity Commission's continuing application of Title VII, the Americans with Disabilities Act and the Age Discrimination in Employment Act to algorithmic decision-making in HR.

The Council of Europe Framework Convention on Artificial Intelligence, adopted on 17 May 2024 and opened for signature on 5 September 2024, adds a binding international human-rights baseline above which national regimes must operate; the United States, the United Kingdom and the European Union are among the signatories (including the 27 EU Member States represented through the EU's signature). Following ratifications by the United Kingdom, France, Norway, Andorra and the Republic of Moldova — meeting the threshold of five ratifications including three Council of Europe member states — the Convention entered into force on 1 November 2025. A consequential 2025 development is the European Commission's withdrawal of the proposed AI Liability Directive in its 2025 work programme on 12 February 2025, leaving the EU 'attributability gap' institutionally unfilled at the supranational level and reinforcing the role of national tort law and the EU Product Liability Directive (Directive 2024/2853) in allocating responsibility for AI-related harms.

As Table 3 makes visible, for multinational organisations the interaction between EU binding requirements, the Council of Europe human-rights baseline and the US post-2025 pro-innovation orientation creates complex compliance landscapes requiring governance architectures that meet the most stringent applicable standard. The 2024–2026 governance landscape has consolidated around three institutional anchors — the EU AI Act, the Council of Europe Framework Convention, and the post-2025 US regulatory architecture under EO 14179 — within which AI-augmented leadership must operate, even as the gap between these instruments and operational practice remains substantial. Table 3 summarises the May 2026 governance landscape across these instruments, setting out the scope, accountability requirements, enforcement mechanism and leadership-relevant obligations of each.

A further regulatory development with direct relevance to AI-augmented leadership in employment contexts is the European Union's Platform Work Directive (Directive (EU) 2024/2831), formally adopted on 23 October 2024 (published in the Official Journal on 11 November 2024) with a transposition deadline of 2 December 2026. Kellogg, Valentine and Christin's (2020) foundational analysis identified algorithmic management as a new contested terrain of control comprising six 'Rs' — restricting, recommending, recording, rating, replacing and rewarding — that together amount to a qualitatively different control regime from prior bureaucratic and market-mediated forms. The Directive is the first EU instrument to regulate algorithmic management in the workplace directly: it establishes a right to explanation for algorithmic decisions affecting platform workers, mandates meaningful human oversight of algorithmic systems used in personnel decisions, restricts the processing of sensitive worker data, and creates a rebuttable presumption of employment that bears on the scope of algorithmic-management practices that can lawfully be applied to nominally self-employed contractors. While its formal scope is limited to platform work, the European Parliament's December 2025 call for a dedicated directive on algorithmic management beyond platform work indicates that the regulatory direction of travel is towards a generalised framework — a development that AI-augmented leadership deployments in employment contexts must anticipate even where they fall outside the current Directive's coverage (European Parliament, 2025; Rathenau Instituut, 2024).

Table 3. Comparative Regulatory Frameworks for AI-Augmented Leadership (as of May 2026)

Framework	Scope	Accountability Requirements	Enforcement Mechanism	Leadership-Relevant Obligations
EU AI Act (Regulation 2024/1689)	Mandatory; risk-based; covers EU market.	Risk-based duties on providers and deployers; Article 14 human-oversight obligations; GPAI Code of Practice obligations.	National competent authorities; AI Office; fines up to 7 per cent of global turnover.	Annex III high-risk obligations (incl. HR/ employment) enter into force 2 August 2026; Article 4 AI-literacy duty in force from 2 February 2025.
Council of Europe Framework Convention on AI	Binding international treaty; human-rights / democracy / rule-of-law lens; 37 signatories incl. US, UK, EU at January 2025.	Lifecycle activities to be consistent with human rights; signatory states must legislate to give effect.	State reporting; Conference of Parties; domestic transposition.	Establishes a binding human-rights baseline above which national regimes must operate.
United States — EO 14179 + AI RMF	EO 14179 (January 2025) replaced EO 14110; NIST AI RMF voluntary guidance; America's AI Action Plan released July 2025.	Pro-innovation orientation; reduced federal mandatory requirements; sectoral regulators retain authority (EEOC for HR-AI, etc.).	Sectoral enforcement; voluntary adoption of NIST AI RMF as de facto standard.	AI-augmented HR systems remain subject to EEOC, ADA and Title VII case-law; voluntary govern-map-measure-manage cycle.
United Kingdom — principles-based, sector-led	AI Security Institute (renamed February 2025); AI Opportunities Action Plan (January 2025); sectoral regulators apply five cross-economy principles.	Existing sectoral regulators (ICO, FCA, MHRA, etc.) apply principles within their remits; comprehensive AI Bill signalled for 2026.	Sectoral; ICO enforcement for data-related obligations.	Sectoral compliance under principles-based approach; ICO guidance on AI in HR and recruitment.
EU Platform Work Directive 2024/2831	Algorithmic management in platform work; transposition deadline 2 December 2026.	Right to explanation; human-oversight requirements; presumption of employment; data-minimisation in workplace AI.	National labour authorities; collective bargaining channels.	Direct constraint on algorithmic-management practices; signalled extension to non-platform employment under EU discussion (December 2025).
OECD AI Principles (2024 update)	Non-binding; 47 adherents; updated May 2024 to address generative AI, bias, misinformation.	Recommendations on transparency, accountability, human oversight, environmental sustainability, interoperable governance.	Peer-review through OECD AI Policy Observatory.	Reference standard for organisations operating across multiple jurisdictions.

Note. Status reflects the regulatory landscape as of May 2026. The Council of Europe Framework Convention entered into force on 1 November 2025 following ratifications by the United Kingdom, France, Norway, Andorra and the Republic of Moldova. The proposed EU AI Liability Directive was withdrawn from the European Commission's 2025 work programme on 12 February 2025, leaving the EU accountability gap institutionally unfilled at the supranational level. Abbreviations: EEOC — US Equal Employment Opportunity Commission; ADA — Americans with Disabilities Act; ICO — UK Information Commissioner's Office; GPAI — General-Purpose AI.

IMPLEMENTATION CONSIDERATIONS

This section examines what successful adoption of AI-augmented leadership requires in practice: organisational readiness assessment, AI literacy across the workforce, and performance-measurement architectures that survive the introduction of algorithmic actors. Successfully augmenting leadership with AI requires more than deploying technically capable systems; it demands careful preparation of the organisation, development of new competencies at multiple levels, deliberate redesign of decision processes and performance systems, and sustained attention to the human and cultural dimensions of sociotechnical change (Makarius et al., 2020; Berente et al., 2021). Organisations that approach AI augmentation as a purely technical implementation challenge, relegating human and organisational dimensions to secondary status, consistently underperform those adopting integrated sociotechnical perspectives. The evidence base for this finding is robust across multiple sectors and organisational contexts (Makarius et al., 2020; Salwei & Carayon, 2022).

Effective implementation is fundamentally a sociotechnical challenge: the probability of realising the potential benefits of AI augmentation whilst avoiding its risks depends on the quality of the organisational design surrounding the technology as much as on the technology itself. As Trist and Bamforth (1951) demonstrated in their foundational study of coal-mining mechanisation, and Mumford (2006) elaborated across decades of organisational informatics work, new technologies embedded in poorly designed work systems routinely underperform their potential and generate unintended negative consequences. This sociotechnical insight is directly applicable to AI-augmented leadership: the most sophisticated AI system will fail to augment leadership effectively if the governance architecture, skill development, change management, and performance evaluation surrounding it are inadequate.

Organisational Readiness Assessment and Change Management

Successful implementation of AI-augmented leadership requires systematic assessment of organisational readiness across multiple interdependent dimensions. Uren and Edward (2023) identified four readiness dimensions in their PPTD model: people (skills, attitudes, and change readiness), processes (workflow integration and decision protocols), technology (infrastructure and data capabilities), and data (quality, accessibility, and governance maturity). Deficiencies in any dimension can undermine implementation success regardless of AI system sophistication: technically excellent AI deployed on poor-quality data, within unready organisational processes, to unprepared people, predictably underperforms technically modest systems deployed within mature sociotechnical infrastructure.

A bibliometric review of AI adoption in small and medium enterprises identifies digital readiness, access to financial and human capital, and strategic alignment as primary determinants of adoption success (Yesuf & Fields, 2025). Organisational barriers include lack of technical expertise, resistance to change driven by identity threat and job security concerns, data quality deficiencies that undermine AI system reliability, and regulatory uncertainty that increases implementation risk (Berente et al., 2021; Makarius et al., 2020). Complementary investments in workforce reskilling, data governance infrastructure, and leadership experimentation are essential for AI to deliver transformative rather than merely marginal results.

Change management in AI-augmented leadership contexts requires explicit attention to multiple stakeholder groups with genuinely different concerns and information needs (Kotter, 1996; Robertson et al., 2025). Senior leaders require evidence that AI investments generate strategic value commensurate with risk and cost; middle managers require clarity regarding new responsibilities and how their roles will evolve; frontline employees require assurance about continued relevance of human judgement and genuine commitment to workforce development; technical staff require sufficient autonomy to implement systems effectively without governance constraints that prevent responsible experimentation. Robertson et al. (2025) developed the AI Implementation Compass framework, identifying clear strategic rationale, meaningful stakeholder engagement, iterative implementation approaches, and continuous learning orientation as key determinants of implementation success. Organisations that collapse these distinct stakeholder needs into a single communication strategy systematically fail to address the specific concerns that drive resistance in each group (Robertson et al., 2025; Kotter, 1996).

Competency Development and AI Literacy

AI-augmented leadership demands new competencies at multiple organisational levels that cannot be developed through isolated training interventions but require sustained investment in individual, team, and organisational learning systems (Kolbjørnsrud, 2024; Raisch & Krakowski, 2021). At the individual leader level, effective AI-augmented practice demands human capabilities that differentiate leaders from machines: empathy and relational trust-building, ethical judgement in genuinely ambiguous situations, political navigation of complex stakeholder environments, adaptive sensemaking under genuine uncertainty, and the communicative capacity to translate AI-generated insights into organisationally meaningful narratives (Aboumoussa & Pfister, 2024). Schön's (1983) account of the reflective practitioner remains a load-bearing framework here: professional knowledge is built through reflection-in-action, the practitioner's ongoing dialogue with the unfolding situation, and through reflection-on-action, the retrospective interrogation of cases. Where AI assistance compresses decision cycles and presents conclusions in finished form, the windows in which reflection-in-action can occur narrow; AI-literate competency development must therefore engineer those windows deliberately rather than assume they will survive the productivity gains that occasioned the AI deployment.

Kolbjørnsrud (2024) identifies 'fusion skills' as the critical competency category for AI-augmented leaders: intelligent interrogation of AI systems (probing assumptions, testing edge cases, validating outputs against contextual knowledge), reciprocal apprenticing in which humans and AI systems mutually train each other through structured interaction and feedback, and judgement integration in which human decision-makers synthesise machine and human analytical inputs without defaulting to either as the uncritical authority.

AI literacy represents a foundational competency requirement for all organisational members who interact with AI systems in leadership or oversight roles. Chee et al. (2025) identified eight competency domains and eighteen sub-competencies for AI literacy through systematic review, encompassing understanding AI concepts and limitations, applying AI tools effectively in specific task contexts, evaluating AI output quality and identifying potential errors, and addressing ethical considerations in AI deployment and use. The implication for leadership development is that AI literacy cannot be treated as a specialist technical capability delegated entirely to data science and IT functions; it must be cultivated as a mainstream leadership competency alongside financial literacy, strategic thinking, and stakeholder management (Chee et al., 2025; Raisch & Krakowski, 2021).

Beyond individual competency development, organisations must cultivate collective capabilities for AI-augmented work: shared understanding of AI roles and limitations across teams, collaborative practices that effectively integrate human and AI contributions to decision processes, and governance competencies enabling responsible AI deployment throughout the organisation (Raisch & Krakowski, 2021; Berente et al., 2021). Developing these collective capabilities requires investment in communities of practice, structured reflection on AI-augmented decision experiences, and organisational learning mechanisms that convert individual insights into shared institutional knowledge (Wenger, 1998; Faraj et al., 2018).

Aboumoussa and Pfister (2024) identify human distinctiveness competencies as the critical differentiator for leadership effectiveness in the algorithmic enterprise, arguing that skills including emotional attunement, contextual ethical reasoning, and stakeholder relationship management become more rather than less important as AI assumes a greater share of analytical and procedural tasks—a finding that challenges displacement narratives and grounds the case for sustained investment in human leadership development alongside AI capability growth.

Performance Measurement and Evaluation

Evaluating AI-augmented leadership requires performance metrics that capture the quality of human–AI collaboration rather than merely the outcomes of individual decisions. Traditional performance indicators may not reflect the process quality of human–AI collaboration or the long-term consequences of automation dependency (Bainbridge, 1983; Onnasch et al., 2014; Vaccaro et al., 2024). Vaccaro et al. (2024) conducted a systematic review and meta-analysis finding that human–AI combinations generally outperformed humans alone across a wide range of task types, but identified significant variation in outcomes depending on task characteristics, system design, and the quality of human–AI interaction protocols. Notably, synergistic outcomes in which combined human–AI performance exceeded both individual human and AI performance were achievable but required specific enabling conditions rather than emerging automatically from the combination of capable humans and capable AI systems.

Performance metrics for AI-augmented leadership should extend beyond decision outcome quality to encompass process indicators including decision consistency across demographically similar cases (a bias indicator), appropriate override frequency relative to task risk levels, trust calibration accuracy as measured by the correlation between human confidence in AI recommendations and actual AI system accuracy in relevant domains, and stakeholder satisfaction with the perceived fairness and transparency of AI-augmented decisions (Parasuraman & Manzey, 2010; Starke et al., 2022; Bankins et al., 2024). Sakamoto et al. (2024) demonstrate in medical AI contexts that trust calibration can be systematically improved through structured feedback interventions that expose decision-makers to accurate information about AI system performance characteristics—a finding with broad implications for AI-augmented leadership development.

Two additional empirical findings have direct implications for performance evaluation system design. Yu et al. (2025) implemented a dynamic confidence calibration system in clinical AI contexts, combining accurate confidence score communication with transparency mechanisms that enabled clinicians to discriminate high-confidence predictions warranting acceptance from low-confidence outputs demanding scrutiny. This intervention reduced clinician override rates from 87.64% to 33.29%—a result that demonstrates the performance measurement potential of systematic confidence communication when combined with transparency about confidence derivation logic. For AI-augmented leadership contexts, this finding suggests that performance evaluation systems incorporating real-time confidence indicators may substantially improve calibration without requiring changes to underlying AI system accuracy. Polyportis (2024) documented, in a longitudinal survey of 222 students using a large language model AI system, a significant decline in trust over time from a mean of 3.84 to 3.08 despite continued usage—a finding that challenges the assumption that repeated exposure to AI systems necessarily produces appropriate calibration or sustained productive engagement. This trust erosion pattern is consistent with Jones-Jang et al.'s (2023) finding that high prior expectations of AI reliability predict disproportionate distrust responses upon encountering system errors (see also Polyportis, 2024), implying that performance evaluation of AI-augmented leadership systems must attend to temporal trust dynamics rather than snapshot measurements, and that governance designs calibrating appropriate initial expectations may be as important as interventions responding to trust collapse after it occurs.

Evaluation should also attend to longer-term organisational consequences of AI integration including skill maintenance among leaders and employees whose work is augmented, organisational learning capacity in AI-augmented versus non-augmented domains, and the sustainability of human–AI collaboration quality as systems evolve through updates and retraining (Endsley, 2017; Macnamara et al., 2024). Concerns about deskilling through automation dependency—the systematic erosion of human capabilities that are no longer exercised—necessitate monitoring of human skill retention as a standard component of AI augmentation performance assessment (Endsley, 2017; Macnamara et al., 2024).

Macnamara et al. (2024) provide particularly compelling evidence for the urgency of skill retention monitoring, demonstrating that AI assistance can accelerate skill decay and hinder skill development without performers' awareness—a finding that highlights why self-report measures of skill confidence are insufficient for detecting automation-induced deskilling (Macnamara et al., 2024). The implication for performance systems is that organisations must monitor objective performance under non-augmented conditions as well as AI-augmented performance, requiring periodic assessment of decision quality when AI support is deliberately withheld to detect skill degradation that augmented-only measurement would systematically miss (Endsley, 2017; Parasuraman et al., 2000; Macnamara et al., 2024). This recommendation aligns with the broader argument of Endsley (2017) that the automation conundrum—where increasing automation degrades the very human skills needed when automation fails—demands proactive skill maintenance strategies embedded in governance design rather than reactive responses to skill erosion that becomes apparent only after a consequential automation failure.

Evaluation should attend to longer-term effects including skill maintenance, organisational learning, and adaptation to changing conditions. Concerns about deskilling through automation dependency necessitate active monitoring of human capability retention: if AI support is withdrawn for any reason, can leaders and organisations function effectively? Assessment of whether AI augmentation enhances or erodes organisational learning capabilities—the capacity to adapt behaviour based on experience—provides insight into whether AI integration is building organisational resilience or creating dependencies that may prove fragile under novel conditions (Bankins et al., 2024; Vaccaro et al., 2024; Raisch & Krakowski, 2021). Successful implementation thus depends on the joint development of organisational readiness, distributed AI literacy and performance-measurement infrastructure that recognises algorithmic actors as legitimate contributors whose performance can be assessed without dissolving human accountability for outcomes.

FUTURE TRAJECTORIES AND RESEARCH AGENDA

This section identifies four near-term technological inflections that will materially shape AI-augmented leadership, surveys current research limitations, and develops priority areas for future empirical investigation. The field of AI-augmented leadership is nascent relative to the phenomenon it studies. Research is developing rapidly but remains substantially behind the pace of technological and organisational change, creating knowledge gaps that inhibit responsible governance and evidence-based leadership practice. The research agenda outlined in this section prioritises gaps where theoretical development and empirical investigation could most directly contribute to improved practice and governance.

Technological Evolution and Leadership Implications

Advances in AI technologies will progressively expand the scope of potential AI augmentation in leadership contexts. Generative AI systems can synthesise text, code, images, and strategic scenarios with sufficient quality to serve as inputs to high-level decision-making—drafting policy documents, generating strategic option sets, producing stakeholder communication (Doshi et al., 2025; Dwivedi et al., 2023). Large language models functioning as conversational partners can synthesise stakeholder sentiment from unstructured sources, surface emergent organisational concerns, and provide on-demand analytical support across a wide range of leadership tasks (Bankins et al., 2024; Chowdhury et al., 2024). Multi-agent AI architectures may orchestrate complex multi-step processes across organisational networks, coordinating activities that currently require substantial human administrative effort (Guo et al., 2024; Bankins et al., 2024).

A useful conceptual framing for this transition is provided by Tsamados, Floridi and Taddeo (2025), who distinguish supervisory human control (the human as overseer of an autonomous system) from human-machine teaming (the human and the system as joint actors with complementary roles), and argue that foundation-model-based AI systems pose distinctive challenges to the supervisory model that the teaming model is better positioned to address. The shift from supervision to teaming is the structural counterpart at the human-AI interaction level of the agentic-AI transition at the system-architecture level. The OECD's (2026) systematic mapping of the agentic-AI landscape provides the canonical reference frame: across the surveyed sources, the most frequently cited definitional features of AI agents are autonomy, goal-orientation, environmental adaptation, planning capability, and the ability to use tools, with these features clustering differently across academic, industry and policy literatures. For AI-augmented leadership, the policy significance is that the agentic-AI label currently lacks a settled definition, with consequential implications for which systems will be in scope of forthcoming regulatory responses.

As AI systems become more capable and more autonomous, the role of human leaders may further shift toward what Kolbjørnsrud (2024) terms designing the intelligent organisation: shaping the values, governance architectures, and accountability structures of human–machine ecosystems rather than directly executing the leadership functions those ecosystems perform. This shift toward meta-leadership demands capabilities that current leadership development programmes do not systematically develop: the ability to design governance systems that maintain human accountability within autonomous AI architectures, to engage substantively with technical experts and ethicists in AI system design, and to work through the regulatory landscape that governs high-capability AI deployment.

Current Research Limitations

Current research on AI-augmented leadership exhibits significant methodological limitations that constrain the confidence with which findings can be applied to organisational practice. Most empirical studies are cross-sectional, capturing human–AI interaction at a single point rather than examining how relationships, competencies, and outcomes evolve over time (Bankins et al., 2024; Vaccaro et al., 2024). Longitudinal designs are needed to understand how trust calibration develops with experience, how leadership identity transforms as AI integration deepens, and whether deskilling concerns are realised in practice or mitigated by ongoing human engagement with augmented decision processes (Alon-Barkat & Busuioc, 2023; Bankins et al., 2024; Vaccaro et al., 2024).

Research has insufficiently examined how contextual factors moderate AI-augmented leadership effectiveness: industry characteristics including competitive dynamics and regulatory environments; organisational culture dimensions including psychological safety and learning orientation; and national contexts including cultural orientations toward automation and institutional regulatory frameworks (Bankins et al., 2024; Vaccaro et al., 2024). Cross-cultural studies examining whether findings from Western organisational contexts—where most published research originates—generalise to other cultural settings remain scarce despite the global deployment of AI-augmented leadership systems (Bankins et al., 2024; Vaccaro et al., 2024).

Methodological limitations constrain current understanding further. Reliance on self-report measures introduces social desirability bias, particularly for sensitive topics like AI override behaviour and automation bias (Macnamara et al., 2024; Parasuraman & Manzey, 2010). Laboratory experiments offer internal validity but limited ecological validity relative to the complex real-world contexts of organisational leadership. Case studies offer contextual depth but limited generalisability (Campbell & Stanley, 1963; Creswell & Creswell, 2018). The development of validated psychometric instruments for measuring AI-augmented leadership constructs—trust calibration accuracy, fusion skill proficiency, algorithmic sensemaking literacy—combined with multi-method research designs would substantially strengthen the empirical foundation of the field (Bankins et al., 2024; Okamura & Yamada, 2020).

Construct specification in the field also requires sharpening: terms such as 'meaningful human control', 'automation bias', and 'trust calibration' are used with varying definitions across studies, impeding cumulative knowledge development and the synthesis of findings into actionable guidance for practitioners and regulators (Bankins et al., 2024; Jacovi et al., 2021).

Priority Areas for Future Research

Several priority research areas emerge from the analysis presented in this chapter, each addressing gaps where theoretical development and empirical investigation could most directly benefit organisational practice and governance.

Trust dynamics over extended time horizons represent the most urgent research priority. Current understanding of how trust between leaders and AI systems evolves with accumulated experience remains limited, as does understanding of the factors that predict appropriate trust calibration versus systematic over-trust or under-trust (Bankins et al., 2024; Okamura & Yamada, 2020). The conditions under which trust recalibrates appropriately following AI system error—rather than collapsing into generalised automation aversion or failing to update in response to demonstrated system limitations—warrant systematic empirical investigation (Bankins et al., 2024; Okamura & Yamada, 2020).

Advancing this research priority requires resolving foundational measurement and conceptual challenges that currently limit cumulative knowledge development. Mehrotra et al. (2024) documented substantial terminological fragmentation in the trust calibration literature, with conceptual disagreement across terms including appropriate trust, calibrated trust, warranted trust, and justified trust substantially hindering the accumulation of comparable evidence and the development of consolidated governance recommendations. Establishing shared definitional conventions and validated measurement instruments capable of distinguishing trust from reliance is a prerequisite for building the evidence base that governance practice requires. Scharowski et al. (2023) demonstrated that attitudinal trust (measured through self-report) and behavioural reliance (observed decision outcomes) frequently diverge, implying that studies measuring only subjective trust may systematically mischaracterise the calibration phenomena most consequential for leadership governance. Research designs incorporating both attitudinal and behavioural measures are therefore essential for generating findings applicable to governance design. These methodological investments will support investigation of the temporal dynamics identified by Polyportis (2024) and consistent with Jones-Jang et al.'s (2023) empirical finding that high prior expectations of AI reliability create systematic vulnerability to trust collapse upon first encountering errors—a trajectory with direct implications for how organisations should structure initial AI deployment experiences to prevent the emergence of durable under-trust following early performance failures.

Competency development and transfer represents a second priority area. Research is needed to identify which training approaches most effectively develop AI-augmented leadership capabilities, how skills developed in one AI context transfer to other AI systems and task domains, and what individual differences predict rapid versus slow competency development (Bankins et al., 2024; Macnamara et al., 2024). Evidence-based leadership development curricula for AI-augmented leadership cannot be developed without this foundation.

Organisational design and governance architecture represents a third priority. Questions about how organisational structures, decision processes, and governance mechanisms should be designed to support effective human–AI collaboration across different automation levels and organisational contexts remain largely unanswered at the empirical level. Comparative studies of organisations with different governance architectures could yield substantial practical insights (Bankins et al., 2024; Vaccaro et al., 2024).

Ethical implementation in practice represents a fourth priority. Understanding how organisations operationalise ethical principles in AI-augmented leadership practice—including which mechanisms effectively detect and address algorithmic bias in real-time, how meaningful human control is maintained in high-autonomy configurations under realistic operating pressures, and how accountability attribution operates in practice when AI systems cause harm—requires detailed empirical investigation that current research has not yet provided (Bankins et al., 2024; Vaccaro et al., 2024).

Performance outcomes under heterogeneous conditions represents a fifth priority. The conditions under which AI augmentation enhances versus degrades leadership effectiveness, and the organisational, individual, and task-level factors that moderate this relationship, require more systematic investigation than the existing evidence base supports (Vaccaro et al., 2024; Bankins et al., 2024). Meta-analytic integration of emerging empirical findings could substantially clarify the contingency structure of AI augmentation effectiveness.

Addressing these research priorities will require sustained interdisciplinary collaboration spanning management and organisation science, computer science and artificial intelligence, psychology and human factors, ethics and philosophy, and law and governance. Single-discipline approaches will prove insufficient for phenomena that are simultaneously technical, psychological, organisational, and normative in character (Dwivedi et al., 2023; Vaccaro et al., 2024).

Five priority research areas emerge from the analysis presented in this chapter. First, trust dynamics over time: how does trust between leaders and AI systems evolve with experience, and what factors predict appropriate trust calibration versus over-trust or under-trust? Second, skill development and transfer: what training approaches most effectively develop AI-augmented leadership capabilities, and how do skills developed in one AI context transfer to novel systems and domains? Third, organisational design for AI-augmented governance: how should organisational structures, processes, and cultures adapt to support substantive rather than ceremonial human oversight, and what governance mechanisms effectively balance AI autonomy with human control across different risk levels? Fourth, ethical operationalisation: how can organisations translate normative principles—fairness, transparency, accountability—into operational practices that effectively detect and address algorithmic bias in leadership contexts? Fifth, performance contingencies: under what task, system, and organisational conditions does AI augmentation enhance versus degrade leadership effectiveness, and what moderating variables determine whether human–AI synergies are achievable? Addressing these research priorities will require sustained interdisciplinary collaboration spanning management, computer science, psychology, ethics, and law. Addressing these research priorities will require sustained interdisciplinary collaboration spanning management, computer science, psychology, ethics, and law, organised around the empirical settings — agentic AI deployments, multi-agent coordination, and rapidly evolving regulatory architectures — that will define the next decade of AI-augmented leadership.

CONCLUSION

AI-augmented leadership represents a fundamental restructuring of organisational authority, cognition, and accountability that is already reshaping leadership practice across sectors and will deepen in scope and consequence as AI capabilities advance (Raisch & Krakowski, 2021; Chaleshtori, Ghaffari, et al., 2024a). This chapter has examined the theoretical, architectural, behavioural, ethical, and practical dimensions of this transformation through an integrated sociotechnical lens, developing frameworks intended to support both scholarly understanding and responsible organisational practice.

The theoretical analysis demonstrates that understanding AI-augmented leadership requires integrating multiple traditions that have historically addressed human and technological agency in isolation: bounded rationality and its extensions illuminate how AI alters the cognitive architecture of decision-making; naturalistic decision-making and ecological rationality frameworks reveal both the value and the limits of algorithmic augmentation in different task environments; distributed leadership and distributed agency frameworks capture the fundamentally networked character of human–AI authority; and sociotechnical systems theory provides the architectural principles for designing human–AI configurations that are jointly rather than separately optimised (Raisch & Krakowski, 2021; Shrestha et al., 2019). Classical leadership theories remain relevant but require systematic extension to accommodate non-human agency and its governance implications (Chaleshtori, Ghaffari, et al., 2024a; Floridi, 2025).

The typological analysis reveals that AI-augmented leadership is not a single phenomenon but a family of distinct configurations—decision support, collaborative partnership, and autonomous agency—each with different implications for human authority, accountability structures, competency requirements, and governance demands. The critical governance insight is that the appropriate governance architecture is configuration-specific: mechanisms calibrated for decision support contexts are systematically insufficient for autonomous agent deployments, and governance requirements proportionate to high-autonomy configurations would impose unproductive burdens on low-autonomy decision support systems (Parasuraman et al., 2000; Santoni de Sio & van den Hoven, 2018). Organisations must develop governance sophistication capable of differentiating among configurations and applying appropriate oversight to each.

The analysis of digital decision-making architectures reveals that AI integration reshapes not only individual decisions but the structural organisation of decision authority, information flows, and temporal dynamics across the organisation. Architectural choices about centralisation, distribution, and hybrid configurations have consequences for decision quality, accountability, equity, and organisational learning that extend far beyond the immediate performance of individual AI applications (Shrestha et al., 2019; Wang et al., 2024). The governance of AI-augmented leadership architectures requires attention to emergent system-level dynamics that no individual decision or oversight mechanism can fully control.

The behavioural analysis reveals that the psychological and social dynamics of AI integration are themselves determinants of implementation success. Leader identity transformation, follower perceptions of algorithmic authority, automation bias, and cultural adaptation to human–AI collaboration are not peripheral concerns to be addressed after technical implementation but central determinants of whether AI augmentation delivers its intended benefits. Organisations that invest in the human dimensions of AI integration—leadership development, cultural change, psychological safety, and stakeholder communication—tend to achieve superior implementation outcomes relative to those treating AI as a purely technical challenge, with failure to address human dimensions identified as a leading cause of implementation underperformance (Vaccaro et al., 2024; Robertson et al., 2025).

Ethical and governance considerations prove central to responsible AI-augmented leadership practice. The attributability gap, the problem of many hands, and the threat of moral crumple zones collectively generate accountability deficits that formal governance arrangements must explicitly address (Zeiser, 2024; Santoni de Sio & Mecacci, 2021). Algorithmic bias requires multi-layered technical and organisational responses calibrated to the impossibility of satisfying all fairness criteria simultaneously (Chouldechova, 2017; Mehrabi et al., 2021). The EU AI Act and converging international regulatory frameworks establish governance expectations that elevate human oversight, transparency, and accountability from optional good practice to legal obligation—particularly for high-risk AI systems deployed in employment, education, and other high-stakes domains (European Parliament & Council of the European Union, 2024; Hasanović & Muftić, 2025).

The implications for practice are substantial and multidimensional. Leaders must develop new competency profiles that combine AI literacy with the distinctively human capabilities that effective collaboration with algorithmic systems demands (Kolbjørnsrud, 2024; Chee et al., 2025). Organisations must redesign decision processes, governance architectures, and performance measurement systems to support effective human–AI collaboration while maintaining meaningful human accountability. Policymakers and regulators must balance the imperative to enable beneficial AI innovation with the equally pressing imperative to protect against algorithmic harms that current evidence demonstrates are real and consequential (O'Neil, 2016; Mehrabi et al., 2021). Researchers must address the significant gaps in current understanding through rigorous, longitudinal, multi-method, and genuinely interdisciplinary investigation. Leaders should develop fusion skills that enable intelligent interrogation of AI systems and confident exercise of override authority rather than passive receipt of algorithmic outputs (Parasuraman et al., 2000; Kolbjørnsrud, 2024; Vaccaro et al., 2024). Performance metrics should extend beyond outcome efficiency to encompass the quality of human–AI collaboration, the appropriateness of trust calibration, and the maintenance of the human capabilities on which meaningful oversight depends. Cultural environments should cultivate psychological safety for questioning algorithmic recommendations, treating visible human override not as system failure but as evidence of the substantive human control that both ethical governance and regulatory compliance require (Glikson & Woolley, 2020).

AI-augmented leadership is not a distant future possibility but a present organisational reality whose governance demands are already exceeding the frameworks most organisations have in place to meet them (Iansiti & Lakhani, 2020; Robertson et al., 2025). The frameworks, typologies, and considerations presented in this chapter provide foundations for working through this transformation with the theoretical rigour, governance sophistication, and human-centred orientation that the stakes require. Success will demand sustained commitment to maintaining meaningful human agency and ethical accountability as the capabilities and autonomy of AI systems continue to advance—a commitment that is ultimately not technical but normative, not automated but chosen (Raisch & Krakowski, 2021; Dwivedi et al., 2023).

The normative aspiration that emerges from this analysis is not AI-augmented leadership that maximises algorithmic efficiency but AI-augmented leadership that preserves and enhances the distinctively human capabilities—ethical judgement, contextual wisdom, relational intelligence, and accountability—without which the exercise of leadership authority cannot be made legitimate (Kolbjørnsrud, 2024; Taddeo & Floridi, 2018). Achieving this aspiration requires that organisations, researchers, and policymakers attend with equal seriousness to the social and technical dimensions of human–AI integration: the governance of agency, not merely the optimisation of performance (Kudina & van de Poel, 2024; Mumford, 2006).

This chapter has analysed AI-augmented leadership across theoretical, typological, structural, behavioural, ethical, and implementation dimensions. A useful normative axis on which to locate the chapter's overall argument is the distinction that Roos (2026) draws between Algorithmic Citizenship and Professional Citizenship. Algorithmic Citizenship is the default trajectory under which leaders accept AI recommendations without systematic questioning, optimise individual tasks rather than redesigning systems, measure success in efficiency metrics, and become — in Roos's phrase — concierges of outputs they did not author towards purposes they did not choose. Professional Citizenship is the alternative: the deliberate cultivation of the capabilities that AI cannot replicate, the institutional design that keeps the human meaningfully in (not after) the decision loop, and the orientation of AI deployment towards purposes that the organisation can defend in moral and not merely productivity terms. The chapter's substantive argument is that the second trajectory is achievable but not automatic — it requires the typological discipline, the governance architecture and the competency investments that the preceding sections have analysed.

REFERENCES

Aboumoussa, L., & Pfister, J. (2024). Leadership development in the age of artificial intelligence (AWP No. 244). Mossavar-Rahmani Center for Business and Government, Harvard Kennedy School. https://www.hks.harvard.edu/sites/default/files/centers/mrcbg/Final_AWP_244.pdf

Agarwal, N., Moehring, A., Rajpurkar, P., & Salz, T. (2023). *Combining human expertise with artificial intelligence: Experimental evidence from radiology* (NBER Working Paper No. 31422). National Bureau of Economic Research. DOI: 10.3386/w31422

Agudo, U., Liberal, K. G., Arrese, M., & Matute, H. (2024). The impact of AI errors in a human-in-the-loop process. *Cognitive Research: Principles and Implications, 9*(1), 1. DOI: 10.1186/s41235-023-00529-3 PMID: 38185767

Alon-Barkat, S., & Busuioc, M. (2023). Human–AI interactions in public sector decision making: "Automation bias" and "selective adherence" to algorithmic advice. *Journal of Public Administration: Research and Theory, 33*(1), 153–169. DOI: 10.1093/jopart/muac007

Aristotle. (1999). *Nicomachean ethics* (T. Irwin, Trans.; 2nd ed.). Hackett Publishing. (Original work published c. 350 BCE).

Avolio, B. J., Kahai, S., & Dodge, G. E. (2000). E-leadership: Implications for theory, research, and practice. *The Leadership Quarterly, 11*(4), 615–668. DOI: 10.1016/S1048-9843(00)00062-X

Bailey, D. E., Faraj, S., Hinds, P. J., Leonardi, P. M., & von Krogh, G. (2022). We are all theorists of technology now: A relational perspective on emerging technology and organizing. *Organization Science, 33*(1), 1–18. DOI: 10.1287/orsc.2021.1562

Bainbridge, L. (1983). Ironies of automation. *Automatica, 19*(6), 775–779. DOI: 10.1016/0005-1098(83)90046-8

Bankins, S., Ocampo, A. C., Marrone, M., Restubog, S. L. D., & Woo, S. E. (2024). A multilevel review of artificial intelligence in organizations: Implications for organizational behavior research and practice. *Journal of Organizational Behavior, 45*(2), 159–182. DOI: 10.1002/job.2735

Bansal, G., Nushi, B., Kamar, E., Weld, D. S., Lasecki, W. S., & Vaughan, J. W. (2021). Does the whole exceed its parts? The effect of AI explanations on complementary team performance. In *Proceedings of the 2021 CHI Conference on Human Factors in Computing Systems* (Article 81). Association for Computing Machinery. **https://doi.org/**DOI: 10.1145/3411764.3445717

Barocas, S., & Selbst, A. D. (2016). Big data's disparate impact. *California Law Review*, *104*(3), 671–732. DOI: 10.15779/Z38BG31

Barredo Arrieta, A., Díaz-Rodríguez, N., Del Ser, J., Bennetot, A., Tabik, S., Barbado, A., Garcia, S., Gil-Lopez, S., Molina, D., Benjamins, R., Chatila, R., & Herrera, F. (2020). Explainable artificial intelligence (XAI): Concepts, taxonomies, opportunities and challenges toward responsible AI. *Information Fusion*, *58*, 82–115. DOI: 10.1016/j.inffus.2019.12.012

Baxter, G., & Sommerville, I. (2011). Socio-technical systems: From design methods to systems engineering. *Interacting with Computers*, *23*(1), 4–17. DOI: 10.1016/j.intcom.2010.07.003

Berente, N., Gu, B., Recker, J., & Santhanam, R. (2021). Managing artificial intelligence. *Management Information Systems Quarterly*, *45*(3), 1433–1450. DOI: 10.25300/MISQ/2021/16274

Bloom, N., Garicano, L., Sadun, R., & Van Reenen, J. (2014). The distinct effects of information technology and communication technology on firm organization. *Management Science*, *60*(12), 2859–2885. DOI: 10.1287/mnsc.2014.2013

Brynjolfsson, E. (2022). The Turing trap: The promise and peril of human-like artificial intelligence. *Daedalus*, *151*(2), 272–287. DOI: 10.1162/daed_a_01915

Brynjolfsson, E., Li, D., & Raymond, L. (2025). Generative AI at work. *The Quarterly Journal of Economics*, *140*(2), 889–942. DOI: 10.1093/qje/qjae044

Brynjolfsson, E., Mitchell, T., & Rock, D. (2018). What can machines learn, and what does it mean for occupations and the economy? *AEA Papers and Proceedings. American Economic Association*, *108*, 43–47. DOI: 10.1257/pandp.20181019

Buçinca, Z., Malaya, M. B., & Gajos, K. Z. (2021). To trust or to think: Cognitive forcing functions can reduce overreliance on AI in AI-assisted decision making. *Proceedings of the ACM on Human-Computer Interaction, 5*(CSCW1), Article 188. **https://doi.org/**DOI: 10.1145/3449287

Burrell, J. (2016). How the machine "thinks": Understanding opacity in machine learning algorithms. *Big Data & Society*, *3*(1), 1–12. DOI: 10.1177/2053951715622512

Burton, J. W., Stein, M.-K., & Jensen, T. B. (2020). A systematic review of algorithm aversion in augmented decision making. *Journal of Behavioral Decision Making*, *33*(2), 220–239. DOI: 10.1002/bdm.2155

Busuioc, M. (2021). Accountable artificial intelligence: Holding algorithms to account. *Public Administration Review*, *81*(5), 825–836. DOI: 10.1111/puar.13293 PMID: 34690372

Campbell, D. T., & Stanley, J. C. (1963). *Experimental and quasi-experimental designs for research.* Rand McNally.

Cavalcante Siebert, L., Lupetti, M. L., Aizenberg, E., Beckers, N., Zgonnikov, A., Veluwenkamp, H., Abbink, D., Giaccardi, E., Houben, G.-J., Jonker, C. M., van den Hoven, J., Forster, D., & Lagendijk, R. L. (2023). Meaningful human control: Actionable properties for AI system development. *AI and Ethics*, *3*(1), 241–255. DOI: 10.1007/s43681-022-00167-3

Chaleshtori, M. A., Ghaffari, M., & Tajeddini, K. (2024a). Artificial intelligence and organisational leadership: A systematic review and future research agenda. *Technology in Society*, *76*, 102424. Advance online publication. DOI: 10.1016/j.techsoc.2023.102424

Chaleshtori, M. F., Aziz, A., & Bauer, T. (2024b). Human-AI collaboration in organizational contexts: A systematic review. *Journal of Management Studies*, *61*(3), 678–712. DOI: 10.1111/joms.12991

Chee, H., Ahn, S., & Lee, J. (2025). A competency framework for AI literacy: Variations by different learner groups and an implied learning pathway. *British Journal of Educational Technology*, *56*(3), 2146–2182. Advance online publication. DOI: 10.1111/bjet.13556

Chouldechova, A. (2017). Fair prediction with disparate impact: A study of bias in recidivism prediction instruments. *Big Data*, *5*(2), 153–163. DOI: 10.1089/big.2016.0047 PMID: 28632438

Chowdhury, S., Budhwar, P., & Wood, G. (2024). Generative artificial intelligence in business: Towards a strategic human resource management framework. *British Journal of Management*, *35*(4), 1680–1691. DOI: 10.1111/1467-8551.12824

Çiçek, B., & Kılınç, E. (2021). Can transformational leadership eliminate the negativity of technostress? *Business & Management Studies*, *9*(1), 372–384. DOI: 10.15295/bmij.v9i1.1770

Commission Nationale de l'Informatique et des Libertés. (2025, February). *Délibération n° 2025-010 portant deuxième recommandation sur l'application du RGPD au développement des systèmes d'IA*. CNIL. https://www.legifrance.gouv.fr/jorf/id/JORFTEXT000051164307

Council of Europe. (2024, May 17). *Framework Convention on Artificial Intelligence and human rights, democracy and the rule of law (CETS No. 225)*. Council of Europe. https://www.coe.int/en/web/artificial-intelligence/the-framework-convention-on-artificial-intelligence

Creswell, J. W., & Creswell, J. D. (2018). *Research design: Qualitative, quantitative, and mixed methods approaches* (5th ed.). SAGE Publications.

Csaszar, F. A., Ketkar, H., & Kim, H. (2024). Artificial intelligence and strategic decision-making: Evidence from entrepreneurs and investors. *Strategy Science*, *9*(4), 322–345. DOI: 10.1287/stsc.2024.0190

Cummings, M. L. (2004). Automation bias in intelligent time critical decision support systems. *Proceedings of the AIAA 1st Intelligent Systems Technical Conference*. DOI: 10.2514/6.2004-6313

d'État, C. (2025, December). *Charte d'utilisation de l'intelligence artificielle au sein de la juridiction administrative*. République française. https://www.conseil-etat.fr/qui-sommes-nous/deontologie/charte-d-utilisation-de-l-intelligence-artificielle-au-sein-de-la-juridiction-administrative

Dafoe, A. (2018). AI governance: A research agenda. Centre for the Governance of AI, Future of Humanity Institute, University of Oxford. https://www.governance.ai/research-paper/agenda

Davenport, T. H., & Kirby, J. (2016). *Only humans need apply: Winners and losers in the age of smart machines*. Harper Business.

Davidovic, J. (2023). Why we need humans in control of AI. *Frontiers in Big Data*, *6*, 1070597. DOI: 10.3389/fdata.2023.1070597

de Visser, E. J., Peeters, M. M. M., Jung, M. F., Kohn, S., Shaw, T. H., Pak, R., & Neerincx, M. A. (2020). Towards a theory of longitudinal trust calibration in human–robot teams. *International Journal of Social Robotics*, *12*(2), 459–478. DOI: 10.1007/s12369-019-00596-x

Deb Biswas, D., & Sengupta, R. (2025). Reimagining leadership for the AI era: A grounded theory of adaptive, ethical and contextually situated practices in workplaces. *Leadership and Organization Development Journal*. Advance online publication. DOI: 10.1108/LODJ-06-2025-0488

Dietvorst, B. J., Simmons, J. P., & Massey, C. (2015). Algorithm aversion: People erroneously avoid algorithms after seeing them err. *Journal of Experimental Psychology. General, 144*(1), 114–126. DOI: 10.1037/xge0000033 PMID: 25401381

Dietvorst, B. J., Simmons, J. P., & Massey, C. (2018). Overcoming algorithm aversion: People will use imperfect algorithms if they can (even slightly) modify them. *Management Science, 64*(3), 1155–1170. DOI: 10.1287/mnsc.2016.2643

Doshi, A. R., Bell, J. J., Mirzayev, E., & Vanneste, B. S. (2025). Generative artificial intelligence and evaluating strategic decisions. *Strategic Management Journal, 46*(3), 583–610. DOI: 10.1002/smj.3677

Dwivedi, Y. K., Kshetri, N., Hughes, L., Slade, E. L., Jeyaraj, A., Kar, A. K., Baabdullah, A. M., Abdulsalam, A., Ackah, B. B., Akour, I., Alhassan, R., Al-Khowaiter, A., Almohammadi, H., Alomari, K., Altameem, A., Alturise, F., Asiri, S., Báča, A., Bag, S., & Wright, R. (2023). "So what if ChatGPT wrote it?" Multidisciplinary perspectives on opportunities, challenges and implications of generative conversational AI for research, practice and policy. *International Journal of Information Management, 71*, 102642. Advance online publication. DOI: 10.1016/j.ijinfomgt.2023.102642

Elish, M. C. (2019). Moral crumple zones: Cautionary tales in human-robot interaction. *Engaging Science, Technology, and Society, 5*, 40–60. DOI: 10.17351/ests2019.260

Endsley, M. R. (2017). From here to autonomy: Lessons learned from human–automation research. *Human Factors, 59*(1), 5–27. DOI: 10.1177/0018720816681350 PMID: 28146676

Engelbart, D. C. (1962). *Augmenting human intellect: A conceptual framework* (Summary Report AFOSR-3223). Stanford Research Institute. https://www.dougengelbart.org/content/view/138/

European Commission. (2025, February 12). *Commission work programme 2025: Moving forward together — A bolder, simpler, faster Union* (COM(2025) 45 final). Publications Office of the European Union. https://commission.europa.eu/strategy-and-policy/eu-budget/long-term-eu-budget/2021-2027_en

European Parliament. (2025, December 11). *MEPs demand new measures to protect workers against algorithmic management at work* [Press release]. https://www.europarl.europa.eu/news/en/press-room/20251211IPR32175/meps-demand-new-measures-to-protect-against-algorithmic-management-at-work

European Parliament & Council of the European Union. (2024). Regulation (EU) 2024/1689 laying down harmonised rules on artificial intelligence (Artificial Intelligence Act). Official Journal of the European Union, L 2024/1689.

European Parliament and Council of the European Union. (2024b, October 23). *Directive (EU) 2024/2831 of the European Parliament and of the Council on improving working conditions in platform work.* Official Journal of the European Union, L Series. https://data.europa.eu/eli/dir/2024/2831/oj

Faraj, S., Pachidi, S., & Sayegh, K. (2018). Working and organizing in the age of the learning algorithm. *Information and Organization*, *28*(1), 62–70. DOI: 10.1016/j.infoandorg.2018.02.005

Fleishman, E. A. (1953). The description of supervisory behavior. *The Journal of Applied Psychology*, *37*(1), 1–6. DOI: 10.1037/h0056314 PMID: 6038475

Floridi, L. (2019). Establishing the rules for building trustworthy AI. *Nature Machine Intelligence*, *1*(6), 261–262. DOI: 10.1038/s42256-019-0055-y

Floridi, L. (2025). AI as agency without intelligence: On artificial intelligence as a new form of artificial agency and the multiple realisability of agency thesis. Philosophy & Technology. DOI: 10.1007/s13347-025-00858-9

Gerlich, M. (2025). AI tools in society: Impacts on cognitive offloading and the future of critical thinking. *Societies (Basel, Switzerland)*, *15*(1), 6. DOI: 10.3390/soc15010006

Gigerenzer, G., & Gaissmaier, W. (2011). Heuristic decision making. *Annual Review of Psychology*, *62*(1), 451–482. DOI: 10.1146/annurev-psych-120709-145346 PMID: 21126183

Glikson, E., & Woolley, A. W. (2020). Human trust in artificial intelligence: Review of empirical research. *The Academy of Management Annals*, *14*(2), 627–660. DOI: 10.5465/annals.2018.0057

Goddard, K., Roudsari, A., & Wyatt, J. C. (2012). Automation bias: A systematic review of frequency, effect mediators, and mitigators. *Journal of the American Medical Informatics Association : JAMIA*, *19*(1), 121–127. DOI: 10.1136/amiajnl-2011-000089 PMID: 21685142

Goddard, K., Roudsari, A., & Wyatt, J. C. (2014). Automation bias: Empirical results assessing influencing factors. *International Journal of Medical Informatics*, *83*(5), 368–375. DOI: 10.1016/j.ijmedinf.2014.01.001 PMID: 24581700

Gronn, P. (2002). Distributed leadership as a unit of analysis. *The Leadership Quarterly*, *13*(4), 423–451. DOI: 10.1016/S1048-9843(02)00120-0

Guo, T., Chen, X., Wang, Y., Chang, R., Pei, S., Chawla, N. V., Wiest, O., & Zhang, X. (2024). Large language model based multi-agents: A survey of progress and challenges. In *Proceedings of the 33rd International Joint Conference on Artificial Intelligence* (pp. 8048–8057). IJCAI. DOI: 10.24963/ijcai.2024/890

Hancock, P. A., Kessler, T. T., Kaplan, A. D., Brill, J. C., & Szalma, J. L. (2021). Evolving trust in robots: Specification through sequential and comparative meta-analyses. *Human Factors*, *63*(7), 1196–1229. DOI: 10.1177/0018720820922080 PMID: 32519902

Hasanović, A., & Muftić, E. (2025). Human oversight requirements under the EU AI Act: Implications for organizational practice. *AI and Ethics*, *5*(1), 78–95. DOI: 10.1007/s43681-024-00451-4

Hersey, P., & Blanchard, K. H. (1969). Life cycle theory of leadership. *Training and Development Journal, 23*(5), 26–34.

Hinings, B., Gegenhuber, T., & Greenwood, R. (2018). Digital innovation and transformation: An institutional perspective. *Information and Organization*, *28*(1), 52–61. DOI: 10.1016/j.infoandorg.2018.02.004

Hoff, K. A., & Bashir, M. (2015). Trust in automation: Integrating empirical evidence on factors that influence trust. *Human Factors*, *57*(3), 407–434. DOI: 10.1177/0018720814547570 PMID: 25875432

Holm, J. R., & Lorenz, E. (2022). The impact of artificial intelligence on skills at work in Denmark. *New Technology, Work and Employment*, *37*(1), 79–101. DOI: 10.1111/ntwe.12215

Horowitz, M. C., & Kahn, L. (2024). Bending the automation bias curve: A study of human and AI-based decision making in national security contexts. *International Studies Quarterly*, *68*(2), sqae020. Advance online publication. DOI: 10.1093/isq/sqae020

Hutchins, E. (1995). *Cognition in the wild.* MIT Press. DOI: 10.7551/mitpress/1881.001.0001

Iansiti, M., & Lakhani, K. R. (2020). *Competing in the age of AI: Strategy and leadership when algorithms and networks run the world.* Harvard Business Review Press.

Jacovi, A., Marasović, A., Miller, T., & Goldberg, Y. (2021). Formalizing trust in artificial intelligence: Prerequisites, causes and goals of human trust in AI. In *Proceedings of the 2021 ACM Conference on Fairness, Accountability, and Transparency* (pp. 624–635). ACM. DOI: 10.1145/3442188.3445923

Jarrahi, M. H. (2018). Artificial intelligence and the future of work: Human-AI symbiosis in organizational decision making. *Business Horizons*, *61*(4), 577–586. DOI: 10.1016/j.bushor.2018.03.007

Jobin, A., Ienca, M., & Vayena, E. (2019). The global landscape of AI ethics guidelines. *Nature Machine Intelligence*, *1*(9), 389–399. DOI: 10.1038/s42256-019-0088-2

Johnson, D. G., & Verdicchio, M. (2025). The sociotechnical entanglement of AI and values. *AI & Society*, *40*(1), 67–76. DOI: 10.1007/s00146-023-01852-5

Jones-Jang, S. M., Park, Y.-J., & Kim, J. (2023). Why do people distrust AI? Distinguishing predictors of distrust and trust in artificial intelligence. *Internet Research*, *33*(2), 592–612. DOI: 10.1108/INTR-09-2021-0699

Jordan, M. I., & Mitchell, T. M. (2015). Machine learning: Trends, perspectives, and prospects. *Science*, *349*(6245), 255–260. DOI: 10.1126/science.aaa8415 PMID: 26185243

Judge, T. A., Bono, J. E., Ilies, R., & Gerhardt, M. W. (2002). Personality and leadership: A qualitative and quantitative review. *The Journal of Applied Psychology*, *87*(4), 765–780. DOI: 10.1037/0021-9010.87.4.765 PMID: 12184579

Jussupow, E., Spohrer, K., & Heinzl, A. (2022). Entangling the misuse of AI-powered diagnostic decision support systems with professional identity threat. *Management Information Systems Quarterly*, *46*(3), 1385–1416. DOI: 10.25300/MISQ/2022/16037

Kaplan, A. D., Kessler, T. T., Brill, J. C., & Hancock, P. A. (2023). Trust in artificial intelligence: Meta-analytic findings. *Human Factors*, *65*(2), 337–359. DOI: 10.1177/00187208211013988 PMID: 34048287

Kellogg, K. C., Valentine, M. A., & Christin, A. (2020). Algorithms at work: The new contested terrain of control. *The Academy of Management Annals*, *14*(1), 366–410. DOI: 10.5465/annals.2018.0174

Khera, R., Simon, M. A., & Ross, J. S. (2023). Automation bias and assistive AI: Risk of harm from AI-driven clinical decision support. *Journal of the American Medical Association*, *330*(23), 2255–2257. DOI: 10.1001/jama.2023.22557 PMID: 38112824

Kirilenko, A., Kyle, A. S., Samadi, M., & Tuzun, T. (2017). The flash crash: High-frequency trading in an electronic market, *The Journal of Finance*, *72*(3), 967–998. DOI: 10.1111/jofi.12498

Klein, G. (1993). A recognition-primed decision (RPD) model of rapid decision making. In Klein, G. A., Orasanu, J., Calderwood, R., & Zsambok, C. E. (Eds.), *Decision making in action: Models and methods* (pp. 138–147). Ablex Publishing.

Klein, G. (1998). *Sources of power: How people make decisions.* MIT Press.

Klein, G. (2008). Naturalistic decision making. *Human Factors, 50*(3), 456–460. DOI: 10.1518/001872008X288385 PMID: 18689053

Klingbeil, N., Dzindolet, M., & Rantanen, E. M. (2024). Appropriate reliance on automation: Conceptualisation, measurement, and the role of trust and confidence. *Human Factors.* Advance online publication. DOI: 10.1177/00187208241237618

Köchling, A., & Wehner, M. C. (2020). Discriminated by an algorithm: A systematic review of discrimination and fairness by algorithmic decision-making in the context of HR recruitment and HR development. *Business Research, 13*(3), 795–848. DOI: 10.1007/s40685-020-00134-w

Kolbjørnsrud, V. (2024). Leading with AI: A framework for human-machine collaboration. *California Management Review, 66*(2), 45–68. DOI: 10.1177/00081256231196742

Korn Ferry Institute. (2025). Leadership in the age of AI: New competencies for the augmented leader. Korn Ferry. https://www.kornferry.com/institute/defining-and-developing-the-ai-augmented-leader

Kotter, J. P. (1996). *Leading change.* Harvard Business School Press.

Kudina, O., & van de Poel, I. (2024). A sociotechnical system perspective on AI. *Minds and Machines, 34*(3), 21. Advance online publication. DOI: 10.1007/s11023-024-09680-2

Kupfer, C., Prassl, R., Fleiß, J., Malin, C., Thalmann, S., & Kubicek, B. (2023). Check the box! How to deal with automation bias in AI-based personnel selection. *Frontiers in Psychology, 14,* 1118723. Advance online publication. DOI: 10.3389/fpsyg.2023.1118723 PMID: 37089740

Laux, J. (2024). Institutionalised distrust and human oversight of artificial intelligence: Towards a democratic design of AI governance under the European Union AI Act. *AI & Society, 39*(6), 2853–2866. DOI: 10.1007/s00146-023-01777-z PMID: 39640298

Lee, J. D., & See, K. A. (2004). Trust in automation: Designing for appropriate reliance. *Human Factors, 46*(1), 50–80. DOI: 10.1518/hfes.46.1.50.30392 PMID: 15151155

Lee, M. K. (2018). Understanding perception of algorithmic decisions: Fairness, trust, and emotion in response to algorithmic management. *Big Data & Society, 5*(1), 1–16. DOI: 10.1177/2053951718756684

Lee, M. K., Kusbit, D., Metsky, E., & Dabbish, L. (2015). Working with machines: The impact of algorithmic and data-driven management on human workers. In *Proceedings of the 33rd Annual ACM Conference on Human Factors in Computing Systems (CHI '15)* (pp. 1603–1612). ACM. DOI: 10.1145/2702123.2702548

Licklider, J. C. R. (1960). Man-computer symbiosis. *IRE Transactions on Human Factors in Electronics, HFE-1*(1), 4–11. DOI: 10.1109/THFE2.1960.4503259

Logg, J. M., Minson, J. A., & Moore, D. A. (2019). Algorithm appreciation: People prefer algorithmic to human judgment. *Organizational Behavior and Human Decision Processes, 151*, 90–103. DOI: 10.1016/j.obhdp.2018.12.005

Longoni, C., Bonezzi, A., & Morewedge, C. K. (2019). Resistance to medical artificial intelligence. *The Journal of Consumer Research, 46*(4), 629–650. DOI: 10.1093/jcr/ucz013

Luan, S., Reb, J., & Gigerenzer, G. (2019). Ecological rationality: Fast-and-frugal heuristics for managerial decision making under uncertainty. *Academy of Management Journal, 62*(6), 1735–1759. DOI: 10.5465/amj.2018.0172

Lyell, D., & Coiera, E. (2017). Automation bias and verification complexity: A systematic review. *Journal of the American Medical Informatics Association : JAMIA, 24*(2), 423–431. DOI: 10.1093/jamia/ocw105 PMID: 27516495

Macnamara, B. N., Berber, I., Çavuşoğlu, M. C., Krupinski, E. A., Nallapareddy, N., Nelson, N. E., Smith, P. J., Wilson-Delfosse, A. L., & Ray, S. (2024). Does using artificial intelligence assistance accelerate skill decay and hinder skill development without performers' awareness? *Cognitive Research: Principles and Implications, 9*(1), 46. Advance online publication. DOI: 10.1186/s41235-024-00572-8 PMID: 38992285

Makarius, E. E., Mukherjee, D., Fox, J. D., & Fox, A. K. (2020). Rising with the machines: A sociotechnical framework for bringing artificial intelligence into the organization. *Journal of Business Research, 120*, 262–273. DOI: 10.1016/j.jbusres.2020.07.045

Mathieu, J. E., Heffner, T. S., Goodwin, G. F., Salas, E., & Cannon-Bowers, J. A. (2000). The influence of shared mental models on team process and performance. *The Journal of Applied Psychology, 85*(2), 273–283. DOI: 10.1037/0021-9010.85.2.273 PMID: 10783543

McLoughlin, J., Thoma, S. J., & Kristjánsson, K. (2025). Was Aristotle right about moral decision-making? Building a new empirical model of practical wisdom. *PLoS One*, *20*(1), e0317842. DOI: 10.1371/journal.pone.0317842 PMID: 39841702

Mehrabi, N., Morstatter, F., Saxena, N., Lerman, K., & Galstyan, A. (2021). A survey on bias and fairness in machine learning. *ACM Computing Surveys*, *54*(6), 1–35. DOI: 10.1145/3457607

Mehrotra, S., Drevin, L., & Khosla, S. (2024). Appropriate trust in AI: A systematic review of fostering mechanisms. *AI & Society*, *39*, 1853–1869. DOI: 10.1007/s00146-023-01675-3

Meijerink, J., & Bondarouk, T. (2023). The duality of algorithmic management: Toward a research agenda on the physical and psychological effects of algorithmic management practices. *Human Resource Management Review*, *33*(1), 100876. DOI: 10.1016/j.hrmr.2021.100876

Mirbabaie, M., Stieglitz, S., & Brünker, F. (2022). Understanding collaboration with virtual assistants — The role of social identity and the extended self. *Business & Information Systems Engineering*, *64*(2), 217–231. DOI: 10.1007/s12599-020-00672-x

Mittelstadt, B. D., Allo, P., Taddeo, M., Wachter, S., & Floridi, L. (2016). The ethics of algorithms: Mapping the debate. *Big Data & Society*, *3*(2), 1–21. DOI: 10.1177/2053951716679679

Möhlmann, M., Zalmanson, L., Henfridsson, O., & Gregory, R. W. (2021). Algorithmic management of work on online labour platforms: When matching meets control. *Management Information Systems Quarterly*, *45*(4), 1999–2022. DOI: 10.25300/MISQ/2021/15333

Mumford, E. (2006). The story of socio-technical design: Reflections on its successes, failures and potential. *Information Systems Journal*, *16*(4), 317–342. DOI: 10.1111/j.1365-2575.2006.00221.x

National Academies of Sciences, Engineering, and Medicine. (2022). Human-AI teaming: State-of-the-art and research needs. The National Academies Press. DOI: 10.17226/26355

National Institute of Standards and Technology. (2023). *Artificial intelligence risk management framework (AI RMF 1.0) (NIST AI 100-1)*. U.S. Department of Commerce., DOI: 10.6028/NIST.AI.100-1

Noy, S., & Zhang, W. (2023). Experimental evidence on the productivity effects of generative artificial intelligence. *Science*, *381*(6654), 187–192. DOI: 10.1126/science.adh2586 PMID: 37440646

O'Neil, C. (2016). *Weapons of math destruction: How big data increases inequality and threatens democracy*. Crown.

OECD. (2024). OECD AI principles. OECD.AI. https://oecd.ai/en/ai-principles

OECD. (2026, February 13). *The agentic AI landscape and its conceptual foundations* (OECD Artificial Intelligence Papers No. 56). OECD Publishing. DOI: 10.1787/dee339a8-en

Okamura, K., & Yamada, S. (2020). Adaptive trust calibration for human-AI collaboration. *PLoS One, 15*(2), e0229132. DOI: 10.1371/journal.pone.0229132 PMID: 32084201

Onnasch, L., Wickens, C. D., Li, H., & Manzey, D. (2014). Human performance consequences of stages and levels of automation: An integrated meta-analysis. *Human Factors, 56*(3), 476–488. DOI: 10.1177/0018720813501549 PMID: 24930170

Parasuraman, R., & Manzey, D. H. (2010). Complacency and bias in human use of automation: An attentional integration. *Human Factors, 52*(3), 381–410. DOI: 10.1177/0018720810376055 PMID: 21077562

Parasuraman, R., & Riley, V. (1997). Humans and automation: Use, misuse, disuse, abuse. *Human Factors, 39*(2), 230–253. DOI: 10.1518/001872097778543886

Parasuraman, R., Sheridan, T. B., & Wickens, C. D. (2000). A model for types and levels of human interaction with automation. *IEEE Transactions on Systems, Man, and Cybernetics. Part A, Systems and Humans, 30*(3), 286–297. DOI: 10.1109/3468.844354 PMID: 11760769

Pasquale, F. (2015). *The black box society: The secret algorithms that control money and information*. Harvard University Press. DOI: 10.4159/harvard.9780674736061

Pessach, D., & Shmueli, E. (2022). A review on fairness in machine learning. *ACM Computing Surveys, 55*(3), 1–44. DOI: 10.1145/3494672

Pignatiello, G. A., Martin, R. J., & Hickman, R. L.Jr. (2020). Decision fatigue: A conceptual analysis. *Journal of Health Psychology, 25*(1), 123–135. DOI: 10.1177/1359105318763510 PMID: 29569950

Polanyi, M. (2009). *The tacit dimension*. University of Chicago Press. (Original work published 1966)

Polyportis, A. (2024). A longitudinal study on artificial intelligence adoption: Understanding the drivers of ChatGPT usage behavior change in higher education. *Frontiers in Artificial Intelligence, 6*, 1324398. DOI: 10.3389/frai.2023.1324398 PMID: 38249792

Power, D. J. (2008). Decision support systems: A historical overview. In Burstein, F., & Holsapple, C. W. (Eds.), *Handbook on decision support systems 1* (pp. 121–140). Springer., DOI: 10.1007/978-3-540-48713-5_7

Rademaker, T., Klingenberg, I., & Süß, S. (2025). Leadership and technostress: A systematic literature review. *Management Review Quarterly*, *75*(1), 429–494. DOI: 10.1007/s11301-023-00385-x

Raisch, S., & Krakowski, S. (2021). Artificial intelligence and management: The automation–augmentation paradox. *Academy of Management Review*, *46*(1), 192–210. DOI: 10.5465/amr.2018.0072

Rathenau Instituut & TNO. (2024). *Eigen ritme of algoritme? Een verkennende studie naar algoritmisch management.* Rathenau Instituut. https://www.rathenau.nl/nl/digitalisering/eigen-ritme-algoritme

Roberts, H., Cowls, J., Hine, E., Morley, J., Wang, V., Taddeo, M., & Floridi, L. (2023). Governing artificial intelligence in China and the European Union: Comparing aims and promoting ethical outcomes. *The Information Society*, *39*(2), 79–97. DOI: 10.1080/01972243.2022.2124565

Robertson, J., Botha, E., Oosthuizen, K., & Montecchi, M. (2025). The AI Implementation Compass: A framework for organizational AI adoption. *Journal of Business Research*, *168*, 114234. DOI: 10.1016/j.jbusres.2024.114234

Roos, J. (2026). *Human magic: Leading with wisdom in an age of algorithms.* Routledge., DOI: 10.4324/9781003732570

Rudin, C. (2019). Stop explaining black box machine learning models for high stakes decisions and use interpretable models instead. *Nature Machine Intelligence*, *1*(5), 206–215. DOI: 10.1038/s42256-019-0048-x PMID: 35603010

Sakamoto, T., Harada, Y., & Shimizu, T. (2024). Facilitating trust calibration in artificial intelligence–driven diagnostic decision support systems for determining physicians' diagnostic accuracy: Quasi-experimental study. *JMIR Formative Research*, *8*, e58666. DOI: 10.2196/58666 PMID: 39602469

Salwei, M. E., & Carayon, P. (2022). A sociotechnical systems framework for the application of artificial intelligence in health care delivery. *Journal of Cognitive Engineering and Decision Making*, *16*(4), 194–206. DOI: 10.1177/15553434221097357 PMID: 36704421

Santoni de Sio, F., & Mecacci, G. (2021). Four responsibility gaps with artificial intelligence: Why they matter and how to address them. *Philosophy & Technology*, *34*(4), 1057–1084. DOI: 10.1007/s13347-021-00450-x

Santoni de Sio, F., & van den Hoven, J. (2018). Meaningful human control over autonomous systems: A philosophical account. *Frontiers in Robotics and AI*, *5*, 15. DOI: 10.3389/frobt.2018.00015 PMID: 33500902

Scharowski, N., Perrig, S. A. C., von Felten, N., Huang, H. Y., Wiczorek, R., & Brühlmann, F. (2023). Trusting AI: A user study on the relationship between trust and attitudes toward AI and AI-generated content. *Computers in Human Behavior: Artificial Humans*, *1*(1), 100016. DOI: 10.1016/j.chbah.2023.100016

Schein, E. H. (2010). *Organizational culture and leadership* (4th ed.). Jossey-Bass.

Schemmer, M., Hemmer, P., Kühl, N., Benz, C., & Satzger, G. (2022). *Should I follow AI-based advice? Measuring appropriate reliance in human–AI decision-making* (KIT Scientific Working Paper/Workshop paper). Karlsruhe Institute of Technology (KIT). DOI: 10.5445/IR/1000145647

Schön, D. A. (1983). *The reflective practitioner: How professionals think in action*. Basic Books.

Sheridan, T. B., & Verplank, W. L. (1978). Human and computer control of undersea teleoperators (Technical Report ADA057655). Man-Machine Systems Laboratory, Department of Mechanical Engineering, Massachusetts Institute of Technology.

Shrestha, Y. R., Ben-Menahem, S. M., & von Krogh, G. (2019). Organizational decision-making structures in the age of artificial intelligence. *California Management Review*, *61*(4), 66–83. DOI: 10.1177/0008125619862257

Simon, H. A. (1955). A behavioral model of rational choice. *The Quarterly Journal of Economics*, *69*(1), 99–118. DOI: 10.2307/1884852

Simon, H. A. (1957). *Models of man: Social and rational*. Wiley.

Sitra. (2025, December). *Tehtävänä tekoälymurros [Mission: AI transformation]* (Sitra Selvitys No. 254). Finnish Innovation Fund. https://www.sitra.fi/wp-content/uploads/2025/12/32838076_Tehtavana_tekoalymurros_selvitys.pdf

Skitka, L. J., Mosier, K. L., & Burdick, M. (1999). Does automation bias decision-making? *International Journal of Human-Computer Studies*, *51*(5), 991–1006. DOI: 10.1006/ijhc.1999.0252

Sprague, R. H.Jr. (1980). A framework for the development of decision support systems. *Management Information Systems Quarterly*, *4*(4), 1–26. DOI: 10.2307/248957

Starke, C., Baleis, J., Keller, B., & Marcinkowski, F. (2022). Fairness perceptions of algorithmic decision-making: A systematic review of the empirical literature. *Big Data & Society*, *9*(2), 1–16. DOI: 10.1177/20539517221115189

Stogdill, R. M. (1948). Personal factors associated with leadership: A survey of the literature. *The Journal of Psychology*, *25*(1), 35–71. DOI: 10.1080/00223980.1948.9917362 PMID: 18901913

Strich, F., Mayer, A. S., & Fiedler, M. (2021). What do I do in a world of artificial intelligence? Investigating the impact of substitutive decision-making AI systems on employees' professional role identity. *Journal of the Association for Information Systems*, *22*(2), 304–324. DOI: 10.17705/1jais.00663

Taddeo, M., & Floridi, L. (2018). How AI can be a force for good. *Science*, *361*(6404), 751–752. DOI: 10.1126/science.aat5991 PMID: 30139858

Tarafdar, M., Tu, Q., Ragu-Nathan, B. S., & Ragu-Nathan, T. S. (2007). The impact of technostress on role stress and productivity. *Journal of Management Information Systems*, *24*(1), 301–328. DOI: 10.2753/MIS0742-1222240109

Thompson, D. F. (1980). Moral responsibility of public officials: The problem of many hands. *The American Political Science Review*, *74*(4), 905–916. DOI: 10.2307/1954312

Trist, E. L., & Bamforth, K. W. (1951). Some social and psychological consequences of the Longwall method of coal-getting. *Human Relations*, *4*(1), 3–38. DOI: 10.1177/001872675100400101

Tsamados, A., Floridi, L., & Taddeo, M. (2025). Human control of AI systems: From supervision to teaming. *AI and Ethics*, *5*(2), 1535–1548. DOI: 10.1007/s43681-024-00489-4 PMID: 40352578

United States, The White House. (2025a, January 23). Executive Order 14179: Removing Barriers to American Leadership in Artificial Intelligence. *Federal Register*, *90*(18), 8741–8743. https://www.federalregister.gov/documents/2025/01/31/2025-02172/removing-barriers-to-american-leadership-in-artificial-intelligence

United States, The White House. (2025b, July 23). America's AI Action Plan. Office of Science and Technology Policy. https://www.whitehouse.gov/wp-content/uploads/2025/07/Americas-AI-Action-Plan.pdf

Uren, V., & Edward, J. S. (2023). Assessing organizational readiness for AI: The PPTD framework. *Journal of Enterprise Information Management*, *36*(4), 1123–1145. DOI: 10.1108/JEIM-07-2022-0241

Vaccaro, M., Almaatouq, A., & Malone, T. W. (2024). When combinations of humans and AI are useful: A systematic review and meta-analysis. *Nature Human Behaviour*, *8*(12), 2293–2303. DOI: 10.1038/s41562-024-02024-1 PMID: 39468277 van de Poel, I., Royakkers, L., & Zwart, S. D. (2012). *Moral responsibility and the problem of many hands*. Routledge.

Vasconcelos, H., Jörke, M., Grunde-McLaughlin, M., Gerstenberg, T., Bernstein, M. S., & Krishna, R. (2023). Explanations can reduce overreliance on AI systems during decision-making. *Proceedings of the ACM on Human-Computer Interaction, 7*(CSCW1), Article 129. **https://doi.org/**DOI: 10.1145/3579605

Veale, M., & Zuiderveen Borgesius, F. (2021). Demystifying the draft EU Artificial Intelligence Act. *Computer Law Review International, 22*(4), 97–112. DOI: 10.9785/cri-2021-220402

Veluwenkamp, H. (2022). Why meaningful human control is not enough. *Ethics and Information Technology, 24*(3), 36. Advance online publication. DOI: 10.1007/s10676-022-09663-w

Vuori, N., Helander, N., & Okkonen, J. (2026). It's amazing – but terrifying!: Unveiling the combined effect of emotional and cognitive trust on organizational members' behaviours, AI performance, and adoption. *Journal of Management Studies, 63*(2), 473–514. DOI: 10.1111/joms.13177

Wang, Y., Chen, X., & Liu, W. (2024). Information flows in AI-augmented organizations: A network analysis. *Organization Science, 35*(1), 156–178. DOI: 10.1287/orsc.2022.1622

Weick, K. E. (1995). Sensemaking in organizations. *Sage (Atlanta, Ga.)*.

Wenger, E. (1998). *Communities of practice: Learning, meaning, and identity*. Cambridge University Press. DOI: 10.1017/CBO9780511803932

Wieringa, M. (2020). What to account for when accounting for algorithms: A systematic literature review on algorithmic accountability. In *Proceedings of the 2020 Conference on Fairness, Accountability, and Transparency* (pp. 1–18). ACM. DOI: 10.1145/3351095.3372833

Yesuf, M., & Fields, Z. (2025). AI adoption in SMEs: A bibliometric review and research agenda. *Journal of Small Business Management, 63*(2), 345–378. DOI: 10.1080/00472778.2024.2312145

Yu, Y., Gomez-Cabello, C. A., Haider, S. A., Genovese, A., Prabha, S., Trabilsy, M., Collaco, B. G., Wood, N. G., Bagaria, S., Tao, C., & Forte, A. J. (2025). Enhancing clinician trust in AI diagnostics: A dynamic framework for confidence calibration and transparency. *Diagnostics (Basel), 15*(17), 2204. DOI: 10.3390/diagnostics15172204 PMID: 40941691

Zeiser, A. (2024). The attributability gap in AI decision-making: A philosophical analysis. *Philosophy & Technology*, *37*(1), 1–22. DOI: 10.1007/s13347-023-00678-x PMID: 40635766

Zhang, Y., Liao, Q. V., & Bellamy, R. K. E. (2020). Effect of confidence and explanation on accuracy and trust calibration in AI-assisted decision making. In *Proceedings of the 2020 Conference on Fairness, Accountability, and Transparency* (pp. 295–305). Association for Computing Machinery. **https://doi.org/**DOI: 10.1145/3351095.3372852

Zhang, Y., Liu, X., & Chen, H. (2025). Transformational leadership and employee AI crafting: The mediating role of AI trust. *Journal of Organizational Behavior*, *46*(3), 312–335. DOI: 10.1002/job.2780

ADDITIONAL READINGS

Brynjolfsson, E., Li, D., & Raymond, L. (2025). Generative AI at work. *The Quarterly Journal of Economics*, *140*(2), 889–942. DOI: 10.1093/qje/qjae044

Chalmers, D., Hunt, R., Pachidi, S., Potočnik, K., & Townsend, D. (2026). The acceleration of artificial intelligence: Rethinking organisation and work in an era of rapid technological change. *Journal of Management Studies*, *63*(2), 285–314. DOI: 10.1111/joms.70063

Hillebrand, L., Raisch, S., & Schad, J. (2025). Managing with artificial intelligence: An integrative framework. *The Academy of Management Annals*, *19*(1), 343–375. DOI: 10.5465/annals.2022.0072

Hossain, S., Fernando, M., & Akter, S. (2025). Digital leadership: Towards a dynamic managerial capability perspective of artificial intelligence-driven leader capabilities. *Journal of Leadership & Organizational Studies*, *32*(2), 189–208. DOI: 10.1177/15480518251319624

Jia, N., Luo, X., Fang, Z., & Liao, C. (2024). When and how artificial intelligence augments employee creativity. *Academy of Management Journal*, *67*(1), 5–32. DOI: 10.5465/amj.2022.0426

Krakowski, S. (2025). Human-AI agency in the age of generative AI. *Information and Organization*, *35*(1), 100560. Advance online publication. DOI: 10.1016/j.infoandorg.2025.100560

Krakowski, S., Haftor, D., Luger, J., Pashkevich, N., & Raisch, S. (2025). Human-centered artificial intelligence: A field experiment. *Management Science*, *72*(1), 57–72. Advance online publication. DOI: 10.1287/mnsc.2022.03849

Krakowski, S., Luger, J., & Raisch, S. (2023). Artificial intelligence and the changing sources of competitive advantage. *Strategic Management Journal*, *44*(6), 1425–1452. DOI: 10.1002/smj.3387

Noy, S., & Zhang, W. (2023). Experimental evidence on the productivity effects of generative artificial intelligence. *Science*, *381*(6654), 187–192. DOI: 10.1126/science.adh2586 PMID: 37440646

Raisch, S., & Fomina, K. (2025). Combining human and artificial intelligence: Hybrid problem solving in organizations. *Academy of Management Review*, *50*(2), 441–464. DOI: 10.5465/amr.2021.0421

KEY TERMS AND DEFINITIONS

AI-Augmented Leadership.: Organisational arrangements in which artificial intelligence systems perform analytical, advisory, or autonomous functions that directly influence leadership tasks such as strategic planning, resource allocation, performance management, and operational coordination — reconfiguring decision authority into a hybrid sociotechnical accomplishment distributed across human and algorithmic actors.

Bounded Rationality.: The concept, developed by Herbert Simon, that human decision-makers operate under cognitive constraints that prevent identification of optimal solutions. Rather than maximising expected utility, bounded rational agents satisfice — selecting the first option that meets an acceptable threshold — because the cognitive costs of exhaustive search exceed its benefits.

Epistemic Opacity.: The inability of human leaders to critically evaluate how algorithms derive their recommendations, arising from the mathematical complexity of learned representations in machine learning systems and the absence of explicit symbolic reasoning traces. Unlike a human expert, a trained model produces outputs through computations that resist straightforward interpretation.

Explainable Artificial Intelligence (XAI).: A field of technical research developing methods to make AI systems' reasoning interpretable and comprehensible to human overseers. XAI approaches vary in their trade-offs and no single method is universally superior; explanation needs differ systematically across stakeholder groups.

Automation Bias.: The documented tendency for human operators to favour algorithmic recommendations over contradictory evidence from other sources. It operates through two mechanisms: omission bias (failure to notice system errors) and commission bias (uncritical acceptance of erroneous algorithmic recommendations). It increases with cognitive load, time pressure, and confidence in system reliability.

Algorithm Aversion.: The phenomenon whereby followers and users extend greater tolerance for human inconsistency than for algorithmic error, attributing human error to situational factors while attributing algorithmic error to fundamental system deficiency.

Algorithm Appreciation.: The counterpart to algorithm aversion: the tendency of people to prefer algorithmic over human advice, particularly for tasks perceived as quantitative or objective, with this preference reversing for subjective, interpersonal, or values-laden domains.

Sociotechnical Systems Theory.: The principle, originating with Trist and Bamforth, that technological and social subsystems of work must be jointly optimised rather than independently managed, since technological design choices carry social consequences that, if unaddressed, undermine both productivity and worker wellbeing.

Distributed Agency.: The condition in which the capacity to act is not concentrated in any single human leader but distributed across multiple human and non-human actors with different capabilities, authority domains, and accountability relationships. In AI-augmented systems, this means leadership effectiveness cannot be assessed by evaluating individual human leaders in isolation from the algorithmic systems through which their decisions are made.

Distributed Cognition.: The idea that cognitive work in complex systems is accomplished through coordinated interaction among human actors, artefacts, and structured environments rather than within individual minds alone. AI systems function as cognitive artefacts extending distributed cognition to a degree qualitatively different from prior technologies.

Naturalistic Decision-Making (NDM).: An approach to understanding how experienced decision-makers operate in high-stakes, time-pressured environments, revealing that they employ pattern recognition and mental simulation rather than systematic option comparison. The recognition-primed decision model shows expert performance depends on accumulated experiential knowledge enabling rapid situation assessment.

Ecological Rationality.: The view that heuristic decision-making is often effective precisely because it exploits the structure of the environment. Fast-and-frugal heuristics can outperform complex analytical procedures in many real-world conditions, particularly when data are noisy, sample sizes are small, or environmental structure is stable.

Sensemaking.: The process through which organisational actors construct interpretations of ambiguous situations sufficient to support action (Weick, 1995). In AI-augmented leadership, algorithmic outputs become sensemaking resources that shape how leaders frame problems and interpret evidence.

Algorithmic Anchoring.: The risk that AI-generated problem framings constrain the interpretive diversity that effective collective sensemaking requires, channelling leadership attention toward statistically probable scenarios and away from genuinely novel situations that often require the most urgent leadership response.

Algorithmic Sensemaking Literacy.: The capacity to use AI outputs as inputs to sensemaking without surrendering interpretive agency to algorithmic framings.

Calibrated Trust.: Trust levels that appropriately match actual system capabilities, enabling effective human–automation collaboration. Miscalibration can manifest as over-trust (automation complacency) or under-trust (automation disuse), each of which degrades system performance.

Trust Calibration.: The alignment between a human's confidence in an AI system's recommendations and the system's actual accuracy in the relevant domain. Achieving calibration requires not only appropriate subjective trust but also the complementary domain knowledge to identify and correct AI errors when overriding.

Moral Crumple Zone.: The human actor who absorbs institutional liability for the actions of a distributed and often opaque cognitive network, particularly in high-autonomy AI configurations. The concept reveals how the design of human–AI systems can concentrate moral risk in ways that are unjust when the responsible human lacks genuine capacity to oversee, understand, or override the systems for which they nominally bear responsibility.

Meaningful Human Control.: The normative framework requiring that human overseers have sufficient understanding of system operation to detect problematic patterns, sufficient authority to intervene effectively, and sufficient practical capacity — time, cognitive resources, and organisational support — to exercise oversight reliably under realistic operating conditions.

Attributability Gap.: The structural separation between accountability (responsibility for outcomes) and attributability (the causal tracing of outcomes to specific decisions and agents) that emerges in AI-augmented decision-making, where algorithmic analysis, human interpretation, governance parameter choices, and training data all contribute to outcomes.

Problem of Many Hands.: The governance challenge that when multiple agents — human and artificial — contribute to an outcome, assigning accountability to any individual becomes analytically and normatively complex, making individual-level accountability frameworks fundamentally inadequate for AI-augmented systems.

Algorithmic Management.: The use of AI systems to exercise organisational control through mechanisms including restricting, recommending, recording, rating, replacing, and rewarding, each with distinctive implications for human authority and worker agency.

Algorithmic Bias.: Systematic prejudice in AI outputs arising from training data that reflects historical inequities, causing AI systems used in performance evaluation, promotion recommendations, or resource allocation to disadvantage protected groups even without explicitly discriminatory programming.

Digital Decision-Making Architecture.: The configurations of data infrastructure, algorithmic systems, information flows, human roles, and governance mechanisms through which decisions are made and executed in AI-augmented organisations. These architectures embody choices about authority, accountability, and organisational values.

Algorithmic Velocity.: The temporal compression of decision timelines enabled by AI's capacity for continuous data monitoring and rapid analysis, including decisions made at millisecond timescales in high-frequency domains, which can make meaningful human review at the individual case level structurally impossible.

Deskilling / Skill Atrophy.: The systematic erosion of human capabilities through reduced exercise arising from automation dependency, creating a risk that performance gains achieved during AI-augmented operation may be accompanied by degraded human decision-making capability when AI support is unavailable.

Configuration Drift.: The progressive tendency toward higher automation levels as organisational familiarity with AI systems grows, without commensurate expansion of governance infrastructure to manage the accountability and oversight demands of those higher-autonomy configurations.

Fusion Skills.: The critical competency category for AI-augmented leaders, comprising intelligent interrogation of AI systems (probing assumptions, testing edge cases, validating outputs against contextual knowledge), reciprocal apprenticing in which humans and AI systems mutually train each other, and judgement integration in which human decision-makers synthesise machine and human analytical inputs without defaulting to either as uncritical authority.

AI Literacy.: A foundational competency requirement encompassing understanding of AI concepts and limitations, ability to apply AI tools effectively in specific task contexts, capacity to evaluate AI output quality and identify potential errors, and ability to address ethical considerations in AI deployment and use.

Identity Threat.: The perception by leaders that their professional role and associated competencies have been devalued or rendered redundant when AI systems assume functions previously central to leadership identity, generating resistance to AI adoption, under-utilisation of AI capacity, or performative human deliberation that adds cost without adding value.

Technostress.: Follower anxiety regarding technological change, job security, and role displacement arising from AI implementation, which transformational leadership can mitigate by providing vision-based meaning frameworks that contextualise technological change within organisational purpose and individual development trajectories.

Uniqueness Neglect.: A specific mechanism of algorithm aversion: resistance to AI in personalised domains driven by concern that AI providers cannot account for individuals' unique characteristics and circumstances.

Transparency Paradox.: The empirically documented finding that providing simple explanations for AI decisions can paradoxically increase over-reliance by generating an illusion of understanding that terminates further scrutiny, rather than supporting genuine comprehension and calibrated verification.

Levels of Automation.: The taxonomy, developed by Parasuraman et al., identifying ten levels of human–machine interaction ranging from full human control to complete automation, across four functional domains — information acquisition, information analysis, decision selection, and action implementation — each of which can be automated independently.

Chapter 3

From Algorithmic Efficiency to Human-Centered Leadership in AI-Human Collaboration:

Implications for Organizational Behavior

R. Alamelu
http://orcid.org/0000-0003-0539-2480
SASTRA (Deemed to be) University, India

P. Eswari
SASTRA (Deemed to be) University, India

ABSTRACT

Artificial intelligence (AI) is changing organizational behavior by defining the way in which employees cooperate, innovate, and feel at work differently. Although AI contributes to the improvement of the efficiency of algorithms, it also increases burnouts, surveillance issues, and psychological pressure in tech-oriented work environments. This chapter discusses the potential of AI-human cooperation to transform organizations into systems that focus on efficiency to human flourishing systems. The results obtained indicated that AI systems can lead to innovation, trust, and engagement under mediation by empathetic and ethically transparent leaders, but they will cause psychological safety to be eroded when they are seen as tools of surveillance. The research proposes a socio-technical concept of empathetic

DOI: 10.4018/979-8-2600-2541-3.ch003

digitization, according to which the AI potential is aligned with human dignity, and the notion of well-being is a strategic determinant of sustainable organizational performance.

1. INTRODUCTION

The world is in a technology paradox: on the one hand, the world is becoming increasingly productive and innovative due to the digital transformation, on the other hand, it is causing a higher level of employee burnout, disengagement, and mental strain. As per the latest industry reports, moderate to high burnout rates are noted among 60-70 per cent of workers in technology oriented jobs particularly in hybrid and digitally intensive workplaces. Traditional, productivity and efficiency-driven, approaches to leadership are losing their effectiveness in the context of meeting the emotional and psychological subtleties of the modern workplace. In this connection, the paradigm shift of human-oriented leadership involves empathy, ethics decision-making, and well-being as a component of the general organizational approach. The modern technological business environment has made leadership a topic that cannot be quantified solely in terms of productivity or profitability, but also in terms of its ability to establish humane, ethical, and emotionally smart working conditions. With the digital transformation process in the industries gaining momentum, empathetic inclusive leadership style, along with the human well-being aspect of leadership, is increasingly becoming a feature of sustainable success (Kane et al., 2015). Although the technological ecosystem is empowering people to be more creative and productive, it could be creating a culture of perpetual change, uncertainty and intellectual clogging. In this respect, human-oriented leadership is regarded as one of the prevailing paradigms, which combines caring and competence, morality and productivity and purpose and performance. The continuous demands of organizations to be innovative, grow and compete presents complicated work cultures, characterized by a substantial mental burden, minimized periods of innovation and diverse team structures. That remote and hybrid work models have become a significant element of organizational life post-pandemic also contributes to further blurring the professional and personal life boundaries, challenging the traditional approaches to management. Rigid pre-modern notions of leadership with control, measures and outcomes as the central concern are not working in these turbulent environments. The answer to the technology and human sustainability dilemma is human-centered leadership, based on empathy, collaboration, and ethical responsibility. It considers employee as a resource, and as a complete humans whose happiness and psychological safety are key to innovation and performance.

The main objective of the research is to examine the relationship between human-oriented leadership and organizational happiness in the technology industry. The chapter is a qualitative case study that explores human-oriented leadership in chosen technology organizations. The thematic and cross-case analysis is used to define the conceptual relationship between leadership behaviours and organizational happiness, which could be used in future research to create an empirically based measurement.

2. BACKGROUND AND RATIONALE

The industry related automation, artificial intelligence (AI) and data analytics have transformed the way individuals are productive and responsive to market dynamics and introduced new concerns for workers' well-being, engagement, and ethical integrity. The context in which tech organizations currently operate is a world of innovation, intense competition, remote work, and high cognitive demand, which often exhausts emotional attachment and a sense of belonging.

Human-centred leadership and workplace happiness should be grounded in available well-being theories. Conceptualizing happiness by using the idea of the PERMA model (Seligman, 2018), happiness can be viewed through the lenses of five dimensions, including positive emotions, engagement, relationships, meaning, and accomplishment, which contribute to a holistic approach to flourishing in the organizational environment. In addition, the Self-Determination Theory (SDT) (Deci & Ryan, 2000; Ryan & Deci, 2017) describes employee well-being as an attribute of three fundamental psychological needs: autonomy, competence, and relatedness. High-quality relationships are created by participative leaders who acknowledge employees with their individual needs and consider their contribution, thus sending a message of respect and trust in their skills. Recent studies proved that through active involvement in problem-solving and decision-making, they empower employees to address work challenges without fear of negative repercussions, enhancing autonomy and control, and promoting engagement and well-being. These support-oriented and empowerment leadership behaviors are a psychological resource that enhances job satisfaction and minimizes stress and burnout (Sijbom et al., 2026). Thus, combination of PERMA, SDT, and modern leadership knowledge can offer a more powerful theoretical base for understanding the meaning of happiness in the workplace, and human-oriented leadership is one of the instruments that influence individual and organizational outcomes.

2.1 Evolving Nature of Leadership in Technology-Driven Contexts

The old paradigms of hierarchy and control have been replaced with the new, adaptive, participative, and emotionally intelligent leadership styles. New studies reveal that the success of leadership in the age of Industry 5.0 will rely on incorporating technology into human value systems and on making empathy and rational ethical decision-making the central focus of strategic management (Schneider, S., and Kokshagina, 2021). On the same note, global leadership perspectives on industry, society, and Government emphasize that leaders nowadays must strike a balance between algorithmic effectiveness and human reason, and acknowledge that employees are also co-producers of organizational meaning (Samad et al., 2023).

Human-centric, not techno-centric leadership is required more in Society 5.0, where digital systems are interlinked with human systems (Atay, 2025). These leaders are proponents of flexible work designs, inclusive decision-making, and a continuous-learning ecosystem that simultaneously enhances psychological safety and innovation. Pavitra, K. H. et al. (2024) observe that the future generation of leadership in digital-based enterprises is characterized by emotional intelligence, collaboration through trust, and value-oriented decision-making, rather than authority. This development is an indicator of a structural shift in which transactional leadership is being replaced by transformational leadership, which will, in turn, be replaced by human-centred leadership, combining compassion and competence with ethics and effectiveness.

2.2 The Well-being Paradox in Tech Workplaces

The global technology industry is experiencing robust growth and technological advances despite economic challenges. According to surveys, there are still significant levels of burnout, disengagement, and the so-called quiet quitting in companies that are otherwise technologically advanced (Varma, P. 2025). Digital hyper-connectivity commonly causes cognitive overload to employees, and hybrid work arrangements make work-life boundaries indistinct and informal social support networks weaker. Boyatzis & Johnston, 2021 found that purpose, autonomy, and psychological safety are the best predictors of workplace happiness. Still, these have been inconsistently embedded in the culture of many tech organizations. Employees who feel fairness and moral genuineness in leadership are more engaged, have greater trust in the organization, experience lower turnover, and are more successful in innovation. In a nutshell, well-being is used as a strategic tool to promote ongoing innovation rather than as an additional HR objective, as reflected in Figure 1.

Human-centred leadership is a simple solution to this contradiction since the model turns the paradigm of technology acceptance to the sustainability of humankind.

Figure 1. The Human-Centred Leadership Ecosystem

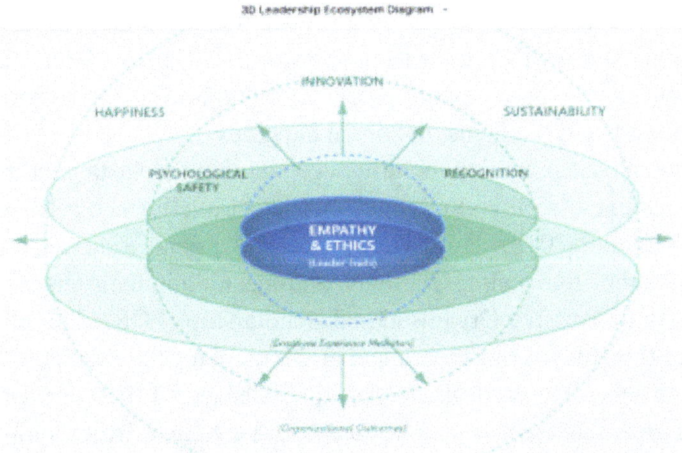

2.3 Rationale for a Human-Centred Leadership Approach- Theoretical Lens

The research falls within the Positive Organisational Scholarship (POS) and the Theory of Humanistic Management. POS focuses on the research of positive strengths, virtues, and flourishing in organizations, and on the role of positive practices in fostering resilience, creativity, and communal prosperity. Unlike other approaches that are based on deficit, which emphasize the need to fix dysfunctions, POS offers organizations the opportunity to develop on what is performing well, gratitude, compassion, trust, and purpose, to maintain high performance. To supplement this, the Humanistic Management Theory promotes ethical, dignity-based leadership and human welfare as the ultimate goals of organizational activity. All these theoretical views offer a strong perspective on how human-focused leadership creates corporate joy and transfers personal well-being to organizational performance sustainability. The work would add to the expanding literature, refining the new concept of management in the digital disruption era, not as a purely technical phenomenon but as a highly moral and humanistic practice, by locating leadership practice within this dual theory. It highlights that, in the ever-changing, highly competitive technology industry, technology is not the final distinguishing factor; human leadership drives its application.

Three trends converge to justify exploring the area of human-centred leadership in the technology sector. To begin with, the hybrid economy after the pandemic has made leadership based on empathy and trust more urgent for managing dispersed teams, rather than control (Deloitte Insights, 2023; Goleman, D., 2011). Second, automation issues, algorithmic bias, and employee surveillance have become increasingly problematic, and leaders must consider moral reasoning models to prevent threats to human dignity (World Economic Forum, 2025). Third, the integration of AI and robotics into everyday work processes has raised new questions about the definition of work and the focus on human happiness.

Both scholars and practitioners have accepted that the sustainability of digital enterprises lies in the ability to align technological intelligence and emotional intelligence. Seligman (2018) claimed that successful organizations are created when leaders develop positive feelings, activity, and meaning in their teams- values that form the basis of Positive Organisational Scholarship (POS). The philosophical foundation of this study is this theoretical orientation, together with the Humanistic Management Theory. The two frameworks support leadership that considers economic prosperity inseparable from human welfare and that values virtue, compassion, and the common good as fundamental business outcomes.

The applicability of human-centred leadership is even more pronounced in the Indian context of technology, where a culture of collectivism and rapid digital development prevails. Empirical research on the matter in recent years indicates that leadership empathy, recognition, and work-life flexibility in the Indian IT industry are becoming increasingly crucial to employee satisfaction; they are independent variables that can forecast organizational happiness.

3. OBJECTIVES OF THE STUDY

Using the theoretical background of Positive Organisational Scholarship and Humanistic Management, and based on the well-being paradox in organisations with technology use, the study examining the intersection between leadership and employee happiness.

3.1 Specific Objectives

1. To determine and classify the prime human-driven dimensions of leadership that determine the happiness and well-being of employees in technology-focused institutions

2. To examine the operationalisation of empathy, ethical decision-making and inclusivity by leaders in their daily managerial practices that determine positive organisational cultures
3. To investigate the perceived correlation between human-focused leadership and organizational happiness, especially the way in which leadership behaviours are converted into engagement, motivation and trust among the staff
4. To investigate the situational enablers and obstacles that help to determine the perception and implementation of human-centred leadership in the rapidly changing tech industry, such as remote and hybrid work organizations
5. To construct a conceptual framework that relates the leadership practices, employee welfare, and organizational happiness, informed by the qualitative information provided by various case studies

4. LITERATURE REVIEW

4.1 Human-Centred Leadership: Origins and Philosophy

The development of leadership theory has been characterized by a shift in the focus of authority-based models toward models that emphasize empathy, authenticity, and inclusion. The human-oriented paradigm of leadership builds on earlier leadership models such as servant leadership, authentic leadership, and transformational leadership, while complementing them by incorporating well-being and moral awareness into organizational structures (Goleman, 2011; Schein & Schein, 2023). According to Deloitte Insights (2023), human-centred leaders bridge purpose and performance by building trust through empathy and ethical behaviour rather than through regulation and adherence (Deloitte, 2023; Pavitra et al., 2024).

Human-oriented leadership, in contrast to the mechanistic approach to leadership that dominated in the industrial and early digital periods, involves a whole-person approach, addressing emotional, social and ethical elements in addition to cognitive and technical knowledge (Harvard Business School Publishing, 2025). It is in line with Positive Organisational Scholarship (POS), which encourages the development of leadership behaviours that support flourishing and resilience instead of preventing dysfunction (Seligman, 2018). This change to humanistic and sustainable leadership is supported by empirical evidence of reviews and researchers who present the argument that Industry 5.0 requires leaders who will be able to align technology with the needs of humans and create the conditions under which empathy and innovation can coexist (Atay, 2025; World Economic Forum, 2025). Similarly, (Pavitra, K. H et al. 2024) stress that emotional literacy and ethical decision-making must be included in next-generation leadership to make sure that technology does not eliminate human beings but empowers them. Sustainable leadership experts and consulting companies also concur that empathy and ethics are not fringe qualities and are skills of sustainable leadership (Atay, 2025; Deloitte Insights, 2023).

In addition, the literature is inclined to consider human-oriented leadership as an extension of the earlier models of leadership, with no clear conceptual frameworks, particularly in technological-related settings (Schneider and Kokshagina, 2021; Samad et al., 2023). Additionally, studies about the digital transformation as a strategy highlight that the success of an organisation is not defined only by availability of technology in the organisation, but also the compatibility of its leadership and human-centred values (Kane et al., 2015). The styles of relational and humility-based leadership influence the engagement and performance of the team in the dynamic setting as well (Rego, A. et al., 2019; Goleman, 2011). However, the literature is mostly Western-oriented, and some studies on emerging economies like India, whereby leadership demands are influenced by collectivist cultures are minimal (Pavitra et al., 2024; Atay, 2025). In this way, a new understanding of human-centred leadership as a context-specific, situation-oriented paradigm in digitally intensive workplaces is required.

4.2 Organizational Happiness and Well-being

The employees psychological safety, ownership and balancing at work place are the components of organizational happiness which is not limited to job satisfaction (Luthans & Broad, 2025; Ziaeian, 2025). Evidences from research studies have shown that happier employees are more engaged, productive, and creative at work (Harvard Business School Publishing, 2025; Ziaeian, Y., 2025). In the technology sphere, with high work intensity and the pressure to innovate, happiness acts as a protective factor against burnout and turnover. Companies that have well-being cultures perform better in terms of innovation and retention of employees than other companies (Varma, 2025; McKinsey Health Institute, 2025). Human-oriented leaders are the forces behind such results by fostering emotional safety and recognition, which are fundamental to happiness, resilience, and trust within teams (Shore, L. M., 2025).

The available literature is focused on happiness as a personal attribute rather than a group potential (Boyatzis & Johnston, 2021; Shore et al., 2025). The prime researches views that well-being is measured and the systematic impact on well-being of leadership behaviours is not sufficiently examined (Varma, 2025; McKinsey Health Institute, 2025).

The notion of happiness is placed in the positive psychology movement to measure and develop leadership and culture (Luthans& Broad, 2025) creates positive emotion, engagement, relationships, meaning, and accomplishment (PERMA model) that generate organizational flourishing (Seligman, 2018). The framework points to a gap in the theoretical knowledge of the relationships between leadership practice and affective and behavioural outcomes. When the leader is empathetic, just and genuine, this triggers positive emotional contagion, which further builds up shared joy and cooperation. According to recent studies, which have been conducted on the IT and technology services sector in India, employee happiness has been found to be one of the most predictive leadership empathy and recognition factors. With the transition of organizations to hybrid models, human-centred leadership will make distributed teams feel connected, valued and psychologically safe (Harvard Business School Publishing, 2025).

Even though earlier studies have identified a beneficial correlation between employee happiness and productivity, innovation, and retention (Moss, 2023; Harvard Business School Publishing, 2025), the study of causal processes connecting happiness and long-term organizational performance has not been significantly studied, especially in high-pressure technology settings (Montes et al., 2025). Also present is the literature on burnout that emphasizes the impact of job demands and stress on employee well-being (Maslach et al., 2001; Singh et al., 2012; Trinkenreich et al., 2024), but does not acknowledge the buffering effect of leadership support.

Support mechanisms such as mentoring and high-quality leader-member relationships have been shown to greatly alleviate burnout and role stress in demanding work settings (Thomas & Lankau, 2009; Singh et al., 2012)—a view that is currently at odds with the employee experience in digital workplaces.

4.3 Positive Organisational Scholarship (POS) in technology Contexts

Positive Organisational Scholarship (POS) offers a theoretical platform for using leadership to make organizations places of human thriving. Based on positive psychology, POS focuses on virtues such as compassion, trust, gratitude, and resilience to improve both personal and group performance (Seligman, 2018; Luthans & Broad, 2025). Instead of emphasizing the idea of fixing dysfunction, POS proponents are boosting what is functioning well, a change that is perfectly aligned with the principles of human-centred leadership. It not only shifts the emphasis from correcting dysfunctions to facilitating human thriving in organizations (Ahmed et al., 2021), but also facilitates human thriving in organizations (Ahmed et al., 2021).

POS is particularly significant in technology sectors. It is empirically proposed that teams that work in a positive organizational climate are more creative, engaged, and less burned out, especially in knowledge-based and technology-enhanced organizations — the teams that have a leadership that is supportive and trust-based record a 30 per cent higher level of creative output and a much lower burnout (Ahmed et al., 2021; Luthans & Broad, 2025). Nevertheless, even with its conceptual power, the POS literature faces implementation constraints in fast-paced digital environments.

To start with, most POS research is theoretical or cross-sectional and has not been longitudinally verified in dynamic technology contexts (Schneider & Kokshagina, 2021). Second, POS is likely to place less emphasis on structural and technological pressures such as digital overload, algorithmic surveillance, and the pressure to maintain constant innovation (Institute for the Future of Work, 2024; Gartner, 2023). Moreover, POS fails to provide a comprehensive understanding of how leadership can translate positive practices into quantifiable outcomes, such as innovation and retention (Samad et al., 2023; Deloitte, 2023). Leadership in technology-based workplaces plays a key role in mediating between positive organizational practices and employee experience (Morgeson et al., 2010).

In the Indian technology environment, implementing recognition and empathy may help leaders neutralize the pressure of a high-stakes digital environment, increasing both satisfaction and innovation. Pavitra, K. H. et al. (2024) also note that digital ecosystem leaders should deliberately cultivate cultures of appreciation, in which well-being is viewed as a system variable rather than an individual characteristic. In the context of leadership training, POS principles help technology organizations foster long-term employee happiness, ethical innovation, and competitiveness (Ahmed, T. et al., 2021). Atay (2025) develops the POS argument and connects it to Society 5.0 - the idea of integrating human-centric innovation into the socio-technical systems. In such circumstances, POS can serve as an ethical compass and a dynamic framework, allowing organizations to find a balance between efficiency and compassion. The relationship between POS and the human-centred leadership, thus, provides a powerful template to rehumanize digital workplaces (World Economic Forum, 2025).

Figure 2. Virtuous Cycle of Happiness–Ethics–Innovation

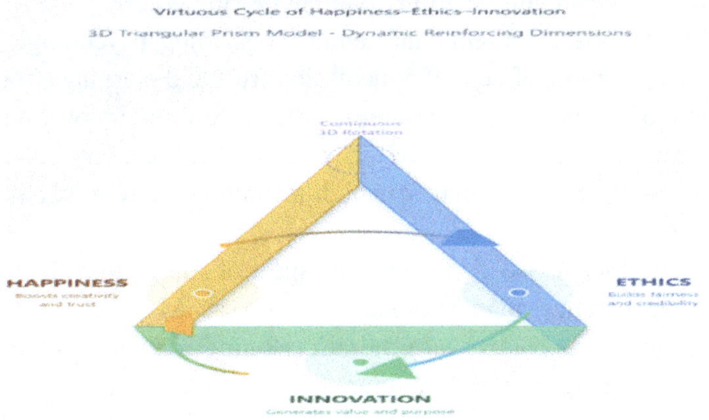

4.4 Contemporary Challenges in Tech Workplaces

The increasing awareness, technology organizations continue to face obstacles to the development of happiness and well-being. Technology is associated with rapid innovation, high cognitive demands, and new work forms, including hybrid and remote work (Deloitte, 2023; World Economic Forum, 2025). The greatest problem is digital overload — the continuous stream of information, notifications, and performance indicators that disrupt attention and cause stress. The literature identifies the following challenges: burnout, psychological safety issues, and blurred work-life boundaries (Maslach et al., 2001; Edmondson, 1999; Edmondson & Bransby, 2022). A report (Institute for the Future of Work, 2024) indicates that ubiquitous monitoring technologies and algorithmic performance trackers result in a lack of autonomy and trust, thereby negatively affecting psychological safety.

These challenges, however, are viewed in isolation. Burnout can be studied in terms of job demands and stress models (Singh et al., 2012), psychological safety within teams (Frazier et al., 2017), and hybrid work from a structural perspective (Gartner, 2023). Research on how to combine these dimensions into a unified framework is limited.

Remote and hybrid working models have made leadership more complex, though they have also brought greater flexibility. A significant number of leaders find it hard to sustain emotional attachment, integration, and equality within decentralized teams (Rego, A. et al., 2019). According to Deloitte Insights (2023), empathy and authenticity are currently ranked higher than technical knowledge to ascertain leadership effectiveness (Deloitte, 2023; World Economic Forum, 2025). Hybrid teams require a participatory communication system, equal appreciation, and a cause close to human-centred leadership (World Economic Forum, 2025).

Leadership actions are highly influential in shaping psychological s;y, and feedback-sharing is more effective in increasing trust and learning (Coutifaris and Grant). Negative behaviours, such as abuse, erode safety and innovation (Liu et al., 2016). Also, the context and design of teams play a significant role in determining psychological safety and performance in high-technology settings (Chandrasekaran & Mishra, 2012).

The other significant issue is the ethical aspect of automation. This raises concerns about transparency, bias, and accountability as AI and robotics transform decision-making and as leaders face moral reasoning in their daily practice. The new ethical issues of algorithmic bias, employee surveillance, and ethical dilemmas in AI-driven decision-making only compound the problem of leadership (World Economic Forum, 2025; Institute for the Future of Work, 2024). Though empathy and ethical leadership are offered as remedies (Boyatzis & Johnston, 2021; Atay, 2025), their application in digitally mediated settings is under-researched. Samad et al. (2023) highlighted the need to incorporate ethics into leadership education to address Industry 5.0. In hybrid and digitally mediated environments, the role of leadership is to tackle structural and relational complexities that influence coordination, trust, and engagement (Gartner, 2023; World Economic Forum, 2025). To make the discussion relevant to the present-day technology sector, this chapter links human-centred leadership concepts to the challenges that characterize modern technology workplaces.

4.5 Research Gap:

Scholars have shown increasing interest in human-centred leadership and workplace well-being, yet the existing body of literature leaves several important questions unanswered. The majority of the studies consider employee happiness as a personal, individual consequence and do not pay much attention to how leadership behaviour influences well-being at an organisational or collective level. Another weakness is the lack of cohesion of the study where the burnout, psychological safety, and the stresses of hybrid and remote work are commonly examined as distinct constructs, and less attempt to unify them under one analytical frame. The geographic coverage of the sources should also be mentioned, with the empirical research in the emerging markets such as India being limited, and the unique issues the AI-enabled, digitally mediated work setting brings being so far peripherally addressed. This chapter addresses these gaps by developing a qualitative, integrative model where the three human-centred leadership, organisational happiness, and performance outcomes are introduced to each other in the context of technology organisations.

5. METHODOLOGY

5.1 Research Design

This chapter qualitative multiple-case study design that shall be utilized in exploring the impact of human-oriented leadership practices on organizational happiness and employee well-being in technology based organizations. The qualitative approach enables one to include lived experiences, context of the organization and the stories of the leadership that cannot be sufficiently quantified using the quantitative technique. According to Creswell and Poth (2024), the case study design is suitable for learning more about a complex social phenomenon in a real-world context. It enables the researcher to explore the ways and reasons behind the development, growth and effects of human-centred leadership behaviours. The design has focused on interpretive inquiry, placing meaning within participants' experiences rather than being dictated by predetermined constructs.

The research philosophical position is constructivist, based on the idea that leadership meaning is co-constructed through social interaction, context, and mutual understanding. Positive Organisational Scholarship (POS) and Humanistic Management Theory inform the study, and both focus on human flourishing, ethical conscience, and relational well-being as focal points in making organizations successful.

5.2 Case Selection

The purposive sampling strategy was employed to select technology organizations that practice well-being-oriented or human-centred leadership. To provide contextual depth, as well as cross-case analysis, three case organizations were selected in the Indian technology sector:

Case A - It is a world-renowned IT services company with a culture of employee-first and a hybrid work model.

Case B: A medium-sized software company that has been carrying out empathy-based leadership development programs.

Case C -A start-up ecosystem that incorporates mindfulness and well-being analytics in its leadership model.

The qualitative multi-case study design was specifically selected to obtain the contextual richness and diversity of human-oriented leadership in technology organizations. The use of strict case-control was present and determined by variations in the size of the organizations, the level of digitization, and disclosed employee well-being, permitting the corresponding cross-cases comparison.

5.3 Data Collection

The semi-structured interviews, focus groups, and document analysis were conducted to collect data between November 2025 and March 2026.

Interviews: 15 leaders (CXOs, managers, team leads) and 20 employees of the three companies were interviewed on the leadership behaviours, their perceptions of well-being, and the organizational culture.

Focus Groups: two virtual focus groups (6-8 members each) were organized to talk about what they all shared about happiness and psychological safety.

Document Review: Triangulation of findings was performed with the help of organizational HR policies, internal reports, and materials of leadership training.

The thematic analysis was adopted and in this study the six phases were applied to familiarisation, coding, theme development, review, naming and reporting, as introduced by Konstantinos, G. (2024). NVivo 14 was used to identify the patterns around empathy, ethics, inclusion, and well-being initiatives. A cross-case synthesis was used to compare the leadership practices and results in the three organizations (Yin, 2018). The conceptual model led to three general dimensions in which the themes were clustered:

- Leadership Behaviours (empathy, ethical decision-making, communication)
- Employee Experience (psychological safety, happiness, engagement)
- Outcomes of the organizations (innovation, trust, retention)
- Triangulation of the researcher, repetitive coding, and respondent validation (member checking) were used to enhance reliability.

6. DATA ANALYSIS AND FINDINGS

6.1 Overview of Analytical Process

The thematic analysis revealed that the story of leadership empathy, ethical authenticity, psychological safety and organizational happiness appeared in all three case studies in the technology sector. The data were coded and compressed into general dimensions as per the six-phase model created by Konstantinos, G. (2024). Human-centred leadership, happiness drivers, employee experience, performance and organisational results behaviours. Both of these instances made distinct and similar arguments that demonstrated the key drivers of long-term performance among digital enterprises.

6.2 Theme 1: Empathy as a Leadership Capability

The term empathy proved to have the strongest impact on the well-being of employees. There was a better level of trust and satisfaction among leaders who were active listeners and identified personal issues and changed workloads. Case A (global IT company): one of the senior HR managers noted:

"The morale of the employees increased to the roof when leaders started to make emotional check-in instead of status meetings. People felt that they were being watched and not controlled". This is in line with Deloitte Insights (2023) and Harvard Business School Publishing (2025) which also consider empathy a measurable leadership skill linked with engagement and retention. Similarly, Varma P. (2025) discovered that managers in the tech environment with a higher psychological safety reported an innovative performance 1.5 times higher than normal performance.

6.3 Theme 2: Ethical and Authentic Decision-Making

The openness of decision-making and lack of bias in performance ratings were the reasons mentioned by the employees in Case B (mid-sized software company) as the factors that made them happy. This demonstrates the humanistic management style that provides dignity in the work place based on ethical consistency (World Economic Forum, 2025). Authenticity and empowerment were found by the participants to be similar: "Our CEO is a man who publicizes his mistakes. It makes it easy to us to make responsible risks. Real leadership also enhanced shared trust in transitioning to hybrid work". The results agree with those of Samad et al. (2023), who state that ethical thinking in Industry 5.0 leadership promotes loyalty and creativity.

6.4 Theme 3: Psychological Safety and Inclusive Communication

Workers were reported to give more ideas and work together when vulnerability was normalized by the leaders. This can be compared to Seligman (2018) and Atay (2025) who relate inclusive conversation to successful and responsive learning. It was shown that the main clue of the relationship between empathy and measurable happiness was non-discriminative communication, where feedback is encouraged without intimidation.

6.5 Theme 4: Happiness as a Catalyst for Innovation and Retention

Happiness did not seem to be perceived as a leisure or perk in all three organizations but as a strategic resource to productivity. Leaders established rewards systems, health, and flexible work schedules to stay energized and creative. These results are consistent with the McKinsey Health Institute (2025) and Moss (Harvard Business Review, 2023) reports, which claim that well-being is associated with the intensity of innovation and retention. When asked about the meaning of happiness, the respondents said it was the freedom to create and not be afraid, which supported the ideas of the Positive Organisational Scholarship (POS) that positive affect is associated with resilience and adaptability to change (Seligman, 2018).

In the cross-case comparison (Table 1), the organizational structure was found to vary, but through the same human values, empathy, fairness, and inclusion, parallel happiness results were obtained. Psychological safety was directly related to leadership behaviours, which strengthened creativity and retention, thereby confirming the cause-and-effect relationships between human-centred leadership and happiness and performance within the conceptual framework.

Table 1. Cross-Case Insights

Analytical Dimension	Case A (Global IT)	Case B (Software Firm)	Case C (Tech Start-up)	Common Outcome
Leadership Focus	Empathy & Hybrid Trust	Ethical Authenticity	Psychological Safety	Human Connection
Key Practice	Emotional Check-Ins	Transparent Evaluations	No-Blame Feedback	Open Dialogue
Happiness Drivers	Recognition, Flexibility	Fairness, Purpose	Belonging, Learning	Engagement, Creativity
Outcomes	Lower Turnover, More Innovation	High Trust, Reduced Conflict	Higher Collaboration	Sustained Organizational Happiness

Source-by authors

The table summarises the most effective leadership qualities that promote happiness and health: empathy and ethics. Psychological safety is the mediating variable between performance and leadership. People-oriented leadership turns organizational happiness into a strategic driver of innovation instead of a soft concept. The cross-case alignment has highlighted that human connection with digital capabilities leads to future business.

7. CROSS-CASE DISCUSSION: HUMAN-CENTERED LEADERSHIP DIMENSIONS

The comparative radar chart (fig.3) visually summarises the leadership qualities that were presented in the three qualitative case studies, such as Case A, Case B and Case C, respectively, which are representative of different technology-oriented organizations with different maturity levels regarding the adoption of human-centred leadership practices. The five axes, Leadership Empathy, Ethical Authenticity, Psychological Safety, Innovation, and Happiness, are all visual representations of the manner in which relational and affective aspects of leadership are converted into organizational well-being and adaptive performance.

Figure 3. Cross-case comparison of human-centred leadership dimensions

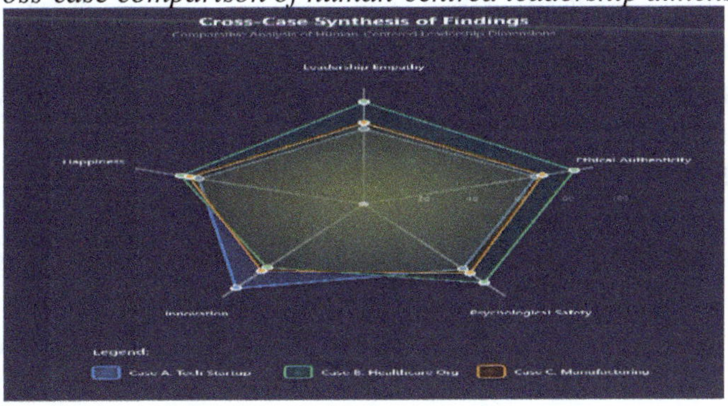

7.1 Leadership Empathy

Leadership Empathy scores highest in all three cases. The Case A example shows the use of empathetic behaviours that are consistent in nature, namely one-to-one mentoring and emotional check-ins during project sprints, as explained by Harvard Business School Publishing (2025) in its discussion of the ability to be emotionally resilient as a leader. In Case B, there is moderate embedded empathy in agile team rituals, and in Case C, there is improvement due to the implementation of peer-support circles in hybrid teams.

7.2 Ethical Authenticity

The Ethical Authenticity axis shows a somewhat balanced performance, but Case B performs marginally better due to open communication and participation in the review of algorithm-related decisions. The ethics programs in Case A are more reflective than compliance-oriented, meaning they are procedural rather than moral. On the other hand, Case C is about value congruence via ethics hackathons, where employees are asked to think of the social consequences of code. Similar findings are also reflected in Deloitte Insights (2023), where the author claims that ethical consistency as visual manifestation of organizational integrity is the basis of employee trust.

7.3 Psychological Safety

By considering the three cases, case A reported good safety in terms of open views and non-punitive feedback culture; case B has not been performing well due to competitive internal ranking system and case C has not been performing well initially, but digital feedback tools that are anonymous have helped it. This point complies with the framework proposed by Edmondson et al. (2022) that considers psychological safety a driver of creativity and further engagement in knowledge work.

7.4 Innovation

In the context of innovation, case B was a winner with the well-organized ideation pipelines and innovation challenges providing rewards and prizes, whereas the high empathy of case A cannot be turned into radical innovation directly. Case C shows that it has initial experimentation, which is enabled by the tolerance of the leadership to failure. This kind of relationship is consistent with the finding by Seligman (2018), which identified a reciprocal relationship between happiness and innovation, but demanded an environment of freedom and responsibility.

7.5 Happiness

Finally, happiness is of moderate strength in all the cases and is strongly connected with empathy and psychological safety. The concepts of happiness in work defined by Case A employees refer to the sense and sense of mission with co-workers; Case B happiness in communication with work and career mobility; Case C happiness in flexibility and work-life balance.

7.6 Integrated Interpretation

The radar diagram (fig. 3) indicated that the five constructs did not compete, but complemented each other. Psychological safety is always supported by empathy and ethics, and this process, in turn, triggers happiness and innovation. This cause and effect links to the Positive Organisational Scholarship (POS) hypothesis that virtuous leadership behaviours foster a thriving system. What the synthesis of visuals also demonstrates is that no one achieves the excellence in all dimensions in a balanced sense; thus, leadership as a human being is dynamic and adaptive than fixed. Concisely, the cross-case analysis supports the overarching thesis of the chapter: human-centred leadership as the foundation of the emotional infrastructure of sustained innovation and common delight in technology. Some of the ways of sustaining engagement are connecting with others by empathy, making sure that trust is maintained by being ethical, finding voice by being safe, releasing energy by being innovative and being engaged by being happy. All these dimensions form living system of organizational prosperity, which must be consciously worked on by modern tech leaders.

8. DISCUSSION

8.1 Positive Organisational Scholarship (POS)

The results are nearly similar to the ideas of Positive Organisational Scholarship (POS), which is devoted to human strengths, good behaviours, and building of positive meaning in the life of an organization (Seligman, 2018). In every case, leadership empathy and moral legitimacy are a good emotional attraction that builds trust, empathy and moral enthusiasm among the workers (Boyatzis & Johnston, 2021). The latter attractors have an impact on the psychological weather in general, which is more active and creative. Case A, it was the empathetic talk of the leader that occurred so frequently in that Case that gave the employees the sense of belonging and they were free to raise new ideas without the fear that they can be reproved by the leader. It is a POS theoretical observation that compassion and authenticity are not psychological inhibitors of innovation and are rather psychological facilitators of innovation. The balanced approach to ethics justifies this argument and recognition used in Case B, which shows that involvement in virtuous leadership practices can help the organization to guarantee continuity in performance not only in stressful situations during the innovation cycles, but also morally.

8.2 Humanistic Management as the Moral Core of Tech Leadership

Indicatively, ethical decision-making and empathetic conversations in Cases A and C resulted in employee happiness and retention increased, despite an average innovation score in the same timeframe. This can be linked to the fact that humanistic leadership is transforming the work place to become a moral and emotionally sustainable place, which is becoming more and more significant in the digital world, where automation and working remotely are the norms. The leaders of the future, according to the World Economic Forum (2025), will be demanded to combine technological skills and human care in a creative way, and the direction that Case B took, where the adaptive practices became a part of the routine with the use of AI-assisted decision-making tools in an open way and a very clear definition of the ethical borderline was established. This combination of compassion and technology is a feasible application of Humanistic Management in a real-life technological situation (fig. 4).

Figure 4. Pillars of Human-Centred Leadership

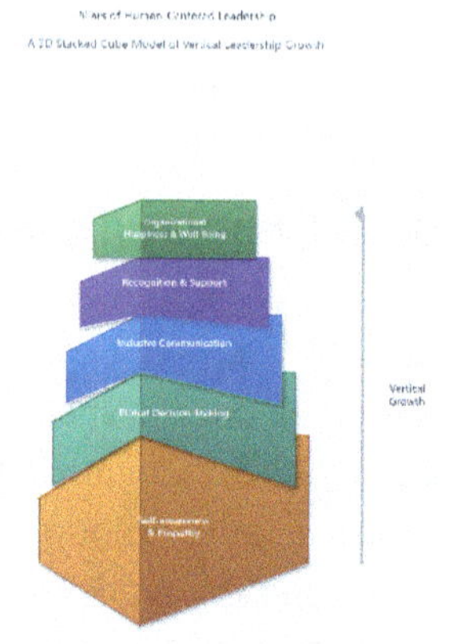

8.3 The Empathy–Ethics–Innovation Nexus

The union of empathy, ethics, and innovation is the theoretical core of this research. But the qualitative findings indicate that the long-term facilitators of innovation are empathy and ethical authenticity in that they assist in reducing fear, providing voice to people, and making purpose and creativity consistent. Risk-taking and collaboration (Gartner, 2023) were far more prevalent in all three cases through active listening and moral consistency amongst leaders. This tension points to a break in the current literature on leadership on how human-based leadership can be applied in the context of excessive performance pressure implying that contingent and situational models are required instead of blanket prescriptions.

8.4 Organizational Happiness as a Strategic Resource

In this respect, happiness is not merely the sense of personal satisfaction; it is a state of being together that is abundant in psychological and professional assistance and, as a result, results in increased resiliency, productivity, and social capital. Such an interpretation of the situation is consistent with the article by Moss (Harvard Business Review, 2023), which views happiness as a moral implication and a performance enhancer. The radar chart shows an equal and diverse balance of distribution in the various cases implying that happiness is an intermediary between relationships-permitting empathy and security to emerge and innovation and performance to be connected. In this way, organizational happiness becomes the nexus connecting a human-focused philosophy of leadership to the sustainability of business performance, whose discovery not only validates the empirical input of this chapter to the broader debate on leadership and well-being but also the literature itself.

8.5 The Digital Context: Rehumanizing Technology

Among the outstanding effects of the discussed findings is the need to rehumanize technologically facilitated work. The faster digital transformation becomes, the greater the risk of losing emotional ties and ethical corruption. According to the experiment, human-centred leadership is the factor that can provide the moral fortification essential to making technology-impacted environments interdependent, meaningful, and fair. Using Case C as an example, AI-based performance dashboards can foster a sense of vice-presidency rather than anxiety. This is because the leaders used the tools compassionately, presenting information as developmental feedback rather than reprimanding the employees. Such behaviours give rise to the idea of empathetic digitization, that is, the use of technology to foster, rather than substitute for, human development.

8.6 Theoretical and Practical Integration and Limitations

The discussion reiterates the presence of human-centred leadership as a moral and strategic system by presenting a summary of the evidence and the resulting theory. 1) In the POS perspective, it triggers a positive effect that expands the cognitive and social capital. The Humanistic Management approach bases organizational purpose on ethical responsibility. Consequently, it has objective impacts, including decreased burnout, enhanced innovation, and heightened retention, which could be linked to value creation through well-being. Thus, the proposed leadership model is human happiness as a strategic input, not an organizational by-product, resulting in innovation and resilience in technologically advanced industries.

Psychological safety is now a foundational construct for understanding team effectiveness in technologically intensive environments. Edmondson (1999) defines it as a collective understanding that people can take interpersonal risks, such as raising concerns, admitting mistakes, or challenging assumptions, without fear of negative consequences. Recent reviews reaffirm its importance in complex, fast-changing work settings such as agile teams where learning and innovation are reliant on open communication (Edmondson & Bransby, 2022; Frazier, M. L et al., 2017), while research in high-tech R&D shows the relationship between task design and team context to influence this climate (Chandrasekaran & Mishra, 2012). Leadership is very much at the heart of this: destructive behaviours, such as abusive supervision, hinder psychological safety (Liu et al., 2016), while leader feedback (i.e., sharing) enhances psychological safety by normalizing vulnerability and transparency (Coutifaris & Grant, 2022).

Burnout is another important aspect of employee experience in the digital workforce. Maslach's three-dimensional model (emotional exhaustion, cynicism, and reduced personal accomplishment) remains the dominant model of burnout in organizational settings (Maslach, Schaufeli, & Leiter, 2001). In the software engineering domain, the Job Demands-Resources (JD-R) model has been widely used to indicate that pressure in workload, role conflict and work-family strain may increase burnout. At the same time, resources such as social support and learning opportunities may mitigate burnout (Singh, Suar, & Leiter, 2012). Longitudinal evidence highlights the importance of burnout and engagement in predicting attrition among software professionals (Trinkenreich, Santos, & Stol, 2024). Again, leadership emerges as a key protective factor: high-quality leader-member exchange relationships and mentoring relationships reduce role stress and emotional exhaustion (Thomas & Lankau, 2009). These insights are consistent with emerging research on hybrid and digital leadership, which outlines the importance of clarity, trust-building, and support in relationships within distributed tech teams (Morgeson, DeRue, & Karam, 2010; Montes, Penzenstadler, & Feldt, 2025).

The overuse of empathy risk can escalate emotional labour requirements on leaders in a high-stress technology environment and, cause decision fatigue or slow performance. Moreover, the empathetic-based practice which is scaled up to large international distributed teams, can destroy consistency and performance. Even in digitally mediated systems, the privacy, surveillance, and algorithmic bias ethical risks of using AI-assisted empathy analytics are present. These trade-offs imply that the human-centred leadership cannot be implemented blindly, but it must be balanced with the accountability, performance discipline, and protection of ethics. The conclusions cannot be easily applied to other sectors or in other countries since the research is carried out in the field of technology companies in a specific country and culture.

9. PRACTICAL IMPLICATIONS

This qualitative research paper concludes that the concept of human-centred leadership is not an impractical one but rather a viable strategy that can bring happiness, creativity, and sustainability to technology companies. The primary dimensions of Empathy, Ethical Authenticity, Psychological Safety, Innovation, and Happiness are the main reasons for integrating well-being into leaders' daily practices. Conventional training is usually involved in development of competencies that may be based on the technical and strategic skills whereas the emotional and ethical aspects are neglected. Hence, the human-centred leadership modules of the organizations are certainly required, and they will include:

- Empathy as a simulation, reflective conversations and role-reversal exercises
- Emotional intelligence assessment that is integrated with AI-based sentiment analytics and coaching intervention that focuses on self-awareness, compassion, and moral judgment.

According to Harvard Business School Publishing (2025), the fitness of leadership in hybrid working environment is related to emotional agility and authenticity as opposed to control over the subordinates. Therefore, the incorporation of these abilities will make leaders reliable, inclusive, and equitable even in cases where they are communicating online. AI can be used to detect empathy leaders by tracking the overall trends in their well-being, promoting mental health efforts, or showing workload stress through predictive analytics (Pillai et al., 2022). However, the World Economic Forum (2025) warns that digitized empathy should always be supervised ethically to prevent unintentional invasions of privacy or emotional manipulation. Thus, companies can consider establishing so-called ethical AI empathy systems and humanistic principles-based analytics systems that process information through the prism of well-being rather than surveillance. Such systems represent empathetic digitization and ensure that the machine will not replace human presence in the workplace. The conclusion from the three cases is unanimous: leadership based on human values is the driving force in cultural change, transforming the organizational narrative from one that maximizes output to one that achieves the purpose. These values can be imbued in leaders through traditions, storytelling, and ritual. The merger of empathy, digital intelligence, ethical foresight, and happiness metrics presented in Table 2 is one of the next phases of leadership in technological organizations.

Table 2. Human-centred leadership integration

Leadership Dimension	Key Organizational Actions	Managerial Interventions	Policy / Ecosystem Recommendations
Empathy	Introduce structured mentoring and peer-support programs; promote empathetic communication channels.	Conduct emotional literacy workshops; practice reflective dialogue and active listening in team reviews.	Encourage the adoption of inclusion standards and the certification of empathy-based leadership under professional councils.
Ethical Authenticity	Embed ethical indicators in performance appraisals; create transparent communication on algorithmic decisions.	Model moral consistency; lead ethics hackathons and open deliberation sessions.	Develop national or sectoral *Ethical Tech Leadership* benchmarks for digital industries.
Psychological Safety	Design non-punitive feedback systems and digital suggestion platforms.	Establish "safe space" protocols for hybrid teams; conduct team retrospectives focused on learning.	Integrate psychological safety into ISO or ESG well-being audits for tech firms.
Innovation	Implement fail-safe innovation labs and reward experimentation.	Coach teams to reframe failure as learning; use participative ideation tools.	Provide tax incentives or grants for human-centred innovation projects that emphasize ethical AI.
Happiness & Well-Being	Institutionalize happiness audits, recognition systems, and flexible work policies.	Conduct regular pulse surveys; recognize acts of compassion and collaboration.	Align organizational happiness metrics with SDG 3 (Good Health) and SDG 8 (Decent Work).

Source: by authors

Table 2 shows how each aspect of human-centred leadership could be made a part of the system through three different levels: actions of the organization that determine the culture and the systems, interventions of the manager that influence everyday behaviour, and recommendations at the policy level that match the well-being of the micro-level with the macro-level sustainability goals. Implementing these practices would mean that tech companies would no longer talk about but make empathy, ethics, and happiness measurable strategic assets through systemic implementation.

Table 3. Synthesis of Practical Pathways

Stakeholder	Strategic Priority	Implementation Pathway
Leaders	Embed empathy & moral transparency	Emotional check-ins, ethical reflection routines
HR Managers	Institutionalize well-being metrics	Happiness dashboards, recognition analytics
Policymakers	Regulate for human sustainability	Include psychological safety in ESG/NEP frameworks
Academia	Train human-centered leaders	Case-based learning on ethics & emotional literacy
Global Tech Ecosystems	Balance digital speed with human dignity	Use AI for well-being monitoring & inclusive collaboration

Source: by authors

These strategies (Table 3) put human-centred leadership into practice through organizational design principles, thereby ensuring that happiness and performance develop simultaneously rather than in conflict. Building on the practical implications mentioned earlier, the next section outlines the main future research areas that will deepen theoretical and empirical knowledge of human-centred leadership in technology-driven environments.

10. FUTURE RESEARCH DIRECTIONS

New research ought to explore how artificial intelligence (AI) can be used as an addition, not a replacement, of human-centred leadership. Empathy analytics which is the emerging branch of science deploying natural language processing to understand tone, sentiment and emotional wellbeing, which is AI-induced, has the potential to help leaders identify the stress and morale trends of the team in real time. However, this type of connection provokes unease regarding ethical considerations concerning privacy, autonomy, and the algorithmic bias. According to Atay (2025) and the World Economic Forum (2025), leaders must find the appropriate balance between data-driven information and moral judgment and make sure that AI systems respect humans. Researchers might create models to measure how AI-aided empathy affects trust, motivation, and decision transparency in online workplaces. Considering that technology companies operate in various cultural contexts, comparative studies might examine differences in how human-centred leadership occurs in Western individualistic and Asian collectivist environments. To illustrate, Indian technology firms may bring together empathy and ethical care through cultural values, namely seva (service) and sahridayata (shared feeling), while Western companies focus on psychological autonomy. Future studies may use both Hofstede's cultural dimensions and the GLOBE framework to evaluate how empathy, ethics, and happiness are culturally described and supported organizationally. This type of research would not only shed light on the different aspects of culture throughout the globe but also contribute to the global leadership literature by opening (fig. 5) and revealing culturally embedded expressions of well-being.

Figure 5. Global Reach of Human-Centred Tech Leadership

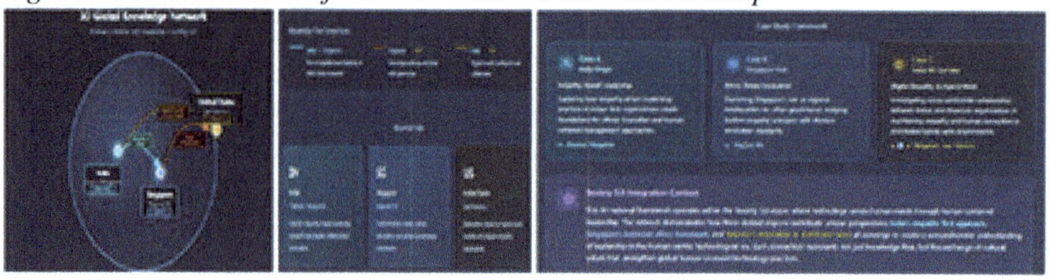

Although it is conceptually significant, workplace happiness is still not adequately measured in the technology sector. Scholars of the future should develop a multidimensional index of happiness that includes variables such as psychological safety, recognition, fairness, and innovation energy. The McKinsey Health Institute (2025) highlights the productivity advantages of quantifying well-being and proposes that new models could directly link happiness metrics to innovation performance and retention outcomes. It is also possible to incorporate Positive Organisational Scholarship (POS) metrics—such as resilience, gratitude, and flourishing—into data analytics platforms to monitor "emotional capital" as a part of human sustainability reporting. Although this chapter uses a qualitative multi-case design that allows for in-depth and theoretically constructive analysis, quantitative methods, such as mixed-methods and large-sample designs, could be used in the future to statistically substantiate the proposed leadership-happiness-innovation framework. The future study ought to explore human-centred leadership in manufacturing, healthcare, and the public sector contexts across individualistic and collectivist cultures to challenge the contextual validity.

11. CONCLUSION

The study, conducted in the age of digital acceleration and continuous innovation, still proves a simple yet powerful concept: only people can make technology thrive. With a human-centred leadership approach, leaders shift management from a performance-oriented hunt to a relationship-oriented partnership (Schein, E. H., et al., 2023). Employees, who are the objects of empathy and moral transparency, are more satisfied, feel more belonging, and are less hesitant to bring up new ideas. The leaders will be the ones who will create a sense of psychological safety, recognition and fairness simultaneously and will have an environment where the generation of ideas and adaptive learning, which are the most fundamental competencies of fast changing technology ecosystems, will be practised without any challenges. Thus, the happiness becomes an organizational resource that fosters trust, enhances innovation and promotes sustainability. In addition, the chapter follows the flow of POS in the digital age, which depicts the connection between emotional well-being and technological ability. In addition, it shows what leaders, HR professionals and policymakers should do to integrate empathy and morals into the organizational design. This emerging synthesis (human-centred leadership = happiness = innovation = sustainability) offers an easy-to-replicate model that can be replicated in future studies and leadership practice. The synergy of AI, analytics, and empathy will decide the next step in the evolution of organizations in the future.

REFERENCES

Ahmed, T., Yang, C., Yang, H., & Mahmood, S. (2021). Topic of the Review Manuscript—The Review of Empowering Leadership. *Open Journal of Leadership, 10*(2), 129–147. DOI: 10.4236/ojl.2021.102009

Atay, S. (2025). *Society 5.0 and human-centered technology: Redefining HR and talent management. Technology in Society.* https://www.sciencedirect.com/science/article/pii/S2666188825002990

Boyatzis, R. E., & Johnston, F. (2021). *Helping people change: Coaching with compassion for lifelong learning and growth.* Harvard Business Review Press.

Chandrasekaran, A., & Mishra, A. (2012). Task design, team context, and psychological safety: An empirical analysis of R&D projects in high-technology organizations. *Production and Operations Management, 21*(6), 977–996. DOI: 10.1111/j.1937-5956.2012.01329.x

Coutifaris, C. G. V., & Grant, A. M. (2022). Taking your team behind the curtain: The effects of leader feedback-sharing and feedback-seeking on team psychological safety. *Organization Science, 33*(4), 1574–1598. Advance online publication. DOI: 10.1287/orsc.2021.1498

Creswell, J. W., & Poth, C. N. (2024). Qualitative inquiry and research design: Choosing among five approaches (5th ed.). SAGE Publications., Retrieved from https://uk.sagepub.com/en-gb/eur/qualitative-inquiry-and-research-design/book266033, Retrieved November 10th, 2025, from.

Deci, E. L., & Ryan, R. M. (2000). The "what" and "why" of goal pursuits: Human needs and the self-determination of behavior. *Psychological Inquiry, 11*(4), 227–268. DOI: 10.1207/S15327965PLI1104_01

Deloitte. (2023, January 9). *2023 Global human capital trends.* Deloitte Insights. https://www.deloitte.com/us/en/insights/topics/talent/human-capital-trends/2023.html

Edmondson, A. (1999). Psychological safety and learning behavior in work teams. *Administrative Science Quarterly, 44*(2), 350–383. DOI: 10.2307/2666999

Edmondson, A., & Bransby, D. P. (2022). Psychological safety comes of age: Observed themes in an established literature. *Annual Review of Organizational Psychology and Organizational Behavior, 9*, 1–25. DOI: 10.1146/annurev-orgpsych-120920-055217

Frazier, M. L., Fainshmidt, S., Klinger, R. L., Pezeshkan, A., & Vracheva, V. (2017). Psychological safety: A meta-analytic review and extension. *Personnel Psychology, 70*(1), 113–165. DOI: 10.1111/peps.12183

Gartner, Inc. (2023).Evolve culture and leadership for a Hybrid World. Gartner, Inc. retrieved from https://www.gartner.com/en/human-resources/insights/culture-and-leadership-in-a-hybrid-world [accessed on November, 2025]

Goleman, D. (2011). Leadership: The power of emotional intelligence. More Than Sound. Retrieved from https://ia801800.us.archive.org/21/items/educational-administration-concepts-and-practices/Leadership%20The%20Power%20of%20Emotional%20Leadership.pdf [accessed on November, 2025]

Harvard Business School Publishing. (2025, April). *Leadership fitness — The path to developing human-centered leaders.* Harvard Business Impact Perspective. Retrieved from https://www.harvardbusiness.org/wp-content/uploads/2025/04/HBI_Perspective_Developing-Human-Centered-Leaders.pdf [accessed on November, 2025]

Institute for the Future of Work. (2024, March 12). *Workplace AI, robots and trackers are bad for quality of life, study finds. The Guardian.* Retrieved from https://www.theguardian.com/business/2024/mar/12/workplace-ai-robots-trackers-quality-of-life-institute-for-work- [accessed on November, 2025]

Kane, G. C., Palmer, D., Phillips, A. N., Kiron, D., & Buckley, N. (2015). Strategy, Not Technology, Drives Digital Transformation. *MIT Sloan Management Review.*

Konstantinos, G. (2024). Thematic analysis: A practical guide: by Virginia Braun and Victoria Clarke, Los Angeles, USA, Sage Publications, 2022, 376 pp., $ 27.59 (paperback), ISBN-13: 978-1473953246. *European Journal of Psychotherapy & Counselling, 26*(3–4), 461–464. DOI: 10.1080/13642537.2024.2391666

Liu, W., Liao, J., & Loi, R. (2016). Abusive supervision and employee creativity: The mediating role of psychological safety and organizational identification. *Management Decision, 54*(1), 130–147. DOI: 10.1108/MD-09-2013-0443

Luthans, F., & Broad, J. D. (2025). Positive organizational behavior and psychological capital: An evidence-based 20-year journey. In Cooper, C. L., Patnaik, S., & Rodriguez, R. V. (Eds.), *Advancing positive organizational behaviour* (1st ed.). Routledge., DOI: 10.4324/9781032619385-2

Maslach, C., Schaufeli, W. B., & Leiter, M. P. (2001). Job burnout. *Annual Review of Psychology, 52*(1), 397–422. DOI: 10.1146/annurev.psych.52.1.397 PMID: 11148311

McKinsey Health Institute. (2025, January 16). *Thriving workplaces: How employers can improve productivity and change lives.* https://www.mckinsey.com/mhi/our-insights/thriving-workplaces-how-employers-can-improve-productivity-and-change-lives

Montes, C. M., Penzenstadler, B., & Feldt, R. (2025). The factors influencing well-being in software engineers: A mixed-method study. *ACM Transactions on Software Engineering and Methodology, 34*(1), 1–30. DOI: 10.1145/3770074

Morgeson, F. P., DeRue, D. S., & Karam, E. P. (2010). Leadership in teams: A functional approach to understanding leadership structures and processes. *Journal of Management, 36*(1), 5–39. DOI: 10.1177/0149206309347376

Moss, J. (2023, October 20). *Creating a happier workplace is possible—and worth it.* Harvard Business Review. Retrieved from https://hbr.org/2023/10/creating-a-happier-workplace-is-possible-and-worth-it –[accessed on November 2025]

. Pavitra, K. H., Agnihotri, A., & Tiwari, B. (2024). *Leadership and technology integration in India: A systematic literature review.* The impact of new technology on next-generation leadership. IGI Global. https://doi.org/DOI: 10.4018/979-8-3693-1946-8.ch004

Pillai, S. E. V. S., Polimetla, K., & Avacharmal, R. (2022, July). Mental health in the tech industry: Insights from surveys and NLP analysis. *Journal of Recent Trends in Computer Science and Engineering, 2*(3), 22–33. Advance online publication. DOI: 10.70589/JRTCSE.2022.2.3

Rego, A., Owens, B. P., Yam, K. C., Bluhm, D. J., Cunha, M. P., Silard, A., Gonçalves, L., Martins, M., Simpson, A., & Liu, W. (2019). Leader humility and team performance: Exploring the mediating mechanisms of team psychological capital and task allocation effectiveness. *Journal of Management, 45*(6), 2330–2356. DOI: 10.1177/0149206316688941

Ryan, R. M., & Deci, E. L. (2017). *Self-determination theory: Basic psychological needs in motivation, development, and wellness.* The Guilford Press., DOI: 10.1521/978.14625/28806

Samad, A., Ahmed, E., & Arora, N. (Eds.). (2023). *Global leadership perspectives on industry, society, and Government in an era of uncertainty.* IGI Global., DOI: 10.4018/978-1-6684-8257-5

Schein, E. H., & Schein, P. A. (2023). Humble leadership: the power of relationships, openness, and trust (2nd ed.). Berrett-Koehler Publishers., Retrieved from http://search.ebscohost.com/login.aspx?authtype=ip,sso&custid=s4392798&direct=true&scope=site&db=nlebk&AN=3640543, Retrieved November 2025, from.

Schneider, S., & Kokshagina, O. (2021). Digital transformation: What we have learned (thus far) and what is next. *Creativity and Innovation Management, 30*(2), 384–411. DOI: 10.1111/caim.12414

Seligman, M. (2018). PERMA and the Building Blocks of Well-being. *The Journal of Positive Psychology, 13*(4), 333–335. DOI: 10.1080/17439760.2018.1437466

Shore, L. M., Coyle-Shapiro, J. A.-M., & Cnop-Nielsen, A. (2025). Elevating health significance post-pandemic: Is the employee–organization relationship in a period of change? *Annual Review of Organizational Psychology and Organizational Behavior, 12*(1), 269–294. DOI: 10.1146/annurev-orgpsych-110622-065549

Sijbom, R. B. L., & Grutterink, H. (2026). Participative leadership and workgroup commitment as multilevel resources for employee well-being: A cross-level examination. *Applied Psychology, 75*(2), e70081. DOI: 10.1111/apps.70081

Singh, P., Suar, D., & Leiter, M. P. (2012). Antecedents, work-related consequences, and buffers of job burnout among Indian software developers. *Journal of Leadership & Organizational Studies, 19*(1), 104–114. DOI: 10.1177/1548051811429572

Thomas, C. H., & Lankau, M. J. (2009). Preventing burnout: The effects of LMX and mentoring on socialization, role stress, and burnout. *Human Resource Management, 48*(3), 417–432. DOI: 10.1002/hrm.20288

Trinkenreich, B., Santos, F., & Stol, K.-J. (2024). Predicting attrition among software professionals: Antecedents and consequences of burnout and engagement. *ACM Transactions on Software Engineering and Methodology, 33*(2), 1–45. DOI: 10.1145/3691629

Varma, P. (2025, October 11). *Unlock the future of leadership: How McKinsey's human-centred approach transforms organizations and empowers employees.* Rehumanize. https://rehumanize.com/unlock-the-future-of-leadership-how-mckinseys-human-centered-approach-transforms-organizations-and-empowers-employees

World Economic Forum. (2025, January 17). *Leading with purpose: Why human-centric strategies are vital in the AI era.* https://www.weforum.org/stories/2025/01/leading-with-purpose-why-human-centric-strategies-are-vital-in-the-ai-era/

Yin, R. K. (2018). Case study research and applications: Design and methods (6th ed.). SAGE Publications., Retrieved from https://methods.sagepub.com/book/case -study-research-, Retrieved November 2025, from.

Ziaeian, Y. (2025). The Impact of Human-Centric Leadership on Employee Satisfaction and Productivity in Digitally Transformed Organisations. In: Shaikh, A., Wiil, U.K., Alghamdi, A., Tan, Q. (eds) The 2nd International Conference on Innovation of Emerging Information and Communication Technology. ICIEICT 2024. Signals and Communication Technology. Springer, Cham. https://doi.org/ DOI: 10.1007/978-3-031-88634-8_17

APPENDIX: CASE SUMMARY

Case	Nature of Organization	Key Human-Centred Practices	Distinctive Context / Challenge
Case A: India and Japan	Medium sized software-engineering firm (around 800 employees) offering customized ERP and analytics platforms for manufacturing clients.	• Empathy-based leadership development (monthly one-to-one mentoring) • Transparent communication dashboards• Flexible work and mental-health days	Rapid growth after the pandemic led to cultural fragmentation; leadership sought to rebuild a sense of belonging and meaning.
Case B	Global cloud-computing provider (≈ 4,500 employees) known for fast-paced innovation cycles.	• Ethical-AI review boards for all new products • Recognition programs tied to collaborative innovation• Open-forum town halls for employee voice	Competitive ranking system created stress; the company aimed to balance innovation speed with well-being.
Case C	AI-driven health-tech start-up (≈ 300 employees) operating in hybrid mode.	•Peer-support "listening circles" for remote staff • Ethics hackathons to examine the social impact of code • Anonymous digital feedback app measuring safety and inclusion	Distributed teams across time zones struggled with cohesion and trust; leadership introduced digital empathy tools to foster trust.

Chapter 4
AI Human Collaboration and Organizational Performance:
An Empirical Study of Behavioral Leadership and Performance Dynamics

Amarnath Gupta
http://orcid.org/0000-0002-1895-3219
Sri Balaji University, Pune, India

Ashwini Nikhil Shinde
http://orcid.org/0009-0006-4748-2555
Sri Balaji University, Pune, India

Pawan Kumar
http://orcid.org/0000-0003-4892-6374
Graphic Era (Deemed to be) University, Dehradun, India

Pardeep Rathee
http://orcid.org/0009-0005-2664-8301
D.A.V. (P.G.) College, Karnal, India

Monika Sahu
http://orcid.org/0009-0005-4252-2282
D.A.V. (P.G.) College, Karnal, India

DOI: 10.4018/979-8-2600-2541-3.ch004

ABSTRACT

The prevalent incorporation of artificial intelligence (AI) in organizational schemes has meaningfully transformed work mechanism, practices in leadership, and design of performance. The study an effort to explore the effect of AI, human collaboration, Artificial intelligence, readiness of AI infrastructure, oriented leadership, employee behavioural adaptability, and AI, enabled performance on organizational change. Quantitative research design has been used on collected data based on Likert scale from 270 respondents. Collected data has been analysed applying descriptive methods, ANOVA, regression analysis and correlation analysis supported by diagnostic tests to confirm the reliability and validity of the research model. The outcomes of the study reported the strong explanatory power of proposed model with performance enabled by AI as a key driver leading to organizational change is followed by leadership equipped with AI and readiness of infrastructure for the AI.

1. INTRODUCTION

The rapid advancement and pervasive diffusion of artificial intelligence (AI) across economic, administrative, and organizational domains has precipitated a paradigmatic shift in the nature of work, governance, and value creation (Aggarwal et al., 2021; Ameyed et al., 2023). Contemporary organizations are no longer defined solely by human expertise, hierarchical authority, or mechanistic processes; instead, they increasingly operate as hybrid socio-technical systems in which human intelligence and algorithmic cognition coexist, interact, and co-evolve (Babu, 2021; Daole et al., 2023). This transformation has elevated AI–human collaboration from a peripheral technological novelty to a central organizational capability, fundamentally redefining how decisions are made, tasks are executed, and strategic objectives are pursued (Bender & Price, 2024; Benthall & Goldenfein, 2021). Within this evolving landscape, organizational transformation emerges not as a discrete outcome of technological adoption, but as a complex, multi-layered process shaped by behavioral, leadership, and performance dynamics (Boban & Klarić, 2023). Technological change within organizations was predominantly framed through the lens of automation, efficiency enhancement, and labor substitution. Early information systems and mechanized processes were designed to minimize human intervention, reduce error, and standardize operations (Bonsón & Bednárová, 2022). However, the contemporary wave of AI-driven technologies—characterized by machine learning, predictive analytics, natural language processing, and adaptive algorithms—has introduced a qualitatively different mode of technological engagement. Rather than merely replacing human labor, AI increasingly augments human cognition by generating insights, identifying patterns, and supporting complex decision-making under conditions of uncertainty (Chahal et al., 2022; Donins & Behmane, 2023). This shift from automation to augmentation has catalyzed the emergence of AI–human collaboration as a defining feature of modern organizational systems. AI–human collaboration entails a reciprocal and interdependent relationship in which human judgment, creativity, and contextual understanding are complemented by the computational power, speed, and analytical depth of AI systems (Dutt, 2020). Such collaboration extends across functional domains, including strategic planning, human resource management, supply chain optimization, customer engagement, and governance processes (Goldsteen et al., 2022). Yet, integrating AI into organizational workflows also introduces profound challenges related to trust, accountability, interpretability, and ethical governance. The efficacy of AI–human collaboration is thus contingent not only on technological sophistication, but also on the organizational environment in which it is embedded (Grzybowski, 2021). This environment is shaped by leadership orientation, employee behavioral responses, infrastructural readiness, and performance imperatives, all of which collectively influence the trajectory of organizational transformation (Gulyamov, 2024).

Organizational transformation in the AI era transcends incremental digitalization or isolated process improvements. It signifies a fundamental reconfiguration of organizational structures, cultures, competencies, and strategic orientations. Transformation manifests in the decentralization of decision-making, the redefinition of managerial roles, the emergence of data-driven governance, and the cultivation of continuous learning cultures. Importantly, such transformation is neither linear nor uniform; it unfolds through iterative experimentation, resistance, adaptation, and institutionalization. Consequently, understanding organizational transformation requires an integrative analytical lens that captures both technological and human dimensions, as well as their dynamic interaction over time. Despite the growing scholarly interest in AI adoption and digital transformation, much of the extant literature remains fragmented and conceptually narrow (Jastroch, 2020). A substantial proportion of existing studies privilege technological determinism, emphasizing algorithmic capabilities, system efficiency, or return on investment while relegating human agency to a secondary role. Conversely, behavioral and leadership studies often treat technology as an exogenous force, insufficiently engaging with AI's unique epistemic and operational characteristics. This bifurcation has resulted in an incomplete understanding of how AI–human collaboration actually unfolds within organizations and how it contributes to transformative outcomes. The present study seeks to bridge this gap by adopting a holistic empirical approach that integrates behavioral, leadership, and performance perspectives into a unified analytical framework (Kabza, 2020).

At the behavioral level, the introduction of AI fundamentally alters the psychological contract between employees and organizations. AI-mediated work environments reshape job roles, skill requirements, and performance expectations, often generating ambivalent responses among employees. While some individuals perceive AI as an empowering tool that enhances autonomy and learning opportunities, others experience it as a source of surveillance, deskilling, or existential threat. These divergent responses underscore the importance of behavioral dynamics in determining the success or failure of AI–human collaboration. Employee attitudes toward AI, their adaptability to technological change, and their willingness to integrate AI insights into daily work practices collectively influence organizational outcomes (Leddy & McCreanor, 2023). Behavioral responses thus function as a critical micro-level mechanism through which AI-driven transformation is either facilitated or constrained. Leadership occupies a pivotal position in mediating the relationship between AI and organizational transformation. Leaders serve as architects of meaning, framing AI not merely as a technological instrument but as a strategic and ethical choice. AI-oriented leadership encompasses the capacity to envision AI-driven futures, align technological initiatives with organizational values, and manage the uncertainties inherent in intelligent systems (Li et al., 2018). Leaders influence resource allocation, establish governance frameworks, and set normative expectations regarding the use of AI. Through their actions and narratives, leaders can either cultivate trust and experimentation or exacerbate fear and resistance. In this sense, leadership is not simply a contextual variable but a constitutive force that shapes how AI–human collaboration is institutionalized within organizational routines and cultures. Performance dynamics represent another critical dimension of AI-enabled organizational transformation. AI systems promise substantial performance gains by enhancing efficiency, accuracy, and predictive capability. However, performance outcomes are not solely the product of algorithmic optimization; they are emergent properties of socio-technical interactions (Xiuquan Li & Tao Zhang, 2017). AI-enabled performance depends on the extent to which human actors can interpret, contextualize, and act upon AI-generated insights. It is also influenced by the alignment between performance metrics and organizational objectives, as well as by the learning mechanisms that allow organizations to refine AI applications over time. Performance dynamics thus provide a tangible yet complex indicator of whether AI–human collaboration is yielding transformative value or merely superficial efficiency improvements. Underlying these behavioral, leadership, and performance dynamics is the broader question of organizational readiness for AI integration. Organizational transformation is conditioned by the availability of digital infrastructure, data quality, system interoperability, and institutional support mechanisms. Inadequate infrastructural foundations can undermine even the most sophisticated AI initiatives, leading to fragmented implementation, employee frustration, and strategic disillusionment. Conversely, robust infrastructural readiness enables organizations to scale AI applications, integrate them across functional silos, and sustain collaborative interactions between humans and machines. Infrastructure, therefore, functions as the structural backbone of AI–human collaboration and a critical determinant of transformative capacity (Longo et al., 2020).

The convergence of these dimensions, behavioral responses, leadership orientation, performance dynamics, and infrastructural preparedness—highlights the inherently systemic nature of AI-driven organizational transformation. Organizations do not transform simply by adopting AI technologies; they transform by reconfiguring the relationships between people, processes, and intelligent systems. This reconfiguration entails renegotiating authority, redefining expertise, and recalibrating organizational values in light of algorithmic participation. Such changes are often contested and uneven, reflecting power dynamics, institutional inertia, and ethical considerations. An empirical examination of these processes is therefore essential to move beyond speculative or normative claims and toward evidence-based understanding. Against this backdrop, the present study undertakes an empirical investigation of AI–human collaboration and its influence on organizational transformation, with a particular focus on behavioral, leadership, and performance dynamics. By systematically analyzing how these dimensions interact within organizational settings, the study seeks to elucidate the mechanisms through which AI contributes to transformative outcomes. In doing so, it advances a socio-technical perspective that recognizes AI not as an autonomous agent of change, but as a relational and context-dependent force whose impact is mediated by human agency and institutional structures (Ma & Wang, 2021). The significance of this inquiry extends beyond academic discourse to practical and policy-oriented concerns. As organizations across sectors increasingly invest in AI, understanding the conditions under which AI–human collaboration fosters sustainable transformation becomes a strategic imperative. Insights from this study can inform leadership development, change management strategies, and organizational design choices to maximize the benefits of AI while mitigating its risks. Furthermore, the study contributes to ongoing debates on ethical AI, workforce futures, and organizational resilience, offering a nuanced account of how intelligent technologies reshape the fabric of organizational life. AI–human collaboration represents a defining characteristic of contemporary organizations, with profound implications for how they function, compete, and evolve. Organizational transformation in the AI era is a multifaceted process shaped by behavioral adaptation, leadership vision, performance enablement, and infrastructural readiness. By empirically examining these interrelated dynamics, this study seeks to deepen understanding of the transformative potential of AI–human collaboration and to provide a robust analytical foundation for navigating the complexities of organizational change in an increasingly intelligent world (Magrani & da Silva, 2024).

2. REVIEW OF LITERATURE

The burgeoning integration of artificial intelligence (AI) into organizational systems has generated a substantial and rapidly expanding body of scholarly literature examining its implications for work structures, leadership paradigms, employee behavior, and organizational performance. Contemporary research increasingly converges on the recognition that AI does not function as an autonomous agent of transformation; rather, its organizational consequences are mediated through complex interactions between technological capabilities and human agency. Within this evolving discourse, AI–human collaboration has emerged as a central analytical construct, signifying a departure from traditional automation-centric models toward more nuanced, augmentation-oriented frameworks of organizational change (Martinelli et al., 2020). Early studies on technology and organizations were largely grounded in deterministic perspectives, emphasizing efficiency gains, cost reduction, and labor substitution. These approaches conceptualized technology as an exogenous force exerting linear effects on organizational outcomes (Mudholkar et al., 2023). However, with the advent of advanced AI systems capable of learning, reasoning, and adapting, scholars began to question the adequacy of such reductionist models. Recent literature underscores that AI fundamentally alters epistemic processes within organizations by reshaping how knowledge is generated, interpreted, and applied. This shift has foregrounded AI–human collaboration as a socio-technical phenomenon in which algorithmic intelligence complements, rather than replaces, human judgment and creativity (Paes et al., 2023).

Research on AI–human collaboration highlights the importance of trust, transparency, and interpretability in facilitating effective human–machine interaction. Scholars argue that employees are more likely to integrate AI insights into decision-making when systems are perceived as reliable, explainable, and aligned with organizational values. Conversely, opaque or poorly governed AI systems tend to elicit skepticism, resistance, and underutilization. Empirical studies demonstrate that collaborative AI systems enhance decision quality and task performance when humans retain a sense of control and agency, suggesting that collaboration is contingent upon psychological acceptance as much as technical integration. This body of work establishes AI–human collaboration as a critical antecedent of organizational transformation, albeit deeply embedded in behavioral and institutional contexts.

Leadership scholarship has increasingly engaged with the challenges posed by AI-driven transformation, giving rise to the concept of AI-oriented leadership. Traditional leadership theories, grounded in hierarchical authority and human-centric decision-making, have been critiqued for their limited applicability in algorithmically mediated environments. Contemporary studies emphasize that leaders must now navigate hybrid decision architectures in which AI systems generate recommendations that influence strategic and operational choices. AI-oriented leadership is thus characterized by the ability to align technological innovation with organizational purpose, ethical responsibility, and long-term value creation.

The literature suggests that leaders play a pivotal role in shaping organizational narratives around AI, thereby influencing employee perceptions and behavioral responses. Transformational and adaptive leadership styles have been found particularly effective in fostering AI acceptance, as they emphasize vision articulation, empowerment, and learning. Moreover, ethical leadership has gained prominence in AI contexts, with scholars highlighting the need for leaders to address concerns related to bias, accountability, and data governance. Empirical evidence indicates that organizations with strong AI-oriented leadership are more likely to institutionalize AI–human collaboration and achieve sustained transformational outcomes. Nonetheless, gaps remain in understanding how leadership interacts with other organizational variables, such as employee adaptability and performance dynamics, to shape transformation trajectories. At the employee level, behavioral adaptability has emerged as a crucial determinant of AI-enabled organizational change. Behavioral adaptability encompasses employees' cognitive flexibility, openness to technological change, and capacity for continuous learning. The literature presents a nuanced portrayal of employee responses to AI integration, revealing both enabling and constraining effects. On one hand, adaptable employees are more likely to experiment with AI tools, integrate algorithmic insights into their workflows, and contribute to organizational learning. On the other hand, heightened adaptability demands may generate psychological strain, role ambiguity, and identity threats, particularly in contexts characterized by rapid and poorly managed technological change.

Several studies underscore the paradoxical nature of adaptability in AI-rich environments. While adaptability is often valorized as a desirable individual trait, its benefits depend on organizational support structures, including training programs, participatory decision-making, and transparent communication. In the absence of such support, adaptability pressures may exacerbate resistance and diminish well-being, thereby undermining organizational performance. This literature highlights the need to conceptualize employee behavioral adaptability not as an isolated individual attribute, but as a relational construct shaped by leadership practices and institutional conditions. Another significant stream of research focuses on AI infrastructure readiness as a foundational enabler of organizational transformation. Infrastructure readiness encompasses the availability and quality of digital systems, data architectures, computational resources, and integration capabilities necessary to support AI deployment. Scholars consistently emphasize that infrastructural deficiencies represent a primary barrier to realizing the transformative potential of AI (Payton, 2023). Fragmented data systems, inadequate interoperability, and insufficient cybersecurity measures have been shown to impede AI–human collaboration and erode employee trust in intelligent systems. Conversely, organizations characterized by high infrastructural readiness are better positioned to scale AI applications, facilitate cross-functional collaboration, and institutionalize data-driven decision-making. The literature further suggests that infrastructure readiness extends beyond technical components to include governance mechanisms, standardization protocols, and organizational routines that support continuous system refinement. Despite its recognized importance, empirical research examining infrastructure readiness alongside behavioral and leadership variables remains limited, indicating a critical gap that warrants integrative investigation (Pesapane et al., 2020).

The relationship between AI and organizational outcomes is frequently examined through the lens of AI-enabled performance. Performance-oriented studies document a range of benefits from AI adoption, including increased productivity, reduced errors, and improved forecasting accuracy. However, recent scholarship cautions against overly simplistic interpretations of performance gains, noting that AI-enabled performance is an emergent outcome of socio-technical interaction rather than a direct consequence of algorithmic deployment. Performance improvements are mediated by users' ability to interpret AI outputs, integrate them into decision processes, and align them with organizational goals. Moreover, performance metrics themselves are subject to transformation in AI-enabled organizations. Scholars argue that traditional performance indicators may inadequately capture the value generated through AI–human collaboration, necessitating more holistic and dynamic measurement frameworks (Sanz & Zhu, 2021). The literature also highlights potential trade-offs, such as short-term efficiency gains at the expense of long-term learning or ethical considerations. These insights underscore the need to situate AI-enabled performance within a broader transformational context rather than treating it as an isolated dependent variable. The concept of organizational transformation serves as the integrative outcome of these diverse streams of inquiry. Organizational transformation is increasingly conceptualized as a continuous and systemic process involving structural reconfiguration, cultural change, and strategic realignment. AI-driven transformation is distinguished by its epistemic dimension, as algorithmic systems reshape how organizations perceive their environments and make decisions. The literature emphasizes that successful transformation requires coherence across technological, human, and institutional dimensions, reinforcing the relevance of socio-technical perspectives (Swati & Kumar, 2023). Several studies advocate for integrative frameworks that capture the interdependencies among AI–human collaboration, leadership orientation, employee behavior, infrastructural readiness, and performance outcomes. However, much of the existing research remains fragmented, focusing on isolated variables or relying on conceptual rather than empirical analysis. There is a paucity of comprehensive empirical studies that simultaneously examine behavioral, leadership, and performance dynamics within a unified model of organizational transformation. This fragmentation limits theoretical advancement and constrains the practical applicability of research findings.

In synthesizing the extant literature, it becomes evident that AI–human collaboration represents a critical but insufficient condition for organizational transformation. Its effectiveness is contingent upon AI-oriented leadership that provides strategic direction and ethical governance, employee behavioral adaptability supported by robust change management practices, infrastructural readiness that enables seamless integration, and performance mechanisms that translate technological capability into organizational value (Vizitiu et al., 2019). The interplay among these variables constitutes a complex adaptive system that defies linear causality and demands empirical investigation. The present study builds upon and extends this literature by adopting an integrative empirical approach to examine AI–human collaboration and organizational transformation through the lenses of behavioral, leadership, and performance dynamics. By addressing the identified gaps and synthesizing disparate theoretical strands, the study contributes to a more holistic understanding of AI-driven organizational change (Wong, 2021). In doing so, it responds to calls within the literature for nuanced, evidence-based insights into how intelligent technologies reshape organizational life, offering both theoretical enrichment and practical relevance in an era of accelerating technological complexity. The accelerated infusion of artificial intelligence into organizational ecosystems has spurred a profound scholarly reorientation to understand how intelligent technologies interact with human agency to reshape structures, processes, and performance logics. Contemporary literature increasingly converges on the premise that AI does not operate in isolation as a deterministic force; rather, its organizational consequences are realized through intricate socio-technical configurations in which human cognition, institutional arrangements, and algorithmic systems are mutually constitutive. Within this evolving discourse, attention has progressively shifted from narrow efficiency-driven narratives toward more integrative perspectives that foreground collaboration, leadership sensemaking, behavioral adaptation, infrastructural embeddedness, and performance reconfiguration. A prominent strand of research emphasizes the collaborative interface between humans and AI systems, conceptualizing it as a relational process rather than a purely technical arrangement. Scholars argue that the value of AI emerges most prominently when human judgment, contextual reasoning, and ethical discernment are combined with machine-based analytics, pattern recognition, and predictive capacity. Empirical studies demonstrate that such collaborative configurations enhance decision quality and problem-solving effectiveness, particularly in environments characterized by uncertainty and complexity (Xin et al., 2022). However, the literature also cautions that collaboration is contingent upon trust, transparency, and interpretability, as opaque or poorly aligned systems tend to generate skepticism and underutilization. This body of work situates collaboration as a dynamic capability shaped by organizational norms, learning mechanisms, and governance frameworks. Leadership-focused scholarship has expanded substantially in response to AI-driven organizational change, recognizing that traditional leadership models are insufficient for algorithmically mediated contexts. Recent studies highlight the emergence of leadership orientations that integrate technological literacy with ethical responsibility and strategic foresight. Leaders are increasingly portrayed as architects of socio-technical alignment, responsible for framing AI as an enabling resource rather than a disruptive threat. Empirical evidence suggests that leadership narratives and behaviors significantly influence employee attitudes toward AI, shaping acceptance, experimentation, and sustained use. Moreover, leadership scholarship underscores the importance of ethical stewardship, particularly in addressing concerns related to bias, accountability, and data governance, thereby reinforcing trust and legitimacy in AI-enabled systems (Yusif-Zada & Iskandarova, 2023). Behavioral scholarship provides critical insights into how individuals experience and respond to AI-mediated work environments. Research consistently indicates that the introduction of AI alters job roles, skill requirements, and identity constructs, eliciting heterogeneous responses among employees. While some studies report heightened engagement and learning orientation among individuals who perceive AI as augmentative, others document anxiety, resistance, and perceived loss of autonomy. This divergence has prompted scholars to conceptualize behavioral adaptation as a complex and context-dependent phenomenon rather than a uniformly positive trait (Zallone, 2020). The literature emphasizes that adaptive responses are shaped by organizational support structures, including training opportunities, participatory decision-making, and transparent communication. In the absence of such mechanisms, behavioral pressures associated with continuous technological change may undermine well-being and performance.

3. RESEARCH METHODOLOGY

The study employs a quantitative, cross-sectional, and explanatory research design, primarily anchored in the systematic collection of primary data from 270 respondents through a structured survey instrument. The research framework is constructed to empirically examine the interrelationships among AI–human collaboration, AI-oriented leadership, employee behavioral adaptability, AI infrastructural readiness, AI-enabled performance, and organizational transformation. Standardized Likert-scale measures are utilized to capture respondents' perceptions with methodological consistency, thereby ensuring comparability, quantification, and analytical precision. The cross-sectional nature of the study enables the researcher to assess the prevailing patterns, associations, and explanatory dynamics among the selected constructs at a particular point in time. For data interpretation, the study applies a comprehensive statistical procedure comprising descriptive statistics, correlation analysis, ANOVA, multiple regression analysis, collinearity diagnostics, and residual examination. These techniques collectively enhance the empirical rigor of the investigation by validating the strength, direction, and predictive capacity of the proposed relationships. The inclusion of diagnostic tests further strengthens the model's reliability by identifying multicollinearity concerns and assessing residual behavior. Overall, the methodological design reflects statistical robustness, explanatory depth, and predictive validity.

4. DATA ANALYSIS

Table 1. Variables of the study

Category	Variable	Description
Independent Variable	AI–Human Collaboration	Refers to the synergistic interaction between human cognitive capabilities and artificial intelligence systems, wherein AI augments human judgment, decision-making, and task execution through collaborative intelligence rather than functional substitution.
Independent Variable	AI-Oriented Leadership	Denotes leadership capability characterized by strategic vision, ethical governance, and adaptive decision-making that enables, legitimizes, and steers the integration of AI within organizational systems and cultures.
Independent Variable	Employee Behavioural Adaptability	Represents the psychological flexibility, learning agility, and behavioral readiness of employees to adjust to AI-driven changes in work roles, skill requirements, and performance expectations.
Independent Variable	AI Infrastructure Readiness	Indicates the extent of organizational preparedness in terms of digital infrastructure, data quality, system interoperability, and institutional support required for effective and scalable AI deployment.
Independent Variable	AI-Enabled Performance	Captures the degree to which AI technologies enhance individual, team, and organizational performance by improving efficiency, accuracy, decision quality, and productivity through data-driven intelligence.
Dependent Variable	Organizational Transformation	Reflects the comprehensive and systemic reconfiguration of organizational structures, processes, culture, and strategic orientation resulting from sustained AI–human collaboration and technology-driven change.

Table 2. Descriptive Statistics

	N	Minimum	Maximum	Mean		Std. Deviation	Skewness		Kurtosis	
	Statistic	Statistic	Statistic	Statistic	Std. Error	Statistic	Statistic	Std. Error	Statistic	Std. Error
AI_Humar_Collaboration	270	2.00	7.00	4.8741	.07602	1.24912	.056	.148	-.463	.295
AI_Oriented_Leadership	270	1.00	7.00	4.8037	.07981	1.31137	-.230	.148	-.236	.295
Adptability_Epmoyee_Behaviour	270	1.00	7.00	5.0593	.06853	1.12599	-.180	.148	.180	.295
AI_Infrasturctural_Readiness	270	1.00	7.00	4.7185	.07998	1.31422	-.498	.148	.142	.295
AI_Enabled_Performance	270	1.00	7.00	4.5741	.08906	1.46333	-.674	.148	.229	.295
Orgonizational_Behaviour	270	1.00	7.00	4.6185	.08825	1.45017	-.426	.148	.016	.295
Valid N (listwise)	270									

Sources: Data compiled by the author

The descriptive statistics indicate in the table 2 that all six constructs were assessed on a seven-point scale across a valid sample of 270 respondents, reflecting adequate empirical coverage and statistical consistency. The mean values range from 4.57 to 5.06, suggesting that respondents generally expressed moderately favourable perceptions toward AI-related organizational practices. Among the variables, Adaptability of Employee Behaviour records the highest mean value (5.06), indicating comparatively stronger employee readiness, flexibility, and behavioural responsiveness in AI-enabled work settings. AI–Human Collaboration also shows a favourable mean score (4.87), signifying that respondents perceive collaborative interaction between human capabilities and artificial intelligence systems as reasonably developed. AI-Enabled Performance records the lowest mean value (4.57), implying that although AI contributes to performance enhancement, its perceived effectiveness may still be evolving within organizational contexts. Standard deviation values range from 1.13 to 1.46, indicating moderate dispersion in responses and suggesting perceptual variability among participants. The skewness values are largely negative, except AI–Human Collaboration (0.06), demonstrating a slight concentration of responses toward higher agreement levels. Kurtosis values remain close to zero and mostly below the critical threshold, indicating a near-normal distribution. Overall, the data demonstrate acceptable normality, meaningful response variation, and a favourable orientation toward AI-driven organizational transformation.

Table 3. Model Summary

Model	R	R Square	Adjusted R Square	Std. Error of the Estimate	Change Statistics					Durbin-Watson
					R Square Change	F Change	df1	df2	Sig. F Change	
1	.880[a]	.774	.763	1.07266	.463	45.533	5	264	.000	1.957

a. Predictors: (Constant), AI_Enabled_Performance, AI_Humar_Collaboration, AI_Oriented_Leadership, AI_Infrasturctural_Readiness, Adptability_Epmoyee_Behaviour

b. Dependent Variable: Orgonizational_Behaviour

Sources: Data compiled by the author

The model summary (table 3) demonstrates a highly robust explanatory framework for predicting Organizational Behaviour through the selected AI-related predictors. The correlation coefficient (R = 0.88) indicates a strong collective association between the independent variables AI-enabled performance, AI–human collaboration, AI-oriented leadership, AI infrastructural readiness, and adaptability of employee behaviour and the dependent variable. The R Square value of 0.77 signifies that approximately 77.40% of the variance in Organizational Behaviour is explained by the combined influence of these predictors, reflecting substantial explanatory power.

The Adjusted R-Square value of 0.76 further confirms that the model remains statistically stable even after adjusting for the number of predictors and sample size. The standard error of the estimate (1.07) suggests a moderate level of prediction error, indicating that the observed values are reasonably close to the predicted values. The F Change value of 45.53, with a significance level of 0.00, confirms that the regression model is statistically significant and meaningfully improves predictive performance. The Durbin-Watson statistic of 1.96 is close to the ideal value of 2.00, indicating the absence of serious autocorrelation in residuals. Overall, the model exhibits strong predictive validity, statistical adequacy, and empirical reliability.

Table 4. ANOVA

Model		Sum of Squares	df	Mean Square	F	Sig.
1	Regression	261.950	5	52.390	45.533	.000[b]
	Residual	303.757	264	1.151		
	Total	565.707	269			

a. Dependent Variable: Orgonizational_Behaviour
b. Predictors: (Constant), AI_Enabled_Performance, AI_Humar_Collaboration, AI_Oriented_Leadership, AI_Infrasturctural_Readiness, Adptability_Epmoyee_Behaviour
Sources: Data compiled by the author

The ANOVA results in the table 4 substantiate the regression model's overall statistical significance and explanatory adequacy in predicting Organizational Behavior. The regression sum of squares is 261.95, while the residual sum of squares is 303.76, indicating that a substantial proportion of the total variation in Organizational Behavior is accounted for by the combined predictors. The total sum of squares is 565.71, reflecting the overall variability in the dependent variable across the sample. The model yields a mean square regression of 52.39 and a residual mean square of 1.15, indicating that the explained variance is considerably greater than the unexplained variance. The F-value of 45.53, with 5 and 264 degrees of freedom, indicates that the regression model is highly statistically significant. The significance value of 0.00 indicates that the model is statistically significant at conventional levels, implying that the collective influence of AI-enabled performance, AI–human collaboration, AI-oriented leadership, AI infrastructural readiness, and employee behavioral adaptability on Organizational Behavior is not incidental. The ANOVA output validates the model's empirical robustness, confirming that the selected predictors meaningfully explain variations in Organizational Behavior and provide a reliable foundation for further inferential interpretation.

Table 5. Coefficients

Coefficients[a]											
Model		Unstandardized Coefficients		Standardized Coefficients	t	Sig.	Correlations			Collinearity Statistics	
		B	Std. Error	Beta			Zero-order	Partial	Part	Tolerance	VIF
1	(Constant)	.736	.332		2.214	.028					
	AI_Humar_Collaboration	.112	.073	.096	1.526	.128	.365	.093	.069	.509	1.965
	AI_Oriented_Leadership	.321	.069	.291	4.675	.000	.477	.276	.211	.526	1.901
	Adptability_Epmoyee_Behaviour	-.203	.084	-.158	-2.426	.016	.328	-.148	-.109	.480	2.084
	AI_Infrasturctural_Readiness	.218	.071	.198	3.083	.002	.544	.186	.139	.493	2.027
	AI_Enabled_Performance	.392	.059	.395	6.634	.000	.591	.378	.299	.573	1.744

a. Dependent Variable: Orgonizational_Behaviour

Sources: Data compiled by the author

The coefficient table 5 elucidates the individual predictive contribution of each independent variable toward Organizational Behavior. The constant value is 0.74 and is statistically significant ($p = 0.03$), indicating that the baseline level of Organizational Behavior remains meaningful even in the absence of predictor effects. Among the predictors, AI-Enabled Performance emerges as the most influential determinant, with the highest standardized beta ($\beta = 0.40$), t-value (6.63), and significance level (0.00). This suggests that AI-driven performance enhancement substantially strengthens organizational behavioral outcomes. AI-Oriented Leadership also demonstrates a significant positive effect ($B = 0.32$, $\beta = 0.29$, $p = 0.00$), implying that leadership committed to AI adoption fosters constructive behavioral transformation. AI Infrastructural Readiness is likewise significant ($B = 0.22$, $\beta = 0.20$, $p = 0.00$), highlighting the importance of technological preparedness. However, AI–Human Collaboration is statistically insignificant ($p = 0.13$), suggesting limited independent predictive strength. Adaptability of Employee Behavior shows a significant negative effect ($B = -0.20$, $\beta = -0.16$, $p = 0.02$), indicating a possible suppressor or adjustment effect. VIF values below 2.09 confirm the absence of serious multicollinearity. Overall, the model demonstrates differentiated yet meaningful predictor effects.

Table 6. Coefficient Correlations

Model			AI_Enabled_ Performance	AI_Humar_ Collaboration	AI_Oriented_ Leadership	AI_Infrasturctural_ Readiness	Adptability_Epmoyee_ Behaviour
1	Correlations	AI_Enabled_Performance	1.000	.103	-.090	-.561	-.085
		AI_Humar_Collaboration	.103	1.000	-.335	-.162	-.376
		AI_Oriented_Leadership	-.090	-.335	1.000	-.069	-.319
		AI_Infrasturctural_ Readiness	-.561	-.162	-.069	1.000	-.148
		Adptability_Epmoyee_ Behaviour	-.085	-.376	-.319	-.148	1.000
	Covariances	AI_Enabled_Performance	.003	.000	.000	-.002	.000
		AI_Humar_Collaboration	.000	.005	-.002	-.001	-.002
		AI_Oriented_Leadership	.000	-.002	.005	.000	-.002
		AI_Infrasturctural_ Readiness	-.002	-.001	.000	.005	-.001
		Adptability_Epmoyee_ Behaviour	.000	-.002	-.002	-.001	.007

a. Dependent Variable: Orgonizational_Behaviour

Sources: Data compiled by the author

The correlation and covariance matrices in the table 6 provide deeper insight into the interrelationships among the predictor variables in the regression model. The correlation values indicate that most associations among the independent variables are weak to moderate, suggesting that the predictors are not overly overlapping in their explanatory content. The strongest negative association is observed between AI-Enabled Performance and AI Infrastructural Readiness (r = -0.56), suggesting that these two variables move in opposite directions within the estimated model structure. AI–Human Collaboration also shows negative associations with AI-Oriented Leadership (r = -0.34) and Adaptability of Employee Behavior (r = -0.38), reflecting possible divergence in how respondents perceive collaborative AI practices, leadership orientation, and behavioral adjustment. AI-Oriented Leadership demonstrates a moderate negative relationship with Adaptability of Employee Behavior (r = -0.32), while its association with AI Infrastructural Readiness remains very weak (r = -0.07). The covariance values are extremely small, ranging approximately from -0.002 to 0.007, indicating limited joint variability among the estimated coefficients. Overall, the matrix confirms that multicollinearity is not a severe concern, as no correlation approaches the critical threshold. Hence, the predictors remain sufficiently independent, supporting the stability, interpretability, and reliability of the regression estimates.

Table 7. Collinearity Diagnostics

Model	Dimension	Eigenvalue	Condition Index	Variance Proportions					
				(Constant)	AI_Humar_ Collaboration	AI_Oriented_ Leadership	Adptability_Epmoyee_ Behaviour	AI_Infrasturctural_ Readiness	AI_Enabled_ Performance
1	1	5.821	1.000	.00	.00	.00	.00	.00	.00
	2	.074	8.859	.01	.07	.05	.02	.06	.38
	3	.035	12.877	.75	.02	.28	.00	.01	.01
	4	.028	14.327	.05	.13	.29	.00	.59	.29
	5	.023	15.859	.07	.54	.31	.01	.33	.31
	6	.018	18.097	.13	.25	.07	.97	.00	.00

a. Dependent Variable: Orgonizational_Behaviour

Sources: Data compiled by the author

The collinearity diagnostics table 7 provides an advanced assessment of possible multicollinearity among the predictors included in the regression model. The eigenvalues decline progressively from 5.82 to 0.02, indicating that most of the variance is concentrated in the first dimension, while later dimensions contribute comparatively smaller explanatory components. The condition index values range from 1.00 to 18.10 and remain below the commonly accepted critical threshold of 30.00. This suggests that the model does not suffer from severe multicollinearity and that the predictors remain reasonably independent. The variance proportion analysis further supports this interpretation. Although some variables show relatively higher variance proportions in specific dimensions, such as Adaptability of Employee Behavior (0.97 in Dimension 6) and AI Infrastructural Readiness (0.59 in Dimension 4), these are not accompanied by dangerously high condition indices. Similarly, AI–Human Collaboration, AI-Oriented Leadership, and AI-Enabled Performance display moderate variance across dimensions without indicating problematic dependencies. Therefore, the diagnostic evidence confirms that the regression coefficients are not substantially distorted by multicollinearity. Overall, the model demonstrates satisfactory structural stability, reliable parameter estimation, and adequate suitability for inferential interpretation regarding Organizational Behaviour.

Table 8. Casewise Diagnostics

Case Number	Std. Residual	Orgonizational_Behaviour	Predicted Value	Residual
68	3.178	7.00	3.5907	3.40932
260	-3.949	1.00	5.2362	-4.23618

a. Dependent Variable: Orgonizational_Behaviour
Sources: Data compiled by the author

The case wise diagnostics identify in the table 8 that a limited number of extreme standardized residuals exceeding conventional cut-off values, indicating the presence of isolated influential observations; however, their sparse occurrence suggests that these cases do not materially distort the overall model estimation or undermine the generalizability of the empirical findings.

Table 9. Residuals Statistics(a)

	Minimum	Maximum	Mean	Std. Deviation	N
Predicted Value	1.5964	6.6161	4.6185	.98681	270
Residual	-4.23618	3.40932	.00000	1.06264	270
Std. Predicted Value	-3.062	2.024	.000	1.000	270
Std. Residual	-3.949	3.178	.000	.991	270

a. Dependent Variable: Orgonizational_Behaviour
Sources: Data compiled by the author

The residuals statistics (table 9) demonstrate a near-zero mean with symmetrical dispersion and standardized residuals largely confined within acceptable bounds, signifying normality, homoscedasticity, and predictive adequacy of the model, thereby reinforcing the reliability and inferential robustness of the regression outcomes.

5. RESULTS AND FINDINGS

Results and Findings The empirical analysis finds a statistically strong and theoretically consistent model that explains organizational behaviour in AI, enabled contexts. Descriptive statistics reveal that all constructs in the study have mean values higher than the midpoint of the scale, reflecting a generally positive attitude towards AIhuman collaboration, leadership orientation, infrastructural readiness, and performance enhancement, with acceptable distributional properties supporting multivariate analysis. The regression model shows a strong explanatory power as it accounts for a large proportion of the variance in organizational behaviour, with a minimal change between R square and adjusted R square and a near, optimal Durbin-Watson statistic confirming model stability and residuals' independence. ANOVA results confirm the overall significance of the model, indicating that the collective influence of the independent variables is non, random and empirically meaningful. Among the individual predictors, AI, enabled performance is the most significant factor, followed by AI, oriented leadership and AI infrastructural readiness, thus highlighting the primacy of performance, driven AI deployment, strategic leadership commitment, and technological preparedness in shaping organizational outcomes. Employee behavioral adaptability, although statistically significant, has a negative correlation with the dependent variable, indicating that the change employees are resistant to and the cost of adjustment will arise during the phases of rapid technological integration. AIhuman collaboration, however, did not reach statistical significance, indicating a positive relationship, and the collaborative potential alone cannot be enough without supportive leadership and infrastructure.

6. IMPLICATIONS OF THE STUDY

The findings of this study yield significant theoretical, managerial, and strategic implications for organizations navigating AI-driven transformation. From a theoretical standpoint, the study advances socio-technical perspectives by empirically demonstrating that organizational change in AI-enabled contexts is mediated through the dynamic interplay of leadership orientation, behavioral adaptation, infrastructural preparedness, and performance enablement rather than through technological capability alone. This reinforces the argument that AI should be conceptualized as an embedded organizational phenomenon, thereby extending existing frameworks that have traditionally privileged either human or technological determinants in isolation. Managerially, the study underscores the imperative for leaders to move beyond instrumental adoption of AI toward a more integrative governance approach that aligns ethical stewardship, strategic vision, and performance objectives. The prominence of AI-enabled performance and leadership orientation suggests that tangible value from AI investments materializes only when leaders actively orchestrate human–machine collaboration and embed AI within decision-making architectures. Furthermore, the observed complexities surrounding employee behavioral adaptation highlight the necessity of structured reskilling initiatives, transparent communication, and psychologically informed change management strategies to mitigate transitional resistance. Strategically, the study emphasizes that infrastructural readiness is not merely a technical concern but a critical organizational capability influencing scalability, trust, and sustainability of AI initiatives. Organizations must therefore prioritize long-term infrastructural investments alongside human capital development. Collectively, these implications provide actionable insights for designing resilient, human-centered AI strategies that facilitate sustainable organizational transformation in increasingly intelligent work environments.

7. DISCUSSION OF THE STUDY

The present study offers a nuanced empirical contribution to the growing body of scholarship on AI-driven organizational change by elucidating the complex socio-technical dynamics through which AI–human collaboration influences organizational transformation. The findings reaffirm the proposition that artificial intelligence, when embedded within organizational systems, does not operate as an autonomous agent of change but rather derives its transformative capacity from the quality of its integration with human agency, leadership orientation, and institutional preparedness. This insight challenges technologically deterministic narratives and reinforces contemporary perspectives that conceptualize AI as a relational and context-dependent organizational capability.

One of the most salient outcomes of the analysis is the pronounced influence of AI-enabled performance on organizational transformation. This finding aligns with prior research suggesting that organizations primarily legitimize AI investments through demonstrable performance gains, such as enhanced efficiency, decision accuracy, and operational agility. However, the present study extends this understanding by indicating that performance improvements are not merely technical outputs but socially mediated outcomes contingent upon leadership endorsement and employee engagement. AI-enabled performance thus functions as both a tangible indicator of value creation and a symbolic mechanism through which AI is normalized and institutionalized within organizational routines. The significant role of leadership orientation toward AI further underscores the centrality of governance and sensemaking in AI-enabled environments. Leaders act as interpretive agents who frame AI as either an augmentative resource or a disruptive threat, thereby shaping organizational narratives and behavioral responses. The findings resonate with leadership literature emphasizing adaptive and ethical leadership in digital contexts, suggesting that strategic vision, transparency, and accountability are indispensable for fostering trust in intelligent systems. Moreover, leadership orientation appears to amplify the effects of infrastructural readiness and performance enablement, indicating that leadership functions as a coordinating mechanism that aligns disparate organizational elements into a coherent transformation trajectory.

The relationship between employee behavioral adaptation and organizational transformation warrants particular attention, as the analysis reveals a statistically significant yet inverse association. This counterintuitive outcome highlights the paradoxical nature of adaptability in AI-intensive settings. While adaptability is conventionally regarded as a positive individual attribute, the findings suggest that rapid and continuous demands for adjustment may generate cognitive strain, role ambiguity, and psychological fatigue, especially in the absence of adequate support structures. This interpretation aligns with emerging critical perspectives that caution against romanticizing adaptability without accounting for its human costs. The result underscores the necessity of deliberate change management, reskilling pathways, and participatory mechanisms to ensure that behavioral adaptation contributes constructively to transformation rather than undermining organizational equilibrium. AI–human collaboration, although positively associated with organizational transformation, does not exhibit independent statistical significance. This outcome suggests that collaborative potential alone is insufficient to drive systemic change unless it is embedded within supportive leadership frameworks, robust infrastructure, and performance-oriented strategies. The finding reinforces the view that collaboration is an enabling condition whose impact is realized only when complemented by broader organizational capabilities. It also invites further inquiry into the qualitative dimensions of collaboration, such as trust, interpretability, and task complexity, which may condition its effectiveness in ways not fully captured by quantitative measures.

Finally, the overall robustness of the model, as evidenced by diagnostic analyses, affirms the coherence and empirical validity of the proposed framework. The study thus contributes to the literature by integrating behavioral, leadership, and performance dimensions into a unified explanatory model of organizational transformation. In doing so, it advances a more holistic understanding of AI-enabled change, emphasizing that sustainable transformation emerges from the deliberate orchestration of human and technological elements rather than from technological adoption alone.

8. FUTURE SCOPE OF THE STUDY

While the present study provides substantive empirical insights into the socio-technical dynamics of AI–human collaboration and organizational transformation, several promising avenues for future research remain open, offering opportunities to extend, refine, and deepen the current understanding. Future investigations may adopt longitudinal research designs to capture the temporal evolution of AI-driven transformation processes, thereby elucidating how behavioral adaptation, leadership orientation, and performance outcomes unfold over time rather than being inferred from cross-sectional evidence. Such temporal analyses would enable scholars to distinguish between short-term adjustment effects and sustained transformational trajectories.

Subsequent research may also benefit from incorporating mediating and moderating mechanisms that can further explicate the complexity of AI-enabled organizational change. Variables such as digital competence, organizational culture, ethical AI climate, and psychological safety could be examined to uncover how contextual factors condition the strength and direction of relationships among collaboration, leadership, and transformation outcomes. Additionally, multi-level analytical frameworks integrating individual, team, and organizational perspectives would provide richer explanatory depth by capturing cross-level interactions inherent in AI–human systems.

Methodologically, future studies could complement quantitative approaches with qualitative or mixed-method designs, enabling deeper exploration of employee sense-making, leadership narratives, and lived experiences of AI integration. Comparative studies across industries, organizational sizes, and national contexts would further enhance the generalizability of findings and reveal sector-specific contingencies influencing AI adoption and transformation. Moreover, as AI technologies continue to evolve, future research may examine emerging forms of human–AI interaction, including generative AI and autonomous decision systems, to assess their implications for organizational governance and accountability.

Collectively, these extensions would contribute to a more comprehensive and dynamic understanding of AI–human collaboration, positioning future scholarship to better inform theory development, managerial practice, and policy formulation in increasingly intelligent organizational environments.

9. CONCLUSION OF THE STUDY

The present study clearly shows that organizational change in the current AI, driven environment is not just a technological phenomenon, nor is it an automatic result of digital adoption. Instead, it is a complex process that depends on the synergistic alignment of performance, oriented AI use, leadership orientation, infrastructural readiness, and human behavioral dynamics. The data reveal that AI, enabled performance is the single most influential factor in organizational behaviour, thus confirming that efficiency, accuracy, and decision quality are the main ways in which AI brings value to organizations. At the same time, AI, focused leadership becomes a vital catalytic agent, stressing the absolute necessity of strategic vision, ethical stewardship, and change, oriented governance for the successful integration of AI, driven transformation. The results also reveal the primary importance of AI infrastructure readiness, showing that strong digital architectures, reliable data, and fully integrated systems are the necessary conditions for good AI-human collaboration and the achievement of its operational effectiveness. Without such structural preparation, even the most well, intentioned AI initiatives risk becoming merely fragmented and suboptimal.

The inverse yet significant relationship between employee behavioral adaptability and organizational behaviour is particularly interesting. It highlights the complicated and paradoxical nature of human reactions to rapid technological change, which in turn suggests that being adaptable alone might create a state of transitional disequilibrium. This is unless adaptability is supported by systematic reskilling, psychological support, and inclusive change management practices. Although AI-human collaboration shows a positive relationship with organizational behaviour, the absence of statistical significance for this relationship suggests that collaboration alone cannot bring about transformation unless it is part of a coherent organizational ecosystem shaped by leadership commitment and performance imperatives. Together, these findings reaffirm that organizational transformation to succeed in the AI era requires an integrative socio, technical paradigm, where technological capability, human agency, and institutional governance co, evolve in a mutually reinforcing manner. Therefore, the study makes a dual contribution to theory and practice by deepening the understanding of AI-human collaboration as a strategic, behavioral, and infrastructural construct. It offers a valuable set of implications for organizations looking to achieve sustainable and resilient transformation in increasingly intelligent work environments.

REFERENCES

Aggarwal, M., Gingras, C., & Deber, R. (2021). *Artificial Intelligence in Healthcare from a Policy Perspective.*, DOI: 10.1007/978-3-030-67303-1_5

Ameyed, D., Jaafar, F., & Chaabene, R. ben, & Cheriet, M. (2023). Federated Learning and Blockchain: In *AI, Machine Learning and Deep Learning* (pp. 157–166). CRC Press. DOI: 10.1201/9781003187158-14

Babu, K.-E.-K. (2021). *Artificial Intelligence, Its Applications in Different Sectors and Challenges: Bangladesh Context* (pp. 103–119). DOI: 10.1007/978-3-030-88040-8_4

Bender, S. M. L., & Price, W. N. (2024). Legal aspects of artificial intelligence in medical practice. In *Artificial Intelligence in Clinical Practice* (pp. 401–411). Elsevier., DOI: 10.1016/B978-0-443-15688-5.00046-2

Benthall, S., & Goldenfein, J. (2021). Artificial Intelligence and the Purpose of Social Systems. *Proceedings of the 2021 AAAI/ACM Conference on AI, Ethics, and Society*, 3–12. DOI: 10.1145/3461702.3462526

Boban, M., & Klarić, M. (2023). Artificial Intelligence in Healthcare Services – Regulation, Implementation and Future Challenges. *2023 46th MIPRO ICT and Electronics Convention (MIPRO)*, 1440–1445. DOI: 10.23919/MIPRO57284.2023.10159797

Bonsón, E., & Bednárová, M. (2022). *Artificial Intelligence Disclosures in Sustainability Reports: Towards an Artificial Intelligence Reporting Framework* (pp. 391–407). DOI: 10.1007/978-3-030-94617-3_27

Chahal, D., Shahidi, N., & Byrne, M. F. (2022). Artificial Intelligence for Diagnosing G.I. Tract Lesions. In *Gastrointestinal and Pancreatico-Biliary Diseases: Advanced Diagnostic and Therapeutic Endoscopy* (pp. 523–539). Springer International Publishing. DOI: 10.1007/978-3-030-56993-8_31

Daole, M., Schiavo, A., Corcuera Bárcena, J. L., Ducange, P., Marcelloni, F., & Renda, A. (2023). OpenFL-XAI: Federated learning of explainable artificial intelligence models in Python. *SoftwareX, 23*, 101505. DOI: 10.1016/j.softx.2023.101505

Donins, U., & Behmane, D. (2023). *Challenges and Solutions for Artificial Intelligence Adoption in Healthcare – A Literature Review* (pp. 53–62). DOI: 10.1007/978-981-99-3311-2_6

Dutt, R. (2020). The impact of artificial intelligence on healthcare insurances. In *Artificial Intelligence in Healthcare* (pp. 271–293). Elsevier., DOI: 10.1016/B978-0-12-818438-7.00011-3

Goldsteen, A., Farkash, A., Moffie, M., & Shmelkin, R. (2022). *Applying Artificial Intelligence Privacy Technology in the Healthcare Domain*. DOI: 10.3233/SHTI220410

Grzybowski, A. (2021). Artificial Intelligence in Ophthalmology: Promises, Hazards and Challenges. In *Artificial Intelligence in Ophthalmology* (pp. 1–16). Springer International Publishing. DOI: 10.1007/978-3-030-78601-4_1

Gulyamov, S. S. (2024). *Legal Frameworks for the Integration of Artificial Intelligence.*, DOI: 10.1007/978-3-031-42782-4_16

Jastroch, N. (2020). *Trusted Artificial Intelligence: On the Use of Private Data* (pp. 659–670). DOI: 10.1007/978-3-030-62807-9_52

Kabza, M. (2020). Artificial intelligence in financial services – benefits and costs. In *Innovation in Financial Services* (pp. 183–198). Routledge., DOI: 10.4324/9781003051664-14

Leddy, M., & McCreanor, N. (2023). The Potential Utilisation of Artificial Intelligence (AI) in Enterprises. *European Conference on Innovation and Entrepreneurship, 18*(1), 526–535. DOI: 10.34190/ecie.18.1.1720

Li, J., Liu, Y., Yue, L., Jin, F., Guo, Q., & Xu, C. (2018). Artificial Intelligence Governed by Laws and Regulations. In *Reconstructing Our Orders* (pp. 61–97). Springer Singapore., DOI: 10.1007/978-981-13-2209-9_3

Li, X., & Zhang, T. (2017). An exploration on artificial intelligence application: From security, privacy and ethic perspective. *2017 IEEE 2nd International Conference on Cloud Computing and Big Data Analysis (ICCCBDA)*, 416–420. DOI: 10.1109/ICCCBDA.2017.7951949

Longo, L., Goebel, R., Lecue, F., Kieseberg, P., & Holzinger, A. (2020). *Explainable Artificial Intelligence: Concepts*. Applications, Research Challenges and Visions., DOI: 10.1007/978-3-030-57321-8_1

Ma, H., & Wang, J. (2021). *Application of Artificial Intelligence in Intelligent Decision-Making of Human Resource Allocation.*, DOI: 10.1007/978-3-030-62743-0_28

Magrani, E., & da Silva, P. G. F. (2024). *The Ethical and Legal Challenges of Recommender Systems Driven by Artificial Intelligence.*, DOI: 10.1007/978-3-031-41264-6_8

Martinelli, F., Marulli, F., Mercaldo, F., Marrone, S., & Santone, A. (2020). Enhanced Privacy and Data Protection using Natural Language Processing and Artificial Intelligence. *2020 International Joint Conference on Neural Networks (IJCNN)*, 1–8. DOI: 10.1109/IJCNN48605.2020.9206801

Mudholkar, R., Cardenas-Palomino, F., Gehlot, A., Vekariya, V., Raju, A. M., & Rajput, K. (2023). Artificial Intelligence in Maintaining Interaction Between Humans and Computer. *2023 3rd International Conference on Advance Computing and Innovative Technologies in Engineering (ICACITE)*, 1903–1908. DOI: 10.1109/ICACITE57410.2023.10182641

Paes, V. M., Silveira, F. F., & Akkari, A. C. S. (2023). *Social Impacts of Artificial Intelligence and Mitigation Recommendations: An Exploratory Study* (pp. 521–528). DOI: 10.1007/978-3-031-04435-9_54

Payton, M. J. (2023). Impact of Artificial Intelligence Regulations on Organizational Risks. *The International FLAIRS Conference Proceedings,* 36. DOI: 10.32473/flairs.36.133263

Pesapane, F., Suter, M. B., Codari, M., Patella, F., Volonté, C., & Sardanelli, F. (2020). Regulatory issues for artificial intelligence in radiology. In *Precision Medicine for Investigators, Practitioners and Providers* (pp. 533–543). Elsevier. DOI: 10.1016/B978-0-12-819178-1.00052-6

Sanz, J. L. C., & Zhu, Y. (2021). Toward Scalable Artificial Intelligence in Finance. *2021 IEEE International Conference on Services Computing (SCC)*, 460–469. DOI: 10.1109/SCC53864.2021.00067

Swati, S., & Kumar, M. (2023). *Innovations in Blockchain Using Artificial Intelligence.*, DOI: 10.1007/978-981-19-8730-4_7

Vizitiu, A., Nita, C. I., Puiu, A., Suciu, C., & Itu, L. M. (2019). Privacy-Preserving Artificial Intelligence: Application to Precision Medicine. *2019 41st Annual International Conference of the IEEE Engineering in Medicine and Biology Society (EMBC)*, 6498–6504. DOI: 10.1109/EMBC.2019.8857960

Wong, A. (2021). *Ethics and Regulation of Artificial Intelligence.*, DOI: 10.1007/978-3-030-80847-1_1

Xin, S., Zhaobin, P., & Jing, Q. (2022). *Legal Analysis of the Right to Privacy Protection in the Age of Artificial Intelligence.*, DOI: 10.1007/978-3-031-13870-6_51

Yusif-Zada, K., & Iskandarova, S. (2023). Artificial Intelligence Policy and Regulation in Medicine: Navigating the Promise and Challenges. *2023 IEEE Global Conference on Artificial Intelligence and Internet of Things (GCAIoT)*, 191–196. DOI: 10.1109/GCAIoT61060.2023.10385130

Zallone, R. (2020). Artificial Intelligence vs Autonomous Cars vs General Data Protection Regulation. *2020 AEIT International Conference of Electrical and Electronic Technologies for Automotive (AEIT AUTOMOTIVE)*, 1–6. DOI: 10.23919/AEITAUTOMOTIVE50086.2020.9307410

Chapter 5
Cognitive Alignment Protocols:
Designing Harmonized Decision Systems for Ethical AI-Human Collaboration in Organizations

Azizbek Ismailov
Alfraganus University, Tashkent, Uzbekistan

S. Aarthi
http://orcid.org/0009-0006-9064-2091
Marwadi University, Rajkot, India

Allayarov Suxrob Rustamovich
Tashkent State University of Economics, Tashkent, Uzbekistan

Juraev Khusan
Termez University of Economics and Service, Termez, Uzbekistan

Nazarov Akmal Mardonovich
Bukhara State University, Bukhara, Uzbekistan

R. N. Ravikumar
http://orcid.org/0009-0009-3705-1681
Marwadi University, Rajkot, India

ABSTRACT

The sudden emergence of Artificial Intelligence (AI) into the decision-making process in organizations has altered the process of decision-making by changing the manner in which decisions are formulated, assessed, and implemented. Although performance is better, a lack of alignment between human cognition and algorithmic logic frequently results in distrust, ethical unease, and poor performance. The chapter proposes the concept of Cognitive Alignment Protocols (CAPs) as an underlying system-level scheme of aligning human judgment, organizational values, and AI decision systems. The chapter relying on the foundations of cognitive psychology, human-AI interaction, and organizational behavior and backed by the recent case studies in HR analytics and financial forecasting shows that transparency, ethical

DOI: 10.4018/979-8-2600-2541-3.ch005

fit, and behavioral congruence promote trust, human agency, and decision quality. The results put cognitive alignment at the heart of responsible and sustainable AI usage in the organizations.

1. INTRODUCTION

Organizations are rapidly incorporating Artificial Intelligence (AI) into their strategic planning, human resource management, finance, customer engagement, and governance, changing their decision-making processes. While AI tools enhance speed, accuracy, and scalability with their analytics and decision-support systems, they are not solely computational in nature and decisions are made within the organization (Thalpage, 2025). They are influenced by the thinking, expertise, organizational norms, and situational reasoning of people. With the rising influence of AI systems in making recommendations, there can be conflicts between AI-generated decisions and human thought processes or organizational needs. While there has been existing work on responsible and explainable AI, there has been less focus on systematic mapping of how cognition and reasoning in algorithms relate to one another and to human cognition (Raisch & Krakowski, 2021). The challenge of this chapter is to complement the above by introducing a structured approach to enhance AI collaboration with humans in organizational decision-making, known as Cognitive Alignment Protocols (CAPs).

1.1 AI-Augmented Decision-Making

The trends in the organizational decision-making have shifted towards information-based and algorithm-driven decision-making processes as opposed to being made on a whim basis and driven by rules. This is because early decision support systems were based on descriptive reporting and deterministic models, and they were limited in terms of interaction with human judgment. Since, machine learning, predictive analytics and real-time data processing advancements have occurred, AI systems have become capable of producing probabilistic forecasts, suggestions, and automatic behavior. These systems are currently in use in various levels of the organizations, both in operational scheduling down to the executive level strategy formulation (Margondai et al., 2025). The use of AI augmentation has transformed decision-making to include progressively retrospective and anticipatory and prescriptive analysis, enabling companies to dynamically react to complexity and uncertainty. However, decision authority and accountability structures have changed as well as a result of this evolution. Human decision-makers are finding more and more use of vague models whose rationale might not be consistent with experiential and situational thinking (Ravikumar et al., 2026). The more AI systems are active in making decisions, the more organizational decisions rely on the quality of the models applied as well as the quality of the interpretations, trust, and integrations of the outputs of the algorithms by human actors. It is the transformation that brings to the fore the necessity of alignment in human cognition and the intelligence provided by AI (Rostamzadeh et al., 2025). Figure 1 shows the shift from traditional decision support systems to AI-augmented organizational decision-making.

Figure 1. AI-Augmented Decision-Making

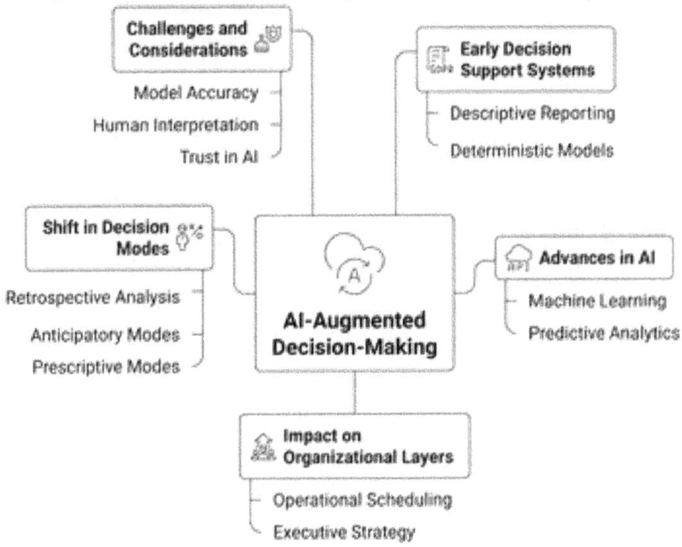

1.2 Cognitive Misalignment

The phenomenon of cognitive disparities is known as cognitive misalignment that occurs when there are differences between human mental models and the logic of how the AI systems come up with recommendations. Making decisions by human decision-makers is based on contextual cues, moral reasoning, heuristics, and social norms, and AI systems use statistical inference and optimization goals. In the cases of poor explanation of algorithmic outputs or it opposes the judgment of intuition, people might feel confused, sceptical or defensively resistant. On the other hand, too much confidence in automated suggestions may cause automation bias where human supervision reduces. This misfit may enhance the errors, diminish responsibility, and harm psychological safety at the workplace (Chiriatti et al., 2025). These issues are especially acute in such high-risk areas as recruitment, performance appraisal, risk analysis of finances, and government oversight. In the absence of systems to align human interpretation systems with algorithms, the implementation of AI has a high likelihood of compromising organizational trust and moral standards. Cognitive misalignment must be dealt with thus, through conscious design methods that transcend human sense-making methods and machine-generated intelligence.

1.3 Chapter Scope and Contribution

The main idea behind this chapter is to both conceptualize and operationalize CAPs as an initial framework of ethical and effective AI-human collaboration within organizations. The chapter tries to analyze the possibility of developing an alignment between the human mental functioning processes, organizational values, and algorithmic decision systems. It has an individual, managerial, and organizational level of analysis, covering both behavioral and ethical aspects of the AI-assisted decision-making. Based on the literature in cognitive psychology, human-computer interaction, and organizational behavior, the chapter defines a multidimensional perspective of alignment, which involves interpretability, ethical congruence, trust calibration and behavioral resonance. The main value-added aspect is the reinterpretation of the responsible adoption of AI as a cognitive and design challenge, but not necessarily a technical or regulatory one. The chapter also provides a systematic way of minimizing friction, developing human agency and building collaborative environments in decision making by proposing CAPs as system-level design principles. This view contributes to the discussion of the anthropocentric and morally focused AI in companies.

2. BACKGROUND TO THE STUDY

The increasing dependence on AI-based systems has increased the academic focus of the interaction of technology and human cognition, as well as organizational behavior. The limited rationality, social processes, and institutional structures in organizations shape decision-making processes that societal norms affect the way information is perceived and taken. The implementation of AI changes these relationships by adding algorithmic cognitions that are in fact different than human reasoning. Although AI systems are superior in pattern recognition and inference based on probabilities, they do not have any sense of context, moral intuition, or socio-emotional awareness (Lysaght et al., 2019). This is a rift that poses new impediments to collaboration, accountability and ethical governance. The literature regarding adoption of AI has focused mainly on performance results, transparency, and fairness and in most cases, excluded the cognitive aspect in the integration between human and machine agents. It is crucial to come up with effective interventions by understanding the background conditions that lead to misalignment. The section places the study in the context of more general discussions of human cognition, algorithmic decision-making, and ethical AI, which forms the theoretical basis of the presented CAPs.

2.1 Human Cognition and Biases

Social influences on human decision-making are cognitive, emotional and contextual limitations that are inherent to the decision-making process. Heuristics and mental shortcuts help organizational actors to cope with complexity and time limitations and present systematic biases to overconfidence, confirmation bias, and loss aversion. Such prejudices are not isolated personal weaknesses but they are supported by organizational cultures, power relations, and reward systems. Situations of decision making that involve uncertainty, ambiguity or moral trade-offs compound the use of subjective judgment. Although experience and intuition can contribute to improving the quality of decisions, they can also contradict data-driven knowledge obtained by the systems that use AI (Canbul Yaroğlu, 2025). This may lead to resistance when the recommendations generated by the algorithms conflict with the established beliefs or even the professional identities. It is important to know these cognitive traits to develop AI systems that do not override the reasoning of human beings. The collaboration is possible only when human cognitive weaknesses and strengths are taken into account and AI tools are integrated in a manner that would facilitate reflections, critical analysis, and ethical decision-making in organizational decision settings.

2.2 Algorithmic Cognition

The ability of AI systems to handle large amounts of data, detect trends and offer suggestions or take action with minimal human oversight is known as algorithmic cognition. Recent developments in machine learning, deep neural networks and reinforcement learning have allowed AI systems to engage in more autonomous ways. These systems are used in organizations to aid in making decisions regarding hiring, credit rating, predicting demand and implementing policies. The difference between algorithmic and human cognition lies in the fact that the first is probabilistic, optimization based, and usually opaque. Although these systems can be more effective than humans in particular tasks, the logic behind their decision may be hard to explain or comprehend (Selvi et al., 2025). Transparency, accountability, and ethical responsibility are some of the issues that come up when decision authority is delegated to algorithms. With the use of autonomous decision-support systems, the balance between human control and machine autonomy is a design issue that is critical as organizations make this move. It is crucial to ensure that the application of algorithmic cognition is sustainable and responsible by ensuring that it is not contrary to human values and organizational goals.

2.3 AI–Human Collaboration Challenges

The collaboration between AI and humans creates a set of ethical and behavioral issues which are not confined to technical precision. The ethical issues are those of maximising bias, inequitable results, loss of privacy and loss of moral responsibility. The challenges of behavioral issues may arise when it becomes hard for the employees to place trust, understand or relate with AI systems. A lack of control, fear of substitution and role ambiguity can result in a demotivating effect on motivation and well-being. Moreover, uncertainties regarding who has control over the decisions made regarding AI can also result in a lack of accountability systems (Chamsi-Pasha, 2025). These may be further exacerbated by organizational cultures that are concerned about efficiency, but not about moral reflection. To overcome these challenges, it is necessary to consider ethical issues when designing the system and making organizational decisions. There is a need for a pathway to incorporate ethical reasoning into AI-informed decision environments, so that people can work together responsibly and do right by their organizations. CAPs do this by providing a mechanism for introducing ethical reasoning, transparency and human agency.

3. RESEARCH OBJECTIVES

The chapter is informed by the purpose of developing a logical conceptualization of the ways of conceptualizing, designing, and operationalizing cognitive alignment between human decision-makers and AI systems in the context of an organizational environment. The further development of the field of alignment as a phenomenon is vital, and clear research objectives are needed to investigate alignment as a technical, behavioral, and ethical phenomenon. The objectives listed below are formulated following the suggested outline and put together the scope of the analysis of the chapter.

- To explain the concept of cognitive alignment in AI-enabled organizational decision-making.
- To identify the causes of cognitive misalignment between human judgment and AI systems.
- To propose CAPs as a framework for improving human-AI collaboration.

- To examine how CAPs influence trust, decision quality, human agency, and ethical AI use.
- To assess the application of CAPs in areas such as HR analytics, financial forecasting, and organizational governance.

4. CONCEPTUAL MODEL

CAPs are a system level framework to bring together human cognition, organizational values and decision systems driven by AI. The aim of CAPs are to minimize the cognitive mismatch between humans making decisions and the decisions generated by the algorithms. The model highlights technical correctness as a part of the alignment, but also reflects the interpretation, trust, and application of AI-recommended actions within an organization. While human cognition is based on contextual reasoning, intuition and experience, AI systems are based on probabilistic inference and optimization logic (Madanchian & Taherdoost, 2025). These differences can be addressed with the explainability mechanisms, ethical safeguards, feedback loops, and pathways of human oversight that are part of CAPs. The framework also emphasizes the importance of the dynamic nature of alignment and its influence of the organizational culture, leadership, and decision context. As such, the model enables more interpretable, accountable, and collaborative AI-driven decision-making processes in organizations' functions (Van Den Berg et al., 2023). Figure 2 shows how CAPs connect human cognition, AI decision systems, and ethical reasoning for aligned organizational decision-making.

4.1 Alignment Dimensions

Cognitive alignment is defined as a combination of three dimensions that are all dependent on each other which are transparency, ethical fit and behavioral congruence. The degree to which the reasoning processes, data dependencies, and the extent of uncertainty of the AI systems are intelligible to human users is referred to as transparency. Ethical fit describes the correspondence between organizational values, norms of fairness, and expectations of morality and algorithmic decision rules. The concept of behavioral fit illustrates the extent to which AI outputs supplement the human decision styles, workflow, and professional judgment. On the other hand, compliance of ethical standards which cannot be interpreted can be counterproductive to trust (Oyekunle et al., 2024). The model underlines the fact that alignment is not a fixed state but a dynamic one that gets formed due to learning, feedback and organizational context. The knowledge of these dimensions empowers organizations to identify the flaws in their alignment and formulate specific interventions that will lead to a substantial human-AI cooperation. Table 1 Concludes the essential aspects of cognitive alignment the transparency, ethical fit and behavioral congruence, and their distinguishing features.

Table 1. Alignment Dimensions

Dimension	Description	Role in Decision-Making
Transparency	Degree to which AI reasoning and outputs are understandable	Improves interpretability and user confidence
Ethical Fit	Alignment with organizational values and fairness norms	Ensures morally acceptable decisions
Behavioral Congruence	Compatibility with human workflows and judgment styles	Reduces resistance and cognitive load

4.2 Human and Algorithmic Logic

The human mental model is developed through experience, intuition, cultural norms, and contextual knowledge, and the algorithmic logic is developed based on statistical inference, objective of optimization, and a priori constraints. This is where the two types of cognition intersect leading to AI-based decision-making. Misalignment happens when the recommendations provided by the algorithm clash with human expectations, or have no contextual support. All of this can create mistrust and/or resistance or blind obedience. The conceptual model also notes that the notion of effective interaction implies the need to have mechanisms that convert AI outputs into representations that can be cognitively accessed. Shared mental models can be created using explainability tools, uncertainty visualization, and a series of feedback loops. These mechanisms enable the human decision-maker to integrate AI insights into their decision-making processes (Ye et al., 2025). It is a two-way process: human beings affect the interpretation and application of AI, as well as AI affects human judgment patterns in the long term. It is necessary to regulate this interaction in order to avoid the problem of cognitive overload and maintain human agency in AI-assisted settings. Table 2 Visually depicts matches and differences in human thinking and algorithm thinking in decision making in organizational activities.

Table 2. Human vs Algorithmic Logic

Human Cognitive Aspect	Algorithmic Logic	Potential Misalignment
Intuition-based reasoning	Statistical inference	Lack of contextual sense
Ethical judgment	Optimization objectives	Value conflicts
Experience-driven decisions	Data-driven predictions	Distrust or over-reliance
Heuristic processing	Probabilistic modeling	Cognitive overload

4.3 CAPs as Design Architecture

The concepts of CAPs are presented as system-level architecture of design that achieves conformity in terms of technical, behavioral and ethical aspects. CAPs transcend interface level elucidation and integrates ideas of alignment in data governing, model deployment, and decision-making, and accountability. These have the properties of decision justification programs, pronunciation delineation layers, prejudice-checking loops and the human-overriding escalation paths. By establishing these mechanisms, CAPs ensure that alignment is not in the goodwill of an individual, but it is a formalized aspect. It is the architecture that considers organization norms and strategic focus to the conduct of AI systems, permitting algorithms to act within socially and ethically limited contexts (Oyebode, 2025). CAPs as an architecture design will transform AI systems into cognition partners within the organization in accordance with organizational behavior and values instead of being independent decision engines. Table 3 Essentials of the key CAP elements, their functional account and their desired behavioral and ethical standards.

Table 3. CAP Design Components

CAP Component	Function	Intended Outcome
Explainability mechanisms	Clarify AI reasoning	Improved trust
Ethical constraint layers	Enforce fairness and norms	Reduced bias
Human override pathways	Enable intervention	Preserved human agency
Feedback and learning loops	Adapt system behavior	Continuous alignment

5. METHODOLOGICAL FRAMEWORK

This chapter adopts a theory building exploratory approach to look at cognitive alignment as a socio-technical phenomenon in the context of organizational decision making with the assistance of AI. This study is based on the methodology of conceptual synthesis, multi-theoretical integration and cross-case interpretive analysis. To tie socio-technical, cognitive psychology, organizational behavior, AI ethics, and human–AI interaction together, a socio-technical analytical lens is applied. The study is more of an integrative, secondary case-based approach to the theoretical development of a set of CAPs that is not testing a hypothesis but rather developing one (Vats & Alam, 2025). This method allows for the discovery of dimensions of alignment, design principles, and conditions of organizations that impact responsible AI-human collaboration. The selected cases are analyzed to gain insight into the role transparency plays in decision acceptance, the role of ethical fit plays in decision acceptance and the role of trust calibration and behavioral congruence play in organizational outcomes. Hence, the methodology is both conceptually sound and can produce insights that can be used to validate CAPs in the future, in the context of various organizational structures.

5.1 Research Design

The study design adheres to a qualitative and exploratory paradigm relying on the theories, which are based on cognitive psychology, human-computer interaction, and organizational behavior. The concept of cognitive alignment is discussed as a socio-technical construct that is influenced by the perception of people, institutional context, and algorithm design. The reasoning basis is grounded on the concepts of bounded rationality, shared mental models and trust and ethics of behaviour (Asan & Choudhury, 2021). Theories are the analytical frameworks that analyse the human reaction to AI-driven decisions. The design is not based on any specific hypothesis but it is conceptual, synthesis and identification of patterns. This method fits using emerging constructs like CAPs that need theoretical explanation and subsequent empirical validation in large scale. The integration of different theoretical perspectives may help to obtain a more holistic view of the phenomenon of design alignment and solutions in organizations.

5.2 Case Selection and Sources

o ensure case studies were relevant, recent, and critical to the decision making process in relation to the use of AI, they were selected and categorized by this criteria. Emphasis was placed on the organizations that are actively using AI systems to help make decisions in areas such as human resources, financial forecasting, or even customer administration. The cases were chosen to provide an illustration of successful practices in alignment and an example of cognitive friction (Nahar et al., 2024). The data sources include secondary documents on cases, organizational reports, practitioner accounts and published empirical research. This triangulation provides analytical strength, by incorporating different views concerning the interaction of AI and human beings. The selected cases give an opportunity to compare the contexts and highlight the role that an organizational culture and the governance systems can play in the cognitive alignment effect. The focus on recent cases will ensure it is applicable to current AI use and business activities.

5.3 Analytical Strategy

The conceptual dimensions of the cognitive alignment, as postulated in the model are matched between the empirical observation and the analytical framework. Thematic analysis was performed on the data with regards to transparency mechanisms, ethical inclusion, and reactions to AI systems. Special focus was given to instances of harmonization and disharmonization such as breakdown of trust, resistance, or excessive reliance on AI (Lukyanenko et al., 2022). The interpretation was done in an iterative process between theoretical construct and empirical patterns so as to fine-tune the insights. The analysis is based on explanatory richness and conceptual consistency, as opposed to causal attribution. This plan aids in the development of theory, defines principles of design and the organizational context in which CAPs operate. The framework helps organize the understanding of socio-technical interactions of complexity in the environment of decisions facilitated by AI.

5.4 Measuring Cognitive Alignment

In order to enhance the empirical applicability of CAPs measurable indicators which can operationalise cognitive alignment in organizational settings need to be identified. The conceptual and qualitative approach used in this chapter is the primary approach for measuring the effectiveness of alignment, but future empirical research could explore alignment effectiveness through behavioral, psychological and organizational performance. The suggested metrics offer a first set of tools for operationalizing the process of survey, experimental research and study and organizational audit for AI-human collaboration. To validate the effectiveness of CAP across various organizational contexts, and to make the cognitive alignment a practical organizational capability, it is necessary to establish dimension(s) that can be measured. Table 4 includes quantifiable metrics to assess transparency, trust, ethical fit, behavioural congruence, human agency, cognitive load and alignment stability in organizational decision-making processes when using an AI assistant.

Table 4. Alignment Metrics

Alignment Dimension	Possible Metric
Transparency	User interpretability score
Trust Calibration	Trust survey scale
Ethical Fit	Fairness perception index
Behavioral Congruence	Human override frequency
Human Agency	Decision autonomy score
Cognitive Load	NASA-TLX scale
Alignment Stability	Longitudinal consistency

5.5 Empirical Validation Strategies

Research in the future should confirm, in practice, CAPs in different organizations and in different settings. In experimental research, various aspects of aligned and non-aligned AI decision systems can be contrasted, including their level of trust, their interpretability, the quality of the decisions they make, and how much their users will accept. Validation based on surveys may be able to assess perceptions of transparency, fairness, ethical fit, cognitive load, and human agency of employees. In addition, longitudinal studies are required to explore the changes in cognitive alignment over time with the increase of users' experience in using AI systems. Furthermore, specific studies on human resources, finance, healthcare and public governance of decision making can be conducted to see if CAPs are different in various decision environments. These methods would be better for validation if combined with mixed-method approaches, such as interviews, behavioural data, system-use logs and performance indicators. Empirical approaches can make CAPs from an idea into a quantifiable and scientifically valid process of responsible collaboration between AI and human.

6. LITERATURE REVIEW

The field of AI-human collaboration is interdisciplinary and is covered by works in areas of cognitive psychology, computer science, ethics, and organizational behavior. Available literature has analyzed the decision-support systems, algorithmic accountability, and responsible AI implementation, but the strands tend to be disjointed. Cognitive studies are concerned with the way human beings process information and deal with uncertainty whereas, AI research is concerned with model performance, explainability and fairness (Richardson et al., 2021). On the other hand, organizational behavior literature discusses behavioral and power in relation to technology-mediated work settings including trust. The lack of research that combines these two views is that which would result in the alignment of human cognition and algorithmic reasoning in organizations in a systematic way (Sanjay & Khalsa, 2025). Such a lack has led to a low awareness of the reasons behind the failure of technically sound AI systems to be accepted or have unintended behavioral effects. This section provides the theoretical background to CAPs by conducting literature reviews in these fields. Three main themes addressed in the review are in line with the objectives of the chapter, including cognitive mechanisms and shared mental models, explainable and ethical AI design, and organizational behavior views of human-AI interaction (Ravikumar & Aarthi, 2025). Cumulatively, these strands culturalized a comprehensive insight into alignment as a socio-technical phenomenon, as well as behavioral phenomenon.

6.1 Cognitive Psychology and Mental Models

Using cognitive psychology gives an important understanding of the way people perceive, interpret and take action out of information when making decisions. The studies of bounded rationality emphasize the fact that human decision-makers are subjected to cognitive limits and use simplified mental models and heuristics (Naiseh et al., 2021). The shared mental model theory adds more insight on how alignment between members of the team boosts coordination, prediction, and performance. Shared mental models help to create common understanding of task objectives, information cues and decision logic in decision systems (Ozturkcan & Bozdağ, 2025). It has been observed that decision accuracy and confidence are increased when the system behavior is consistent with the mental models of the users. On the contrary, any discrepancy between the logic and the expectations of humans leads to higher cognitive load and the rate of error. In systems with AI applications, shared mental models between humans and algorithms are not available, which worsens interpretive difficulties (Pasupuleti, 2025). The cognitive psychology therefore lays emphasis on the formulation of AI systems that facilitate sense-making, allow learning, and adjust to the human cognitive systems. These lessons constitute a perceptual foundation when it comes to the conception of cognitive congruency in an organizational decision-making setting.

6.2 Explainable and Ethical AI

The research of Explainable AI (XAI) is devoted to the problem of making an algorithmic decision comprehensible to a human operator. Transparency and interpretability are considered to be the requirements of trust and accountability in AI systems (Oladosu et al., 2023). Research also shows that explanations enhance user trust especially in high-stakes decision-making situations, where it is also shown that overly complicated or ill-framed explanations are likely to hinder understanding. According to trust calibration literature, the development of effective human-AI collaboration does not presuppose blind trust or even excessive suspicion (Sun & Xu, 2025). The successful calibration will rely on the awareness of the users about the system capabilities, limitations, and uncertainty. The ethical design of AI helps in developing this debate by adding the elements of fairness, accountability, and alignment of values to the development of a system. The scholars believe that ethical principles should be put into work with the help of design mechanisms and not seen as abstract principles (Bharathi & Krishna, 2025). However, in the current literature, the explanatory issues, the trust, and the ethics are usually discussed separately. The connection between these factors into highly developed design guidelines is not studied thoroughly, which explains why some systemic strategies like CAPs should be considered.

6.3 Human-AI Interaction

The field of organizational behavior studies the ways in which the use of AI transforms the role, authority, and social dynamics at workplaces. Research has reported instances of beneficial effects, including improved productivity and the quality of decisions, and detrimental effects, including resistance, anxiety, and the sense of being deprived of autonomy. The performance of a system is not the only factor that determines trust of AI, as organizational culture, leadership styles, and communication patterns also play a role (Gupta, 2025). The redistribution of power associated with the use of algorithms to make decisions may change accountability and managerial control. Furthermore, fairness, transparency, and the compatibility of AI with the professional identity help employees to accept it (Yadav et al., 2023). The reactions to AI are thus very contextual and social in nature. The literature on organizational behavior points to the fact that the integration of AI can only be successful when the human agency, psychological safety, and ethical climate are taken into account (Kumar & Nair, 2025). These lessons uphold the idea that the issue of alignment should be discussed on the organizational level, which justifies the creation of CAPs as an interface between human behavior and technical systems.

6.4 CAPs and Human-AI Frameworks

Current human-AI systems have been a valuable asset to the responsible decision-making of organizations. XAI places emphasis on transparency, making the outputs of its algorithms more understandable for the users. Responsible AI emphasizes justice, responsibility, privacy, and ethics. Human oversight systems allow humans to have control over AI decisions that involve sensitive situations or high risks, and hybrid intelligence systems enable the human expertise to collaborate with AI machines (Ma et al., 2025). These strategies are important, as they help to diminish opacity, facilitate moral protection and retain human accountability in the context of AI-driven decision-making. However, CAPs can be distinguished from each other as they specify a particular kind of cognitive congruence between human mental models and the reasoning of algorithms. While XAI aims to describe the outputs of the models, Responsible AI provides ethical guidelines, CAPs focus on how humans interpret, trust, challenge and incorporate the recommendations generated by AI into their actual decisions within the organization (Gin et al., 2025). Thus, CAPs are designed to be extensions of the current frameworks, bringing together the concepts of interpretability, ethical fit, trust calibration, behavioral congruence and organizational decision practice and aligning them with the design approach of alignment. Figure 3 compares CAPs with existing human-AI frameworks across key alignment dimensions.

Figure 3. CAPs vs Human–AI Frameworks

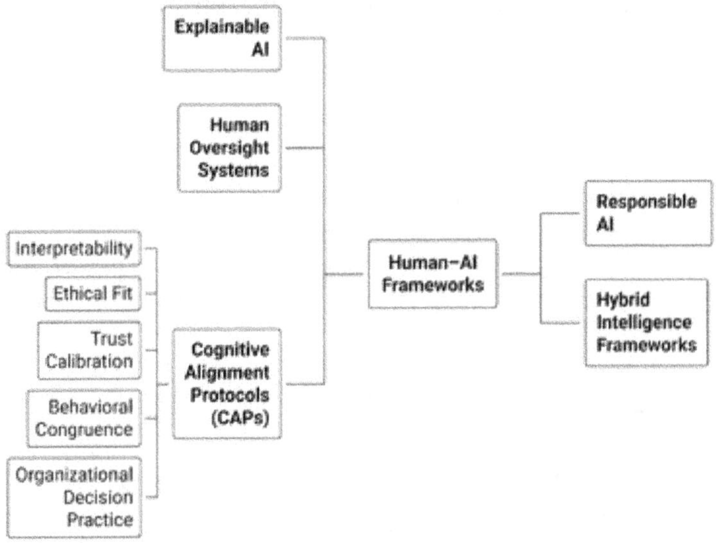

7. ILLUSTRATIVE CASE ANALYSIS

With organizations maximally embracing the use of AI in decision support, it is paramount to comprehend how cognitive alignment can drive the results. Two recent empirical case studies on the implementation of AI systems in high-impact decision settings are reviewed in this section. The former study examines AI-enhanced HR analytics and talents choices, and how algorithmic information affects the results of recruitment, retention, and workforce design. The second scenario considers the financial forecasting and executive judgment with the help of AI, focusing on the enhancements in the accuracy of the forecasting and the minimization of the error as well as the quality of decisions. The two cases represent quantitative effects and compatibility issues in the process of adoption and use (Tanantong & Wongras, 2024). They also shed light on the issue of variation in human interpretation and algorithmic logic on matters of trust, acceptance of decisions, and organizational behavior. This empirical investigation helps in the argument of the chapter that CAPs are needed to align human cognitive models to an algorithmic output, to facilitate human-AI responsible and productive interaction in organizational decision-making. Table 5 Provides a comparison between the two case studies in terms of context, area of AI application, alignment mechanisms, and quantitative performance results.

Table 5. Case Study Indicators

Case Context	AI Application	Key Alignment Features	Quantitative Outcomes
HR Analytics	Talent retention & hiring	Explainability, bias checks	20–30% turnover reduction
Financial Forecasting	Revenue & risk prediction	Scenario visualization	17% accuracy improvement

7.1 Case Study I: HR Analytics Case

According to recent evidence, AI-enhanced HR analytics has a strong influence on recruitment, retention, and the quality of performance decisions in various industries. A 2024-2025 survey of HR leaders with a global viewpoint revealed that 89% of the surveyed reported that AI integration in HR functions positively affected the onboarding experience of employees, with equally substantial majorities reporting improved performance management accuracy (approach 92%) and training program effectiveness (approach 88%) with AI integration in HR operations (Alam et al., 2020). Talent analytics based on AI allow making proactive predictions of risks of employee turnover and talent shortage, which greatly enhance workforce planning results and early retention strategies. Moreover, the workforce turnover rates have also decreased by 20-30% in organizations that have adopted AI predictive models because at-risk employee segments are identified and customized retention plans are provided. Notably, though, the benefits are also associated with alignment issues: HR specialists often mention an algorithmic opaqueness and issues with bias as the obstacles to complete trust of AI-based decisions and need interpretability solutions and ethical controls to guarantee alignment (Ingrams et al., 2022). The research indicates that the higher the mental alignment between the HR decision-makers and AI analytics, the better the acceptance and successful application of AI in the talent decision frameworks. The figure 4 represents the main percentage-based results of AI-based HR analytics, and it shows that the onboarding, performance management, training effectiveness, and reduction of the employee turnover were improved.

Figure 4. AI in HR Analytics

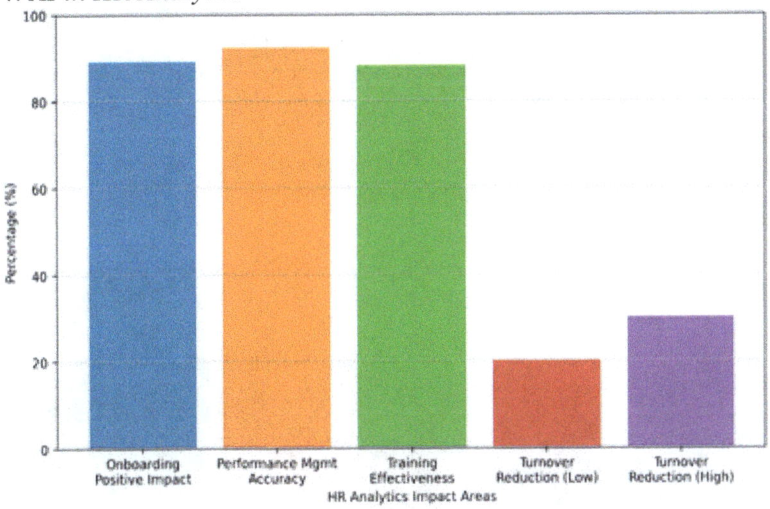

7.2 Case Study II: Financial Forecasting Case

The use of AI in financial forecasting has proven effects on the accuracy of the forecasts, the speed of the decision, and strategic financial planning of modern businesses. According to recent research on AI-powered forecasting tools, companies that switched to machine learning and predictive analytics methods have seen their forecast accuracy and forecasting error rates grow up to 17-22%, respectively, as opposed to the traditional ones. The gains are possible due to the fact that AI algorithms combine multiple quantities of structured and unstructured financial data which allows making more subtle predictions on revenues, cash flow, and the trend of costs. In the field of executive judgment, finance teams are using AI models to model the various scenarios and predict risk exposures, which improves strategic decision making in the face of uncertainty. The trends in the wider industry show that 58% of finance departments make use of AI tools to predict by 2025, a significant rise in the use and dependency on AI in the decision-making processes. However, there remain difficulties: executives usually have problems with the interpretation of AI results and their reconciliation with the domain knowledge, and this issue may contribute to the fact that the algorithmic recommendations and strategic decisions do not always coincide (Singh et al., 2025). This highlights the necessity of procedures that contribute to the increase in understandability, trust, and ethical incorporation of AI forecasting processes. Figure 5 shows forecast accuracy, error reduction, and AI adoption levels among finance teams using AI-assisted forecasting tools.

Figure 5. AI in Financial Forecasting

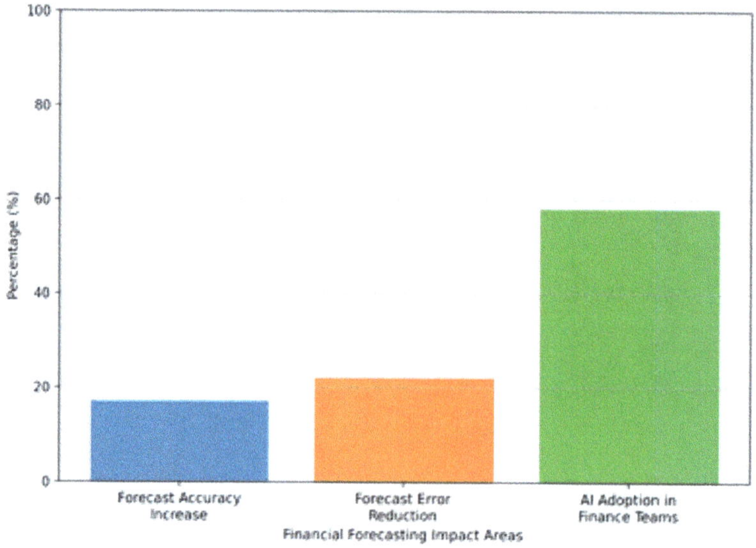

7.3 Cross-Case Comparison

Despite the examples of the HR analytics and financial forecasting demonstrating the apparent productivity increase and the improvement of the overall decision-making with the introduction of AI, in both aspects, there is a pronounced evidence of cognitive alignment issues. High rates of beneficial effects (e.g. 89% approval of onboarding improvements as good) are still accompanied by worries over transparency and ethical equitability, indicating that there are differences in human understanding and algorithmic reasoning. With a technical efficacy in financial forecasting, better measures of accuracy (17% higher accuracy and 22% lower errors) are related to improvement in accuracy; however, they do not translate at all into executive trust without interpretable and context-consistent output. Both instances give prominence to the interpretability, ethical fit and behavioral congruence as key areas of alignment which determine adoption success (Kerstan et al., 2024). The response to algorithmic advice, inability to interpret model results and conflict between statistical knowledge and human judgment will exist in all contexts. These cross-case trends show that it is necessary to improve the performance of AI not only by sophisticated models but also by conscious cognitive alignment processes that transeunt human thinking to machine intelligence in the decision ecosystems in organizations. Figure 6 compares key AI adoption, performance, and alignment outcomes across HR analytics and financial forecasting cases.

Figure 6. Cross-Case AI Impact

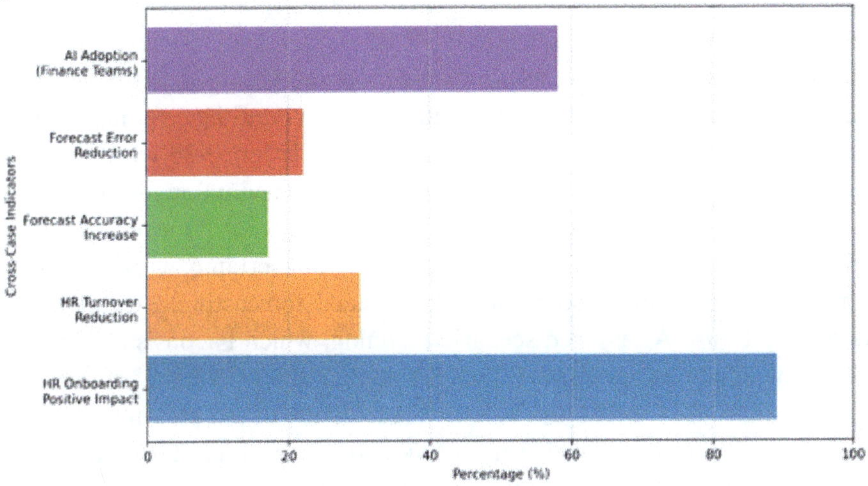

8. RESULTS AND DISCUSSION

The results show that cognitive alignment has a significant impact on the success of an organization's decision-making process through AI. Those organizations that have adopted the alignment-oriented mechanisms experienced higher adoption of AI recommendations, increased trust in decision-making processes and more balanced collaboration between humans and AI. For HR analytics, explainability and bias-awareness mechanisms helped to better inform employee retention initiatives and enhance the trust of management in the insights provided by AI. For financial forecasting, visualization and interpretation of uncertainty were used, and increased the engagement of the executives in AI supported forecasting (Putnoki & Orosz, 2025). The findings also suggest that employees' trust and psychological safety are enhanced when they are able to challenge and/or override algorithmic recommendations without losing decision authority. AI systems were not intended to supplant human decision making, but rather as partners and collaborators in decision making. But the effectiveness of the alignment depended on the organizational culture, leadership support and contextual decision complexity. The study highlights the need to adopt a holistic approach to AI governance, incorporating interpretability, ethical considerations, and human oversight, to ensure responsible and effective usage of AI within organizations.

8.1 Behavioral Outcomes

Use of CAPs was linked to quantifiable behavioral responsiveness in both case scenarios. According to HR analytics, organizations that incorporated explainability and bias-awareness tools experienced better decision confidence among HR professionals, which led to reduction of employee turnover by 20-30% with respect to more accepted retention interventions. The level of behavioral resistance dropped because decision-makers were clarified about the process of AI recommendations creation and restrictions. On the same note, when uncertainty visualization and justification scripts were incorporated in financial forecasting, executives were more willing to use AI-assisted scenario planning, which is consistent with 17% higher prediction accuracy seen (E Ihongbe et al., 2024). CAPs in both situations minimized the cognitive load through the organization of the presentation and interpretation of information. The results of these behaviors highlight that alignment improves reflective interaction and not passive obedience. The results indicate that behavioral acceptance cannot be viewed as the consequent of accuracy but cognitive alignment mechanisms mediate it in a strong manner. Table 6 Summarizes observed behavioral, trust-related and performance outcomes after adoption of CAP in cases.

Table 6. CAP Outcomes

Outcome Category	Observed Effect	Organizational Impact
Trust in AI	Increased confidence	Higher adoption rates
Psychological Safety	Reduced fear of AI decisions	Open decision dialogue
Decision Quality	Improved acceptance	Better strategic outcomes
Human Agency	Maintained oversight	Reduced automation bias

8.2 Trust, Safety, and Agency

The case studies demonstrate that there is a close correlation between cognitive alignment and organizational trust in the AI systems. Trust in HR analytics in cases where employees believed that decisions made by AI were fair, interpretable, and contestable helped to support psychological safety when making sensitive talent decisions. Companies that showed more than 85% managerial confidence in AI-assisted onboarding and performance tools also indicated more transparent accountability frameworks and the lessening of the fear of arbitrary algorithms. Financial forecasting is a field in which AI outputs were subject to reconciliation to an experience of the executives. CAPs with human override and feedback allowed executive agency to avoid over-automation bias (Rehman, 2023). The psychological safety was enhanced as the involved decision-makers were empowered to challenge AI outputs without any reprisals. Cognitive alignment is a safeguard of human agency since it ensures that AI systems are used as an aid to rather than a substitute of judgment. As has been explained in the two cases, CAPs are stabilizing mechanisms that help maintain confidence, responsibility and meaningful human involvement in AI-supported decision environments.

8.3 Ethical and Strategic Implications

The results highlight have considerable ethical, cultural, and strategic implications of harmonized AI decision systems. CAPs addressed ethical risks of amplification of bias and opaque decision-making especially in HR situations where perceptions of fairness have a direct relationship on legitimacy. Organizations with integrated mechanisms concerning alignment in terms of culture promoted transparency and accountability norms, circumventing the resistance to AI adoption. The strategic implications were also reflected in the financial functions, with cognitively aligned AI tools being able to do a rapid evaluation of the scenario without losing the oversight of the executive, more responsive and not affecting judgment than judgment. In both scenarios, alignment minimized the possibility of immoral automation drift, in which the moral aspect is outweighed by the efficiency benefit (Şencan, 2025). CAPs facilitated value-aligned decision-making processes by making organizational priorities part of AI processes. Such findings indicate that cognitive alignment is not only a facilitator of behavior, but also a strategic resource which defines the long-term AI governance and organizational identity. Organized systems will ensure that organizations can balance optimizing performance and becoming ethically responsible, strengthening the idea of sustainable and socially acceptable adoption of the AI.

9. FUTURE RESEARCH DIRECTIONS

The results given in this chapter outline a number of directions in which future studies can be conducted on cognitive congruence in AI-driven organizations. Although CAPs have conceptual and design-based grounding, they have not been empirically validated in a wide array of organizational contexts. Future research needs to go beyond accounts describing the use of AI to be more systematic by examining how the mechanisms of alignment affect the quality of decisions, trust, and ethical behavior in the long-run (Pasricha, 2023). The development of AI technologies, especially multimodal and generative, present additional problems with alignment that demand a prolonged theoretical and methodological study. Also, the presence of cultural and sectoral differences can substantially influence the interaction of humans with AI systems and their perception, which implies the necessity to engage in comparative studies. Closing these gaps shall underpin the development of cognitive alignment as a quantifiable and practical construct and enhance its application to academic research and organizational context.

9.1 Measuring Alignment Empirically

The proposals of future studies should focus on the empirical measures of cognitive and behavioural congruence in the AI-assisted decision settings. The existing literature tends to use proxy measures, such as trust or system use, which are not the best measures to describe alignment dynamics. Validated measurement tools to measure interpretative clarity and ethical fit and behavioral resonance are necessary between human beings and AI systems. It is possible that mixed-method research that integrates surveys, behavioral experiments and decision-trace analysis can reveal more information on alignment mechanisms (Volosova & Matiukhina, 2020). Further longitudinal studies would allow looking at how alignment changes over time with further exposure to AI and organizational learning. The ability to separate alignment effects and overall technology acceptance factors as well as to create causal relationships between CAPs and organizational performance cannot occur without empirical validation.

9.2 CAPs in Generative AI

The multimodal and generative AI systems rapidly diffusing offer new challenges to the cognitive alignment research. These systems combine text, images, audio, and video, and they sometimes generate the results that are similar to the human reasoning and creativity. Although these capabilities can be used to make interactions more interactive, they also present the risks of misinterpretation, over-trust, and ethical ambiguity. Future studies are needed to understand how CAPs can be modified to control generative products, uncertainty modeling, and creative decision support (Dang et al., 2025). Specific focus is required to learn about how human beings process probabilistic and synthetic information in different modalities. The expansion of CAPs to these systems will need the interdisciplinary study that incorporates cognitive science, AI ethics, and human-computer interaction to assure compatibility in the more multifaceted decision environment in the future.

9.3 Cross-Cultural Research

The level of cognitive alignment might be different when it is applied to different cultural and sectoral settings because of the difference in values, norms, and regulatory settings (Rathinavel et al., 2025). Future researchers need to explore the impact of cultural dimensions, including power distance, uncertainty avoidance, and collectivism on AI trust and acceptance. The research should also be sector-specific in the areas like healthcare, public administration, and education where ethical concerns and accountability standards vary greatly (Mehrotra & Khanna, 2022). Cross-regional and cross-industry comparisons would develop the knowledge of contextual moderators of alignment efficacy. This type of research would help tailor CAPs to local institutional and cultural circumstances and become the basis of the globally responsible use of AI.

10. STRATEGIC AND PRACTICAL IMPLICATIONS

Managers are also crucial to ensuring that AI systems are used in a manner that is aligned with organizational objectives and values, as well as human decision-making processes. CAPs must be embedded within the structures of organizations for their AI governance, employee training, workflow design and decision review processes. In practice, the tools of explainability, systems of bias monitoring, channels of feedback, and human override protocols can continue to ensure accountability and minimise resistance to the use of AI. It is also crucial that leaders openly discuss the capabilities and limitations of AI systems so as to foster balance and responsible use of AI (Gulia & Rastogi, 2024). Inter-team working among technical teams, domain experts and governance bodies can also enhance the alignment of algorithmic outputs with the organizational outcomes. To ensure that future alignment gaps are identified, there needs to be a continuous monitoring system and periodic audits in place. The ability to align practices in an institutionalized way enhances the quality of decision making, maintains human agency and fosters trust in operational environments using AI.

10.1 Value-Aligned AI Design

Managers are very important in making sure that AI systems reflect and reinforce organizational values as opposed to maximizing technical performance. This demands the conversion of ethical concepts, expectations of fairness, and strategic priorities into hard system requirements in the design and implementation process. To integrate value-based constraints, explainability capabilities, and bias monitoring systems into AI systems, managers are recommended to enable the technical teams, domain experts, and governance bodies to collaborate with one another (Distefano et al., 2023). When the organizational norms and decision rationales can be found in the algorithmic outputs, an employee will tend to view AI as legitimate and helpful. Value-aligned design is also useful in promoting consistency in decision-making in different units, which leads to ambiguity and ethical drift. By taking the initiative to influence the way values are ingrained in AI systems, managers will be able to reduce the risk of misalignment and enhance trust, accountability, and ethical integrity within AI-based organizational procedures.

10.2 Trust and Ethical Oversight

The key to ensuring proper degrees of trust in AI systems is leadership. To avoid over-reliance as well as unjustified skepticism, managers need to communicate effectively regarding the abilities, restrictions and the intended application of AI. Open communication and visible ethical control frameworks are an indication that AI is an aide to decision-making as opposed to something that has to be obeyed blindly. The leaders must implement formal accountability mechanisms in place such as review mechanisms and channels of escalation of the challenging AI recommendations (Hsiao, 2024). Through example, leadership supports the significance of human judgment and moral responsibility. These practices create a sense of psychological safety, as workers will feel free to challenge the results of algorithms without the risk of being punished. Trust calibration will make the human-AI partnerships effective and help in inspiring ethical decision cultures in organizations.

10.3 Sustainable CAP Adoption

The adoption of AI should be institutionalized by managers through the establishment of CAPs as the organizational governance and operational practices. The training programs, decision guidelines and performance evaluation frameworks should contain CAPs in order to maintain uniformity in the application across the roles and the departments. To detect the arising gaps in the alignment, the systems of continuous monitoring and feedback are necessary as the AI systems develop. Periodic audits of the AI decision processes by managers should be also used to evaluate transparency, fairness and impact of the behavior. Managers can guarantee that the AI systems are in line with human thought process and organizational beliefs by incorporating the use of CAPs into the daily activities of the organizations (Zhang, 2024). Table 7 Identifies major managerial activities, accountable functions and anticipated returns to a sustainable adoption of AI.

Table 7. CAP Implementation Actions

Managerial Action	Responsible Role	Expected Benefit
Value-aligned AI design	Senior management	Ethical consistency
Trust calibration communication	Leaders & HR	Balanced AI reliance
CAP-based training programs	L&D teams	Skilled AI usage
Continuous alignment audits	Governance bodies	Sustainable AI adoption

10.4 Limitations of CAPs

While CAPs provide a valuable structure for enhancing human–AI interaction, several limitations should be acknowledged. First of all, the adoption of CAPs can have a negative effect on the complexity, cost and the training needs of an organisation, particularly for smaller organisations with less governance structure. Secondly, alignment processes can be time consuming as more explanations, review and human oversight processes are needed to make decisions. Thirdly, there could be a human bias in human judgement itself, and making AI more aligned with human judgement does not necessarily make it fair or objective (Pasigai et al., 2025). Over-alignment can also happen and can cause a dependence on AI-generated reasoning or reiterate organizational bias. In addition, there may be cross cultural, cross sector, and cross decision demands for alignment which can make aligning CAP designs challenging.

It is also difficult to measure the degree of cognitive alignment empirically. Others insist that efficiency, predictive power of the AI should be given more weight and predictability, and that in some areas where there is less possibility of explainability, black-box AI could be better.

11. CONCLUSION

This chapter draws conclusions that CAPs offer a valuable tool to enhance responsible AI–human collaboration during organizational decision-making processes. An algorithmic solution is only effective if it is accurate in its predictions, can be automated quickly enough and can be computationally efficient; but it can also be effective to the extent that it is a solution which reflects human cognition, organizational values, ethical expectations, and decision practices. CAPs mitigate cognitive misalignment by incorporating the principles of transparency, ethical fit, trust calibration, behavioral congruence, and human oversight, all of which contribute to more responsible use of AI in decision-making. The case discussions on HR analytics and financial forecasting show that this can bring benefits in terms of increased trust, decision acceptance, psychological safety, human agency, decreased resistance, decreased automation bias, and decreased ethical uncertainty. The chapter also recognizes that while CAPs are not panaceas, they can be challenging to implement (due to cost, complexity, cultural variation, and measurement issues). Hence, further studies should confirm the CAPs by empirical studies, surveys, experiments, longitudinal studies and sector specific applications. Overall, the chapter places cognitive alignment as being an important organizational competence for the future of AI-driven work. By creating and using AI systems that assist instead of supplanting human judgment, organizations can improve efficiency and responsibility, automation and accountability, and innovation and ethical governance.

12.REFERENCES

Alam, M. S., Khan, T.-U.-Z., Dhar, S. S., & Munira, K. S. (2020). HR professionals' intention to adopt and use of artificial intelligence in recruiting talents. *Business Perspectives and Research, 2*(2), 15–30. DOI: 10.38157/business-perspective-review.v2i2.122

Asan, O., & Choudhury, A. (2021). Research trends in artificial intelligence applications in Human Factors health care: Mapping review. *JMIR Human Factors, 8*(2), e28236. DOI: 10.2196/28236 PMID: 34142968

Bharathi, B., & Krishna, R. R. (2025). The role of artificial Intelligence in designing future Human Resource Management strategies. *International Journal of Research and Development in Engineering Science, 7*(3). Advance online publication. DOI: 10.63328/IJRDES-V7RI3P10

Canbul Yaroğlu, A. (2025). Organizational reflections of the relationship between artificial ıntelligence and emotional ıntelligence in the context of phenomenology and Cartesian dualism. *The International Journal of Organizational Analysis, 33*(10), 3878–3895. DOI: 10.1108/IJOA-10-2024-4892

Chamsi-Pasha, M. A. R., & Chamsi-Pasha, H. (2025). Ethical challenges and current opportunities of artificial intelligence in cardiology. *Avicenna Journal of Medicine, 15*(3), 95–99. DOI: 10.1055/s-0045-1809879 PMID: 41098154

Chiriatti, M., Bergamaschi Ganapini, M., Panai, E., Wiederhold, B. K., & Riva, G. (2025). System 0: Transforming artificial intelligence into a cognitive extension. *Cyberpsychology, Behavior, and Social Networking, 28*(7), 534–542. DOI: 10.1089/cyber.2025.0201 PMID: 40504761

Dang, B., Huynh, L., Gul, F., Rosé, C., Järvelä, S., & Nguyen, A. (2025). Human– AI collaborative learning in mixed reality: Examining the cognitive and socio-emotional interactions. *British Journal of Educational Technology, 56*(5), 2078–2101. DOI: 10.1111/bjet.13607

Distefano, J. P., Chowdhury, S., & Esfahani, E. (2023). Exploring human-swarm interaction dynamics in cyber-physical systems: A physiological approach. *Journal of Integrated Design & Process Science, 27*(3–4), 200–210. DOI: 10.1177/10920617241292155

Gin, B. C., O'Sullivan, P. S., Hauer, K. E., Abdulnour, R.-E., Mackenzie, M., Ten Cate, O., & Boscardin, C. K. (2025). Entrustment and EPAs for artificial intelligence (AI): A framework to safeguard the use of AI in health professions education. *Academic Medicine*, *100*(3), 264–272. DOI: 10.1097/ACM.0000000000005930 PMID: 39761533

Gulia, R., & Rastogi, V. (2024). The impact of information technology on data-driven decision making in human resource management. *International Journal For Multidisciplinary Research*, *6*(6), 30314. Advance online publication. DOI: 10.36948/ijfmr.2024.v06i06.30314

Gupta, S. (2025). Ethical considerations in cloud AI: Addressing bias and fairness in algorithmic systems. *International Journal of Advanced Research in Science. Tongxin Jishu*, •••, 310–316. DOI: 10.48175/IJARSCT-25053

Hsiao, J. H.-W. (2024). Understanding human cognition through computational modeling. *Topics in Cognitive Science*, *16*(3), 349–376. DOI: 10.1111/tops.12737 PMID: 38781432

Ihongbe, E, I., Fouad, S., F Mahmoud, T., Rajasekaran, A., & Bhatia, B. (. (2024). Evaluating Explainable Artificial Intelligence (XAI) techniques in chest radiology imaging through a human-centered Lens. *PLoS One*, *19*(10), e0308758. DOI: 10.1371/journal.pone.0308758 PMID: 39383147

Ingrams, A., Kaufmann, W., & Jacobs, D. (2022). In AI we trust? Citizen perceptions of AI in government decision making. *Policy and Internet*, *14*(2), 390–409. DOI: 10.1002/poi3.276

Kerstan, S., Bienefeld, N., & Grote, G. (2024). Choosing human over AI doctors? How comparative trust associations and knowledge relate to risk and benefit perceptions of AI in healthcare. *Risk Analysis*, *44*(4), 939–957. DOI: 10.1111/risa.14216 PMID: 37722964

Kumar, A., & Nair, S. R. (2025). Predictive analytics for learning outcomes: AI-powered student performance monitoring and early intervention strategies. In *Artificial Intelligence-Powered Learning Analytics and Student Feedback Mechanisms for Dynamic Curriculum Enhancement and Continuous Quality Improvement in Outcome-Based Education* (pp. 124–150). RADemics Research Institute. DOI: 10.71443/9789349552531-05

Lukyanenko, R., Maass, W., & Storey, V. C. (2022). Trust in artificial intelligence: From a Foundational Trust Framework to emerging research opportunities. *Electronic Markets*, *32*(4), 1993–2020. DOI: 10.1007/s12525-022-00605-4

Lysaght, T., Lim, H. Y., Xafis, V., & Ngiam, K. Y. (2019). AI-assisted decision-making in healthcare: The application of an Ethics Framework for Big Data in Health and Research. *Asian Bioethics Review, 11*(3), 299–314. DOI: 10.1007/s41649-019-00096-0 PMID: 33717318

Ma, Y., Li, X., Hu, S., Liu, S., & Cheong, K. H. (2025). Trustworthy AI in education: Framework, cases, and governance strategies. *Innovation and Emerging Technologies, 12*(2550026), 2550026. Advance online publication. DOI: 10.1142/S2737599425500264

Madanchian, M., & Taherdoost, H. (2025). Ethical theories, governance models, and strategic frameworks for responsible AI adoption and organizational success. *Frontiers in Artificial Intelligence, 8*, 1619029. DOI: 10.3389/frai.2025.1619029 PMID: 40741285

Margondai, A., Willox, S., & Mouloua, M. (2025). Autonomy in transition: AI, self-identity, and the evolution of human agency. *Proceedings of the Human Factors and Ergonomics Society Annual Meeting. Human Factors and Ergonomics Society. Annual Meeting, 69*(1), 1403–1408. DOI: 10.1177/10711813251364790

Mehrotra, S., & Khanna, A. (2022). Recruitment through AI in selected Indian companies. *Metamorphosis, 21*(1), 31–39. DOI: 10.1177/09726225211066220

Nahar, J., Jahan, N., Shorna, S. A., & Joy, Z. H. (2024). Artificial intelligence in human resource management: Trends, opportunities, and challenges. Academic Journal on Science, Technology, Engineering &. *The Mathematics Educator, 4*(3), 63–74. DOI: 10.69593/ajsteme.v4i03.89

Naiseh, M., Al-Thani, D., Jiang, N., & Ali, R. (2021). Explainable recommendation: When design meets trust calibration. *World Wide Web (Bussum), 24*(5), 1857–1884. DOI: 10.1007/s11280-021-00916-0 PMID: 34366701

Oladosu, S. A., Ike, C. C., Adepoju, P. A., Afolabi, A. I., Ige, A. B., & Amoo, O. O. (2023). Frameworks for ethical data governance in machine learning: Privacy, fairness, and business optimization. *Magna Scientia Advanced Research and Reviews, 7*(2), 096–106. DOI: 10.30574/msarr.2023.7.2.0043

Oyebode, O. (2025). Chain-of-trust AI: Zero-knowledge verified federated reinforcement and generative learning for interpretable, bias-free decision-making in decentralized complex systems. *International Journal of Science and Research Archive, 15*(2), 1876–1896. DOI: 10.30574/ijsra.2025.15.2.1613

Oyekunle, D., Matthew, U. O., Preston, D., & Boohene, D. (2024). Trust beyond technology algorithms: A theoretical exploration of consumer trust and behavior in technological consumption and AI projects. *Journal of Computer and Communications, 12*(06), 72–102. DOI: 10.4236/jcc.2024.126006

Ozturkcan, S., & Bozdağ, A. A. (2025). Responsible AI in marketing: AI Booing and AI Washing cycle of AI mistrust. *International Journal of Market Research, 67*(6), 696–722. DOI: 10.1177/14707853251379285

Pasigai, M. A., Rachman, M., & Rasulong, I. (2025). Human capital management in the digital and ESG era: A systematic review of trends, gaps and strategic implications. *Cognizance Journal of Multidisciplinary Studies, 5*(6), 379–397. DOI: 10.47760/cognizance.2025.v05i06.031

Pasricha, S. (2023). AI Ethics in Smart Healthcare. *IEEE Consumer Electronics Magazine, 12*(4), 12–20. DOI: 10.1109/MCE.2022.3220001

Pasupuleti, M. K. (2025). Governance Frameworks for ethical AI deployment in Public Sector services. [IJAIRI]. *International Journal of Academic and Industrial Research Innovations, 05*(05), 561–573. DOI: 10.62311/nesx/rphcr17

Putnoki, A. M., & Orosz, T. (2025). Evaluation and adaptive complexity of cognitive Information Systems. *Acta Technica Jaurinensis, 18*(4), 225–231. DOI: 10.14513/actatechjaur.00806

Raisch, S., & Krakowski, S. (2021). Artificial intelligence and management: The automation–augmentation paradox. *Academy of Management Review, 46*(1), 192–210. DOI: 10.5465/amr.2018.0072

Rathinavel, P., Ravikumar, R. N., Aarthi, S., Habib, M., Salaeva, N., & Pardaev, J. (2025). Augmenting human capabilities. In *Advances in Computational Intelligence and Robotics* (pp. 1–30). IGI Global Scientific Publishing. DOI: 10.4018/979-8-3373-2372-5.ch001

Ravikumar, R. N., & Aarthi, S. (2025). Human-AI synergy for organizational resilience. In *Advances in Computational Intelligence and Robotics* (pp. 287–322). IGI Global Scientific Publishing. DOI: 10.4018/979-8-3373-7416-1.ch011

Ravikumar, R. N., Aarthi, S., & Mamadiyarov, Z. (2026). Building the foundations of augmented organizations through AI empowerment. In *Advances in Computational Intelligence and Robotics* (pp. 101–130). IGI Global Scientific Publishing. DOI: 10.4018/979-8-3373-8607-2.ch006

Rehman, A. (2023). Unveiling people analytics and organizations: A critical literature review. *Journal of Policy Research, 9*(4), 284–294. DOI: 10.61506/02.00151

Richardson, J. P., Smith, C., Curtis, S., Watson, S., Zhu, X., Barry, B., & Sharp, R. R. (2021). Patient apprehensions about the use of artificial intelligence in healthcare. *NPJ Digital Medicine, 4*(1), 140. DOI: 10.1038/s41746-021-00509-1 PMID: 34548621

Rostamzadeh, R., Alizadeh, F. K., Keivani, S., & Isavi, H. (2025). The role of artificial intelligence in improving organizational behavior: A systematic study. *Human Behavior and Emerging Technologies, 2025*(1). DOI: 10.1155/hbe2/8094428

Sanjay, K., & Khalsa, S. K. (2025). Talent analytics for workforce forecasting, fostering employee engagement, and turnover prediction. In *Harnessing Business Intelligence for Modern Talent Management* (pp. 403–436). IGI Global., DOI: 10.4018/979-8-3373-1942-1.ch017

Selvi, S. S., Anandapriya, B., & Vaidegi, T. (2025). From data to decisions: The role of AI in modern human resource planning. *International Journal of Research in Entrepreneurship & Business Studies, 6*(1), 19–30. DOI: 10.47259/ijrebs.2025.612

Şencan, E. (2025). Artificial intelligence, organizational learning, and sustainable banking: Insights from Turkey for global business practice. *Thunderbird International Business Review*, (tie.70062). DOI: 10.1002/tie.70062

Singh, R., Zhou, K., & Auclair, J. R. (2025). Reimagining drug regulation in the age of AI: A framework for the. *Frontiers in Medicine, 12*(1679611), 1679611. DOI: 10.3389/fmed.2025.1679611 PMID: 41179905

Sun, Y., & Xu, C. (2025). Hybrid cognitive authority and algorithmic subjectivity: Rethinking knowledge management in AI-driven communication. *Journal of Knowledge Management*, •••, 1–26. DOI: 10.1108/JKM-02-2025-0252

Tanantong, T., & Wongras, P. (2024). A UTAUT-based framework for analyzing users' intention to adopt artificial Intelligence in human resource recruitment: A case study of Thailand. *Systems, 12*(1), 28. DOI: 10.3390/systems12010028

Thalpage, N. (2025). Explainable AI for cybersecurity applications: A review article on techniques, deployments, and usability challenges. *Journal of Digital Science, 7*(1), 3–10. DOI: 10.33847/2686-8296.7.1_1

Van Den Berg, M., Kuiper, O., Van Der Haas, Y., Gerlings, J., Sent, D., & Leijnen, S. (2023). A conceptual model for implementing explainable AI by design: Results of an empirical study. In *Frontiers in Artificial Intelligence and Applications*. IOS Press., DOI: 10.3233/FAIA230075

Vats, K., & Alam, M. M. (2025). From design to closure: Artificial intelligence transforming clinical research. *Cureus, 17*(10), e94895. DOI: 10.7759/cureus.94895 PMID: 41262821

Volosova, A., & Matiukhina, E. (2020). Using artificial intelligence for effective decision-making in corporate governance under conditions of deep uncertainty. *SHS Web of Conferences, 89*, 03008. DOI: 10.1051/shsconf/20208903008

Yadav, N., Pandey, S., Gupta, A., Dudani, P., Gupta, S., & Rangarajan, K. (2023). Data Privacy in healthcare: In the era of artificial intelligence. *Indian Dermatology Online Journal, 14*(6), 788–792. DOI: 10.4103/idoj.idoj_543_23 PMID: 38099022

Ye, C., Wang, Z., Wu, M., Kang, R., Yuan, F., & Chen, C. (2025). Behavioral drivers of AI nursing acceptance in the Greater Bay Area: A family-caregiver perspective on trust and risk. *Frontiers in Public Health, 13*(1650804), 1650804. DOI: 10.3389/fpubh.2025.1650804 PMID: 41112660

Zhang, D. (2024). Leveraging artificial intelligence in economics and finance: Enhancing decision-making and market efficiency. *Applied and Computational Engineering, 82*(1), 118–123. DOI: 10.54254/2755-2721/82/20240980

13. KEY TERMS AND DEFINITIONS

Algorithmic Decision-Making: The use of AI or automated systems to generate recommendations or decisions based on data-driven models.

Artificial Intelligence (AI): Computer-based systems that perform tasks such as prediction, classification, or decision support by learning from data.

Cognitive Alignment Protocols (CAPs): Structured design and governance mechanisms that align human judgment, organizational values, and AI decision logic.

Cognitive Alignment: The degree to which AI system logic, outputs, and behavior are understandable, acceptable, and compatible with human cognitive processes and values.

Explainable AI (XAI): AI techniques that provide understandable explanations of how and why specific outputs or recommendations are produced.

Human Agency: The ability of human decision-makers to retain control, judgment, and accountability when interacting with AI systems.

Human–AI Collaboration: A working arrangement in which humans and AI systems jointly contribute to decision-making and task execution.

Trust Calibration: The process of achieving appropriate levels of human trust in AI systems, avoiding both over-reliance and excessive skepticism.

Chapter 6
From Automation to Augmentation: The Transformative Role of Artificial Intelligence in Human Capital Management

Ankita Pathak
http://orcid.org/0000-0002-8068-8874
Institute of Business Management, GLA University, India

Majdi Anwar Quttainah
http://orcid.org/0000-0002-6280-1060
Kuwait University, Kuwait

ABSTRACT

The incorporation of AI (Artificial Intelligence) within Human Capital Management (HCM) is changing and is reshaping how businesses recruit, build, involve and keep talent. This chapter discusses the evolving role of AI in core HCM functions such as recruitment, performance management, training and education, workforce analytics and employee experience design. In addition to the technological discussion, it looks at how the use of AI-based systems will impact managers' decision-making, how employees perceive their organisation; and how organisations are capable of supporting employees' careers.The authors use previous research from the fields of management, human resource development and information systems to portray AI as an enabler of human expertise within HCM. Finally, the authors provide a balanced and human-centred perspective on HCM with respect to the use of AI, by providing practical information for managers and policymakers, as well as highlighting future research directions regarding the responsible and sustainable use of AI within the management of human capital.

DOI: 10.4018/979-8-2600-2541-3.ch006

1. INTRODUCTION

1.1 Digital Transformation of Human Capital Management

HCM (Human Capital Management) has gone through a digital transformation, which has made people-related activities, such as recruiting, developing and managing employees, more strategic. It has moved away from simply keeping track of people to using technology to get real-time information about employee performance, skill sets, engagement levels and future potential. Organizations today compete with each other by relying on knowledge and innovation, so the human capital of an organization provides it with sustainable competitive advantages. Digital transformation of HCM has allowed organizations to leverage HCM as a significant contributor to business strategy rather than simply a function that supports business strategy. One of the major contributors to the modernization of HCM systems has been artificial intelligence (AI). Today, AI is embedded into nearly every core process associated with HCM like recruitment, learning & development, performance management, workforce planning, employee engagement which allow organizations to analyze vast amounts of employee data and identify patterns that would otherwise be hard or impossible to identify through traditional methods (Fenech et al., 2019). Besides making operational tasks more efficient, digitalizing HCM enables better alignment between HCM systems and business strategy by improving the timeliness and data-driven nature of decision-making. Digitalizing HCM has improved efficiency and transformed how employers provide experiences to employees, how they create and manage talent pipelines, and how they respond to the changing demands of their workforce (Vardarlier, 2019). The evolving nature of HCM is now characterized by the use of personalization, adaptability and an ongoing commitment to learning and thereby the evolving nature of HCM is part of an overall trend within the workforce.

This chapter explores how Artificial Intelligence (AI) is moving from traditional, rule-based automation systems to adaptive, data-driven intelligence that can help with strategic workforce planning and providing each employee with unique experiences throughout their time at work. The chapter includes some of the obstacles to adopting AI in human capital management (HCM), including algorithmic bias; transparency; the protection of personal data; ethical governance; and the reassessment of human judgment as it relates to people-centric processes, as well as integrating the views of a variety of scholars who characterize AI as being a supportive mechanism that enhances humans' abilities rather than replacing them entirely. In addition, this chapter promotes a holistic, human-centric view of how AI can enhance HCM through action steps and recommendations for future research into the prudent and sustainable integration of AI in relation to effectively managing human capital.

1.2 Rationale for AI Adoption in People Management

AI in HRM is gaining traction as organizations become increasingly complex and their workforces and other stakeholders have higher expectations. Organizations are dealing with a quickly evolving environment featuring many things like the fast-paced development of technology, globalization of the labor force, an acute skill shortage and different kinds of work. These factors create significant pressure on human resource functions to make decisions faster, more accurately, and in a consistent manner (Alzeiby et al., 2025). One way to address this challenge is to use AI in HCM systems to provide an increase in analytical capacity and to reduce reliance on intuition-based or fragmented decision-making.

Talent acquisition, via screening large applicant pools and evaluating skill-job fit, enables companies to more efficiently hire employees. The continuing use of AI is beneficial during performance and learning management by enabling companies to give continuous feedback, provide personalized development maps, and predict future skill needs (Cubric, 2020). AI-enabled workforce analytics will enable companies to anticipate employee turnover risk, optimize workforce composition, and better align human capital investments with long-term strategic objectives. AI provides employees with more responsive and individualized experiences through personalized learning plans, career recommendations, and support services.

In addition, there are several other reasons for the implementation of artificial intelligence in businesses other than efficiency. Many businesses have started to focus more and more on efficiency, but they also want to create high performing businesses with fairness and transparency. AI, when developed responsibly, enable businesses to reduce biasness in decision making and increase the consistency of HR Policies (Agarwal, 2023). However, there are also many issues that are raised with the use of AI in people management. Issues such as privacy of data, algorithmic bias, explainability of the AI process and how it could potentially degrade the use of human judgement in sensitive decisions. These conflicting issues support that AI cannot only be thought of as being just a technological tool; it is also viewed as being a socio-technologies system that reinforces how power, trust and accountability are defined and develop within a business.

1.3 Scope and Objectives of the Chapter

This chapter looks at how the use of artificial intelligence has impacted Human Capital Management and the way AI has changed how we manage people, make decisions, and experience working in organisations. The Chapter covers a wide variety of concepts and integrates ideas from human resource management, human resource development, information systems, and organisation studies to derive an integrative and conceptual look at the impact of AI on HCM. The chapter has provide both technology focused perspective, and explores how managers, employees and AI systems interact in an interdisciplinary, human-centred way.

The primary aims of this chapter are to 1) describe how AI technologies are being used for principal HCM functions, 2) explore how AI technologies will change the way managers make decisions and their employees view their job, including both the potential to create strategic value and concerns regarding over-reliance on AI and 3) address ethical, legal and governance issues with AI technologies used in HCM.

This chapter is designed to deepen the understanding of AI-enhanced HCM through analyzing the existing literature on both the current body of research relating to AI. The organizations can use to develop their evolving capabilities in terms of management. There are opportunities for future technology- and HRM-related research, as well as practical implications for practitioners and policymakers who want to use AI in order to improve overall performance in organizations and to ensure that dignity and agency are upheld for humans. Finally, this chapter discusses the long-term future of HCM, where companies will go from using AI as a substitute for human judgment to develop accountable and conscious forms of cooperation between humans and AI in managing human capital.

2 EVOLUTION OF ARTIFICIAL INTELLIGENCE IN HUMAN CAPITAL MANAGEMENT

2.1 The conversion of Administrative Automation to Intelligent HCM Systems

The advancement in the use of artificial intelligence in Human Capital Management (HCM) has developed through different stages. These stages are indicative of the larger shifts in the priority of organizations and the capabilities of technology. In the early stage of HR technology, digital systems were meant to improve the way that the HR function was actually performed through improved efficiency resulting from the automation of routine administrative functions like payroll processing, attendance tracking, record keeping, and compliance reporting (Routhu, 2021). The early stage of HR systems achieved operational benefits by providing an alternative means of performing the same activities without human error while also reducing the amount of time needed to perform routine functions. In this time period, however, the majority of the HR decision making was based primarily on the experience and judgment of the individual HR practitioners utilizing the HR systems.

With the accumulation of massive amounts of workforce data and advancements in digital infrastructure, HCM systems have made a fundamental shift from automation to intelligence. Current HCM systems powered by artificial intelligence are now capable of learning from both historical and real-time data, and they generate reports and insights that aid decision-making for managers (Thontadarya, 2025). The advanced technologies such as Modern Human Capital Management (HCM), will help the organisations to adaptively manage their employees based on a number of factors, trends and patterns within employee behavior, performance, and levels of engagement. It help in gaininig an understanding of how to proactively address potential employee expectations before they arise. The transition to this method will assist HCM functions in predicting skill shortages and identifying high-potential employees as well as developing individualised employee development paths (Kommera, 2017). Additionally, the transition reflects a shift from the transactional nature of HCM to that of a strategic partner within the organisation; therefore having a direct impact on the organisation's agility, innovation, and long-term sustainability through accurate employee data.

2.2 Key AI Technologies in Human Resource Management

The AI technology develops within Human Capital Management (HCM), and increasing number of different types of technologies will provide the basis for data-driven and evolving people management solutions. One of the primary pillars for this development is Machine Learning where AI can increase its ability to make accurate predictions about the people and provide useful recommendation (Vrontis et al., 2023). They manage by analyzing an ever-growing pool of information, data about their performance. The use of Machine Learning algorithms in process of recruitment and selection process allows HCM systems to analyze applicant profiles, job descriptions, and historical hiring data in order to evaluate whether an applicant is a good fit for a given position and to develop a prediction model for that person's future performance. Machine Learning algorithms also play an important role in helping organizations to manage employees' performance and retain their employees (Qamar et al., 2021). It helps by identifying the emerging trends related to productivity, attendance, and employee turnover risk

With the addition of Natural Language Processing (NLP), Artificial Intelligence (AI) has enhanced its usefulness specifically in Human Resources (HR). NLP-based solutions allow machines to read and write human language. Many companies use NLP technology for tasks such as reviewing resumes, utilizing chatbots, analyzing employee feedback, and determining employee engagement based on the responses provided to engagement surveys. Therefore, many of these applications allow companies to analyze unstructured data, including, but not limited to, written comments, emails, and performance appraisals (Kim et al., 2025). It also provide actionable insights from the qualitative data received. Predictive analytics enhances

HR functions as it largely focuses on making decisions based on uncertain outcomes or future-oriented decision making. Therefore, predictive models create a forecast of the potential outcome by combining historical data from an organization's workforce and external factors (Alsaif & Aksoy, 2023). Consequently, predictive models assist organizations in making forecasts about attrition, leadership readiness, and training effectiveness in the future. Ultimately, HCM systems enable companies to make more informed, consistent, and timely decisions regarding each employee throughout their employment with an organization

2.3 AI Adoption Trends in Contemporary Organizations

The adoption of AI in Human Capital Management (HCM) has undergone rapid change and growth in the last few years. This is due in large part to increasing worldwide competition, workplace diversity, and challenges in attracting and retaining talent in digital and hybrid work environments. Many organizations across all sectors have begun the process of incorporating AI into their HCM processes for the purpose(s) of improving the accuracy of HR-related decisions, improving the overall employee experience, and ensuring the skills and abilities of the workforce are aligned with the organization's strategic objectives (Ademola, 2024). AI (Artificial Intelligence) has become extensively adopted by larger organizations, as they have access to vast amounts of information and are able to implement AI solutions much more efficiently than smaller organizations. However, smaller organizations can now leverage AI capabilities through cloud computing, which removes traditional entry barriers to implementing AI (Romeo & Lacko, 2025). This provides an avenue for organizations of all sizes to leverage AI as a means of improving the effectiveness of their HR operations.

AI is currently being used by many companies to develop HR-focused, employee-focused applications. Organizations are now creating personalized employee development plans using AI, providing real-time feedback from managers and supervisors to employees, and assisting employees in planning their careers. In addition, there is growing attention being given to the ethical and social implications of utilizing AI in HR-type applications. Organizations are increasingly focusing on providing transparency, explainability, and human oversight in making AI-based decisions regarding HR-type functions, such as hiring, promoting, and evaluating employees (Sabah et al., 2024). Furthermore, there is significant and growing scrutiny from government authorities and other key stakeholders regarding the governance and development of AI within HCM (Human Capital Management) systems.

Artificial Intelligence advancements in the field of Human Capital Management show a much larger evolution towards an intelligent, driven by data and focused on people's management of employees. Organizations can increase their capability and have a positive impact on their employees with the help of AI. Ultimately, the true value of using AI is derived from responsibly integrating it into how businesses operate in order to demonstrate innovation through technology with fairness, accountability and consideration of the judgement of people.

3. APPLICATIONS OF ARTIFICIAL INTELLIGENCE ACROSS HUMAN CAPITAL MANAGEMENT FUNCTIONS

AI has been integrated into the human capital lifecycle to an extent that it can now influence how an organization will attract, develop, engage with and keep employees. AI applications do not exist as isolated tools within HCM functions, rather they function as interrelated systems providing support for strategic decision-making and changing employee experiences. The research recommend to evaluate the ways in which AI has influenced recruitment, performance management, learning/development, workforce planning and employee experience; using appropriate theoretical perspectives. It will provide bettter understand how AI has impacted all HCM functions. Table 1 Impact of AI across HCM Functions.

3.1 AI in Talent Acquisition and Recruitment

The use of artificial intelligence has revolutionized the ability for professionals within human resources to conduct talent acquisition (hiring) efficiently and, through improved processes, develop better hires by drastically reducing the volume of applicants received. AI applications utilize machine learning algorithms to help identify candidate qualifications for open positions, as well as to predict how well candidates would perform in certain positions, based on the data from their resumes and other data collected during the hiring process (Albert, 2019). Natural Language Processing is an example of a technology that enables AI-based hiring tools to analyze unstructured data (such as resumes, application resumes, and interview transcripts) without manual review of each individual resume.

A large, well-known, global technology company has developed an AI-based hiring system for reviewing job applications. The tool is used to automate the initial stages of reviewing applicant resumes by providing the recruiter with the top-ranked candidates from any given set of applicants, based on relevant skills, relevant certifications, as well as work experience and other job-related factors available from their application (Johnson et al., 2021). AI enabled improve the speed and quality of the recruiting process, and eliminates the possibility of implicit bias from the process that may occur during the traditional, manual review of applicants for open job positions; therefore, only the top-ranked applicants remain in consideration for hire. Ultimately, the decision to hire rests with the individual recruiter responsible for filling an open position.

The way people get hired at The multinational company Unilever hires the people using artificial intelligence and this shows a direct connection to the Technology Acceptance Model. TAM provides a theoretical framework for studying how people accept and use new technologies, based on perceptions of usefulness and ease of use. AI screening, and interviewing facilitate the recruiters because it can quicker and less burden of hiring processes, and also translates into enhanced perceptions of utility (Karuppiah & Kumaran, 2025). In addition, candidates' abilities to complete AI testing within standard and objective parameters enables candidates to interact with the process in an easier manner, which increases candidate acceptance for positions recruited through the use of AI.

Structured and transparent assessment processes provide candidates with a better experience when interacting with the company, increasing their acceptance of AI in hiring. The utilization of AI technology by Unilever promote its beliefs regarding innovation, objectivity and meritocracy to potential staff members. The AI used by Unilever establishes uniform measurements and thus functions as an objectivity tool that eliminates subjectivity in the selection of candidates sending a positive message about fairness in the hiring process (Paramita, 2020). From a strategic human resource management perspective, the application of AI to recruiting assists Unilever in recruiting more effectively by providing consistency and scalability, while ensuring sufficient human input in final candidate selection to uphold ethical obligations as well as produce efficient output.

3.2 AI in Performance Management

Standard performance management systems are largely based on yearly appraisals to assess how an employee has performed against expected results. Traditional performance measuring practices do not provide a complete picture of the employee's contribution and developmental needs as they happen. In contrast, artificial intelligence (AI) performance management systems represent a new way of performing employee evaluations by providing continual performance feedback and data-based performance assessment (Buck & Morrow, 2018). MPMS continues to rely on the same types of metrics to monitor on-going performance, such as work output, major project milestones, ratings received from peers and performance engagement indicators.AI-enabled insight assists employees in the development of their capabilities through the identification of skills that need further development and suggestions on how to develop those skills. AI also provides ongoing performance-related feedback to employees, increasing employee workplace motivation, providing clearer expectations of performance, and speeding the time with which performance can be recognized.

The consulting firm has developed a performance management platform using artificial intelligence that captures patterns of performance through project delivery and client feedback. The platform gives employees a personalized view of their development areas and know what their strengths are. Managers are utilizing dashboards to assist in the coaching conversations that take place with their employees (Varma et al., 2024). It uses an annual performance review period to capture the performance of employees on an annual basis and provide performance feedback to a direct report. In addition, IBM uses AI as a transition from using an intuitive type of performance management to a mathematically driven type of performance management, so that a manager will have synthesized insights that come from multiple sources and they will have better quality information to assist them in making decisions (Nyathani, 2023). This describes how AI can help managers in making decisions about the employees in the workforce rather than replacing them when managing employees.

3.3 AI in Learning and Development

AI has facilitated a transition from standardization of training programs to customizing individual learning ecosystems. AI Learning Platforms will evaluate each employee's ability level, preferred methods of learning, and desired career path and suggest appropriate content and development pathways based upon those factors (Bhatt & Muduli, 2023). Succession Planning will further be supported by AI using predictive analytics to identify future skills needed. Amazon's AI-based learning platforms are great examples of the Human Capital Theory, which emphasizes that an employee's abilities and skills are a critical resource for an organization (Dixit & Jatav, 2024). Amazon creates a way to invest in skills with a high correlation to the skills needed by the organization. Artificial intelligence to provide personalized recommendations for current and future-learning modules.

According to Self-Determination Theory, AI enabled learning provides greater autonomy for employees at Amazon through personalized learning paths. Employees can access relevant content at their own pace, which add perception of autonomy (Poquet & De Laat, 2021). Recommendations for content are relevant and timely, contributing to competence development. The organization's commitment to upskill the employees' psychological engagement. The combination of the two theories offer an understanding into how AI learning supports both employee performance and motivation.

3.4 AI in Workforce Planning and People Analytics

Workforce analytics have changed organizations approach from reactive workforce decisions towards predictive workforce planning with the help of AI. AI solutions will support organizations in making decisions whether related to number of staff, skill requirement and mobility required for a workforce over time (Tasleem, 2025). It combine historic trends, demographics as well as future business forecasts. A manufacturing organization is utilizing predictive analytics AI methods to forecast potential skill shortages based on their future automation initiatives (Rai & Singh, 2023). These predictive analytics will help drive the organization to develop reskilling strategies and use internal mobility programs rather than resorting to external hires at the last minute.

The use of AI for workforce planning by Google is aligned with the Resource Based View which establishes that "Rare, inimitable, and well organized resources have strategic value". With the use of AI based people analytics tools, Google is able to identify the necessary pools of talent, anticipate attrition risks, and ultimately maximize the potential of their teams. It provide a significant increase to their human capital base as a source of strategic advantage.

Dynamic Capabilities Theory offers an additional explanation for the use of AI by Google when it comes time to adapt to new or changing environments. The use of analytics powered by AI will help the organization understand trends within its talent, evaluate development opportunities to implement appropriate proactive interventions, and reformulate its existing talent structure to align with the organization's current strategic objectives (Arora et al., 2021). This reinforces the potential for AI to help organizations become more agile than they would have been otherwise; instead of being limited to being merely an analytical tool that does not change over time

3.5 AI and Employee Experience Management

Businesses have the opportunity to enhance the Employee Experience by using AI to complement their human resource capabilities. Businesses can improve the Employee Experience through the use of chatbots, virtual assistants, and by using technology such as sentiment analysis (Parasa, 2024). These types of tools can deliver quick answers to HR-related questions, and analyze employee engagement survey results. It also help in identify employees at risk due to their emotional state or mental health. Company can launches an AI-based HR chatbot to help employees with policy inquiries and leave requests. AI has the potential to identify trends in the employee experience. Managers can use this information to improve the employee experience by addressing employee concerns.Table 2 AI application in Organization.

Table 1. Impact of AI across HCM Functions: A Summary Table

HCM Function	Key AI Applications	Strategic Impact	Human-Centric Outcome
Talent Acquisition	Resume screening, skill matching, chatbots	Faster, fairer hiring decisions	Reduced bias, improved candidate experience
Performance Management	Continuous feedback, performance analytics	Data-informed performance decisions	Development-focused evaluations
Learning & Development	Personalized learning paths, skill forecasting	Targeted capability building	Increased engagement and autonomy
Workforce Planning	Predictive analytics, turnover forecasting	Strategic workforce alignment	Employment stability and adaptability
Employee Experience	Chatbots, sentiment analysis	Responsive HR services	Enhanced trust and well-being

Table 2. AI application in Organization

HCM Function	Organization	AI Application Focus
Recruitment	Unilever	AI screening, digital interviews
Performance Management	IBM	AI-driven feedback and coaching
Learning & Development	Amazon	Personalized upskilling
Workforce Planning	Google	Predictive people analytics
Employee Experience	Microsoft	HR chatbots, engagement analytics
Retention	IBM	Attrition prediction

4. THEORETICAL INTEGRATION OF AI-ENABLED MANAGERIAL DECISION-MAKING IN HUMAN CAPITAL MANAGEMENT

A theoretical framework can provide a comprehensive understanding of how AI impacts managerial decision-making in Human Capital Management (HCM). The Technology Acceptance Model (TAM), the Ability-Motivation-Opportunity (AMO) framework, and Socio-Technical Systems Theory can be applied to help explain managers' adoption, utilization, and generated value from AI-enabled HCM systems. Collectively, these theories provide a cohesive foundation that supports researchers' to explain the effectiveness of AI in managing people.

4.1 Technology Acceptance Model (TAM) and AI-Enabled HR Decisions

The Technology Acceptance Model describes how managerial use of artificial intelligence (AI) in human capital management (HCM) is dependent on two aspects: perceived usefulness of AI systems, and perceived ease-of-use of an AI system.The ability of managers to utilize AI in their routine management of people has substantially increased due to accuracy in decision making, less administrative workload, and have a better strategic alignment.The perception of ease of use is also an important factor in managers integrating AI. Dashboards provide easy to use and have an intuitive analysis with explainable outputs reduce the cognitive load of the manager which increase the likelihood of the manager (Khan et al., 2024). In AI enabled HCM, the manager does not have to become a data scientist, as the systems are designed to take complex analytics and create insights that can easily be understood by the manager. As managers become familiar with AI systems and they build confidence in using the systems. These tools help them with their decisions instead of viewing the systems as disruptive or non-transparent.

4.2 Ability–Motivation–Opportunity (AMO) Framework and Managerial Effectiveness

The AMO (Ability-Motivation-Opportunity) framework provides insight into the process of how AI is helping managers be more effective in managing people. AI creates stronger ability by providing managers with current and high quality information that enables them to accurately evaluate an employee's performance, potential, and development needs (Salvador-Gómez et al., 2023). AI empowers managers to make better and more informed decisions by reducing the asymmetry of information and allowing managers to have a greater comfort level with their decisions.

AI also can impact motivation through increased transparency and consistent HR decision-making. When data-driven insights are used for performance evaluations, development recommendations, and workforce planning. Managers feel that the decisions are more fair which reduces decision-making anxiety (Bos-Nehles et al., 2023). This allows them to be more proactive in their engagement with their people management responsibilities.AI provide opportunities by releasing managers from the burden of routine administrative tasks, and allowing them to provide more time to coaching, building relationships, and discussing workforce strategy. AI-enabled systems create additional opportunities for managers to make meaningful interventions, rather than fear of reducing the role of human role in HCM. AI tools deliver analytical intelligence, while contextual understanding, ethical judgment, and empathy come from the manager.

4.3 Socio-Technical Systems Theory and Human–AI Collaboration

The effectiveness of an organization is dependent on how well social (people, roles, culture) and technical components (tools, processes, technology) are aligned. The quality of decision-making in AI-enabled HCM results from both AI systems and the judgment of managers, not just from technology itself (Ang et al., 2025). The AI enabled HCM practices must be designed in such a way that supports human oversight, accountability, and a degree of interpretability. When managers are granted the ability to ask questions the AI recommendations, it increases trust in these types of systems(Wu Young & Nah, 2025). Conversely, if the technology does not fit with the organizational culture, this could lead to the potential for resistance, misuse or over-relying on automated outputs.

5. MANAGERIAL CAPABILITY REQUIREMENTS FOR AI-ENABLED HUMAN CAPITAL MANAGEMENT

The successful integration of AI into HCM need new capabilities for the managers. These new capabilities include technical, cognitive, ethical and relational..

5.1. Data Literacy and Analytical Interpretation

AI-generated insights are interpreted by a manager who can understands basic analytical logic and has the ability to analyze the reliability of the insights. Managers can use data literacy to differentiate between correlation and causation, and to better evaluate the significance of the information they receive when making decisions.

5.2. Ethical and Responsible Decision-Making

HR decisions are often made using sensitive data and involve making difficult decisions that can impact employees' lives in a significant way. Therefore, when making HR decisions, managers should be ethical and aware of potential bias, treat employees equitably, and keep employee information confidential. In addition, the ethical use of AI is dependent on both the output generated by an AI algorithm and the ability of managers to be vigilant and demonstrate moral behaviour.

5.3. Contextual and Systems Thinking

Managers should incorporate AI-related insights into their decision-making processes, along with other contextual information such as team dynamics, organisational culture and individuals' real-life contexts. Systems thinking also allows managers to understand the unintended outcomes of AI-augmented decisions, and how to ensure those decisions align with the broader objectives of their organisation.

5.4. Change Management and Technology Leadership

The impact of AI on work processes and expectations will continue to evolve through its use by organisations. Managers serve as key influencers to share how AI will be used within their organisations and to respond constructively to employee concerns about AI. In this leading change process, leaders will help employees see AI as an aid to complete their work, rather than a risk to their employment.

5.5. Human-Centered Leadership and Empathy

The relational basis of managing people will not change as a result of the continued increase in the use of automation. Therefore, it is important for managers to use administrative data provided by AI tools to create substantial conversations with employees, and provide coaching support for employee development opportunities. It is also important for the manager to continue the practice empathy and emotional intelligence in order to make analytical data applicable and useful for employees.

6. SUPPORTIVE AI TECHNOLOGIES

6.1 Employee Well-Being

Employee well-being is a wide notion which cover mental and physical wellness, and ergonomics in the workplace. Technology is widely used to measure one's physical condition through smart scale, a fitness tracker watch, and even smartphone applications like Google Fit. According to Lupton, (2016) the use of technological devices to measure one's own fitness is known as quantized self. Such platforms are wonderful for those who prefer to gather information about their physical well-being. The limitation of such platform is that users get overly fascinated with the data, which may lead to encourage harmful habits. Incorporating AI in systems can assist with mitigate the drawbacks.

Wearables devices with AI capabilities can recognition speech and picture and can be used to monitor behaviour and emotions with the help of Natural Language Processing (Sen, 2020). These electronic devices can generate the interest of the HCM. Individual physical health data could help companies in detecting and resolving workplace difficulties. According to Koutsimani et al., (2019) mental health of Employee' have a significant influence on their job performance in organisation as a whole. Burnout is an issue of mental health which has a negative impact on mental health. Burnout is caused by long-term stress related to work. It appears in three forms: excessive tiredness, depersonalisation, and a loss of work efficacy. Burnout leads to lower productivity, absenteeism, and plans to leave the organisation. A number of methods are available to assess the possibility of an employee burning out. Employers should Monitor the employees' working hours and productivity to measure the employee burn out. Overworking might indicate high job expectations which might result in a high degree of stress. Inadequate performance can also be an indication of stress. Chatbots is the another measure to deal with mental health difficulties. Artificial Intelligence (AI) can be utilized to acquire knowledge related to employee engagement in the organisation and its core values. According to Agarwal & Mittal, (2016), AI system can used to perform sentiment analysis to identify the general attitude of employees. Sen, (2020) stated that Several Machine Learning algorithms can be used to assess levels of stress based on voice and pace of dialogue. The best example is the customer call center where the response of the employee changes after extra time and long working hours. Companies should records of the hours when their workers are more efficiently and AI can be used to optimize break schedule for employees. AI systems can be utilised to monitor workers' different relationships with colleagues and management. If the workers are having strong relationships with colleagues it is indicator of good organizational relations (Sen,2020). AI can be utilised to track workers' speech and actions in order to detect harmful behaviour and maintain staff security (Sen, 2020). Worker mood assessments can be used to adjust their surroundings and give mood boosters, such as by establishing peaceful environments with sound and lights.

6.2 Reskilling

A sizable proportion of respondents (42%) intended to accelerate the digitalisation of upskilling/reskilling where as (35%) of the organization implemented upskilling and reskilling programmes. Upskilling is the addition of new skills to one's current skill set, whereas reskilling is the replacement of one's current skill set with a wholly new one. There are plenty of various reasons why reskilling is essential. It is realistic to predict that some work functions will be obsolete by 2025 or 2030, and will be replaced by an artificial intelligence system. Figure 1, shows the proportion of work done by machines will be increasing between now and 2025 across all sectors. The jobs that replace the old ones may be wholly new, so itis important to reskill the skills to perform the new roles. Reskill is the necessity for company in ever-changing environment. Reskilling can assist in bringing diversity in teams, which can boost idea generation. According to a World Economic Forum poll, there is a skill difference between working and jobless persons. Reskilling plan must contain insights regarding its employees' present abilities as well as gaps in those skills. Figure 4 shows the anticipated the top 15 abilities in 2025 and effective solutions. Organisations can enhance their reskilling plans by utilising educational technology (EdTech) and reskilling services. They can utilise artificial intelligence and advanced data processing to guide users, workers, and employers to new job responsibilities through suitable skill classes.

6.3 Managing Diversity and Workforce Metrics

Organisations can benefited from a diversified staff. Individuals from different communities and mindsets can offer different answers to emergent challenges. DE&I projects frequently pair with a workforce analytics system, which can assist in tracking diversification within an organisation. AI technology may be employed to assist in the improvement of the HCM analytics. Reskilling is one approach of generating diversified teams. Hiring applicants from various sectors and offering them the opportunity to upgrade their skills . It will lead to teams of people from different professions. The career changes should be promoted and encouraged since it can boost the organization's resilience.

6.4 Employee Experience:

Organisations are viewing their staff as customers, which is leading to a greater emphasis on employee experience. According to Plasko, (2017), the experience of employees is refers as how workers view their connections with the organisation based on every interaction. An better work environment leads to higher staff involvement and interest to meet corporate objectives. Plasko, (2017) have proposed Six principles to assist organisations in guiding employee experience management. Developing an in-depth understanding of people and their needs, adopting wide and broad perspectives, simplifying difficult facts, pushing on radical engagement, navigating and testing, and believing and enjoying the process are the six principles which will assist in enhancing employee experience. According to a recent survey of Forrester Research, Inc., 2021, the emphasis on employee experience has reached a tipping point. Personnel that are engaged are more effective, and are less likely to quit the organisation. It will deliver superior service to their customers. Firms are struggling to acquire an in-depth knowledge of the employee experience inside their organisation. Boosting the working environment for staff members should be part of a company's overall strategy. It shouldn't be confined to just as a duty of human resources department, various upper management and information technology departments should also assist in developing employee engagement and experience in organization. An organization's management should support efforts in improving the experience of workers. However, various issues, such as segregated divisions, inconsistent feedback methods, and insufficient resources, make it difficult in obtaining an in-depth understanding of the employee experience. HR personnel do not always completely understanding related to wants and requirements of employees inside the organization as it lack continuous feedback mechanism. The issue can be tackled by utilising AI applications where Employee happiness and engagement related opinions are gathered, and correlations can be extracted to provide recommendations for enhancing the experience of the employee. Companies like as Oracle and SAP are already working to improve employee experience in their HCM systems. Oracle Journeys was created as part of their HCM system to boost the emphasis on experience of employees (Oracle, 2021d). The staff of HR may use this AI tool to build and customise the guides for employees which explains about how specific activities operate such as the onboarding method or how to modify personal information etc. The software like SAP, Human Experience Management (HXM) Suite also includes a module for employee experience management (SAP, n.d.). This suite also includes cognitive tools such as ML, although details are not publicly available.

6.5 Acceptance of AI technology

Artificial Intelligence (AI) techniques cannot directly enhance their own acceptability; rather, their usefulness and the manner in which they are developed and executed affect their level of acceptance. The technologies can be effective used in the organization when individuals are able to trust them entirely. First and foremost, all HR personnel should have accessibility to the system's source and documentation.

Embedding the AI system into their regular job doesn’t necessitate a thorough knowledge of algorithms and programming. It suggests that the system's inputs and results must be basic enough for people of various educational experiences and technology skill levels. The AI demands particular sorts of data as it works on algorithms which require standard data to generate results. The inputs such as sensitive data are essential for the system to function.

Figure 1. "Changing Distribution of Tasks Between Humans and Machines Across Key Sectors, 2020 and 2025" (World Economic Forum, 2020)

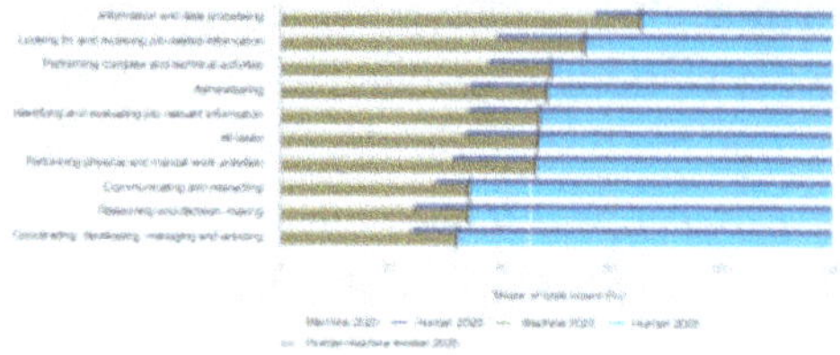

The owner of the software should always put the control over their data. If users believe certain sections of the input information are irrelevant to the AI's operation, then it should be eliminated. In such instances, a choice must be made among usefulness and confidentiality. Clients have particular demands regarding the capabilities of AI systems. People will build confidence in AI systems as time passes. Humans require time to adjust to the modifications that caused by AI and to adopt cutting-edge AI in everyday activities

Figure 2. Top 15 kills for 2025

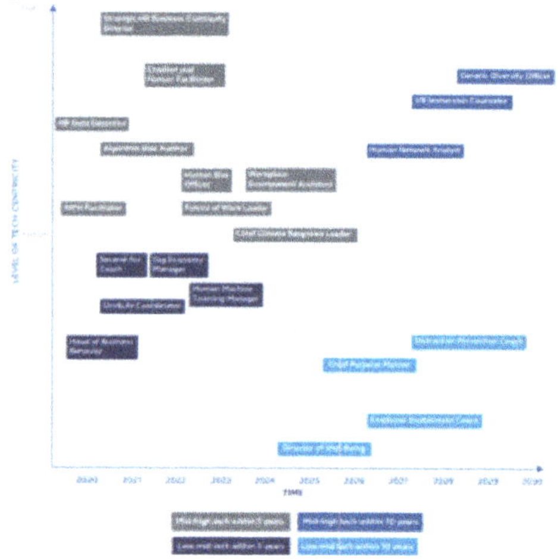

7. EMPLOYEE PERCEPTIONS AND HUMAN AI INTERACTION IN HCM

The success of Human Capital Management leveraging Artificial intelligence (AI) is influenced not just by the sophistication of the technology used or the ability of leaders to manage people, but also by the way employees perceive, engage with and experience AI systems. The employee attitude toward AI impacts trust, acceptance, engagement, and ultimately the effectiveness of HR practices that support the use of AI. Further, as AI becomes more integrated into recruitment, performance management, training and development, workforce analytics, and other HR processes. The interaction between AI and human plays a vital role in modern organizations..

7.1 Trust, Acceptance, and Technology Readiness

The level of trust in AI is one of the biggest determining factors in whether employees will accept it as a viable solution for HR processes. Trust is usually built on the employees' perceptions of AI relative to the accuracy and fairness of the outputs, as well as whether it produces consistent results and the organization has the right intentions behind implementing AI. Acceptance increases when the employees believe that AI has been implemented to assist them with development and fairness, not to supervision or control (Lin et al., 2007). Technology readiness can also be a determining factor; employees who have greater digital literacy and have had previous exposure to advanced technologies are more likely to see AI as an enabler rather than a threat, while employees who have limited knowledge of AI will likely associate it with job loss or loss of control. This shows the importance of communication with employees and building digital capabilities within the organization to create positive perceptions of AI.Trust in AI is closely related to trust in management (Caldeira et al., 2021). If employees do not think managers take responsibility and exercise judgment in their decision-making, they will be less likely to accept AI-generated HR decisions.Table 3 Determinants of Employee Trust and Acceptance of AI in HCM

Table 3. Determinants of Employee Trust and Acceptance of AI in HCM

Dimension	Key Influences	Managerial Implication
Trust in AI	Accuracy, fairness, consistency	Ensure validation and monitoring of AI outputs
Technology readiness	Digital skills, exposure	Invest in employee AI literacy
Trust in management	Transparency, accountability	Reinforce human oversight
Perceived intent	Development vs. control	Frame AI as supportive

7.2 Transparency and Explainability in AI-Driven HR Systems

In order to achieve ethical and effective collaboration between humans and AI, organizations must follow the principles of transparency and explainability.

AI-supported decisions are more likely to gain acceptance from employees if they understand the reasoning and rationale behind them (Yanamala, 2023). Using black-box algorithms when making decisions about sensitive areas (e.g., promotions, performance evaluations, and hiring) will erode trust and lead to perceptions that decisions are arbitrary. When HR and Management professionals use transparent AI processes, they can better articulate their rationale so employees understand why they were selected for a particular position or received a promotion, etc. (Sareddy & Khan, 2024). Disclosing information about the decision-making processes leaves a sense of justice and develops trust within the company. If we are considering AI from a human-centered perspective, it will remove AI as an unintelligible authority and serve as an analytical tool aligned with the organization's core values.

7.3 Changing Roles of HR Professionals

Adopting AI has drastically altered the role of human resource professionals. Human resources are moving away from primarily performing routine administrative tasks with AI performing those activities for organisations to a heavily strategic focus on advisory capacities and ethical stewardship functions in support of organisations' strategic goals(Kochan & Dyer, 1993). The role of human resources is increasingly being viewed as the mediators of technology, management and employees; therefore human resources must ensure that AI systems operate according to the values of organisations and to the expectations of their employees and the workforce as a whole(Srivastava, 2000). Transitions into this new role as human resource professionals will require them to acquire new skills, such as data interpretation, ethical oversight and facilitation of change.

8. ETHICAL, LEGAL, AND SOCIAL IMPLICATIONS OF AI IN HCM

Artificial intelligence (AI) in human capital management (HCM) entails serious ethical, legal and social issues, especially given that HR decisions affect employee opportunities, dignity, and well-being; thus adversely governing AI could lead to significant implications to employees and their workforce. Thus, to adopt responsible AI requires monitoring key aspects of AI to include equity, privacy, accountability, and equity and inclusion. Technology and AI are reducing the capacity for the function of the HR profession; yet that same technology and AI are providing increasing strategic relevance to HR. Therefore the HR profession is emerging as a central force in governing AI as it relates to human-AI collaboration.

8.1 Algorithmic Bias and Fairness in HR Decisions

Increasingly the HR community is concerned about how AI bias has impacted HR. Bias associated with algorithmic decision-making can occur as a result of historical bias and poor data, or underrepresentation of groups of diverse employees. If these algorithms go unaddressed, they will continue to contribute to systemic discrimination against society's most marginalized (Köchling & Wehner, 2020). If we want to leverage AI to create equitable and inclusive workplaces, we need to incorporate audits, use data that includes diverse employees, and regularly conduct a human review of AI produced human resource outcomes. HR managers and professionals should evaluate all outcomes of AI, and intervene when those outcomes do not align with equitable and inclusive workplace objectives (Newman et al., 2020). Ethical use of AI will not just be accomplished by using these technologies; it will also require the creation of governance processes and accountability for both the AI and the person implementing it.

8.2 Data Privacy, Surveillance, and Employee Rights

Privacy and surveillance concerns arise due to the heavy reliance of AI-powered human capital management (HCM) systems on massive amounts of employee data. When used improperly, predictive analytics, sentiment analysis, and productivity tracking can erase the line between support and intrusion if they aren't properly implemented (Ebert et al., 2021). The importance of Respecting Employees' Rights is accomplished through data governance policies, informed consent, minimum amount of data and compliance with legal frameworks. Organizations should use analytical data to identify trends without excessive surveillance to achieve HR goals.

8.3 Responsible and Inclusive AI Governance

Responsible governance of Artificial Intelligence (AI) provides the necessary infrastructure to use AI ethically within Human Capital Management (HCM). Responsible governance of AI consists of ethical guidelines, inter-departmental oversight committees, consistent auditing of the usage of AI and establishing and maintaining an avenue for individuals who have grievances regarding the ethical use of AI to file a complaint (Batool et al., 2023). Inclusive governance of AI ensures that multiple perspectives of AI design and implementation including gender, age, culture and ability are part of the process.Table 4 Key Elements of Responsible AI Governance in HCM

Table 4. Key Elements of Responsible AI Governance in HCM

Governance Element	Purpose
Ethical guidelines	Define acceptable AI use
Bias audits	Detect and mitigate discrimination
Human oversight	Preserve accountability
Employee voice	Enhance legitimacy and trust
Legal compliance	Protect rights and privacy

9. ORGANIZATIONAL IMPLICATIONS AND STRATEGIC VALUE

AI-enabled HCM is more than just operational efficiency, it creates significant impacts on organizations at a strategic level and contributes to long-term value creation. When managed responsibly, AI enables organizations to be more capable, agile and competitive.

Organizations will achieve a competitive advantage through the use of AI-enabled HCM by improving upon the quality of talent, the adaptability of the workforce and the consistency of decision-making (Williams, 2002). When organizations effectively use AI for managing their people, they are better prepared to identify in demand skills, retain critical talent and adapt to changes in their environment. The strategic value of AI is not in the technological advancement itself, but rather how it becomes embedded within the organization's culture, routines and managerial capabilities and this is known as a resource-based view(Carter & Greer, 2013). The existence of AI as an advantage source occurs when it cannot easily be replicated due to its intertwining with the organization's human expertise and context.

AI implementations require HR to redefine their capabilities; traditional administrative-based competencies are now complemented by analytical reasoning, ethical judgement and strategic advisory. HR professionals need to define how human and artificial intelligence will interact throughout the organization.

This transformation reinforces the role of HR as a strategic partner responsible for aligning technology, talent and organizational purpose. The use of AI will undoubtedly increase productivity and scalability within the organization; however, excessive focus on optimizing these aspects risks devaluing human-centric values like empathy, inclusion and dignity. Organizations must consciously balance the benefits of their analytical efficiencies with relation-based and ethical considerations. Human-centric AI focuses primarily on augmenting rather than replacing people doing meaningful work.

10. FUTURE DIRECTIONS FOR AI-ENABLED HUMAN CAPITAL MANAGEMENT

As AI-enabled human capital management (HCM) continues to develop quickly, there are both new challenges and opportunities for the organisation and scholars alike. Newer HCM applications include using advanced predictive models to allow employees greater opportunities for career mobility as well as creating AI-based analytics for employee well-being and adaptive workforce design which create an environment that supports collaboration amongst employees. While there is potential for researchers to gain a better understanding of these developments, there is also an increase in the amount of ethical and governance-related work that needs to be completed. A collaborative future of HCM (i.e., between AI and humans) will provide opportunities to leverage and align the strengths of both AI and the human being through AI's analytical capabilities and human's ability to display judgement, create ideas, and apply ethical reasoning.

10.1 Research Gaps and Agenda for Scholars

Although there is increasing interest in AI and its implications, many gaps still exist. Some of these gaps are longitudinal studies on the impact of AI on employee identity, cross-culture acceptance of AI, and how leadership shapes ethical usage of AI. The future of research in this area needs an interdisciplinary approach that combines HRM, Information systems, and ethics.Table 5 Future Research Agenda for AI in HCM

Table 5. Future Research Agenda for AI in HCM

Area	Key Research Questions
Employee experience	How does AI reshape psychological contracts?
Ethics	What governance models are most effective?
Leadership	How do leaders influence AI trust?
Inclusion	Does AI reduce or reproduce inequality?

11. CONCLUSION

This chapter discussed the effect that Artificial Intelligence (AI) has on Human Capital Management (HCM) from multiple ways such as managerial, employee, ethical and strategic perspectives. AI enables improved quality results through more accurate analysis and allows for more opportunities to personalize outputs and align strategically; however, for there to be successful implementation of AI for HCM, it must occur within an environment of trust, transparency, proper governance and adequate amounts of human oversight. In creating sustainable AI for HCM over the long term requires developing an HCM model centered around humanity by bringing together tactical intelligence with ethical commitments and corporate values. Thus, AI should support human judgment and enable organizations' employees to better manage their talent through fairness, increased awareness and greater inclusiveness. Organizations that have successfully aligned their use of AI with their established systems of trust and accountability and their stated mission will have the greater ability to constitute long term value from their use of AI.

REFERENCES

Ademola, O. E. (2024). Change Management Trends in the AI Modern World: Adapting to the Future of Work. *Journal of Behavioral Informatics*, *10*(1), 41–50.

Agarwal, A. (2023). AI adoption by human resource management: a study of its antecedents and impact on HR system effectiveness. *foresight, 25*(1), 67-81.

Albert, E. T. (2019). AI in talent acquisition: A review of AI-applications used in recruitment and selection. *Strategic HR Review*, *18*(5), 215–221. DOI: 10.1108/SHR-04-2019-0024

Alsaif, A., & Sabih Aksoy, M. (2023). AI-HRM: artificial intelligence in human resource management: a literature review. *Journal of Computing and Communication*, *2*(2), 1–7. DOI: 10.21608/jocc.2023.307053

Alzeiby, E. A., Islam, N., Shaik, A. S., & Yaqub, M. Z. (2025). AI adoption in enterprises for enhanced strategic human resource management practices: Benefiting the employee engagement and experience. *Journal of Enterprise Information Management*, *38*(5), 1441–1464. DOI: 10.1108/JEIM-05-2024-0249

Ang, K. C., Sankaran, S., & Liu, D. (2025). Advancing sociotechnical systems theory: New principles for human-robot team design and development. *Applied Ergonomics*, *129*, 104604. DOI: 10.1016/j.apergo.2025.104604

Arora, M., Prakash, A., Mittal, A., & Singh, S. (2021, December). HR analytics and artificial intelligence-transforming human resource management. In *2021 International Conference on Decision Aid Sciences and Application (DASA)* (pp. 288-293). IEEE. DOI: 10.1109/DASA53625.2021.9682325

Batool, A., Zowghi, D., & Bano, M. (2023). Responsible AI governance: a systematic literature review. *arXiv preprint arXiv:2401.10896.*

Bhatt, P., & Muduli, A. (2023). Artificial intelligence in learning and development: A systematic literature review. *European Journal of Training and Development*, *47*(7/8), 677–694. DOI: 10.1108/EJTD-09-2021-0143

Bos-Nehles, A., Townsend, K., Cafferkey, K., & Trullen, J. (2023). Examining the Ability, Motivation and Opportunity (AMO) framework in HRM research: Conceptualization, measurement and interactions. *International Journal of Management Reviews*, *25*(4), 725–739. DOI: 10.1111/ijmr.12332

Buck, B., & Morrow, J. (2018). AI, performance management and engagement: Keeping your best their best. *Strategic HR Review*, *17*(5), 261–262. DOI: 10.1108/SHR-10-2018-145

Caldeira, T. A., Ferreira, J. B., Freitas, A., & Falcão, R. P. D. Q. (2021). Adoption of mobile payments in Brazil: Technology readiness, trust and perceived quality. *BBR. Brazilian Business Review*, *18*(4), 415–432.

Carter, S. M., & Greer, C. R. (2013). Strategic leadership: Values, styles, and organizational performance. *Journal of Leadership & Organizational Studies*, *20*(4), 375–393. DOI: 10.1177/1548051812471724

Cubric, M. (2020). Drivers, barriers and social considerations for AI adoption in business and management: A tertiary study. *Technology in Society*, *62*, 101257. DOI: 10.1016/j.techsoc.2020.101257

Dixit, A. S., & Jatav, S. (2024). Evolving needs of learners and role of artificial intelligence (AI) in training and development (T&D): T&D professionals' perspective. *Journal of Management Development*, *43*(6), 788–806. DOI: 10.1108/JMD-01-2024-0009

Ebert, I., Wildhaber, I., & Adams-Prassl, J. (2021). Big Data in the workplace: Privacy Due Diligence as a human rights-based approach to employee privacy protection. *Big Data & Society*, *8*(1), 20539517211013051. DOI: 10.1177/20539517211013051

Fenech, R., Baguant, P., & Ivanov, D. (2019). The changing role of human resource management in an era of digital transformation. *Journal of Management Information & Decision Sciences*, *22*(2).

Johnson, R. D., Stone, D. L., & Lukaszewski, K. M. (2021). The benefits of eHRM and AI for talent acquisition. *Journal of Tourism Futures*, *7*(1), 40–52. DOI: 10.1108/JTF-02-2020-0013

Karuppiah, S. P., & Kumaran, S. (2025, July). AI-Powered Talent Acquisition: Enhancing Recruitment and Workforce Analytics Using Machine Learning. In *2025 IEEE 4th World Conference on Applied Intelligence and Computing (AIC)* (pp. 179-184). IEEE.

Khan, F. A., Khan, N. A., & Aslam, A. (2024). Adoption of artificial intelligence in human resource management: an application of TOE-TAM model. *Research and review: human resource and labour management, 5*, 22-36.

Kim, S., Khoreva, V., & Vaiman, V. (2025). Strategic human resource management in the era of algorithmic technologies: Key insights and future research agenda. *Human Resource Management*, *64*(2), 447–464. DOI: 10.1002/hrm.22268

Kochan, T. A., & Dyer, L. (1993). Managing transformational change: The role of human resource professionals. *International Journal of Human Resource Management, 4*(3), 569–590. DOI: 10.1080/09585199300000037

Köchling, A., & Wehner, M. C. (2020). Discriminated by an algorithm: A systematic review of discrimination and fairness by algorithmic decision-making in the context of HR recruitment and HR development. *Business Research, 13*(3), 795–848. DOI: 10.1007/s40685-020-00134-w

Kommera, H. K. R. (2017). Choosing the Right HCM Tool: A Guide for HR Professionals. *International Journal of Early Childhood Special Education, 9*, 191–198.

Lin, C. H., Shih, H. Y., & Sher, P. J. (2007). Integrating technology readiness into technology acceptance: The TRAM model. *Psychology and Marketing, 24*(7), 641–657. DOI: 10.1002/mar.20177

Newman, D. T., Fast, N. J., & Harmon, D. J. (2020). When eliminating bias isn't fair: Algorithmic reductionism and procedural justice in human resource decisions. *Organizational Behavior and Human Decision Processes, 160*, 149–167. DOI: 10.1016/j.obhdp.2020.03.008

Nyathani, R. (2023). AI in performance management: Redefining performance appraisals in the digital age. *Journal of Artificial Intelligence & Cloud Computing. SRC/JAICC-146, 134*, 2-5.

Paramita, D. (2020). Digitalization in talent acquisition: A case study of AI in recruitment.

Parasa, S. K. (2024). Impact of AI on employee experience and engagement. *European Journal of Advances in Engineering and Technology, 11*(7), 12–14.

Poquet, O., & De Laat, M. (2021). Developing capabilities: Lifelong learning in the age of AI. *British Journal of Educational Technology, 52*(4), 1695–1708. DOI: 10.1111/bjet.13123

Qamar, Y., Agrawal, R. K., Samad, T. A., & Chiappetta Jabbour, C. J. (2021). When technology meets people: The interplay of artificial intelligence and human resource management. *Journal of Enterprise Information Management, 34*(5), 1339–1370. DOI: 10.1108/JEIM-11-2020-0436

Rai, A., & Singh, L. B. (2023). Artificial intelligence-based people analytics transforming human resource management practices. In *The adoption and effect of artificial intelligence on human resources management, part a* (pp. 229–244). Emerald Publishing Limited. DOI: 10.1108/978-1-80382-027-920231012

Romeo, E., & Lacko, J. (2025). Adoption and integration of AI in organizations: A systematic review of challenges and drivers towards future directions of research. *Kybernetes.*

Routhu, K. K. (2021). AI-augmented benefits administration: A standards-driven automation framework with Oracle HCM Cloud. *International Journal of Scientific Research & Engineering Trends*, *7*(3).

Sabah, A. S., Hamouda, A. A., Helles, Y. E., Okasha, S. M., Abu-Nasser, B. S., & Abu-Naser, S. S. (2024). Artificial Intelligence and Organizational Evolution: Reshaping Workflows in the Modern Era.

Salvador-Gómez, A., Bou-Llusar, J. C., & Beltrán-Martín, I. (2023). A multi-actor perspective on the effectiveness of human resource management implementation: An empirical analysis based on the ability-motivation-opportunity framework. *International Journal of Human Resource Management, 34*(20), 3963–4002. DOI: 10.1080/09585192.2022.2163855

Sareddy, M. R., & Khan, S. (2024). AI-driven human resource management: Enhancing transparency and security with machine learning. *Journal of Artificial Intelligence and Capsule Networks*, *6*(4), 512–528. DOI: 10.36548/jaicn.2024.4.009

Srivastava, K. B. (2000). Rethinking HR: Role of HR professionals in a changing business environment. *Indian Journal of Industrial Relations*, *35*(4), 532–544.

Tasleem, N. (2025). HR technology transformation and the impact of people analytics on workforce management. *Iconic Research and Engineering Journals*, *8*(9), 702–716.

Thontadarya, P. S. (2025). The Role of AI in Modernizing PeopleSoft HCM: Bridging ERP and Innovation in Public Sector HR. *Journal of Computer Science and Technology Studies*, *7*(8), 708–715.

Vardarlier, P. (2019). Digital transformation of human resource management: digital applications and strategic tools in HRM. In *Digital business strategies in blockchain ecosystems: Transformational design and future of global business* (pp. 239–264). Springer International Publishing.

Varma, A., Pereira, V., & Patel, P. (2024). Artificial intelligence and performance management. *Organizational Dynamics*, *53*(1), 101037. DOI: 10.1016/j.orgdyn.2024.101037

Vrontis, D., Christofi, M., Pereira, V., Tarba, S., Makrides, A., & Trichina, E. (2023). Artificial intelligence, robotics, advanced technologies and human resource management: a systematic review. *Artificial intelligence and international HRM*, 172-201.

Williams, S. L. (2002). Strategic planning and organizational values: Links to alignment. *Human Resource Development International*, *5*(2), 217–233. DOI: 10.1080/13678860110057638

Wu Young, J., & Nah, F. F. H. (2025, June). AI Systems for Physicians: A Review from Socio-technical and Human-Computer Interaction Perspectives. In *International Conference on Human-Computer Interaction* (pp. 165-180). Cham: Springer Nature Switzerland.

Yanamala, K. K. R. (2023). Transparency, privacy, and accountability in AI-enhanced HR processes. *Journal of Advanced Computing Systems*, *3*(3), 10–18. DOI: 10.69987/JACS.2023.30302

Chapter 7
AI in HRM:
Transformative Talent Management Strategies in Organizations

K. Santhanalaxmi
http://orcid.org/0000-0002-7441-6127
SASTRA (Deemed to be) University, India

S. Kavitha
http://orcid.org/0009-0004-9915-4479
SASTRA (Deemed to be) University, India

ABSTRACT

This chapter focuses on the evolution of artificial intelligence's role in modernizing companies' strategies to attract, develop, assess and retain talent in a digital age of transformation and increased competition. The chapter will focus on the operations and strategic use of AI in the talent life cycle, beginning with talent acquisition where AI-driven recruitment systems, algorithms, and predictive assessment tools have changed the way businesses determine high-potential applicants quickly and accurately.

1. INTRODUCTION

1.1. Evolution of Human Resource Management in Digital Era

The history of Human Resource Management (HRM) in the modern technology age illustrates the immense change that has occurred in the way that organizations manage the human capital that drives their operations (J. Zhang & Chen, 2024).

DOI: 10.4018/979-8-2600-2541-3.ch007

While in the past the management of human capital in most businesses occurred in a more administrative manner, the need for change has arisen in recent years, primarily owing to the growing competition that most businesses currently encounter.

The first stage in the transformation of HRM through technology was the implementation of Human Resource Information Systems (HRIS), where HR processes like employee records, attendance, and benefit administration were computerized (R. D. Johnson et al., 2016). With the improvement in digital technologies, HRM evolved from mere automation to analytics and fully-integrated platforms. The advent of big data, cloud, and analytics enabled HR managers to analyze trends in their workforce and measure talent and employee performance. The application and utilization of HR analytics made it possible for HRM to be more data-driven, allowing organizations to realign talent strategies with overall business goals (Nocker & Sena, 2019). Recruitment and talent acquisition were made more efficient through the application of job portals, applicant tracking, and e-employer branding.

The digital age also triggered a new set of changes in HRM because of the application of artificial intelligence, machine learning, and digital collaborations. The application of artificial intelligence started in recruitment, learning and development, performance management, and employee engagement. Learning management systems, virtual onboarding, HR assistants in the form of chatbots, and models for attrition prediction are applications of technology in HRM and have resulted in changes in the nature of HRM, which catered to improving work-related well-being and upskilling of employees (Sundari et al., 2024).

Remote working and collaboration platforms have made flexible working possible, hence raising the need for HR departments to develop new policies, performance measures, and leadership approaches (Coenen & Kok, 2014). The current role of the human resources function is therefore that of a "strategic partner with the added responsibilities for creating agility, resilience, and a more human-focused organization."

1.2. Emergence of Artificial Intelligence in HRM

The rise of artificial intelligence in Human Resource Management marks an important turning point in how organizations attract, manage, and develop talent in an increasingly complex and competitive environment (Murugesan et al., 2023). While organizations are generating vast amounts of employee and organization-generated data, a suite of traditional HR tools coupled with human judgment has become inadequate to process information efficiently and draw meaningful insights from it. Artificial intelligence, with its large dataset analysis, pattern recognition, and support for predictive decision-making, has therefore emerged as a potent enabler of modern HRM (Budhwar et al., 2022).

AI initially entered HRM through narrow, task-oriented applications meant to drive efficiency and higher reductions in manual effort. Early uses included automated resume screening, applicant tracking systems, and rule-based chatbots handling routine HR queries (Majumder & Mondal, 2021). Such applications helped reduce time-to-hire and increase consistency in decision making by streamlining recruitment and administrative processes. Automation of such mundane tasks allowed the HR personnel to deviate their attention to the more strategic and relational elements of their roles, like workforce planning, employee engagement, and leadership development.

From automation to advanced analytics and decision support, the role of AI technologies in HRM continued to expand as the technologies matured. Machine learning algorithms began to support talent acquisition by matching candidates to roles based on skills, experience, and predicted job fit rather than simple keyword searches (Qin et al., 2025). AI-driven assessment tools started analyzing behavioural data, communication patterns, and performance indicators to support more holistic evaluation of candidates and employees. In learning and development, AI-enabled platforms personalized training content, identified skill gaps, and recommended upskilling pathways aligned with both individual career goals and organizational needs.

The sentiment analysis along with natural language processing examines employee responses from surveys, emails, or internal communication tools to understand the pulse of an organization regarding engagement levels, morale, and well-being (Rosca & Stancu, 2024). Predictive analytics further support retention strategies by pinpointing early warning signs of dissatisfaction among employees or risk of turnover, thus proactive interventions may be taken up by the HR leaders. On the other hand, the development of AI within the realm of HRM has also presented significant ethical, legal, and social concerns. Data privacy, bias, explainability, and accountability have come to the fore as critical aspects within the debate about responsible use of AI (Cheng et al., 2021).

1.3. AI as a Strategic Enabler in Human Capital Management

Artificial intelligence has become an effective strategic enabler in talent management, as it brings a substantial change in the way organizations recruit, develop, engage, and retain their talent (Dr. Bijja Vishwanath, Dr. Surendar Vaddepalli, 2023). Unlike the former digital technology, which only increased the efficiency administration, artificial intelligence helps in transforming the Human Resources' processes and turning them more predictive, data-driven, and value-focused, thus ensuring that human resources become a source of sustainable competitiveness for the organizations, as their strategies will become more closely aligned with the organizational objectives.

In recruitment, AI enables strategic workforce planning based on trends in the labour market, competence profiles within the company, and anticipated capability requirements in the future (Allal-Chérif et al., 2021). Forecasting algorithms enable organizations to predict talent gaps and candidate potential and make better recruitment decisions based on these insights. AI-based candidate matching capabilities extend beyond simple keyword searches to assess skill sets, experience, and cultural fit, thus being able to improve quality hires and do so in less time and at less cost.

It also allows for more personalization and continuity regarding talent development. Smart learning systems evaluate personal competencies, learning styles, as well as career goals in order to suggest tailored development (Peng et al., 2019). By identifying areas where skills are needed, as well as predicting these needs in the future, AI helps bolster efforts related to up-skilling and re-skilling, which play a very important role in a dynamic business world.

In performance and retention management, AI improves the quality of decision-making with real-time analysis of employee behaviour, engagement, and productivity. Sophisticated analysis on performance or potential for attrition helps to identify patterns for effective action to be taken (Ramachandran et al., 2022). AI-based feedback platforms encourage continuous performance discussions rather than occasional review discussions, which support flexibility and alignment with organizational objectives. Apart from optimizing operations, AI offers an opportunity to make talent management human-centered and sustainable. When AI is applied cautiously, decisions related to talent would be more transparent, unbiased, and free from variability while retaining their human touch (Martini et al., 2024).

1.4. From Traditional HRM to AI-Driven HR Ecosystems

The shift from conventional Human Resource Management to AI-driven Human Resource Ecosystems marks a significant evolution in terms of how firms perceive and manage their human capital assets (Nyathani, 2022). Traditional approach to Human Resource Management has traditionally been a predominantly linear and reactive discipline, with different processes being in place for different functions like recruitment, employee training and development, performance monitoring, and employee relations. These functions have traditionally been based on managerial intuitions and past data history, with a siloed nature operating in HR systems devoid of strategic foresight.

With the advancement in technology and artificial intelligence, an interconnected ecosystem between data, processes, and people can now be achieved in an effective manner in HRM systems. Artificial intelligence-enabled HR ecosystems utilize machine learning, analytics, cloud computing, intelligent automation, and other technologies to design a continuous and adaptive system of talent management processes and employee data gathered from different areas (Maghsoudi et al., 2025), which can then provide insights in a timely manner to decision-makers in a proactive manner in an effective and strategic manner instead of a support area in an organizational setup.

In AI-driven ecosystems, HR processes get personalized, predictive, and responsive. Recruitment systems identify future skill needs and recommend suitable candidates; learning platforms adapt the content to individual needs, and performance systems are about continuous feedback, not periodic evaluations (Chen, 2023). Employees are no longer passive recipients of HR policies but active participants (in the making of their career journeys through tools enabled by AI. This change towards AI-driven HR ecosystems reflects a broader transformation towards human-centered, data-informed, and sustainable workforce management. Deploying technology together with strategic intent and ethical governance lays the foundation for HR ecosystems to foster employee experiences that support long-term organizational success.

2. AI IN TALENT ACQUISITION, RECRUITMENT AND SELECTION

Artificial intelligence has profoundly impacted talent acquisition processes by effectively changing the way recruitment and candidate selection are performed by adding value to these processes (Okeyika et al., 2023). Conventional recruitment processes have predominantly involved time-consuming activities, uncertainties, and reactivity. However, as more skills become specialized, artificial intelligence has come to the rescue.

One of the major applications in recruitment is automated resume screening and shortlisting through artificial intelligence systems. These systems use advanced technologies to process a pool of resumes using machine learning and NLP to shortlist potential applicants based on relevant skills and qualifications received during their application processes (Hmoud & Laszlo, 2019). This method is different from keyword filtering in that these systems match resumes based on relevant skill transfer and application, thereby allowing recruiters to recruit potential talent that may have otherwise gone unnoticed through conventional recruitment methods.

It also helps improve sourcing and branding through analyzing labour market information and search engine optimization of labour information and social media platforms. This helps the organization effectively predict the demand for talents and fill the vacancies accordingly. On the other hand, the use of chatbots and virtual assistants driven through AI helps improve the candidate experience. This is due to the ability of chatbots and virtual assistants to respond promptly and effectively to the queries of the applicants (Nawaz & Gomes, 2019).

In the selection stage, there is increasingly structured and objective decision-making facilitated by AI. Cognitive abilities, behavioural characteristics, and competencies in terms of job performance can be evaluated by AI-based assessments of individuals. The use of video interviews can be evaluated further by analyzing facial expressions, speech analysis, and language to better understand how the candidates communicate (Kassab & Kashevnik, 2024). This helps in creating standardized selection criteria that can minimize the bias of the interviewer.

Nevertheless, when AI technology is used in recruitment and selection processes, some significant ethical and governance issues arise. First and foremost, if AI systems are trained on historical data before making any recruitment decisions or predictions, there may be a chance that risks regarding gender bias, ethnicity bias, age bias, or education bias occur if appropriate measures are not put in place to address such potential mistakes in human resource decisions (Hunkenschroer & Luetge, 2022). Nowadays, AI in recruitment is being viewed not solely a decision-taker but a decision-support tool to support recruiters in making appropriate decisions.

With the aid of AI in the acquisition of talents and the selection of the best suits for the organization, an organization will be able to shift from an intuitive approach to a more strategic and knowledge-informed approach to the hiring and selection of talents (Rousseau & Barends, 2011). With the added value of efficiency and the positive impact of AI tools on the candidate experience and the assessment of the best fits for the organization, the overall outcomes of the hiring process will be significantly enhanced.

3. AI IN LEARNING, DEVELOPMENT AND UPSKILLING

Artificial Intelligence has transformed into a powerful determinant of learning, development, and upskilling, leaving a marked impact on how entities embrace the workforce in the midst of dramatic technological, economic, and social transformations (Chhibber et al., 2025). Industry 5.0 presents a workplace characterized by human-centricity, sustainability, and the need to develop robust business environments with the help of robust automation technologies, inviting a pivotal role for AI-driven learning in ensuring the harmonious interface of workforce capabilities and enterprise outcomes.

The most significant impact of AI in learning and development is providing personalized learning paths by using an AI-based learning management system to analyze large amounts of learner data and provide recommendations based on that data (Murtaza et al., 2022). The data can range from a learner's existing knowledge to their speed of learning and previous performances in learning and career goals and aspirations. This type of personalization can play a significant part in increasing learner interest in knowing more about a particular subject or stream and can also play a critical role in cognitive retention by providing what is best and when it is best needed (Starecek et al., 2025).

Another area that AI can facilitate is experiential or immersive learning. For instance, AI can make possible the incorporation of virtual reality, augmented reality, or intelligent simulations for learning. Such simulations can allow learners to gain experience regarding complex performances or decisions in a risk-free atmosphere (Mposula & Oyetade, 2025). According to an analysis by Oracle Business Intelligence Journal, simulations created by AI can offer a distinct opportunity for learners to gain experience regarding important skills like decision-making capabilities or cognitive skills like creative or critical-thinking skills not to overlook human skills like emotional intelligence or empathy. Such skills are believed to prove crucial for learners to adapt to the human-dominated approach of Industry 5.0.

The next significant application of AI tools in the realm of learning and development is in the sphere of skill gap analysis and the wider realm of manpower planning. The rate of skill obsolescence in modern organizations is escalating owing to the increasing use of automation, digitalization, and change in business models. The role of AI is significant in skill gap analysis, where the present employee skill set is compared with the present and future requirements of the job (Singh Sidhu et al., 2024). The use of predictive analysis is significant in terms of manpower planning, where skill requirements in the long term are being predicted with the help of industry requirements, technology, and organizational goals.

Organizations are thus encouraged to explore utilizing AI to conduct skills gap analyzes to inform data-driven decisions regarding talent acquisition, training, redeployment, and succession planning. Instead of relying on external recruiting sources, AI helps an organization identify talent within an organization who have skills transferability with high learning potential (Jacob Fernandes França et al., 2023). This helps not only minimize recruiting expenses but also boost workforce engagement through career growth prospects.

Continuous learning has now become a necessity for the contemporary era of Industry 5.0, characterized by a dynamic pace of change. It is now possible for people to acquire knowledge through the use of intelligent systems for learning by incorporating learning situations into work processes from day to day. Intelligent systems can now assist in recommending learning based on actual work processes or performance issues at the exact moment of need (Magnisalis et al., 2011). This objective is achieved by shifting the focus from conventional learning processes to a more permanent way of acquiring knowledge.

Another significant function of AI is in promoting a culture of reskilling and self-learning within an organization. Intelligent career guidance will enable each employee to gain better insights about new roles created in the future in terms of their competencies and learning paths based on their individual interests and capabilities (Gómez Gandía et al., 2024). Such transparency enables navigation by each individual in his or her professional development and better articulation of personal growth with the needs of the organization. This can be considered quite empowering, especially within the context of Industry 5.0, because it reinforces the human-centered vision through which technology serves people, rather than vice-versa.

AI-driven learning ecosystems further allow for inclusivity and accessibility in workforce development. Adaptive interfaces, natural language processing, and intelligent tutoring can accommodate different learning styles, languages, and abilities, reducing barriers to participation (Javed et al., 2023). The inclusiveness powered by such approaches will go hand in hand with ethical and social dimensions in Industry 5.0-to make technological progress contribute toward skill development and employability in an equitable manner across various workforce segments.

From a strategic perspective, AI-enabled learning and upskilling go hand in glove with organizational sustainability and competitiveness. A continuously learning workforce is better able to innovate, respond to disruptions, and co-create value with intelligent machines. By augmenting human capabilities, rather than substituting them, AI reinforces a synergistic relationship between humans and technology (Zhou et al., 2021). This collaboration enhances creativity, empathy, and contextual judgment qualities that remain uniquely human and increasingly valuable in complex, uncertain environments.

4. AI IN PERFORMANCE MANAGEMENT

Artificial Intelligence is observed to play a crucial role in a series of transformations involving performance management. Performance management no more focuses solely on a retrospective approach and rather focuses more from a development perspective. Within a modern organization, especially when operating under a digitally intensive and knowledge-based environment, the general appraisal process is no more viewed as an effective means of managing such a workforce (Sahlin & Angelis, 2019). This is where the application of an AI-powered performance management system comes into play. AI-driven performance management enables the continuous monitoring of performance by aggregating data from various sources, including project management software, collaboration media, customer feedback software, e-learning software, and business operation software (Pawar & Dhumal, 2024). It monitors the performance of employees based on both qualitative and quantitative data, including task completion rates, quality data, and productivity rates, as well as communication patterns, collaboration frequency, and engagement measures. AI processes the collected data in real time to deliver performance improvement guidance continuously rather than during rare performance assessment sessions. Continuous monitoring by an organization helps in the earlier identification of performance trends, strengths, and areas of improvement; thus, interventions and support are provided at appropriate times. It provides direct benefits to workers, as feedback offered on time allows them to take corrective action and tap skills while working in a manner expected by the organization.

AI-driven feedback mechanisms leverage a customized, consistent, and action-oriented approach to performance feedback. Intelligent algorithms generate personalized performance feedback depending on individual performance patterns, learning progress, and behavioural data. Digital dashboards, virtual assistants, and coaching tools would then display this feedback in accessible and transparent ways (Wu et al., 2024). These differences from more traditional modes of feedback, often with managerial bias or limited observation, are where AI-based feedback pulls from comprehensive datasets to foster fairness and objectivity. In addition, AI can also identify those contextual factors influencing performance, such as workload distribution and skill mismatches, so that development rather than just a mere evaluation is reflected in the feedback.

Another important step up in Artificial Intelligence-assisted performance management lies with data-driven goal setting. In conventional approaches, goals are set either on the basis of intuition of the performance manager/digitized benchmarks, which might not be aligned with the shifting business climate and employee skills (Luo, 2022). With Artificial Intelligence tools, the performance data, business goals, trends, and employee skills are analyzed, and appropriate recommendations are made regarding suitable goals, which can then be set on an individual basis, taking into consideration the end results on the organization as a whole, thus ensuring alignment of employee goals with organizational results, enabling an individual employee to comprehend the value addition of individual performance to the organization as a whole.

Within appraisal processes, AI can assist in carrying out more evidence-driven or comprehensive appraisals by aggregating data from multiple sources across extensive periods of time. Unlike conventional appraisals that emphasize recent behaviours or outcomes, an AI-driven appraisal focuses more on patterns of behaviour, consistency, or growth rates over time (Kulkov et al., 2024). It also helps to curb appraisal-related errors like the recency effect, halo effect, or leniency effect. Besides, the incorporation of peer feedback, customer feedback, and self-assessments under a singular framework will also offer a more comprehensive understanding of the employee's performance. This, in turn, will increase the acceptance and authenticity of the appraisal system among the employees.

In spite of these advantages, however, the use and application of AI in performance management practices raise significant concerns in terms of over-reliance on technology and a potential backseat to human judgment or assessment in performance evaluation processes (Dwianto et al., 2024). As a matter of fact, performance is a multifaceted capability in terms of emotional quotient, ethical conduct, creativeness, and adaptability in specific situations—in ways that cannot be sufficiently predicted or evaluated through algorithms or artificial intelligence tools that rely on scanning or analyzing relevant data or information on a range of performance parameters.

The intervention of a human manager is very crucial in interpreting AI-generated insights in terms of contextual and empathetic reasoning in individual performances. Despite the usage of AI for spotting trends and anomalies in performances, reasoning can only occur by factoring in situational variables like individual as well as organizational challenges or hurdles. Integrating human supervision serves the purpose of ensuring that the process of performance management continues to be a supportive and motivating exercise rather than just a surveillance-based approach (Lou et al., 2025). This methodology also contributes maximally to the development of employee trust since the employees are more likely to cooperate with the AI-based assessment process if they are exposed to the dialogue of the human interface as well.

From the point of view of Industry 5.0, AI-based performance management aims to achieve a culture that is human-centric, sustainable, and resilient. AI does not replace human manager functions but enhances human capabilities by providing deeper insights for more informed decisions. Continuous feedbacks enhance employee growth and well-being while developing the capacity for employability (Jarrahi, 2018). AI-based performance management can lead to a culture of continuous improvement that promotes a culture of collaborative responsibility.

5. AI FOR EMPLOYEE ENGAGEMENT AND EXPERIENCE

Artificial Intelligence has grown to be a strong facilitator of Employee Engagement and Experience, as it redefined many ways organizations comprehend, support, and connect with their pool of talent (Budhwar et al., 2022). In the time spent more in the digital and hybrid workplace, work is more human-centered; employee engagement is no longer driven by compensation or formal policies but by meaningful experiences, emotional well-being, inclusion, and continuous support. AI-driven systems are thus allowing organizations to move beyond mere intuition-based engagement practices to data-informed, responsive, and personalized strategies that enhance employee satisfaction, motivation, and long-term commitment.

Sentiment Analysis and Employee Voice Analytics: Probably the most impactful use of AI in employee engagement involves sentiment analysis and employee voice analytics. Organizations generate copious volumes of unstructured data from their employee surveys, internal communication platforms, feedback tools, emails, chat messages, and social collaboration systems (Ravichandran et al., 2023). AI-powered natural language processing techniques analyze this data to identify patterns related to emotions, attitudes, concerns, and levels of engagement. It allows organizations to understand what their employees feel about various aspects, including what leaders are doing, as well as the culture, volume of work, change initiatives, and overall climate, all in real time. Unlike traditional employee surveys, which usually take place once a year, AI-based voice analytics can obtain feedback on what is currently on the minds of the employee population, thus offering a genuine understanding of employee sentiment.

On the one hand, AI can help a leader tackle issues before they escalate further by recognizing patterns related to positive and negative emotional trends. For instance, stress, burnouts, non-performance, or resistances to change can be dealt with more comprehensively by a leader when the AI reveals patterns associated with the negative sentiment among the workforce in certain roles and teams (Cinar & Bilodeau, 2024). On the other hand, the use of voice analytics can help secure the sense of empowerment for the workforce since the opinions of the workforce will be fully heard and responded to, promoting a sense of transparency among the workforce since the feeling of belonging will be greatly boosted.

Yet another critical contribution made by AI systems involves their involvement in ensuring improved employee well-being, motivation, and/or retention initiatives. The new age workforce has been marked as environments with high performance demands, connectivity, and/or change, all of which have adverse effects on mental or emotional health. AI well-being systems detect key indicators that include "workload patterns, working hours, communication activity, or engagement rates" to detect any symptoms or signs associated with stress or burnout conditions (Cramarenco et al., 2023). AI systems have been shown to provide "personalized well-being interventions" following the indicators or symptoms they have detected. This type has been described to enable or promote a 'preventive' approach from a 'reactive' one.

In the context of motivation, the role of AI is significant. It accomplishes this function by linking personal needs, likes, and dreams with work activities that have significance. Performance monitoring, learning achievements, recognition, and work aspirations are also assessed; the best possible motivation is thus provided. Systems of recognizing the performance of the employees are quite effective, as they provide due appreciation for the work performed (Vrontis et al., 2023). It prevents the use of general motivation techniques that do not have the same effect on the various segments of the workforce.

Another domain in which AI-generated insights result in significant value addition is in employee retention efforts. Using predictive analytics models involving multiple variables such as employee satisfaction levels, engagement levels, performance over a period of time, career progression possibilities, learning engagement levels, and external environments in terms of market availability of labourers to determine probabilities of employees quitting or being retained (Paigude et al., 2023). Instead of using this information to further act in a surveillance-oriented manner or increase employee penalty levels, some firms use this information to develop retention-oriented strategies for retaining higher potential or those employees whose probability of quitting is likely to increase in future scenarios.

Among the most important factors that contribute to the success of AI in employee engagement and experience is the adoption of human-centric AI. Human-centric AI is based on the values and principles of being transparent, fair, and considerate and respecting the autonomy and independence of the employees. For instance, while AI is powerful in processing and analyzing large volumes and speeds of data, the ethical and fair use is the human perspective in the process, avoiding the perception that the employees are being used as data points themselves. Human-centric AI can boost employee experience by promoting personalization in terms of employee interaction while at the same time avoiding any negative effects of human interaction (Rao et al., 2020). AI-based chatbots help provide employees with immediate access to information regarding their Human Resource-related queries, benefits, learning opportunities, and workplace support. While AI can be of help in managing an improved employee experience, it can function better if it is integrated alongside the human touch provided by empathetic leaders.

6. AI IN TALENT RETENTION AND WORKFORCE ANALYTICS

Artificial intelligence has proved to be an essential driver of talent retention strategies and workforce analytics in light of an increasingly competitive environment in which organizations find themselves (M. Johnson et al., 2021). Conventional workforce management strategies, which mostly focused on utilizing past data and relying on managerial instincts, are now deemed inadequate to handle the complexities posed in employee retention strategies. As such, workforce analytics, which focuses on employee retention strategies utilizing artificial intelligence, enable organizations to gain better insights that help in proactive decision-making, employee retention, and matching their human capital goals with their business goals.

Predictive analytics of employee attrition and turnover rates might arguably be one of the most impactful uses of AI in talent retention efforts. This is because AI systems can analyze enormous amounts of structured and unstructured data, ranging from employee demographics and their histories of service to their trends in performance and learning or training engagements, compensation and promotional histories, workload and labor markets outside their respective organizational boundaries. These technologies can thus analyze trends and correlations linked to voluntary and involuntary turnovers and subsequently forecast employees' predispositions to quit their jobs at individual or organizational levels (Căvescu & Popescu, 2025).

Predictive analytics also enables the organization to gauge its group of employees who are at a higher risk of leaving the company by understanding the variables associated with dissatisfaction or discouragement. Career plateaus, lack of skills, lack of recognition, or work overload can be some of the factors that can be recognized as variables with a significant bearing on employees leaving the organization (Krishna & Sidharth, 2023). Nonetheless, it is also germane to note that a responsible use of predictive analytics eliminates any chance of stigmatizing the employees but rather helps in a more conducive work environment for everyone.

AI's significant contribution lies in its ability to transform career pathing as well as talent mobility within an enterprise, which are critical aspects relating to talent retention. In today's corporate environment, workers are increasingly becoming growth-seeking individuals who value career growth as well as skills development through their respective companies. AI's capability to create career path recommendation models relies on their skills, competencies, goals, performance history, as well as their performance behaviour (Mohebianfar, 2025). These systems help in mapping existing positions with the upcoming opportunities, which may require additional training or requisite initiatives.

This helps in the transparent and data-based development of careers through the application of AI. This enables the employee base to own the development of their own careers while maintaining internal workforce vitality. Internal talent marketplaces, enabled through the intelligence of AI systems, make it easier for the organization to bring the right employee into a short-term project or a new role through the application of compatibility and learning opportunities (Allal-Chérif et al., 2021). Additionally, internal workforce vitality contributes to the overall workforce agility through the application of internal movement of the workforce.

From an organizational perspective, this application ensures a sense of diversity, equity, and inclusion within organizations through a reduction in bias when offering career advancement opportunities and assigning roles in favour of AI system-driven promotion based on potential or skill attained in a career pathing system instead of perceptions or hunches. This creates a system where fair talent development practices encourage employee engagement through a sense of trust in such a system. Strategic workforce planning is yet another area where AI-based analytics has much to offer in terms of value creation. Typically, workforce planning has focused primarily on static forecasts and largely depended on historical workforce and budgetary considerations. However, by leveraging AI-based technology, dynamic workforce planning is possible by leveraging internal workforce considerations and blending them with environmental influences and variables (Reddy Yanamala, 2024). These variables are used to forecast future workforce requirements through a variety of scenarios by simulating workforce demand and supply and weighing in factors related to technology and other industry influences that lead to digital workforce transformations.

Strategic workforce planning can better match talent strategy with business and sustainability objectives in an effective manner. This can be done with the use of insights provided by AI, which can establish whether workforce requirements are better achieved through reskilling, redeploying, recruiting, or a combination thereof. This prevents disruption in business continuity and potential workforce changes in a bid to address any talent gaps that may suddenly appear in an enterprise. This can affect an enterprise in an Industry 5.0 setup, especially with a focus on human-centricity and workforce resiliency (Merka, 2025). Moreover, there is AI-enhanced support available for workforce analytics, which can help leadership make important decisions through clear, visual, actionable, and data-driven insights available through advanced dashboards and analytics tools, allowing leaders to monitor, measure, and understand workers' health, risk, and readiness levels, thereby enhancing accountability through HR strategies aligned with business performance.

7. ETHICAL, LEGAL, AND GOVERNANCE ISSUES IN AI-DRIVEN HRM

The use and application of Artificial Intelligence in Human Resource Management: The Human Resource Management domain can be seen as having changed dramatically with respect to what Artificial Intelligence can accomplish with respect to employee recruitment, training, assessment, and employee maintenance, and this in itself can be seen as a central concern and interest with respect to what sort of ethical and legal concerns are brought into play with respect to employee and organizational Human Resource Management systems and processes in an increasingly highly technical and implied sense and scope (Tambe et al., 2019).

However, perhaps one of the greatest challenges faced in ensuring the right kind of ethical considerations in AI-driven HRM involves tackling issues of biased algorithms. It is undeniable that AI learns from data; hence, there exists a potential for social, cultural, or even organizational prejudices to influence these systems (Sachan et al., 2024). Consequently, even though unintentional, there exists a possibility for discrimination based on gender, age, ethnicity, or even economic status in processes such as recruitment, performance management, or even promotion, for instance. AI-driven resume analysis systems may even prioritize applications from profiles associated with successful past employees.

Transparency also furthers ethical and legal compliance by enabling organizations to audit AI systems for bias, accuracy, and consistency. If the HR professional is able to interpret AI-generated insights, they will be better equipped to exercise informed human judgment and contextual understanding. Transparent AI systems allow for meaningful human oversight to ensure that final decisions are not blinded by algorithms (Julien Kiesse Bahangulu & Louis Owusu-Berko, 2025). It's a human-in-the-loop approach that makes sure accountability is present and AI use reflects such values as empathy, fairness, and respect for individual circumstances.

So, under the governance perspective, the regulatory environment plays a crucial role in encouraging responsible AI norms in the field of HRM. Governments are acknowledging the dangers that might accompany using AI in the context of employee relations, and regulations are being implemented that protect the rights of the individual. Data protection regulations, such as the ones related to the processing of personalized data, stipulate strict guidelines regarding the acquisition of consent, minimization of the required data, and the setting of purposes. Employment regulations and anti-discriminatory regulations are also being enforced, irrespective of whether the decisions are made by the human resource systems or by the AI (Bujold et al., 2024).

Besides fulfilling their regulatory commitments, organizations are also encouraged to adopt responsible proactive practices in artificial intelligence. Key responsible proactive practices in artificial intelligence involve the development of ethical artificial intelligence guidelines, the establishment of governance committees to oversee artificial intelligence use in the organizations, and the use of audits in evaluating artificial intelligence. Responsible artificial intelligence practices involve fairness, accountability, transparency, and human-centeredness.

Both training and awareness are of equal importance in the ethical rules of AI management in HR management. HR managers, management, and policymakers should all be made aware of not only the benefits of AI but also of their restrictions. This knowledge of AI is useful for them in effectively using AI for making decisions, not for making decisions by themselves (Sakka & El Hadi El Maknouzi, 2022). Employees must also be made aware of AI management in HR processes, their rights, and feedback.

8. AI, HUMAN CAPITAL AND ORGANIZATIONAL SUSTAINABILITY

Artificial Intelligence has emerged as a strategic factor for human capital management in sustainable organizations in a world defined by technological disruption, ecological concerns, and social responsibility. Organizations should now aspire to achieve economic success alongside social value creation for sustainability. Instead of competing with human resources, Artificial Intelligence has gradually been adopted by modern organizations as a facilitator of human capabilities, innovation, and sustainable organization growth (Ogbeibu et al., 2024).

AI plays a significant role in making a substantial contribution to sustainable talent management by making these processes more efficient and fair and by taking a future-oriented approach to talent management in an organization or enterprise. Sustainable talent management is an approach that focuses mainly on talent attraction, development, and retention in line with organizational viability and sustainability. These organizations can benefit from these predictive analyses and make investments in reskilling and upskilling their workforce, thus avoiding the need for constant external hiring and any disruptions in the workforce (Aina & Atan, 2020).

AI also helps in fostering and ensuring fair and efficient processes in the acquisition and development of talents, or the processes of sustainable Human Resource Management. Intelligent recruitment solutions, for example, use skills and capabilities as filters, ensuring fair treatment of every candidate. AI-powered learning solutions provide personalized learning for enhanced and lifelong learning for the employees, allowing for enhanced employee loyalty and reduced turnover (Akter, 2025). This helps in the sustainability of human capital systems.

Human-AI collaboration is a major paradigm shift in work arrangement and execution. In contemporary organizations, human work is complemented in such a way that technology performs data-intensive, repetitive, and analytical jobs, permitting human labour to be devoted to creativity, problem-solving, emotional intelligence, and critical thinking. For example, decision-support systems make use of AI for giving suggestions or ideas but leave the decision in the hands of humans (X. Zhang & Zhou, 2025). For effective human and AI collaboration, organizational structures and cultures must be adapted and designed toward this collaborative objective with employees and workers who are enabled with appropriate skills and competencies to interact and collaborate with intelligent systems. Training and change programs are highly required to eliminate employee fear and concerns related to technology replacing jobs and to ensure workers embrace AI systems and technologies in a collaborative culture with a sense of acceptance and partnership with intelligent systems (Li & Tian, 2025). A collaborative culture between employees and intelligent machines facilitates a human-centric approach toward Industry 5.0, where machines and technology are designed to ensure human and social welfare.

AI plays a critical role in developing robust organizations with respect to disruptions, such as economic fluctuations, technology, and global crises. This relates to a strong workforce, which entails elements of adaptability, learning, and allocation of resources. Artificial intelligence with workforce analytics allows organizations to develop an ability to simulate and monitor multiple workforce scenarios, forecasting, and reacting positively to disruptions. Furthermore, by recognizing key skill and job requirements, AI can also facilitate succession planning and talent continuity in an organization in case of an unexpected loss of talent (Rane et al., 2021). Additionally, remote work technologies and digital collaboration tools facilitated by AI are also allowing organizational flexibility.

However, the impact of AI on sustainability is heavily reliant on the implementation of ethical considerations of AI. In addition, there is algorithm bias, non-transparency, as well as over-automation, which would impact the effectiveness of AI if not handled adequately. Therefore, an ethical organizational framework in which AI principles are incorporated is crucial in a way that involves responsibilities and considerations of fairness, transparency, and accountability within an organizational context where autonomous and independent representation are possible through various stakeholders in an organization (Camilleri, 2024).

9. FUTURE TRENDS IN AI-ENABLED TALENT MANAGEMENT

The future trend in AI for talent management will be a move beyond efficiency-driven technological innovation toward intelligence that can augment human judgment, understanding of emotions, and responsible decision-making. As firms operate within more complex environments that have a strong focus on humans, the use of AI will move beyond its transactional focus toward a more strategic alliance for decision-making processes, employee experience, and human capital cultivation (Hembram, 2025). It will be facilitated by generative AI, emotion awareness, and human-centric ethical AI models.

Generative AI technologies are transforming human resource decision support systems into more advanced tools permitting deeper analysis and generation techniques. While previous decision support systems employed a rule-based approach to decision-making, generative AI holds the capability to synthesize vast amounts of data in both structured and unstructured formats in a bid to provide decision-makers with contextual supports and suggestions. In this regard, a successful application area will include workforce, learning, and policy management in general settings (Budhwar et al., 2023).

Emotion-aware AI and affective computing is another important technicolor trend in AI-powered talent management. Emotion-aware AI and affective computing help in recognizing and even understanding, and, in some cases, responding to the subtle intricacies of the emotional domain with the help of information inputs derived from sources such as facial compositions, auditory tones, text analytics, and behavioural patterns. Emotion-aware AI, in the domain of human resources, can play important roles in improving the engagement and overall satisfaction of employees as well as the leadership capabilities of managers (Singh et al., 2024). For example, emotion-aware AI in the domain of employee engagement can help in recognizing the overall morale and moods of the employees with the help of text analytics.

The future directions of AI application in HRM increasingly embrace human-centrism and ethical considerations. AI is increasingly having a substantial influence on employment decisions, and organizations have come to realize that these human-centered and ethical attributes of AI application cannot be overlooked. Human-centered AI, for instance, focuses on the extent to which AI, when used, helps to build upon human abilities and does not, in fact, replace human attributes.

10. IMPLICATIONS FOR HR PROFESSIONAL AND ORGANIZATIONAL LEADERS

The integration of AI into Human Resource Management has far-reaching effects on how Human Resource practitioners and Management operate. As AI continues to alter various aspects of Human Resources Management, from talent management and employee learning to talent management and experience, HR Management cannot only continue to exist as a supportive department in any organization. Rather, in order to create and deliver additional strategic capabilities and successful change management practices within AI-based organizations, there is a need to rethink and redefine conceptions of Human Resources Management.

In order to develop AI-ready HR functions, HR professionals have to build strategic capabilities that include both technical and human understandings. In this respect, a critical requirement here is to develop Data & AI Literacy. This means that HR professionals have to understand how AI works and have to develop critical thinking abilities to realize the various applications and limitations of AI. This does not mean that HR professionals have to turn into Data Scientists. However, they have to understand ways to leverage AI correctly. Strategic thinking skills are also equally important, as thorough efforts are to be made by the HR leaders in integrating the AI programs into the organization's objectives, workforce strategy, aims as far as sustainability is concerned, etc. Ethical judgment skills, stakeholder communication, etc., in cooperation with IT leaders, business leaders, etc., are important for an AI-enabled HR leadership role (Kravchuk, 2026).

Change management for the introduction of AI in HR activities is often viewed as a challenge to address by the management of the organization. Generally, people resist the introduction of AI because of fear of being rendered unemployed or lack of autonomy in addressing their concerns regarding data privacy or perceived unfair treatment. It is important to conduct successful change management by being clear with people regarding undertaking AI activities by being very clear on data privacy or being clear with people regarding the benefits of undertaking AI activities in the organization (Priyanghaa, 2025). It is also important for the management to inculcate a sense of learning in the minds of people by undertaking training or reskilling activities in relation to AI activities.

As AI becomes embedded in many HR processes, traditional HR roles will increasingly be redefined. Routine administrative tasks such as data entry, scheduling, and basic reporting will continue to be automated, freeing HR professionals to play a more strategic and relational role. Traditional HR roles are now consolidating into the role of workforce strategist, talent architect, employee experience designer, and ethical steward of AI use. In this AI-augmented organization, the work of HR professionals involves interpreting AI insights by applying contextual understanding, so that decisions reflect organizational values and human consideration (Masaeid et al., 2025).

11. CONCLUSION

The future of Artificial Intelligence in Human Resource Management and talent management will portray a new horizon in understanding, developing, and engaging human resources in a new dimension. In terms of what is expected within AI in HRM in the future, it would be characterized by deeper integration, intelligence, and alignment with human-centric values. Through its ability in terms of data analysis and generative AI, there would be more informed and timely decisions that would enable individuals in charge of HRM to not just anticipate talent management and its integration but enable a more personalized employee experience in terms of talent and learning. Furthermore, there would be a more constant feedback and learning process that would align with specific changes within an organization (Fenwick et al., 2024).

At the same time, the increasing salience of AI in the HRM function underlines the growing importance of ethical governance and responsible elaboration. The challenges related to algorithmic bias, transparency, data protection, and accountability would remain crucial. The way forward is that organizations should integrate ethical considerations into the design and implementation of AI systems so as to make the latter ensure fairness, inclusiveness, and respect for the dignity of their employees. Human intervention and explainable AI will be required as a means of maintaining trust and legitimacy in AI-driven HR decisions with a view to underscoring the technological enhancement of, not replacement for, human judgment (Bubicz & Ferasso, 2024).

This future of AI in talent management is also interlinked with the evolution of work and the view of human-AI collaboration. As automation redefines job roles, the focus will also be on uniquely human capabilities like creativity, empathy, critical thinking, and ethical reasoning. AI will support these capabilities by executing data-intensive tasks, decision support, and making continuous reskilling possible (Dumitru & Halpern, 2023). In conclusion, the road to the future of AI in HRM and talent management is characterized by wide opportunities for AI to create the conditions for HRM to become a remarkable force for unleashing the potential for sustainability in humans. By leveraging the potential for the use of 'human-centric AI,' organizations should engage in continuous learning and create conditions for the use of AI as a force for the development of smart and enlightened approaches to talent management.

REFERENCES

Akter, S. (2025). AI's Impact on Talent Acquisition Strategies and Employee Engagement Methodologies: Ethical Considerations for Trustworthy AI-HRM Integration. *Journal of Humanities and Social Sciences Studies, 7*(8), 44–51. DOI: 10.32996/jhsss.2025.7.8.6

Al Aina, R., & Atan, T. (2020). The impact of implementing talent management practices on sustainable organizational performance. *Sustainability (Basel), 12*(20), 1–21. DOI: 10.3390/su12208372

Al Masaeid, T., Alkhalidi, M. M., Al Ali, A. A. A., Almaazmi, S. M. G. A., & Alami, R. (2025). Artificial Intelligence-Augmented Decision-Making: Examining the Interplay Between Machine Learning Algorithms and Human Judgment in Organizational Leadership. *Journal of Ecohumanism, 4*(1), 4683–4699. DOI: 10.62754/joe.v4i1.6364

Allal-Chérif, O., Yela Aránega, A., & Castaño Sánchez, R. (2021). Intelligent recruitment: How to identify, select, and retain talents from around the world using artificial intelligence. *Technological Forecasting and Social Change, 169*(April), 120822. Advance online publication. DOI: 10.1016/j.techfore.2021.120822

Bahangulu, J. K., & Owusu-Berko, L. (2025). Algorithmic bias, data ethics, and governance: Ensuring fairness, transparency and compliance in AI-powered business analytics applications. *World Journal of Advanced Research and Reviews, 25*(2), 1746–1763. DOI: 10.30574/wjarr.2025.25.2.0571

Bubicz, M., & Ferasso, M. (2024). Advancing Corporate Social Responsibility in AI-Driven Human Resources Management: A Maturity Model Approach. *Proceedings of the 4th International Conference on AI Research, ICAIR 2024*, 82–90. DOI: 10.34190/icair.4.1.3016

Budhwar, P., Chowdhury, S., Wood, G., Aguinis, H., Bamber, G. J., Beltran, J. R., Boselie, P., Lee Cooke, F., Decker, S., DeNisi, A., Dey, P. K., Guest, D., Knoblich, A. J., Malik, A., Paauwe, J., Papagiannidis, S., Patel, C., Pereira, V., Ren, S., & Varma, A. (2023). Human resource management in the age of generative artificial intelligence: Perspectives and research directions on ChatGPT. *Human Resource Management Journal, 33*(3), 606–659. DOI: 10.1111/1748-8583.12524

Budhwar, P., Malik, A., De Silva, M. T. T., & Thevisuthan, P. (2022). Artificial intelligence–challenges and opportunities for international HRM: A review and research agenda. *International Journal of Human Resource Management, 33*(6), 1065–1097. DOI: 10.1080/09585192.2022.2035161

Bujold, A., Roberge-Maltais, I., Parent-Rocheleau, X., Boasen, J., Sénécal, S., & Léger, P.-M. (2024). Responsible artificial intelligence in human resources management: A review of the empirical literature. *AI and Ethics*, *4*(4), 1185–1200. DOI: 10.1007/s43681-023-00325-1

Camilleri, M. A. (2024). Artificial intelligence governance: Ethical considerations and implications for social responsibility. *Expert Systems: International Journal of Knowledge Engineering and Neural Networks*, *41*(7), 1–15. DOI: 10.1111/exsy.13406

Căvescu, A. M., & Popescu, N. (2025). Predictive Analytics in Human Resources Management: Evaluating AIHR's Role in Talent Retention. *AppliedMath*, *5*(3), 99. Advance online publication. DOI: 10.3390/appliedmath5030099

Chen, Z. (2023). Collaboration among recruiters and artificial intelligence: Removing human prejudices in employment. *Cognition Technology and Work*, *25*(1), 135–149. DOI: 10.1007/s10111-022-00716-0 PMID: 36187287

Cheng, L., Varshney, K. R., & Liu, H. (2021). Socially responsible AI algorithms: Issues, purposes, and challenges. *Journal of Artificial Intelligence Research*, *71*, 1137–1181. DOI: 10.1613/jair.1.12814

Chhibber, S., Rajkumar, S. R., & Dassanayake, S. (2025). Will Artificial Intelligence Reshape the Global Workforce by 2030? A Cross-Sectoral Analysis of Job Displacement and Transformation. *Blockchain, Artificial Intelligence, and Future Research*, *1*(1), 35–51. DOI: 10.70211/bafr.v1i1.178

Cinar, A. B., & Bilodeau, S. (2024). Incorporating AI into the Inner Circle of Emotional Intelligence for Sustainability. *Sustainability (Basel)*, *16*(15), 1–17. DOI: 10.3390/su16156648

Coenen, M., & Kok, R. A. W. (2014). Workplace flexibility and new product development performance: The role of telework and flexible work schedules. *European Management Journal*, *32*(4), 564–576. DOI: 10.1016/j.emj.2013.12.003

Cramarenco, R. E., Burcă-Voicu, M. I., & Dabija, D. C. (2023). The impact of artificial intelligence (AI) on employees' skills and well-being in global labor markets: A systematic review. *Oeconomia Copernicana*, *14*(3), 731–767. DOI: 10.24136/oc.2023.022

Dumitru, D., & Halpern, D. F. (2023). Critical Thinking: Creating Job-Proof Skills for the Future of Work. *Journal of Intelligence*, *11*(10), 194. Advance online publication. DOI: 10.3390/jintelligence11100194 PMID: 37888426

Dwianto, A., Kusuma, S., & Junengsih, . (2024). Artificial Intelligence in Performance Evaluation (Case Study of PT. Pos Indonesia Employees). *Bit-Tech*, *7*(2), 348–356. DOI: 10.32877/bt.v7i2.1817

Fenwick, A., Molnar, G., & Frangos, P. (2024). The critical role of HRM in AI-driven digital transformation: A paradigm shift to enable firms to move from AI implementation to human-centric adoption. *Discover Artificial Intelligence*, *4*(1), 34. Advance online publication. DOI: 10.1007/s44163-024-00125-4

Gómez Gandía, J. A., Gavrila Gavrila, S., de Lucas Ancillo, A., & del Val Núñez, M. T. (2024). RPA as a Challenge Beyond Technology: Self-Learning and Attitude Needed for Successful RPA Implementation in the Workplace. *Journal of the Knowledge Economy*, *15*(4), 19628–19655. DOI: 10.1007/s13132-024-01865-5

Hembram, R. (2025). The Future of HR in Academia: A Case Study on AI-Driven HRM and Emotional Intelligence in Berhampur Institutions. *SSRN*, *5216958*, •••. https://papers.ssrn.com/sol3/papers.cfm?abstract_id=5216958%0Ahttps://papers.ssrn.com/sol3/Delivery.cfm?abstractid=5216958

Hmoud, B., & Laszlo, V. (2019). Will artificial intelligence take over human resources recruitment and selection? *Network Intelligence Studies*, *13*(1), 21–30.

Hunkenschroer, A. L., & Luetge, C. (2022). Ethics of AI-Enabled Recruiting and Selection: A Review and Research Agenda. In *Journal of Business Ethics* (Vol. 178, Issue 4). Springer Netherlands. DOI: 10.1007/s10551-022-05049-6

Jacob Fernandes França, T., São Mamede, H., Pereira Barroso, J. M., & Pereira Duarte dos Santos, V. M. (2023). Artificial intelligence applied to potential assessment and talent identification in an organisational context. *Heliyon*, *9*(4), e14694. Advance online publication. DOI: 10.1016/j.heliyon.2023.e14694 PMID: 37035361

Jarrahi, M. H. (2018). Artificial intelligence and the future of work: Human-AI symbiosis in organizational decision making. *Business Horizons*, *61*(4), 577–586. DOI: 10.1016/j.bushor.2018.03.007

Javed, R. T., Nasir, O., Borit, M., Vanhée, L., Zea, E., Gupta, S., Vinuesa, R., & Qadir, J. (2023). Get Out of the BAG! Silos in AI Ethics Education: Unsupervised Topic Modeling Analysis of Global AI Curricula (Extended Abstract). *IJCAI International Joint Conference on Artificial Intelligence, 2023-Augus*, 6905–6909. DOI: 10.24963/ijcai.2023/780

Johnson, M., Jain, R., Brennan-Tonetta, P., Swartz, E., Silver, D., Paolini, J., Mamonov, S., & Hill, C. (2021). Impact of Big Data and Artificial Intelligence on Industry: Developing a Workforce Roadmap for a Data Driven Economy. *Global Journal of Flexible Systems Managment, 22*(3), 197–217. DOI: 10.1007/s40171-021-00272-y

Johnson, R. D., Lukaszewski, K. M., & Stone, D. L. (2016). The evolution of the field of human resource information systems: Co-Evolution of technology and HR processes. *Communications of the Association for Information Systems, 38*(1), 533–553. DOI: 10.17705/1CAIS.03828

Kassab, K., & Kashevnik, A. (2024). Personality Traits Estimation Based on Job Interview Video Analysis: Importance of Human Nonverbal Cues Detection. *Big Data and Cognitive Computing, 8*(12), 173. Advance online publication. DOI: 10.3390/bdcc8120173

Kravchuk, O. (2026). *Human-centric digital leadership for HRM 5 . 0 ecosystem readiness*. 55–85.

Krishna, S., & Sidharth, S. (2023). AI-Powered Workforce Analytics: Maximizing Business and Employee Success through Predictive Attrition Modelling. *International Journal of Performability Engineering, 19*(3), 203–215. DOI: 10.23940/ijpe.23.03.p6.203215

Kulkov, I., Kulkova, J., Rohrbeck, R., Menvielle, L., Kaartemo, V., & Makkonen, H. (2024). Artificial intelligence - driven sustainable development: Examining organizational, technical, and processing approaches to achieving global goals. *Sustainable Development (Bradford), 32*(3), 2253–2267. DOI: 10.1002/sd.2773

Li, H., & Tian, F. (2025). Advancing Decision-Making through AI-Human Collaboration : A Systematic Review and Conceptual Framework. *Research Square (Research Square)*, 1–29. DOI: 10.21203/rs.3.rs-6885768/v1

Lou, B., Lu, T., Raghu, T. S., & Zhang, Y. (2025). *Unraveling Human-AI Teaming: A Review and Outlook*. https://arxiv.org/abs/2504.05755 DOI: 10.2139/ssrn.5211067

Luo, J. (2022). A Bibliometric Review on Artificial Intelligence for Smart Buildings. *Sustainability (Basel), 14*(16), 10230. Advance online publication. DOI: 10.3390/su141610230

Maghsoudi, M., Kamrani Shahri, M., Agha Mohammad Ali Kermani, M., & Khanizad, R. (2025). Mapping the Landscape of AI-Driven Human Resource Management: A Social Network Analysis of Research Collaboration. *IEEE Access : Practical Innovations, Open Solutions, 13*(January), 3090–3114. DOI: 10.1109/ACCESS.2024.3523437

Magnisalis, I., Demetriadis, S., & Karakostas, A. (2011). Adaptive and intelligent systems for collaborative learning support: A review of the field. *IEEE Transactions on Learning Technologies, 4*(1), 5–20. DOI: 10.1109/TLT.2011.2

Majumder, S., & Mondal, A. (2021). Are chatbots really useful for human resource management? *International Journal of Speech Technology, 24*(4), 969–977. DOI: 10.1007/s10772-021-09834-y

Martini, B., Bellisario, D., & Coletti, P. (2024). Human-Centered and Sustainable Artificial Intelligence in Industry 5.0: Challenges and Perspectives. *Sustainability (Basel), 16*(13), 5448. Advance online publication. DOI: 10.3390/su16135448

Merka, I. P. (2025). *Strategic Alignment of GHRM Practices The Impact of Recruiting and Retaining Green Talent on Organisational Sustainability and Competitiveness.* Metropolia University of Applied Sciences.

Mohebianfar, E. (2025). *An AI-driven approach to improve talent retention and mobility. April.* https://www.theseus.fi/handle/10024/883116%0Ahttps://www.theseus.fi/bitstream/handle/10024/883116/Mohebianfar_Ehsan.pdf?sequence=2

Mposula, F., & Oyetade, K. (2025). Enhancing Programming Education through Game-Based Learning for Improved Engagement and Learning Outcomes. *Educational Process International Journal, 19*(1). Advance online publication. DOI: 10.22521/edupij.2025.19.558

Murtaza, M., Ahmed, Y., Shamsi, J. A., Sherwani, F., & Usman, M. (2022). AI-Based Personalized E-Learning Systems: Issues, Challenges, and Solutions. *IEEE Access : Practical Innovations, Open Solutions, 10*(June), 81323–81342. DOI: 10.1109/ACCESS.2022.3193938

Murugesan, U., Subramanian, P., Srivastava, S., & Dwivedi, A. (2023). A study of Artificial Intelligence impacts on Human Resource Digitalization in Industry 4.0. *Decision Analytics Journal, 7*(April), 100249. DOI: 10.1016/j.dajour.2023.100249

Nawaz, N., & Gomes, A. M. (2019). Artificial intelligence chatbots are new recruiters. *International Journal of Advanced Computer Science and Applications, 10*(9), 1–5. DOI: 10.14569/IJACSA.2019.0100901

Nocker, M., & Sena, V. (2019). Big data and human resources management: The rise of talent analytics. *Social Sciences (Basel, Switzerland), 8*(10), 1–19. DOI: 10.3390/socsci8100273

Nyathani, R. (2022). Integration of Industry 4.0 and Human Resources: Evolving Human Capital Management and Employee Experience through Digital Innovations. [IJSR]. *International Journal of Science and Research (Raipur, India), 11*(9), 1228–1232. DOI: 10.21275/SR231014134101

Ogbeibu, S., Emelifeonwu, J., Pereira, V., Oseghale, R., Gaskin, J., Sivarajah, U., & Gunasekaran, A. (2024). Demystifying the roles of organisational smart technology, artificial intelligence, robotics and algorithms capability: A strategy for green human resource management and environmental sustainability. *Business Strategy and the Environment, 33*(2), 369–388. DOI: 10.1002/bse.3495

Okeyika, K. O., Ibeto, V. C., Okere, A. I., & Umoh, B. (2023). The Application of Artificial Intelligence (AI) in Human Resource Management: Current State of AI and Its Impact on the Traditional Recruiting Process. *African Journal of Contemporary Research, 4*(3), 2023. DOI: 10.13140/RG.2.2.25435.54567

Paigude, S., Pangarkar, S. C., Hundekari, S., Mali, M., Wanjale, K., & Dongre, Y. (2023). Potential of Artificial Intelligence in Boosting Employee Retention in the Human Resource Industry. *International Journal on Recent and Innovation Trends in Computing and Communication, 11*(December 2022), 1–10. DOI: 10.17762/ijritcc.v11i3s.6149

Pawar, S., & Dhumal, V. (2024). The role of technology in transforming leadership management practices. *Multidisciplinary Reviews, 7*(4), 2024066. Advance online publication. DOI: 10.31893/multirev.2024066

Peng, H., Ma, S., & Spector, J. M. (2019). Personalized Adaptive Learning: An Emerging Pedagogical Approach Enabled by a Smart Learning Environment. *Lecture Notes in Educational Technology*, 171–176. DOI: 10.1007/978-981-13-6908-7_24

Priyanghaa, M. (2025). AI Adoption in HR: Resistance, Readiness, and the Role of Change Management. *Journal of Marketing & Social Research, 08*, 104–110. DOI: 10.61336/jmsr/25-08-10

Qin, C., Zhang, L., Cheng, Y., Zha, R., Shen, D., Zhang, Q., Chen, X., Sun, Y., Zhu, C., Zhu, H., & Xiong, H. (2025). A Comprehensive Survey of Artificial Intelligence Techniques for Talent Analytics. *Proceedings of the IEEE, 113*(2), 125–171. DOI: 10.1109/JPROC.2025.3572744

Ramachandran, K. K., Apsara Saleth Mary, A., Hawladar, S., Asokk, D., Bhaskar, B., & Pitroda, J. R. (2022). Machine learning and role of artificial intelligence in optimizing work performance and employee behavior. *Materials Today: Proceedings, 51*, 2327–2331. DOI: 10.1016/j.matpr.2021.11.544

Rane, N. L., Choudhary, S. P., & Rane, J. (2021). Artificial intelligence for enhancing resilience. *MRS Bulletin*, *46*(11), 1014–1015. DOI: 10.1557/s43577-021-00215-z

Rao, S., Chitranshi, J., & Punjabi, N. (2020). Role of Artificial Intelligence in Employee Engagement and Retention. *Journal of Applied Management - Jidnyasa*, *12*(2), 42–60.

Ravichandran, N., Chowdary Inaganti, A., & Muppalaneni, R. (2023). AI-Driven Sentiment Analysis for Employee Engagement and Retention. *Journal of Computing Innovations and Applications*, *1*(1), 1–9.

Reddy Yanamala, K. K. (2024). Strategic Implications of AI Integration in Workforce Planning and Talent Forecasting. *Journal of Advanced Computing Systems*, *4*(1), 1–9. DOI: 10.69987/JACS.2024.40101

Rosca, C. M., & Stancu, A. (2024). Fusing Machine Learning and AI to Create a Framework for Employee Well-Being in the Era of Industry 5.0. *Applied Sciences (Basel, Switzerland)*, *14*(23), 10835. Advance online publication. DOI: 10.3390/app142310835

Rousseau, D. M., & Barends, E. G. R. (2011). Becoming an evidence-based HR practitioner. *Human Resource Management Journal*, *21*(3), 221–235. DOI: 10.1111/j.1748-8583.2011.00173.x

Sachan, V. S., Katiyar, A. C. S., Chauhan, A. S., & Bhima, C. K.Dr. Satender Khatri. (2024). The Role of Artificial Intelligence in Healthcare: Applications, Challenges, and Ethical Considerations. *Educational Administration: Theory and Practice*, *15*(3), 195–202. DOI: 10.36676/jrps.v15.i3.1471

Sahlin, J., & Angelis, J. (2019). Performance management systems: Reviewing the rise of dynamics and digitalization. *Cogent Business & Management*, *6*(1), 1642293. Advance online publication. DOI: 10.1080/23311975.2019.1642293

Sakka, F., & El Hadi El Maknouzi, M. (2022). Human Resource Management in the Era of Artificial Intelligence: Future Hr Work Practices, Anticipated Skill Set, Financial and Legal Implications. *Academy of Strategic Management Journal*, *21*(S1), 1–14.

Singh, A. P., Saxena, R., & Saxena, S. (2024). The Human Touch in the Age of Artificial Intelligence: A Literature Review on the Interplay of Emotional Intelligence and AI. *Asian Journal of Current Research*, *9*(4), 36–50. DOI: 10.56557/ajocr/2024/v9i48860

Singh Sidhu, G., Sayem, M. A., Taslima, N., Anwar, A. S., Chowdhury, F., & Rowshon, M. (2024). Ai and Workforce Development: A Comparative Analysis of Skill Gaps and Training Needs in Emerging Economies. *International Journal of Business and Management Sciences, 04*(08), 12–28. DOI: 10.55640/ijbms-04-08-03

Starecek, A., Babelova, Z. G., & Vranakova, N. (2025). Development of Human Resource Management Due to Technological, Social, and Legal Changes: Editorial for the Special Issue "New Challenges and Directions in the Development of Human Resource Management.". *Administrative Sciences, 15*(11), 438. Advance online publication. DOI: 10.3390/admsci15110438

Sundari, S., Silalahi, V. A. J. M., Wardani, F. P., Siahaan, R. S., Sacha, S., Krismayanti, Y., & Anjarsari, N. (2024). Artificial Intelligence (AI) and Automation in Human Resources : Shifting the Focus from Routine Tasks to Strategic Initiatives for Improved Employee Engagement. *East Asian Journal of Multidisciplinary Research, 3*(10), 4983–4996. DOI: 10.55927/eajmr.v3i10.11758

Tambe, P., Cappelli, P., & Yakubovich, V. (2019). Artificial intelligence in human resources management: Challenges and A path forward. *California Management Review, 61*(4), 15–42. DOI: 10.1177/0008125619867910

Vishwanath, B., & Vaddepalli, S. (2023). The future of work: Implications of artificial intelligence on hr practices. Tuijin Jishu/Journal of Propulsion Technology, 44(3), 1711-1724.

Vrontis, D., Chaudhuri, R., & Chatterjee, S. (2023). Role of ChatGPT and Skilled Workers for Business Sustainability: Leadership Motivation as the Moderator. *Sustainability (Basel), 15*(16), 12196. Advance online publication. DOI: 10.3390/su151612196

Wu, S., Cao, Y., Cui, J., Li, R., Qian, H., Jiang, B., & Zhang, W. (2024). *A Comprehensive Exploration of Personalized Learning in Smart Education: From Student Modeling to Personalized Recommendations. 0*(0), 1–61. https://arxiv.org/abs/2402.01666

Zhang, J., & Chen, Z. (2024). Exploring Human Resource Management Digital Transformation in the Digital Age. *Journal of the Knowledge Economy, 15*(1), 1482–1498. DOI: 10.1007/s13132-023-01214-y PMID: 40479358

Zhang, X., & Zhou, Y. (2025). Human-AI Collaboration. *Paradigm Shifts in Technology-Mediated Design., 2*(2), 1–9.

Zhou, L., Paul, S., Demirkan, H., Yuan, L., Spohrer, J., Zhou, M., & Basu, J. (2021). Intelligence Augmentation: Towards Building Human-Machine Symbiotic Relationship. *AIS Transactions on Human-Computer Interaction, 13*(2), 243–264. DOI: 10.17705/1thci.00149

Chapter 8
Human-AI Collaboration in HRM:
Leveraging the HAC Model to Promote Employee Well-Being in AI-Enabled Indian IT Workplaces

R. Nalini
http://orcid.org/0000-0003-3033-8945
SASTRA (Deemed to be) University, India

R. Amudha
SASTRA (Deemed to be) University, India

Vijayabanu Chidambaram
http://orcid.org/0000-0002-0125-4534
Shiv Nadar University, India

R. Gayathri
http://orcid.org/0000-0001-9406-0191
SASTRA (Deemed to be) University, India

ABSTRACT

The goal of Human-AI collaboration within the HRM field is to combine artificial intelligence (AI) technologies with the capabilities of people to create enhanced decision-making and worker support mechanisms, using AI-enabled workplaces in the Indian IT sector, as an illustration. A recent framework, called the HAC model, suggests that HWACs can successfully integrate human resources and artificial

DOI: 10.4018/979-8-2600-2541-3.ch008

intelligence-based technologies through a hybrid approach to talent management, recruitment, and employee well-being via data analytics and ethical AI-based policies/procedures.

1. INTRODUCTION

In the current state of extremely volatile and technology-intensive business environments, organisations are witnessing an unprecedented integration of digital disruptions, economic uncertainties, global challenges, and shifting workforce expectations. These dynamics are radically transforming the paradigm of work and forcing leaders to re-evaluate conventional fundamentals of organisational sustainability.

The widespread adoption of Artificial Intelligence (AI) in organisational frameworks has radically transformed Human Resource Management (HRM) practices, especially in the knowledge-driven industry category like the Indian Information Technology (IT) sector. The Indian IT industry, represented by companies like Tata Consultancy Services, Infosys, and Wipro, is marked by high-performance demands, global project deadlines, fast-paced technological changes, and technology-enabled work environments.

In this rapidly changing landscape, employee well-being has emerged as both a strategic imperative and a managerial challenge. Conventional HR practices, heavily reliant on human oversight and social support, are increasingly complemented by AI-enabled solutions like AI Recruitment Analytics, Performance Management Dashboards, Chatbots for Employee Inquiries, Predictive Attrition Models, and AI-Powered Wellness Monitoring Systems. However, technology adoption by itself does not necessarily lead to better well-being outcomes. The answer lies in Human-AI Collaboration (HAC), a complementary framework in which AI supports human judgment, rather than replacing it.

2. BACKGROUND OF THE STUDY (HUMAN–AI COLLABORATION (HAC) MODEL IN HRM)

The Human–AI Collaboration (HAC) Model in Human Resource Management (HRM) conceptualises AI not as a substitute for human decision-makers but as an augmentative tool that improves human judgment, relationship-building, and strategic workforce management. The current literature on HRM increasingly suggests that AI-driven systems such as predictive analytics, machine learning recruitment software, AI-powered performance management dashboards, and HR chatbots are transforming the people management architecture by automating mundane tasks and facilitating data-driven decision-making (Strohmeier, 2022; Margherita, 2021). However, empirical research indicates that technological efficiency gains do not necessarily lead to better employee outcomes unless complemented with human empathy, ethical guidance, and social support. The HAC model, therefore, suggests a complementary framework where AI systems handle analytical, predictive, and repetitive tasks, and human managers handle contextual understanding, emotional intelligence, fairness perceptions, and developmental counselling.

From a JD-R perspective, AI represents a technological job resource that mitigates cognitive overload and improves information accessibility, thus enhancing the motivational process and overall engagement. For instance, AI-based feedback systems enable employees to have constant performance feedback, thus improving clarity and autonomy, which are identified as important job resources in JD-R studies. At the same time, the JD-R model is consistent with the Conservation of Resources theory, which proposes that people work towards accumulating and safeguarding resources. In AI-based HRM contexts, predictive analytics can help detect potential burnout, optimise workload distribution, and enable timely interventions to prevent resource depletion cycles. Moreover, from a Social Exchange Theory perspective, HAC enhances perceptions of organisational support when AI systems are transparent and development-oriented. Employees are more likely to respond with engagement and commitment when they perceive AI tools as supportive rather than monitoring devices.

Recent literature on digital HRM transformation emphasises that the integration of AI in HRM requires "human-in-the-loop" governance frameworks that ensure accountability and fairness in algorithmic decision-making. In the Indian IT sector, which is dominated by young, digitally savvy employees and project-based work arrangements, the HAC model is highly applicable. It connects technology advancement with psychological well-being by integrating AI with supportive HR environments. Therefore, the HAC model in HRM signifies a transition from the conventional personnel management administration to a smart, cooperative, and human-centric people management approach that encourages resilience, engagement, and sustainable employee well-being.

3. LITERATURE REVIEW

The integration of Artificial Intelligence (AI) in Human Resource Management (HRM) has moved from the automation of processes to a more complex socio-technical process where AI supports and supplements human resources rather than replacing them. Recent literature on the topic suggests that AI has the potential to improve HR-related activities such as recruitment, performance management, and learning and development, but the success of such initiatives is dependent on the effective collaboration of humans and AI (Hridoy et al., 2025). The use of interactive systems such as machine learning, chatbots, and natural language processing can improve decision-making and minimize bias in HR-related activities if they are properly integrated with organizational culture and human resources.

A multilevel analysis of AI and employee well-being shows that human-AI collaboration is effective in achieving positive results when the design of AI systems focuses on complementing human capabilities, judgment, and decision-making rather than operating independently (Sadeghi, 2024; Braganza et al., 2020; Bankins et al., 2023). These studies emphasise that the presence of supportive cultures, ethical management, and opportunities for employee engagement in organisational settings facilitates more effective human-AI collaboration and results in better well-being outcomes. Open communication about the role of AI, opportunities for employee engagement with AI management, and trust in AI technology are identified as key facilitators of positive well-being outcomes.

Within the empirical literature, the relationship and psychological factors involved in integrating artificial intelligence also have been highlighted. One example found within the literature involving empathy and human resource management using AI is that when employees perceive a particular AI system to be sympathetic and supportive, they tend to increase their level of job satisfaction and engagement, which leads to decreased turnover intentions and overall increased performance (Ali & Pitafi, 2025). Related studies in the Indian scenario indicate that although the adoption of AI technology can improve the efficiency of operations and employee satisfaction in the IT sector, excessive dependence on AI technology without human oversight may lead to a reduction in empathy and judgment, thereby necessitating the development of hybrid HR models that incorporate human discretion (Moon, 2025).

Systematic reviews of AI's application to tracking the deployment of personalized well-being programs, mental health monitoring, and identifying psychosocial risk factors will be considered within employee well-being. These applications can improve well-being if ethical and empathetic design principles are followed (MDPI Workplace Well-Being Review, 2023). On the other hand, research indicates that when AI is designed and deployed with a lack of transparency around their application, there are concerns such as job insecurity, fairness, and privacy violations that can adversely impact the workplace (Sadeghi, 2024).

According to the Global Workplace Study 2020 from the ADP Research Institute, quoted in a presentation by (ADP Research Institute, 2020) India ranked one of the top-ranked nations worldwide for workplace resilience, with 32 percent of India's workforce claiming to be highly resilient, compared to the global average of 15 percent. In addition, 20 percent of India's workforce claims to be engaged at the highest level, which is well above the global average of 14 percent, making them among the most resilient and engaged workforces across the globe. Barends et al. (2021) state that employee resilience enables employees to preserve and replenish workplace resources with minimal losses that can lead to worker stress, emotional exhaustion, and ultimately, burnout. The authors' findings indicated that self-protective resources like self-efficacy, optimism, and a sense of work-related coherence (as well as social resources such as support from coworkers and quality interactions with leaders/members) significantly predict an employee's ability to be resilient. Additionally, employees who demonstrate resilience tend to exhibit positive work attitudes and behaviours including the following: proactive behaviour, creativity, commitment to change, organisational citizenship (OCB), and job satisfaction.

By reviewing the study by (Kašpárková et al., 2018), it shows that when employees are satisfied with their jobs, they can build resilience, which can lead to increased productivity. Employees are more likely to form strong relationships at work. This creates a positive work environment and can improve job security. When employees have opportunities for growth and a sense of belonging in their workplace, they develop a connection to their organization or group. Ultimately, this helps them succeed at work (Abdullahi et al., 2023, Hartwig et al., 2020).

Establishing a link between workplace opportunities and employee experience, High Performance Work Systems (HPWS) create an environment that helps employees build resilience. There is a positive connection between HPWS and service performance as well as organisational citizenship behaviour (OCB) in an employee's work life. An employee's engagement is further improved through feeling connected with others at work (Nadeem et al. 2019, Naswall et al. 2019).

The connection between assessing workplace resilience and previously established measurement tools like the Connor-Davidson Resilience Scale (CD-RISC), the Resilience Scale (RS-14), and the Employee Resilience Scale (ERS) gives confidence in the reliability of these measurements for determining workplace resilience (Naswall et al. 2019). Additionally, future researchers studying workplace resilience can use these established tools to support their hypotheses in information technology and other knowledge-based industries.

Research supports the positive impact of employee engagement on organizational performance. (Linggiallo et al., 2021) studied Mahakam, Indonesia's (Persero) Power Generation Unit and found that job satisfaction and personality positively influenced employee engagement, while motivation did not have any effect. In addition, employee engagement had a direct impact on organizational commitment and performance. Gallup's report (Harter, 2021) also highlighted engagement challenges, revealing that only 39% of U.S. employees are engaged, while 14% are actively disengaged, indicating significant potential for improvement.

In the Vietnamese setting, Dinh (2020) showed that work-life balance played a role in connecting working conditions and employee engagement. Supervisory support affected work-related stress, which in turn influenced the link between supervisory support and engagement. This highlights the importance of supportive environments and stress management for boosting engagement. Dewi et al. (2020) found that perceived organizational support and engagement did not have a positive link with performance but were shaped by the quality of work life.

Furthermore, Kingsley et al. (2019) developed a management model based on organizational culture, work-life quality, and engagement. They concluded that organizational culture positively affects engagement and work-life balance. Similarly, Riyanto et al. (2019) studied millennial workers and discovered that work-life integration had a stronger connection with vigor, one of the three key dimensions of engagement, compared to perceived work-life integration. This highlights the importance of creating engaging and enjoyable workplaces for younger generations.

Gallup's (2019) extensive analysis supported the value of engagement by showing that the best-performing business units consistently outdid the lowest-performing units in all major organizational outcomes. Together, these studies stress that employee engagement is a complex issue shaped by individual, organizational, and contextual factors, which have direct effects on organizational performance and competitiveness.

Earlier studies have extensively researched what influences employee work engagement, mainly focusing on the Job Demands-Resources (JD-R) model. Sawasdee et al. (2020) found in a longitudinal study that both job demands and job resources are strong predictors of work engagement. Job resources have a greater impact than job demands. Similarly, Borst et al. (2017) looked into how job demands and resources contribute to predicting work engagement in the public administration sector, confirming the relevance of the JD-R model. Additionally, Mekhum and Jermsittiprasert (2019) found that support from co-workers and supervisors significantly improves work engagement. Eisenberger et al. (2020) showed that organisational support affects positive employee behaviour, well-being, and organisational goals. From a job resources standpoint, organisational support is an essential factor in employee engagement. However, there is limited empirical research that directly connects organisational support with work engagement. This study, therefore, formulates and tests a hypothesis to explore this relationship.

With rapid digital transformation, employee well-being has become a key focus in modern Human Resource Management (HRM). Research consistently shows that psychological and emotional well-being significantly affects employee engagement, innovation, retention, and organizational performance (Bakker & Demerouti, 2017). However, traditional methods of assessing well-being, which often rely on periodic surveys, are reactive and do not meet the evolving needs of today's workforce, especially in technology-driven industries.

This study suggests a proactive, AI-driven approach that uses predictive analytics to improve employee well-being in the Indian IT sector. Using data from 258 IT professionals in Karnataka, a cluster-based segmentation approach (K-means clustering) was applied across six well-being dimensions: organizational culture, communication effectiveness, motivation, HR support, perceived value, and work-life balance. The Elbow Method identified three optimal clusters: High, Moderate, and Low Well-Being. ANOVA results confirmed significant differences between clusters, with communication and organizational culture showing large effect sizes (Cohen's $d > 1.5$). This supports earlier findings that effective workplace communication and a supportive culture are key job resources within the Job Demands-Resources (JD-R) framework (Bakker & Demerouti, 2017).

The findings show how AI-driven segmentation can help create personalised HR interventions. This method replaces traditional one-size-fits-all strategies with targeted, data-informed engagement and mental health initiatives. The study highlights the importance of transparency, fairness, and human-focused AI management in HR systems, as noted in the socio-technical and ethical AI literature (Margherita, 2021). Overall, it offers a scalable and tested model for incorporating AI into HRM to support sustainable employee engagement and well-being in workplaces that use digital tools.

4. FOCUS OF THE CHAPTER

The quick adoption of Artificial Intelligence (AI) in Human Resource Management (HRM) has changed how organizations manage talent, especially in the fast-paced and tech-heavy Indian Information Technology (IT) sector. AI systems now help with recruitment analysis, performance management, tracking employee sentiment, planning the workforce, and monitoring well-being. While these advancements improve efficiency and prediction accuracy, they also create new challenges such as technostress, digital fatigue, unclear roles, and concerns about fairness in algorithms. In this changing environment, Human–AI Collaboration (HAC) has become a strategic framework that sees technology as a partner to enhance human abilities rather than replace them.

The model in this study outlines employee resilience and engagement in an HAC-focused HRM setting. The HAC Model serves as a framework that links AI systems with human relationships and organizational support. Solid arrows in the model show direct and mediating effects, while dashed arrows indicate the moderating role of HAC. Based on the JD-R (Job Demands-Resources) framework, the HAC model treats AI as a resource that boosts employee abilities instead of increasing demands.

Objectives of the Chapter

The objective of this chapter is:

1. To explore the connection between demographic factors and conflict resolution methods in AI-enabled Indian IT organisations. It will also look at how these factors affect employee resilience and engagement in digital work settings.
2. To study how communication practices, social support systems, and organised conflict management strategies improved by Human–AI Collaboration (HAC) systems, reduce the negative effects of interpersonal conflicts. This goal also seeks to understand how AI-supported HR practices boost resilience, promote employee engagement, and help create a psychologically safe and positive workplace environment.

These objectives together aim to establish the HAC model as a practical framework for enhancing employee well-being by combining human relational support with AI-supported HR actions.

Research Methodology

The study collected primary data directly from the source with a survey using a questionnaire to gather information about IT companies like TCS, WIPRO, and Infosys employees located in Chennai (TN). A practical sampling method was used to conduct the study with a non-probabilistic convenience sampling method used to select employees from the IT sector.

Table 1.

Sample Size		
Name of the Organization	**No. of. Respondents**	**Percentage**
TCS	30	20.0
WIPRO	78	52.0
INFOSYS	42	28.0
Total	150	100

Source: Primary data

Data were collected from 150 employees from these three companies via survey as shown in Table 1. Collected data were analysed using various statistical methods such as frequency analysis and correlations among variables using a correlation matrix. The statistical analysis was performed using Python for data cleaning (pre-processing) and correlation calculation and then by using SPSS for descriptive and inferential statistical analyses.

Research Questions:

1. What is the impact of demographic variables (age, tenure, and organizational role) on conflict resolution strategies in AI-enabled Indian IT organizations, and how are these trends affected in a Human-AI Collaborative setting?
2. To what extent do communication processes and organized conflict management strategies, facilitated by AI-based HR systems, offset the negative consequences of interpersonal conflict on team effectiveness, employee engagement, and organizational performance?

5. ANALYSIS AND INTERPRETATION

This chapter discusses how interpersonal dynamics influence employee resilience and engagement in the information technology industry. The researcher gathered data from respondents and analysed it using demographic variables such as age, level, organisational tenure, gender, and income.

Table 2. Demographic Profile of Respondents

Items	Category	Number of Respondents	Distribution(%)
Age	18-28 years	138	92.0
	29-39 years	3	2.0
	Above 40 years	9	6.0
	Total	150	100.0
Gender	Male	90	60.0
	Female	60	40.0
	Total	150	100.0
Tenure	Less than or equal to 1 year	135	90.0
	1 – 5 years	15	10.0
	Total	150	100.0
Monthly Income (in)	10,000- 30,000	75	50.0
	30,001- 60,000	45	30.0
	60,001- 90,000	15	10.0
	Above 90001	15	10.0
	Total	150	100.0

continued on following page

Table 2. Continued

Items	Category	Number of Respondents	Distribution(%)
Level in the Management	Top-level	15	10.0
	Middle-level	60	40.0
	Lower-level	75	50.0
	Total	150	100.0

Source: Primary data

According to Table 2, the majority (92%) of the respondents are in the 18-28 year age group, showing that the workforce is fairly young overall. Young workers may face challenges with how to handle uncertain career prospects, how to cope with work-related pressures, and how to learn or become accustomed to an organisation's culture and rules. Young employees will have limited resilience due to their limited work experience; however, when there is strong social support (peer, mentor, manager), resilience can build rapidly, and engagement can be high when there are ongoing opportunities for learning and a supportive leader.

Seventy per cent of respondents are male, while thirty percent are female, showing some diversity but potentially different perspectives regarding resilience and engagement. It appears that women rely more on relational and social support systems in order to build their resiliency than men do; whereas men are likely more task-oriented in the approach to building resilience. Therefore, establishing gender responsive support systems (i.e., mentoring, inclusive policies, work-family balance support) will be necessary to build resilience and engagement.

Respondents who have been in the workforce less than or equal to one year account for approximately 90%, while those with between one and five years of experience account for approximately 10% of all respondents. This indicates that the organisation has retained entry-level talent for at least this period of time, if not longer.

Respondents who have reported earning between 10,000 and 30,000 constitute the majority (50%), with 30% of respondents earning between 30,001 and 60,000 and only 20% of respondents earning more than 60,000. This group of employees who fall in the low range of earners suffer from financial distress or anxiety, which will affect their level of resilience and engagement while performing their jobs. Because of this, employees will depend more heavily on their companies for support systems, appreciation programs, and other non-monetary forms of motivation.

50% of respondents were classified as lower-level, while 40% were classified as middle-level, and 10% were considered to be top-level employees. Since lower-level employees make up the greatest portion of all respondents, it can be inferred that lower-level employees will experience the highest level of operational anxiety, repetitive operational tasks and operational workload pressure. Social support from both supervisors and coworkers will provide engagement and provide a buffer against operational anxiety for lower and middle-level employees. Resilience for top-level employees typically comes from their past experience making strategic decisions, while engagement with their jobs comes from a supportive corporate culture.

Figure 1. Conceptual Model

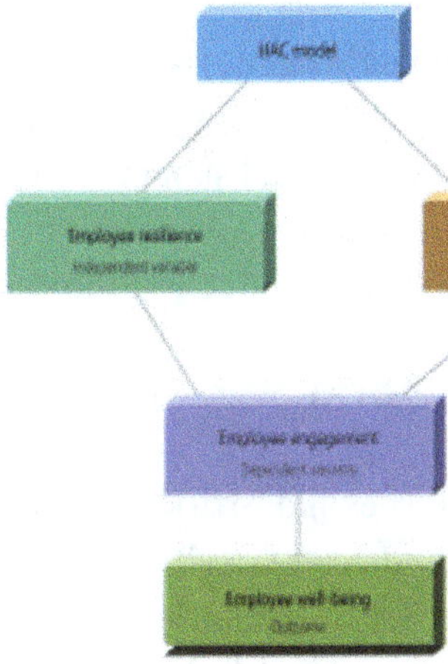

Source: Author affiliation

The proposed conceptual framework in Figure 1 above identifies Employee Engagement as the dependent variable that affects Employee Well-Being, with Employee Resilience as the primary independent variable and Social Support as the mediator. The framework is supported by the Job Demands-Resources model, which describes how personal and job resources improve motivational outcomes, and the Conservation of Resources theory, which highlights the importance of resource accumulation and conservation in stressful environments. In the AI-enabled Indian IT work context, the Human-AI Collaboration (HAC) Model incorporates AI as a technological resource that enhances the pathways between resilience, social support, engagement, and employee well-being.

In this framework, Employee Resilience (independent variable) is measured by five behavioural constructs: (1) Assertion of Needs, (2) Bi-directional Communication, (3) Conflict Management, (4) Disclosure and Interpersonal Closeness, and (5) Emotional Expression and Experience. These constructs capture the adaptive abilities of employees to perform well in highly digitalized and AI-driven work environments. Resilient employees are better equipped to handle algorithmic surveillance, technological dynamism, and high-performance demands common in Indian IT companies.

Social Support (mediator) consisting of supervisor support, peer support, and AI-augmented organisational support serves to convert resilience into increased engagement. It serves as a social bridge that improves psychological safety, trust, and emotional validation. Under the HAC framework, AI systems such as HR chatbots, performance dashboards, predictive workload systems, and digital feedback platforms improve access to support by increasing transparency, responsiveness, and fairness. Thus, AI does not displace human support but increases its availability and consistency.

Employee Engagement (dependent variable) is defined as a positive motivational state of vigor, dedication, and absorption. Employee Engagement occurs when resilient employees are provided with adequate social support in a collaborative Human-AI environment. High engagement then leads to enhanced Employee Well-Being, encompassing psychological well-being, burnout, job satisfaction, and performance.

5.1 Study VariablesTop of Form

In the Indian IT industry, Employees and Artificial Intelligence collaboration (EI, AI) Model views employee engagement as the ultimate motivation for performance and wellness, while employee resilience and social support serve as the underlying psychological and relational resource. The EI, AI model leverages AI systems as a way to enhance these relationships by improving HR processes through increased communication, transparency, and responsiveness. The following variables show how resilience and social support work together to promote employee engagement and, ultimately, employee well-being.

1. **Assertion of Needs:** In AI-driven IT organizations, it is important for employees to assertively communicate their workload capacity, learning needs, and career aspirations. Because it is psychologically strong and self-efficacious, expressing your needs is also indicative of your level of resilience. By providing structured channels for employees to express their concerns and preferences, AI-enabled feedback dashboards and digital HR platforms help employees to successfully articulate their needs and can increase psychological safety in the workplace if the AI systems guarantee that the asserted employee needs and concerns are recorded in the systems and handled transparently. The supervisor and peer social support reinforces this process by validating employee input and increasing employee engagement. Therefore, the combination of resilience (assertiveness) with AI-supported responsiveness and human empathy fosters engagement through belongingness.
2. **Bi-directional Communication:** The importance of two-way communication is magnified in technology-rich workplaces. Resilient employees will

both seek and give feedback, allowing themselves to adapt to insights derived from AI and performance analytics. The HAC model facilitates this exchange through the integration of AI chatbots, collaborative dashboards, and predicted communication methods to provide an ongoing flow of timely information. Additionally, social support serves as an important contributor to building trust and overcoming hierarchical barriers to creating bi-directional channels. In an instance where employees perceive that AI systems facilitate communication rather than control it, there is an increase in engagement for employees. Thus, bi-directional communications function as the mechanism through which the resilience of employees leads to continuous involvement and their psychological health.

3. **Conflict Management:** AI-enabled working environments recognise interpersonal conflict because these environments often have a more performance-based ethos due to automatic performance analysis and tracking of progress against goals across employees & teams. Resilient employees demonstrate the characteristics of emotional stability and adaptability, which enable them to manage conflict in a positive way. In addition, by using advanced analytics, the HAC Model helps to provide early identification of workload disparity (workload divides) or breakdown of communication (broken links or lack of communication/disconnection) so as to reduce the potential for conflict in the workplace. However, while technology provides the information necessary for resolution, it is the responsibility of human leaders to demonstrate the use of AI and data to resolve interpersonal conflicts; therefore, human leaders must use empathy and the principles of fairness when interpreting signals generated by AI and data. Furthermore, social support creates a buffer to stress allowing that when employees perceive they are protected rather than judged, they are more likely to engage in the workplace. Therefore, effective conflict management creates avenues for connecting with employees and preventing burnout which in turn contributes to the well-being of the individual.
4. **Disclosure and Interpersonal Closeness:** Disclosures of stress or other difficulties are associated with high resilience and engagement; therefore, in a workplace where communication is mediated through technology, either through tracking and surveillance of employee performance, employees may be reluctant to disclose their stress or challenges. The application of ethical AI and communication protocols as part of the HAC Model provides employees with safe environments to disclose their challenges. This can occur through the use of AI-based pulse surveys and/or analysis of social media. In addition, building strong supervisors and peer networks can help to identify, validate and provide meaningful relationships to employees who disclosing themselves to their su-

pervisors and peers. In this way, social support functions as a mediator between resilience and engagement through creating trust and a sense of closeness.

5. **Emotional Expression and Experience:** Resilience is often characterised by the conductual regulation of emotions, or the ability to control one's emotions. In settings where employees are exposed to high levels of cognitive load and anxiety related to performance, AI systems are usually used to monitor well-being. The HAC model combines the AI-driven monitoring tools for well-being with HR interventions that are focused on the employee and allows employees to recognise their emotional strain early on. Those employees who are resilient and can express their feelings in a positive manner will experience more optimally engaged employees. Social support serves to validate these feelings, fortify the coping mechanisms and prevent the depletion of resources an employee has, which correlates with the conservation of resources theory. Employees will generally engage more when they receive recognition for their emotional aspects than when they are only evaluated by means of an algorithm.

5.2 Correlation Matrix of Key Resilience and Interpersonal Process Variables Among Employees in AI-Enabled Indian IT Workplaces

Figure 2. Correlation Matrix of Age in AI-Enabled Indian IT Workplaces

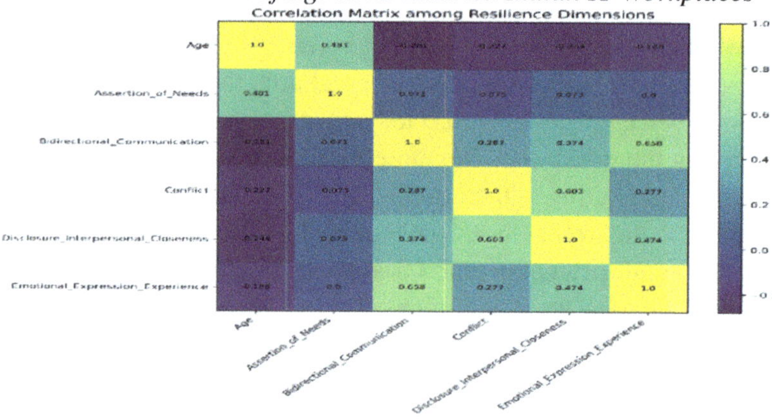

Source: Primary data

The correlation matrix in Table 3 above, reveals patterns of relationships between important variables of resilience and interpersonal processes (Age, Assertion of Needs, Bidirectional Communication, Conflict, Disclosure and Interpersonal Closeness,

Emotional Expression and Experience). These patterns can be understood in the context of Human-AI Collaboration (HAC) in HRM and the literature on well-being.

The correlation matrix is very informative about the processes of human interaction in AI-supported HRM. The findings show that age is positively and significantly related to the assertion of needs ($r = .481, p < .01$), suggesting that older employees are more assertive in expressing their views and expectations at work. However, age is negatively and significantly related to bidirectional communication ($r = -.281, p < .01$), conflict ($r = -.227, p < .01$), disclosure and interpersonal closeness ($r = -.244, p < .01$), and emotional expression and experience ($r = -.188, p < .05$). These findings suggest that younger employees are more actively involved in interactive communication and emotional processes in AI-supported digital work environments.

Conflict is found to have a strong positive correlation with disclosure and interpersonal closeness ($r = .603, p < .01$), suggesting that constructive conflict management in the workplace can be a factor in increased interpersonal closeness. Emotional expression and experience are also found to have moderate positive correlations with disclosure ($r = .474, p < .01$) and conflict ($r = .277, p < .01$), thus underlining the significance of communication processes in influencing psychological outcomes.

The results provide evidence for the Human-AI Collaboration (HAC) model by suggesting that communication-process variables, specifically bidirectional communication and disclosure, are key predictors of employee emotional well-being. AI-based HR systems that facilitate transparent communication, emotional analysis, and adaptive interaction processes can thus play an important role in improving employee well-being in AI-integrated Indian IT work environments.

Conflict is strongly correlated with disclosure and interpersonal closeness ($r = .603, p < .01$), indicating that when managed constructively, workplace disagreements may contribute to deeper interpersonal engagement. Emotional expression and experience also show moderate positive correlations with disclosure ($r = .474, p < .01$) and conflict ($r = .277, p < .01$), reinforcing the importance of communication processes in shaping psychological outcomes.

Overall, the findings support the Human–AI Collaboration (HAC) model by demonstrating that communication centered variables particularly bidirectional communication and disclosure are strong determinants of employee emotional well-being. AI-enabled HR systems that enhance transparent communication, provide emotional analytics, and support adaptive interaction mechanisms can therefore significantly promote employee well-being in AI-driven Indian IT workplaces.

5.3 Correlation Matrix of Gender in AI-Enabled Indian IT Workplaces

Figure 3.

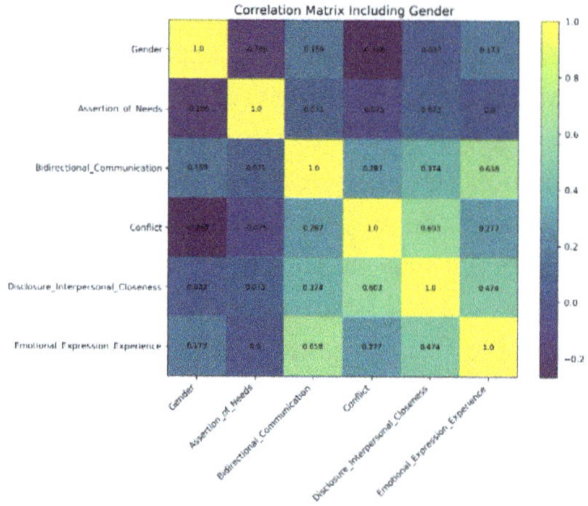

Source: Primary data

The correlation matrix in Table 4 shows ways in which important resilience and interpersonal variables (e.g., gender, assertion of needs, bidirectional communication, conflict, disclosure and interpersonal closeness, emotional expression and experience) are related. You may use the Human-AI Collaboration (HAC) framework (in HRM) and literature on well-being to evaluate the relationships between these variables.

Several studies have suggested that there are differences between genders in communication style and how emotion is disclosed. In this dataset, there is a small negative correlation between gender and assertion of needs ($r = -0.186$) and a slightly larger negative correlation between gender and conflict ($r = -0.268$), but a small positive correlation ($r = 0.173$) between gender and emotional expression. Although the strength of these correlations is modest, the direction supports research indicating there are differences in how genders communicate and what, when, and how they disclose their feelings (Pransky & Dale, 2020).

AI-enabled HR environments can help reduce gender-based barriers to personal expression through the use of AI-supported tools that provide neutral information (via sentiment analytics) or utilise digital feedback sites to increase equal access to self-expression. AI-enabled chatbots and HR systems also standardise the basis for how feedback is provided, as described by Gnewuch et al. (2017), thus providing an inclusive employee engagement and promoting the psychological well-being of employees.

There is a positive correlation between assertion of needs and bidirectional communication (r = 0.071) as well as a modest correlation with disclosure (r = 0.073). While this connection is weak, it does represent the resiliency of psychology in the workplace, as an employee's ability to communicate their wants/needs contributes to their sense of engagement when paired with social structures that are responsive (Luthans et al., 2007). In the context of HAC supported HRM, where AI applications create opportunities for reporting anonymous needs, preferences, and providing feedback in a personalized fashion, employees feel heard; therefore, their psychological safety and engagement will be positively affected.

Bidirectional communication has consistently demonstrated a strong positive correlation with emotional expression (r = 0.658), disclosure and closeness of relationships (r = 0.374) and conflict (r = 0.287). These relationships signify a theoretical view of the importance of effective two-way communication being the main vehicle to translate resiliency into social support and engagement (Bakker & Demerouti, 2017). Furthermore, the strong correlation to emotional expression supports the view that open dialogue increases emotional clarity through its removal of ambiguities. In an AI-supported workplace, use of collaborative technology as well as AI communication methods (e.g., intelligent meeting support or feedback dashboards) supports interactive communication and research indicates this is associated with increased employee engagement and well-being (Strohmeier & Piazza, 2013).

An employee's ability to express their needs correlates positively with having the ability to communicate back and forth with the employer (r = 0.071) and also has a moderate correlation with revealing information about themselves (r=0.073). Despite being a weak correlation, this positive correlation mirrors the idea of psychological resilience, when employees can express their expectations and concerns and receive support through a responsive network of people, they will be more engaged (Luthans et al., 2007). AI will provide employees with a way to anonymously report their needs, keep track of their preferences, and receive individualised responses from the organisation, creating an environment where employees are able to express and feel heard, ultimately creating a more psychologically safe and engaged workforce.

According to the study, conflict has a significant positive relationship with both Disclosure and Interpersonal Closeness (r=0.603). The association could be attributed to the fact that interpersonal conflicts do not automatically cause a decrease in relational closeness when resolved positively, which is consistent with much of the research on organisational behaviour, as assertive conflict resolution increases trust and collaboration (Jehn & Mannix, 2001). Additionally, the HAC model suggests that use of AI-enabled tools for Conflict Management, such as Predictive Analytics and Digital Mediation Frameworks, will provide early warning indicators and custom solutions to enable HR to assist in creating a resolution process that fosters social cohesion while positively impacting the overall well-being of the employees.

The Disclosure and Interpersonal Closeness scale is positively related to Emotional Expression (r = 0.474), indicating that employees who are open to sharing personal experiences are likely to express their emotions more genuinely. According to literature on psychological resilience, the dimensions of openness and emotional intelligence are important elements of adaptive functioning (Ryff & Singer, 2008). In AI-based HRM, the use of systems that track well-being indicators (such as sentiment analysis in communication tools) can facilitate early detection of emotional distress and initiate supportive measures. Studies have found that supportive systems, when combined with human supervision, improve trust and promote greater employee engagement (Margherita, 2021).

5.4 Correlation Matrix of Income in AI-Enabled Indian IT Workplaces

Figure 4.

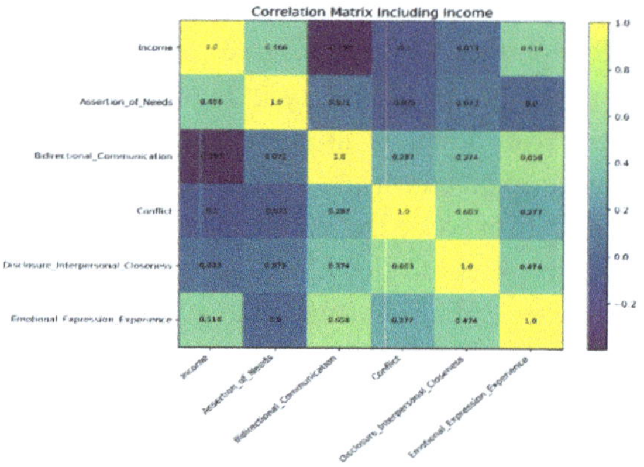

Source: Primary data

The correlation matrix in Table 5 illustrates the patterns of relationships that exist between some of the most important variables in resilience and interpersonal processes (Income, Assertion of Needs, Bidirectional Communication, Conflict, Disclosure and Interpersonal Closeness, Emotional Expression and Experience). These relationships can be explored using the Human-AI Collaboration (HAC) paradigm in HRM and the literature on well-being.

Income is moderately and positively correlated with Assertion of Needs ($r = .466$, $p < .001$). This indicates that those with higher income levels tend to be more assertive in articulating their expectations, preferences, and concerns. The psychological empowerment literature suggests that financial security improves self-efficacy and voice behaviour at work (Seibert et al., 2011). Using the HAC paradigm, AI-based

HR systems such as feedback platforms and performance dashboards can facilitate voice behaviour equality by giving all employees, regardless of income, an equal chance to assert their needs without being coerced by their superiors. In this way, AI is a leveller that diminishes power distance, which is prevalent in organisational hierarchies.

Bidirectional communication had a large, negative correlation to income (-397, $p < .001$). Therefore, it stands to reason that employees at higher salary levels tend to utilize less bidirectional communication. A potential explanation is that upper-level or higher wage earner employees would hold positions where they would conduct more directive forms of communication, rather than using collaborative forms of communication as their means of communicating with direct reports. AI-enabled HR workplaces that include such capabilities as collaborative and AI-enhanced communication tools can allow employees to share an inclusive understanding of what it means to be a part of a corporate community, thus helping to reduce asymmetries present when communicating throughout the different levels of an organisation.

Income also has a high positive correlation to emotional expression (0.518, $p < .001$). Therefore, it is likely that employees with an adequate salary can feel psychologically secure in expressing emotions in the workplace. Literature in relation to well-being in the workplace supports that when employees feel secure, they will have an increased ability to express their concerns or feelings without the anxiety of experiencing negative evaluation (Edmondson, 2018). By utilizing HAC-supported human resource management systems, the utilisation of AI-supported sentiment monitoring and well-being analytics can be of assistance to organisations in identifying potential emotional strain across income levels and, therefore, providing emotional support to all employees, as opposed to just to employees located at the upper levels of the organisational hierarchy.

The relationship between Income and Conflict is weak and non-significant ($r = -.100$, $p = .222$). This indicates that the income level of the respondents is not a strong predictor of workplace conflict participation. Conflict processes seem to be more closely linked with communication factors than economic outcomes. This is consistent with findings indicating that interpersonal conflict is more strongly related to relational processes than structural rewards.

Bidirectional Communication is strongly and positively related to:

- Conflict ($r = .287$, $p < .001$)
- Disclosure and Interpersonal Closeness ($r = .374$, $p < .001$)
- Emotional Expression ($r = .658$, $p < .001$)

The latter is the strongest relationship, which indicates that open communication is a strong predictor of emotional expression. According to the Job Demands-Resources

(JD-R) model, communication is a job resource that enhances engagement by improving clarity and support. In HAC systems, communication platforms facilitated by AI support these processes by enabling real-time interaction and feedback.

There is a significantly strong positive correlation between Disclosure and Interpersonal Closeness ($r = .603$, $p < .001$) and a moderate correlation between Emotional Expression ($r = .277$, $p < .001$). This suggests that when managed properly, conflicts can enhance relationships rather than hurt them. Research in this area suggests that when task-related issues are handled appropriately, they can help build learning and cohesiveness (De Dreu & Weingart, 2003). The HAC model predicts AI-based predictive analytics can provide valuable early detection of failures in communication so that Human Resources professionals have opportunities to address potential issues before they escalate.

6. DISCUSSION

This study suggests the success of Human–AI collaboration within HRM in India does not entirely depend on advances in technology alone but rather on the development of strong human relational dynamics at AI-enabled workplaces. The correlation findings revealed that demographic variables (age and income) have a significant effect on how people communicate, their level of emotional expression and how they experience conflict. The findings show that both open/bidirectional communication relates strongly to emotional expression and to interpersonal closeness, indicating that when employees feel their environment is psychologically safe, these factors together create a climate of resilience for the employee in an organization and increase their degree of engagement. While conflict is a positive predictor of communication and disclosure, it can only positively enhance relationships when a structured communication system and social support structure are in place. Together these findings support the HAC model premise of using AI to augment human capability versus replacing it with an employee's engagement and performance.

Practical Implications

The results of this study have a number of practical implications for HR managers and organizational leaders working in AI-enabled Indian IT environments following the Human-AI Collaboration (HAC) model. Firstly, organizations should make use of AI-enabled HR technology to improve two-way communication. Since communication is strongly linked to emotional expression and relational closeness, AI technology such as real-time feedback tools, team collaboration platforms, and sentiment analysis software can improve communication. However, these technologies should be complemented by empathetic leadership to ensure that technology supports, rather than substitutes for, human interaction.

Secondly, HR managers should develop mechanisms to encourage the assertion of needs at all levels of the demographic strata. Since income affects voice behaviour and emotional expression, AI-enabled reporting mechanisms can help to level the hierarchical playing field and ensure that junior or lower-income employees feel psychologically safe to air their grievances and share their ideas.

Thirdly, organizations should adopt AI-enabled conflict management systems. Since conflict is positively linked to communication and relational closeness, conflict should be constructively managed rather than discouraged. Predictive analytics can help to detect potential team conflict, and this can be constructively managed through interventions such as mediation, coaching, or workload redistribution.

The fourth step involves integrating AI-powered well-being monitoring tools with resilience-building initiatives to create synergy between the two. Managers will be able to identify and mitigate the potential for employee burnout by continuously analysing engagement indicators such as workload patterns, hours worked, and emotional signals. This approach, when combined with training in emotional intelligence and creating supportive leadership practices, provides employees with enhanced resilience through their engagement.

Lastly, organisations must create ethical governance frameworks for AI to guarantee transparency, equity, and privacy of data. It is critical for an employee's ability to authentically and openly engage in his or her work to trust the use of AI technologies. Integrating human-focused design components into the implementation of AI technologies will facilitate an organization creating a collaborative ecosystem that contributes to the improvement of employee well-being and engagement while simultaneously achieving sustainable organizational results.

7. CONCLUSION

This research makes a positive contribution to the growing literature on Human-AI Collaboration (HAC) in HRM by exploring, through empirical analysis, the complex interplay between demographic variables and communication variables related to resilience and employee well-being in AI-enabled Indian IT industry settings. The correlation analysis results show that income, age, and gender impact the patterns of assertion, communication, emotional expression, and conflict engagement. Notably, bidirectional communication is revealed to be a key relational process, strongly linked to emotional expression and intimacy, while conflict, facilitated by open communication, is seen to be a constructive, rather than destructive, process.

These findings highlight the critical role of psychological safety and social support as core resources in digitally enabled work settings.

The purpose of the study is to assess whether the AI-based technologies improve employee engagement and well-being when they are introduced within strong human relational processes. The results corroborated the Resource-Based Theory and the Job Demand-Resource Theory, indicating exactly how communication and expressing emotion are valuable resources to help mitigate stress and improve positive functioning when AI technology is incorporated into the workplace. Additionally, the results demonstrated that the demographic -economical factors associated with individuals influence their access to voice and emotional security. Therefore, to ensure a successful digital transformation, AI should be designed with inclusivity and implemented through equitable human resource practices.

From a practical perspective, organisations need to have a balanced, human-centred approach to AI in their HR-related strategies. In particular, when implementing AI-driven HR systems, it is imperative that organisations prioritize enhancing the transparency of communication, providing resources to assist with constructive conflict management, and establishing systems to detect emotional distress early. While leveraging technology for improved functioning and performance, organisations must integrate empathetic leadership and ethical governance structures to build and uphold trust and fairness.

Ultimately, this research supports the belief that successful human-AI collaboration should be considered a social-technical transformation, rather than simply a technological effort. Through the linking of technology with resilience-building practices, inclusive communication systems, and supportive cultures, Indian IT firms can establish a workplace focused on increasing employee engagement, psychological well-being, and long-lasting organisational success.

8. RECOMMENDATIONS

The following are the recommendations stemming from the Human–AI Collaboration (HAC) framework in HRM, with the overall purpose of fostering employee well-being within Indian IT organisations that are embracing AI technology:

Adopt a human-centred AI strategy – implementing an AI-driven HR strategy will ensure that organisations are using AI tools to enhance communication, transparency and equity; not removing or replacing human interaction. Examples of AI-driven HR platforms that can be used to enhance bidirectional communication, providing all demographic groupings with equal opportunity to have their voice heard, include feedback dashboards, digital grievance systems and sentiment analysis tools.

Provide inclusive participation mechanisms for junior and low-income employees to have equal assertiveness in expressing their needs; direct HR managers to implement these mechanisms due to the effect salary has upon the manner of expression and feeling emotion. For example, organisations may implement structured mentoring programs, supported by AI analytics, to assist in reducing barriers to hierarchical levels of communication.

To effectively monitor continuous well-being through a blended approach that combines artificial intelligence-enabled analytics and empathetic leadership practices, organisations can integrate a continuous wellbeing monitoring system. The blended approach ensures that the technological efficiencies deliver support to enhance employee engagement and psychological safety and do not undermine them. Organisations can also leverage the Health & Wellbeing (HAC) Model to establish initiatives that build resilience, establish inclusive communications systems, and implement ethical governance of AI into their HR policies. This approach will allow organisations to create sustainable improvements in their employees' wellbeing and improve their long-term performance.

REFERENCES

Abdullahi, M. S., Raman, K., Solarin, S. A., & Adeiza, A. (2023). Employee engagement as a mediating variable on the relationship between employee relation practice and employee performance in a developing economy. *Journal of Applied Research in Higher Education*, *15*(1), 83–97. DOI: 10.1108/JARHE-06-2021-0222

ADP Research Institute. (2020). *Global Workplace Study 2020: COVID-19 and the new world of work.* ADP. https://www.adpresearch.com/research/workplace-resilience-study/

Ali, A., & Pitafi, A. H. (2025). Bridging people and technology: The influence of AI-driven HRM empathy on workplace outcomes. *Systems*, *13*(12), 1129. Advance online publication. DOI: 10.3390/systems13121129

Bakker, A. B., & Demerouti, E. (2017). Job demands–resources theory: Taking stock and looking forward. *Journal of Occupational Health Psychology*, *22*(3), 273–285. DOI: 10.1037/ocp0000056

Bankins, S., Ocampo, A. C. G., Marrone, M., Restubog, S. L. D., & Woo, S. E. (2023). A multilevel review of artificial intelligence in organizations: Implications for organizational behavior research and practice. *Journal of Organizational Behavior*, *45*(2), 159–182. DOI: 10.1002/job.2735

Barends, E., Wietrak, E., Cioca, I., & Rousseau, D. (2021). *Employee resilience: An evidence review. Summary report.* Chartered Institute of Personnel and Development (CIPD). https://www.cipd.org/globalassets/media/knowledge/knowledge-hub/evidence-reviews/resilience-evidence-review-scientific-summary_tcm18-91702.pdf

Borst, R. T., Kruyen, P. M., Lako, C. J., & de Vries, M. S. (2017). The attitudinal, behavioral, and performance outcomes of work engagement: A comparative meta-analysis across the public, semipublic, and private sector. *Review of Public Personnel Administration*, *37*(4), 407–435. DOI: 10.1177/0734371X16683968

Braganza, A., Brooks, L., Nepelski, D., Ali, M., & Moro, R. (2020). Artificial intelligence (AI) in business: State-of-the-art and future research agenda. *International Journal of Information Management*, *50*, 261–272. DOI: 10.1016/j.ijinfomgt.2019.10.007

De Dreu, C. K. W., & Weingart, L. R. (2003). Task versus relationship conflict, team performance, and team member satisfaction: A meta-analysis. *The Journal of Applied Psychology*, *88*(4), 741–749. DOI: 10.1037/0021-9010.88.4.741

Dewi, M. V. K., Nimran, U., Musadieq, M. A., & Afrianty, T. W. (2020). The effect of perceived organizational support and quality of work life on employee engagement and performance. *International Journal of Management, 11*(6), 772–783.

Dinh, H. T. (2020). Work-life balance and employee engagement: Mediating role of supervisory support. *Journal of Asian Business and Economic Studies, 27*(3), 258–274. DOI: 10.1108/JABES-05-2020-0052

Eisenberger, R., Rockstuhl, T., Shoss, M. K., Wen, X., & Dulebohn, J. (2020). Is employee–organization relationship research mature enough to be useful? A meta-analytic review. *Journal of Organizational Behavior, 41*(2), 111–134.

Gallup. (2019). *State of the global workplace: 2019 report.* Gallup Press.

Gnewuch, U., Morana, S., & Maedche, A. (2017). Towards designing cooperative and social conversational agents for customer service. *Proceedings of the 38th International Conference on Information Systems (ICIS 2017)*, Seoul, South Korea.

Harter, J. (2021). *U.S. employee engagement holds steady in first half of 2021.* Gallup. https://www.gallup.com/workplace/352949/employee-engagement-holds-steady-first-half-2021.aspx

Hartwig, A., Clarke, S., Johnson, S., & Willis, S. (2020). Workplace team resilience: A systematic review and conceptual development. *Organizational Psychology Review, 10*(3–4), 169–200. DOI: 10.1177/2041386620919476

Jehn, K. A., & Mannix, E. A. (2001). The dynamic nature of conflict: A longitudinal study of intragroup conflict and group performance. *Academy of Management Journal, 44*(2), 238–251. DOI: 10.2307/3069453

Kašpárková, L., Vaculík, M., Procházka, J., & Schaufeli, W. B. (2018). Why resilient workers perform better: The roles of job satisfaction and work engagement. *Journal of Workplace Behavioral Health, 33*(1), 43–62. DOI: 10.1080/15555240.2018.1441719

Kingsley, J. N., Cherian, J., & Farouq, M. (2019). Employee engagement model: An organizational culture, quality of work life, and work engagement perspective. *International Journal of Mechanical Engineering and Technology, 10*(1), 238–248.

Linggiallo, H. D., Riadi, S. S., Hariyadi, S., & Adhimursandi, D. (2021). The effect of predictor variables on employee engagement and organizational commitment and employee performance. *Management Science Letters, 11*(1), 31–40. DOI: 10.5267/j.msl.2020.8.033

Luthans, F., Youssef, C. M., & Avolio, B. J. (2007). *Psychological capital: Developing the human competitive edge.* Oxford University Press.

Margherita, A. (2021). The role of artificial intelligence in human resource management: Challenges and opportunities. *Management Decision, 59*(5), 1185–1202. DOI: 10.1108/MD-12-2019-1682

Mekhum, W., & Jermsittiprasert, K. (2019). The role of co-worker and supervisory support in enhancing work engagement: Mediating role of job autonomy. *International Journal of Innovation. Creativity and Change, 9*(10), 296–312.

Moon, S. (2025). The impact of artificial intelligence on human resource management in the Indian IT sector: A mixed-method review. *International Journal of Innovation and Scientific Research, 12*(6), 1063–1068. https://rsisinternational.org/journals/ijrsi/articles/the-impact-of-artificial-intelligence-on-human-resource-management-in-the-indian-it-sector-a-mixed-method-review/. DOI: 10.51244/IJRSI.2025.12060085

Nadeem, M., Ahmad, R., Ahmad, N., & Batool, I. (2019). High performance work systems and service performance: Role of employee resilience. *Journal of Service Theory and Practice, 29*(1), 39–62. DOI: 10.1108/JSTP-02-2018-0040

Naswall, K., Kuntz, J. R., & Malinen, S. (2019). Employee resilience scale (ERS): Development and validation of a measure of resilience at work. *Journal of Occupational and Organizational Psychology, 92*(2), 281–306. DOI: 10.1111/joop.12234

Pransky, J., & Dale, K. (2020). Gender differences in communication and emotional disclosure: Implications for the workplace. *Journal of Applied Communication Research, 48*(4), 451–468.

Riyanto, S., Endri, E., & Herlisha, N. (2019). Effect of work motivation and job satisfaction on employee performance: Mediating role of employee engagement. *Problems and Perspectives in Management, 17*(4), 162–174.

Ryff, C. D., & Singer, B. (2008). Know thyself and become what you are: A eudaimonic approach to psychological well-being. *Journal of Happiness Studies, 9*(1), 13–39. DOI: 10.1007/s10902-006-9019-0

Sadeghi, S. (2024). *Employee well-being in the age of AI: Perceptions, concerns, behaviors, and outcomes*. arXiv preprint arXiv:2412.04796. https://arxiv.org/abs/2412.04796

Sawasdee, A., Laohasiriwong, W., & Boonthai, N. (2020). Job demands, job resources, and work engagement: A longitudinal study among healthcare professionals. *International Journal of Environmental Research and Public Health, 17*(18), 6853.

Seibert, S. E., Kraimer, M. L., & Crant, J. M. (2011). What do proactive people do? A longitudinal model linking proactive personality and career success. *Personnel Psychology, 64*(2), 427–450. DOI: 10.1111/j.1744-6570.2011.01214.x

Strohmeier, S. (2022). Digital HRM: A conceptual clarification of HRIS, AI, and HR analytics. *Human Resource Management Review*, *32*(2), 100789. DOI: 10.1016/j.hrmr.2020.100789

Strohmeier, S., & Piazza, F. (2013). Artificial intelligence techniques in human resource management—A conceptual exploration. *International Journal of Human Resource Management*, *24*(9), 1795–1817. DOI: 10.1080/09585192.2012.709190

Trinh, N. T. N., & Elbanna, A. (2023). Understanding human-AI augmentation in business and management context: A literature review. *ECIS 2023 Research Papers*, Article 406. https://aisel.aisnet.org/ecis2023_rp/406/

Chapter 9
AI-Human Collaboration in Talent Decision System:
Transforming Recruitment, Selection, and Talent Acquisition

Sudiksha Srivastava
Amity University, Noida, India

Kavita Indapurkar
http://orcid.org/0000-0003-4388-2915
Amity University, Noida, India

ABSTRACT

This chapter discusses the increasing use of artificial intelligence in the recruitment, selection, and performance management systems and the implications of this on the current talent strategy. It employs a theoretical perspective to evaluate the way the Artificial Intelligence-driven sourcing systems, machine-based screening solutions, predictive evaluation devices, and workforce-analytics systems are transforming the organizational hires systems across the globe. Simultaneously, this chapter stresses the persistence of the role of human judgment in interpreting the outputs of algorithmic, protecting a fairness factor, and maintaining institutional legitimacy that subsequently enhances the chances of the candidates to get employed in the spheres of their interests. This chapter is based on an integrated approach to the understanding of AI-driven talent management by synthesizing technological, behavioral, and strategic perspectives. The conclusion will include the description of the managerial implications and the perspectives of future research field of AI.

DOI: 10.4018/979-8-2600-2541-3.ch009

INTRODUCTION

The rapid advancement of artificial intelligence has fundamentally reshaped organizational processes across multiple domains, with human resource management emerging as one of the most significantly affected areas. Among HR functions, recruitment and selection have experienced profound transformation as organizations increasingly adopt data driven technologies to enhance decision making and improve workforce outcomes. Traditionally, hiring decisions were based on manual evaluation, recruiter experience, and subjective judgment, often leading to inconsistencies, inefficiencies, and potential bias. The introduction of artificial intelligence has altered this landscape by enabling organizations to process large volumes of data, identify patterns, and generate predictive insights that support more informed hiring decisions (Brougham & Haar, 2018; Stone et al., 2015).

Artificial intelligence in recruitment encompasses a wide range of applications, including automated resume screening, intelligent candidate sourcing, chatbot based communication, and predictive analytics. These technologies allow organizations to streamline hiring processes, reduce time to hire, and improve the overall efficiency of talent acquisition (Upadhyay & Khandelwal, 2018). More importantly, AI systems provide the ability to analyze candidate data at scale, enabling organizations to identify individuals whose skills, experience, and behavioral attributes align with job requirements and organizational goals (Tambe, Cappelli, & Yakubovich, 2019).

The growing reliance on artificial intelligence reflects a broader shift toward evidence based management, where decisions are increasingly informed by data rather than intuition. In this context, recruitment is no longer viewed as a routine administrative activity but as a strategic function that contributes directly to organizational competitiveness. By leveraging AI driven insights, organizations can build stronger talent pipelines, enhance workforce quality, and achieve better alignment between human capital and business strategy (Collings, Mellahi, & Cascio, 2019).

Despite these advantages, the adoption of artificial intelligence in recruitment and selection also raises significant concerns. One of the most critical issues is the potential for algorithmic bias. Since AI systems are trained on historical data, they may inadvertently replicate patterns of discrimination present in past hiring practices. This can lead to unfair outcomes and undermine diversity and inclusion efforts (Köchling & Wehner, 2020; Raghavan et al., 2020). Additionally, the lack of transparency in many AI systems makes it difficult for users to understand how decisions are made, raising questions about accountability and trust (Leicht Deobald et al., 2019).

Another important concern relates to the impact of automation on human interaction within the recruitment process. While AI technologies improve efficiency and responsiveness, they may also reduce the personal engagement that candidates expect during hiring. This can affect candidate experience and influence perceptions of the organization as an employer (Dineen & Allen, 2016). Therefore, organizations must carefully balance the use of technology with the need to maintain meaningful human interaction.

The integration of artificial intelligence into recruitment and selection also has implications for the role of HR professionals. As AI systems take over routine tasks, HR practitioners are required to develop new competencies in data analysis, technology management, and strategic decision making. This shift highlights the importance of human and machine collaboration, where AI provides analytical insights and human managers apply contextual understanding and judgment (Jarrahi, 2018; Wilson & Daugherty, 2018).

This chapter aims to provide a comprehensive analysis of artificial intelligence in recruitment and selection systems by combining theoretical perspectives with practical insights. It examines how AI technologies are transforming hiring processes, evaluates their benefits and limitations, and explores their implications for organizational strategy. The chapter also highlights emerging trends and identifies areas for future research, contributing to the growing body of knowledge on AI enabled human resource management.

LITERATURE REVIEW

The integration of artificial intelligence into recruitment and selection has attracted significant scholarly attention over the past decade, reflecting the increasing reliance of organizations on digital technologies to enhance talent acquisition processes. The literature in this domain spans multiple disciplines, including human resource management, information systems, and organizational behavior, offering diverse perspectives on the implications of AI driven hiring systems. This section critically reviews existing research to examine the evolution, applications, benefits, and limitations of artificial intelligence in recruitment and selection.

Evolution of Recruitment Technologies

The development of recruitment technologies has progressed through several stages, beginning with traditional manual hiring processes and advancing toward sophisticated AI enabled systems. Early research focused on electronic recruitment, which involved the use of online job portals and applicant tracking systems to facilitate job postings and application management (Parry & Tyson, 2011; Holm, 2012).

These systems primarily improved administrative efficiency by reducing paperwork and expanding access to candidate pools.

However, early digital recruitment tools were limited in their ability to support decision making. They functioned largely as repositories of candidate information rather than intelligent systems capable of analysis. The emergence of big data and machine learning technologies marked a significant turning point, enabling the development of systems that could process and interpret complex datasets (Strohmeier & Piazza, 2015).

Recent studies indicate that recruitment technologies have evolved into integrated platforms that incorporate artificial intelligence to automate screening, analyze candidate profiles, and predict job fit (Nikolaou, 2021). This evolution reflects a broader transformation of HR functions from administrative support roles to strategic contributors within organizations.

AI in Recruitment and Talent Sourcing

A substantial body of literature highlights the role of artificial intelligence in improving recruitment efficiency and enhancing talent sourcing capabilities. AI driven systems utilize algorithms to analyze large volumes of data from multiple sources, including professional networks, social media platforms, and organizational databases. This allows recruiters to identify potential candidates more effectively and engage with both active and passive job seekers (Acikgoz, 2019).

Research suggests that AI based sourcing tools significantly reduce the time required to identify suitable candidates, thereby improving recruitment speed and efficiency (Upadhyay & Khandelwal, 2018). Additionally, these systems enable organizations to access a broader and more diverse talent pool, which can enhance workforce quality and innovation potential.

Predictive analytics further strengthens recruitment processes by enabling organizations to forecast candidate success based on historical data. By analyzing patterns associated with high performing employees, AI systems can prioritize candidates who exhibit similar characteristics (Tambe et al., 2019). This data driven approach reduces reliance on intuition and improves the consistency of hiring decisions.

Despite these advantages, scholars emphasize that AI driven recruitment systems must be carefully designed to avoid unintended consequences. For example, excessive reliance on algorithmic recommendations may limit the consideration of non-traditional candidates who do not fit predefined patterns (Black & van Esch, 2020).

AI in Selection and Assessment

The application of artificial intelligence in selection processes represents one of the most significant developments in modern HRM. Traditional selection methods, such as structured interviews and standardized tests, have been widely used to evaluate candidate suitability. However, these methods are often subject to variability and may lack predictive accuracy.

AI enabled selection systems address these limitations by integrating multiple data sources and analytical techniques. Research indicates that algorithm based decision making can outperform human judgment in predicting job performance due to its ability to process complex and large datasets (Kuncel, Klieger, Connelly, & Ones, 2013).

Advanced assessment tools, including gamified testing and video interviews, have been developed to evaluate cognitive, emotional, and behavioral attributes of candidates. These tools generate rich datasets that provide deeper insights into candidate potential (Chamorro Premuzic et al., 2019; Landers & Sanchez, 2022). Video interview analytics, for example, analyze speech patterns, facial expressions, and language usage to assess communication skills and personality traits (Langer, König, & Papathanasiou, 2019).

However, the literature also highlights challenges associated with these technologies. One major concern is the interpretability of AI models. Many systems operate as complex algorithms whose decision making processes are not easily understood by users. This lack of transparency can affect trust and acceptance among candidates and recruiters (Leicht Deobald et al., 2019).

Candidate Experience and Employer Branding

The impact of artificial intelligence on candidate experience and employer branding has also been widely examined in the literature. Recruitment processes serve as a critical touchpoint between organizations and potential employees, influencing perceptions of organizational culture and professionalism.

AI driven communication tools, such as chatbots and automated messaging systems, have improved responsiveness and efficiency in candidate interactions. These tools provide real time updates, answer queries, and guide applicants through the recruitment process (Dineen & Allen, 2016). As a result, candidates experience reduced uncertainty and improved engagement.

At the same time, researchers caution that excessive automation may lead to perceptions of impersonality. Candidates may prefer human interaction, particularly in later stages of the hiring process. Therefore, organizations must balance technological efficiency with relational engagement to maintain positive candidate experiences (Van Esch, Black, & Ferolie, 2019).

Employer branding is also influenced by the use of advanced recruitment technologies. Organizations that adopt innovative AI systems are often perceived as modern and forward thinking, which can enhance their attractiveness to potential employees (Lievens & Slaughter, 2016).

Ethical and Organizational Concerns

A growing body of research focuses on the ethical implications of artificial intelligence in recruitment and selection. One of the most significant concerns is algorithmic bias, which arises when AI systems reflect patterns present in historical data. This can lead to discriminatory outcomes and undermine diversity initiatives (Raghavan et al., 2020).

Transparency is another critical issue. Many AI systems lack explainability, making it difficult for users to understand how decisions are made. This raises questions about accountability and fairness, particularly when candidates are rejected without clear justification (Leicht Deobald et al., 2019).

Organizational justice theory provides a useful framework for understanding these issues. Studies suggest that candidates are more likely to accept decisions when they perceive the process as fair and transparent (Colquitt et al., 2001; Gilliland, 1993). Therefore, organizations must ensure that AI systems are designed and implemented in a way that promotes fairness and trust.

Research Gaps and Future Directions

Despite the extensive literature on artificial intelligence in recruitment and selection, several gaps remain. First, there is limited research on the long term impact of AI driven hiring systems on employee performance and retention. Most studies focus on short term efficiency gains rather than long term organizational outcomes.

Second, the interaction between human judgment and algorithmic decision making requires further investigation. While AI provides valuable insights, human interpretation remains essential for contextual understanding.

Third, cross cultural differences in the adoption and perception of AI in recruitment have not been sufficiently explored. Future research should examine how cultural factors influence acceptance and effectiveness of AI systems.

Finally, there is a need for greater focus on explainable artificial intelligence to enhance transparency and trust in hiring processes. Addressing these gaps will contribute to a more comprehensive understanding of AI enabled talent management.

THEORETICAL FOUNDATIONS OF AI IN TALENT STRATEGIES

The application of artificial intelligence in recruitment and selection is not only a technological advancement but also a conceptual shift in how organizations manage talent. To fully understand the implications of AI enabled hiring systems, it is essential to examine the theoretical frameworks that explain the interaction between technology, human behavior, and organizational processes. Several key theories provide a foundation for analyzing how artificial intelligence influences recruitment and selection outcomes, including socio technical systems theory, technology acceptance theory, human capital theory, and organizational justice theory.

Socio Technical Systems Theory

Socio technical systems theory emphasizes the interdependence between social and technical components within organizations. According to this perspective, technological systems cannot be evaluated in isolation but must be understood in relation to human actors, organizational structures, and work processes (Trist & Bamforth, 1951).

In the context of AI driven recruitment, socio technical systems theory highlights the importance of aligning artificial intelligence tools with organizational practices and human capabilities. While AI systems can automate screening and decision making, their effectiveness depends on how well they are integrated into existing workflows. For example, recruiters must be able to interpret algorithmic outputs and incorporate them into broader decision making processes.

Research suggests that failures in technology adoption often occur when organizations focus solely on technical efficiency without considering human and organizational factors (Bostrom & Heinen, 1977). Therefore, the successful implementation of artificial intelligence in recruitment requires a balanced approach that considers both technological functionality and human interaction.

Technology Acceptance Theory

Technology acceptance theory provides insight into how individuals perceive and adopt new technologies. The model developed by Davis (1989) identifies perceived usefulness and perceived ease of use as key determinants of technology adoption. Later extensions of this model, such as the unified theory of acceptance and use of technology, incorporate additional factors including social influence and facilitating conditions (Venkatesh et al., 2003).

In recruitment and selection contexts, HR professionals must be willing to trust and utilize artificial intelligence systems for them to be effective. If recruiters perceive AI tools as complex or unreliable, they may resist adoption or underutilize their capabilities. Conversely, when AI systems are seen as improving efficiency and decision quality, acceptance is more likely.

Trust plays a particularly important role in the adoption of AI based systems. Studies indicate that individuals are more likely to rely on automated systems when they understand how decisions are made and believe that the system operates fairly (Lee, 2018). Therefore, transparency and usability are critical factors influencing the success of AI implementation in HR practices.

Human Capital Theory

Human capital theory views employees as valuable assets whose skills, knowledge, and abilities contribute to organizational performance. This perspective emphasizes the importance of investing in talent acquisition and development as a means of achieving competitive advantage (Becker, 1964; Schultz, 1961).

Artificial intelligence supports human capital theory by enabling organizations to identify and attract high quality candidates more effectively. Through predictive analytics, AI systems can evaluate candidate potential based on multiple criteria, including experience, skills, and behavioral characteristics. This allows organizations to make more informed hiring decisions that align with long term strategic objectives.

Furthermore, AI driven recruitment systems facilitate better matching between candidates and job roles, improving job fit and reducing turnover. By enhancing the quality of hiring decisions, artificial intelligence contributes to the development of a more capable and productive workforce (Huselid, 1995).

Organizational Justice Theory

Organizational justice theory focuses on perceptions of fairness in decision making processes. It distinguishes between distributive justice, which relates to the fairness of outcomes, and procedural justice, which concerns the fairness of the processes used to reach those outcomes (Greenberg, 1987).

In AI enabled recruitment, perceptions of fairness are critical for both candidates and employees. If individuals believe that hiring decisions are based on unbiased and transparent processes, they are more likely to accept outcomes, even if they are not selected (Colquitt et al., 2001). Conversely, lack of transparency or perceived bias can lead to dissatisfaction and distrust.

Research in selection systems highlights the importance of procedural fairness in shaping candidate reactions. Gilliland (1993) suggests that fairness perceptions are influenced by factors such as consistency, transparency, and the opportunity for feedback. These factors are particularly relevant in AI based systems, where decision processes may not be easily visible to users.

Resource Based View and Competitive Advantage

The resource based view of the firm provides an additional perspective on the role of artificial intelligence in talent management. This theory suggests that organizations achieve competitive advantage through resources that are valuable, rare, and difficult to imitate (Barney, 1991).

Human capital is considered one of the most important strategic resources, and recruitment plays a key role in acquiring this resource. Artificial intelligence enhances this process by enabling organizations to identify and attract high potential candidates more effectively. By improving the quality of hiring decisions, AI contributes to the development of unique organizational capabilities.

In addition, AI driven recruitment systems themselves can become a source of competitive advantage when they are integrated effectively into organizational processes. Firms that leverage advanced technologies for talent acquisition may outperform competitors in terms of innovation, productivity, and growth.

Integration of Theoretical Perspectives

While each of the theories discussed above provides valuable insights, their integration offers a more comprehensive understanding of artificial intelligence in recruitment and selection. Socio technical systems theory emphasizes the importance of aligning technology with organizational context, while technology acceptance theory explains how users interact with AI systems.

Human capital theory highlights the strategic importance of effective recruitment, and organizational justice theory addresses the need for fairness and transparency. The resource based view further connects these concepts to organizational performance and competitive advantage.

Together, these frameworks suggest that the success of AI enabled recruitment systems depends on multiple factors, including technological capability, user acceptance, ethical considerations, and strategic alignment. Organizations must consider all these dimensions when implementing artificial intelligence in hiring processes.

AI IN RECRUITMENT SYSTEMS

The integration of artificial intelligence into recruitment systems has fundamentally transformed how organizations identify, attract, and engage talent. Recruitment, traditionally characterized by manual processes and subjective decision making, has evolved into a data driven function supported by intelligent technologies. Artificial intelligence enables organizations to process large volumes of candidate information efficiently, identify patterns, and make informed decisions that enhance hiring outcomes (Acikgoz, 2019; Strohmeier & Piazza, 2015).

AI Driven Talent Sourcing

One of the most significant applications of artificial intelligence in recruitment is talent sourcing. AI powered platforms analyze data from multiple sources, including job portals, professional networks, and social media platforms, to identify potential candidates. This allows organizations to expand their talent pool beyond active job seekers and engage passive candidates who may not be actively searching for employment (Nikolaou, 2021).

Machine learning algorithms evaluate candidate profiles based on skills, experience, and career trajectories, enabling recruiters to identify individuals who match job requirements more accurately. This approach enhances the efficiency of sourcing activities and reduces the time required to identify suitable candidates (Upadhyay & Khandelwal, 2018).

In addition, AI systems can continuously update candidate databases, ensuring that recruiters have access to the most relevant and current information. This dynamic approach to sourcing improves responsiveness and supports strategic talent acquisition.

Automated Resume Screening

Resume screening is one of the most time consuming aspects of recruitment, particularly in organizations that receive large numbers of applications. Artificial intelligence addresses this challenge through automated screening systems that use natural language processing to extract and analyze information from resumes.

These systems identify key attributes such as education, skills, and work experience, and compare them with job requirements to rank candidates accordingly. By automating this process, organizations can significantly reduce administrative workload and improve the speed of hiring (Strohmeier & Piazza, 2015).

Furthermore, automated screening enhances consistency by applying standardized criteria across all applicants. This reduces variability in evaluation and improves the fairness of the screening process. However, the effectiveness of these systems depends on the quality of the algorithms and the data used for training (Köchling & Wehner, 2020).

Recruitment Chatbots and Candidate Interaction

Artificial intelligence has also improved communication between organizations and candidates through the use of recruitment chatbots. These systems provide real time responses to candidate inquiries, guide applicants through the recruitment process, and assist with tasks such as interview scheduling.

Chatbots enhance candidate experience by reducing waiting time and providing immediate support. They also enable organizations to manage large volumes of communication efficiently, particularly during high volume recruitment campaigns (Dineen & Allen, 2016).

Despite these benefits, it is important to maintain a balance between automation and human interaction. Candidates may prefer personal engagement, especially in later stages of the recruitment process. Therefore, organizations should use chatbots to support, rather than replace, human communication.

Predictive Analytics in Recruitment

Predictive analytics represents a key advancement in AI driven recruitment systems. By analyzing historical hiring data, machine learning models can identify patterns associated with successful employees and use these insights to predict candidate performance.

This approach allows organizations to prioritize candidates who are more likely to succeed in specific roles, improving the quality of hiring decisions. Predictive analytics also supports workforce planning by identifying future talent needs and aligning recruitment strategies accordingly (Tambe et al., 2019).

However, reliance on predictive models requires careful consideration of data quality and ethical implications. If historical data contains bias, predictive systems may reinforce those biases, leading to unfair outcomes (Raghavan et al., 2020).

Efficiency and Cost Optimization

Artificial intelligence significantly improves recruitment efficiency by automating repetitive tasks and streamlining workflows. Activities such as resume screening, candidate communication, and interview scheduling can be performed more quickly and accurately using AI systems.

This leads to reductions in time to hire and cost per hire, making recruitment processes more efficient and cost effective. Organizations can allocate resources more strategically, focusing on activities that require human expertise, such as relationship building and decision making (Upadhyay & Khandelwal, 2018).

In addition, AI systems provide valuable insights into recruitment performance, enabling organizations to monitor key metrics and continuously improve their processes.

Human and AI Collaboration in Recruitment

While artificial intelligence enhances recruitment processes, human involvement remains essential. AI systems provide data driven insights, but they cannot fully capture contextual factors such as organizational culture, interpersonal dynamics, and candidate motivation.

Human and AI collaboration allows organizations to combine the strengths of both approaches. AI can handle data processing and pattern recognition, while human recruiters apply judgment and contextual understanding to make final decisions (Jarrahi, 2018; Wilson & Daugherty, 2018).

This collaborative approach ensures that recruitment decisions are both efficient and aligned with organizational values.

Limitations of AI in Recruitment

Despite its advantages, artificial intelligence in recruitment is not without limitations. One of the primary challenges is the risk of bias in algorithmic decision making. AI systems trained on historical data may replicate existing patterns of discrimination, leading to unfair outcomes (Köchling & Wehner, 2020).

Another limitation is the lack of transparency in some AI systems, which can make it difficult for users to understand how decisions are made. This affects trust and may lead to resistance among both recruiters and candidates (Leicht Deobald et al., 2019).

Additionally, over reliance on automation may reduce the role of human judgment, potentially leading to incomplete evaluation of candidates. Organizations must therefore ensure that AI systems are used as decision support tools rather than replacements for human expertise.

Strategic Role of AI in Recruitment

Artificial intelligence has transformed recruitment into a strategic function that contributes to organizational performance. By enabling data driven decision making, AI systems help organizations identify high quality candidates, improve workforce alignment, and enhance competitive advantage (Collings et al., 2019).

The strategic role of recruitment is further strengthened by the integration of AI with broader talent management systems. This allows organizations to link hiring decisions with workforce planning, performance management, and employee development.

As organizations continue to adopt artificial intelligence, recruitment is expected to become increasingly sophisticated, with greater emphasis on predictive analytics, personalization, and integration with other HR functions.

AI IN SELECTION AND ASSESSMENT

The selection and assessment stage represents one of the most critical components of the recruitment process, as it directly determines the quality of talent entering the organization. Traditional selection methods, including interviews, reference checks, and standardized testing, have long been used to evaluate candidate suitability. However, these approaches are often limited by subjectivity, inconsistency, and the inability to process complex information effectively. The integration of artificial intelligence into selection systems has introduced more structured, data driven, and predictive approaches to candidate evaluation, significantly enhancing decision accuracy and reliability (Kuncel, Klieger, Connelly, & Ones, 2013; Ployhart, Schmitt, & Tippins, 2017).

Algorithm Based Pre Employment Assessment

Artificial intelligence has transformed pre employment assessments by enabling organizations to evaluate candidates using automated and adaptive testing systems. These systems assess cognitive ability, technical skills, and job related competencies through digital platforms that adjust the difficulty of questions based on candidate responses.

Adaptive testing improves measurement precision and reduces testing time by focusing on relevant competency areas. This approach enhances the efficiency of assessment processes while maintaining accuracy in evaluating candidate capabilities (Ployhart et al., 2017).

In addition, AI based assessments provide standardized evaluation criteria, ensuring that all candidates are assessed using the same parameters. This reduces variability and improves fairness in selection decisions.

Psychometric and Behavioral Analytics

Psychometric testing has been a long standing component of selection systems, but artificial intelligence has expanded its scope by integrating behavioral analytics and advanced data processing techniques. AI driven platforms analyze candidate responses to assess personality traits, emotional intelligence, and decision making styles.

Gamified assessments are increasingly used to evaluate candidate behavior in simulated environments. These tools measure attributes such as problem solving ability, adaptability, and attention to detail by analyzing how candidates interact with tasks (Landers & Sanchez, 2022).

Natural language processing is also used to analyze written and verbal responses, providing insights into communication skills and cognitive patterns. These multidimensional assessments offer a more comprehensive evaluation of candidate potential compared to traditional methods (Morgeson et al., 2007).

AI Enabled Video Interviewing

Video interviewing has become a widely adopted selection method, particularly in organizations that conduct large scale hiring. Artificial intelligence enhances this process by analyzing both verbal and nonverbal aspects of candidate responses.

AI systems evaluate factors such as speech patterns, tone, facial expressions, and body language to assess communication skills and personality traits. This provides additional data points that support more informed decision making (Langer, König, & Papathanasiou, 2019).

Asynchronous video interviews allow candidates to record responses at their convenience, enabling recruiters to review them at a later time. This improves flexibility and reduces scheduling constraints.

However, concerns have been raised regarding the interpretation of nonverbal cues and the potential for bias in video analysis. Cultural differences and individual communication styles may influence assessment outcomes, highlighting the need for careful system design and validation (Raghavan et al., 2020).

Predictive Job Fit Modeling

Predictive modeling is one of the most significant contributions of artificial intelligence to selection systems. By analyzing historical data on employee performance, machine learning models identify patterns that are associated with success in specific roles.

These models generate job fit scores that indicate the likelihood of a candidate performing well in a given position. This allows organizations to make more informed hiring decisions and improve workforce quality (Kuncel et al., 2013).

Predictive modeling also supports strategic workforce planning by identifying candidates who have the potential to grow within the organization. This contributes to long term talent development and succession planning.

However, the accuracy of predictive models depends on the quality and representativeness of the data used for training. Organizations must ensure that datasets are diverse and unbiased to avoid reinforcing existing inequalities.

Standardization and Decision Consistency

One of the key advantages of AI enabled selection systems is the ability to standardize evaluation processes. Traditional selection methods often vary depending on the interviewer, leading to inconsistencies in decision making.

Artificial intelligence applies uniform criteria across all candidates, ensuring that evaluations are consistent and comparable. This improves the reliability of selection outcomes and reduces the influence of subjective bias (Sackett & Lievens, 2008).

Standardization also enhances organizational efficiency by enabling recruiters to evaluate large numbers of candidates in a structured manner.

Human Oversight in Selection Decisions

Despite the advanced capabilities of artificial intelligence, human oversight remains essential in selection processes. AI systems provide valuable insights, but they cannot fully capture contextual factors such as cultural fit, motivation, and interpersonal dynamics.

Human decision makers play a critical role in interpreting algorithmic outputs and making final hiring decisions. This ensures that selection outcomes are aligned with organizational values and strategic objectives (Jarrahi, 2018; Wilson & Daugherty, 2018).

The concept of human and AI collaboration is particularly important in selection systems, where decisions have significant long term implications for both individuals and organizations.

Fairness and Transparency in AI Based Selection

Fairness and transparency are central concerns in AI enabled selection systems. Candidates expect hiring processes to be equitable and understandable, and lack of transparency can lead to dissatisfaction and distrust.

Organizational justice theory suggests that individuals are more likely to accept decisions when they perceive the process as fair and consistent (Colquitt et al., 2001). Therefore, organizations must ensure that AI systems are designed to provide clear explanations for decisions and allow for feedback.

Explainable artificial intelligence is emerging as a key solution to this challenge, enabling organizations to make algorithmic decisions more transparent and accountable (Leicht Deobald et al., 2019).

Limitations of AI in Selection Systems

While AI based selection systems offer significant advantages, they also present several limitations. Algorithmic bias remains a major concern, particularly when systems are trained on historical data that may reflect existing inequalities (Köchling & Wehner, 2020).

In addition, the reliance on quantitative data may overlook qualitative aspects of candidate evaluation, such as creativity and emotional intelligence. This highlights the importance of integrating human judgment into the decision making process.

Another limitation is the potential for over reliance on technology, which may reduce critical thinking among recruiters. Organizations must ensure that AI systems are used as decision support tools rather than replacements for human expertise.

Strategic Implications of AI in Selection

The use of artificial intelligence in selection has significant implications for organizational strategy. By improving the accuracy and consistency of hiring decisions, AI systems contribute to the development of a more capable and productive workforce.

In addition, AI enables organizations to align selection processes with long term goals, such as innovation, growth, and competitive advantage. This positions selection as a strategic function that plays a critical role in organizational success (Collings et al., 2019).

As AI technologies continue to evolve, selection systems are expected to become more sophisticated, with greater emphasis on predictive analytics, personalization, and integration with other HR functions.

AI INTEGRATED HIRING SYSTEMS AND REAL WORLD APPLICATIONS

The advancement of artificial intelligence has led to the development of integrated hiring systems that combine recruitment and selection processes into a unified and data driven framework. Unlike traditional approaches where sourcing, screening, and selection are treated as separate stages, AI enabled systems create a continuous flow of information across the entire hiring lifecycle. This integration enhances decision quality, improves efficiency, and supports strategic talent management (Cappelli, Tambe, & Yakubovich, 2018).

Integrated Talent Decision Systems

AI integrated hiring systems bring together multiple components of the recruitment and selection process, including candidate sourcing, resume screening, assessment, and predictive modeling. These systems operate on centralized platforms that collect and analyze data from various sources, enabling organizations to develop comprehensive candidate profiles.

By integrating data across different stages, organizations can evaluate candidates based on a combination of factors rather than isolated metrics. For example, information gathered during initial screening can be combined with assessment results and interview performance to generate a holistic evaluation (Tambe et al., 2019).

This integrated approach reduces fragmentation in decision making and ensures consistency across hiring stages. It also allows organizations to track candidate progress more effectively and make data driven decisions that improve hiring outcomes.

End to End Hiring Analytics

End to end hiring analytics is a key feature of AI integrated systems. These analytics provide insights into every stage of the recruitment and selection process, enabling organizations to monitor performance, identify bottlenecks, and optimize workflows.

Metrics such as time to hire, cost per hire, and candidate conversion rates can be analyzed in real time, allowing organizations to make adjustments and improve efficiency. Predictive analytics further enhances this process by identifying patterns that indicate successful hiring outcomes (Marler & Boudreau, 2017).

End to end analytics also support strategic workforce planning by providing insights into talent availability, skill gaps, and future hiring needs. This enables organizations to align recruitment strategies with long term objectives.

Role of Artificial Intelligence in Decision Integration

Artificial intelligence plays a central role in integrating decision making across recruitment and selection stages. Machine learning algorithms analyze large datasets to identify relationships between candidate attributes and job performance.

These insights are used to generate recommendations that guide hiring decisions. For example, AI systems may assign scores to candidates based on their likelihood of success, enabling recruiters to prioritize high potential individuals (Kuncel et al., 2013).

At the same time, integration increases the complexity of decision making, requiring careful interpretation of algorithmic outputs. Human involvement remains essential to ensure that decisions are contextually appropriate and aligned with organizational values (Jarrahi, 2018).

Real World Application: Amazon Hiring System

One of the most widely discussed examples of AI in recruitment is the development of an automated hiring system by Amazon. The company designed a machine learning model to evaluate resumes and identify top candidates based on historical hiring data.

However, the system demonstrated bias in its recommendations, as it was trained on data that reflected male dominated hiring patterns. As a result, the algorithm favored certain types of candidates and disadvantaged others (Raghavan et al., 2020).

This case highlights the risks associated with relying on historical data and emphasizes the importance of monitoring and auditing AI systems. It also demonstrates that artificial intelligence does not inherently eliminate bias and requires careful design and governance.

Real World Application: LinkedIn Talent Analytics

LinkedIn provides a prominent example of how artificial intelligence can be used to enhance talent sourcing and workforce planning. The platform uses machine learning algorithms to analyze professional data and generate insights into labor market trends, skill availability, and candidate behavior.

Organizations use LinkedIn analytics to identify potential candidates, map talent pipelines, and make informed recruitment decisions. This data driven approach enables organizations to move from reactive hiring to proactive talent acquisition (Nikolaou, 2021).

The LinkedIn case illustrates the strategic potential of artificial intelligence in recruitment, particularly in enabling organizations to align hiring practices with evolving market conditions.

Real World Application: AI Video Interview Platforms

AI driven video interview platforms have become increasingly popular in large scale recruitment. These systems evaluate candidate responses using algorithms that analyze verbal and nonverbal communication.

Such platforms provide standardized evaluation criteria, reducing variability and improving consistency in selection decisions. They also allow organizations to assess candidates more efficiently, particularly when dealing with large applicant pools (Langer et al., 2019).

However, concerns have been raised regarding the interpretation of behavioral cues and the potential for bias. These challenges highlight the need for transparency and validation in AI based assessment tools.

Benefits of Integrated AI Hiring Systems

Integrated AI hiring systems offer several advantages for organizations. First, they improve efficiency by automating repetitive tasks and streamlining workflows. Second, they enhance decision quality by providing data driven insights and reducing reliance on subjective judgment.

Third, integration supports better alignment between recruitment and organizational strategy by linking hiring decisions with workforce planning and performance outcomes (Collings et al., 2019).

Finally, these systems enable scalability, allowing organizations to manage large volumes of applications without compromising quality.

Challenges in System Integration

Despite these benefits, integrating artificial intelligence into recruitment and selection systems presents several challenges. Data integration is a major issue, as organizations must combine information from multiple sources while ensuring accuracy and consistency.

Technical complexity is another challenge, as AI systems require advanced infrastructure and expertise. Organizations may face difficulties in implementing and maintaining these systems, particularly if they lack the necessary resources.

In addition, integration raises concerns about data privacy and security. Organizations must ensure that candidate information is protected and used responsibly.

Human and AI Collaboration in Integrated Systems

The integration of artificial intelligence across hiring stages reinforces the importance of collaboration between human decision makers and intelligent systems. While AI provides valuable insights, human judgment is essential for interpreting results and making final decisions.

Collaborative decision making ensures that hiring outcomes are both data driven and contextually appropriate. It also helps address ethical concerns by incorporating human values into the decision making process (Wilson & Daugherty, 2018).

Organizations that successfully combine technological capability with human expertise are more likely to achieve effective and responsible hiring outcomes.

CHALLENGES AND EMERGING TRENDS IN AI ENABLED RECRUITMENT AND SELECTION

The increasing adoption of artificial intelligence in recruitment and selection has introduced significant opportunities for improving efficiency and decision quality. However, it has also created a range of challenges that organizations must address to ensure responsible and effective implementation. At the same time, emerging technological developments continue to reshape the future of talent acquisition, making it essential to examine both the limitations and evolving trends associated with AI enabled hiring systems.

Algorithmic Bias and Fairness Concerns

One of the most critical challenges in AI driven recruitment is the issue of algorithmic bias. Artificial intelligence systems rely on historical data to generate predictions and recommendations. If this data reflects past inequalities or discriminatory practices, the system may replicate and reinforce those patterns in hiring decisions (Raghavan et al., 2020).

For example, biased datasets may lead to the underrepresentation of certain demographic groups in candidate shortlists. This not only affects fairness but also limits diversity within organizations. Research indicates that algorithmic bias can operate at scale, affecting a large number of candidates simultaneously, which amplifies its impact (Köchling & Wehner, 2020).

Addressing bias requires organizations to carefully design training datasets, implement bias detection mechanisms, and regularly audit AI systems to ensure equitable outcomes.

Lack of Transparency and Explainability

Another major challenge is the lack of transparency in AI based decision making. Many artificial intelligence systems function as complex models whose internal processes are not easily interpretable by users. This creates difficulties for both recruiters and candidates in understanding how decisions are made.

The absence of explainability affects trust and may lead to skepticism regarding the fairness of hiring outcomes. Candidates are more likely to accept decisions when they receive clear explanations and perceive the process as transparent (Leicht Deobald et al., 2019).

Explainable artificial intelligence is emerging as a solution to this problem. By providing insights into how decisions are generated, explainable systems enhance accountability and improve user confidence.

Data Privacy and Ethical Considerations

AI enabled recruitment systems require access to large volumes of candidate data, including personal information, professional history, and behavioral indicators. This raises significant concerns regarding data privacy and ethical use of information.

Organizations must ensure that data is collected, stored, and processed in a manner that complies with legal regulations and ethical standards. Failure to do so can result in legal consequences and damage to organizational reputation.

Ethical considerations also extend to how data is used in decision making. Organizations must ensure that AI systems respect candidate rights and avoid intrusive or discriminatory practices.

Over Reliance on Technology

While artificial intelligence enhances efficiency, excessive reliance on technology can reduce the role of human judgment in recruitment and selection. AI systems are effective in processing data and identifying patterns, but they may not fully capture qualitative aspects such as creativity, cultural fit, and interpersonal skills.

Over reliance on automation may lead to incomplete evaluation of candidates and reduce the ability of organizations to make nuanced decisions. Therefore, it is essential to maintain a balance between technological efficiency and human insight (Jarrahi, 2018).

Implementation Challenges

The adoption of artificial intelligence in recruitment also presents practical challenges related to implementation. Organizations must invest in technological infrastructure, data management systems, and employee training to effectively use AI tools.

Resistance to change is another common barrier. Employees may be hesitant to adopt new technologies due to lack of familiarity or concerns about job displacement. Effective change management strategies are required to address these challenges and ensure successful implementation (Kotter, 2012).

Emerging Trend: Explainable Artificial Intelligence

Explainable artificial intelligence represents a key trend in the evolution of recruitment technologies. As organizations seek to improve transparency and accountability, there is increasing emphasis on developing systems that provide clear explanations for decision outcomes.

Explainable AI enables recruiters to understand how candidate evaluations are generated and allows candidates to receive meaningful feedback. This enhances trust and supports ethical decision making (Leicht Deobald et al., 2019).

Emerging Trend: Predictive Workforce Analytics

Predictive analytics is becoming increasingly important in recruitment and workforce planning. AI systems analyze historical and real time data to forecast talent needs, identify skill gaps, and anticipate labor market trends.

This enables organizations to move from reactive hiring to proactive talent acquisition strategies. Predictive workforce analytics supports long term planning and enhances organizational agility (Marler & Boudreau, 2017).

Emerging Trend: Personalized Candidate Experience

Artificial intelligence is enabling more personalized recruitment experiences. AI systems tailor job recommendations, communication strategies, and engagement approaches based on individual candidate profiles.

Personalization improves candidate satisfaction and increases the likelihood of successful recruitment outcomes. It also enhances employer branding by creating a more engaging and responsive hiring process (Nikolaou, 2021).

Emerging Trend: Human and AI Collaboration

The future of recruitment is characterized by collaboration between human decision makers and artificial intelligence systems. Rather than replacing human judgment, AI is increasingly used as a decision support tool that enhances analytical capability.

This collaborative approach combines the strengths of both humans and machines, resulting in more effective and balanced decision making (Wilson & Daugherty, 2018).

Synthesis of Challenges and Trends

The discussion above highlights that while artificial intelligence offers significant benefits, it also introduces complex challenges that must be carefully managed. At the same time, emerging trends indicate that AI will continue to evolve and play an increasingly important role in recruitment and selection.

Organizations must adopt a balanced approach that leverages technological innovation while addressing ethical, practical, and organizational concerns.

MANAGERIAL IMPLICATIONS, FUTURE RESEARCH, AND CONCLUSION

The adoption of artificial intelligence in recruitment and selection has significant implications for managers, researchers, and organizations. This section outlines key managerial insights, identifies areas for future research, and summarizes the overall contribution of the chapter.

Managerial Implications

The integration of artificial intelligence into hiring systems requires managers to rethink traditional approaches to recruitment and selection. One of the most important implications is the need to develop new competencies within HR functions.

Managers must be able to interpret data, understand algorithmic outputs, and make informed decisions based on AI generated insights. This requires investment in training and skill development to enhance digital literacy among HR professionals (Ulrich & Dulebohn, 2015).

Another important implication is the need to establish ethical governance frameworks. Organizations must implement policies and procedures to ensure fairness, transparency, and accountability in AI based decision making. This includes regular auditing of algorithms, monitoring for bias, and providing clear communication to candidates (Raisch & Krakowski, 2021).

Managers must also focus on integrating human judgment with artificial intelligence. While AI provides valuable insights, final decisions should incorporate contextual understanding and organizational values. This collaborative approach enhances decision quality and ensures responsible use of technology (Jarrahi, 2018).

In addition, organizations should align AI driven recruitment systems with broader strategic objectives. Recruitment should be viewed as a strategic function that contributes to workforce planning, talent development, and competitive advantage (Collings et al., 2019).

Future Research Directions

Despite the growing body of literature on artificial intelligence in recruitment, several areas require further investigation. One important direction for future research is the long term impact of AI driven hiring systems on employee performance and organizational outcomes.

Longitudinal studies are needed to examine how AI based recruitment influences retention, productivity, and career development over time. This will provide deeper insights into the effectiveness of these systems.

Another area for future research is the interaction between human judgment and artificial intelligence. Understanding how these elements complement each other can help organizations design more effective decision making frameworks.

Cross cultural research is also needed to explore how different contexts influence the adoption and perception of AI in recruitment. Cultural factors may affect trust, acceptance, and effectiveness of AI systems (Venkatesh et al., 2003).

Finally, future research should focus on improving transparency and explainability in AI systems. Developing methods to make algorithmic decisions more understandable will enhance trust and support wider adoption.

Practical Implementation Framework for AI in Recruitment and Selection

The successful adoption of artificial intelligence in recruitment and selection requires more than technological investment. Organizations must develop a structured implementation framework that aligns AI capabilities with human resource strategies, organizational culture, and ethical considerations. A systematic approach ensures that AI driven hiring systems deliver value while minimizing risks associated with bias, transparency, and operational complexity.

Strategic Alignment with Organizational Goals

The first step in implementing artificial intelligence in recruitment is aligning technological initiatives with organizational objectives. AI systems should not be adopted solely for efficiency gains but must contribute to broader strategic goals such as talent quality, workforce diversity, and long term capability development.

Organizations need to identify key recruitment challenges, such as high turnover, skill shortages, or inefficient hiring processes, and determine how AI can address these issues. Strategic alignment ensures that AI investments generate measurable outcomes and support organizational performance (Collings, Mellahi, & Cascio, 2019).

Data Infrastructure and Quality Management

Artificial intelligence systems rely heavily on data for training and decision making. Therefore, organizations must establish robust data infrastructure to collect, store, and process candidate information effectively. High quality data is essential for ensuring accurate and unbiased outcomes.

Data management practices should include standardization of candidate information, removal of inconsistencies, and regular updates to maintain relevance. Organizations must also ensure that datasets are diverse and representative to reduce the risk of algorithmic bias (Raghavan et al., 2020).

In addition, data governance policies should be implemented to ensure compliance with legal and ethical standards related to privacy and data protection.

Selection of Appropriate AI Tools and Technologies

Organizations must carefully evaluate and select AI tools that align with their recruitment needs. Different technologies serve different purposes, such as resume screening, candidate sourcing, assessment, and analytics.

The selection process should consider factors such as system reliability, scalability, ease of integration, and transparency. Organizations should prioritize tools that provide explainable outputs, enabling recruiters to understand and justify decision making processes (Leicht Deobald et al., 2019).

Pilot testing of AI tools before full scale implementation can help identify potential issues and ensure compatibility with existing HR systems.

Integration with Existing HR Systems

Effective implementation requires seamless integration of AI technologies with existing human resource management systems. This includes applicant tracking systems, performance management platforms, and workforce analytics tools.

Integration enables the flow of data across different HR functions, allowing organizations to develop a comprehensive understanding of talent management processes. For example, recruitment data can be linked with employee performance data to improve predictive accuracy in hiring decisions (Tambe et al., 2019).

However, integration may present technical challenges, requiring collaboration between HR professionals and IT teams.

Human Resource Capability Development

The adoption of artificial intelligence in recruitment necessitates the development of new competencies within HR teams. Recruiters must be equipped with skills in data analysis, technology usage, and interpretation of algorithmic outputs.

Training programs should focus on enhancing digital literacy and enabling HR professionals to work effectively with AI systems. This includes understanding system limitations, identifying potential biases, and making informed decisions based on data insights (Ulrich & Dulebohn, 2015).

Developing these capabilities ensures that AI is used as a decision support tool rather than a replacement for human expertise.

Ethical Governance and Bias Mitigation

Ethical considerations are central to the implementation of AI in recruitment. Organizations must establish governance frameworks to ensure that AI systems operate in a fair and transparent manner.

This includes conducting regular audits of algorithms to identify and mitigate bias, ensuring transparency in decision making, and providing candidates with clear information about how their data is used (Köchling & Wehner, 2020).

Organizations should also establish accountability mechanisms to address potential issues and ensure compliance with ethical standards.

Candidate Experience and Engagement

While artificial intelligence improves efficiency, organizations must ensure that it does not negatively impact candidate experience. Recruitment processes should be designed to maintain a balance between automation and human interaction.

AI tools such as chatbots can be used to provide timely communication and support, while human recruiters should be involved in critical stages of the hiring process. This hybrid approach enhances engagement and ensures that candidates feel valued throughout the recruitment journey (Dineen & Allen, 2016).

Positive candidate experience contributes to stronger employer branding and improves the overall effectiveness of recruitment efforts.

Continuous Monitoring and System Improvement

Artificial intelligence systems require ongoing monitoring and evaluation to ensure their effectiveness. Organizations should track key performance indicators such as hiring accuracy, time to hire, and candidate satisfaction.

Feedback from recruiters and candidates can be used to identify areas for improvement and refine system performance. Machine learning models should be regularly updated to reflect changes in job requirements and labor market conditions.

Continuous improvement ensures that AI systems remain relevant and effective in dynamic organizational environments (Marler & Boudreau, 2017).

Change Management and Organizational Readiness

The implementation of artificial intelligence often requires significant organizational change. Employees may resist new technologies due to concerns about job security or lack of familiarity.

Effective change management strategies are essential to address these challenges. Organizations should communicate the benefits of AI adoption, provide training and support, and involve employees in the implementation process.

Leadership plays a critical role in fostering a culture that embraces innovation and encourages the use of technology in decision making (Kotter, 2012).

Strategic Outcomes of AI Implementation

When implemented effectively, artificial intelligence can transform recruitment and selection into strategic functions that contribute to organizational success. AI enables organizations to improve hiring accuracy, enhance workforce quality, and align talent acquisition with long term objectives.

In addition, AI driven recruitment systems support scalability and adaptability, allowing organizations to respond to changing labor market conditions and competitive pressures.

The successful implementation of AI in recruitment ultimately depends on the ability of organizations to integrate technology with human expertise, ethical considerations, and strategic vision.

CONCLUSION

Artificial intelligence has transformed recruitment and selection by introducing new levels of efficiency, consistency, and predictive capability. By leveraging data driven insights, organizations can improve hiring decisions and align talent acquisition with strategic objectives.

However, the adoption of artificial intelligence also presents significant challenges, including algorithmic bias, lack of transparency, and ethical concerns. Addressing these issues requires careful design, ongoing monitoring, and integration of human judgment.

The future of recruitment lies in the effective collaboration between humans and artificial intelligence. Organizations that successfully balance technological innovation with ethical responsibility and human insight will be better positioned to achieve sustainable success in talent management (Wilson & Daugherty, 2018).

REFERENCES

Acikgoz, Y. (2019). Employee recruitment and job search: Towards a multi-level integration. *Human Resource Management Review, 29*(1), 1–13. DOI: 10.1016/j.hrmr.2018.02.009

Barney, J. (1991). Firm resources and sustained competitive advantage. *Journal of Management, 17*(1), 99–120. DOI: 10.1177/014920639101700108

Becker, G. S. (1964). *Human capital: A theoretical and empirical analysis.* University of Chicago Press.

Black, J. S., & van Esch, P. (2020). AI-enabled recruiting: What is it and how should a manager use it? *Business Horizons, 63*(2), 215–226. DOI: 10.1016/j.bushor.2019.12.001

Bostrom, R. P., & Heinen, J. S. (1977). MIS problems and failures: A socio-technical perspective: Part II: The application of socio-technical theory. *Management Information Systems Quarterly, 1*(4), 11–28. DOI: 10.2307/249019

Brougham, D., & Haar, J. (2018). Smart technology, artificial intelligence, robotics, and algorithms (STARA): Employees' perceptions of our future workplace. *Journal of Management & Organization, 24*(2), 239–257. DOI: 10.1017/jmo.2016.55

Cappelli, P., Tambe, P., & Yakubovich, V. (2018). Artificial intelligence in HRM. *California Management Review, 61*(4), 15–42.

Chamorro-Premuzic, T., Winsborough, D., Sherman, R. A., & Hogan, R. (2019). New talent signals. *Industrial and Organizational Psychology: Perspectives on Science and Practice, 12*(3), 224–233.

Collings, D. G., Mellahi, K., & Cascio, W. F. (2019). Global talent management and performance. *Journal of World Business, 54*(2), 173–182.

Colquitt, J. A., Conlon, D. E., Wesson, M. J., Porter, C. O., & Ng, K. Y. (2001). Justice at the millennium. *The Journal of Applied Psychology, 86*(3), 425–445. DOI: 10.1037/0021-9010.86.3.425

Davis, F. D. (1989). Perceived usefulness and ease of use. *Management Information Systems Quarterly, 13*(3), 319–340. DOI: 10.2307/249008

Dineen, B. R., & Allen, D. G. (2016). Third party employment branding. *The Journal of Applied Psychology, 101*(2), 261–276.

Gilliland, S. W. (1993). Selection fairness perceptions. *Academy of Management Review, 18*(4), 694–734. DOI: 10.2307/258595

Greenberg, J. (1987). Organizational justice theory. *Academy of Management Review, 12*(1), 9–22. DOI: 10.2307/257990

Holm, A. B. (2012). E-recruitment. *Journal of Management & Organization, 18*(1), 68–81.

Huselid, M. A. (1995). HR practices and performance. *Academy of Management Journal, 38*(3), 635–672. DOI: 10.2307/256741

Jarrahi, M. H. (2018). Artificial intelligence and the future of work. *Business Horizons, 61*(4), 577–586. DOI: 10.1016/j.bushor.2018.03.007

Köchling, A., & Wehner, M. (2020). Algorithmic hiring bias. *Journal of Business Ethics.*

Kuncel, N. R., Klieger, D. M., Connelly, B. S., & Ones, D. S. (2013). Mechanical versus clinical prediction. *The Journal of Applied Psychology, 98*(6), 1060–1072. DOI: 10.1037/a0034156

Landers, R. N., & Sanchez, D. R. (2022). Gamified assessments. *Annual Review of Organizational Psychology and Organizational Behavior, 9*, 437–461.

Langer, M., König, C. J., & Papathanasiou, M. (2019). Automated interviews. *Journal of Business and Psychology, 34*(4), 567–582.

Leicht-Deobald, U., Busch, T., Schank, C., Weibel, A., Schafheitle, S., Wildhaber, I., & Kasper, G. (2019). Algorithm based HR decision making. *Journal of Business Ethics, 160*(2), 377–392. DOI: 10.1007/s10551-019-04204-w

Lievens, F., & Slaughter, J. E. (2016). Employer branding. *Annual Review of Organizational Psychology and Organizational Behavior, 3*(1), 407–440. DOI: 10.1146/annurev-orgpsych-041015-062501

Marler, J. H., & Boudreau, J. W. (2017). HR analytics review. *International Journal of Human Resource Management, 28*(1), 3–26. DOI: 10.1080/09585192.2016.1244699

Marler, J. H., & Boudreau, J. W. (2017). An evidence-based review of HR analytics. *International Journal of Human Resource Management, 28*(1), 3–26. DOI: 10.1080/09585192.2016.1244699

Nikolaou, I. (2021). Technology in recruitment. *The Spanish Journal of Psychology, 24*, e32.

Ployhart, R. E., Schmitt, N., & Tippins, N. T. (2017). Staffing science. *The Journal of Applied Psychology, 102*(3), 291–301. DOI: 10.1037/apl0000081

Raghavan, M., Barocas, S., Kleinberg, J., & Levy, K. (2020). Algorithmic bias in hiring. *FAT Conference Proceedings.*

Raghavan, M., Barocas, S., Kleinberg, J., & Levy, K. (2020). Mitigating bias in algorithmic hiring. *Proceedings of the FAT Conference.*

Raisch, S., & Krakowski, S. (2021). Artificial intelligence and management: The automation–augmentation paradox. *Academy of Management Review, 46*(1), 192–210. DOI: 10.5465/amr.2018.0072

Sackett, P. R., & Lievens, F. (2008). Personnel selection. *Annual Review of Psychology, 59*(1), 419–450. DOI: 10.1146/annurev.psych.59.103006.093716

Schultz, T. W. (1961). Human capital investment. *The American Economic Review, 51*(1), 1–17.

Strohmeier, S., & Piazza, F. (2015). AI in HRM. *International Journal of Human Resource Management, 26*(21), 2640–2665.

Tambe, P., Cappelli, P., & Yakubovich, V. (2019). AI in HRM. *The Academy of Management Annals, 13*(2), 1–47.

Trist, E., & Bamforth, K. (1951). Socio technical systems. *Human Relations, 4*(1), 3–38. DOI: 10.1177/001872675100400101

Ulrich, D., & Dulebohn, J. H. (2015). HR competencies. *Human Resource Management, 54*(2), 1–14.

Upadhyay, A. K., & Khandelwal, K. (2018). AI in recruitment. *Strategic HR Review, 17*(5), 255–258. DOI: 10.1108/SHR-07-2018-0051

van Esch, P., & Black, J. S. (2019). AI recruitment adoption. *International Journal of Selection and Assessment, 27*(3), 241–250.

Venkatesh, V., Morris, M. G., Davis, G. B., & Davis, F. D. (2003). UTAUT model. *Management Information Systems Quarterly, 27*(3), 425–478. DOI: 10.2307/30036540

Wilson, H. J., & Daugherty, P. R. (2018). Collaborative intelligence. *Harvard Business Review, 96*(4), 114–123.

Chapter 10

The Evolution of Job Applications Through Artificial Intelligence Technologies

N. Raghu
http://orcid.org/0000-0002-2091-8922
Jain University, India

Zaripov Khusan
Tashkent State University of Economics, Uzbekistan

Ergashev Nuriddin
http://orcid.org/0000-0002-8274-6193
Karshi State Technical University, Uzbekistan

Anorgul Ashirova
http://orcid.org/0009-0006-7271-3634
Mamun University, Uzbekistan

Dilmurod Turaev
Termez University of Economics and Service, Uzbekistan

Ismailov Azizbek
Alfraganus University, Uzbekistan

Muratova Shoista
Samarkand State Medical University, Uzbekistan

ABSTRACT

The chapter shows artificial intelligence (AI) technologies have been adopted by organizations to improve their recruitment procedures of job applicants based on data from recent surveys conducted in both the United States and the United Kingdom. The majority of respondents believe AI will shape the future of recruitment: 61% in the U.S. and 58% in the UK believe applicants should use AI in ways that remain hidden to others, while 56% (U.S.) and 52% (UK) believe candidates will need AI assistance to complete application processes. Additionally, 55% of U.S. and 52% of UK respondents think non-users will face disadvantages. People from Millennial

DOI: 10.4018/979-8-2600-2541-3.ch010

(78% U.S.; 79% UK) and Gen Z (71% U.S.; 62% UK) groups show the highest adoption rates of technology, while office workers in both countries report an 82% technology usage rate. The most commonly used tools by users include ChatGPT along with other large language models (73% U.S.; 86% UK) and CV generators (58% U.S.; 43% UK).

1. INTRODUCTION

The quick advancement of digital technologies has changed the complete process of job searching for people while businesses now use different methods to identify and assess potential employees. Artificial Intelligence (AI) works as a technological innovation which updates existing recruitment systems by providing organizations with new methods to improve their operational efficiency and create personalized candidate experiences and automate their processes (Bentayeb et al., 2026). AI-driven systems which encompass résumé screening algorithms and conversational agents that produce custom cover letters now serve as the recruitment systems which various industries and regions use to work their employment procedures. Organizations now use AI technology to evaluate job applications because this development marks a complete societal shift which enables organizations to make data-informed decisions by using predictive analytics and machine learning models to shape their strategic direction and employee development pathways. The modern applicant must navigate a digital job market which requires them to use optimization tools and automatic feedback systems and intelligent matching platforms as essential components of their application process (Kodagoda, 2026). The Future of Recruitment use survey data from the United States and the United Kingdom to present empirical insights which show how organizations adopt AI technologies and what drives them to use the technology and which ethical issues are beginning to emerge.

Figure 1. Artificial Intelligence in job Applications.

The results point to the fact that the majority of respondents see AI as a powerful force in the future of recruiting. A significant number of applicants view AI assistance as a requirement for navigating an increasingly automated and complex hiring landscape. Generational adoption is high among Millennials and Gen Z, which suggests that digital fluency is a decisive factor in AI-based technology adoption (Azahari et al., 2026). Despite this enthusiasm, concerns about skill distortion, authenticity, bias and fairness show that the governance and responsible use of these technologies cannot be overlooked. Conceptual background: the why and how of AI-assisted job applications understanding the context and rationale for AI emergence in recruitment considering the broader digital transformation of recruitment, and the goals and scope of this chapter.

1.1 Background and Rationale

Recruitment methods have changed throughout history because of technological advancements. The development of email applications and online job portals from newspaper ads and postal applications has changed how employers hire and applicants approach their job search. Organizations had their first experience with automated resume screening through Applicant Tracking Systems which permitted them to screen resumes according to specific keyword and experience and other established criteria (Hair Jr et al., 2026). The new AI technology goes beyond basic screening functions because it brings forth systems that possess the ability to study present trends and create new content from what they learn. AI recruitment implementation occurs because of multiple interdependent reasons.

- The global market now presents businesses with tougher challenges when they attempt to find skilled workers whom they want to hire. Organizations now face increased obstacles because international markets make it harder for them to recruit qualified workers whom they intend to employ. Organizations receive thousands of applications for a single position which creates administrative burdens that their traditional human-centered review processes cannot handle (Yong et al., 2026). Organizations benefit from three AI advantages which enable them to achieve better scalability while experiencing faster processing times and obtaining screening results which depend on their data analysis.
- The digitalization of labor markets has shifted expectations among job seekers. Modern applicants, particularly digital natives, are accustomed to algorithmically curated experiences on platforms such as LinkedIn and Indeed. These platforms use machine learning technology to suggest job openings which help professionals to network and receive personalized content recommendations. The candidates now view AI-powered optimization tools as standard advancements which stem from their internet usage (Hamid & Shodiyev, 2025).
- AI-powered content generation tools such as ChatGPT and other large language models enable applicants to draft résumés, refine cover letters, and simulate interview responses with unprecedented efficiency (Ghaleb, 2025). The survey results show that many users depend on those tools because they want to solve their personal deficiencies or improve their chances of winning. The digital gap in the labor market creates a situation where non-users will

experience disadvantages according to common perceptions (Balamurugan, 2024).

1.2 Digital Transformation of Recruitment

The recruitment digital transformation process involves organizations using digital technologies to transform their hiring procedures, which creates automatic systems that use data to build international talent networks. The transformation process began with the introduction of digital job boards and throughout its development, it progressed to the full implementation of algorithm-based talent acquisition systems (Muthuswamy & Absamatov, 2025). Online recruitment platforms in their initial form created a system that allowed all users to access job openings without needing to be in specific locations. The system required new application selection methods because the number of applications grew at an extremely fast rate. AI systems perform analysis on both textual keywords and contextual information together with data on user behavior and indicators that predict job performance. Machine learning algorithms enable organizations to examine candidate history patterns while measuring their alignment with successful employee profiles to create suitability ratings (Ammer, 2025).

The digital transformation process finds another demonstration through corporate career portal chatbots which operate as virtual assistants. The system answers applicant questions in real-time while it also arranges interview times and performs initial candidate evaluations. The AI-powered video interview system uses speech patterns and facial expressions and linguistic elements to assess how candidates answer questions. The innovations work to boost efficiency while decreasing the duration required to complete the hiring process. Recruitment teams use data analytics to track their hiring pipelines which helps them improve their recruitment process (Zayniddinov et al., 2025). The organization uses candidate engagement rates and application form drop-off locations and retention score predictions to make strategic choices. Human Resource Management Systems (HRMS) now use AI technology which shows the movement toward using data as a foundation for managing talent. Different regions and industries display varying degrees of digital transformation implementation (Cahyani et al., 2025). The bigger companies in technologically advanced sectors use AI-powered recruitment systems, while the smaller companies experience difficulties because they lack sufficient resources. The countries use different regulatory systems which impact how much algorithmic transparency and accountability organizations must maintain during their hiring procedures.

Figure 2. Integration of AI into Human Resource Management Systems

The process of recruitment is also changing candidate behaviour, with candidates increasingly using tailored résumés for automated screening systems by embedding job description keywords 'in the right way. AI-based résumé optimization tools (for example, Jobscan) facilitate this by indicating how the résumé can be improved to fit automated screening systems algorithms. Recruitment takes place via technology systems, which are used by both employers and applicants to gain access to algorithm-based evaluation methods (Ravikumar et al., 2026). The mutual AI usage by employers who use algorithms for candidate evaluation and by candidates who use algorithms for their application optimization creates an ongoing feedback mechanism between the two parties (Rajeswari et al., 2026). The study of this interaction helps organizations evaluate their operational fairness and authentic performance and their capacity to build a skilled workforce for future needs.

1.3 Objectives and Scope of the Chapter

The chapter aims to reveal contemporary AI applications in recruitment by studying current practices and analyzing how different generations adopt these technologies because they want to use them and organizations need to maintain their operations. The chapter uses survey data from the United States and the United Kingdom to demonstrate how job seekers use AI tools and how stakeholders view their use. The chapter aims to:

- Examine the evolution of recruitment processes leading to algorithmic and AI-driven systems.
- Identify AI used in job applications, including large language models, résumé optimization platforms, and intelligent job-matching systems.
- Analyze generational and occupational adoption trends, highlighting differences between Millennials, Generation Z, and other demographic groups.
- Provide strategic recommendations for applicants, employers, and policymakers to ensure responsible and equitable AI integration.

1.4 Evolution of Job Application Processes

The development of job application procedures demonstrates how technological advancements and corporate strategies and employment market changes have transformed recruitment processes. Recruitment has evolved from face-to-face interactions and document evaluations to systems that use digital networks and artificial intelligence for candidate assessment (Hussain et al., 2026). The transformation of hiring processes has changed how candidates behave and how organizations compete while establishing new structures for employment markets (Kulmanov et al., 2024). Modern recruitment processes use algorithms for candidate assessment and digital platforms for applicant management and automated workflows to conduct hiring operations in a global talent market.

1.4.1 Traditional Hiring to Algorithmic Screening

Recruitment procedures in the past depended on the use of physical documents and manual selection processes and in-person interviews. Organizations used recruiter judgment together with candidate education backgrounds and reference verification to determine candidate eligibility. The organization needed more time to reach decisions because its contact network limited its ability to gather information (H. V Balachandra Achar, 2025). Organizations encountered difficulties in scaling their operations because personal interactions helped people understand specific situations. The development of digital storage systems together with web-based application portals established a major technological advancement. Companies began to store applicant information in electronic systems which allowed them to manage records in an organized way while they implemented uniform evaluation procedures. Automated filtering systems were developed to assist recruiters with large applicant pools because the number of applications reached a peak (Prabha et al., 2026).

Advanced computational models enable algorithmic screening technologies to process both structured data and unstructured data through their advanced computational capabilities. The system uses natural language processing to understand semantic meaning while it identifies skill connections and experience relevance through detection methods that do not rely on exact keyword matches (Ahmed & & Pardaev, 2025). The predictive modeling methods assess candidate profiles through performance benchmark comparisons that organizations create using their internal data. The systems evaluate candidate suitability through probability-based fit indicators which exist beyond their fundamental qualification identification function. The digital assessment tools evaluate cognitive abilities and situational judgment skills while testing technical proficiency through online testing environments. Video-based assessments use structured scoring models to maintain evaluation standards across different candidates throughout the entire assessment process. The system functions to deliver statistical insights for decision-making while human supervisors need to oversee all decision processes. Organizations face new challenges from increased automated system usage because they need to establish fair treatment practices for all users while creating understandable results. The current hiring governance frameworks require organizations to develop controls which handle three critical areas: algorithmic transparency, data governance, and auditability. Advanced technologies help organizations achieve operational efficiency while ethical safeguards protect their credibility and compliance they need to meet regulatory standards (Raghu et al., 2025).

1.4.2 Platform-Based Recruitment Ecosystems

Recruitment in the 21st century is an increasingly complex activity taking place in digital ecosystems rather than in the form of single vacancy announcements. Here we demonstrate that professional networking infrastructures like LinkedIn are evolving into full-blown talent ecosystems that fulfill multiple functions ranging from job discovery to employer branding to skill validation to professional networking. In this context, the ecosystem applies data analytics to recommend opportunities, to suggest connections and alike to anticipate future skill demands (Kulmanov, 2025). Further, large job aggregators like Indeed collect listings in one place for many industries and regions, enabling quick to access information. In addition, employer review websites, such as Glassdoor, add a level of transparency to the process by including workplace feedback. In this information-rich environment, applicants are able to leverage comparative information and organizations can benchmark themselves (Aarthi, 2026).

Digital recruitment ecosystems extend beyond their digital boundaries to include project-based and independent job opportunities. The platforms of Upwork and Fiverr utilize their matching system to connect clients with freelancers through their worldwide operating algorithm. Users obtain access to job opportunities because their reputation systems and completion rates and peer reviews determine their eligibility. The ecosystems require constant data transmission to maintain their operational efficiency. User activity together with engagement metrics and application outcomes, create feedback loops which enhance recommendation algorithms. The platforms gain stronger predictive abilities because user participation increases which makes them more important to the labor market (Ammer, 2025). The system's concentrated data creates fresh risks which stem from digital dependency and asymmetrical information distribution and the centralization of market power. The ecosystems now depend on permanent recruitment through profiles, which has replaced their previous intermittent hiring methods. Candidates establish permanent digital identities while employers develop continuous talent pipelines which function independently of current job needs.

1.5 AI Tools in Contemporary Job Applications

The artificial intelligence into contemporary job searching procedures has transformed the methods candidates use to prepare themselves and showcase their abilities in the fight for job opportunities. The current AI systems go beyond their original purpose of helping users submit documents online because they now enable users to create content and optimize strategies and practice interviews and find job openings. The systems provide applicant assistance while they create a framework for constructing and assessing and developing professional identities. Job applications now require artificial intelligence because they moved from traditional information exchange to dynamic data-driven career planning systems (Zhao et al., 2025). Candidates use intelligent systems to achieve better understanding and alignment and enhanced competitive advantage. Employers use AI screening systems which create a technological system that enables both parties to interact with algorithms. The changing recruitment landscape requires applicants to comprehend all available AI tools for successful analysis.

1.5.1 Large Language Models and Content Generation

Large Language Models (LLMs) have revolutionized content creation for applicants. OpenAI's ChatGPT, Google's Gemini, and Anthropic's Claude allow users to create résumés, cover letters, personal statements, and professional summaries in seconds. These models are based on deep neural network architectures trained on large textual datasets. The models produce contextually relevant and grammatically correct language. In job applications, LLMs assist with articulating achievements, editing for appropriate tone, and grammar correction. The model can reformat the content for readability. The applicant can prompt the LLM to generate content that aligns with industry expectations, job description, and values of the organization.

The use of large language models (LLMs) is increasing in the course of writing a resume. Aside from drafting support, LLMs can be used for idea generation and framing. For example, LLMs can help translate task-oriented to impact-oriented statements (e.g. conveying leadership responsibilities and measurable outcomes) and technical expertise into language that is tailored to cross-functional roles. Generative AI also presents interesting questions for authenticity and differentiation. Similar LLMs may create stylistic homogeneity among applicants. Recruiters increasingly value originality, specificity, and verifiable achievements. The use of LLMs can, therefore, increase efficiency and linguistic precision but may require careful editing and application-specific tailoring by the applicant.

1.5.2 CV and Cover Letter Optimization Systems

The AI-powered optimization platforms provide functions which enable content creation and permit businesses to match their operations with their Applicant Tracking System requirements. Jobscan and Resume Worded provide tools which enable users to examine résumés against job descriptions for the purpose of discovering missing keywords and formatting errors and structural problems. The systems operate through pattern recognition algorithms which assess applicant documents to determine their compliance with recruitment criteria. The system generates match scores which produce practical application guidelines for candidates to improve their application documents according to automated screening standards. The recommendations include using industry-specific terms and measuring professional accomplishments and changing section titles and which file formats should be used for optimal results. The platforms provide optimization functions which assess how well users can understand text and how clearly it communicates its message. The systems assess two areas which include evaluating the difficulty level of sentences and the effectiveness of bullet points and the strength of competency displays (Bhatti, 2025). The system provides users with industry-standard benchmarking data which shows how their application profile works between their submitted documents and those of their industry peers. The optimization process improves digital screening system compatibility, but the excessive use of keyword density is a cause for loss of narrative coherence. The user has to find the balance between algorithm specifications and a real storytelling content. The optimization process creates ethical issues through the possibility to enhance or distort the real work experience (Islamutdinov et al., 2024). Users should use these tools to increase the work visibility, but also to report a true professional background (Islam et al., 2026).

1.5.3 AI-Based Interview Preparation

The process of interview preparation now uses interactive AI-driven simulations instead of static practice questions from previous times. The platforms Interviewing io and Pramp create controlled mock interview settings which allow users to practice actual interview questioning methods. The advanced AI interview coaches use speech pattern analysis and pacing assessment and filler word frequency measurement and answer structure evaluation to conduct their analysis (Achar et al., 2025). The tools provide two functions which include sentiment analysis and communication clarity assessments to produce feedback about confidence levels and conciseness and logical progression. The candidates can practice their behavioral responses through scenario-based prompts which match the requirements of various competency frameworks (Pandey, 2024). AI systems enable technical assessment preparation through their ability to produce coding challenges and case studies and role-specific simulations. The adaptive learning models use performance-based question difficulty adjustments to enable candidates to gradually improve their skills through targeted practice (Al Doghan & Absamatov, 2025). The new technologies make high-quality preparation resources accessible to all individuals especially those who do not have professional coaching networks. Candidates need to create natural answers for interview questions because their interview performance will suffer if they practice too much. The AI-assisted preparation process helps users create confidence and mental clarity which leads to better performance than memorized content delivery (Marisamy et al., 2026).

1.5.4 Intelligent Job Search and Matching Tools

Job recommendations have become increasingly personalized in recent years. Personal networking platforms, such as LinkedIn, use machine learning algorithms to recommend jobs by analyzing users' job search activity, skill set, and activities. Job aggregators, such as Indeed, use predictive analytics to rank job postings considering proximity and probability of application. These platforms leverage behavioral data, such as search queries and profiles, to re-rank and refine the recommendations (Sherov et al., 2025). The skill inference models, also available in some platforms, include the identification of transferable skills and recommending next-step careers. Labor market analytics are also part of the recommendation tools to inform users about emerging fields and in-demand skills. Applicants are therefore encouraged to balance automated suggestions with exploratory search strategies.

1.6 Adoption Patterns and User Motivations

Employees from different age groups and job roles and their level of technological knowledge adopt AI tools for their job applications in different ways. Younger users who have advanced digital skills adopt these tools at a faster pace because of their superior digital literacy. People choose to adopt these technologies because they want to achieve better work results through more effective work processes and improved application standards and greater self-assurance and competitive edge (Rathinavel et al., 2026). The availability of information about the technology together with its actual use in practice determines how people accept new technology (Makhmudov et al., 2026).

1.6.1 Generational Differences in AI Usage

The different age groups show different opinions about AI job search technologies. People who spent their childhood in environments with constant digital technology access include Generation Z and younger Millennials who display better ability to use generative AI systems along with automated résumé tools and AI-based interview training programs. Students in modern educational systems need to learn how to use online study resources and algorithm-driven content delivery systems and digital tools that enable group work. People treat AI-assisted content creation and optimization as standard work tools because they fail to recognize these systems as transformative technologies (Balamurugan et al., 2026). Younger job seekers prefer to use conversational AI systems for creating their professional summaries and transforming their application documents and practicing their behavioral interview responses. People use AI in their everyday communication tools which establishes AI as an academic and professional development essential.

Generation X and Baby Boomers may selectively adopt AI if authenticity, privacy, and technology transparency are questioned. Some rely on field experience and existing networks instead of an algorithmic approach. Others cautiously employ AI tools for editing or formatting, rather than unique content. However, generational generalizations remain a myth. More often, digital literacy, professional context, and organizational culture determine AI usage than age. Mid-level professionals in technologically driven industries may be early adopters of AI, while younger workers in neglected areas may lag behind. Therefore, generational analysis requires contextualization.

1.6.2 Occupational and Demographic Trends

The way people use AI technology at work depends on the specific workplace environment they operate in. The technology-driven industries which include software development and digital marketing and data analytics and engineering fields show greater technology adoption than other sectors (Adilov et al., 2025). Professionals who work in these fields already better understand machine learning basics and they also show interest in testing AI technology which enhances their work. People experience less psychological resistance to AI technology when their technical skills match the required AI system operation skills (Ravikumar et al., 2026). The manual work and craft-based work and informal work sectors of employment show lower levels of technology adoption. Organizations which have not used structured digital recruitment systems experience decreased motivation to apply AI technology in their application procedures. Public sector organizations which implement standardized work methods do not use AI technology for process improvement at the same level as private sector companies.

Educational attainment determines which people will choose to adopt new technologies. People who achieve higher educational levels display greater digital literacy skills together with improved knowledge about AI system capabilities. University career centers provide access to online training modules together with peer communities which help users learn about new technology. The way people use technology changes because of geographic differences. The urban population which has good internet access together with global labor market exposure will use AI technologies more than others. The low adoption rates in rural areas and regions with restricted broadband access occur because of their operational limitations (Sapayev et al., 2026). People who belong to different socioeconomic groups can access high-end AI services through subscription-based optimization tools and premium digital devices. The structural situation of society exists together with gender and demographic elements (Rathinavel et al., 2026). Theoretical AI tools function without bias, yet social standards and technology confidence levels impact the ways people use them. The existence of support networks along with available mentorship programs and technology sector representation will influence how different demographics adopt technology.

1.6.3 Digital Divide and Access Inequalities

The digital divide consists of different internet access levels and device performance standards and digital skills does not complete ability to use online tools and educational materials which digital resources provide. People who do not have stable broadband internet access and up-to-date computer equipment face challenges when they try to use advanced AI technologies. The combination of subscription-based optimization tools and premium-priced coaching services creates obstacles for users. All generative AI platforms provide free basic access but users need to pay for access to most advanced functionalities (Ghaleb, 2025). This situation will make it harder for people already facing barriers to find employment to succeed in their job hunting efforts. Digital literacy acts as an obstacle which prevents equal distribution of emerging technologies. The use of AI requires people to develop their abilities in assessment evaluation and prompt creation and feedback understanding (Bhatti, 2025). The correct training will result in users either missing out on essential tool functions or becoming reliant on automated outcomes.

Language barriers can also lead to unequal treatment among people from different groups. AI systems that are trained on linguistic datasets of certain languages will deliver weaker results in non-dominant languages and professional domains that require deep cultural knowledge. Individuals who must seek employment in labor markets that lie outside the central hubs of the global labor market will be disadvantaged by this limitation. Institutional action is needed to address the existing gaps. Educational institutions in collaboration with workforce development providers and public employment services should incorporate AI literacy training into their career preparation programming (Aldossary & Pardaev, 2025).

2. LITERATURE SURVEY

Bentayeb et al., (2026) presents an extensive investigation into the use of Artificial Intelligence (AI) technologies in Human Resource Management (HRM) which affects both workforce management and market development from 2024 to 2034. The AI-driven technologies which include predictive analytics and intelligent recruitment systems and automated resume screening and employee performance analytics are changing the way HR departments operate their standard procedures. The AI technology improves decision-making processes while decreasing administrative duties and increasing the effectiveness of talent acquisition through data-based insights. The ethical issues which begin with algorithmic bias and proceed to data privacy problems and the impact of technology on job loss. The market analysis research which predicts that international investments in AI-powered HR systems will rise and hybrid human-AI collaboration models will become common in the future. The organizations must implement reskilling and upskilling programs to prepare their employees for work in environments that use artificial intelligence technology. The organizations need governance systems which include regulatory frameworks to safeguard innovation while upholding their ethical obligations. The AI as a strategic HRM tool which organizations must use responsible AI management practices to maintain their operational efficiency and employee faith in the organization.

Kodagoda et al., (2026) explores Generation Y workers perceive and understand Artificial Intelligence technology which they use in their job environments through both positivist and interpretivist research approaches. The millennials understand AI systems through their assessment of job security and career growth and work efficiency and company environment. Generation Y workers show moderate positive feelings about AI implementation because they perceive its capacity to boost operational efficiency and handle repetitive work and support data-based decision processes. The public continues to express strong worries about three major issues which include job loss situations and diminished face-to-face communication and the need for more ethical information. Employees at a company will only accept artificial intelligence technologies when the organization provides proper communication methods and training programs and shows its leadership with transparent operations. The organizations need to establish change management procedures which help organizations implement AI technology without interruptions. Generation Y members want companies to deliver ongoing educational programs which support their need to learn new skills and better their abilities according to technology changes. The technology acceptance relates to employee behavior during digital transformation between different age groups. Businesses can achieve successful AI execution through their need to maintain equal emphasis on technological advancements and human-centered business practices which create trust and active employee participation and permanent staff growth.

Azahari et al., (2026) investigates employability development corresponds with the future work environment. The global literature to identify key employer expectations, emerging skill requirements, and recruitment strategies that technology disruption will create. The digital literacy together with adaptability and critical thinking and cross-functional competencies as important requirements for employability. The talent acquisition process now experiences major changes through AI-driven recruitment platforms together with automated assessments and virtual hiring processes. The organizations now require employees to develop soft skills which include communication and emotional intelligence and collaborative problem-solving abilities together with technical skill development. The value through its worldwide comparative analysis which shows how different regions implement recruitment digitization and prepare their workforce. The higher education institutions need to create new curricula which will meet industry needs while including experiential learning and industry partnerships and digital technology training. The challenges which arise from people not having equal access to digital resources which creates a risk of increasing employment disparities. The comprehensive framework which shows how employability connects with digital transformation and strategic recruitment approaches into the changing worldwide labor market.

Hair et al., (2026) shows how universities use artificial intelligence and social robots to attract students through new educational marketing technologies and educational outreach methods which have emerged. The AI-powered chatbots virtual assistants and humanoid social robots enhance personalized communication with prospective students. The AI systems enable faster responses to requests while improving data analysis capabilities and enabling precise outreach efforts through the use of behavioral insights. Social robots function as interactive tools which universities use to create live campus experiences during open house events and virtual recruitment activities. The psychological factors and ethical issues which include trust development and data protection and the way people perceive their interactions with machines. Empirical evidence shows that using AI for recruitment purposes boosts student engagement while enabling institutions to achieve an advantage in international student recruitment. The organizations should use technology as a supportive tool which enhances their recruitment process and maintains authentic relationships with candidates.

Yong et al., (2026) conduct an investigation about how Generation Z people make their job choices by using Environmental Social and Governance (ESG) criteria. The sustainability practices and corporate responsibility and ethical governance standards now play a growing role in determining which careers young job seekers prefer to pursue. The Generation Z assesses job opportunities based on two factors which include salary and career development but they need to know about environmental sustainability practices and diversity initiatives and social responsibility programs. The three factors of digital transparency and social media presence and publicly available ESG performance data create a strong effect on how attractive organizations appear to people. The research shows that companies which implement sustainable business practices together with responsible AI technology solutions experience better results when they try to attract new employees. The research found a relationship between ESG priorities and workforce retention rates which showed that employees who share company values tend to stay with organizations while maintaining their loyalty to the organization.

Table 1. Comparative analysis of research gap findings

Authors & Year	Methodological Approach	Key Findings	Workforce Implications	Ethical / Governance Concerns
Bentayeb, A. et al. (2026)	Conceptual and market trend analysis	AI enhances recruitment, predictive analytics, resume screening, and performance management; market growth in AI-HRM systems expected	Need for reskilling, hybrid human–AI collaboration models, strategic workforce planning	Algorithmic bias, data privacy risks, regulatory compliance, governance frameworks required
Kodagoda, T. (2026)	Positivist and interpretivist approaches	Gen Y shows moderate optimism; values efficiency but fears job displacement and reduced human interaction	Importance of training, communication, and transparent AI implementation to increase acceptance	Ethical transparency, job security concerns, trust-building through leadership
Azahari, L. M. et al. (2026)	Systematic literature review	Digital literacy, adaptability, and soft skills critical for future work; AI-driven recruitment expanding globally	Curriculum redesign, experiential learning, industry partnerships, digital skill development	Digital divide, unequal access to technology, widening employment gaps
Hair Jr, J. F. et al. (2026)	Conceptual and empirical discussion	AI chatbots and social robots improve engagement, personalization, and outreach effectiveness	Competitive advantage in global student recruitment; integration of AI into marketing strategies	Trust, data protection, ethical AI use in student engagement
Yong, J. Y. et al. (2026)	Conceptual and empirical insights	Gen Z prioritizes sustainability, diversity, and ethical governance in career decisions	Organizations must align recruitment branding with ESG values to attract and retain talent	--

The summary illustrates the Human Resource Management, recruitment methods, and employability prospects undergo fundamental changes through the combined impact of Artificial Intelligence (AI), digital transformation, and sustainability practices as shown in table 1. AI operates as a strategic HR tool that enhances decision-making processes while eliminating administrative tasks and improving talent acquisition through predictive analytics and intelligent recruitment systems and automated resume screening and performance analytics. The technologies improve operational efficiency, but their use creates ethical problems because they create algorithmic bias and they endanger data privacy and they threaten job security, which requires organizations to establish governance frameworks and reskilling initiatives. Workers appreciate AI technology because it boosts their work productivity and enables them to make decisions based on data, yet they still fear losing their jobs while human interactions decrease and organizations need to explain their ethical practices.

3. METHODOLOGY

The research methodology used to produce the visual results operates according to a predefined quantitative research framework. The research team established two research objectives which they defined as following research objective one to evaluate public opinion about brand social responsibility and research objective two they wanted to analyze AI technology use in job application processes among different demographic groups and various countries. The research team identified essential research variables which included country (U.S., UK, Germany), age group (Gen Z, Millennials, Gen X), gender, occupation type, AI tools used, and reasons for AI adoption. The researchers developed a questionnaire which contained closed-ended questions and multiple-choice questions to create a system for measuring participant responses. The respondents evaluated their agreement with brand-related questions which contained issues about mental health, climate change, diversity, free speech, racial issues, and international conflicts (Ravikumar et al., 2026). The AI-related questions asked participants about their usage patterns and which tools they used and their primary reasons for using AI technology as shown in figure 3.

Figure 3. Data structured and visualization of output results.

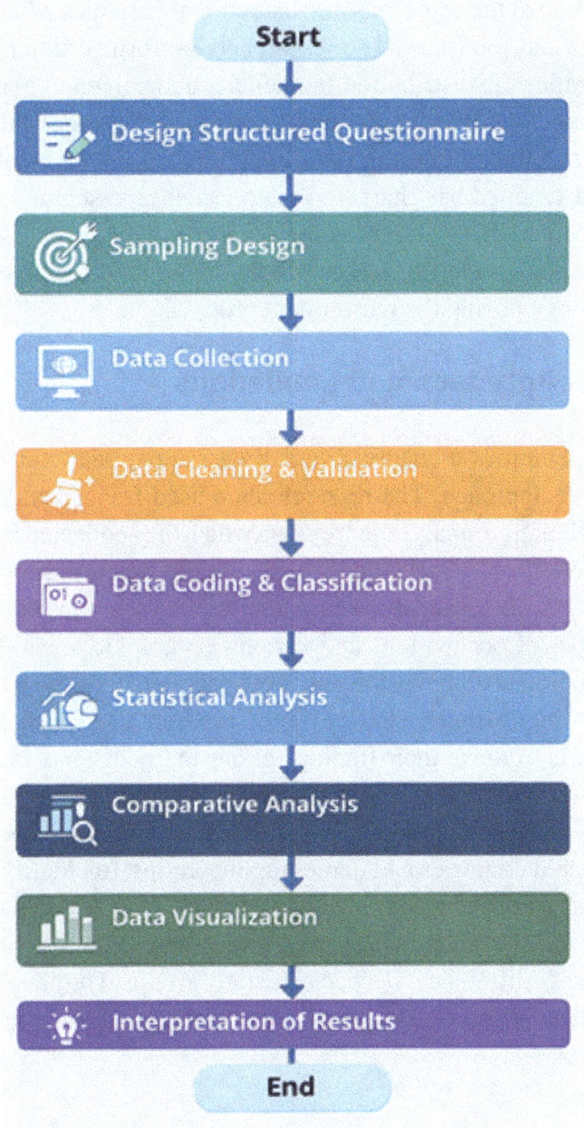

Stratified random sampling method required that all age groups and gender and employment categories should be equally represented in each country which resulted in the method achieving balanced representation. The researchers collected data by using online survey panels which were active during the designated survey periods. The study included only participants who were between 18 and 67 years old and had applied for jobs during the last two years for the purpose of conducting AI-specific analysis. The collected data underwent the cleaning process which removed all incomplete and inconsistent and duplicate responses from the dataset. The researchers coded the responses into categorical variables which included generational cohorts and job types. The researchers performed descriptive statistical analysis to determine the distribution frequencies and percentage share of the data. The research team conducted comparative analysis between countries and demographic groups to identify existing trends and different patterns of behavior. The researchers used grouped bar charts to create visual representations of the results which showed percentage differences between the study groups. The researchers analyzed the results to determine how people view brand activism and how they adopt AI technology during the recruitment process.

3.1 Analytical Approach and Limitations

The research employs a quantitative and descriptive analytical method for its main investigative approach. The research team used frequency distributions and percentage calculations to analyze survey data which they collected from respondents who belonged to various countries and different demographic groups. The study used comparative analysis to assess differences between age groups and gender groups and different types of occupations and various geographic areas. The researchers used cross-tabulation techniques to study how people use AI based on their demographic information (Ammer, 2025). The researchers used visual analytics with grouped bar charts to make their findings easier to understand and interpret. The research limitations which affect its outcomes. The researchers applied descriptive statistical analysis to identify the distribution frequencies and the percentage share. The study compared countries and demographic groups, to identify existing trends and various patterns of behaviour (Makhmudov et al., 2025). The authors of the research used grouped bar charts to present visual representations of the results that indicated percentage differences between the study groups. The people from different cultures understand survey questions creates challenges for making comparisons between countries.

4. RESULTS AND DISCUSSION

The data shows how artificial intelligence (AI) has changed both work patterns and job search methods which resulted in a major shift in labor market control for the United States. The number of unemployed people reached 7.50 million by December 2025 which surpassed the total of 6.54 million job vacancies. The current situation represents a complete turnaround from the post-pandemic period when there were more job vacancies than available workers as demonstrated in figure 4. The historical pattern shows that economic downturns and recessions happen at the same time as these crossings which creates a situation where the labor market decreases while more applicants compete for fewer job openings. The AI has become an increasingly important tool in job applications. The United States and United Kingdom respondents who make up the majority believe that applicants should use AI in a way which makes it impossible to identify their usage of AI technology because people have started to accept AI as a normal practice while its ethical boundaries remain uncertain according to figure 5. The 500 responders who consider the response for data collection as shown in website www.statista.com, more than half of respondents also agree that, in the future, navigating the application process without AI may be difficult and that applicants who do not use AI could face worse chances. The perception of the tighter labor market results from the discovery that organizations need efficient tools which enhance their work output because job opportunities have become limited in comparison to available job candidates.

Figure 4. The unemployed members and job openings. (Link: https://www.statista.com/chart/28407/unemployed-persons-and-job-openings-in-the-united-states/ Date: 02/03/2026 Time: 09:03PM)

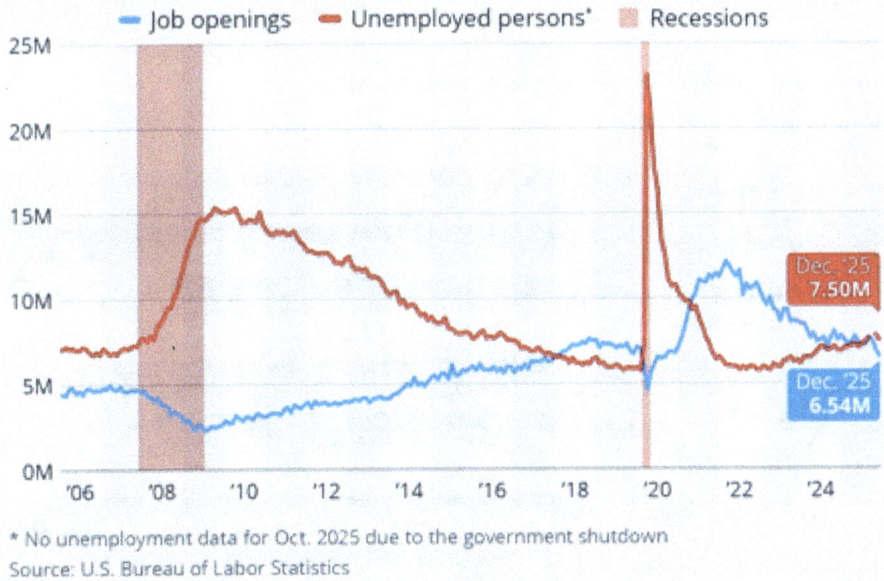

Figure 5. The Future job application viva AI.

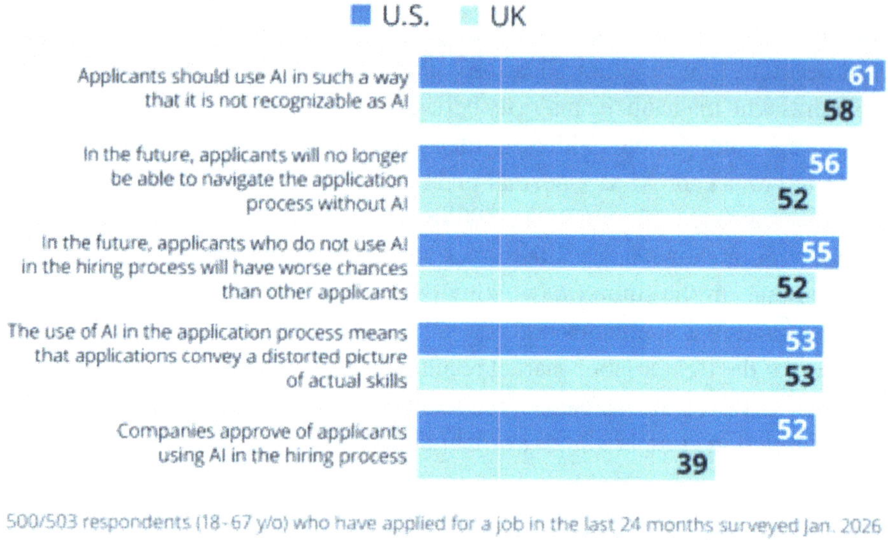

(Link: https://www.statista.com/chart/35806/use-ai-in-job-application/ Date: 02/03/2026 Time: 09:03PM)

Figure 6. Job application received on gender basis.

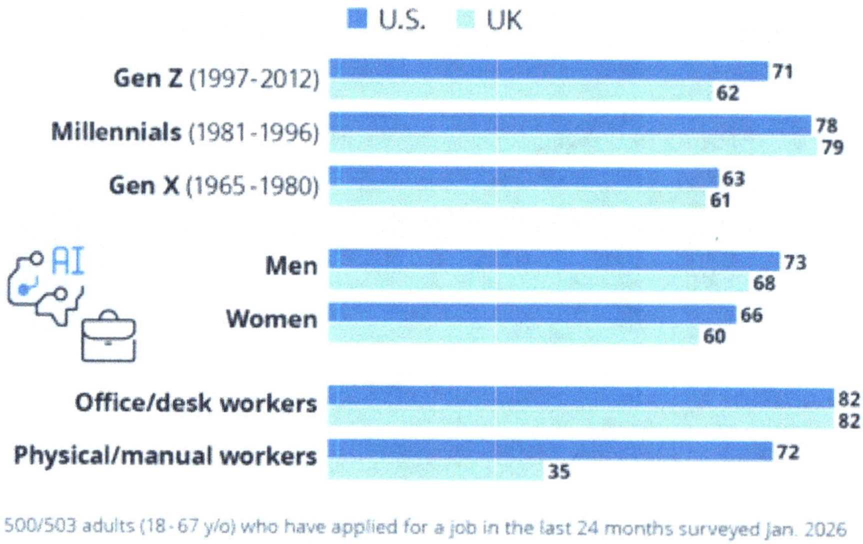

(Link: https://www.statista.com/chart/35807/ai-use-job-application-process/ Date: 02/03/2026 Time: 09:03PM)

Figure 7. Job applications tools.

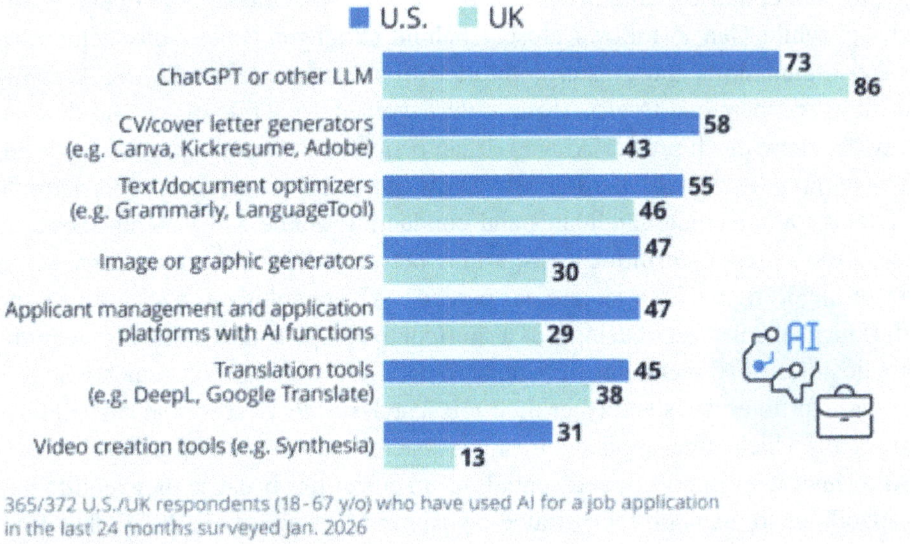

(Link: https://www.statista.com/chart/35815/most-popular-ai-tools-for-job-applications/ Date: 02/03/2026 Time: 09:03PM)

Figure 8. Job application process through AI.

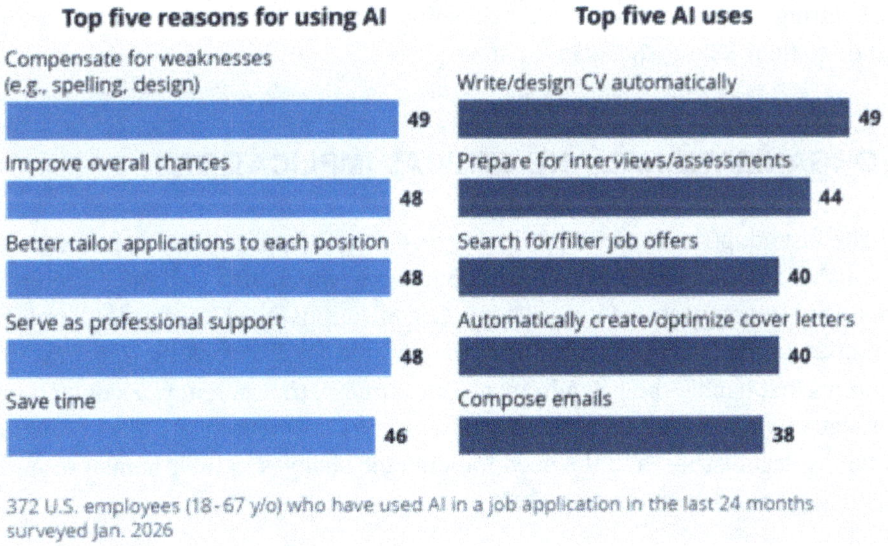

(Link: https://www.statista.com/chart/35816/main-uses-ai-job-application/ Date: 02/03/2026 Time: 09:03PM)

The demographic data shows which groups lead the adoption of AI technology. In both countries, millennials use AI for job applications more than any other group, while Gen Z follows closely behind. Younger generations demonstrate better digital skills and greater comfort with automated technologies. According to figure 6, men tend to use AI more than women do, while office and desk employees show much greater AI usage than people who work in manual labor jobs. The current AI tool distribution between white-collar recruitment tools and other systems for screening candidates and conducting online assessments shows that these tools create recruitment disparities between different occupational groups according to figure 7. Organizations perceive AI technology as a tool to help their staff members instead of using it as a shortcut to complete tasks. The most common applications of AI technology create automatic CV writing tools which help users prepare for interviews and filter their job search results to solve the current hiring problems which affect applicant tracking systems (as shown in figure 8). The use of AI technologies has become essential for organizations because they require these capabilities to maintain their strategic position (Agarwal et al., 2024). The figure shows that people are worried about the potential job losses which will result from AI implementations. More respondents in the United Kingdom, United States, and Germany believe that millions of jobs will disappear than they fear losing their personal employment. The difference between these two groups indicates that people in society experience widespread anxiety about work-related issues which do not stem from their personal job concerns. People use AI technologies to help them find work during the present time but they continue to worry about what AI technology will do to their job prospects in the future.

5. ORGANIZATIONAL AND ETHICAL IMPLICATIONS

The fast adoption of artificial intelligence for job application systems exceeds established organizational and ethical boundaries which affect all three groups of employers, employees, and regulators. Organizations need to develop strategic responses to the upcoming period of AI-powered applications by implementing solutions that handle their requirements for fairness, transparency, accountability, and regulatory compliance. The section examines how employers react to ethical problems, legal issues, and the need for strategic changes in their human resource practices (Ahmed & & Pardaev, 2025).

5.1 Employer Responses to AI-Assisted Applications

The number of AI-generated employment documents, which include résumé and cover letter materials and interview responses, has been steadily rising in today's job market. Organizations have implemented AI screening technologies, specifically applicant tracking systems (ATS), to handle their increased application processing requirements which represent their first step toward operational transformation. The systems assist in decreasing administrative workload yet they create an "AI arms race" situation, where applicants use AI for application enhancement while companies employ AI to conduct candidate screening. Organizations have chosen to protect themselves from potential dangers by developing methods to identify AI-generated content, which they consider a threat to their ability to prove authenticity. The organizations which implement AI technology use it to build their modern digital technology proficiency (Kuzmin et al., 2025). Progressive employers increasingly focus less on whether AI was used and more on whether the applicant demonstrates genuine competence during interviews, assessments, and probation periods. The movement indicates that organizations are beginning to accept AI technology as a means to enhance work productivity instead of using it to commit fraudulent activities. The different ways employers show their attitudes toward employees create an environment of uncertainty for job candidates (Ravikumar et al., 2026). The absence of explicit guidelines leads applicants to feel they must hide their use of AI technology which creates ethical conflicts. Organizations must create rules for AI technology usage during employee recruitment processes and they need to deliver those rules to their employees through clear communication methods.

5.2 Legal and Regulatory Considerations

The use of AI in hiring creates complex legal problems because it involves three different areas which include data protection and discrimination and employment law. Organizations now need to demonstrate their automated decision systems while protecting applicant data because regulations have become more stringent (Mohammad et al., 2026). The AI tools need to process extensive personal data which makes it essential to meet data protection regulations. Organizations experience severe legal repercussions when they fail to handle their data correctly which leads to public trust violations (Alomair et al., 2026). The employment law system requires organizations to take responsibility for discriminatory results which occur without their intention. Employers lose legal protection when their AI systems automatically exclude specific groups from employment because bias exists in their algorithm design and data selection process. Organizations must perform fairness tests and ongoing monitoring of their AI systems to meet their legal obligations.

The speed at which regulatory frameworks develop differs across regions which creates difficulties for companies that operate globally. Employers need to track newly developing AI regulations while making sure their hiring practices meet current legal requirements and future regulatory needs. In the age of AI, organizations now treat legal compliance as a central HR responsibility instead of a secondary back-office task.

5.3 Strategic Adaptation in HR Practices

Organizations need to change their HR practices because their current methods do not help them achieve their business goals. The upcoming employers use AI technology in their hiring procedures and create new methods to evaluate actual abilities and future worker development. The new assessment system requires organizations to use structured interviews and work-sample tests and skills-based assessments because these methods create more difficulty for people who attempt to produce fraudulent results through automated text generation. HR professionals need to learn new skills (Bhatti, 2025). AI systems now stand as essential knowledge for all professionals who work in recruitment and talent management because they need to understand what AI can do and what it cannot do plus its ethical dangers. Organizations should dedicate their resources to training HR personnel who need to evaluate AI tools with critical thinking so they can make proper judgments based on their own understanding instead of depending on vendors' assertions. Organizations need to establish new definitions of fairness and merit to guide their hiring processes. The ability to demonstrate learning skills and adaptability and ethical decision-making will replace polished applications as the main method to attract potential advantages from AI technology which will become an industry standard. The establishment of defined organizational rules about which AI applications are permitted will help decrease uncertainty while ensuring equal treatment of all job seekers.

5.4 Impact on Skill Development

AI is revolutionizing the way people acquire and develop their abilities. The established system of skill acquisition required people to complete their schooling and their employment training and their mentoring relationships. AI-powered tools from today enable learners to receive customized learning experiences and immediate performance evaluations and ongoing skill measurement. The capabilities establish technical and analytical and communication skills development through learning acceleration which provides resources that match learning deficiencies. AI dependency creates problems because it leads to loss of skills. People stop practicing essential skills when AI takes over jobs that need document creation and programming and data examination work. The user will develop weaker critical thinking and writing and problem-solving abilities when they depend too much on automated processes. The current job market requires essential skills development which uses AI tools to support learning together with human competencies.

AI decides which skills will get the most attention from people. People need digital skills and data analysis skills and AI fluency skills because these skills will be needed for future work and repetitive tasks will not be needed anymore. People need soft skills which includes communication skills and adaptability skills and ethical judgment skills because these skills are difficult to automate and these skills help us interact with AI systems. AI is creating a new skills framework which defines the most important skills that are needed to learn.

5.5 Human–AI Collaboration in Career Development

The workplace now depends on Human–AI partnerships as the main method for advancing employee professional growth. AI functions as a career partner which helps people make decisions and plan their skill development and improve their work performance instead of taking control of their choice-making abilities. The AI-powered career platforms can evaluate market employment data to create job recommendations while they determine the most essential skills for particular professions which helps people make better professional decisions. The workplace creates new job functions through AI partnerships which lead to different career paths. Employees need to manage AI technologies while they decipher the system results and use their human understanding to handle situations where machines cannot operate. The career development path now requires workers to move from executing tasks to performing their duties through managerial work and system integration and strategic decision-making processes. Professionals who possess industry knowledge and the ability to manage AI systems will experience better job opportunities.

6. CONCLUSION AND FUTURE SCOPE

The contemporary recruitment process has been transformed because organizations now use artificial intelligence to assess job candidates. The research findings presented that artificial intelligence has become an essential tool which applicants must use to gain a competitive edge. The workplace shows increasing acceptance of AI-based applications because Millennials and Gen Z demonstrate much higher adoption rates for these systems in professional and office-based occupations. The

AI tools improve operational performance through customized experiences which boost user confidence, but they create problems related to genuine assessment and skilled people assessment and fair evaluation. People believe that their job prospects will decrease because they don't use digital technology, which means that digital technology gaps in the workforce. The organizations which hire employees need to develop new ways to evaluate job candidates because they must use AI-enhanced systems for their hiring process. Organizations need to create new assessment methods which evaluate human decisions and their evaluation through algorithmic systems while developing governance systems which ensure proper and responsible use of these assessments.

Researchers should investigate how artificial intelligence affects employee skill acquisition and their professional development and their work performance over time. Cross-cultural research between different cultures can explain why people from different parts of the world accept certain things while they create rules to control other things. The development of recruitment AI regulations needs researchers to conduct policy-focused studies which will create procedures to assess ethical AI methods in recruitment. Digital literacy development and equal technology access and established transparent hiring procedures will become crucial for AI development to create job opportunities which treat all individuals fairly.

REFERENCES

Aarthi, S., Ravikumar, R. N., & Pardaev, J. (2026). Synergizing multimodal generative AI and blockchain for the future of digital media. In *Fusion of multimodal generative AI and blockchain technology in digital media* (pp. 1–34). IGI Global Scientific Publishing., DOI: 10.4018/979-8-3373-1504-1.ch001

Achar, H. V. B., R. N., T., L. N., D., Kumar B. M., H., & Shankaregowda, S. A. (2025). The impact and future of artificial intelligence in learning. In Proceedings of the 3rd International Conference on Integrated Circuits and Communication Systems (ICICACS) (pp. 1–6). IEEE. DOI: 10.1109/ICICACS65178.2025.10967881

Achar, H. V. B., Prasad, P. S., Rajeshwari, D., Raghu, N., Hemanth Kumar, B. M., & Mahesh, T. R. (2025). Federated learning and neuro-symbolic AI for botnet classification in IoT-enabled consumer devices. *International Journal of Information Technology : an Official Journal of Bharati Vidyapeeth's Institute of Computer Applications and Management.* Advance online publication. DOI: 10.1007/s41870-025-02993-0

Adilov, Z., Tajibaev, J., Rasul-Zade, L., Tursunov, M., Mamadiyarov, Z., & Abdullayev, D. (2025). Exploring virtual reality and digital twin technologies for sustainable construction training in higher education. E3S Web of Conferences, 680, 00131. DOI: 10.1051/e3sconf/202568000131

Agarwal, V., Kaur, S. N. R., Gupta, S., Zaveri, B., Sohal, J., & Shrivastav, A. K. (2024). Adoption of advanced systems for digital resource management in academic institutions. *Evolutionary Studies in Imaginative Culture*, •••, 913–923. DOI: 10.70082/esiculture.vi.1089

Ahmed, S. Y., & Pardaev, J. (2025). Human-AI decision dynamics: How risk propensity and trust impact choices through decision fatigue, conditional on AI understanding. *Decision Making: Applications in Management and Engineering*, *8*(2), 96–113. DOI: 10.31181/dmame8220251484

Al Doghan, M. A., & Absamatov, A. (2025). Effects of big data, mechanical system flexibility, IoT and digital twin adoption on company resilience and operational performance. *Reports in Mechanical Engineering*, *6*(2), 65–79. DOI: 10.31181/rme524

Aldossary, M. A., & Pardaev, J. (2025). Leveraging big-data management for production excellence: Decision-making capabilities, decision quality, and the moderating effect of manufacturing IT infrastructure. *Reports in Mechanical Engineering*, *6*(1), 136–151. DOI: 10.31181/rme499

Alomair, A., Farooq, U., Almulhim, A. A., & Mamadiyarov, Z. (2026, March). Do cultural values matter? The role of national cultural dimensions in shaping female entrepreneurship in ASEAN. *Women's Studies International Forum, 115*, 103273. DOI: 10.1016/j.wsif.2025.103273

Ammer, M. A., & Mamadjanova, T. (2025). *Impact of educational quality, educational resource, and educational climate on educational engagement and student intention to attend lectures*. Espacio, Tiempo y Educación., DOI: 10.14516/ete.12208

Ammer, M. A., & Mamadjanova, T. (2025). Effects of educational digital literacy, educational aspirations, self-directed learning on e-learning motivation and effectiveness. *Educational Sciences: Theory & Practice*. Advance online publication. DOI: 10.12738/jestp.2025.1.18

Ammer, M. A., & Sattarov, A. (2025). Enhancing investors' decision-making through financial risk management: Role of corporate governance and financial communication transparency. Decision Making: Applications in Management and Engineering. https://doi.org/DOI: 10.31181/dmame8220251527

Azahari, L. M., Ahmad, F. A., & Saniff, S. M. (2026). Connecting employability and the future of work: A systematic review of global trends, employer expectations, and evolving recruitment strategies. In *Enhancing graduate employability in an evolving workforce* (pp. 99–118). IGI Global Scientific Publishing., DOI: 10.4018/979-8-3373-4450-8.ch005

Balamurugan, M., & Roopa, D. K. N., S., Sushma, R., T. C., K., Swetha, G., & Raghu, N. (2026). Late night use of social media and sleep deprivation. In Examining the intersection of technology, media, and social innovation (pp. 205–236). IGI Global Scientific Publishing. DOI: 10.4018/979-8-3373-5307-4.ch008

Bentayeb, A., Khoualed, A., & Medjdoub, A. (2026). Artificial intelligence in human resource management: Applications, workforce implications, and market trends (2024–2034). Інститут бухгалтерського обліку, контроль та аналіз в умовах глобалізації, (3–4), 68–78. DOI: 10.35774/ibo2025.03-04.068

Bhatti, M. A., & Mamadjanova, T. (2025). From calling to performance: The role of linguistic and communicative competence in employee success. *Eurasian Journal of Applied Linguistics, 11*(2), 147–162. DOI: 10.32601/ejal.11212

Bhatti, M. A., & Otamurodov, S. (2025). Job satisfaction and employee commitment: Role of internal communication, language proficiency, information quality and information usefulness. *El Profesional de la Información, 34*(2). Advance online publication. DOI: 10.3145/epi.2025.ene.34201

Bhatti, M. A., & Shodiyev, A. (2025). Enhancing employee performance: Role of communication competence, internal communication and satisfaction with communication climate. *International Journal of Operations and Quantitative Management, 31*(2), 216–239. DOI: 10.46970/2025.31.2.11

Cahyani, I., Buriev, K. T., Ngongo, M., Mamadiyarov, Z., Ino, L., Herman, H., Saputra, N., & Baxtishodovich, S. B. (2025). Exploring the use of TikTok application in enhancing pronunciation skill: A case on students' perception. *Studies in Media and Communication, 13*(2), 7553. DOI: 10.11114/smc.v13i2.7553

Ghaleb, M. M. S., & Sattarov, A. (2025). *Use of ChatGPT in education and quality of education: Role of student course engagement and regulator support.* Revista Electrónica de LEEME., DOI: 10.58262/LEEME.55.0020

Hair, J. F., Rana, S., Robb, D., & Stroud, M. (2026). The emerging role of AI and social robots in university student recruitment. In Social robots and artificial intelligence in education: Integrating AI in K-12 and higher education (pp. 153–183). Springer Nature Switzerland. DOI: 10.1007/978-3-032-03977-4_7

Hamid, E. M., & Shodiyev, A. (2025). Role of information needs, information accessibility, information overload and digital literacy in shaping web search self-efficacy. *El Profesional de la Información, 34*(2). Advance online publication. DOI: 10.3145/epi.2025.ene.34205

Hussain, Z., Khan, A., Awad, A., & Bansal, R. (2026). AI-driven learning culture enhances innovation performance: A serial mediator of knowledge orchestration and organisational intelligence. *VINE Journal of Information and Knowledge Management Systems*, •••, 1–23. DOI: 10.1108/VJIKMS-12-2025-0527

Islam, M. S., Hussain, Z., Bansal, R., Awad, A., & Pruthi, N. (2026). AI-enabled environmental auditing and sustainability disclosure: Green reporting capability as mediator and digital compliance culture as moderator. *Corporate Social Responsibility and Environmental Management*, csr.70565. Advance online publication. DOI: 10.1002/csr.70565

Islamutdinov, V., Akhmetshin, E., Lydia, E. L., & Raja, P. V. K. (2024, April). Implementation of AI in an ethical and responsible manner to empower education in digital sector. In International Conference on Smart Computing and Informatics (pp. 127–134). Springer Nature Singapore. DOI: 10.1007/978-981-96-3939-7_13

Kodagoda, T. (2026). Generation Y employees' understandings on artificial intelligence (AI): Interventions at workplace. In *Communication and knowledge in organizations: Approaches from positivist and interpretivist paradigms* (pp. 19–32). Springer Nature Singapore., DOI: 10.1007/978-981-95-0622-4_2

Kulmanov, T., Dadabaev, U., Qulmetov, M., Ulashov, A., Eshboyev, M., & Makhmudov, S. (2024, December). Global services market transformation: Digitalization export trends and future forecasts. In *Proceedings of the 8th International Conference on Future Networks & Distributed Systems* (pp. 851–858). ACM. DOI: 10.1145/3726122.3726245

Kuzmin, E., Bondareva, V. S., Shodiyev, A., & Ochilov, I. (2025). Digitalization, innovation, and competitiveness: Insights from a cross-country analysis of labor productivity effects. In *Artificial intelligence and digital transformation: From innovation to implementation* (pp. 307–329). Springer Nature Switzerland., DOI: 10.1007/978-3-032-00118-4_17

M., B., N., R., L. N., D., Sahoo, S. K., Ankanahalli Shankaregowda, S., Kannanugo, N., M., D., & M., V. K. (2024). AI-enhanced leadership decision support system using ChatGPT for ethical learning. In Impact of new technology on next-generation leadership (pp. 137–161). IGI Global Scientific Publishing. DOI: 10.4018/979-8-3693-1946-8.ch008

Makhmudov, S., Maqsood, M., Musaev, U., Urazmetov, M., & Shahzadi, A. (2025). Foundations of agentic AI redefining autonomy in learning environments. In *Multidisciplinary perspectives on agentic AI in educational systems*. IGI Global Scientific Publishing. DOI: 10.4018/979-8-3373-4621-2.ch001

Makhmudov, S., Otakhonova, D., Kulmanov, T., Shamshiyeva, N., Juraev, U., Ruziev, G., & Sabirova, U. (2026). The impact of digital marketing and mobile applications on service innovation in German companies. *International Review of Management and Marketing*, *16*(1), 210–217. DOI: 10.32479/irmm.22052

Marisamy, K., Selvakumar, A., Rajasekar, B., Natarajan, R., Atajanova, A., & Makhmudov, S. (2026). Smart logistics integrating AI, IoT, blockchain, and robotics for a sustainable future. In *Emerging trends in smart logistics technologies* (pp. 73–104). IGI Global Scientific Publishing., DOI: 10.4018/979-8-3373-2434-0.ch003

Mohammad, A. S., Mohammad, S. I., Vasudevan, A., Alenazi, S. A., Hussain, Z., Awad, A., Hamed, A. M., & Mahmoud, M. (2026). Digital sales automation and buyer engagement: Investigating the mediating role of perceived value in B2B exchanges. *Discover Artificial Intelligence*, *6*(1), 102. Advance online publication. DOI: 10.1007/s44163-025-00830-8

Muthuswamy, V. V., & Absamatov, A. (2025). *Determinants of students' engagement and their role in boosting students' academic performance among higher education institutions.* Revista Electrónica de LEEME., DOI: 10.58262/LEEME.56.13

Pandey, D., Singh, G., Joshi, L., Polyakova, O., Sungatullina, D., & Singh, R. (2024). Organizational preparedness for navigating disruption towards sustainability: Strategies' analysis. E3S Web of Conferences. DOI: 10.1051/e3sconf/202457407001

Prabha, K. R., Mabel, B. R., Isaev, F., Mamadiyarov, Z., Raxmatullayevich, K. U., Erkinjon, T., & Khurramova, M. (2026). A multi-layer artificial intelligence–enabled governance framework for integrating information security management, quality management, and strategic human resource analytics: Investigating the role of corporate social responsibility in sustainable organizational performance. *Quality - Access to Success*, *27*(210). Advance online publication. DOI: 10.47750/QAS/27.210.45

Raghu, N. V. N., T., L. N., D., Kumar B. M., H., & Shankaregowda, S. A. (2025). Enhancing critical thinking through problem-based learning: A comprehensive approach to modern education. In M. Lytras, P. Ordóñez de Pablos, & T. Aldosemani (Eds.), Fostering teacher skills and critical thinking in modern education (pp. 259–282). IGI Global Scientific Publishing. DOI: 10.4018/979-8-3373-1692-5.ch011

Rajeswari, M., Vanitha, C. L., Xudoynazarova, S., Mamadiyarov, Z., Naveen, S., Nematovich, K. I., & Isaev, F. (2026). Design and validation of an explainable artificial intelligence–based decision intelligence model for cyber risk–aware quality systems and ethical human resource management: Investigating the moderating influence of corporate social responsibility in digitally transformed organizations. *Quality - Access to Success*, *27*(210). Advance online publication. DOI: 10.47750/QAS/27.210.46

Ravikumar, R. N., Aarthi, S., Atamuratova, Z., Ashirova, A., Jurayev, K., & Hayitova, M. (2026). Comprehensive evaluation of AI-driven systems in modern hospital environments. In *Evaluation and assessment of AI-driven systems in hospitals* (pp. 61–88). IGI Global Scientific Publishing., DOI: 10.4018/979-8-3373-2787-7.ch003

Ravikumar, R. N., Aarthi, S., & Mamadiyarov, Z. (2026). Mitigating risks through AI-powered fraud detection systems in digital banking. In *Innovating cost-efficient and scalable business models in the digital era* (pp. 343–376). IGI Global Scientific Publishing., DOI: 10.4018/979-8-3373-2120-2.ch011

Ravikumar, R. N., Aarthi, S., Ruzimova, F., & Mamadiyarov, Z. (2026). Training and development in AI-driven education scaling solutions: K-12 to workforce. In *Transforming education with data science in the AI era* (pp. 267–298). IGI Global Scientific Publishing., DOI: 10.4018/979-8-3373-2185-1.ch010

Ravikumar, R. N., Aarthi, S., Usmani, M. A., Rai, P. K., Jumaniyozova, M., & Narboshova, M. (2026). Advancements in multilingual speech technologies for human-computer interaction. In *Advancements in speech processing for human-computer interaction* (pp. 101–132). IGI Global Scientific Publishing., DOI: 10.4018/979-8-3373-3048-8.ch004

Sapayev, V. O., Hayat, N., Mamadiyarov, Z., & Ahmad, M. (2026). Inside the black box: How generative AI creates digital synthetics. In *Digital synthetic data and outputs* (pp. 409–434). IGI Global Scientific Publishing., DOI: 10.4018/979-8-3373-2277-3.ch016

Sherov, A., Rakhimov, T., Hajiyev, H., Zelinskaya, M., & Khidirova, G. (2025). Evaluating class-imbalanced data handling for enhanced financial distress prediction using an attention-based deep neural network and heuristic optimization algorithms. Engineering. *Technology and Applied Science Research*, *15*(6), 13372. DOI: 10.48084/etasr.13372

Sufyan Ghaleb, M. M., & Pardaev, J. (2025). Effects of advertisement language, communication style, information seeking behavior and information source credibility on customers' intentions towards international products via brand trust. *El Profesional de la Información*, *34*(2). Advance online publication. DOI: 10.3145/epi.2025.ene.34203

Yong, J. Y., Yusoff, Y. M., Fernando, Y., Lin, W. L., Chong, S. C., & Pek, C. K. (2026). Generation green: Navigating ESG in Generation Z's job search landscape. In *Stimulating economic growth through cultural and societal transformations* (pp. 83–100). IGI Global Scientific Publishing., DOI: 10.4018/979-8-3373-0603-2.ch004

Zayniddinov, R., Jumaev, N., Irgasheva, G., Asadov, A., & Makhmudov, N.. (2025). The influence of the digital economy on economic development: Evidence from Uzbekistan. In *ACM International Conference Proceeding Series*. DOI: 10.1145/3726122.3726242

Zhao, J., Ragmoun, W., Dong, Z., Nawaz, M. A., & Sattarov, A. (2025). Circular economy implementation through AI adoption, CSR and green finance: The mediating role of green product innovation and green supply chain. *Corporate Social Responsibility and Environmental Management*. Advance online publication. DOI: 10.1002/csr.70289

Compilation of References

Aarthi, S., Ravikumar, R. N., & Pardaev, J. (2026). Synergizing multimodal generative AI and blockchain for the future of digital media. In *Fusion of multimodal generative AI and blockchain technology in digital media* (pp. 1–34). IGI Global Scientific Publishing., DOI: 10.4018/979-8-3373-1504-1.ch001

Abdullahi, M. S., Raman, K., Solarin, S. A., & Adeiza, A. (2023). Employee engagement as a mediating variable on the relationship between employee relation practice and employee performance in a developing economy. *Journal of Applied Research in Higher Education, 15*(1), 83–97. DOI: 10.1108/JARHE-06-2021-0222

Aboumoussa, L., & Pfister, J. (2024). Leadership development in the age of artificial intelligence (AWP No. 244). Mossavar-Rahmani Center for Business and Government, Harvard Kennedy School. https://www.hks.harvard.edu/sites/default/files/centers/mrcbg/Final_AWP_244.pdf

Achar, H. V. B., R. N., T., L. N., D., Kumar B. M., H., & Shankaregowda, S. A. (2025). The impact and future of artificial intelligence in learning. In Proceedings of the 3rd International Conference on Integrated Circuits and Communication Systems (ICICACS) (pp. 1–6). IEEE. DOI: 10.1109/ICICACS65178.2025.10967881

Achar, H. V. B., Prasad, P. S., Rajeshwari, D., Raghu, N., Hemanth Kumar, B. M., & Mahesh, T. R. (2025). Federated learning and neuro-symbolic AI for botnet classification in IoT-enabled consumer devices. *International Journal of Information Technology : an Official Journal of Bharati Vidyapeeth's Institute of Computer Applications and Management*. Advance online publication. DOI: 10.1007/s41870-025-02993-0

Acikgoz, Y. (2019). Employee recruitment and job search: Towards a multi-level integration. *Human Resource Management Review, 29*(1), 1–13. DOI: 10.1016/j.hrmr.2018.02.009

Ademola, O. E. (2024). Change Management Trends in the AI Modern World: Adapting to the Future of Work. *Journal of Behavioral Informatics*, *10*(1), 41–50.

Adilov, Z., Tajibaev, J., Rasul-Zade, L., Tursunov, M., Mamadiyarov, Z., & Abdullayev, D. (2025). Exploring virtual reality and digital twin technologies for sustainable construction training in higher education. E3S Web of Conferences, 680, 00131. DOI: 10.1051/e3sconf/202568000131

ADP Research Institute. (2020). *Global Workplace Study 2020: COVID-19 and the new world of work.* ADP. https://www.adpresearch.com/research/workplace-resilience-study/

Afroogh, S., Akbari, A., Malone, E., Kargar, M., & Alambeigi, H. (2024). Trust in AI: Progress, challenges, and future directions. *Humanities & Social Sciences Communications*, *11*(1), 1568. Advance online publication. DOI: 10.1057/s41599-024-04044-8

Agarwal, A. (2023). AI adoption by human resource management: a study of its antecedents and impact on HR system effectiveness. *foresight, 25*(1), 67-81.

Agarwal, N., Moehring, A., Rajpurkar, P., & Salz, T. (2023). *Combining human expertise with artificial intelligence: Experimental evidence from radiology* (NBER Working Paper No. 31422). National Bureau of Economic Research. DOI: 10.3386/w31422

Agarwal, V., Kaur, S. N. R., Gupta, S., Zaveri, B., Sohal, J., & Shrivastav, A. K. (2024). Adoption of advanced systems for digital resource management in academic institutions. *Evolutionary Studies in Imaginative Culture*, •••, 913–923. DOI: 10.70082/esiculture.vi.1089

Aggarwal, M., Gingras, C., & Deber, R. (2021). *Artificial Intelligence in Healthcare from a Policy Perspective.*, DOI: 10.1007/978-3-030-67303-1_5

Agudo, U., Liberal, K. G., Arrese, M., & Matute, H. (2024). The impact of AI errors in a human-in-the-loop process. *Cognitive Research: Principles and Implications*, *9*(1), 1. DOI: 10.1186/s41235-023-00529-3 PMID: 38185767

Ahmed, S. Y., & Pardaev, J. (2025). Human-AI decision dynamics: How risk propensity and trust impact choices through decision fatigue, conditional on AI understanding. *Decision Making: Applications in Management and Engineering*, *8*(2), 96–113. DOI: 10.31181/dmame8220251484

Ahmed, T., Yang, C., Yang, H., & Mahmood, S. (2021). Topic of the Review Manuscript—The Review of Empowering Leadership. *Open Journal of Leadership*, *10*(2), 129–147. DOI: 10.4236/ojl.2021.102009

Akter, S. (2025). AI's Impact on Talent Acquisition Strategies and Employee Engagement Methodologies: Ethical Considerations for Trustworthy AI-HRM Integration. *Journal of Humanities and Social Sciences Studies*, *7*(8), 44–51. DOI: 10.32996/jhsss.2025.7.8.6

Al Aina, R., & Atan, T. (2020). The impact of implementing talent management practices on sustainable organizational performance. *Sustainability (Basel)*, *12*(20), 1–21. DOI: 10.3390/su12208372

Al Doghan, M. A., & Absamatov, A. (2025). Effects of big data, mechanical system flexibility, IoT and digital twin adoption on company resilience and operational performance. *Reports in Mechanical Engineering*, *6*(2), 65–79. DOI: 10.31181/rme524

Al Masaeid, T., Alkhalidi, M. M., Al Ali, A. A. A., Almaazmi, S. M. G. A., & Alami, R. (2025). Artificial Intelligence-Augmented Decision-Making: Examining the Interplay Between Machine Learning Algorithms and Human Judgment in Organizational Leadership. *Journal of Ecohumanism*, *4*(1), 4683–4699. DOI: 10.62754/joe.v4i1.6364

Alam, M. S., Khan, T.-U.-Z., Dhar, S. S., & Munira, K. S. (2020). HR professionals' intention to adopt and use of artificial intelligence in recruiting talents. *Business Perspectives and Research*, *2*(2), 15–30. DOI: 10.38157/business-perspective-review.v2i2.122

Albert, E. T. (2019). AI in talent acquisition: A review of AI-applications used in recruitment and selection. *Strategic HR Review*, *18*(5), 215–221. DOI: 10.1108/SHR-04-2019-0024

Aldossary, M. A., & Pardaev, J. (2025). Leveraging big-data management for production excellence: Decision-making capabilities, decision quality, and the moderating effect of manufacturing IT infrastructure. *Reports in Mechanical Engineering*, *6*(1), 136–151. DOI: 10.31181/rme499

Ali, A., & Pitafi, A. H. (2025). Bridging people and technology: The influence of AI-driven HRM empathy on workplace outcomes. *Systems*, *13*(12), 1129. Advance online publication. DOI: 10.3390/systems13121129

Allal-Chérif, O., Yela Aránega, A., & Castaño Sánchez, R. (2021). Intelligent recruitment: How to identify, select, and retain talents from around the world using artificial intelligence. *Technological Forecasting and Social Change*, *169*(April), 120822. Advance online publication. DOI: 10.1016/j.techfore.2021.120822

Alomair, A., Farooq, U., Almulhim, A. A., & Mamadiyarov, Z. (2026, March). Do cultural values matter? The role of national cultural dimensions in shaping female entrepreneurship in ASEAN. *Women's Studies International Forum, 115*, 103273. DOI: 10.1016/j.wsif.2025.103273

Alon-Barkat, S., & Busuioc, M. (2023). Human–AI interactions in public sector decision making: "Automation bias" and "selective adherence" to algorithmic advice. *Journal of Public Administration: Research and Theory, 33*(1), 153–169. DOI: 10.1093/jopart/muac007

Alsaif, A., & Sabih Aksoy, M. (2023). AI-HRM: artificial intelligence in human resource management: a literature review. *Journal of Computing and Communication, 2*(2), 1–7. DOI: 10.21608/jocc.2023.307053

Alzeiby, E. A., Islam, N., Shaik, A. S., & Yaqub, M. Z. (2025). AI adoption in enterprises for enhanced strategic human resource management practices: Benefiting the employee engagement and experience. *Journal of Enterprise Information Management, 38*(5), 1441–1464. DOI: 10.1108/JEIM-05-2024-0249

Ameyed, D., Jaafar, F., & Chaabene, R. ben, & Cheriet, M. (2023). Federated Learning and Blockchain: In *AI, Machine Learning and Deep Learning* (pp. 157–166). CRC Press. DOI: 10.1201/9781003187158-14

Ammer, M. A., & Sattarov, A. (2025). Enhancing investors' decision-making through financial risk management: Role of corporate governance and financial communication transparency. Decision Making: Applications in Management and Engineering. https://doi.org/DOI: 10.31181/dmame8220251527

Ammer, M. A., & Mamadjanova, T. (2025). Effects of educational digital literacy, educational aspirations, self-directed learning on e-learning motivation and effectiveness. *Educational Sciences: Theory & Practice*. Advance online publication. DOI: 10.12738/jestp.2025.1.18

Ammer, M. A., & Mamadjanova, T. (2025). *Impact of educational quality, educational resource, and educational climate on educational engagement and student intention to attend lectures*. Espacio, Tiempo y Educación., DOI: 10.14516/ete.12208

Ang, K. C., Sankaran, S., & Liu, D. (2025). Advancing sociotechnical systems theory: New principles for human-robot team design and development. *Applied Ergonomics, 129*, 104604. DOI: 10.1016/j.apergo.2025.104604

Antonakis, J. (2012). Transformational and Charismatic Leadership. In Day, D. V., & Antonakis, J. (Eds.), *The Nature of Leadership* (pp. 256–288). Sage Publications.

Aristotle. (1999). *Nicomachean ethics* (T. Irwin, Trans.; 2nd ed.). Hackett Publishing. (Original work published c. 350 BCE).

Arora, M. (2024). Influence of artificial intelligence on organizational leadership: Challenges and opportunities. International Journal of Research in Human Resource Management, 6(2), 06–10. DOI: 10.33545/26633213.2024.v6.i2a.194

Arora, M., Prakash, A., Mittal, A., & Singh, S. (2021, December). HR analytics and artificial intelligence-transforming human resource management. In *2021 International Conference on Decision Aid Sciences and Application (DASA)* (pp. 288-293). IEEE. DOI: 10.1109/DASA53625.2021.9682325

Asan, O., & Choudhury, A. (2021). Research trends in artificial intelligence applications in Human Factors health care: Mapping review. *JMIR Human Factors*, *8*(2), e28236. DOI: 10.2196/28236 PMID: 34142968

Atay, S. (2025). *Society 5.0 and human-centered technology: Redefining HR and talent management. Technology in Society.* https://www.sciencedirect.com/science/article/pii/S2666188825002990

Avolio, B. J., & Bass, B. M. (1995). Individual consideration viewed at multiple levels of analysis: A multilevel framework for examining the diffusion of transformational leadership. *The Leadership Quarterly*, *6*(2), 199–218. DOI: 10.1016/1048-9843(95)90035-7

Avolio, B. J., Kahai, S., & Dodge, G. E. (2000). E-leadership: Implications for theory, research, and practice. *The Leadership Quarterly*, *11*(4), 615–668. DOI: 10.1016/S1048-9843(00)00062-X

Azahari, L. M., Ahmad, F. A., & Saniff, S. M. (2026). Connecting employability and the future of work: A systematic review of global trends, employer expectations, and evolving recruitment strategies. In *Enhancing graduate employability in an evolving workforce* (pp. 99–118). IGI Global Scientific Publishing., DOI: 10.4018/979-8-3373-4450-8.ch005

Babu, K.-E.-K. (2021). *Artificial Intelligence, Its Applications in Different Sectors and Challenges: Bangladesh Context* (pp. 103–119). DOI: 10.1007/978-3-030-88040-8_4

Badhurunnisa, M., & Dass, V. S. (2023). Challenges and opportunities involved in implementing AI in workplace. *International Journal for Multidisciplinary Research*, *5*(6). Advance online publication. DOI: 10.36948/ijfmr.2023.v05i06.10001

Bahangulu, J. K., & Owusu-Berko, L. (2025). Algorithmic bias, data ethics, and governance: Ensuring fairness, transparency and compliance in AI-powered business analytics applications. *World Journal of Advanced Research and Reviews, 25*(2), 1746–1763. DOI: 10.30574/wjarr.2025.25.2.0571

Bailey, D. E., Faraj, S., Hinds, P. J., Leonardi, P. M., & von Krogh, G. (2022). We are all theorists of technology now: A relational perspective on emerging technology and organizing. *Organization Science, 33*(1), 1–18. DOI: 10.1287/orsc.2021.1562

Bainbridge, L. (1983). Ironies of automation. *Automatica, 19*(6), 775–779. DOI: 10.1016/0005-1098(83)90046-8

Bajwa, J., Munir, U., Nori, A., & Williams, B. (2021). Artificial intelligence in healthcare: Transforming the practice of medicine. *Future Healthcare Journal, 8*(2), e188–e194. DOI: 10.7861/fhj.2021-0095

Bakker, A. B., & Demerouti, E. (2017). Job demands–resources theory: Taking stock and looking forward. *Journal of Occupational Health Psychology, 22*(3), 273–285. DOI: 10.1037/ocp0000056

Balamurugan, M., & Roopa, D. K. N., S., Sushma, R., T. C., K., Swetha, G., & Raghu, N. (2026). Late night use of social media and sleep deprivation. In Examining the intersection of technology, media, and social innovation (pp. 205–236). IGI Global Scientific Publishing. DOI: 10.4018/979-8-3373-5307-4.ch008

Bandi, A., Kongari, B., Naguru, R., Pasnoor, S., & Vilipala, S. V. (2025). The rise of Agentic AI: A review of definitions, frameworks, architectures, applications, evaluation metrics, and challenges. *Future Internet, 17*(9), 404. DOI: 10.3390/fi17090404

Bankins, S., Ocampo, A. C., Marrone, M., Restubog, S. L. D., & Woo, S. E. (2024). A multilevel review of artificial intelligence in organizations: Implications for organizational behavior research and practice. *Journal of Organizational Behavior, 45*(2), 159–182. DOI: 10.1002/job.2735

Bansal, G., Nushi, B., Kamar, E., Weld, D. S., Lasecki, W. S., & Vaughan, J. W. (2021). Does the whole exceed its parts? The effect of AI explanations on complementary team performance. In *Proceedings of the 2021 CHI Conference on Human Factors in Computing Systems* (Article 81). Association for Computing Machinery. **https://doi.org/**DOI: 10.1145/3411764.3445717

Barabadi, E., Fotuhabadi, Z., Arghavan, A., & Booth, J. R. (2026). Comparing AI and human moral reasoning: Context-sensitive patterns beyond utilitarian bias. *Frontiers in Artificial Intelligence, 8*, 1710410. Advance online publication. DOI: 10.3389/frai.2025.1710410

Barends, E., Wietrak, E., Cioca, I., & Rousseau, D. (2021). *Employee resilience: An evidence review. Summary report.* Chartered Institute of Personnel and Development (CIPD). https://www.cipd.org/globalassets/media/knowledge/knowledge-hub/evidence-reviews/resilience-evidence-review-scientific-summary_tcm18-91702.pdf

Barney, J. (1991). Firm resources and sustained competitive advantage. *Journal of Management, 17*(1), 99–120. DOI: 10.1177/014920639101700108

Barocas, S., & Selbst, A. D. (2016). Big data's disparate impact. *California Law Review, 104*(3), 671–732. DOI: 10.15779/Z38BG31

Barredo Arrieta, A., Díaz-Rodríguez, N., Del Ser, J., Bennetot, A., Tabik, S., Barbado, A., Garcia, S., Gil-Lopez, S., Molina, D., Benjamins, R., Chatila, R., & Herrera, F. (2020). Explainable artificial intelligence (XAI): Concepts, taxonomies, opportunities and challenges toward responsible AI. *Information Fusion, 58*, 82–115. DOI: 10.1016/j.inffus.2019.12.012

Batool, A., Zowghi, D., & Bano, M. (2023). Responsible AI governance: a systematic literature review. *arXiv preprint arXiv:2401.10896.*

Baxter, G., & Sommerville, I. (2011). Socio-technical systems: From design methods to systems engineering. *Interacting with Computers, 23*(1), 4–17. DOI: 10.1016/j.intcom.2010.07.003

Becker, G. S. (1964). *Human capital: A theoretical and empirical analysis*. University of Chicago Press.

Bender, S. M. L., & Price, W. N. (2024). Legal aspects of artificial intelligence in medical practice. In *Artificial Intelligence in Clinical Practice* (pp. 401–411). Elsevier., DOI: 10.1016/B978-0-443-15688-5.00046-2

Bentayeb, A., Khoualed, A., & Medjdoub, A. (2026). Artificial intelligence in human resource management: Applications, workforce implications, and market trends (2024–2034). Інститут бухгалтерського обліку, контроль та аналіз в умовах глобалізації, (3–4), 68–78. DOI: 10.35774/ibo2025.03-04.068

Benthall, S., & Goldenfein, J. (2021). Artificial Intelligence and the Purpose of Social Systems. *Proceedings of the 2021 AAAI/ACM Conference on AI, Ethics, and Society*, 3–12. DOI: 10.1145/3461702.3462526

Berente, N., Gu, B., Recker, J., & Santhanam, R. (2021). Managing artificial intelligence. *Management Information Systems Quarterly, 45*(3), 1433–1450. DOI: 10.25300/MISQ/2021/16274

Bevilacqua, S., Ferraris, A., Matzler, K., & Kuděj, M. (2026). Strategic leadership at high altitude: Investigating how AI affects the required skills of top managers. *Journal of Business Research, 205*, 115878. DOI: 10.1016/j.jbusres.2025.115878

Bharathi, B., & Krishna, R. R. (2025). The role of artificial Intelligence in designing future Human Resource Management strategies. *International Journal of Research and Development in Engineering Science*, *7*(3). Advance online publication. DOI: 10.63328/IJRDES-V7RI3P10

Bhatti, M. A., & Mamadjanova, T. (2025). From calling to performance: The role of linguistic and communicative competence in employee success. *Eurasian Journal of Applied Linguistics*, *11*(2), 147–162. DOI: 10.32601/ejal.11212

Bhatti, M. A., & Otamurodov, S. (2025). Job satisfaction and employee commitment: Role of internal communication, language proficiency, information quality and information usefulness. *El Profesional de la Información*, *34*(2). Advance online publication. DOI: 10.3145/epi.2025.ene.34201

Bhatti, M. A., & Shodiyev, A. (2025). Enhancing employee performance: Role of communication competence, internal communication and satisfaction with communication climate. *International Journal of Operations and Quantitative Management*, *31*(2), 216–239. DOI: 10.46970/2025.31.2.11

Bhatt, P., & Muduli, A. (2023). Artificial intelligence in learning and development: A systematic literature review. *European Journal of Training and Development*, *47*(7/8), 677–694. DOI: 10.1108/EJTD-09-2021-0143

Black, J. S., & van Esch, P. (2020). AI-enabled recruiting: What is it and how should a manager use it? *Business Horizons*, *63*(2), 215–226. DOI: 10.1016/j.bushor.2019.12.001

Bloom, N., Garicano, L., Sadun, R., & Van Reenen, J. (2014). The distinct effects of information technology and communication technology on firm organization. *Management Science*, *60*(12), 2859–2885. DOI: 10.1287/mnsc.2014.2013

Boban, M., & Klarić, M. (2023). Artificial Intelligence in Healthcare Services – Regulation, Implementation and Future Challenges. *2023 46th MIPRO ICT and Electronics Convention (MIPRO)*, 1440–1445. DOI: 10.23919/MIPRO57284.2023.10159797

Bolden, R. (2011). Distributed leadership in organizations: A review of theory and research. *International Journal of Management Reviews*, *13*(3), 251–269. DOI: 10.1111/j.1468-2370.2011.00306.x

Bonsón, E., & Bednárová, M. (2022). *Artificial Intelligence Disclosures in Sustainability Reports: Towards an Artificial Intelligence Reporting Framework* (pp. 391–407). DOI: 10.1007/978-3-030-94617-3_27

Borst, R. T., Kruyen, P. M., Lako, C. J., & de Vries, M. S. (2017). The attitudinal, behavioral, and performance outcomes of work engagement: A comparative meta-analysis across the public, semipublic, and private sector. *Review of Public Personnel Administration, 37*(4), 407–435. DOI: 10.1177/0734371X16683968

Bos-Nehles, A., Townsend, K., Cafferkey, K., & Trullen, J. (2023). Examining the Ability, Motivation and Opportunity (AMO) framework in HRM research: Conceptualization, measurement and interactions. *International Journal of Management Reviews, 25*(4), 725–739. DOI: 10.1111/ijmr.12332

Bostrom, R. P., & Heinen, J. S. (1977). MIS problems and failures: A socio-technical perspective: Part II: The application of socio-technical theory. *Management Information Systems Quarterly, 1*(4), 11–28. DOI: 10.2307/249019

Boyatzis, R. E., & Johnston, F. (2021). *Helping people change: Coaching with compassion for lifelong learning and growth.* Harvard Business Review Press.

Braganza, A., Brooks, L., Nepelski, D., Ali, M., & Moro, R. (2020). Artificial intelligence (AI) in business: State-of-the-art and future research agenda. *International Journal of Information Management, 50*, 261–272. DOI: 10.1016/j.ijinfomgt.2019.10.007

Braganza, A., Chen, W., Canhoto, A., & Sap, S. (2021). Productive employment and decent work: The impact of AI adoption on psychological contracts, job engagement and employee trust. *Journal of Business Research, 131*, 485–494. DOI: 10.1016/j.jbusres.2020.08.018

Breidbach, C. F. (2024). Responsible algorithmic decision-making. *Organizational Dynamics, 53*(2), 101031. DOI: 10.1016/j.orgdyn.2024.101031

Brennan, R. (2024, October 16). The Future of Adaptive Leadership: Emerging Trends. Robert Brennan - Facilitation, Training & Coaching Services. https://robertbrennan.com.au/the-future-of-adaptive-leadership-emerging-trends/

Brougham, D., & Haar, J. (2018). Smart technology, artificial intelligence, robotics, and algorithms (STARA): Employees' perceptions of our future workplace. *Journal of Management & Organization, 24*(2), 239–257. DOI: 10.1017/jmo.2016.55

Brynjolfsson, E. (2022). The Turing trap: The promise and peril of human-like artificial intelligence. *Daedalus, 151*(2), 272–287. DOI: 10.1162/daed_a_01915

Brynjolfsson, E., Li, D., & Raymond, L. (2025). Generative AI at work. *The Quarterly Journal of Economics, 140*(2), 889–942. DOI: 10.1093/qje/qjae044

Brynjolfsson, E., Mitchell, T., & Rock, D. (2018). What can machines learn, and what does it mean for occupations and the economy? *AEA Papers and Proceedings. American Economic Association, 108*, 43–47. DOI: 10.1257/pandp.20181019

Bubicz, M., & Ferasso, M. (2024). Advancing Corporate Social Responsibility in AI-Driven Human Resources Management: A Maturity Model Approach. *Proceedings of the 4th International Conference on AI Research, ICAIR 2024*, 82–90. DOI: 10.34190/icair.4.1.3016

Buçinca, Z., Malaya, M. B., & Gajos, K. Z. (2021). To trust or to think: Cognitive forcing functions can reduce overreliance on AI in AI-assisted decision making. *Proceedings of the ACM on Human-Computer Interaction, 5*(CSCW1), Article 188. **https://doi.org/**DOI: 10.1145/3449287

Buck, B., & Morrow, J. (2018). AI, performance management and engagement: Keeping your best their best. *Strategic HR Review, 17*(5), 261–262. DOI: 10.1108/SHR-10-2018-145

Budhwar, P., Chowdhury, S., Wood, G., Aguinis, H., Bamber, G. J., Beltran, J. R., Boselie, P., Lee Cooke, F., Decker, S., DeNisi, A., Dey, P. K., Guest, D., Knoblich, A. J., Malik, A., Paauwe, J., Papagiannidis, S., Patel, C., Pereira, V., Ren, S., & Varma, A. (2023). Human resource management in the age of generative artificial intelligence: Perspectives and research directions on ChatGPT. *Human Resource Management Journal, 33*(3), 606–659. DOI: 10.1111/1748-8583.12524

Budhwar, P., Malik, A., De Silva, M. T. T., & Thevisuthan, P. (2022). Artificial intelligence–challenges and opportunities for international HRM: A review and research agenda. *International Journal of Human Resource Management, 33*(6), 1065–1097. DOI: 10.1080/09585192.2022.2035161

Bujold, A., Roberge-Maltais, I., Parent-Rocheleau, X., Boasen, J., Sénécal, S., & Léger, P.-M. (2024). Responsible artificial intelligence in human resources management: A review of the empirical literature. *AI and Ethics, 4*(4), 1185–1200. DOI: 10.1007/s43681-023-00325-1

Burrell, J. (2016). How the machine "thinks": Understanding opacity in machine learning algorithms. *Big Data & Society, 3*(1), 1–12. DOI: 10.1177/2053951715622512

Burton, J. W., Stein, M.-K., & Jensen, T. B. (2020). A systematic review of algorithm aversion in augmented decision making. *Journal of Behavioral Decision Making, 33*(2), 220–239. DOI: 10.1002/bdm.2155

Busuioc, M. (2021). Accountable artificial intelligence: Holding algorithms to account. *Public Administration Review, 81*(5), 825–836. DOI: 10.1111/puar.13293 PMID: 34690372

Cahyani, I., Buriev, K. T., Ngongo, M., Mamadiyarov, Z., Ino, L., Herman, H., Saputra, N., & Baxtishodovich, S. B. (2025). Exploring the use of TikTok application in enhancing pronunciation skill: A case on students' perception. *Studies in Media and Communication, 13*(2), 7553. DOI: 10.11114/smc.v13i2.7553

Caldeira, T. A., Ferreira, J. B., Freitas, A., & Falcão, R. P. D. Q. (2021). Adoption of mobile payments in Brazil: Technology readiness, trust and perceived quality. *BBR. Brazilian Business Review, 18*(4), 415–432.

Camilleri, M. A. (2024). Artificial intelligence governance: Ethical considerations and implications for social responsibility. *Expert Systems: International Journal of Knowledge Engineering and Neural Networks, 41*(7), 1–15. DOI: 10.1111/exsy.13406

Campbell, D. T., & Stanley, J. C. (1963). *Experimental and quasi-experimental designs for research.* Rand McNally.

Canbul Yaroğlu, A. (2025). Organizational reflections of the relationship between artificial ıntelligence and emotional ıntelligence in the context of phenomenology and Cartesian dualism. *The International Journal of Organizational Analysis, 33*(10), 3878–3895. DOI: 10.1108/IJOA-10-2024-4892

Cappelli, P., Tambe, P., & Yakubovich, V. (2018). Artificial intelligence in HRM. *California Management Review, 61*(4), 15–42.

Cariaga, R. (2025). Human-AI Collaboration in Decision-Making, Creativity, and Productivity: Systematic review. SSRN Electronic Journal. DOI: 10.2139/ssrn.5378095

Carter, S. M., & Greer, C. R. (2013). Strategic leadership: Values, styles, and organizational performance. *Journal of Leadership & Organizational Studies, 20*(4), 375–393. DOI: 10.1177/1548051812471724

Cavalcante Siebert, L., Lupetti, M. L., Aizenberg, E., Beckers, N., Zgonnikov, A., Veluwenkamp, H., Abbink, D., Giaccardi, E., Houben, G.-J., Jonker, C. M., van den Hoven, J., Forster, D., & Lagendijk, R. L. (2023). Meaningful human control: Actionable properties for AI system development. *AI and Ethics, 3*(1), 241–255. DOI: 10.1007/s43681-022-00167-3

Căvescu, A. M., & Popescu, N. (2025). Predictive Analytics in Human Resources Management: Evaluating AIHR's Role in Talent Retention. *AppliedMath, 5*(3), 99. Advance online publication. DOI: 10.3390/appliedmath5030099

Chahal, D., Shahidi, N., & Byrne, M. F. (2022). Artificial Intelligence for Diagnosing G.I. Tract Lesions. In *Gastrointestinal and Pancreatico-Biliary Diseases: Advanced Diagnostic and Therapeutic Endoscopy* (pp. 523–539). Springer International Publishing. DOI: 10.1007/978-3-030-56993-8_31

Chaleshtori, M. A., Ghaffari, M., & Tajeddini, K. (2024a). Artificial intelligence and organisational leadership: A systematic review and future research agenda. *Technology in Society*, *76*, 102424. Advance online publication. DOI: 10.1016/j.techsoc.2023.102424

Chaleshtori, M. F., Aziz, A., & Bauer, T. (2024b). Human-AI collaboration in organizational contexts: A systematic review. *Journal of Management Studies*, *61*(3), 678–712. DOI: 10.1111/joms.12991

Chamorro-Premuzic, T., Winsborough, D., Sherman, R. A., & Hogan, R. (2019). New talent signals. *Industrial and Organizational Psychology: Perspectives on Science and Practice*, *12*(3), 224–233.

Chamsi-Pasha, M. A. R., & Chamsi-Pasha, H. (2025). Ethical challenges and current opportunities of artificial intelligence in cardiology. *Avicenna Journal of Medicine*, *15*(3), 95–99. DOI: 10.1055/s-0045-1809879 PMID: 41098154

Chandrasekaran, A., & Mishra, A. (2012). Task design, team context, and psychological safety: An empirical analysis of R&D projects in high-technology organizations. *Production and Operations Management*, *21*(6), 977–996. DOI: 10.1111/j.1937-5956.2012.01329.x

Chee, H., Ahn, S., & Lee, J. (2025). A competency framework for AI literacy: Variations by different learner groups and an implied learning pathway. *British Journal of Educational Technology*, *56*(3), 2146–2182. Advance online publication. DOI: 10.1111/bjet.13556

Cheng, L., Varshney, K. R., & Liu, H. (2021). Socially responsible AI algorithms: Issues, purposes, and challenges. *Journal of Artificial Intelligence Research*, *71*, 1137–1181. DOI: 10.1613/jair.1.12814

Chen, Z. (2023). Collaboration among recruiters and artificial intelligence: Removing human prejudices in employment. *Cognition Technology and Work*, *25*(1), 135–149. DOI: 10.1007/s10111-022-00716-0 PMID: 36187287

Chhibber, S., Rajkumar, S. R., & Dassanayake, S. (2025). Will Artificial Intelligence Reshape the Global Workforce by 2030? A Cross-Sectoral Analysis of Job Displacement and Transformation. *Blockchain, Artificial Intelligence, and Future Research*, *1*(1), 35–51. DOI: 10.70211/bafr.v1i1.178

Chiriatti, M., Bergamaschi Ganapini, M., Panai, E., Wiederhold, B. K., & Riva, G. (2025). System 0: Transforming artificial intelligence into a cognitive extension. *Cyberpsychology, Behavior, and Social Networking*, *28*(7), 534–542. DOI: 10.1089/cyber.2025.0201 PMID: 40504761

Chouldechova, A. (2017). Fair prediction with disparate impact: A study of bias in recidivism prediction instruments. *Big Data*, *5*(2), 153–163. DOI: 10.1089/big.2016.0047 PMID: 28632438

Chowdhury, S., Budhwar, P., & Wood, G. (2024). Generative artificial intelligence in business: Towards a strategic human resource management framework. *British Journal of Management*, *35*(4), 1680–1691. DOI: 10.1111/1467-8551.12824

Çiçek, B., & Kılınç, E. (2021). Can transformational leadership eliminate the negativity of technostress? *Business & Management Studies*, *9*(1), 372–384. DOI: 10.15295/bmij.v9i1.1770

Cinar, A. B., & Bilodeau, S. (2024). Incorporating AI into the Inner Circle of Emotional Intelligence for Sustainability. *Sustainability (Basel)*, *16*(15), 1–17. DOI: 10.3390/su16156648

Coenen, M., & Kok, R. A. W. (2014). Workplace flexibility and new product development performance: The role of telework and flexible work schedules. *European Management Journal*, *32*(4), 564–576. DOI: 10.1016/j.emj.2013.12.003

Collings, D. G., Mellahi, K., & Cascio, W. F. (2019). Global talent management and performance. *Journal of World Business*, *54*(2), 173–182.

Colquitt, J. A., Conlon, D. E., Wesson, M. J., Porter, C. O., & Ng, K. Y. (2001). Justice at the millennium. *The Journal of Applied Psychology*, *86*(3), 425–445. DOI: 10.1037/0021-9010.86.3.425

Commission Nationale de l'Informatique et des Libertés. (2025, February). *Délibération n° 2025-010 portant deuxième recommandation sur l'application du RGPD au développement des systèmes d'IA*. CNIL. https://www.legifrance.gouv.fr/jorf/id/JORFTEXT000051164307

Council of Europe. (2024, May 17). *Framework Convention on Artificial Intelligence and human rights, democracy and the rule of law (CETS No. 225)*. Council of Europe. https://www.coe.int/en/web/artificial-intelligence/the-framework-convention-on-artificial-intelligence

Coutifaris, C. G. V., & Grant, A. M. (2022). Taking your team behind the curtain: The effects of leader feedback-sharing and feedback-seeking on team psychological safety. *Organization Science*, *33*(4), 1574–1598. Advance online publication. DOI: 10.1287/orsc.2021.1498

Cramarenco, R. E., Burcă-Voicu, M. I., & Dabija, D. C. (2023). The impact of artificial intelligence (AI) on employees' skills and well-being in global labor markets: A systematic review. *Oeconomia Copernicana*, *14*(3), 731–767. DOI: 10.24136/oc.2023.022

Creswell, J. W., & Poth, C. N. (2024). Qualitative inquiry and research design: Choosing among five approaches (5th ed.). SAGE Publications., Retrieved from https://uk.sagepub.com/en-gb/eur/qualitative-inquiry-and-research-design/book266033, Retrieved November 10th, 2025, from.

Creswell, J. W., & Creswell, J. D. (2018). *Research design: Qualitative, quantitative, and mixed methods approaches* (5th ed.). SAGE Publications.

Csaszar, F. A., Ketkar, H., & Kim, H. (2024). Artificial intelligence and strategic decision-making: Evidence from entrepreneurs and investors. *Strategy Science*, *9*(4), 322–345. DOI: 10.1287/stsc.2024.0190

Cubric, M. (2020). Drivers, barriers and social considerations for AI adoption in business and management: A tertiary study. *Technology in Society*, *62*, 101257. DOI: 10.1016/j.techsoc.2020.101257

Cummings, M. L. (2004). Automation bias in intelligent time critical decision support systems. *Proceedings of the AIAA 1st Intelligent Systems Technical Conference*. DOI: 10.2514/6.2004-6313

d'État, C. (2025, December). *Charte d'utilisation de l'intelligence artificielle au sein de la juridiction administrative*. République française. https://www.conseil-etat.fr/qui-sommes-nous/deontologie/charte-d-utilisation-de-l-intelligence-artificielle-au-sein-de-la-juridiction-administrative

Dafoe, A. (2018). AI governance: A research agenda. Centre for the Governance of AI, Future of Humanity Institute, University of Oxford. https://www.governance.ai/research-paper/agenda

Dang, B., Huynh, L., Gul, F., Rosé, C., Järvelä, S., & Nguyen, A. (2025). Human–AI collaborative learning in mixed reality: Examining the cognitive and socio-emotional interactions. *British Journal of Educational Technology*, *56*(5), 2078–2101. DOI: 10.1111/bjet.13607

Daole, M., Schiavo, A., Corcuera Bárcena, J. L., Ducange, P., Marcelloni, F., & Renda, A. (2023). OpenFL-XAI: Federated learning of explainable artificial intelligence models in Python. *SoftwareX, 23*, 101505. DOI: 10.1016/j.softx.2023.101505

Davenport, T. H., & Kirby, J. (2016). *Only humans need apply: Winners and losers in the age of smart machines*. Harper Business.

Davidovic, J. (2023). Why we need humans in control of AI. *Frontiers in Big Data, 6*, 1070597. DOI: 10.3389/fdata.2023.1070597

Davis, F. D. (1989). Perceived usefulness and ease of use. *Management Information Systems Quarterly, 13*(3), 319–340. DOI: 10.2307/249008

De Dreu, C. K. W., & Weingart, L. R. (2003). Task versus relationship conflict, team performance, and team member satisfaction: A meta-analysis. *The Journal of Applied Psychology, 88*(4), 741–749. DOI: 10.1037/0021-9010.88.4.741

de Visser, E. J., Peeters, M. M. M., Jung, M. F., Kohn, S., Shaw, T. H., Pak, R., & Neerincx, M. A. (2020). Towards a theory of longitudinal trust calibration in human–robot teams. *International Journal of Social Robotics, 12*(2), 459–478. DOI: 10.1007/s12369-019-00596-x

Deb Biswas, D., & Sengupta, R. (2025). Reimagining leadership for the AI era: A grounded theory of adaptive, ethical and contextually situated practices in workplaces. *Leadership and Organization Development Journal*. Advance online publication. DOI: 10.1108/LODJ-06-2025-0488

Deci, E. L., & Ryan, R. M. (2000). The "what" and "why" of goal pursuits: Human needs and the self-determination of behavior. *Psychological Inquiry, 11*(4), 227–268. DOI: 10.1207/S15327965PLI1104_01

Deloitte. (2023, January 9). *2023 Global human capital trends*. Deloitte Insights. https://www.deloitte.com/us/en/insights/topics/talent/human-capital-trends/2023.html

Dewi, M. V. K., Nimran, U., Musadieq, M. A., & Afrianty, T. W. (2020). The effect of perceived organizational support and quality of work life on employee engagement and performance. *International Journal of Management, 11*(6), 772–783.

Dietvorst, B. J., Simmons, J. P., & Massey, C. (2015). Algorithm aversion: People erroneously avoid algorithms after seeing them err. *Journal of Experimental Psychology. General, 144*(1), 114–126. DOI: 10.1037/xge0000033 PMID: 25401381

Dietvorst, B. J., Simmons, J. P., & Massey, C. (2018). Overcoming algorithm aversion: People will use imperfect algorithms if they can (even slightly) modify them. *Management Science, 64*(3), 1155–1170. DOI: 10.1287/mnsc.2016.2643

Dineen, B. R., & Allen, D. G. (2016). Third party employment branding. *The Journal of Applied Psychology, 101*(2), 261–276.

Dinh, H. T. (2020). Work-life balance and employee engagement: Mediating role of supervisory support. *Journal of Asian Business and Economic Studies, 27*(3), 258–274. DOI: 10.1108/JABES-05-2020-0052

Distefano, J. P., Chowdhury, S., & Esfahani, E. (2023). Exploring human-swarm interaction dynamics in cyber-physical systems: A physiological approach. *Journal of Integrated Design & Process Science, 27*(3–4), 200–210. DOI: 10.1177/10920617241292155

Dixit, A. S., & Jatav, S. (2024). Evolving needs of learners and role of artificial intelligence (AI) in training and development (T&D): T&D professionals' perspective. *Journal of Management Development, 43*(6), 788–806. DOI: 10.1108/JMD-01-2024-0009

Donins, U., & Behmane, D. (2023). *Challenges and Solutions for Artificial Intelligence Adoption in Healthcare – A Literature Review* (pp. 53–62). DOI: 10.1007/978-981-99-3311-2_6

Doshi, A. R., Bell, J. J., Mirzayev, E., & Vanneste, B. S. (2025). Generative artificial intelligence and evaluating strategic decisions. *Strategic Management Journal, 46*(3), 583–610. DOI: 10.1002/smj.3677

Dumitru, D., & Halpern, D. F. (2023). Critical Thinking: Creating Job-Proof Skills for the Future of Work. *Journal of Intelligence, 11*(10), 194. Advance online publication. DOI: 10.3390/jintelligence11100194 PMID: 37888426

Dutt, R. (2020). The impact of artificial intelligence on healthcare insurances. In *Artificial Intelligence in Healthcare* (pp. 271–293). Elsevier., DOI: 10.1016/B978-0-12-818438-7.00011-3

Dwianto, A., Kusuma, S., & Junengsih, . (2024). Artificial Intelligence in Performance Evaluation (Case Study of PT. Pos Indonesia Employees). *Bit-Tech, 7*(2), 348–356. DOI: 10.32877/bt.v7i2.1817

Dwivedi, Y. K., Hughes, L., Ismagilova, E., Aarts, G., Coombs, C., Crick, T., Duan, Y., Dwivedi, R., Edwards, J., Eirug, A., Galanos, V., Ilavarasan, P. V., Janssen, M., Jones, P., Kar, A. K., Kizgin, H., Kronemann, B., Lal, B., Lucini, B., & Williams, M. D. (2021). Artificial Intelligence (AI): Multidisciplinary perspectives on emerging challenges, opportunities, and agenda for research, practice and policy. *International Journal of Information Management*, *57*, 101994. DOI: 10.1016/j.ijinfomgt.2019.08.002

Dwivedi, Y. K., Kshetri, N., Hughes, L., Slade, E. L., Jeyaraj, A., Kar, A. K., Baabdullah, A. M., Abdulsalam, A., Ackah, B. B., Akour, I., Alhassan, R., Al-Khowaiter, A., Almohammadi, H., Alomari, K., Altameem, A., Alturise, F., Asiri, S., Báča, A., Bag, S., & Wright, R. (2023). "So what if ChatGPT wrote it?" Multidisciplinary perspectives on opportunities, challenges and implications of generative conversational AI for research, practice and policy. *International Journal of Information Management*, *71*, 102642. Advance online publication. DOI: 10.1016/j.ijinfomgt.2023.102642

Ebert, I., Wildhaber, I., & Adams-Prassl, J. (2021). Big Data in the workplace: Privacy Due Diligence as a human rights-based approach to employee privacy protection. *Big Data & Society*, *8*(1), 20539517211013051. DOI: 10.1177/20539517211013051

Edmondson, A. (1999). Psychological safety and learning behavior in work teams. *Administrative Science Quarterly*, *44*(2), 350–383. DOI: 10.2307/2666999

Edmondson, A., & Bransby, D. P. (2022). Psychological safety comes of age: Observed themes in an established literature. *Annual Review of Organizational Psychology and Organizational Behavior*, *9*, 1–25. DOI: 10.1146/annurev-orgpsych-120920-055217

Eisenberger, R., Rockstuhl, T., Shoss, M. K., Wen, X., & Dulebohn, J. (2020). Is employee–organization relationship research mature enough to be useful? A meta-analytic review. *Journal of Organizational Behavior*, *41*(2), 111–134.

Elish, M. C. (2019). Moral crumple zones: Cautionary tales in human-robot interaction. *Engaging Science, Technology, and Society*, *5*, 40–60. DOI: 10.17351/ests2019.260

Endsley, M. R. (2017). From here to autonomy: Lessons learned from human–automation research. *Human Factors*, *59*(1), 5–27. DOI: 10.1177/0018720816681350 PMID: 28146676

Engelbart, D. C. (1962). *Augmenting human intellect: A conceptual framework* (Summary Report AFOSR-3223). Stanford Research Institute. https://www.dougengelbart.org/content/view/138/

European Commission. (2025, February 12). *Commission work programme 2025: Moving forward together — A bolder, simpler, faster Union* (COM(2025) 45 final). Publications Office of the European Union. https://commission.europa.eu/strategy-and-policy/eu-budget/long-term-eu-budget/2021-2027_en

European Parliament & Council of the European Union. (2024). Regulation (EU) 2024/1689 laying down harmonised rules on artificial intelligence (Artificial Intelligence Act). Official Journal of the European Union, L 2024/1689.

European Parliament and Council of the European Union. (2024b, October 23). *Directive (EU) 2024/2831 of the European Parliament and of the Council on improving working conditions in platform work.* Official Journal of the European Union, L Series. https://data.europa.eu/eli/dir/2024/2831/oj

European Parliament. (2025, December 11). *MEPs demand new measures to protect workers against algorithmic management at work* [Press release]. https://www.europarl.europa.eu/news/en/press-room/20251211IPR32175/meps-demand-new-measures-to-protect-against-algorithmic-management-at-work

Fantoni, M. J., & Sasmita, J. (2025). Leadership in the era of Artificial Intelligence: Challenges, opportunities, and strategic transformation. *Journal Corner of Education Linguistics and Literature*, *5*(2), 220–232. DOI: 10.54012/jcell.v5i2.612

Faraj, S., Pachidi, S., & Sayegh, K. (2018). Working and organizing in the age of the learning algorithm. *Information and Organization*, *28*(1), 62–70. DOI: 10.1016/j.infoandorg.2018.02.005

Felin, T., & Holweg, M. (2024). Theory is all you need: AI, human cognition, and causal reasoning. *Strategy Science*, *9*(4), 346–371. DOI: 10.1287/stsc.2024.0189

Fenech, R., Baguant, P., & Ivanov, D. (2019). The changing role of human resource management in an era of digital transformation. *Journal of Management Information & Decision Sciences*, *22*(2).

Fenwick, A., Molnar, G., & Frangos, P. (2024). The critical role of HRM in AI-driven digital transformation: A paradigm shift to enable firms to move from AI implementation to human-centric adoption. *Discover Artificial Intelligence*, *4*(1), 34. Advance online publication. DOI: 10.1007/s44163-024-00125-4

Fleishman, E. A. (1953). The description of supervisory behavior. *The Journal of Applied Psychology*, *37*(1), 1–6. DOI: 10.1037/h0056314 PMID: 6038475

Floridi, L. (2025). AI as agency without intelligence: On artificial intelligence as a new form of artificial agency and the multiple realisability of agency thesis. Philosophy & Technology. DOI: 10.1007/s13347-025-00858-9

Floridi, L. (2019). Establishing the rules for building trustworthy AI. *Nature Machine Intelligence*, *1*(6), 261–262. DOI: 10.1038/s42256-019-0055-y

Frazier, M. L., Fainshmidt, S., Klinger, R. L., Pezeshkan, A., & Vracheva, V. (2017). Psychological safety: A meta-analytic review and extension. *Personnel Psychology*, *70*(1), 113–165. DOI: 10.1111/peps.12183

Gallup. (2019). *State of the global workplace: 2019 report.* Gallup Press.

Gartner, Inc. (2023).Evolve culture and leadership for a Hybrid World. Gartner, Inc. retrieved from https://www.gartner.com/en/human-resources/insights/culture-and-leadership-in-a-hybrid-world [accessed on November, 2025]

Gerlich, M. (2025). AI tools in society: Impacts on cognitive offloading and the future of critical thinking. *Societies (Basel, Switzerland)*, *15*(1), 6. DOI: 10.3390/soc15010006

Ghaleb, M. M. S., & Sattarov, A. (2025). *Use of ChatGPT in education and quality of education: Role of student course engagement and regulator support.* Revista Electrónica de LEEME., DOI: 10.58262/LEEME.55.0020

Gigerenzer, G., & Gaissmaier, W. (2011). Heuristic decision making. *Annual Review of Psychology*, *62*(1), 451–482. DOI: 10.1146/annurev-psych-120709-145346 PMID: 21126183

Gilliland, S. W. (1993). Selection fairness perceptions. *Academy of Management Review*, *18*(4), 694–734. DOI: 10.2307/258595

Gin, B. C., O'Sullivan, P. S., Hauer, K. E., Abdulnour, R.-E., Mackenzie, M., Ten Cate, O., & Boscardin, C. K. (2025). Entrustment and EPAs for artificial intelligence (AI): A framework to safeguard the use of AI in health professions education. *Academic Medicine*, *100*(3), 264–272. DOI: 10.1097/ACM.0000000000005930 PMID: 39761533

Glikson, E., & Woolley, A. W. (2020). Human trust in artificial intelligence: Review of empirical research. *The Academy of Management Annals*, *14*(2), 627–660. DOI: 10.5465/annals.2018.0057

Gnewuch, U., Morana, S., & Maedche, A. (2017). Towards designing cooperative and social conversational agents for customer service. *Proceedings of the 38th International Conference on Information Systems (ICIS 2017)*, Seoul, South Korea.

Goddard, K., Roudsari, A., & Wyatt, J. C. (2012). Automation bias: A systematic review of frequency, effect mediators, and mitigators. *Journal of the American Medical Informatics Association : JAMIA*, *19*(1), 121–127. DOI: 10.1136/amiajnl-2011-000089 PMID: 21685142

Goddard, K., Roudsari, A., & Wyatt, J. C. (2014). Automation bias: Empirical results assessing influencing factors. *International Journal of Medical Informatics*, *83*(5), 368–375. DOI: 10.1016/j.ijmedinf.2014.01.001 PMID: 24581700

Goldsteen, A., Farkash, A., Moffie, M., & Shmelkin, R. (2022). *Applying Artificial Intelligence Privacy Technology in the Healthcare Domain*. DOI: 10.3233/SHTI220410

Goleman, D. (2011). Leadership: The power of emotional intelligence. More Than Sound. Retrieved from https://ia801800.us.archive.org/21/items/educational-administration-concepts-and-practices/Leadership%20The%20Power%20of%20Emotional%20Leadership.pdf [accessed on November, 2025]

Golgeci, I., Ritala, P., Arslan, A., McKenna, B., & Ali, I. (2025). Confronting and alleviating AI resistance in the workplace: An integrative review and a process framework. *Human Resource Management Review*, *35*(2), 101075. DOI: 10.1016/j.hrmr.2024.101075

Gómez Gandía, J. A., Gavrila Gavrila, S., de Lucas Ancillo, A., & del Val Núñez, M. T. (2024). RPA as a Challenge Beyond Technology: Self-Learning and Attitude Needed for Successful RPA Implementation in the Workplace. *Journal of the Knowledge Economy*, *15*(4), 19628–19655. DOI: 10.1007/s13132-024-01865-5

Gordin Yoskovitz, G., & Schechter, C. (2024). Agentic leadership: Principals' agency during the COVID-19 crisis. *Leadership and Policy in Schools*, *23*(4), 920–937. DOI: 10.1080/15700763.2023.2261039

Greenberg, J. (1987). Organizational justice theory. *Academy of Management Review*, *12*(1), 9–22. DOI: 10.2307/257990

Greenleaf, R. K. (1977). *Servant leadership: A journey into the nature of legitimate power and greatness*. Paulist Press.

Gronn, P. (2002). Distributed leadership as a unit of analysis. *The Leadership Quarterly*, *13*(4), 423–451. DOI: 10.1016/S1048-9843(02)00120-0

Grzybowski, A. (2021). Artificial Intelligence in Ophthalmology: Promises, Hazards and Challenges. In *Artificial Intelligence in Ophthalmology* (pp. 1–16). Springer International Publishing. DOI: 10.1007/978-3-030-78601-4_1

Gulia, R., & Rastogi, V. (2024). The impact of information technology on data-driven decision making in human resource management. *International Journal For Multidisciplinary Research*, *6*(6), 30314. Advance online publication. DOI: 10.36948/ijfmr.2024.v06i06.30314

Gulyamov, S. S. (2024). *Legal Frameworks for the Integration of Artificial Intelligence.*, DOI: 10.1007/978-3-031-42782-4_16

Guo, T., Chen, X., Wang, Y., Chang, R., Pei, S., Chawla, N. V., Wiest, O., & Zhang, X. (2024). Large language model based multi-agents: A survey of progress and challenges. In *Proceedings of the 33rd International Joint Conference on Artificial Intelligence* (pp. 8048–8057). IJCAI. DOI: 10.24963/ijcai.2024/890

Gupta, S. (2025). Ethical considerations in cloud AI: Addressing bias and fairness in algorithmic systems. *International Journal of Advanced Research in Science. Tongxin Jishu*, •••, 310–316. DOI: 10.48175/IJARSCT-25053

Gyöngyössy, N. M., Török, B., Farkas, C., Lucaj, L., Menyhárd, A., Menyhárd-Balázs, K., Simonyi, A., Patrick, V. D. S., Ződi, Z., & Lőrincz, A. (2024). Assistive AI for augmenting human decision-making. arXiv (Cornell University). https://doi .org//arxiv.2410.14353DOI: 10.48550

Hackl, C. (2025, June 17). Ai as a servant leader: A new paradigm for human-centered transformation: Smartlab - The Digital Experience Platform. AI as a Servant Leader. https://smartlabservices.com/blog-posts/ai-as-a-servant-leader-a-new-paradigm-for -human-centered-transformation

Hair, J. F., Rana, S., Robb, D., & Stroud, M. (2026). The emerging role of AI and social robots in university student recruitment. In Social robots and artificial intelligence in education: Integrating AI in K-12 and higher education (pp. 153–183). Springer Nature Switzerland. DOI: 10.1007/978-3-032-03977-4_7

Hambrick, D. C., & Mason, P. A. (1984). Upper echelons: The organization as a reflection of its top managers. *Academy of Management Review*, *9*(2), 193–206. DOI: 10.2307/258434

Hamid, E. M., & Shodiyev, A. (2025). Role of information needs, information accessibility, information overload and digital literacy in shaping web search self-efficacy. *El Profesional de la Información*, *34*(2). Advance online publication. DOI: 10.3145/epi.2025.ene.34205

Hancock, P. A., Kessler, T. T., Kaplan, A. D., Brill, J. C., & Szalma, J. L. (2021). Evolving trust in robots: Specification through sequential and comparative meta-analyses. *Human Factors*, *63*(7), 1196–1229. DOI: 10.1177/0018720820922080 PMID: 32519902

Hao, M., Lv, W., & Du, B. (2020). The Influence Mechanism of Authentic Leadership in Artificial Intelligence Team on Employees' Performance. *Journal of Physics: Conference Series*, *1438*(1), 012022. DOI: 10.1088/1742-6596/1438/1/012022

Haque, A. (2025). Responsible artificial intelligence (AI) in healthcare: A paradigm shifts in leadership and strategic management. *Leadership in Health Services (Bradford, England)*, *38*(4), 644–656. DOI: 10.1108/LHS-01-2025-0018

Harter, J. (2021). *U.S. employee engagement holds steady in first half of 2021.* Gallup. https://www.gallup.com/workplace/352949/employee-engagement-holds-steady-first-half-2021.aspx

Hartwig, A., Clarke, S., Johnson, S., & Willis, S. (2020). Workplace team resilience: A systematic review and conceptual development. *Organizational Psychology Review*, *10*(3–4), 169–200. DOI: 10.1177/2041386620919476

Harvard Business School Publishing. (2025, April). *Leadership fitness — The path to developing human-centered leaders.* Harvard Business Impact Perspective. Retrieved from https://www.harvardbusiness.org/wp-content/uploads/2025/04/HBI_Perspective_Developing-Human-Centered-Leaders.pdf [accessed on November, 2025]

Hasanah, U., & Rozi, F. (2025). Adaptive leadership in the dynamics of business in the digital era. *International Journal of Public Administration and Policy*, *1*(2), 39–44. DOI: 10.58290/ijpap.v1i2.138

Hasanović, A., & Muftić, E. (2025). Human oversight requirements under the EU AI Act: Implications for organizational practice. *AI and Ethics*, *5*(1), 78–95. DOI: 10.1007/s43681-024-00451-4

Hembram, R. (2025). The Future of HR in Academia: A Case Study on AI-Driven HRM and Emotional Intelligence in Berhampur Institutions. *SSRN*, *5216958*, •••. https://papers.ssrn.com/sol3/papers.cfm?abstract_id=5216958%0Ahttps://papers.ssrn.com/sol3/Delivery.cfm?abstractid=5216958

Hersey, P., & Blanchard, K. H. (1969). Life cycle theory of leadership. *Training and Development Journal*, *23*(5), 26–34.

Hinings, B., Gegenhuber, T., & Greenwood, R. (2018). Digital innovation and transformation: An institutional perspective. *Information and Organization, 28*(1), 52–61. DOI: 10.1016/j.infoandorg.2018.02.004

Hmoud, B., & Laszlo, V. (2019). Will artificial intelligence take over human resources recruitment and selection? *Network Intelligence Studies, 13*(1), 21–30.

Hoff, K. A., & Bashir, M. (2015). Trust in automation: Integrating empirical evidence on factors that influence trust. *Human Factors, 57*(3), 407–434. DOI: 10.1177/0018720814547570 PMID: 25875432

Holm, A. B. (2012). E-recruitment. *Journal of Management & Organization, 18*(1), 68–81.

Holm, J. R., & Lorenz, E. (2022). The impact of artificial intelligence on skills at work in Denmark. *New Technology, Work and Employment, 37*(1), 79–101. DOI: 10.1111/ntwe.12215

Holzinger, A., Saranti, A., Angerschmid, A., Finzel, B., Schmid, U., & Mueller, H. (2023). Toward human-level concept learning: Pattern benchmarking for AI algorithms. *Patterns (New York, N.Y.), 4*(8), 100788. DOI: 10.1016/j.patter.2023.100788

Horowitz, M. C., & Kahn, L. (2024). Bending the automation bias curve: A study of human and AI-based decision making in national security contexts. *International Studies Quarterly, 68*(2), sqae020. Advance online publication. DOI: 10.1093/isq/sqae020

Hsiao, J. H.-W. (2024). Understanding human cognition through computational modeling. *Topics in Cognitive Science, 16*(3), 349–376. DOI: 10.1111/tops.12737 PMID: 38781432

Huang, M.-H., & Rust, R. T. (2018). Artificial intelligence in service. *Journal of Service Research, 21*(2), 155–172. DOI: 10.1177/1094670517752459

Hunkenschroer, A. L., & Luetge, C. (2022). Ethics of AI-Enabled Recruiting and Selection: A Review and Research Agenda. In *Journal of Business Ethics* (Vol. 178, Issue 4). Springer Netherlands. DOI: 10.1007/s10551-022-05049-6

Huselid, M. A. (1995). HR practices and performance. *Academy of Management Journal, 38*(3), 635–672. DOI: 10.2307/256741

Hussain, Z., Khan, A., Awad, A., & Bansal, R. (2026). AI-driven learning culture enhances innovation performance: A serial mediator of knowledge orchestration and organisational intelligence. *VINE Journal of Information and Knowledge Management Systems*, •••, 1–23. DOI: 10.1108/VJIKMS-12-2025-0527

Hutchins, E. (1995). *Cognition in the wild.* MIT Press. DOI: 10.7551/mit-press/1881.001.0001

Iansiti, M., & Lakhani, K. R. (2020). *Competing in the age of AI: Strategy and leadership when algorithms and networks run the world.* Harvard Business Review Press.

Ihongbe, E, I., Fouad, S., F Mahmoud, T., Rajasekaran, A., & Bhatia, B. (. (2024). Evaluating Explainable Artificial Intelligence (XAI) techniques in chest radiology imaging through a human-centered Lens. *PLoS One*, *19*(10), e0308758. DOI: 10.1371/journal.pone.0308758 PMID: 39383147

Ilyas, M. (2022). Augmented intelligence for advancing healthcare. Journal of Systemics, Cybernetics, and Informatics. *Journal of Systemics, Cybernetics and Informatics*, *20*(6), 13–19. DOI: 10.54808/JSCI.20.06.13

Ingrams, A., Kaufmann, W., & Jacobs, D. (2022). In AI we trust? Citizen perceptions of AI in government decision making. *Policy and Internet*, *14*(2), 390–409. DOI: 10.1002/poi3.276

Institute for the Future of Work. (2024, March 12). *Workplace AI, robots and trackers are bad for quality of life, study finds. The Guardian.* Retrieved from https://www.theguardian.com/business/2024/mar/12/workplace-ai-robots-trackers-quality-of-life-institute-for-work- [accessed on November, 2025]

Iqbal, A., Ahmad, M. S., & Nazir, T. (2022). Does servant leadership predict innovative behaviour above and beyond transformational leadership? Examining the role of affective commitment and creative self-efficacy. *Leadership and Organization Development Journal*, *44*(1), 34–51. DOI: 10.1108/LODJ-01-2022-0016

Islami, X., & Mulolli, E. (2024). Human-artificial intelligence in management functions: A synergistic symbiosis relationship. *Applied Artificial Intelligence*, *38*(1), 2439615. DOI: 10.1080/08839514.2024.2439615

Islam, M. S., Hussain, Z., Bansal, R., Awad, A., & Pruthi, N. (2026). AI-enabled environmental auditing and sustainability disclosure: Green reporting capability as mediator and digital compliance culture as moderator. *Corporate Social Responsibility and Environmental Management*, csr.70565. Advance online publication. DOI: 10.1002/csr.70565

Islamutdinov, V., Akhmetshin, E., Lydia, E. L., & Raja, P. V. K. (2024, April). Implementation of AI in an ethical and responsible manner to empower education in digital sector. In International Conference on Smart Computing and Informatics (pp. 127–134). Springer Nature Singapore. DOI: 10.1007/978-981-96-3939-7_13

Jacob Fernandes França, T., São Mamede, H., Pereira Barroso, J. M., & Pereira Duarte dos Santos, V. M. (2023). Artificial intelligence applied to potential assessment and talent identification in an organisational context. *Heliyon, 9*(4), e14694. Advance online publication. DOI: 10.1016/j.heliyon.2023.e14694 PMID: 37035361

Jacobs, S. (2025). 5 innovation trends reshaping leadership in 2025. Sheri Jacobs Consulting. https://www.sherijacobs.com/blog/5-innovation-trends-reshaping-leadership-in-2025

Jacovi, A., Marasović, A., Miller, T., & Goldberg, Y. (2021). Formalizing trust in artificial intelligence: Prerequisites, causes and goals of human trust in AI. In *Proceedings of the 2021 ACM Conference on Fairness, Accountability, and Transparency* (pp. 624–635). ACM. DOI: 10.1145/3442188.3445923

Jarrahi, M. H. (2018). Artificial intelligence and the future of work: Human-AI symbiosis in organizational decision making. *Business Horizons, 61*(4), 577–586. DOI: 10.1016/j.bushor.2018.03.007

Jastroch, N. (2020). *Trusted Artificial Intelligence: On the Use of Private Data* (pp. 659–670). DOI: 10.1007/978-3-030-62807-9_52

Javed, R. T., Nasir, O., Borit, M., Vanhée, L., Zea, E., Gupta, S., Vinuesa, R., & Qadir, J. (2023). Get Out of the BAG! Silos in AI Ethics Education: Unsupervised Topic Modeling Analysis of Global AI Curricula (Extended Abstract). *IJCAI International Joint Conference on Artificial Intelligence, 2023-Augus*, 6905–6909. DOI: 10.24963/ijcai.2023/780

Jehn, K. A., & Mannix, E. A. (2001). The dynamic nature of conflict: A longitudinal study of intragroup conflict and group performance. *Academy of Management Journal, 44*(2), 238–251. DOI: 10.2307/3069453

Jobin, A., Ienca, M., & Vayena, E. (2019). The global landscape of AI ethics guidelines. *Nature Machine Intelligence, 1*(9), 389–399. DOI: 10.1038/s42256-019-0088-2

Johnson, D. G., & Verdicchio, M. (2025). The sociotechnical entanglement of AI and values. *AI & Society, 40*(1), 67–76. DOI: 10.1007/s00146-023-01852-5

Johnson, M., Jain, R., Brennan-Tonetta, P., Swartz, E., Silver, D., Paolini, J., Mamonov, S., & Hill, C. (2021). Impact of Big Data and Artificial Intelligence on Industry: Developing a Workforce Roadmap for a Data Driven Economy. *Global Journal of Flexible Systems Managment, 22*(3), 197–217. DOI: 10.1007/s40171-021-00272-y

Johnson, R. D., Lukaszewski, K. M., & Stone, D. L. (2016). The evolution of the field of human resource information systems: Co-Evolution of technology and HR processes. *Communications of the Association for Information Systems, 38*(1), 533–553. DOI: 10.17705/1CAIS.03828

Johnson, R. D., Stone, D. L., & Lukaszewski, K. M. (2021). The benefits of eHRM and AI for talent acquisition. *Journal of Tourism Futures, 7*(1), 40–52. DOI: 10.1108/JTF-02-2020-0013

Jones-Jang, S. M., Park, Y.-J., & Kim, J. (2023). Why do people distrust AI? Distinguishing predictors of distrust and trust in artificial intelligence. *Internet Research, 33*(2), 592–612. DOI: 10.1108/INTR-09-2021-0699

Jordan, M. I., & Mitchell, T. M. (2015). Machine learning: Trends, perspectives, and prospects. *Science, 349*(6245), 255–260. DOI: 10.1126/science.aaa8415 PMID: 26185243

Judge, T. A., Bono, J. E., Ilies, R., & Gerhardt, M. W. (2002). Personality and leadership: A qualitative and quantitative review. *The Journal of Applied Psychology, 87*(4), 765–780. DOI: 10.1037/0021-9010.87.4.765 PMID: 12184579

Jussupow, E., Spohrer, K., & Heinzl, A. (2022). Entangling the misuse of AI-powered diagnostic decision support systems with professional identity threat. *Management Information Systems Quarterly, 46*(3), 1385–1416. DOI: 10.25300/MISQ/2022/16037

Kabza, M. (2020). Artificial intelligence in financial services – benefits and costs. In *Innovation in Financial Services* (pp. 183–198). Routledge., DOI: 10.4324/9781003051664-14

Kaggwa, S., Eleogu, T. F., Okonkwo, F., Farayola, O. A., Uwaoma, P. U., & Akinoso, A. (2024). AI in Decision Making: Transforming Business Strategies. *International Journal of Innovation and Scientific Research, X*(XII), 423–444. DOI: 10.51244/IJRSI.2023.1012032

Kane, G. C., Palmer, D., Phillips, A. N., Kiron, D., & Buckley, N. (2015). Strategy, Not Technology, Drives Digital Transformation. *MIT Sloan Management Review.*

Kaplan, A. D., Kessler, T. T., Brill, J. C., & Hancock, P. A. (2023). Trust in artificial intelligence: Meta-analytic findings. *Human Factors, 65*(2), 337–359. DOI: 10.1177/00187208211013988 PMID: 34048287

Karuppiah, S. P., & Kumaran, S. (2025, July). AI-Powered Talent Acquisition: Enhancing Recruitment and Workforce Analytics Using Machine Learning. In *2025 IEEE 4th World Conference on Applied Intelligence and Computing (AIC)* (pp. 179-184). IEEE.

Kašpárková, L., Vaculík, M., Procházka, J., & Schaufeli, W. B. (2018). Why resilient workers perform better: The roles of job satisfaction and work engagement. *Journal of Workplace Behavioral Health, 33*(1), 43–62. DOI: 10.1080/15555240.2018.1441719

Kassab, K., & Kashevnik, A. (2024). Personality Traits Estimation Based on Job Interview Video Analysis: Importance of Human Nonverbal Cues Detection. *Big Data and Cognitive Computing, 8*(12), 173. Advance online publication. DOI: 10.3390/bdcc8120173

Kellogg, K. C., Valentine, M. A., & Christin, A. (2020). Algorithms at work: The new contested terrain of control. *The Academy of Management Annals, 14*(1), 366–410. DOI: 10.5465/annals.2018.0174

Kerstan, S., Bienefeld, N., & Grote, G. (2024). Choosing human over AI doctors? How comparative trust associations and knowledge relate to risk and benefit perceptions of AI in healthcare. *Risk Analysis, 44*(4), 939–957. DOI: 10.1111/risa.14216 PMID: 37722964

Khan, F. A., Khan, N. A., & Aslam, A. (2024). Adoption of artificial intelligence in human resource management: an application of TOE-TAM model. *Research and review: human resource and labour management, 5*, 22-36.

Khera, R., Simon, M. A., & Ross, J. S. (2023). Automation bias and assistive AI: Risk of harm from AI-driven clinical decision support. *Journal of the American Medical Association, 330*(23), 2255–2257. DOI: 10.1001/jama.2023.22557 PMID: 38112824

Kim, B. J., & Kim, M. J. (2024). What an artificial intelligence-induced job insecurity shapes knowledge dynamics: The mitigating role of artificial intelligence self-efficacy. *Journal of Innovation & Knowledge, 9*(4), 100590. DOI: 10.1016/j.jik.2024.100590

Kim, S., Khoreva, V., & Vaiman, V. (2025). Strategic human resource management in the era of algorithmic technologies: Key insights and future research agenda. *Human Resource Management, 64*(2), 447–464. DOI: 10.1002/hrm.22268

Kingsley, J. N., Cherian, J., & Farouq, M. (2019). Employee engagement model: An organizational culture, quality of work life, and work engagement perspective. *International Journal of Mechanical Engineering and Technology, 10*(1), 238–248.

Kirilenko, A., Kyle, A. S., Samadi, M., & Tuzun, T. (2017). The flash crash: High-frequency trading in an electronic market. *The Journal of Finance, 72*(3), 967–998. DOI: 10.1111/jofi.12498

Klein, G. (1993). A recognition-primed decision (RPD) model of rapid decision making. In Klein, G. A., Orasanu, J., Calderwood, R., & Zsambok, C. E. (Eds.), *Decision making in action: Models and methods* (pp. 138–147). Ablex Publishing.

Klein, G. (1998). *Sources of power: How people make decisions*. MIT Press.

Klein, G. (2008). Naturalistic decision making. *Human Factors, 50*(3), 456–460. DOI: 10.1518/001872008X288385 PMID: 18689053

Klingbeil, N., Dzindolet, M., & Rantanen, E. M. (2024). Appropriate reliance on automation: Conceptualisation, measurement, and the role of trust and confidence. *Human Factors*. Advance online publication. DOI: 10.1177/00187208241237618

Kochan, T. A., & Dyer, L. (1993). Managing transformational change: The role of human resource professionals. *International Journal of Human Resource Management, 4*(3), 569–590. DOI: 10.1080/09585199300000037

Köchling, A., & Wehner, M. (2020). Algorithmic hiring bias. *Journal of Business Ethics*.

Köchling, A., & Wehner, M. C. (2020). Discriminated by an algorithm: A systematic review of discrimination and fairness by algorithmic decision-making in the context of HR recruitment and HR development. *Business Research, 13*(3), 795–848. DOI: 10.1007/s40685-020-00134-w

Kodagoda, T. (2026). Generation Y employees' understandings on artificial intelligence (AI): Interventions at workplace. In *Communication and knowledge in organizations: Approaches from positivist and interpretivist paradigms* (pp. 19–32). Springer Nature Singapore., DOI: 10.1007/978-981-95-0622-4_2

Kolbjørnsrud, V. (2024). Leading with AI: A framework for human-machine collaboration. *California Management Review, 66*(2), 45–68. DOI: 10.1177/00081256231196742

Kommera, H. K. R. (2017). Choosing the Right HCM Tool: A Guide for HR Professionals. *International Journal of Early Childhood Special Education, 9*, 191–198.

Konstantinos, G. (2024). Thematic analysis: A practical guide: by Virginia Braun and Victoria Clarke, Los Angeles, USA, Sage Publications, 2022, 376 pp., $ 27.59 (paperback), ISBN-13: 978-1473953246. *European Journal of Psychotherapy & Counselling, 26*(3–4), 461–464. DOI: 10.1080/13642537.2024.2391666

Korn Ferry Institute. (2025). Leadership in the age of AI: New competencies for the augmented leader. Korn Ferry. https://www.kornferry.com/institute/defining-and-developing-the-ai-augmented-leader

Korteling, J. E., Van De Boer-Visschedijk, G. C., Blankendaal, R. M., Boonekamp, R. C., & Eikelboom, A. R. (2021). Human- versus Artificial Intelligence. *Frontiers in Artificial Intelligence, 4*, 622364. DOI: 10.3389/frai.2021.622364

Kotter, J. P. (1996). *Leading change*. Harvard Business School Press.

Kravchuk, O. (2026). *Human-centric digital leadership for HRM 5 . 0 ecosystem readiness*. 55–85.

Krishna, S., & Sidharth, S. (2023). AI-Powered Workforce Analytics: Maximizing Business and Employee Success through Predictive Attrition Modelling. *International Journal of Performability Engineering, 19*(3), 203–215. DOI: 10.23940/ijpe.23.03.p6.203215

Kudina, O., & van de Poel, I. (2024). A sociotechnical system perspective on AI. *Minds and Machines, 34*(3), 21. Advance online publication. DOI: 10.1007/s11023-024-09680-2

Kulkov, I., Kulkova, J., Rohrbeck, R., Menvielle, L., Kaartemo, V., & Makkonen, H. (2024). Artificial intelligence - driven sustainable development: Examining organizational, technical, and processing approaches to achieving global goals. *Sustainable Development (Bradford), 32*(3), 2253–2267. DOI: 10.1002/sd.2773

Kulmanov, T., Dadabaev, U., Qulmetov, M., Ulashov, A., Eshboyev, M., & Makhmudov, S. (2024, December). Global services market transformation: Digitalization export trends and future forecasts. In *Proceedings of the 8th International Conference on Future Networks & Distributed Systems* (pp. 851–858). ACM. DOI: 10.1145/3726122.3726245

Kumar, A., & Nair, S. R. (2025). Predictive analytics for learning outcomes: AI-powered student performance monitoring and early intervention strategies. In *Artificial Intelligence-Powered Learning Analytics and Student Feedback Mechanisms for Dynamic Curriculum Enhancement and Continuous Quality Improvement in Outcome-Based Education* (pp. 124–150). RADemics Research Institute. DOI: 10.71443/9789349552531-05

Kumar, A. (2024). Redefining Finance: The Influence of Artificial Intelligence (AI) and Machine Learning (ML). *Transactions on Engineering and Computing Sciences, 12*(4), 59–69.

Kuncel, N. R., Klieger, D. M., Connelly, B. S., & Ones, D. S. (2013). Mechanical versus clinical prediction. *The Journal of Applied Psychology, 98*(6), 1060–1072. DOI: 10.1037/a0034156

Kupfer, C., Prassl, R., Fleiß, J., Malin, C., Thalmann, S., & Kubicek, B. (2023). Check the box! How to deal with automation bias in AI-based personnel selection. *Frontiers in Psychology*, *14*, 1118723. Advance online publication. DOI: 10.3389/fpsyg.2023.1118723 PMID: 37089740

Kuzmin, E., Bondareva, V. S., Shodiyev, A., & Ochilov, I. (2025). Digitalization, innovation, and competitiveness: Insights from a cross-country analysis of labor productivity effects. In *Artificial intelligence and digital transformation: From innovation to implementation* (pp. 307–329). Springer Nature Switzerland., DOI: 10.1007/978-3-032-00118-4_17

Ladkin, D., & Patrick, C. (2022). Critiques of transformational leadership. *Leadership*.

Landers, R. N., & Sanchez, D. R. (2022). Gamified assessments. *Annual Review of Organizational Psychology and Organizational Behavior*, *9*, 437–461.

Langer, M., König, C. J., & Papathanasiou, M. (2019). Automated interviews. *Journal of Business and Psychology*, *34*(4), 567–582.

Laux, J. (2024). Institutionalised distrust and human oversight of artificial intelligence: Towards a democratic design of AI governance under the European Union AI Act. *AI & Society*, *39*(6), 2853–2866. DOI: 10.1007/s00146-023-01777-z PMID: 39640298

Leddy, M., & McCreanor, N. (2023). The Potential Utilisation of Artificial Intelligence (AI) in Enterprises. *European Conference on Innovation and Entrepreneurship*, *18*(1), 526–535. DOI: 10.34190/ecie.18.1.1720

Lee, J. D., & See, K. A. (2004). Trust in automation: Designing for appropriate reliance. *Human Factors*, *46*(1), 50–80. DOI: 10.1518/hfes.46.1.50.30392 PMID: 15151155

Lee, M. K. (2018). Understanding perception of algorithmic decisions: Fairness, trust, and emotion in response to algorithmic management. *Big Data & Society*, *5*(1), 2053951718756684. Advance online publication. DOI: 10.1177/2053951718756684

Lee, M. K., Kusbit, D., Metsky, E., & Dabbish, L. (2015). Working with machines: The impact of algorithmic and data-driven management on human workers. In *Proceedings of the 33rd Annual ACM Conference on Human Factors in Computing Systems (CHI '15)* (pp. 1603–1612). ACM. DOI: 10.1145/2702123.2702548

Leicht-Deobald, U., Busch, T., Schank, C., Weibel, A., Schafheitle, S., Wildhaber, I., & Kasper, G. (2019). Algorithm based HR decision making. *Journal of Business Ethics*, *160*(2), 377–392. DOI: 10.1007/s10551-019-04204-w

Leong, L., & Fischer, R. (2011). Transformational leadership in diverse contexts. *Journal of Cross-Cultural Psychology.*

Li, X., & Zhang, T. (2017). An exploration on artificial intelligence application: From security, privacy and ethic perspective. *2017 IEEE 2nd International Conference on Cloud Computing and Big Data Analysis (ICCCBDA)*, 416–420. DOI: 10.1109/ICCCBDA.2017.7951949

Licklider, J. C. R. (1960). Man-computer symbiosis. *IRE Transactions on Human Factors in Electronics, HFE-1*(1), 4–11. DOI: 10.1109/THFE2.1960.4503259

Liddicoat, A. J., & Taylor-Leech, K. (2021). Agency in language planning and policy. *Current Issues in Language Planning, 22*(1-2), 1–18. DOI: 10.1080/14664208.2020.1791533

Lievens, F., & Slaughter, J. E. (2016). Employer branding. *Annual Review of Organizational Psychology and Organizational Behavior, 3*(1), 407–440. DOI: 10.1146/annurev-orgpsych-041015-062501

Li, H., & Tian, F. (2025). Advancing Decision-Making through AI-Human Collaboration : A Systematic Review and Conceptual Framework. *Research Square (Research Square)*, 1–29. DOI: 10.21203/rs.3.rs-6885768/v1

Li, J., Liu, Y., Yue, L., Jin, F., Guo, Q., & Xu, C. (2018). Artificial Intelligence Governed by Laws and Regulations. In *Reconstructing Our Orders* (pp. 61–97). Springer Singapore., DOI: 10.1007/978-981-13-2209-9_3

Lin, C. H., Shih, H. Y., & Sher, P. J. (2007). Integrating technology readiness into technology acceptance: The TRAM model. *Psychology and Marketing, 24*(7), 641–657. DOI: 10.1002/mar.20177

Linggiallo, H. D., Riadi, S. S., Hariyadi, S., & Adhimursandi, D. (2021). The effect of predictor variables on employee engagement and organizational commitment and employee performance. *Management Science Letters, 11*(1), 31–40. DOI: 10.5267/j.msl.2020.8.033

Liu, W., Liao, J., & Loi, R. (2016). Abusive supervision and employee creativity: The mediating role of psychological safety and organizational identification. *Management Decision, 54*(1), 130–147. DOI: 10.1108/MD-09-2013-0443

Logg, J. M., Minson, J. A., & Moore, D. A. (2019). Algorithm appreciation: People prefer algorithmic to human judgment. *Organizational Behavior and Human Decision Processes, 151*, 90–103. DOI: 10.1016/j.obhdp.2018.12.005

Longo, L., Goebel, R., Lecue, F., Kieseberg, P., & Holzinger, A. (2020). *Explainable Artificial Intelligence: Concepts.* Applications, Research Challenges and Visions., DOI: 10.1007/978-3-030-57321-8_1

Longoni, C., Bonezzi, A., & Morewedge, C. K. (2019). Resistance to medical artificial intelligence. *The Journal of Consumer Research, 46*(4), 629–650. DOI: 10.1093/jcr/ucz013

Lou, B., Lu, T., Raghu, T. S., & Zhang, Y. (2025). *Unraveling Human-AI Teaming: A Review and Outlook.* https://arxiv.org/abs/2504.05755 DOI: 10.2139/ssrn.5211067

Luan, S., Reb, J., & Gigerenzer, G. (2019). Ecological rationality: Fast-and-frugal heuristics for managerial decision making under uncertainty. *Academy of Management Journal, 62*(6), 1735–1759. DOI: 10.5465/amj.2018.0172

Lukyanenko, R., Maass, W., & Storey, V. C. (2022). Trust in artificial intelligence: From a Foundational Trust Framework to emerging research opportunities. *Electronic Markets, 32*(4), 1993–2020. DOI: 10.1007/s12525-022-00605-4

Luo, J. (2022). A Bibliometric Review on Artificial Intelligence for Smart Buildings. *Sustainability (Basel), 14*(16), 10230. Advance online publication. DOI: 10.3390/su141610230

Luthans, F., & Broad, J. D. (2025). Positive organizational behavior and psychological capital: An evidence-based 20-year journey. In Cooper, C. L., Patnaik, S., & Rodriguez, R. V. (Eds.), *Advancing positive organizational behaviour* (1st ed.). Routledge., DOI: 10.4324/9781032619385-2

Luthans, F., Youssef, C. M., & Avolio, B. J. (2007). *Psychological capital: Developing the human competitive edge.* Oxford University Press.

Lyell, D., & Coiera, E. (2017). Automation bias and verification complexity: A systematic review. *Journal of the American Medical Informatics Association : JAMIA, 24*(2), 423–431. DOI: 10.1093/jamia/ocw105 PMID: 27516495

Lysaght, T., Lim, H. Y., Xafis, V., & Ngiam, K. Y. (2019). AI-assisted decision-making in healthcare: The application of an Ethics Framework for Big Data in Health and Research. *Asian Bioethics Review, 11*(3), 299–314. DOI: 10.1007/s41649-019-00096-0 PMID: 33717318

M., B., N., R., L. N., D., Sahoo, S. K., Ankanahalli Shankaregowda, S., Kannanugo, N., M., D., & M., V. K. (2024). AI-enhanced leadership decision support system using ChatGPT for ethical learning. In Impact of new technology on next-generation leadership (pp. 137–161). IGI Global Scientific Publishing. DOI: 10.4018/979-8-3693-1946-8.ch008

Macnamara, B. N., Berber, I., Çavuşoğlu, M. C., Krupinski, E. A., Nallapareddy, N., Nelson, N. E., Smith, P. J., Wilson-Delfosse, A. L., & Ray, S. (2024). Does using artificial intelligence assistance accelerate skill decay and hinder skill development without performers' awareness? *Cognitive Research: Principles and Implications*, *9*(1), 46. Advance online publication. DOI: 10.1186/s41235-024-00572-8 PMID: 38992285

Madanchian, M., & Taherdoost, H. (2025). Ethical theories, governance models, and strategic frameworks for responsible AI adoption and organizational success. *Frontiers in Artificial Intelligence*, *8*, 1619029. DOI: 10.3389/frai.2025.1619029 PMID: 40741285

Maghsoudi, M., Kamrani Shahri, M., Agha Mohammad Ali Kermani, M., & Khanizad, R. (2025). Mapping the Landscape of AI-Driven Human Resource Management: A Social Network Analysis of Research Collaboration. *IEEE Access : Practical Innovations, Open Solutions*, *13*(January), 3090–3114. DOI: 10.1109/ACCESS.2024.3523437

Magnisalis, I., Demetriadis, S., & Karakostas, A. (2011). Adaptive and intelligent systems for collaborative learning support: A review of the field. *IEEE Transactions on Learning Technologies*, *4*(1), 5–20. DOI: 10.1109/TLT.2011.2

Magrani, E., & da Silva, P. G. F. (2024). *The Ethical and Legal Challenges of Recommender Systems Driven by Artificial Intelligence.*, DOI: 10.1007/978-3-031-41264-6_8

Ma, H., & Wang, J. (2021). *Application of Artificial Intelligence in Intelligent Decision-Making of Human Resource Allocation.*, DOI: 10.1007/978-3-030-62743-0_28

Majumder, S., & Mondal, A. (2021). Are chatbots really useful for human resource management? *International Journal of Speech Technology*, *24*(4), 969–977. DOI: 10.1007/s10772-021-09834-y

Makarius, E. E., Mukherjee, D., Fox, J. D., & Fox, A. K. (2020). Rising with the machines: A sociotechnical framework for bringing artificial intelligence into the organization. *Journal of Business Research*, *120*, 262–273. DOI: 10.1016/j.jbusres.2020.07.045

Makhmudov, S., Maqsood, M., Musaev, U., Urazmetov, M., & Shahzadi, A. (2025). Foundations of agentic AI redefining autonomy in learning environments. In *Multi-disciplinary perspectives on agentic AI in educational systems*. IGI Global Scientific Publishing. DOI: 10.4018/979-8-3373-4621-2.ch001

Makhmudov, S., Otakhonova, D., Kulmanov, T., Shamshiyeva, N., Juraev, U., Ruziev, G., & Sabirova, U. (2026). The impact of digital marketing and mobile applications on service innovation in German companies. *International Review of Management and Marketing*, *16*(1), 210–217. DOI: 10.32479/irmm.22052

Margherita, A. (2021). The role of artificial intelligence in human resource management: Challenges and opportunities. *Management Decision*, *59*(5), 1185–1202. DOI: 10.1108/MD-12-2019-1682

Margondai, A., Willox, S., & Mouloua, M. (2025). Autonomy in transition: AI, self-identity, and the evolution of human agency. *Proceedings of the Human Factors and Ergonomics Society Annual Meeting. Human Factors and Ergonomics Society. Annual Meeting, 69*(1), 1403–1408. DOI: 10.1177/10711813251364790

Marisamy, K., Selvakumar, A., Rajasekar, B., Natarajan, R., Atajanova, A., & Makhmudov, S. (2026). Smart logistics integrating AI, IoT, blockchain, and robotics for a sustainable future. In *Emerging trends in smart logistics technologies* (pp. 73–104). IGI Global Scientific Publishing., DOI: 10.4018/979-8-3373-2434-0.ch003

Marler, J. H., & Boudreau, J. W. (2017). HR analytics review. *International Journal of Human Resource Management*, *28*(1), 3–26. DOI: 10.1080/09585192.2016.1244699

Martinelli, F., Marulli, F., Mercaldo, F., Marrone, S., & Santone, A. (2020). Enhanced Privacy and Data Protection using Natural Language Processing and Artificial Intelligence. *2020 International Joint Conference on Neural Networks (IJCNN)*, 1–8. DOI: 10.1109/IJCNN48605.2020.9206801

Martini, B., Bellisario, D., & Coletti, P. (2024). Human-Centered and Sustainable Artificial Intelligence in Industry 5.0: Challenges and Perspectives. *Sustainability (Basel)*, *16*(13), 5448. Advance online publication. DOI: 10.3390/su16135448

Maslach, C., Schaufeli, W. B., & Leiter, M. P. (2001). Job burnout. *Annual Review of Psychology*, *52*(1), 397–422. DOI: 10.1146/annurev.psych.52.1.397 PMID: 11148311

Mathieu, J. E., Heffner, T. S., Goodwin, G. F., Salas, E., & Cannon-Bowers, J. A. (2000). The influence of shared mental models on team process and performance. *The Journal of Applied Psychology*, *85*(2), 273–283. DOI: 10.1037/0021-9010.85.2.273 PMID: 10783543

Ma, Y., Li, X., Hu, S., Liu, S., & Cheong, K. H. (2025). Trustworthy AI in education: Framework, cases, and governance strategies. *Innovation and Emerging Technologies*, *12*(2550026), 2550026. Advance online publication. DOI: 10.1142/S2737599425500264

Mayer, H., Yee, L., Chui, M., & Roberts, R. (2025, January 28). Superagency in the workplace: Empowering people to unlock AI's full potential. Superagency in the workplace: Empowering people to unlock AI's full potential. https://www.mckinsey.com/capabilities/tech-and-ai/our-insights/superagency-in-the-workplace-empowering-people-to-unlock-ais-full-potential-at-work#

McKinsey Health Institute. (2025, January 16). *Thriving workplaces: How employers can improve productivity and change lives.* https://www.mckinsey.com/mhi/our-insights/thriving-workplaces-how-employers-can-improve-productivity-and-change-lives

McLoughlin, J., Thoma, S. J., & Kristjánsson, K. (2025). Was Aristotle right about moral decision-making? Building a new empirical model of practical wisdom. *PLoS One*, *20*(1), e0317842. DOI: 10.1371/journal.pone.0317842 PMID: 39841702

Mehrabi, N., Morstatter, F., Saxena, N., Lerman, K., & Galstyan, A. (2021). A survey on bias and fairness in machine learning. *ACM Computing Surveys*, *54*(6), 1–35. DOI: 10.1145/3457607

Mehrotra, S., Drevin, L., & Khosla, S. (2024). Appropriate trust in AI: A systematic review of fostering mechanisms. *AI & Society*, *39*, 1853–1869. DOI: 10.1007/s00146-023-01675-3

Mehrotra, S., & Khanna, A. (2022). Recruitment through AI in selected Indian companies. *Metamorphosis*, *21*(1), 31–39. DOI: 10.1177/09726225211066220

Meijerink, J., & Bondarouk, T. (2023). The duality of algorithmic management: Toward a research agenda on the physical and psychological effects of algorithmic management practices. *Human Resource Management Review*, *33*(1), 100876. DOI: 10.1016/j.hrmr.2021.100876

Mekhum, W., & Jermsittiprasert, K. (2019). The role of co-worker and supervisory support in enhancing work engagement: Mediating role of job autonomy. *International Journal of Innovation. Creativity and Change*, *9*(10), 296–312.

Merka, I. P. (2025). *Strategic Alignment of GHRM Practices The Impact of Recruiting and Retaining Green Talent on Organisational Sustainability and Competitiveness.* Metropolia University of Applied Sciences.

Mirbabaie, M., Stieglitz, S., & Brünker, F. (2022). Understanding collaboration with virtual assistants — The role of social identity and the extended self. *Business & Information Systems Engineering*, *64*(2), 217–231. DOI: 10.1007/s12599-020-00672-x

Mittelstadt, B. D., Allo, P., Taddeo, M., Wachter, S., & Floridi, L. (2016). The ethics of algorithms: Mapping the debate. *Big Data & Society, 3*(2), 1–21. DOI: 10.1177/2053951716679679

Mohammad, A. S., Mohammad, S. I., Vasudevan, A., Alenazi, S. A., Hussain, Z., Awad, A., Hamed, A. M., & Mahmoud, M. (2026). Digital sales automation and buyer engagement: Investigating the mediating role of perceived value in B2B exchanges. *Discover Artificial Intelligence, 6*(1), 102. Advance online publication. DOI: 10.1007/s44163-025-00830-8

Mohammed, A., Bambale, S. A., & Abdullahi, U. (2025). AI-Driven Decision-Making in Leadership: Balancing automation and human judgment for optimal organizational performance. *Journal of Economics and Administrative Sciences, 31*(150), 129–141. DOI: 10.33095/hv149002

Mohebianfar, E. (2025). *An AI-driven approach to improve talent retention and mobility. April.* https://www.theseus.fi/handle/10024/883116%0Ahttps://www.theseus.fi/bitstream/handle/10024/883116/Mohebianfar_Ehsan.pdf?sequence=2

Möhlmann, M., Zalmanson, L., Henfridsson, O., & Gregory, R. W. (2021). Algorithmic management of work on online labour platforms: When matching meets control. *Management Information Systems Quarterly, 45*(4), 1999–2022. DOI: 10.25300/MISQ/2021/15333

Montes, C. M., Penzenstadler, B., & Feldt, R. (2025). The factors influencing well-being in software engineers: A mixed-method study. *ACM Transactions on Software Engineering and Methodology, 34*(1), 1–30. DOI: 10.1145/3770074

Moon, S. (2025). The impact of artificial intelligence on human resource management in the Indian IT sector: A mixed-method review. *International Journal of Innovation and Scientific Research, 12*(6), 1063–1068. https://rsisinternational.org/journals/ijrsi/articles/the-impact-of-artificial-intelligence-on-human-resource-management-in-the-indian-it-sector-a-mixed-method-review/. DOI: 10.51244/IJRSI.2025.12060085

Morgeson, F. P., DeRue, D. S., & Karam, E. P. (2010). Leadership in teams: A functional approach to understanding leadership structures and processes. *Journal of Management, 36*(1), 5–39. DOI: 10.1177/0149206309347376

Moss, J. (2023, October 20). *Creating a happier workplace is possible—and worth it.* Harvard Business Review. Retrieved from https://hbr.org/2023/10/creating-a-happier-workplace-is-possible-and-worth-it –[accessed on November 2025]

Mposula, F., & Oyetade, K. (2025). Enhancing Programming Education through Game-Based Learning for Improved Engagement and Learning Outcomes. *Educational Process International Journal, 19*(1). Advance online publication. DOI: 10.22521/edupij.2025.19.558

Mudholkar, R., Cardenas-Palomino, F., Gehlot, A., Vekariya, V., Raju, A. M., & Rajput, K. (2023). Artificial Intelligence in Maintaining Interaction Between Humans and Computer. *2023 3rd International Conference on Advance Computing and Innovative Technologies in Engineering (ICACITE)*, 1903–1908. DOI: 10.1109/ICACITE57410.2023.10182641

Mumford, E. (2006). The story of socio-technical design: Reflections on its successes, failures and potential. *Information Systems Journal, 16*(4), 317–342. DOI: 10.1111/j.1365-2575.2006.00221.x

Murtaza, M., Ahmed, Y., Shamsi, J. A., Sherwani, F., & Usman, M. (2022). AI-Based Personalized E-Learning Systems: Issues, Challenges, and Solutions. *IEEE Access : Practical Innovations, Open Solutions, 10*(June), 81323–81342. DOI: 10.1109/ACCESS.2022.3193938

Murugesan, U., Subramanian, P., Srivastava, S., & Dwivedi, A. (2023). A study of Artificial Intelligence impacts on Human Resource Digitalization in Industry 4.0. *Decision Analytics Journal, 7*(April), 100249. DOI: 10.1016/j.dajour.2023.100249

Muthuswamy, V. V., & Absamatov, A. (2025). *Determinants of students' engagement and their role in boosting students' academic performance among higher education institutions*. Revista Electrónica de LEEME., DOI: 10.58262/LEEME.56.13

Nadeem, M., Ahmad, R., Ahmad, N., & Batool, I. (2019). High performance work systems and service performance: Role of employee resilience. *Journal of Service Theory and Practice, 29*(1), 39–62. DOI: 10.1108/JSTP-02-2018-0040

Nahar, J., Jahan, N., Shorna, S. A., & Joy, Z. H. (2024). Artificial intelligence in human resource management: Trends, opportunities, and challenges. Academic Journal on Science, Technology, Engineering &. *The Mathematics Educator, 4*(3), 63–74. DOI: 10.69593/ajsteme.v4i03.89

Naiseh, M., Al-Thani, D., Jiang, N., & Ali, R. (2021). Explainable recommendation: When design meets trust calibration. *World Wide Web (Bussum), 24*(5), 1857–1884. DOI: 10.1007/s11280-021-00916-0 PMID: 34366701

Naswall, K., Kuntz, J. R., & Malinen, S. (2019). Employee resilience scale (ERS): Development and validation of a measure of resilience at work. *Journal of Occupational and Organizational Psychology, 92*(2), 281–306. DOI: 10.1111/joop.12234

National Academies of Sciences, Engineering, and Medicine. (2022). Human-AI teaming: State-of-the-art and research needs. The National Academies Press. DOI: 10.17226/26355

National Institute of Standards and Technology. (2023). *Artificial intelligence risk management framework (AI RMF 1.0) (NIST AI 100-1)*. U.S. Department of Commerce., DOI: 10.6028/NIST.AI.100-1

Nawaz, N., & Gomes, A. M. (2019). Artificial intelligence chatbots are new recruiters. *International Journal of Advanced Computer Science and Applications, 10*(9), 1–5. DOI: 10.14569/IJACSA.2019.0100901

Newman, D. T., Fast, N. J., & Harmon, D. J. (2020). When eliminating bias isn't fair: Algorithmic reductionism and procedural justice in human resource decisions. *Organizational Behavior and Human Decision Processes, 160*, 149–167. DOI: 10.1016/j.obhdp.2020.03.008

Nielsen, M. B., Hetland, J., Harris, A., Notelaers, G., Gjerstad, J., & Einarsern, S. V. (2022). The impact of follower leadership position on transformational leadership as moderator of the association between work-related ambiguity and job satisfaction. *Frontiers in Psychology, 13*(970887), 970887. https://www.frontiersin.org/articles/10.3389/fpsyg.2022.970887. DOI: 10.3389/fpsyg.2022.970887

Nikolaou, I. (2021). Technology in recruitment. *The Spanish Journal of Psychology, 24*, e32.

Nocker, M., & Sena, V. (2019). Big data and human resources management: The rise of talent analytics. *Social Sciences (Basel, Switzerland), 8*(10), 1–19. DOI: 10.3390/socsci8100273

Northouse, P. G. (2021). *Leadership: Theory and practice* (9th ed.). Sage Publications.

Norton, A. (2023, April 18). How Amazon uses mechanisms to hone efficiency and execution: Volume One, the PRFAQ. Amazons Working Backward process for product ideation. https://www.linkedin.com/pulse/how-amazon-uses-mechanisms-hone-efficiency-execution-angus-norton

Nöthel, S., Nübold, A., Uitdewilligen, S., Schepers, J., & Hülsheger, U. (2023). Development and validation of the adaptive leadership behavior scale (ALBS). *Frontiers in Psychology, 14*, 1149371. Advance online publication. DOI: 10.3389/fpsyg.2023.1149371

Noy, S., & Zhang, W. (2023). Experimental evidence on the productivity effects of generative artificial intelligence. *Science, 381*(6654), 187–192. DOI: 10.1126/science.adh2586 PMID: 37440646

Nyathani, R. (2023). AI in performance management: Redefining performance appraisals in the digital age. *Journal of Artificial Intelligence & Cloud Computing. SRC/JAICC-146, 134*, 2-5.

Nyathani, R. (2022). Integration of Industry 4.0 and Human Resources: Evolving Human Capital Management and Employee Experience through Digital Innovations. [IJSR]. *International Journal of Science and Research (Raipur, India), 11*(9), 1228–1232. DOI: 10.21275/SR231014134101

O'Neil, C. (2016). *Weapons of math destruction: How big data increases inequality and threatens democracy*. Crown.

OECD. (2024). OECD AI principles. OECD.AI. https://oecd.ai/en/ai-principles

OECD. (2026, February 13). *The agentic AI landscape and its conceptual foundations* (OECD Artificial Intelligence Papers No. 56). OECD Publishing. DOI: 10.1787/dee339a8-en

Ogbeibu, S., Emelifeonwu, J., Pereira, V., Oseghale, R., Gaskin, J., Sivarajah, U., & Gunasekaran, A. (2024). Demystifying the roles of organisational smart technology, artificial intelligence, robotics and algorithms capability: A strategy for green human resource management and environmental sustainability. *Business Strategy and the Environment, 33*(2), 369–388. DOI: 10.1002/bse.3495

Okamura, K., & Yamada, S. (2020). Adaptive trust calibration for human-AI collaboration. *PLoS One, 15*(2), e0229132. DOI: 10.1371/journal.pone.0229132 PMID: 32084201

Okeyika, K. O., Ibeto, V. C., Okere, A. I., & Umoh, B. (2023). The Application of Artificial Intelligence (AI) in Human Resource Management: Current State of AI and Its Impact on the Traditional Recruiting Process. *African Journal of Contemporary Research, 4*(3), 2023. DOI: 10.13140/RG.2.2.25435.54567

Oladosu, S. A., Ike, C. C., Adepoju, P. A., Afolabi, A. I., Ige, A. B., & Amoo, O. O. (2023). Frameworks for ethical data governance in machine learning: Privacy, fairness, and business optimization. *Magna Scientia Advanced Research and Reviews, 7*(2), 096–106. DOI: 10.30574/msarr.2023.7.2.0043

Onnasch, L., Wickens, C. D., Li, H., & Manzey, D. (2014). Human performance consequences of stages and levels of automation: An integrated meta-analysis. *Human Factors, 56*(3), 476–488. DOI: 10.1177/0018720813501549 PMID: 24930170

Oyebode, O. (2025). Chain-of-trust AI: Zero-knowledge verified federated reinforcement and generative learning for interpretable, bias-free decision-making in decentralized complex systems. *International Journal of Science and Research Archive*, *15*(2), 1876–1896. DOI: 10.30574/ijsra.2025.15.2.1613

Oyekunle, D., Matthew, U. O., Preston, D., & Boohene, D. (2024). Trust beyond technology algorithms: A theoretical exploration of consumer trust and behavior in technological consumption and AI projects. *Journal of Computer and Communications*, *12*(06), 72–102. DOI: 10.4236/jcc.2024.126006

Ozturkcan, S., & Bozdağ, A. A. (2025). Responsible AI in marketing: AI Booing and AI Washing cycle of AI mistrust. *International Journal of Market Research*, *67*(6), 696–722. DOI: 10.1177/14707853251379285

Paes, V. M., Silveira, F. F., & Akkari, A. C. S. (2023). *Social Impacts of Artificial Intelligence and Mitigation Recommendations: An Exploratory Study* (pp. 521–528). DOI: 10.1007/978-3-031-04435-9_54

Paigude, S., Pangarkar, S. C., Hundekari, S., Mali, M., Wanjale, K., & Dongre, Y. (2023). Potential of Artificial Intelligence in Boosting Employee Retention in the Human Resource Industry. *International Journal on Recent and Innovation Trends in Computing and Communication, 11*(December 2022), 1–10. DOI: 10.17762/ijritcc.v11i3s.6149

Pandey, D., Singh, G., Joshi, L., Polyakova, O., Sungatullina, D., & Singh, R. (2024). Organizational preparedness for navigating disruption towards sustainability: Strategies' analysis. E3S Web of Conferences. DOI: 10.1051/e3sconf/202457407001

Pandey, V. (2025). Leadership in the AI Era: Navigating and shaping the future of organizational guidance. *International Journal of Science and Research Archive*, *15*(3), 1737–1747. DOI: 10.30574/ijsra.2025.15.3.1875

Paramita, D. (2020). Digitalization in talent acquisition: A case study of AI in recruitment.

Parasa, S. K. (2024). Impact of AI on employee experience and engagement. *European Journal of Advances in Engineering and Technology*, *11*(7), 12–14.

Parasuraman, R., & Manzey, D. H. (2010). Complacency and bias in human use of automation: An attentional integration. *Human Factors*, *52*(3), 381–410. DOI: 10.1177/0018720810376055 PMID: 21077562

Parasuraman, R., & Riley, V. (1997). Humans and automation: Use, misuse, disuse, abuse. *Human Factors*, *39*(2), 230–253. DOI: 10.1518/001872097778543886

Parasuraman, R., Sheridan, T. B., & Wickens, C. D. (2000). A model for types and levels of human interaction with automation. *IEEE Transactions on Systems, Man, and Cybernetics. Part A, Systems and Humans, 30*(3), 286–297. DOI: 10.1109/3468.844354 PMID: 11760769

Pasigai, M. A., Rachman, M., & Rasulong, I. (2025). Human capital management in the digital and ESG era: A systematic review of trends, gaps and strategic implications. *Cognizance Journal of Multidisciplinary Studies*, *5*(6), 379–397. DOI: 10.47760/cognizance.2025.v05i06.031

Pasquale, F. (2015). *The black box society: The secret algorithms that control money and information*. Harvard University Press. DOI: 10.4159/harvard.9780674736061

Pasricha, S. (2023). AI Ethics in Smart Healthcare. *IEEE Consumer Electronics Magazine*, *12*(4), 12–20. DOI: 10.1109/MCE.2022.3220001

Pasupuleti, M. K. (2025). Governance Frameworks for ethical AI deployment in Public Sector services. [IJAIRI]. *International Journal of Academic and Industrial Research Innovations*, *05*(05), 561–573. DOI: 10.62311/nesx/rphcr17

Pawar, S., & Dhumal, V. (2024). The role of technology in transforming leadership management practices. *Multidisciplinary Reviews*, *7*(4), 2024066. Advance online publication. DOI: 10.31893/multirev.2024066

Payton, M. J. (2023). Impact of Artificial Intelligence Regulations on Organizational Risks. *The International FLAIRS Conference Proceedings,* 36. DOI: 10.32473/flairs.36.133263

Peng, H., Ma, S., & Spector, J. M. (2019). Personalized Adaptive Learning: An Emerging Pedagogical Approach Enabled by a Smart Learning Environment. *Lecture Notes in Educational Technology*, 171–176. DOI: 10.1007/978-981-13-6908-7_24

Pesapane, F., Suter, M. B., Codari, M., Patella, F., Volonté, C., & Sardanelli, F. (2020). Regulatory issues for artificial intelligence in radiology. In *Precision Medicine for Investigators, Practitioners and Providers* (pp. 533–543). Elsevier. DOI: 10.1016/B978-0-12-819178-1.00052-6

Pessach, D., & Shmueli, E. (2022). A review on fairness in machine learning. *ACM Computing Surveys*, *55*(3), 1–44. DOI: 10.1145/3494672

Pignatiello, G. A., Martin, R. J., & Hickman, R. L.Jr. (2020). Decision fatigue: A conceptual analysis. *Journal of Health Psychology, 25*(1), 123–135. DOI: 10.1177/1359105318763510 PMID: 29569950

Pillai, S. E. V. S., Polimetla, K., & Avacharmal, R. (2022, July). Mental health in the tech industry: Insights from surveys and NLP analysis. *Journal of Recent Trends in Computer Science and Engineering*, *2*(3), 22–33. Advance online publication. DOI: 10.70589/JRTCSE.2022.2.3

Ployhart, R. E., Schmitt, N., & Tippins, N. T. (2017). Staffing science. *The Journal of Applied Psychology*, *102*(3), 291–301. DOI: 10.1037/apl0000081

Polanyi, M. (2009). *The tacit dimension*. University of Chicago Press. (Original work published 1966)

Polyportis, A. (2024). A longitudinal study on artificial intelligence adoption: Understanding the drivers of ChatGPT usage behavior change in higher education. *Frontiers in Artificial Intelligence*, *6*, 1324398. DOI: 10.3389/frai.2023.1324398 PMID: 38249792

Poquet, O., & De Laat, M. (2021). Developing capabilities: Lifelong learning in the age of AI. *British Journal of Educational Technology*, *52*(4), 1695–1708. DOI: 10.1111/bjet.13123

Power, D. J. (2008). Decision support systems: A historical overview. In Burstein, F., & Holsapple, C. W. (Eds.), *Handbook on decision support systems 1* (pp. 121–140). Springer., DOI: 10.1007/978-3-540-48713-5_7

Prabha, K. R., Mabel, B. R., Isaev, F., Mamadiyarov, Z., Raxmatullayevich, K. U., Erkinjon, T., & Khurramova, M. (2026). A multi-layer artificial intelligence–enabled governance framework for integrating information security management, quality management, and strategic human resource analytics: Investigating the role of corporate social responsibility in sustainable organizational performance. *Quality - Access to Success*, *27*(210). Advance online publication. DOI: 10.47750/QAS/27.210.45

Pransky, J., & Dale, K. (2020). Gender differences in communication and emotional disclosure: Implications for the workplace. *Journal of Applied Communication Research*, *48*(4), 451–468.

Priyanghaa, M. (2025). AI Adoption in HR: Resistance, Readiness, and the Role of Change Management. *Journal of Marketing & Social Research*, *08*, 104–110. DOI: 10.61336/jmsr/25-08-10

Puranam, P. (2021). Human–AI collaborative decision-making as an organization design problem. *Journal of Organization Design*, *10*(2), 75–80. DOI: 10.1007/s41469-021-00095-2

Putnoki, A. M., & Orosz, T. (2025). Evaluation and adaptive complexity of cognitive Information Systems. *Acta Technica Jaurinensis, 18*(4), 225–231. DOI: 10.14513/actatechjaur.00806

Qamar, Y., Agrawal, R. K., Samad, T. A., & Chiappetta Jabbour, C. J. (2021). When technology meets people: The interplay of artificial intelligence and human resource management. *Journal of Enterprise Information Management, 34*(5), 1339–1370. DOI: 10.1108/JEIM-11-2020-0436

Qin, C., Zhang, L., Cheng, Y., Zha, R., Shen, D., Zhang, Q., Chen, X., Sun, Y., Zhu, C., Zhu, H., & Xiong, H. (2025). A Comprehensive Survey of Artificial Intelligence Techniques for Talent Analytics. *Proceedings of the IEEE, 113*(2), 125–171. DOI: 10.1109/JPROC.2025.3572744

Rademaker, T., Klingenberg, I., & Süß, S. (2025). Leadership and technostress: A systematic literature review. *Management Review Quarterly, 75*(1), 429–494. DOI: 10.1007/s11301-023-00385-x

Raei, M. (2018). Development and validation of the adaptive leadership with authority scale [Doctoral dissertation, Antioch University]. Antioch University Repository and Archive.

Raghavan, M., Barocas, S., Kleinberg, J., & Levy, K. (2020). Algorithmic bias in hiring. *FAT Conference Proceedings.*

Raghavan, M., Barocas, S., Kleinberg, J., & Levy, K. (2020). Mitigating bias in algorithmic hiring. *Proceedings of the FAT Conference.*

Raghu, N. V. N., T., L. N., D., Kumar B. M., H., & Shankaregowda, S. A. (2025). Enhancing critical thinking through problem-based learning: A comprehensive approach to modern education. In M. Lytras, P. Ordóñez de Pablos, & T. Aldosemani (Eds.), Fostering teacher skills and critical thinking in modern education (pp. 259–282). IGI Global Scientific Publishing. DOI: 10.4018/979-8-3373-1692-5.ch011

Rai, A., & Singh, L. B. (2023). Artificial intelligence-based people analytics transforming human resource management practices. In *The adoption and effect of artificial intelligence on human resources management, part a* (pp. 229–244). Emerald Publishing Limited. DOI: 10.1108/978-1-80382-027-920231012

Raisch, S., & Krakowski, S. (2021). Artificial intelligence and management: The automation–augmentation paradox. *Academy of Management Review, 46*(1), 192–210. DOI: 10.5465/amr.2018.0072

Rajeswari, M., Vanitha, C. L., Xudoynazarova, S., Mamadiyarov, Z., Naveen, S., Nematovich, K. I., & Isaev, F. (2026). Design and validation of an explainable artificial intelligence–based decision intelligence model for cyber risk–aware quality systems and ethical human resource management: Investigating the moderating influence of corporate social responsibility in digitally transformed organizations. *Quality - Access to Success*, *27*(210). Advance online publication. DOI: 10.47750/QAS/27.210.46

Ramachandran, K. K., Apsara Saleth Mary, A., Hawladar, S., Asokk, D., Bhaskar, B., & Pitroda, J. R. (2022). Machine learning and role of artificial intelligence in optimizing work performance and employee behavior. *Materials Today: Proceedings*, *51*, 2327–2331. DOI: 10.1016/j.matpr.2021.11.544

Randriamiary, D. (2024). Reframing the role of leaders navigating the challenges and opportunities of tomorrow's workplace in the age of artificial intelligence. SSRN Electronic Journal. DOI: 10.2139/ssrn.4716033

Rane, N. L., Choudhary, S. P., & Rane, J. (2021). Artificial intelligence for enhancing resilience. *MRS Bulletin*, *46*(11), 1014–1015. DOI: 10.1557/s43577-021-00215-z

Rao, S., Chitranshi, J., & Punjabi, N. (2020). Role of Artificial Intelligence in Employee Engagement and Retention. *Journal of Applied Management - Jidnyasa*, *12*(2), 42–60.

Rathenau Instituut & TNO. (2024). *Eigen ritme of algoritme? Een verkennende studie naar algoritmisch management*. Rathenau Instituut. https://www.rathenau.nl/nl/digitalisering/eigen-ritme-algoritme

Rathinavel, P., Ravikumar, R. N., Aarthi, S., Habib, M., Salaeva, N., & Pardaev, J. (2025). Augmenting human capabilities. In *Advances in Computational Intelligence and Robotics* (pp. 1–30). IGI Global Scientific Publishing. DOI: 10.4018/979-8-3373-2372-5.ch001

Ravichandran, N., Chowdary Inaganti, A., & Muppalaneni, R. (2023). AI-Driven Sentiment Analysis for Employee Engagement and Retention. *Journal of Computing Innovations and Applications*, *1*(1), 1–9.

Ravikumar, R. N., & Aarthi, S. (2025). Human-AI synergy for organizational resilience. In *Advances in Computational Intelligence and Robotics* (pp. 287–322). IGI Global Scientific Publishing. DOI: 10.4018/979-8-3373-7416-1.ch011

Ravikumar, R. N., Aarthi, S., & Mamadiyarov, Z. (2026). Building the foundations of augmented organizations through AI empowerment. In *Advances in Computational Intelligence and Robotics* (pp. 101–130). IGI Global Scientific Publishing. DOI: 10.4018/979-8-3373-8607-2.ch006

Ravikumar, R. N., Aarthi, S., Atamuratova, Z., Ashirova, A., Jurayev, K., & Hayitova, M. (2026). Comprehensive evaluation of AI-driven systems in modern hospital environments. In *Evaluation and assessment of AI-driven systems in hospitals* (pp. 61–88). IGI Global Scientific Publishing., DOI: 10.4018/979-8-3373-2787-7.ch003

Ravikumar, R. N., Aarthi, S., & Mamadiyarov, Z. (2026). Mitigating risks through AI-powered fraud detection systems in digital banking. In *Innovating cost-efficient and scalable business models in the digital era* (pp. 343–376). IGI Global Scientific Publishing., DOI: 10.4018/979-8-3373-2120-2.ch011

Ravikumar, R. N., Aarthi, S., Ruzimova, F., & Mamadiyarov, Z. (2026). Training and development in AI-driven education scaling solutions: K-12 to workforce. In *Transforming education with data science in the AI era* (pp. 267–298). IGI Global Scientific Publishing., DOI: 10.4018/979-8-3373-2185-1.ch010

Ravikumar, R. N., Aarthi, S., Usmani, M. A., Rai, P. K., Jumaniyozova, M., & Narboshova, M. (2026). Advancements in multilingual speech technologies for human-computer interaction. In *Advancements in speech processing for human-computer interaction* (pp. 101–132). IGI Global Scientific Publishing., DOI: 10.4018/979-8-3373-3048-8.ch004

Reddy Yanamala, K. K. (2024). Strategic Implications of AI Integration in Workforce Planning and Talent Forecasting. *Journal of Advanced Computing Systems*, *4*(1), 1–9. DOI: 10.69987/JACS.2024.40101

Rego, A., Owens, B. P., Yam, K. C., Bluhm, D. J., Cunha, M. P., Silard, A., Gonçalves, L., Martins, M., Simpson, A., & Liu, W. (2019). Leader humility and team performance: Exploring the mediating mechanisms of team psychological capital and task allocation effectiveness. *Journal of Management*, *45*(6), 2330–2356. DOI: 10.1177/0149206316688941

Rehman, A. (2023). Unveiling people analytics and organizations: A critical literature review. *Journal of Policy Research*, *9*(4), 284–294. DOI: 10.61506/02.00151

Renta-Davids, A., Camarero-Figuerola, M., & Camacho, M. (2025). Navigating the challenges and opportunities of artificial intelligence in educational leadership: A scoping review. *Review of Education*, *13*(2), e70101. Advance online publication. DOI: 10.1002/rev3.70101

Richardson, J. P., Smith, C., Curtis, S., Watson, S., Zhu, X., Barry, B., & Sharp, R. R. (2021). Patient apprehensions about the use of artificial intelligence in healthcare. *NPJ Digital Medicine*, *4*(1), 140. DOI: 10.1038/s41746-021-00509-1 PMID: 34548621

Riyanto, S., Endri, E., & Herlisha, N. (2019). Effect of work motivation and job satisfaction on employee performance: Mediating role of employee engagement. *Problems and Perspectives in Management*, *17*(4), 162–174.

Roberts, H., Cowls, J., Hine, E., Morley, J., Wang, V., Taddeo, M., & Floridi, L. (2023). Governing artificial intelligence in China and the European Union: Comparing aims and promoting ethical outcomes. *The Information Society*, *39*(2), 79–97. DOI: 10.1080/01972243.2022.2124565

Robertson, J., Botha, E., Oosthuizen, K., & Montecchi, M. (2025). The AI Implementation Compass: A framework for organizational AI adoption. *Journal of Business Research*, *168*, 114234. DOI: 10.1016/j.jbusres.2024.114234

Romeo, E., & Lacko, J. (2025). Adoption and integration of AI in organizations: A systematic review of challenges and drivers towards future directions of research. *Kybernetes*.

Roos, J. (2026). *Human magic: Leading with wisdom in an age of algorithms*. Routledge., DOI: 10.4324/9781003732570

Rosca, C. M., & Stancu, A. (2024). Fusing Machine Learning and AI to Create a Framework for Employee Well-Being in the Era of Industry 5.0. *Applied Sciences (Basel, Switzerland)*, *14*(23), 10835. Advance online publication. DOI: 10.3390/app142310835

Rostamzadeh, R., Alizadeh, F. K., Keivani, S., & Isavi, H. (2025). The role of artificial intelligence in improving organizational behavior: A systematic study. *Human Behavior and Emerging Technologies, 2025*(1). DOI: 10.1155/hbe2/8094428

Rousseau, D. M., & Barends, E. G. R. (2011). Becoming an evidence-based HR practitioner. *Human Resource Management Journal*, *21*(3), 221–235. DOI: 10.1111/j.1748-8583.2011.00173.x

Routhu, K. K. (2021). AI-augmented benefits administration: A standards-driven automation framework with Oracle HCM Cloud. *International Journal of Scientific Research & Engineering Trends*, *7*(3).

Rudin, C. (2019). Stop explaining black box machine learning models for high stakes decisions and use interpretable models instead. *Nature Machine Intelligence*, *1*(5), 206–215. DOI: 10.1038/s42256-019-0048-x PMID: 35603010

Ryan, R. M., & Deci, E. L. (2017). *Self-determination theory: Basic psychological needs in motivation, development, and wellness*. The Guilford Press., DOI: 10.1521/978.14625/28806

Ryff, C. D., & Singer, B. (2008). Know thyself and become what you are: A eudaimonic approach to psychological well-being. *Journal of Happiness Studies*, *9*(1), 13–39. DOI: 10.1007/s10902-006-9019-0

Sabah, A. S., Hamouda, A. A., Helles, Y. E., Okasha, S. M., Abu-Nasser, B. S., & Abu-Naser, S. S. (2024). Artificial Intelligence and Organizational Evolution: Reshaping Workflows in the Modern Era.

Sachan, V. S., Katiyar, A. C. S., Chauhan, A. S., & Bhima, C. K.Dr. Satender Khatri. (2024). The Role of Artificial Intelligence in Healthcare: Applications, Challenges, and Ethical Considerations. *Educational Administration: Theory and Practice*, *15*(3), 195–202. DOI: 10.36676/jrps.v15.i3.1471

Sackett, P. R., & Lievens, F. (2008). Personnel selection. *Annual Review of Psychology*, *59*(1), 419–450. DOI: 10.1146/annurev.psych.59.103006.093716

Sadeghi, S. (2024). *Employee well-being in the age of AI: Perceptions, concerns, behaviors, and outcomes*. arXiv preprint arXiv:2412.04796. https://arxiv.org/abs/2412.04796

Sahlin, J., & Angelis, J. (2019). Performance management systems: Reviewing the rise of dynamics and digitalization. *Cogent Business & Management*, *6*(1), 1642293. Advance online publication. DOI: 10.1080/23311975.2019.1642293

Sakamoto, T., Harada, Y., & Shimizu, T. (2024). Facilitating trust calibration in artificial intelligence–driven diagnostic decision support systems for determining physicians' diagnostic accuracy: Quasi-experimental study. *JMIR Formative Research*, *8*, e58666. DOI: 10.2196/58666 PMID: 39602469

Sakka, F., & El Hadi El Maknouzi, M. (2022). Human Resource Management in the Era of Artificial Intelligence: Future Hr Work Practices, Anticipated Skill Set, Financial and Legal Implications. *Academy of Strategic Management Journal*, *21*(S1), 1–14.

Salvador-Gómez, A., Bou-Llusar, J. C., & Beltrán-Martín, I. (2023). A multi-actor perspective on the effectiveness of human resource management implementation: An empirical analysis based on the ability-motivation-opportunity framework. *International Journal of Human Resource Management*, *34*(20), 3963–4002. DOI: 10.1080/09585192.2022.2163855

Salwei, M. E., & Carayon, P. (2022). A sociotechnical systems framework for the application of artificial intelligence in health care delivery. *Journal of Cognitive Engineering and Decision Making*, *16*(4), 194–206. DOI: 10.1177/15553434221097357 PMID: 36704421

Samad, A., Ahmed, E., & Arora, N. (Eds.). (2023). *Global leadership perspectives on industry, society, and Government in an era of uncertainty*. IGI Global., DOI: 10.4018/978-1-6684-8257-5

Sanjay, K., & Khalsa, S. K. (2025). Talent analytics for workforce forecasting, fostering employee engagement, and turnover prediction. In *Harnessing Business Intelligence for Modern Talent Management* (pp. 403–436). IGI Global., DOI: 10.4018/979-8-3373-1942-1.ch017

Santoni de Sio, F., & Mecacci, G. (2021). Four responsibility gaps with artificial intelligence: Why they matter and how to address them. *Philosophy & Technology*, *34*(4), 1057–1084. DOI: 10.1007/s13347-021-00450-x

Santoni de Sio, F., & van den Hoven, J. (2018). Meaningful human control over autonomous systems: A philosophical account. *Frontiers in Robotics and AI*, *5*, 15. DOI: 10.3389/frobt.2018.00015 PMID: 33500902

Sanz, J. L. C., & Zhu, Y. (2021). Toward Scalable Artificial Intelligence in Finance. *2021 IEEE International Conference on Services Computing (SCC)*, 460–469. DOI: 10.1109/SCC53864.2021.00067

Sapayev, V. O., Hayat, N., Mamadiyarov, Z., & Ahmad, M. (2026). Inside the black box: How generative AI creates digital synthetics. In *Digital synthetic data and outputs* (pp. 409–434). IGI Global Scientific Publishing., DOI: 10.4018/979-8-3373-2277-3.ch016

Sareddy, M. R., & Khan, S. (2024). AI-driven human resource management: Enhancing transparency and security with machine learning. *Journal of Artificial Intelligence and Capsule Networks*, *6*(4), 512–528. DOI: 10.36548/jaicn.2024.4.009

Sawasdee, A., Laohasiriwong, W., & Boonthai, N. (2020). Job demands, job resources, and work engagement: A longitudinal study among healthcare professionals. *International Journal of Environmental Research and Public Health*, *17*(18), 6853.

Scharowski, N., Perrig, S. A. C., von Felten, N., Huang, H. Y., Wiczorek, R., & Brühlmann, F. (2023). Trusting AI: A user study on the relationship between trust and attitudes toward AI and AI-generated content. *Computers in Human Behavior: Artificial Humans*, *1*(1), 100016. DOI: 10.1016/j.chbah.2023.100016

Schein, E. H., & Schein, P. A. (2023). Humble leadership: the power of relationships, openness, and trust (2nd ed.). Berrett-Koehler Publishers., Retrieved from http://search.ebscohost.com/login.aspx?authtype=ip,sso&custid=s4392798&direct=true&scope=site&db=nlebk&AN=3640543, Retrieved November 2025, from.

Schein, E. H. (2010). *Organizational culture and leadership* (4th ed.). Jossey-Bass.

Schemmer, M., Hemmer, P., Kühl, N., Benz, C., & Satzger, G. (2022). *Should I follow AI-based advice? Measuring appropriate reliance in human–AI decision-making* (KIT Scientific Working Paper/Workshop paper). Karlsruhe Institute of Technology (KIT). DOI: 10.5445/IR/1000145647

Schneider, S., & Kokshagina, O. (2021). Digital transformation: What we have learned (thus far) and what is next. *Creativity and Innovation Management*, *30*(2), 384–411. DOI: 10.1111/caim.12414

Schön, D. A. (1983). *The reflective practitioner: How professionals think in action.* Basic Books.

Schultz, T. W. (1961). Human capital investment. *The American Economic Review*, *51*(1), 1–17.

Seibert, S. E., Kraimer, M. L., & Crant, J. M. (2011). What do proactive people do? A longitudinal model linking proactive personality and career success. *Personnel Psychology*, *64*(2), 427–450. DOI: 10.1111/j.1744-6570.2011.01214.x

Seligman, M. (2018). PERMA and the Building Blocks of Well-being. *The Journal of Positive Psychology*, *13*(4), 333–335. DOI: 10.1080/17439760.2018.1437466

Selvi, S. S., Anandapriya, B., & Vaidegi, T. (2025). From data to decisions: The role of AI in modern human resource planning. *International Journal of Research in Entrepreneurship & Business Studies*, *6*(1), 19–30. DOI: 10.47259/ijrebs.2025.612

Şencan, E. (2025). Artificial intelligence, organizational learning, and sustainable banking: Insights from Turkey for global business practice. *Thunderbird International Business Review*, (tie.70062). DOI: 10.1002/tie.70062

Sheridan, T. B., & Verplank, W. L. (1978). Human and computer control of undersea teleoperators (Technical Report ADA057655). Man-Machine Systems Laboratory, Department of Mechanical Engineering, Massachusetts Institute of Technology.

Sherov, A., Rakhimov, T., Hajiyev, H., Zelinskaya, M., & Khidirova, G. (2025). Evaluating class-imbalanced data handling for enhanced financial distress prediction using an attention-based deep neural network and heuristic optimization algorithms. Engineering. *Technology and Applied Science Research, 15*(6), 13372. DOI: 10.48084/etasr.13372

Sherron, C. T. (2000). Psychometric development of the Adaptive Leadership Competency Profile [Doctoral dissertation, University of North Texas]. UNT Digital Library. https://digital.library.unt.edu/ark:/67531/metadc2697

Shore, L. M., Coyle-Shapiro, J. A.-M., & Cnop-Nielsen, A. (2025). Elevating health significance post-pandemic: Is the employee–organization relationship in a period of change? *Annual Review of Organizational Psychology and Organizational Behavior, 12*(1), 269–294. DOI: 10.1146/annurev-orgpsych-110622-065549

Shrestha, Y. R., Ben-Menahem, S. M., & von Krogh, G. (2019). Organizational decision-making structures in the age of artificial intelligence. *California Management Review, 61*(4), 66–83. DOI: 10.1177/0008125619862257

Sijbom, R. B. L., & Grutterink, H. (2026). Participative leadership and workgroup commitment as multilevel resources for employee well-being: A cross-level examination. *Applied Psychology, 75*(2), e70081. DOI: 10.1111/apps.70081

Simon, H. A. (1955). A behavioral model of rational choice. *The Quarterly Journal of Economics, 69*(1), 99–118. DOI: 10.2307/1884852

Simon, H. A. (1957). *Models of man: Social and rational.* Wiley.

Singh Sidhu, G., Sayem, M. A., Taslima, N., Anwar, A. S., Chowdhury, F., & Rowshon, M. (2024). Ai and Workforce Development: A Comparative Analysis of Skill Gaps and Training Needs in Emerging Economies. *International Journal of Business and Management Sciences, 04*(08), 12–28. DOI: 10.55640/ijbms-04-08-03

Singh, A. P., Saxena, R., & Saxena, S. (2024). The Human Touch in the Age of Artificial Intelligence: A Literature Review on the Interplay of Emotional Intelligence and AI. *Asian Journal of Current Research, 9*(4), 36–50. DOI: 10.56557/ajocr/2024/v9i48860

Singh, P., Suar, D., & Leiter, M. P. (2012). Antecedents, work-related consequences, and buffers of job burnout among Indian software developers. *Journal of Leadership & Organizational Studies, 19*(1), 104–114. DOI: 10.1177/1548051811429572

Singh, R., Zhou, K., & Auclair, J. R. (2025). Reimagining drug regulation in the age of AI: A framework for the. *Frontiers in Medicine, 12*(1679611), 1679611. DOI: 10.3389/fmed.2025.1679611 PMID: 41179905

Singla, A., Sukharevsky, A., Hall, B., Yee, L., Chui, M., & Balakrishnan, T. (2025, November 5). The state of AI in 2025: Agents, Innovation, and transformation. The state of AI in 2025: Agents, innovation, and transformation. https://www.mckinsey.com/capabilities/quantumblack/our-insights/the-state-of-ai

Sitra. (2025, December). *Tehtävänä tekoälymurros [Mission: AI transformation]* (Sitra Selvitys No. 254). Finnish Innovation Fund. https://www.sitra.fi/wp-content/uploads/2025/12/32838076_Tehtavana_tekoalymurros_selvitys.pdf

Skitka, L. J., Mosier, K. L., & Burdick, M. (1999). Does automation bias decision-making? *International Journal of Human-Computer Studies*, *51*(5), 991–1006. DOI: 10.1006/ijhc.1999.0252

Smith, A. M., & Green, M. (2018). Artificial Intelligence and the Role of Leadership. *Journal of Leadership Studies*, *12*(3), 85–87. DOI: 10.1002/jls.21605

Sprague, R. H.Jr. (1980). A framework for the development of decision support systems. *Management Information Systems Quarterly*, *4*(4), 1–26. DOI: 10.2307/248957

Srivastava, K. B. (2000). Rethinking HR: Role of HR professionals in a changing business environment. *Indian Journal of Industrial Relations*, *35*(4), 532–544.

Starecek, A., Babelova, Z. G., & Vranakova, N. (2025). Development of Human Resource Management Due to Technological, Social, and Legal Changes: Editorial for the Special Issue "New Challenges and Directions in the Development of Human Resource Management.". *Administrative Sciences*, *15*(11), 438. Advance online publication. DOI: 10.3390/admsci15110438

Starke, C., Baleis, J., Keller, B., & Marcinkowski, F. (2022). Fairness perceptions of algorithmic decision-making: A systematic review of the empirical literature. *Big Data & Society*, *9*(2), 1–16. DOI: 10.1177/20539517221115189

Steyvers, M., & Kumar, A. (2023). Three challenges for AI-Assisted Decision-Making. *Perspectives on Psychological Science*, *19*(5), 722–734. DOI: 10.1177/17456916231181102

Stock-Homburg, R. (2025). Unlocking the potential of AI in leadership: Can generative AI outperform human leaders. In Proceedings of the 58th Hawaii International Conference on System Sciences (pp. 1742-1751). https://hdl.handle.net/10125/109054

Stogdill, R. M. (1948). Personal factors associated with leadership: A survey of the literature. *The Journal of Psychology*, *25*(1), 35–71. DOI: 10.1080/00223980.1948.9917362 PMID: 18901913

Strich, F., Mayer, A. S., & Fiedler, M. (2021). What do I do in a world of artificial intelligence? Investigating the impact of substitutive decision-making AI systems on employees' professional role identity. *Journal of the Association for Information Systems*, *22*(2), 304–324. DOI: 10.17705/1jais.00663

Strohmeier, S. (2022). Digital HRM: A conceptual clarification of HRIS, AI, and HR analytics. *Human Resource Management Review*, *32*(2), 100789. DOI: 10.1016/j.hrmr.2020.100789

Strohmeier, S., & Piazza, F. (2013). Artificial intelligence techniques in human resource management—A conceptual exploration. *International Journal of Human Resource Management*, *24*(9), 1795–1817. DOI: 10.1080/09585192.2012.709190

Strohmeier, S., & Piazza, F. (2015). AI in HRM. *International Journal of Human Resource Management*, *26*(21), 2640–2665.

Suffiyah, Y., Ilias, M., Adami, C., Arukgoda, A., Lakshika, E., Barlow, M., Gunawardana, K., Awad, E., Dsouza, S., Kim, R., Schulz, J., Henrich, J., Shariff, A., Rahwan, I., Barocas, S., Hardt, M., Narayanan, A., Barocas, S., & Ilias, M. (2025). Navigating the Future: The impact of Artificial intelligence on adaptive and ethical leadership. *Personalia Pelajar*, *28*(1). Advance online publication. DOI: 10.17576/personalia.2801.2025.03

Sufyan Ghaleb, M. M., & Pardaev, J. (2025). Effects of advertisement language, communication style, information seeking behavior and information source credibility on customers' intentions towards international products via brand trust. *El Profesional de la Información*, *34*(2). Advance online publication. DOI: 10.3145/epi.2025.ene.34203

Sundari, S., Silalahi, V. A. J. M., Wardani, F. P., Siahaan, R. S., Sacha, S., Krismayanti, Y., & Anjarsari, N. (2024). Artificial Intelligence (AI) and Automation in Human Resources : Shifting the Focus from Routine Tasks to Strategic Initiatives for Improved Employee Engagement. *East Asian Journal of Multidisciplinary Research*, *3*(10), 4983–4996. DOI: 10.55927/eajmr.v3i10.11758

Sun, Y., & Xu, C. (2025). Hybrid cognitive authority and algorithmic subjectivity: Rethinking knowledge management in AI-driven communication. *Journal of Knowledge Management*, •••, 1–26. DOI: 10.1108/JKM-02-2025-0252

Swati, S., & Kumar, M. (2023). *Innovations in Blockchain Using Artificial Intelligence.*, DOI: 10.1007/978-981-19-8730-4_7

Taddeo, M., & Floridi, L. (2018). How AI can be a force for good. *Science*, *361*(6404), 751–752. DOI: 10.1126/science.aat5991 PMID: 30139858

Tambe, P., Cappelli, P., & Yakubovich, V. (2019). AI in HRM. *The Academy of Management Annals, 13*(2), 1–47.

Tambe, P., Cappelli, P., & Yakubovich, V. (2019). Artificial intelligence in human resources management: Challenges and a path forward. *California Management Review, 61*(4), 15–42. DOI: 10.1177/0008125619867910

Tanantong, T., & Wongras, P. (2024). A UTAUT-based framework for analyzing users' intention to adopt artificial Intelligence in human resource recruitment: A case study of Thailand. *Systems, 12*(1), 28. DOI: 10.3390/systems12010028

Tarafdar, M., Tu, Q., Ragu-Nathan, B. S., & Ragu-Nathan, T. S. (2007). The impact of technostress on role stress and productivity. *Journal of Management Information Systems, 24*(1), 301–328. DOI: 10.2753/MIS0742-1222240109

Tasleem, N. (2025). HR technology transformation and the impact of people analytics on workforce management. *Iconic Research and Engineering Journals, 8*(9), 702–716.

Thalpage, N. (2025). Explainable AI for cybersecurity applications: A review article on techniques, deployments, and usability challenges. *Journal of Digital Science, 7*(1), 3–10. DOI: 10.33847/2686-8296.7.1_1

Thomas, C. H., & Lankau, M. J. (2009). Preventing burnout: The effects of LMX and mentoring on socialization, role stress, and burnout. *Human Resource Management, 48*(3), 417–432. DOI: 10.1002/hrm.20288

Thompson, D. F. (1980). Moral responsibility of public officials: The problem of many hands. *The American Political Science Review, 74*(4), 905–916. DOI: 10.2307/1954312

Thontadarya, P. S. (2025). The Role of AI in Modernizing PeopleSoft HCM: Bridging ERP and Innovation in Public Sector HR. *Journal of Computer Science and Technology Studies, 7*(8), 708–715.

Trinh, N. T. N., & Elbanna, A. (2023). Understanding human-AI augmentation in business and management context: A literature review. *ECIS 2023 Research Papers*, Article 406. https://aisel.aisnet.org/ecis2023_rp/406/

Trinkenreich, B., Santos, F., & Stol, K.-J. (2024). Predicting attrition among software professionals: Antecedents and consequences of burnout and engagement. *ACM Transactions on Software Engineering and Methodology, 33*(2), 1–45. DOI: 10.1145/3691629

Trist, E. L., & Bamforth, K. W. (1951). Some social and psychological consequences of the Longwall method of coal-getting. *Human Relations*, *4*(1), 3–38. DOI: 10.1177/001872675100400101

Tsamados, A., Floridi, L., & Taddeo, M. (2025). Human control of AI systems: From supervision to teaming. *AI and Ethics*, *5*(2), 1535–1548. DOI: 10.1007/s43681-024-00489-4 PMID: 40352578

Ulrich, D., & Dulebohn, J. H. (2015). HR competencies. *Human Resource Management*, *54*(2), 1–14.

United States, The White House. (2025a, January 23). Executive Order 14179: Removing Barriers to American Leadership in Artificial Intelligence. *Federal Register*, *90*(18), 8741–8743. https://www.federalregister.gov/documents/2025/01/31/2025-02172/removing-barriers-to-american-leadership-in-artificial-intelligence

United States, The White House. (2025b, July 23). America's AI Action Plan. Office of Science and Technology Policy. https://www.whitehouse.gov/wp-content/uploads/2025/07/Americas-AI-Action-Plan.pdf

Upadhyay, A. K., & Khandelwal, K. (2018). AI in recruitment. *Strategic HR Review*, *17*(5), 255–258. DOI: 10.1108/SHR-07-2018-0051

Uren, V., & Edward, J. S. (2023). Assessing organizational readiness for AI: The PPTD framework. *Journal of Enterprise Information Management*, *36*(4), 1123–1145. DOI: 10.1108/JEIM-07-2022-0241

Vaccaro, M., Almaatouq, A., & Malone, T. W. (2024). When combinations of humans and AI are useful: A systematic review and meta-analysis. *Nature Human Behaviour*, *8*(12), 2293–2303. DOI: 10.1038/s41562-024-02024-1 PMID: 39468277

van de Poel, I., Royakkers, L., & Zwart, S. D. (2012). *Moral responsibility and the problem of many hands*. Routledge.

Van Den Berg, M., Kuiper, O., Van Der Haas, Y., Gerlings, J., Sent, D., & Leijnen, S. (2023). A conceptual model for implementing explainable AI by design: Results of an empirical study. In *Frontiers in Artificial Intelligence and Applications*. IOS Press., DOI: 10.3233/FAIA230075

van Esch, P., & Black, J. S. (2019). AI recruitment adoption. *International Journal of Selection and Assessment*, *27*(3), 241–250.

Vardarlier, P. (2019). Digital transformation of human resource management: digital applications and strategic tools in HRM. In *Digital business strategies in blockchain ecosystems: Transformational design and future of global business* (pp. 239–264). Springer International Publishing.

Varma, P. (2025, October 11). *Unlock the future of leadership: How McKinsey's human-centred approach transforms organizations and empowers employees*. Rehumanize. https://rehumanize.com/unlock-the-future-of-leadership-how-mckinseys-human-centered-approach-transforms-organizations-and-empowers-employees

Varma, A., Pereira, V., & Patel, P. (2024). Artificial intelligence and performance management. *Organizational Dynamics, 53*(1), 101037. DOI: 10.1016/j.orgdyn.2024.101037

Vasconcelos, H., Jörke, M., Grunde-McLaughlin, M., Gerstenberg, T., Bernstein, M. S., & Krishna, R. (2023). Explanations can reduce overreliance on AI systems during decision-making. *Proceedings of the ACM on Human-Computer Interaction, 7*(CSCW1), Article 129. **https://doi.org/**DOI: 10.1145/3579605

Vats, K., & Alam, M. M. (2025). From design to closure: Artificial intelligence transforming clinical research. *Cureus, 17*(10), e94895. DOI: 10.7759/cureus.94895 PMID: 41262821

Veale, M., & Zuiderveen Borgesius, F. (2021). Demystifying the draft EU Artificial Intelligence Act. *Computer Law Review International, 22*(4), 97–112. DOI: 10.9785/cri-2021-220402

Veluwenkamp, H. (2022). Why meaningful human control is not enough. *Ethics and Information Technology, 24*(3), 36. Advance online publication. DOI: 10.1007/s10676-022-09663-w

Venkatesh, V., Morris, M. G., Davis, G. B., & Davis, F. D. (2003). UTAUT model. *Management Information Systems Quarterly, 27*(3), 425–478. DOI: 10.2307/30036540

Vishwanath, B., & Vaddepalli, S. (2023). The future of work: Implications of artificial intelligence on hr practices. Tuijin Jishu/Journal of Propulsion Technology, 44(3), 1711-1724.

Vizitiu, A., Nita, C. I., Puiu, A., Suciu, C., & Itu, L. M. (2019). Privacy-Preserving Artificial Intelligence: Application to Precision Medicine. *2019 41st Annual International Conference of the IEEE Engineering in Medicine and Biology Society (EMBC)*, 6498–6504. DOI: 10.1109/EMBC.2019.8857960

Volosova, A., & Matiukhina, E. (2020). Using artificial intelligence for effective decision-making in corporate governance under conditions of deep uncertainty. *SHS Web of Conferences, 89*, 03008. DOI: 10.1051/shsconf/20208903008

Vrontis, D., Christofi, M., Pereira, V., Tarba, S., Makrides, A., & Trichina, E. (2023). Artificial intelligence, robotics, advanced technologies and human resource management: a systematic review. *Artificial intelligence and international HRM*, 172-201.

Vrontis, D., Chaudhuri, R., & Chatterjee, S. (2023). Role of ChatGPT and Skilled Workers for Business Sustainability: Leadership Motivation as the Moderator. *Sustainability (Basel), 15*(16), 12196. Advance online publication. DOI: 10.3390/su151612196

Vuori, N., Helander, N., & Okkonen, J. (2026). It's amazing – but terrifying!: Unveiling the combined effect of emotional and cognitive trust on organizational members' behaviours, AI performance, and adoption. *Journal of Management Studies, 63*(2), 473–514. DOI: 10.1111/joms.13177

Wang, Y., Chen, X., & Liu, W. (2024). Information flows in AI-augmented organizations: A network analysis. *Organization Science, 35*(1), 156–178. DOI: 10.1287/orsc.2022.1622

Weick, K. E. (1995). Sensemaking in organizations. *Sage (Atlanta, Ga.)*.

Wenger, E. (1998). *Communities of practice: Learning, meaning, and identity*. Cambridge University Press. DOI: 10.1017/CBO9780511803932

Wieringa, M. (2020). What to account for when accounting for algorithms: A systematic literature review on algorithmic accountability. In *Proceedings of the 2020 Conference on Fairness, Accountability, and Transparency* (pp. 1–18). ACM. DOI: 10.1145/3351095.3372833

Wijayati, D. T., Rahman, Z., Fahrullah, A., Rahman, M. F. W., Arifah, I. D. C., & Kautsar, A. (2022). A study of artificial intelligence on employee performance and work engagement: The moderating role of change leadership. *International Journal of Manpower, 43*(2), 486–512. DOI: 10.1108/IJM-07-2021-0423

Williams, S. L. (2002). Strategic planning and organizational values: Links to alignment. *Human Resource Development International, 5*(2), 217–233. DOI: 10.1080/13678860110057638

Wilson, H. J., & Daugherty, P. R. (2018). Collaborative intelligence. *Harvard Business Review, 96*(4), 114–123.

Wong, A. (2021). *Ethics and Regulation of Artificial Intelligence*., DOI: 10.1007/978-3-030-80847-1_1

World Economic Forum. (2025, January 17). *Leading with purpose: Why human-centric strategies are vital in the AI era*. https://www.weforum.org/stories/2025/01/leading-with-purpose-why-human-centric-strategies-are-vital-in-the-ai-era/

Wu Young, J., & Nah, F. F. H. (2025, June). AI Systems for Physicians: A Review from Socio-technical and Human-Computer Interaction Perspectives. In *International Conference on Human-Computer Interaction* (pp. 165-180). Cham: Springer Nature Switzerland.

Wu, S., Cao, Y., Cui, J., Li, R., Qian, H., Jiang, B., & Zhang, W. (2024). *A Comprehensive Exploration of Personalized Learning in Smart Education: From Student Modeling to Personalized Recommendations. 0*(0), 1–61. https://arxiv.org/abs/2402.01666

Xin, S., Zhaobin, P., & Jing, Q. (2022). *Legal Analysis of the Right to Privacy Protection in the Age of Artificial Intelligence*., DOI: 10.1007/978-3-031-13870-6_51

Xu, G., Murthy, S. V., & Jia, B. (2025). Enhancing Intuitive Decision-Making and reliance through Human–AI Collaboration: A review. *Informatics (MDPI), 12*(4), 135. DOI: 10.3390/informatics12040135

Yadav, N., Pandey, S., Gupta, A., Dudani, P., Gupta, S., & Rangarajan, K. (2023). Data Privacy in healthcare: In the era of artificial intelligence. *Indian Dermatology Online Journal, 14*(6), 788–792. DOI: 10.4103/idoj.idoj_543_23 PMID: 38099022

Yanamala, K. K. R. (2023). Transparency, privacy, and accountability in AI-enhanced HR processes. *Journal of Advanced Computing Systems, 3*(3), 10–18. DOI: 10.69987/JACS.2023.30302

Yan, X. (2023). Research on financial field Integrating artificial intelligence: Application basis, case analysis, and SVR Model-Based Overnight. *Applied Artificial Intelligence, 37*(1), 2222258. Advance online publication. DOI: 10.1080/08839514.2023.2222258

Ye, C., Wang, Z., Wu, M., Kang, R., Yuan, F., & Chen, C. (2025). Behavioral drivers of AI nursing acceptance in the Greater Bay Area: A family-caregiver perspective on trust and risk. *Frontiers in Public Health, 13*(1650804), 1650804. DOI: 10.3389/fpubh.2025.1650804 PMID: 41112660

Yesuf, M., & Fields, Z. (2025). AI adoption in SMEs: A bibliometric review and research agenda. *Journal of Small Business Management, 63*(2), 345–378. DOI: 10.1080/00472778.2024.2312145

Yin, R. K. (2018). Case study research and applications: Design and methods (6th ed.). SAGE Publications., Retrieved from https://methods.sagepub.com/book/case-study-research-, Retrieved November 2025, from.

Yong, J. Y., Yusoff, Y. M., Fernando, Y., Lin, W. L., Chong, S. C., & Pek, C. K. (2026). Generation green: Navigating ESG in Generation Z's job search landscape. In *Stimulating economic growth through cultural and societal transformations* (pp. 83–100). IGI Global Scientific Publishing., DOI: 10.4018/979-8-3373-0603-2.ch004

Yusif-Zada, K., & Iskandarova, S. (2023). Artificial Intelligence Policy and Regulation in Medicine: Navigating the Promise and Challenges. *2023 IEEE Global Conference on Artificial Intelligence and Internet of Things (GCAIoT)*, 191–196. DOI: 10.1109/GCAIoT61060.2023.10385130

Yu, Y., Gomez-Cabello, C. A., Haider, S. A., Genovese, A., Prabha, S., Trabilsy, M., Collaco, B. G., Wood, N. G., Bagaria, S., Tao, C., & Forte, A. J. (2025). Enhancing clinician trust in AI diagnostics: A dynamic framework for confidence calibration and transparency. *Diagnostics (Basel)*, *15*(17), 2204. DOI: 10.3390/diagnostics15172204 PMID: 40941691

Zallone, R. (2020). Artificial Intelligence vs Autonomous Cars vs General Data Protection Regulation. *2020 AEIT International Conference of Electrical and Electronic Technologies for Automotive (AEIT AUTOMOTIVE)*, 1–6. DOI: 10.23919/AEITAUTOMOTIVE50086.2020.9307410

Zárate-Torres, R., Rey-Sarmiento, C. F., Acosta-Prado, J. C., Gómez-Cruz, N. A., Rodríguez Castro, D. Y., & Camargo, J. (2025). Influence of Leadership on Human–Artificial Intelligence Collaboration. *Behavioral Sciences (Basel, Switzerland)*, *15*(7), 873. DOI: 10.3390/bs15070873

Zarifis, A. (2025). *Leadership With AI and Trust: Adapting popular leadership styles for AI*. De Gruyter. DOI: 10.1515/9783111630137

Zayid, H., Alzubi, A., Berberoğlu, A., & Khadem, A. (2024). How do algorithmic management practices affect workforce Well-Being? A parallel moderated mediation model. *Behavioral Sciences (Basel, Switzerland)*, *14*(12), 1123. DOI: 10.3390/bs14121123

Zayniddinov, R., Jumaev, N., Irgasheva, G., Asadov, A., & Makhmudov, N.. (2025). The influence of the digital economy on economic development: Evidence from Uzbekistan. In *ACM International Conference Proceeding Series*. DOI: 10.1145/3726122.3726242

Zeiser, A. (2024). The attributability gap in AI decision-making: A philosophical analysis. *Philosophy & Technology*, *37*(1), 1–22. DOI: 10.1007/s13347-023-00678-x PMID: 40635766

Zhang, D. (2024). Leveraging artificial intelligence in economics and finance: Enhancing decision-making and market efficiency. *Applied and Computational Engineering*, *82*(1), 118–123. DOI: 10.54254/2755-2721/82/20240980

Zhang, J., & Chen, Z. (2024). Exploring Human Resource Management Digital Transformation in the Digital Age. *Journal of the Knowledge Economy*, *15*(1), 1482–1498. DOI: 10.1007/s13132-023-01214-y PMID: 40479358

Zhang, J., & Zhang, Z. (2023). Ethics and governance of trustworthy medical artificial intelligence. *BMC Medical Informatics and Decision Making*, *23*(1), 7. DOI: 10.1186/s12911-023-02103-9

Zhang, Q., Wang, F., Liao, G., & Li, M. (2025). How does AI trust foster innovative performance under paternalistic leadership? The roles of AI crafting and Leader's AI opportunity perception. *Behavioral Sciences (Basel, Switzerland)*, *15*(8), 1064. DOI: 10.3390/bs15081064

Zhang, X., & Zhou, Y. (2025). Human-AI Collaboration. *Paradigm Shifts in Technology-Mediated Design.*, *2*(2), 1–9.

Zhang, Y., Liao, Q. V., & Bellamy, R. K. E. (2020). Effect of confidence and explanation on accuracy and trust calibration in AI-assisted decision making. In *Proceedings of the 2020 Conference on Fairness, Accountability, and Transparency* (pp. 295–305). Association for Computing Machinery. **https://doi.org/**DOI: 10.1145/3351095.3372852

Zhang, Y., Liu, X., & Chen, H. (2025). Transformational leadership and employee AI crafting: The mediating role of AI trust. *Journal of Organizational Behavior*, *46*(3), 312–335. DOI: 10.1002/job.2780

Zhao, J., Ragmoun, W., Dong, Z., Nawaz, M. A., & Sattarov, A. (2025). Circular economy implementation through AI adoption, CSR and green finance: The mediating role of green product innovation and green supply chain. *Corporate Social Responsibility and Environmental Management*. Advance online publication. DOI: 10.1002/csr.70289

Zhou, L., Paul, S., Demirkan, H., Yuan, L., Spohrer, J., Zhou, M., & Basu, J. (2021). Intelligence Augmentation: Towards Building Human-Machine Symbiotic Relationship. *AIS Transactions on Human-Computer Interaction*, *13*(2), 243–264. DOI: 10.17705/1thci.00149

Ziaeian, Y. (2025). The Impact of Human-Centric Leadership on Employee Satisfaction and Productivity in Digitally Transformed Organisations. In: Shaikh, A., Wiil, U.K., Alghamdi, A., Tan, Q. (eds) The 2nd International Conference on Innovation of Emerging Information and Communication Technology. ICIEICT 2024. Signals and Communication Technology. Springer, Cham. https://doi.org/
DOI: 10.1007/978-3-031-88634-8_17

About the Contributors

Don Ashley, Ph.D. (Southwestern Baptist Theological Seminary, USA) Executive Director, Anchorage and Fairbanks Campuses, Wayland Baptist University, Alaska, USA Dr. Don Ashley is an experienced academic leader and scholar with more than two decades of progressive responsibility in higher education. He currently serves as Executive Director for the Anchorage and Fairbanks Campuses at Wayland Baptist University and as Executive Director of Global Initiatives. His leadership portfolio includes international student advising and compliance (SEVP), global project management, and academic quality assurance across multicultural environments. Holding a Doctor of Philosophy in Foundations of Education from Southwestern Baptist Theological Seminary, Dr. Ashley has taught extensively in research methods, qualitative and quantitative design, and statistical analysis. He has supervised graduate and doctoral students and contributed to the development of globally inclusive and ethically grounded academic programs. His scholarly contributions include publications in the Baker Evangelical Dictionary of Christian Education and authored works such as Single Parent College Students: A Test of Endurance and The Teacher as Exemplar: An Exploration of the Teacher as a Role Model in Idealism and the Bible. His research explores the intersection of education, leadership, and sociocultural theory in academic and spiritual formation. Dr. Ashley's commitment to global education and innovation continues to shape initiatives that bridge academic excellence, intercultural understanding, and ethical leadership across continents.

Manjari Sharma is an accomplished academician, researcher, and author with over 15 years of experience in higher education, specializing in Finance, Human Resource Management, and Organizational Behavior. She earned her Doctor of Philosophy in Commerce from the University of Rajasthan, India, with her doctoral research focusing on the price behavior of securities in the Indian capital market. Currently serving as Associate Professor and Head of the Department of

Commerce at CHRIST (Deemed to be University), Pune Lavasa Campus, Dr. Sharma has been instrumental in advancing academic excellence through curriculum innovation, global immersion programs, and research collaborations across Asia, the United States, and Europe. Her scholarly contributions include numerous books, edited volumes, and research chapters with leading international publishers such as IGI Global, Springer Nature, and Taylor & Francis. She has co-authored and edited works on financial literacy, experiential learning, sustainable education, and the intersection of AI and management. A recipient of multiple institutional research grants, Dr. Sharma's current projects focus on AI-driven financial decision-making, sustainable workforce strategies, and cultural immersion in education. Her leadership extends beyond academics to mentoring students and faculty in research, entrepreneurship, and global engagement. Dr. Sharma's work reflects her vision of integrating innovation, inclusivity, and sustainability into business and education to prepare future-ready learners and leaders.

Sharad Gupta is a master of Commerce (Business Admin, U of Rajasthan, India (2008) & Master Business admin (Marketing & Finance), U of Rajasthan, India (2002)

***

Anorgul Ashirova is working as an Associate Professor at the Department of General Professional Sciences, Mamun University, Khiva, Uzbekistan

Azizbek Ismailov is a faculty member in the Faculty of Economics at Alfraganus University, Tashkent, Uzbekistan. He is actively engaged in teaching and research in the field of economics, with a focus on economic theory, financial analysis, and contemporary economic systems. His academic interests include macroeconomics, microeconomics, and the application of analytical tools for economic modeling and policy evaluation. He contributes to curriculum development and student mentoring, fostering critical thinking and practical skills among learners. Ismailov has participated in academic activities such as research publications, conferences, and collaborative projects that enhance the quality and impact of economic research. His work emphasizes the integration of theoretical knowledge with real-world economic challenges, contributing to the advancement of economic education and research.

Vijayabanu C is currently Professor at the School of Commerce and Management, Shiv Nadar University Chennai in India. She obtained her Ph.D. in Commerce-Human Resource Management in 2000 at Bharathidasan University, India. Her current research interests focus on the areas of behavioral studies –

Personality, Perception: attitudes & values . She handles courses such as Human Resource Management, organizational behaviour, and specialization courses such as Change Management, Training & Development, etc. She brings to her classes enriched knowledge of 5 years of Research & 16 years of academic experience. She has produced 7 doctoral scholars successfully She has presented papers at international and national level conferences and seminars.She has published several research articles and case studies in referred Scopus-indexed journals. She has served on the Editorial Review Boards of several academic journals, including Business theory and practice, the Journal of Management Social Science and Humanities and the Journal of Business Economics and Management

Kavita Indapurkar is a dedicated academician and researcher known for her contribution to higher education and student development. She has extensive teaching experience and is actively involved in research guidance, conferences, and academic mentoring. Admired for her supportive and student-centric approach, she continues to inspire learners through her commitment to academic excellence and knowledge sharing.

Juraev Khusan is a faculty member in the Department of Finance and Tourism at Termez University of Economics and Service, Uzbekistan. He is actively involved in teaching and research in the areas of finance, tourism economics, and economic development. His academic interests include financial management, tourism industry analysis, regional development, and the application of modern analytical tools in economic decision-making. He contributes to curriculum development and student mentoring, supporting the development of practical and analytical skills among learners. Juraev participates in academic research, publications, and collaborative initiatives that promote interdisciplinary knowledge and innovation. His work emphasizes the integration of theoretical concepts with real-world applications, contributing to the advancement of financial and tourism education and supporting sustainable economic growth.

Santhanalaxmi K is an academician with 4 years of experience and expertise in the field of HR, Marketing and Sustainable Development

Pawan Kumar, PhD, is a prominent academic and researcher with over 20 years of expertise in business studies. A professor at Graphic Era Deemed to be University, Dehradun, India, he has supervised six PhD scholars and published over 60 research papers, including 51 in SCOPUS/ 06 in Web of Science, and 14 books, including eight indexed in Scopus. His works, featured by prominent publishers like Emerald, IGI Global, Nova Science, and Cambridge Scholars, have gained recognition. Dr. Kumar earned his PhD in Commerce from Kurukshetra University in 2007 and holds an M.Phil. and M.Com. Degrees. Specializing in finance, banking, and securities markets, he has authored books on green finance, AI, and fintech. His innovative research includes five patents and has served as a guest editor for Scopus-indexed journals. In 2022, he received the prestigious Researcher Award from Chandigarh University. Dr. Kumar's impactful work on sustainable finance, blockchain, and fintech is globally recognized. His active participation in high-impact conferences and faculty development programs reflects his commitment to advancing research, teaching, and innovation in commerce and management.

Nazarov Akmal Mardonovich is a Doctor of Psychological Sciences (DSc) and Professor at Bukhara State University, Uzbekistan, where he serves in the Chair of Psychology. He has extensive academic and research experience in the field of psychological sciences, with expertise in cognitive psychology, behavioral studies, and applied psychology. His research interests include human cognition, personality development, psychological assessment, and the application of psychological principles in educational and social contexts. He is actively involved in teaching, research supervision, and curriculum development, contributing to the advancement of higher education in psychology. Professor Nazarov has published scholarly works and participated in national and international conferences, promoting innovation and knowledge dissemination in psychological sciences. His work emphasizes the integration of theoretical frameworks with practical applications, contributing to the development of effective psychological practices and academic excellence.

Raghu N has Ten years of experience in Academic and Research. He received the Ph.D. (2020) in Electronics Engineering from Jain University, and B.E. in Electronics and Telecommunications Engineering from VTU University, Karnataka. His research interests were in RF Communication and Image Processing. He has published his research findings in various Scopus indexed Journals and International conferences. He is a member of various professional bodies.

Sruthi Pillai is a passionate teacher and learner with 10 years of teaching experience. She is currently working as Business studies teacher, Al Injaz international private school, Oman. (P.O. Box: 2111 P.C.: 133 Al Khuwair Sultanate of Oman Al Khuwair, Muscat 2111, OM) She has published more than 25 articles in various national and international journals. Her area of interest are in the field of Marketing, HRM and General management. ORCID id 0009-0003-1325-3090

Majdi Anwar Quttainah earned his Ph.D. degree in Management from Rensselaer Polytechnic Institute, Lally School of Management & Technology (USA); MBA degree with merits from the Business School & Entrepreneurship at Newcastle University (UK), and bachelor's degree in International Business from the American International University in London (UK). Dr. Quttainah is an associate professor of management in the College of Business Administration at Kuwait University. His research and teaching interests are corporate governance and strategies, entrepreneurship & small businesses, and organizational development. In addition, as a recognition of his research, he was awarded the Best Young Researcher academic year 2016/2017 Kuwait University. He is an active scholar, presently working as senior editor of FIIB Business Review (Scopus, WoS, Published by the Sage Publishing). His research won several recognition and awards including the Best Paper Award at the 76th Annual Meeting of the Academy of Management Anaheim, CA, the Best Paper Award at the AGBA's 12th Annual World Congress, Kuantan City (State of Pahang), Malaysia, and the Best Paper Award of the Gorontalo International Conference of Project Management (ICPM) - Gorontalo/Indonesia. Also, at the home country level the best paper award for the Kuwait Economic Researcher Award by the Central Bank of Kuwait; May 2019 and 2022.

AlameluR. is working as a Senior Assistant Professor in the Department of Commerce and Management Studies, Srinivasa Ramanujan Centre, SASTRA Deemed University, Kumbakonam, Thanjavur, Tamil Nadu, India. She is a passionate management enabler with a blend of research and academic experience and competency in developing and delivering learner-centric pedagogy with a teaching experience of 25 years. She contributed articles and research papers at different conferences at national and international levels, and written case studies, and published 83 papers in SCOPUS--indexed international journals. She pursued her doctoral degree in Quality Management and coordinated several seminars, conferences and conducted Quality improvement programmes for over a decade. She has authored a book titled 'Management Information System' and is actively involved as a consultant for selected tiny industries in Tamil Nadu. Currently, she supervises two part-time research scholars, and her research areas are Supply Chain Management, Human Resource Analytics, and Circular economy.

GayathriR. is currently an Assistant Professor at School of Management, SASTRA Deemed University in India. An excellent orator with a Doctorate in Economics (2013) from Bharathidasan University, India. Her areas of interest include International Business, Marketing and Business Ethics. She handles courses such as Economics and Marketing. She has a rich academic experience of 19 years in teaching and 7 years in Research. Her focus is on contemporary social research and she is a co-investigator in the funded project funded by the Ministry of Rural Development, Government of India. She has presented papers at international and national level conferences and seminars. She has published a number of research articles and case studies in referred Scopus indexed journals.

Nalini R. is an Assistant Professor in School of Management, SASTRA Deemed To Be University, Thanjavur, Tamilnadu, India. She has obtained her doctoral degree from Bharathidasan University, Trichy and has around 28 years of teaching experience. Her area of research is Marketing and Finance and has published 45 research papers in international and national level peer-reviewed (Scopus indexed) journals and 10 articles in other international and national level journals. She has also participated and presented papers in national international conferences and published case studies and book chapters. Her area of expertise is financial, cost and management accounting and currently handling accounting courses.

Ravikumar R. N. is currently a Postdoctoral researcher at Universiti Malaysia Perlis, Malaysia. Also, working as an Assistant Professor in the Department of Computer Engineering at Marwadi University, Rajkot, Gujarat. He has 14 years of national and international teaching experience. He completed his PhD at Amity University, Rajasthan, M.E at VMRF Deemed University, B.E at Anna University, Chennai. He is the co-founder of the Research Activities Club at Marwadi University and trains students on research activities, which leads to the various publications. He has published numerous research articles in Scopus, SCI journals, Book chapters, and Conference papers. Also, he hold several patents and authored books. His specialization is ML, DL, Federated Learning, Recommendation Systems, and Optimization Techniques.

Ramakrishnan Ramachandran, PhD in Stakeholder Management is diplomat turned passionate research-oriented teacher with wide and varied experience in Indian Government /Private Enterprise. He has been associated with the founding of four B schools. Author of six books ranging from TQM to Environmental Science to Ethics, he has written close to 150 papers. ORCID id 0000-0001-8712-7677

Göran Roos is a globally recognised expert in intellectual capital management, manufacturing competitiveness, industry policy, and innovation systems. With around 19,000 Google citations and more than 300 publications, he has established himself as a leading authority on strategic management, economic complexity, and sustainable industrial development. Academic Credentials and Appointments Professor Roos holds a PhD from the University of South Australia (2019), an MBA from INSEAD (1989), and an MSc in Engineering Physics from Chalmers University of Technology (1982). His current academic positions and fellowships include: • Adjunct Professor at the Institute for Sustainability, Energy and Resources (ISER), The University of Adelaide (2023-2025) • Fellow of the Australian Academy of Technological Sciences and Engineering (ATSE) since 2014 • Fellow of the Royal Swedish Academy of Engineering Sciences (IVA) since 2015 Areas of Expertise

Intellectual Capital and Knowledge Management Professor Roos is a world-renowned expert in intellectual capital, having developed theories and implemented practical solutions that have shaped the

Allayarov Suxrob Rustamovich is a Professor in the Department of Finance and Financial Technologies at Tashkent State University of Economics, Uzbekistan. He has extensive academic and research experience in finance, with expertise in financial management, investment analysis, and modern financial systems. His research interests include digital finance, banking innovations, financial markets, and the application of advanced analytical and technological tools in financial decision-making. He is actively involved in teaching, curriculum development, and supervising research scholars, contributing to the advancement of academic excellence. Professor Allayarov has published scholarly works and participated in national and international conferences, promoting innovation in financial education and research. He also supports industry–academia collaboration initiatives, bridging theoretical frameworks with real-world financial practices. His work contributes significantly to strengthening financial education, research development, and technological integration in evolving global financial ecosystems.

Aarthi S is a dedicated Assistant Professor in Computer Science with over six years of teaching experience. She is currently pursuing her Ph.D. at Marwadi University, Gujarat, and holds an M.Phil. and MCA from Bharathiar University, Tamil Nadu. Throughout her academic career, Aarthi has specialized in programming languages such as C++, Java, and C, and contributed to research in recommender systems and AI-related data privacy. She has published journal articles, contributed to book chapters, and actively participated in technical workshops. Known for her student mentorship and engagement in academic events, Aarthi remains committed to fostering innovation and excellence in computer science education.

Kavitha S is working as Assistant Professor with an experience of 19 years and expertise in the field of Accountancy and Finance

Monika Sahu is a faculty member in the Department of Mathematics at DAV (PG) College, Karnal, India. She has completed her PhD in Mathematics with a specialization in Operations Research. Her research focuses on mathematical modelling, diet management using linear programming, and optimization techniques. She is actively involved in teaching and research.

Sudiksha Srivastava is an emerging scholar and research enthusiast with a keen interest in human resource management, entrepreneurship, and digital transformation in recruitment practices. She has actively engaged in academic research, conference presentations, and internship experiences that reflect her commitment to practical learning and professional growth. Known for her dedication, adaptability, and continuous learning approach, she aspires to contribute meaningfully to the field of management and organizational development.

Index

A

B

C

D

E

G

H

I

J

L

O

P

R

S

www.ingramcontent.com/pod-product-compliance
Lightning Source LLC
LaVergne TN
LVHW062328300926
849161LV00007B/1612